P9-EMO-574

THE INSIDERS' GUIDE TO

The Twin Cities

THE INSIDERS' GUIDE TO
The Twin Cities

by
Barbara DeGroot
and
Jack El-Hai

The Insiders' Guides® Inc.

Co-published and marketed by:
Saint Paul Pioneer Press
Northwest Publications, Inc.
345 Cedar St.
St. Paul, MN 55101
(612)222-5011

Co-published and distributed by:
The Insiders' Guides Inc.
The Waterfront • Suites 12 &13
P.O. 2057
Manteo, NC 27954
(919) 473-6100

•

SECOND EDITION
1st printing

•

Copyright ©1995
by Northwest Publications

•

Printed in the United States
of America

•

All rights reserved. No part of this
book may be reproduced in any form
without permission, in writing, from
the publisher, except by a reviewer
who wishes to quote brief passages
in connection with a review in a
magazine or newspaper.

ISBN 0-912367-85-7

Saint Paul Pioneer Press

Director of New Ventures
David A. Fryxell

Researchers
**Rob Hubbard, Debra Nygren,
Kathleen Rysgaard**

The Insiders' Guides® Inc.

Publisher/Managing Editor
Beth P. Storie

President/General Manager
Michael McOwen

Vice President/Advertising
Murray Kasmenn

Creative Services Director
Mike Lay

Partnership Services Director
Giles Bissonnette

Project Editor
Eileen Myers

Project Artist
David Haynes

On Line Services Director
David Haynes

Fulfillment Director
Gina Twiford

Sales and Marketing Director
Julie Ross

Managing Editor
Theresa Chavez

Controller
Claudette Forney

Preface

This *Insiders' Guide®* *to the Twin Cities* is for you if you're thinking of visiting Minneapolis-St. Paul, considering relocating there or simply if you're a current Twin Cities resident who wants to learn more about the rich and complex place in which you live. It's undoubtedly the most complete guide to life in the Twin Cities ever published — and if you use it to its fullest, it will be dog-eared, scribbled upon, highlighted and riddled with bookmarks within a few weeks. You can also use it to introduce others to the area's riches.

As you'll learn in this book, the Twin Cities is a changing place, one quite unlike the quiet and homogenous community that existed only a few decades ago. Today it is an artistic center, a vibrant business region, a good place to work and a great place to live.

This is the second edition of this *Insiders' Guide®*, and we have fully updated the book. Although this guide is not intended to be encyclopedic, you'll find an incredible amount of information in its pages. If you don't find your own favorite place or event listed here, let us know. We'll undoubtedly make changes and additions in future editions.

Although writing this book has been a fun project, using it should prove even more enjoyable. That part of this guide's life is now in your hands.

Photo: Buzz Magnuson, Pioneer Press

Minnehaha Falls inspired Longfellow's "The Song of Hiawatha."

About the Authors

Barbara DeGroot...

Barbara DeGroot is a free-lance writer whose articles have appeared in the *St. Paul Pioneer Press* newspaper and local magazines, such as *Mpls.St. Paul* and *Minnesota Parent*.

A graduate of the University of Minnesota, Barbara worked as a feature writer/editor for newspapers in Lubbock, Texas; Wausau, Wisconsin; and Las Vegas, Nevada, before returning home to the land of loons in the 1980s. While in Wisconsin, she wrote an award-winning column for the *Wausau Daily Herald* newspaper.

A Minneapolis native who grew up in the western suburbs, Barbara fondly remembers a childhood filled with trips to the lake cabin, Aquatennial parades, Lake Harriet band concerts, pickled herring and crackers on Sunday afternoon, family ice-fishing excursions and Dayton's sales. Today, she lives in St. Louis Park with her husband, Bob; 13-year-old daughter, Leigh; and a Brittany spaniel named Larry. Barbara also works as a school secretary at Cedar Manor Intermediate Center in St. Louis Park. Her free time is spent enjoying family, playing tennis, traveling and, of course, exploring these ever-fascinating cities.

She may be reached, via e-mail, at bbldegroot@aol.com.

Jack El-Hai...

Jack El-Hai said farewell to Los Angeles and became a Twin Cities resident in 1980. A freelancer who works from a Minneapolis warehouse-district office, he has written more than 300 articles on the arts, history, business, current events and interesting personalities for such publications as *American Heritage*, *Avenues*, *Minnesota Monthly*, *City Pages*, the *Star Tribune* and the *St. Paul Pioneer Press*. He is also a contributing editor to *Mpls.St.Paul Magazine* and a member of the National Writers Union and the American Society of Journalists and Authors. The Minnesota Historical Society Press published his book *Minnesota Collects* in 1992.

A writer of fiction as well, he is featured in the anthology *26 Minnesota Writers* (Nodin Press) and has published short stories in the *Star Tribune*, *Twin Cities Magazine* and *Northern Lit Quarterly*, among other publications. He's a winner of a Loft-McKnight Award, the Loft's Mentor Series and Creative Non-Fiction competitions, the Great Lakes Regional Writers Competition, and a Travel and Study Grant from the Center for Arts Criticism.

Fond of music in many forms, he plays mandolin, mandola and mandocello and is the founder of the Minnesota Mandolin Orchestra. He lives in Minneapolis with his wife, Ann Aronson.

El-Hai can be contacted by e-mail at jelhai@maroon.tc.umn.edu.

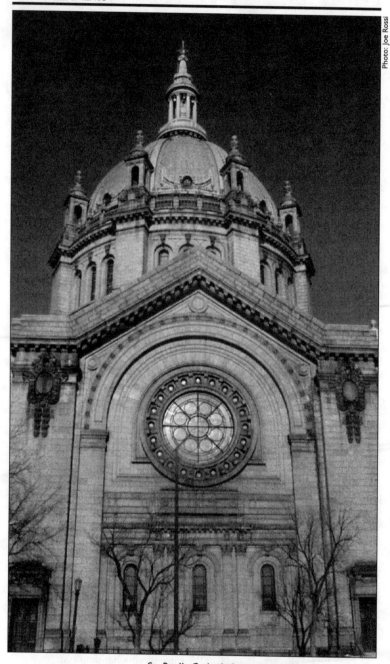

St. Paul's Cathedral.

Acknowledgments

Jack...

Diane Hellekson contributed most of the information in the Restaurants section, and we also thank the people at all of the libraries, government agencies, community organizations and businesses who provided arcane data of all sorts.

Barbara...

wishes to thank Rob Hubbard. The Nightlife chapter was based on information supplied by Rob, and we are most grateful. She also thanks the staff members of local chambers of commerce, tourism and visitors bureaus and government offices who so generously shared their expertise. Gratitude also to: Eileen Myers and David Fryxell, for the editorial assistance; to Betty Lundquist and Harris Smith, for the encouragement; to Brad Brinkworth, for the photo; and most importantly, to Bob and Leigh for putting up with all of this craziness.

Twin Cities
and
metro area

Minnesota

Downtown St. Paul

Minnesota

Rice St.

University Ave.

State Capitol

Constitution Ave.

Ramsey Hosp.

12th St.

94

7th St.

John Ireland Blvd.

Robert St.

St. Paul

Cedar St.

Wabasha St.

St. Peter St.

St. Joseph Hosp.

5th St.

4th St.

Kellogg Blvd.

Shepard Rd.

35E

Civic Center

Market

City Hall

Mississippi River

Ridder Cir.

Harriet Island

Nagasaki Rd.

Fillmore Ave.

Plato Blvd.

State St.

Lafayette Fwy.

Florida St.

Chester St.

St. Paul Downtown Airport

N

Downtown

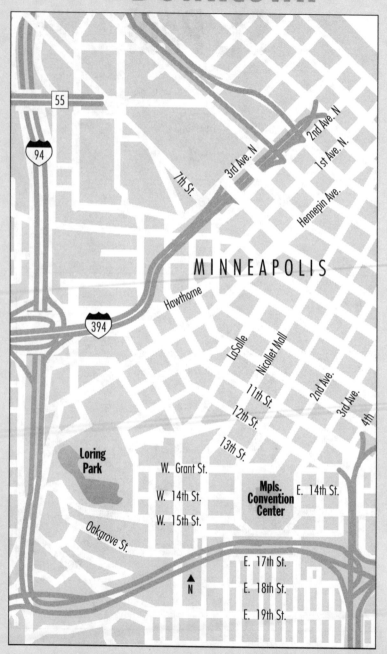

MINNEAPOLIS

55

94

394

7th St.

3rd Ave. N

2nd Ave. N

1st Ave. N

Hennepin Ave.

Hawthorne

LaSalle

Nicollet Mall

2nd Ave.

3rd Ave.

4th

11th St.

12th St.

13th St.

Loring Park

W. Grant St.

W. 14th St.

W. 15th St.

Mpls. Convention Center

E. 14th St.

Oakgrove St.

N

E. 17th St.

E. 18th St.

E. 19th St.

Minneapolis

St. Paul skyway

Minnesota

10th St.

Science Museum

Exchange St.

Skyways

Ninth St.

City Walk

Downtown ST. PAUL

World Trade Center

Seventh St.

Town Square

Hemar Bldg.

Metro Square

St. Peter St.

Dayton's

Bremer Tower

Mears Park Place

Control Data

Hamm Bldg.

Wabasha St.

Norwest Center

American Bank

Sixth St.

Galtier Plaza

Mears Park

The St. Paul Co.

First National

Fifth St.

Lowry Square

Victory Ramp

First Trust Center

Fourth S

City Hall

Radisson

Cedar St.

Minnesota St.

Kellogg Square

Robert St.

Federal Courts Bldg.

Jackson St.

KTCA

Sibley St.

Kellogg Blvd.

N

2nd St.

Shepard Rd.

Minneapolis
skyway

Make An Educated Move.

A Woman with Unique Properties.

Welcome to our wonderful Twin City area! It is a warm and friendly area waiting to welcome you into the fold of a rich arts culture, many corporate headquarters, ethnic festivals, good schools where students can excel and - where people care about one another. There is a wonderful variety of seasons, places, things & joys to experience; from Minnesotas' famous Northern reaches along magnificent Lake Superior to the Twin Cities.

Eva J is a name in real estate recognized and respected for being knowledgeable, hearing & satisfying buyers & seller's needs. Eva J is a trained relocation specialist who has been recognized in the Who's Who.

EVA J.

Specialist

MLS

2950 White Bear Ave.
Maplewood, MN 55109

(612) 429-7777

Table of Contents

Directory of Maps

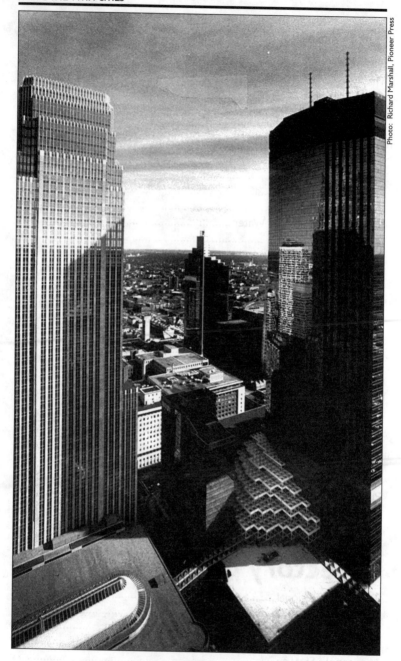

Photo: Richard Marshall, Pioneer Press

This view of the Norwest and IDS buildings is from the Multifoods Tower in downtown Minneapolis.

Inside
The Twin Cities

The overhead honking of Canada geese in flight. The hot, sticky scent of the Minnesota State Fair. The head of a parking meter impudently protruding from a pile of snow. A deer gliding across headlight beams on a suburban road. The house lights dimming and the crowd hushing at a Guthrie Theater performance. The clatter of a bicycle careening down Grand Avenue Hill.

Like every other place in the world, the Twin Cities is a unique mixture of sights, smells and sounds — a distinctive coming together of earth, water, sky and people. In our case the earth is fertile, the water plentiful, the sky often cold and the people generous and friendly (with a deep-down reluctance to draw too close too quickly).

The Personality of the Twin Cities

Can a metropolitan area consisting of more than 2 million souls even have an identifiable personality? You bet it can, because a city's character is built as much from public perception as from truth.

Take a poll of people around the country and you'll discover that certain images and qualities recur when they think about the Twin Cities:

• Cultural richness. There are a lot of facts to back up this perception. Here's a metropolitan area that has four major art museums, two big orchestras, the nation's foremost regional theater, bookstores galore, a wealth of talent in jazz, pop and gospel music, a pair of the finest science and history museums in the country, unusually strong public radio and TV, and a rapidly diversifying ethnic mix that keeps the area's culture in a healthy flux.

• An involved community. It's true — a lot of companies reinvest in the community, an extremely strong group of local foundations feed money to area nonprofits of all kinds, and people are unusually supportive of neighborhood associations and other community organizations.

• Cold. There's no getting around this one. The only cities in the continental United States that can claim a colder climate are Duluth, Bismarck and Great Falls, and they probably won't. To imagine the Twin Cities as a metropolitan Siberia, however, is to forget about the months of May through October, when snow is unlikely.

When the Civil War erupted, Minnesota was the first state to offer troops to President Abraham Lincoln.

Insiders' Tips

• Flat. This perception is demonstrably false. Much of St. Paul is actually hilly; try the walk from the riverfront to the State Capitol. Minneapolis is significantly flatter, but the areas near the Mississippi River in both cities (and some suburbs) contain high bluffs.

• Ethnically homogeneous. The image of the Twin Cities as a mini-Scandinavia was never truly accurate. St. Paul, in fact, has drawn most of its population from such places as Ireland, Canada, Germany, Great Britain, Southeast Asia and Mexico. Minneapolis, which always has had a larger number of Norwegians, Finns, Danes and Swedes and their descendants, now boasts increasing numbers of African Americans, Russian Jews, Ethiopians and American Indians. At the same time, the suburbs — particularly those north and south of Minneapolis — are growing richer with residents of varied cultural backgrounds. The Twin Cities, although it remains the least racially mixed of the nation's top 25 metropolitan areas, is white bread no more.

• Crime free. There is actually a division of opinion here, with outsiders perceiving the Twin Cities as a haven free of murders, muggings and carjackings, while residents often believe the crime rate is soaring. Comparative statistics show that the Twin Cities' overall crime rate is lower than that of most of the other largest metropolitan areas, with significantly lower violent crime figures and relatively high property crime figures.

• Nice. See the discussion of "Minnesota nice" later in this chapter.

It is a good mixture of people and qualities we have here, one that keeps the Twin Cities economically and culturally healthy while spurring its people to steadily and painfully leave behind this metropolitan area's origins as a group of isolated settlements perched on the windy plains of the Upper Midwest.

Looking Through the Mists of Time

Long before those settlements sprouted, perhaps 10,000 years before any European settlers set eyes upon the land that would become the Twin Cities, the first people arrived. It was good food that brought them here. These Paleo-Indians, a big-game hunting people, probably came from the south, following herds of mammoths and bison that roamed plains leveled by earlier advances of ice. The mammoths eventually vanished, and the people who hunted them left the region.

Some time after, another people migrated to the area. They ate berries, nuts, fish and small animals. These people — now known as the Late Woodland people — grew in number, becoming some of the first North Americans to fashion tools and weapons out of metal. Other innovations arrived in succeeding years: the atlatl, a hinged pole that gave spear-throwers greater range and speed; the ability to weave baskets and floor mats from plant stalks; techniques of harvesting wild rice, an abundant plant that became an important food source; and the use of clay to produce pots and jars. They fished, decorated their pottery, smoked tobacco, traded with other people to the south and buried their dead in some 10,000 mounds that once dotted the land of Minnesota. Most of the mounds are now gone.

For reasons not completely understood, the Late Woodland people left the region by about 500 or 1000 A.C.E. (After the Common Era). Over the course of centuries, the Dakota Indians, part of a great community of people who lived throughout much of the Midwest, arrived and occupied the land upon which the Twin Cities now stands. The Dakota were hunters of game, planters of gardens, harvesters of corn and wild rice, and traders. Dakota bands established villages at Lake Calhoun and elsewhere in the area.

To the north and east were the Ojibwa Indians (sometimes called the Chippewa), whose roots lay among the Algonquin tribes of eastern North America. The Ojibwa and Dakota were in frequent conflict over hunting and fishing grounds, and it was the Ojibwa who coined the pejorative name "Nadouessioux" (later shortened to "Sioux"), meaning "little snakes," for the Dakota.

By the middle of the 17th century, Frenchmen had entered the region via Lake Superior and moved as far west as Lake Mille Lacs. These Europeans could more properly be called prospectors than explorers, because their main aim was to investigate and eventually exploit the potential of the fur trade. The year 1680 marked the arrival of the Franciscan missionary Louis Hennepin, who ventured from the south, up the Mississippi River. Held captive for a time by the Dakota, Hennepin became perhaps the first European to view the Mississippi River's Falls of St. Anthony (which are now at the heart of downtown Minneapolis). Hennepin returned to France and wrote a largely fictitious account of his Minnesota sojourn.

The French built stockades in several locations south and west of the Twin Cities, but the English were steadily weakening the French influence in the region. A handful of large English trading companies opened posts and directed the fur trade, including the Hudson Bay Company and the North West Company. In 1763 the French gave up their claim to land in North America, and three years later Jonathan Carver, a native New Englander working for the British government, arrived in Minnesota territory to survey and explore. He scrutinized much of the land in present-day Minneapolis and St. Paul and wrote a best-selling account of his adventures.

The next big-name explorer to set foot in the Twin Cities area was Zebulon Pike, the U.S. Army officer whose name later went to Pike's Peak in Colorado. In 1805, with the territory now supposedly under United States control after the Louisiana Purchase of 1803, he came north from St. Louis to survey the upper reaches of the Mississippi River. He bargained with the Dakota to gain rights to a military site at the confluence of the Mississippi and Minnesota rivers, hoisting the U.S. flag at the future location of Fort Snelling. After Pike's departure, however, the British fur trading concerns refused to recognize any U.S. jurisdiction over the area. Not until the United States and Britain signed the treaty of Ghent in 1814 did the territory become indisputably American.

With all the international jockeying for the territory now completed, the U.S. government moved to strengthen its control. In 1820 Capt. Josiah Snelling and a garrison of Army troops began constructing a fort on the land that Pike had acquired for a military post years earlier. Initially called Fort St. Anthony, the military installation became known as Fort Snelling in 1825. Now crowded between freeways, federal buildings and the Minneapolis-St. Paul International Airport, the fort dominated the area in the 19th century in ways that are unimaginable today.

Starting in 1823, for instance, the fort was the docking area for the first steamboats to arrive up the river from St. Louis. Its soldiers constructed the first flour mill and sawmill at the Falls of St. Anthony, thus sparking the birth of Minneapolis. The fort also served as a refuge for some of the region's first farm families, who arrived in 1821. In 1840, these people were finally evicted from the fort reservation, and they moved across the Mississippi and several miles north to establish a new community.

They found another character already squatting on that land: Pierre Parrant, a French Canadian whisky seller. Parrant's trading post was nicknamed Pig's Eye by the soldiers who proved its most dedicated customers. Only the arrival in 1841 of the French priest Lucian Galtier, who built a humble log chapel at the riverboat landing near Parrant's buildings and consecrated it to Saint Paul, prevented Minnesota's second-largest city from the humiliation of having Pig's Eye as its official moniker.

The population of this fledgling city of St. Paul grew rapidly. By 1847, the town had a school, enjoyed the regular visits of steamboats carrying passengers and freight and boasted the headquarters of the American Fur Company. Two years later, when the U.S. Congress created the Territory of Minnesota, St. Paul's population stood at 840.

Meanwhile, upriver at the mills the soldiers had built to tap the power of the Mississippi at the Falls of St. Anthony, another settlement (although an initially smaller one) was taking shape. Two men — the merchant Franklin Steele and the eccentric, part-Indian guide Pierre Bottineau — bought land at the east bank of the falls in the late 1830s and early '40s. In 1847 Steele started building his own sawmill there, an undertaking that attracted workers of all kinds, including a sizable number of freed African-American slaves. This dusty settlement grew into the village of St. Anthony, which numbered 250 people by 1850. Five years later illegal squatters on the west bank of the Falls acquired official status as landowners, and they got fancy, joining the Dakota word for "water" with the Greek word for "city" and naming their town Minneapolis.

And so began a unique rivalry and interdependence between burgeoning communities separated from one another by the vast Fort Snelling reservation. At the start, St. Paul, to the east, had the political and commercial power, along with the greater population. Minneapolis, which absorbed St. Anthony in 1872, had the strength of the Falls, industrial smarts and a reckless Western spirit. They both mushroomed, supported armies of land speculators, survived financial panics, and, after Minnesota achieved statehood in 1858, promoted themselves tirelessly as the leading representatives of civilization in a rough-and-tumble state.

Slowly, and with much vicious spilling of ink in the newspapers, Minneapolis began to attain a certain kind of dominance. The rapid growth of the milling industry, spawning such giant businesses as Pillsbury, Cargill and General Mills, gave it a clear industrial lead over St. Paul. And by 1890, after a scandalous U.S. census fiasco in which enumerators from both cities counted dead and imaginary people to boost their figures, Minneapolis claimed an indisputable supremacy in population. Minneapolis boosters also crowed over the placement of the University of Minnesota's main campus in their city.

St. Paul, on the other hand, early on

Talking Minnesotan

Minnesotan term	English translation
dale	shopping center
that's interesting	that's stupid
cool	freezing
hot dish	casserole
rusty bucket	rusty car
ish	yuk
pop	soda
rubber binder	rubber band
salad	Jell-O
Scandahoovian	Scandinavian
uff da	oy vey
Strib	Star Tribune newspaper
outstate	Outside the Twin Cities but inside Minnesota ("Greater Minnesota" is a term some outstaters prefer.)

became the state capital and won the Minnesota State Fair, an institution enormously prestigious as a showcase of the state's agricultural and industrial wealth. It also was the home of a genteel class of the rich, people who made their money from such refined enterprises as banking, insurance and commercial transportation, not by chopping down trees and grinding up grain. No residential area in Minneapolis could match St. Paul's elegant Summit Hill neighborhood, where the palatial Cathedral of Saint Paul presided over one of the nation's grandest collections of oversize Victorian-style houses. (Nevermind that during the Prohibition era, St. Paul also was a popular refuge for notorious gangsters!)

Seen through the mists of time, the old rivalry between Minneapolis and St. Paul now seems ridiculous and destructive. A favorite joke from the turn of the century sums up its silliness: A visiting minister, the story goes, was preaching at a church in Minneapolis. He rose to the pulpit and declared that he would draw the text of his sermon from Saint Paul. To his astonishment, the congregation walked out en masse.

One of the reasons why Minneapolis and St. Paul never melded into a "Minneapaul" megacity is that each had

In its first official census (1850), Minnesota had only 6,077 people.

Insiders' Tips

a different vision of what a large city should be like. To this day, St. Paul prides itself on its distinct neighborhoods, its small-town atmosphere and its resistance to pointless glitz. (Drive through certain sections of north St. Paul, for instance, and you'll see stretches of commercial and residential blocks that look virtually unchanged from the 1950s.) Minneapolis, on the other hand, makes a big deal of its glamorous music and film industries, its major-league sports teams (none plays in St. Paul) and its nightlife. It's a cliche, but nonetheless true, to observe that St. Paul is a small town grown large, while Minneapolis is a metropolis on a small scale. (Another oft-repeated cliche maintains that "St. Paul is the westernmost city of the East, while Minneapolis is the easternmost city of the West." What exactly that means, who knows?)

What Really Are "the Twin Cities"?

To focus on the cities' differences, though, is to ignore that Minneapolis and St. Paul grew quite alike as they matured. Both developed outstanding park systems. Both sponsored good public schools. Both became progressive and generally veered to the left politically. And, perhaps most telling, both lost big chunks of their populations to the suburbs during the last half of this century, and that migration created the "metropolitan area" that now constitutes the real Twin Cities.

Nowadays, most people in the Twin Cities live outside the city limits of Minneapolis and St. Paul. Some live far outside — the toll-free local telephone calling area, which stretches from New Prague in the southwest to Isanti in the northeast, is reportedly the largest in the world. Officially, the metropolitan area

includes seven counties: Hennepin, Ramsey, Anoka, Washington, Dakota, Scott and Carver. Hennepin and Ramsey counties contain Minneapolis and St. Paul, respectively, and they are growing only slowly in population. The other five are exploding.

Much that's worth seeing and experiencing in the Twin Cities, in fact, is outside Minneapolis and St. Paul. Restrict yourself to the big twin towns and you'll miss the Mall of America, the Minnesota Zoo and many of the best restaurants, hotels and historic sites. The reverse side of the coin, of course, is that if you shy away from the urban centers you'll never see the Minnesota State Capitol, the Minneapolis Institute of Arts, the Como Park Zoo and Basilica of St. Mary.

Yes, in the Twin Cities you'll find people from Minneapolis who couldn't think of a reason to go to Coon Rapids, folks from Eagan who don't set foot in Minneapolis, people in Roseville who most contentedly get everything they need from their own community and residents of St. Paul who have never seen Chaska. Get to know these people, if you can, and share with them the parts of this book that will encourage them to enjoy the Twin Cities in its entirety.

The Cost of Living

It's hard to categorize the Twin Cities as either expensive or inexpensive. After all, so many factors conspire to set prices: geography, supply, demand, climate, trendiness and the area's general financial health, to name a few.

Take housing costs, for instance. Like other metropolitan centers in the Midwest, the Twin Cities enjoys a housing market that is less expensive than the national average. In many parts of the area,

A Gallery of Famous Twin Citians

Eddie Albert: The actor eventually found his green acres in Hollywood.

Loni Anderson: That "WKRP" femme fatale grew up in suburban St. Paul.

Richard Dean Anderson: TV's "McGyver" also hails from the Twin Cities.

The Andrews Sisters: Patty, Maxine and LaVerne sang their way to fame and fortune in the 1930s and '40s.

Twin Cities native Loni Anderson.

Harry Blackmun: This U.S. Supreme Court judge who grew up in St. Paul wrote the opinion for Roe vs. Wade.

Carol Bly: She's one of the nation's best spinners of stories and promoters of social conscience.

Robert Bly: A leading figure of the men's movement, accomplished poet and author of the book *Iron John*. He lives in Minneapolis.

Warren Burger: This St. Paul native became Chief Justice of the United States Supreme Court.

John Camp/"John Sandford": The best-selling author of *The Empress File* and a series of "prey" novels — *Silent Prey, Eyes of Prey,* etc. — lives in St. Paul and was for years a local newspaperman. He won a Pulitzer Prize at the *St. Paul Pioneer Press.*

Joel and Ethan Coen: They learned how to direct such films as *Raising Arizona* and *Barton Fink* while growing up with a home movie camera in St. Louis Park.

Arlene Dahl: The glamorous Hollywood actress is from Minneapolis.

William Demarest: He excelled as Uncle Charley in *My Three Sons* and as a series of irascible characters in many film comedies of the 1940s.

Amelia Earhart: The famed aviatrix was a St. Paul schoolgirl.

F. Scott Fitzgerald: The author of *The Great Gatsby,* born in St. Paul, used Minnesota locales for some of his early stories and novels.

Al Franken: The comedian, screenwriter, political satirist and original writer for *Saturday Night Live* grew up in St. Louis Park.

J. Paul Getty: The billionaire was a native of Minneapolis.

Peter Graves: Along with his brother James Arness, the star of *Mission: Impossible* grew up in Minneapolis.

Judith Guest: The author of *Ordinary People* is from Edina.

Kent Hrbek: The Minnesota Twins' recently retired star first baseman is a hometown boy.

Hubert Humphrey: He served as mayor of Minneapolis, U.S. senator, vice president, the Democratic nominee for president in 1968 and the embodiment of political progressivism in Minnesota.

Jimmy Jam and Terry Lewis: These Grammy Award-winning music producers are both Twin Cities natives.

Garrison Keillor: A humorist par excellence, he's involved in a love-hate relationship with the Twin Cities press.

Sister Elizabeth Kenny: For three decades, this native Australian ran a trailblazing polio clinic in Minneapolis.

Greg LeMond: The two-time Tour de France-winning bicyclist lives in suburban Medina.

Meridel Le Sueur: The writer of fiction, leftist activist and social-justice worker lives in St. Paul.

Harvey Mackay: The businessman and book author has spent most of his years swimming with the sharks in the Twin Cities.

Paul Molitor: The great Milwaukee Brewers and Toronto Blue Jays baseball player is a St. Paul native.

Walter Mondale: U.S. senator, vice president to Jimmy Carter, wager of an unsuccessful campaign for the presidency against Ronald Reagan in 1984, he's now the U.S. ambassador to Japan.

Jack Morris: The World Series-winning pitcher (for both the Twins and the Blue Jays) is a St. Paul lad.

Gordon Parks: This photographer, author of *The Learning Tree* and film director (*Shaft* is among his credits) grew up in St. Paul.

Prince: Except for his own staff, nobody calls him by the unpronounceable graphic symbol he recently adopted as his new name. (His original name was Prince Rogers Nelson.) But forget the name — the rock star, music producer and film director is the most influential popular artist ever to come from these parts.

Harry Reasoner: The *60 Minutes* newsman attended West High in Minneapolis.

Maria Sanford: The first woman in the United States ever to become a full professor of history (at Swarthmore) later joined the faculty of the University of Minnesota.

Charles Schulz: The man behind "Peanuts" is a St. Paul native.

Nadine Strossen: The president of the American Civil Liberties Union is from Hopkins.

Robert Vaughn: The Man from U.N.C.L.E. was originally a man from Minneapolis.

Roy Wilkins: The former director of the NAACP was raised in St. Paul.

Dave Winfield: The 3,000-hit man of baseball also has St. Paul roots.

Twin Cities Statistics: A Random Selection

Population (1993 figures)

Seven-county metropolitan area: 2,383,725
   (15th-largest in the United States)
Minneapolis: 367,924
St. Paul: 272,242
Metro area growth rate, 1980 to 1990: 15.2 percent
Twin Cities' percentage of Minnesota population: 52.7

Twin Cities racial diversity (1992)

White 91.6 percent
African American 3.9 percent
Asian/Pacific Islander 2.8 percent
American Indian/Eskimo/Aleut 1.0 percent
Other 0.6 percent
(The U.S. Census Bureau believes that people of Hispanic
   origin can be of any race.)

Weather

Coldest month: January, 11.8 degree average
Warmest month: July, 73.6 degree average
Annual mean temperature: 44.9 degrees
Snowiest month: March, 9.6 inches average
Rainiest month: June, 3.9 inches average
Driest month: October, 1.8 inches of precipitation average
Sunniest month: July
Cloudiest month: December

within the cities or in the suburbs, you can find good houses in respectable areas for well under $100,000. But once you move in, what's it going to cost to heat that place? There's a winter here, in case you haven't heard, and you'll be amazed at how quickly your new home will absorb gas, electricity or heating oil. As a result, the cost of home ownership is hard to meaningfully categorize.

Rents are in the intermediate range, lower than New York City and higher than Fargo. A continuing surplus of rental

properties has kept rent increases moderate in recent years. For details on the renting and home-buying market, see our Real Estate chapter.

What about another necessity, food? Again, the verdict is split. If you're a glutton for meat, milk, cheese and butter, you'll get off easy here, thanks to the proximity of meat and dairy producing operations. (You'll also likely have to take advantage of the region's oft-praised medical facilities; see the chapter on Health Care.) If instead you graze upon fruits and vegetables, watch out for high prices in the produce department, especially during the winter when locally grown goods are not available in farmers markets.

Because of lower than average crime rates, car and property insurance rates come as a relief to people used to the going prices on the coasts. But watch out for property taxes. Even more, watch out for income taxes! That money for government-supplied services has to come from somewhere. During the 1970s and '80s, taxation critics were fond of calling the state "The People's Republic of Minnesota."

It costs $6.75 to see a first-run movie, $1.15 to buy a gallon of gas, a quarter to make a phone call and $400 to get a recreation membership at the YMCA. And if you lose track of your expenses, a bounced check could run you $22.

Minnesota Nice

If your memory stretches back more than a few years, you'll recall that the term "politically correct" was once a phrase of praise used to indicate tact, courtesy or social diplomacy. Nowadays, of course, it's a slur, a label indicating a lock-step conformity of thought and an unwillingness to risk offending anyone. The term "Minnesota nice" has undergone a similar metamorphosis.

Through the 1980s, Twin Citians liked hearing that their culture was imbued with "Minnesota nice." It meant that store clerks were sincerely helpful, strangers smiled at each other on the street, and such commercial establishments as movie theaters and fast-food restaurants took checks. It indicated that you would rarely encounter someone who was habitually rude, boastful, vulgar or boorish. It characterized the efforts of good Samaritans who would appear from nowhere to assist snow-stuck drivers, direct lost tourists (the lost ones always seem to be from Iowa), and guard ducklings attempting to cross busy streets.

All those nice things still happen in the Twin Cities, much more often than they do in other metropolitan areas of comparable size. (Syndicated newspaper columnist Molly Ivins recently described Minnesotans as the nicest people in the United States.) But don't try to praise a Twin Citian by referring to "Minnesota nice" any more. Over time, the term has come to mean something not so nice.

These days, "Minnesota nice" evokes different images: people who offer a false smile instead of telling you what they really think, folks who avoid talking about unpleasant things, those who avert their eyes from troubling sights and cooks who prepare bland, inoffensive food. These flaws are by no means unique to Minnesotans. But be forewarned: The term "nice" is becoming bad. Try another term if you want to extend praise: "kind," "generous," "thoughtful," whatever. And, remember: If you avoid the problem entirely by ceasing to offer praise altogether, you're exemplifying "Minnesota nice" yourself.

Inside
Getting Around

Not all that long ago, the Twin Cities boasted one of the nation's finest streetcar systems, a network of tracks that could carry you from neighborhoods far east of St. Paul to the shores of Lake Minnetonka, 20 miles west of Minneapolis. Destroyed in the 1950s by corrupt public officials and the machinations of various bus manufacturers, the streetcar system is now reduced to a single line, a thread of rails that connects Lake Harriet and Lake Calhoun in Minneapolis. Volunteer conductors operate it out of love, riders board the cars out of nostalgia, and people stop to watch it as it chimes its bell and clatters by. As charming as the old streetcar is, it's more an attraction than a means of transport.

Even if the streetcars had remained, however, it is doubtful that the system could have kept up with the Twin Cities' urban and suburban growth during the past 40 years. (Yes, some light-rail plans are currently creeping forward, particularly corridors to link Minneapolis and St. Paul and to serve Minneapolis' southern suburbs, but it will be years before they materialize.) Unfettered by the mountains, basins and large bodies of water that confine some other metropolitan areas, Minneapolis-St. Paul has sprawled in all directions. Only the snaking of the Mississippi and Minnesota rivers has lent a natural hindrance to the growth, and even that hasn't done much to slow it.

In the old days, when the streetcars whisked you out to Snelling Avenue in St. Paul or to Lake Street in Minneapolis, they were carrying you to the edge of

Photo: Scott Takushi, Pioneer Press

A view of downtown St. Paul showing I-94 and I-35E.

town. Now those streets run through the inner cities. In the 1990s, the Twin Cities cover a geographic region that technically spans seven counties, and it can take some ingenuity to get from one place to another in the most efficient and fun manner. Never despair — there's always a way.

Doing It By Car

Minnesota is not the world's easiest place in which to operate a car. Winter not only causes the awesome automotive demands that car battery commercials are so fond of showing, but it also coats the roads with ice, narrows the roads with piles of snow, breaks apart asphalt to form vertigo-inducing potholes and forces fuel suppliers to oxygenate gasoline to levels that not all cars enjoy.

But winter's only half the year, right? The other half, according to Minnesota highway veterans, is road construction season. It does seem as if all major roads are under construction when you need them most, but all that work has resulted in a metropolitan highway system that functions well when the orange construction cones go away.

Like many major urban centers, the Twin Cities is served by a "ring" system of interstate highways. Interstate 35 — with a 35W fork that runs through Minneapolis and a 35E fork that runs through St. Paul — is the main north-south artery. Interstate 94 (a coast-to-coast highway that connects Minneapolis and St. Paul) and Interstate 394 (from Minneapolis going west) carry much of the east-west traffic. Forming a ring around most of the metro area is Interstate 494/694 (494 is the designation for the southern half of the ring; 694 is the northern segment). These interstates connect with many state and county highways that fill the gaps. In general, north-south routes bear odd numbers, while east-west highways have even numbers.

Rush-hour traffic has picked up noticeably during the past decade, with the most consistent trouble spots being I-394 approaching downtown Minneapolis; the I-35W/Minn. 62 interchange south of Minneapolis, known as the "Crosstown Commons"; and "Spaghetti Junction" in downtown St. Paul, where I-35E and I-94 cross paths. Gawkers anywhere, however, can turn a minor accident into a major slowdown. Although many radio stations offer traffic updates, the best source of highway information is KBEM 88.5 FM, which taps the resources of the Minnesota Department of Transportation.

The Department of Transportation also maintains a set of phone numbers for traffic information. Call 296-3076 to hear about Minnesota highway road conditions, 297-4103 to keep up on highway lane closings and 296-3000 (TDD 296-9930) for general transportation information.

While on the highways, you'll notice a full complement of Minnesota driving styles. The Speed Limit Enforcer, for example, drives at a steady 55, even in the left lane, and refuses to move over for speedier traffic. (Some would argue that this civilian enforcement is necessary, because the Minnesota State Patrol is more lax in enforcing speed limits than its counterparts in other states.) When two Speed Limit Enforcers cruise alongside each other they form the famous Minnesota Wedge, which can slow traffic for miles.

You also may find yourself behind the Surprise Decelerator, a nervous driver who slows down on highway entrances rather than accelerating to merge with traffic. Or maybe you'll encounter the Disintegrator, who pilots a car so eroded by rust and salt that at least one part falls off every trip.

All drivers should be on guard for "black ice," the exhaust of autos that freezes and camouflages itself on the roadway, as well as potholes and the raccoons and deer that stray onto the roads in suburban areas. Do not underestimate the ability of snow and ice to make you slip and slide. Slow down! Despite these hazards, Minnesota has one of the lowest rates of highway fatalities of all the states, and Twin Cities drivers are safe and often surprisingly courteous.

Natives of Minneapolis and St. Paul both claim to get lost in each other's cities. In the downtown area, where some streets follow the trail of old footpaths and the barrier of the Mississippi River dictates some peculiarities, navigating in St. Paul can be somewhat confusing. Street addresses often do not follow the course that logically minded visitors would prefer, with numbers in the 800s, say, sometimes jumping an intervening cross-street to appear on the next block. Still, the uninitiated will get around just fine with a map or by asking for directions.

On the surface, the street layout of Minneapolis seems better ordered. In general, avenues run east-west and streets run north-south. In addition, many thoroughfares are numbered, and some areas have alphabetical sequences of streets, based on the names of former residents, presidents and even chemical elements. But some drivers become confused by the existence of pairs of numbered avenues with the same name (Second Avenue N. lies northwest of Nicollet Avenue, while Second Avenue S. lies southeast of that dividing line) and by identical addresses on numbered streets north or south of Nicollet. Also perplexing to some are the numbered streets east of the Mississippi River that run diagonally compared with the rest of the street grid (they bear the designation "northeast" or "southeast"). You'll get used to it.

Traffic laws and customs in the Twin Cities are pretty normal. You can turn right on red, except at the frustratingly high number of Minneapolis intersections where signs prohibit it. Motorcyclists don't have to wear a helmet (but they should anyway). If you're using your windshield wipers at any time of the day, turn on your headlights. Don't even think about driving close to the Aquatennial Parade in Minneapolis and the Winter Carnival Parade in St. Paul. Watch out for one-way streets in downtown Minneapolis and St. Paul. And if you try to drive on the Nicollet Mall in Minneapolis (reserved for pedestrians, buses, bicyclists and taxis) someone will call out and ask what part of Iowa you're from. If you're in the front seat of your car, you must wear your seat belt. Don't drive drunk.

Parking

Suburbanites tremble at the idea of parking in downtown Minneapolis and St. Paul, but the parking situation isn't

Consider carpooling, riding the bus or pedaling a bike to the University of Minnesota campus, because the parking is difficult at best.

Insiders' Tips

too bad in either place because of an ample supply of lots and ramps. It's just expensive: Daily rates can top $12 for a stall in a primo heated ramp. Downtown street parking is regulated by meters, which vary considerably in hours and allotted time. Meters in Minneapolis take only quarters, and down by the Metrodome the meter cops remain vigilant until 10 PM, even on Sundays.

Other troublesome parking areas are the neighborhood near St. Thomas University and the Grand Avenue area in St. Paul, anywhere near the University of Minnesota (although new ramps have eased the problem) and the Uptown area of Minneapolis.

The parking situation becomes greatly complicated when a heavy snowfall occurs. If city officials declare a genuine snow emergency, which you'll hear about in all the news media, special parking rules go into effect. St. Paul's snow emergency parking system is the simplest: Plows first attack snow emergency routes and the labeled side of streets bearing special signs, where parking is prohibited until the work is completed. Drivers then move their cars to the cleared portions of the streets as the plows dig into the other side of the street.

Minneapolis' snow emergency system is a devilish scheme in which citizens need to move their cars from odd to even sides of the street, or vice versa, in a manner that changes in alternate years. Call 348-SNOW for details on the current year's system.

In suburban areas where off-street parking is more plentiful, some municipalities simply prohibit street parking until the plows clear the roads of snow.

If you leave your car where it shouldn't be, there's a good chance it will be towed. In Minneapolis, your car will likely end up in the municipal impound lot at 51 Colfax Avenue N.; call 673-5777 to find out if your car is really there. St. Paul's impound lot is at 830 Bard's Channel Road, just east of Minn. 3; call 292-3642.

Share A Ride

Commuting to work solo in a car can be expensive, environmentally unsound, tiresome and lonely, so many drivers take advantage of Minnesota Rideshare (call 348-RIDE or TDD 349-7746), a government-funded service that helps people set up or join carpools and vanpools. About 16,000 people are currently on the Rideshare database. Poolers enjoy many benefits: shared expenses, the use of designated highway express lanes, special highway access ramps, free or reduced-cost parking in downtown Minneapolis and St. Paul, and preferential parking granted by many employers.

Hail a Cab

Except at the Minneapolis-St. Paul International Airport, trying to hail a taxi in the Twin Cities can be a time-consuming, if not impossible, effort. Phone the taxi services instead, well in advance. Check the Yellow Pages for the latest listing or ask a hotel desk clerk for recommendations. Some cab companies provide smoke-free taxis. Rates vary somewhat by municipality, as do special fares for seniors.

Take the Bus

The Twin Cities boasts some 145 bus routes that run 903 peak-hour and 277 midday buses on any given weekday. Since many of the riders are commuters who want to go to downtown Minneapolis or downtown St. Paul, service into the central corridors is strongest. Metropoli-

If It's Tuesday,
It Must Be . . .

When some Twin Citians think about getting around, that activity extends outside the area, especially to warmer climes during those long winter months. That's where charter vacations come in. Most such excursions from the Twin Cities are packaged by two companies. The most easily accessible is **Trans Global Tours**, 8200 Normandale Boulevard in Bloomington, 831-1980 or 948-8333 for the 24-hour recorded hotline. The other is **MLT Vacations**, which is not open directly to the public. Check the ads in Sunday newspaper travel sections for details of current tours offered by both these companies, then call your travel agent for booking.

tan Council Transit Operations is by far the biggest provider of public bus service, but a number of other bus companies meet the needs of riders in suburban areas.

Municipal Bus Service

METROPOLITAN COUNCIL
TRANSIT OPERATIONS
373-3333

During a typical year, fully one-third of all Twin Cities residents take an MCTO bus for one reason or another, and its buses carry more than 60 million passengers a year. Local service most often radiates from downtown Minneapolis or downtown St. Paul, while express service carries commuters on highways (often traveling in special lanes designated for buses). There is also special service to such locations as the Minnesota State Fairgrounds and the Mall of America.

Call the number above for bus schedules, help in planning a route to your destination, customer relations and other services. Although an increase is expected soon, the fare is currently $1; it goes up to $1.25 during the peak hours of 6 to 9 AM

and 3:30 to 6:30 PM. Express bus rides cost $1.50 and $1.75 (peak hours). Adults 65 and older, people with disabilities and kids ages 6 to 17 pay only 25¢ during non-peak hours. Up to three kids 5 and younger can ride free with a paid fare at any time. Rides within special downtown zones in Minneapolis and St. Paul cost only 25¢ (50¢ during peak hours). Transfers are free. Monthly passes and discounted ride tickets are available, and the fare boxes accept dollar bills, automatically count the money you drop into them (sometimes inaccurately; they don't easily recognize Canadian coins) and do not make change. In general, bus service ceases between 1 and 4:30 AM.

The drivers are a varied bunch, ranging from friendly folks who call out the names of streets and tell jokes ("Attention ladies and gentlemen: The letters MCTO stand for Metropolitan Council Transit Operations, not My Cafeteria Travels On — please don't eat or drink on the bus") to behind-the-wheel drudges who consider it a strain to grunt hello. Most, though, are real people who can rise to such heroic heights as navigating snow-clogged streets, gently guiding a bus down an icy hill and waiting out a light to let a patron cross the street and board.

The MCTO employs 187 police officers, and on-board crime is uncommon on most routes. Some of the express routes, in fact, are known for commuter camaraderie, and riders have enjoyed bus-bound celebrations of anniversaries and birthdays. Some of the most interesting routes are the 16, connecting downtown Minneapolis and downtown St. Paul via the University of Minnesota and the State Capitol; the 21, linking Minneapolis' chic Uptown neighborhood, several St. Paul residential neighborhoods and downtown St. Paul; St. Paul's route 12, heading far out into the countryside east of the city; and Minneapolis' route 7, running through north Minneapolis and the city's warehouse district on the way, at some times of the day, to the Minneapolis-St. Paul International Airport. Compared with the buses in other large cities, the MCTO's fleet is very clean.

Six transit hubs in the Twin Cities — at Rosedale Center, Mall of America, downtown St. Paul, Plymouth Road, Louisiana Avenue and downtown Minneapolis — let riders make transfers and await their buses in climate-controlled comfort. Many streetside bus stops also have shelters that will keep the snow, sleet and rain off your head. You can recognize bus stops by the red sign with a "T" enclosed in a circle.

For commuters in outlying areas, the Park & Ride lots can be convenient. Sprinkled throughout the metro area, the 148 lots hold more than 7,000 cars and allow their occupants to easily hop aboard at a nearby bus stop.

OTHER PUBLIC BUS SERVICES

The MCTO claims the lion's share of bus passengers, but other smaller companies provide local transit, dial-a-ride trips and otherwise unavailable services.

Anoka County Transit	422-7088
Medicine Lake Bus Co.	545-9417
Carver Area Rural Transit	361-1631
Columbia Heights Shared Ride	782-2800
Dakota Area Referral and Transportation Service	455-1560
Dakota County Volunteer Transportation Services	450-2874
Hopkins Hop-A-Ride	935-8474
Human Services Inc. "Transporter" (Washington County)	777-5222
Maple Grove Transit System	420-4000
Minnesota Valley Transit Authority	431-4311
Mound Westonka Rides	472-0349
North Suburban Lines	784-7196
Northeast Suburban Transit	777-1872
Plymouth Metro Link	550-5072
Roseville Area Circulator	645-1959
St. Louis Park Emergency Program	925-4899
Scott County Transportation Program	496-8277
Senior Community Services (Minnetonka)	541-1019
Senior Community Services (Westonka)	472-0340
Senior Transportation Program (Champlin)	323-9017
Shakopee Area Transit	445-3650
Southwest Metro Transit Commission	949-8544
University of Minnesota Transit Service (Route 52)	625-9000
Lake (White Bear) Area Transit	770-1872

METRO MOBILITY
221-1928

As the Twin Cities' public transit service for people with disabilities who are unable to use regular route bus service, Metro Mobility operates a fleet of 150 vans specially designed to be comfortable and safe for disabled passengers and equipped with wheelchair lifts and tie-downs. The program provides door-to-door service, helping passengers through the first set of doors at both the pickup point and at the destination. About 100,000 riders make use of the service each month.

Riders can schedule their trips up to 14 days in advance by calling the number above. Fares and hours are similar to those for regular bus service.

Intercity Bus Service

GREYHOUND BUS STATIONS
29 N. Ninth St., Minneapolis   371-3323
25 W. Seventh St., St. Paul   222-0509

Greyhound (which began in Minnesota in the early decades of the century) and Jefferson Lines, a bus carrier that serves many towns throughout the Upper Midwest, share passenger stations in the Twin Cities. Neither one is the kind of place you'd want to visit all day, but they're clean and quiet as far as bus stations go. There are also suburban Greyhound pickup points in Anoka, Bloomington and Shakopee, as well as at the Minneapolis-St. Paul International Airport.

Train Service

AMTRAK TWIN CITIES PASSENGER STATION
730 Transfer Rd., St. Paul   644-1127

The Twin Cities are at mile 418 on the 2,209-mile route of the *Empire Builder*, running from Chicago's Union Station to Seattle. Other Minnesota cities with stops along the route are Winona, Red Wing, St. Cloud, Staples, and Detroit Lakes. Overall, though, Amtrak keeps a low profile in the Twin Cities, and few people use the train to get around.

Air Travel

MINNEAPOLIS/ST. PAUL INTERNATIONAL AIRPORT - WOLD CHAMBERLAIN FIELD
Near Bloomington at I-494 and
Minn. 5 intersection   726-8100

Even beyond the transatlantic heroics of Charles Lindbergh (who grew up in Little Falls, Minnesota, about an hour's drive north of the Twin Cities), aviation has a distinguished history in the region. In 1926 the Twin Cities-based Northwest Airways (now Northwest Airlines) won the government's air mail contract and began using the only hangar within an abandoned car race track that had been converted to an air field three years before, south of Minneapolis-St. Paul. Northwest inaugurated passenger service in 1929, and the airport's rapid growth was on. Soon the U.S. Weather Bureau opened a station there, a control tower rose over the field, and paved runways replaced the grass strips. The airport took its present ungainly name in 1948 (Ernest Wold and Cyrus Chamberlain were early Minnesota aviators killed in France during World War I).

To this day, the airport is dominated by the presence of Northwest, which uses it as a major hub. During a recent year, the airline accounted for 77 percent of all the passenger boardings. Nineteen other major and regional airlines also serve the airport, along with an additional 35 charter and cargo carriers. Each year, the airport serves 21 million passengers bound

Hennepin County alone spends about $2 million annually to clear snow from roads and apply salt to streets.

Insiders' Tips

Downtown St. Paul skyway.

Photo: Mark Morson, Pioneer Press

for 100 domestic and 13 international nonstop destinations. The Hubert H. Humphrey Terminal, a separate facility on 34th Avenue S. that handles charter and international flights, is linked with the main terminal (called the Lindbergh Terminal) by a shuttle bus that runs frequently.

Outside of rush-hour times, it takes about 20 minutes to drive to the airport from either downtown Minneapolis or downtown St. Paul. Bus service is available on five MCTO lines (call 373-3333 for schedule information), but none has luggage racks. The taxi stand is across the street from the baggage pickup area; a cab fare into town could run as high as $30, although the average fare is around $20. Airport Express, 726-6400, provides van transportation to downtown Minneapolis, downtown St. Paul and many suburbs, and other companies connect the airport with towns outside the Twin Cities.

Recent improvements have made parking more pleasant. An enclosed skyway joins the parking ramp with the main terminal. Options include short-term, general, valet and long-term parking (the latter available in the EconoLot just north of the Humphrey Terminal). All areas have handicapped parking, and people with disabilities can use the valet parking at general parking rates.

ST. PAUL DOWNTOWN AIRPORT
644 Bayfield St., St. Paul   224-4306

This airport, just minutes from downtown St. Paul and also known as Holman Field, is becoming increasingly popular among business and corporate travelers. It has a new 6,700-foot runway, a restaurant and catering facilities. The airport also offers fuel service, no tie-down fees in front of the main terminal and transportation into town via taxis and rental cars.

OTHER AIRPORTS
Several other airports handle the Twin Cities' business and general aviation needs. These include:
- Flying Cloud Airport in Eden Prairie, 941-3545
- Crystal Airport in Minneapolis' northern suburbs, 537-2058

• Anoka County/Blaine
Airport, 786-9490
• Lake Elmo Airport, 777-6300
• AirLake Airport near
Lakeville, 469-4040.

Pedals and Spokes

Minnesotans bicycle at nearly twice the national average, and our 4.3 bikes per capita leads the country. Many of the hearty pedalers use their bikes to commute to work and just generally get around. Even in the dead of winter, it's not unusual to see a helmeted and bundled cyclist atop a pair of spinning wheels, wrapped head to toe in protective garb, peering out from a narrow scarf opening. Aside from their penchant for riding on sidewalks along busy streets, they're a welcome sight.

The city of Minneapolis recently gave bicycle commuting a huge boost by creating 93 blocks of on-street bike lanes downtown, including a specially graded set of lanes that barrels right down the middle of main drag Hennepin Avenue. Plans are underway to connect the 53 miles of bike trails in Minneapolis to St. Paul and metro-area suburbs by filling the gaps between existing trails. A new 3.8-mile bicycle and walking trail, running from Minn. Highway 100 in St. Louis Park to downtown Minneapolis, opened in 1995. In addition, new bike paths will soon accommodate University of Minnesota commuters. While some of the new paths will be dedicated solely to cyclists, others will run along city streets

in designated bike lanes. For information on using a bike to commute, contact the Minnesota Extension Service Bicycle Program at 625-5737.

In 1994 Metropolitan Council Transit Operations began a new program to rent bicycle lockers to people who want to commute with their bikes in conjunction with bus trips. The lockers are placed throughout the Twin Cities at Park & Ride lots and other areas where bus traffic is heavy. Each location has four to six lockers available for rent seasonally or annually. Rental rates are $5 monthly plus a refundable deposit. For more information, call Minnesota Rideshare at 349-RIDE.

For decades, Minnesota has been a leader in the development of off-the-road bike trails. An extensive bike path system is a renowned feature of the Minneapolis parks system; its 38 miles of linked bike paths provide views of city lakes, downtown, Minnehaha Creek and Minnehaha Falls and the Mississippi River. St. Paul offers 5 miles of paved trails at Hidden Falls-Crosby Farm Regional Park and the 17-mile Gateway Trail starting at Arlington Avenue and I-35E north of downtown. In addition, many of the Hennepin Park reserves, including Baker Park Reserve, Carver Park Reserve, Cleary Lake Regional Park, Elm Creek Park Reserve and Hyland Park Reserve, each contain 3 to 9 miles of bike paths, and the 7-mile North Hennepin Trail Corridor connects Elm Creek Park Reserve with Coon Rapids Dam Regional Park.

The movie *Airport* was filmed at Minneapolis-St. Paul International Airport.

Insiders' Tips

Finally, one of Minnesota's fabulous state bike trails, developed by the Department of Natural Resources, lies within the Twin Cities area. The Luce Line Trail, built along a 30-mile-long former railbed, connects Plymouth with the town of Winsted. Following a route used long ago by Dakota Indians, it skirts tree groves, pastures, lake beaches and farmland. You can find its Plymouth trailhead on Vicksburg Lane between county roads 6 and 15.

Color maps outlining bicycle routes throughout the Twin Cities and the entire state are available from the map sale office of the Minnesota Department of Transportation, 395 John Ireland Boulevard, St. Paul, 296-2216.

On Foot Via the Skyways

Visitors to Minneapolis and St. Paul stare up at them in amazement, searching for the right word to describe them. Some newcomers try to call them "bridges," "connectors" or "walkways." One or two even try to call them "tunnels," which is emphatically wrong. They are, in fact, skyways — enclosed, second-story sidewalks that link most of the major buildings in the two downtowns.

For more than 40 years they've crisscrossed the sky above our heads. The first Twin Cities skyway was built in the mid '50s in St. Paul and connected the old Golden Rule department store to a parking ramp. That first proposal to build an enclosed elevated pedestrian bridge was so unusual that the St. Paul City Council had to pass a special resolution enabling its construction. In 1962 the first Minneapolis skyway was built across Marquette Avenue to connect the Northstar Center and the old Northwestern National Bank Building in Minneapolis. Skyways have forever altered the dynamics and atmosphere of Minneapolis and St. Paul. Many of the healthiest retail establishments in the downtowns are now on the skyway-served second floors, and buildings have to deal with the benefits and problems of essentially having two main floors. In both cities, landlords often charge higher rents for skyway-level space than for first-floor space. During the cold season, when people most heavily use the climate-controlled skyways, the street-level foot traffic can dwindle to practically nothing.

As a result, many of the sights and sounds of street life have moved upstairs. The skyways have their own beat police officers, musical buskers strumming their hearts out for quarters, flower stands, Salvation Army bell-ringers and even parades.

St. Paul eventually began its own skyways, and they now cover about 4 miles, making it the world's largest publicly owned system. It connects department stores, office buildings, apartment and condo residences, and parking ramps.

In Minneapolis, the system is actually larger, but each skyway is separately owned and maintained by building owners. Via skyway you can avoid the frigid winds that hurtle through the downtown

Insiders' Tips

Locals pronounce "Nicollet" like "Nick-o-let" — to the dismay of francophiles everywhere.

canyons, and travel all the way from the municipal parking ramps on the north end of downtown to the Minneapolis Convention Center — a distance of 12 blocks. Along the way, you'll pass through (or have the opportunity to pass through) virtually every building of importance in the downtown core. Minneapolis' busiest skyway, the one spanning Marquette Avenue from the IDS Center to the Baker Building, carries something like 20,000 people each day.

In both cities, the skyway hours vary somewhat, depending on the hours of the buildings they connect. But most open early in the morning and remain navigable into the evening.

Additions to the systems are built every few months, as a new building rises or a structure undergoes renovation. You can find the most up-to-date skyway maps in the Minneapolis and St. Paul editions of the *Skyway News*, a weekly publication (available free in downtown racks) that serves as the community newspapers of the downtowns.

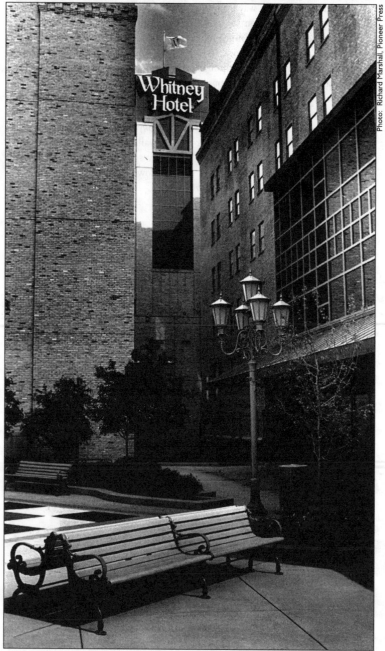

Photo: Richard Marshall, Pioneer Press

Whitney Hotel, a converted flour mill, in the Minneapolis riverfront area.

Inside
Accommodations

"To sleep, perchance to dream."

A good hotel room is a traveler's necessity that too often is simply taken for granted. But that's as it should be.

The best hotels are hospitable yet non-intrusive, quiet and serviceable — like a good pair of shoes.

But, just as squeaky soles or pinched toes can ruin one's day, so too can thin walls, a lumpy bed or sourpuss desk clerk spoil even the most well-planned vacation or business trip.

Travelers to the Twin Cities needn't despair of finding good-quality lodging in a range of price brackets. Downtown Minneapolis alone has around 4,500 hotel rooms, boosting its position as a magnet for national conventions.

While hotels are less numerous in downtown St. Paul, those that are there are as fine as can be found in any major U.S. city — most notably the peerless St. Paul Hotel and the St. Paul Radisson.

The southern suburb of Bloomington, home to the Mall of America and close neighbor to the Minneapolis/St. Paul International Airport, is teeming with convenient and comfortable hotels and motels, all within a stone's throw of a major freeway and, therefore, minutes from any Twin Cities attraction.

Many business travelers opt for suburban hotels, because many corporate headquarters have moved to the suburbs and suburban lodgings offer free parking, a rarity in the cities.

Here's a listing of the major hotels, motels, inns and bed and breakfasts in the Twin Cities, broken down into geographical areas. The rates quoted here do not include hotel tax, which is 12 percent in Minneapolis and Bloomington, 13 percent in St. Paul.

Room rates (double occupancy) are indicated as follows:

Less than $75	$
$75 to $95	$$
$95 to $115	$$$
$115 to $150	$$$$
More than $150	$$$$$

Hotels and Motels

Minneapolis

CROWN PLAZA NORTHSTAR
618 Second Ave. S.   338-2288
$$

The Crown Plaza Northstar, built above a six-story parking ramp, may be hard to locate, but it's worth the search. This high-quality, 17-story hotel with 224 rooms underwent a $4 million renovation last year. The result is a lush, rich look of deep greens, burgundies, dark woods and Victorian accents. Several floors for nonsmokers were created as part of the overhaul. This is the home of an award-winning restaurant. While the hotel has no on-site pool, guests have access to the pool in the nearby Minneapolis Club via an underground tunnel. The hotel offers several package deals.

CROWN STERLING SUITES

425 S. Seventh St.   *333-3111*
$$$$

For those who feel cramped in the conventional hotel room, this facility offers expansive suites comprising a living room, bedroom and small kitchen area with a refrigerator, a microwave and a wet bar. Each suite also has two TVs and two telephones. Guests are served a complimentary cooked-to-order breakfast in the hotel's atrium area. Recreational facilities include an indoor pool, a sauna, a steam room and a weight-lifting area, plus guest privileges at the nearby Arena Athletic Club for a nominal extra charge. This six-story hotel has 218 suites and, for fine dining at a reasonable price, the on-premises Cornell's Restaurant.

MINNEAPOLIS HILTON HOTEL AND TOWERS

1001 Marquette Ave., Minneapolis   *376-1000*
$$$$

From it crystal chandeliers and fine wallpaper to the handsome bronze statue that graces its lobby, the Minneapolis Hilton has brought a touch of luxury and elegance to the Minneapolis hospitality scene. Frequent patrons praise its "New York feel." Built in 1992, this huge facility has 814 guest rooms, including 51 suites, an in-house health club with a swimming pool, two acclaimed restaurants and 43,000 feet of retail and specialty shops. Primarily a conventioneer's hotel, the Hilton has several large meeting rooms and a 2,500-square-foot ballroom. Special attention is paid to guests who stay on the concierge level, where each room has a fax machine. Skyways connect the hotel to the nearby Minneapolis Convention Center and Nicollet Mall stores.

HOLIDAY INN-METRODOME

1500 Washington Ave. S.   *333-4646*
$$$

This local branch of the national chain is in Minneapolis' Seven Corners area and within walking distance of several theaters, such as Theater in the Round and Mixed Blood, not to mention nightlife from blues bars to folk houses. You have a choice of a handful of good restaurants within a block of this hotel, plus the Holiday Inn's own Grill Room. Hotel amenities here include a small indoor pool, whirlpool, sauna and exercise room. The famous Hubert H. Humphrey Metrodome is six blocks away, and the Nicollet Mall is eight more beyond that. (Hint: Ask for a "great rate" special.) The hotel has 265 rooms on 14 stories.

HYATT REGENCY MINNEAPOLIS

1300 Nicollet Mall   *370-1234*
$$$$ *(800) 233-1234*

This luxury hotel in the heart of downtown has 532 comfortable rooms and 21 suites with city views, complimentary HBO and cable news. Some rooms are grouped on nonsmoking floors. A nice extra here is the Regency Athletic Club, a private athletic facility with enclosed tennis and racquetball courts, a running track, weight room, sauna and Jacuzzi, which hotel guests may use for a nomi-

Insiders' Tips

Be forewarned: St. Paul hotels may be booked to capacity in mid-March during state hockey and basketball tournaments. Plan ahead.

Burnsville
MINNESOTA

CONVENTION & VISITORS BUREAU

We're bursting with exciting things to do and see when you visit Mpls./St. Paul...Mall of America and more! Burnsville offers lower room tax rates, comfortable surroundings and friendly, hometown atmosphere.
Burnsville hotels and motels provide 700 rooms, close to all the fun!
Call or write today for your free Burnsville visitors guide and lodging discount coupons.

Burnsville
Convention & Visitors Bureau
101 West Burnsville Parkway, Suite 150
Burnsville, MN 55337

1-612-435-6000
or 1-800-521-6055 (Toll Free)

STPP

nal daily fee. All guests have access to a large on-premises swimming pool.

The Hyatt is also home to three good restaurants: Manny's Steakhouse, Pronto (Italian fare) and Taxxi (American bistro), plus Spike's sports bar. The Hyatt is near the Minneapolis Convention Center (via the skyway), Nicollet Mall shops and Orchestra Hall.

For a "luxury-level rate," guest amenities include a private lounge, an honor bar, a complimentary continental breakfast and refreshments. The Hyatt offers discounts for AAA members, senior citizens and convention groups and runs frequent specials, especially on weekends. City-run parking ramps are nearby.

HOTEL LUXEFORD SUITES
1101 LaSalle Ave.   *332-6800*
$$

Oriental vases, classical columns and elegant furniture fill the small lobby of this cozy, all-suites hotel. Each of the 230 suites contains a sitting room (with a queen-size sleeper-sofa), a bedroom, kitchenette, phone and TV. The hotel offers discounts to AAA members and runs

frequent specials. Guests also have access to an in-house fitness center with whirlpool and sauna. Cafe Luxeford, on the main floor, specializes in live jazz by local and nationally known musicians.

THE MARQUETTE
Seventh St. and Marquette Ave.   *332-2351*
$$$$

President Clinton slept here during a whistle-stop visit in 1994. The 19-story luxury hotel, part of the Hilton International chain, has 277 rooms, including 13 suites. The Marquette is in the IDS building, Minneapolis' tallest skyscraper, and, because of the building's design, all rooms are corner rooms, with about 20 percent more space than the average hotel room. Amenities include steam baths in some rooms and basic cable TV in all rooms. Guests may use the fifth-floor workout facility, sans pool.

The hotel restaurant is moderately priced Basil's, specializing in traditional fare — from Angus beef to specialty pizzas — prepared with fresh herbs. There's also a ritzy bar, the Mark 7. Discount room rate packages are available.

MARRIOTT CITY CENTER

30 S. Seventh St.   *349-4000*
$$$$

The Marriott, a deluxe hotel above the bustling City Center indoor shopping complex, offers 584 rooms, including suites, in 31 stories. There's also an on-premises health club with hot tub, sauna and weight rooms, but no swimming pool. For those who simply can't be separated from Ma Bell, some rooms have phones in the bathroom. Hotel restaurants are Gustino's, featuring singing waiters and Northern Italian fare, and Papaya's, for family dining. An advantage to staying here — apart from the sheer indulgence — is the proximity to downtown shopping via the skyway system. The Cinnebar Lounge is a pleasant hotel bar. The Marriott offers a special weekend package.

NICOLLET ISLAND INN

95 Merriam St., Nicollet Island   *331-1800*
$$$

This classy, cozy 24-room inn on an island in the Mississippi River is only a block from downtown, yet in atmosphere it's worlds removed. Built in an old sash and door factory, the Inn boasts an award-winning gourmet restaurant, awesome river views, individually decorated rooms (some with four-poster beds), a roaring fireplace in the lobby and charm aplenty. You'll never want to go home! The Inn offers several getaway packages.

MINNEAPOLIS REGAL

1313 Nicollet Ave.   *332-0371*
$-$$$$

A midsize, 14-story hotel near the Minneapolis Convention Center, the Regal has an indoor pool, a Jacuzzi, sauna and 325 rooms, including suites. Group discounts and packages are available. George's in the Park, a restaurant and bar, is on the premises, and several restaurants and cultural and shopping venues are within a few blocks.

RADISSON PLAZA

35 S. Seventh St.   *339-4900*
$$$$

A Minneapolis landmark, this flagship hotel of the locally owned Radisson chain was virtually rebuilt in the 1980s, and the result is an elegant, grand hotel with amenities for the 20th-century traveler. The Radisson is in a prime shopping locale, next-door to Dayton's and within easy walking distance to the Conservatory, City Center and Gaviidae Common. A stunning focal point in the lobby is a huge marble ball suspended on a fountain. Tucked away on the third floor is Festival, a top-notch restaurant with an adjoining intimate, hushed bar, where you can escape the madding crowd.

Rooms are designed for business executives, with generous desks and bedside and bathroom phones. There's an on-site fitness center with classes and aerobic and weight-training equipment. Ask about special package deals. Higher rates apply to the hotel's upper three floors which comprise the Plaza Club. Here, guests stay in more luxurious rooms and receive complimentary drinks and continental breakfast.

WHITNEY HOTEL

150 Portland Ave.   *339-9300*
$$$$ *(800) 248-1879*

A stately lobby with a spiral staircase and a grand piano sets the tone for this elegant hotel near the banks of the Mississippi. First-class meals are served in the intimate Whitney Grill or outdoors on the Garden Plaza. The Whitney has 94 richly decorated rooms and 40 suites in its eight stories. Some suites are bilevel,

Photo: Joe Oden, Pioneer Press

Thorwood Inn in Hastings.

with spiral staircases and breathtaking views of the Mississippi. If you want to pull out all the stops, rent the three-bedroom penthouse with two living rooms, a grand piano, fireplaces, whirlpools and a deck overlooking the river — it goes for a mere $1,500 a night. Five private meeting rooms provide an elegant setting for meetings or dinners for up to 200 people. The hotel also offers several weekend package deals.

BEST WESTERN REGENCY PLAZA
41 N. 10th St.   *339-9311*
$

This no-nonsense downtown motel has more than 200 rooms, an indoor pool, a whirlpool, Harrigan's restaurant and coffee shop and, best of all, free parking. This motel isn't as centrally located as the other hotels, but for the price it's a good deal. And you can take the free shuttle service to a variety of downtown destinations.

BEST WESTERN NORMANDY INN
405 S. Eighth St.   *370-1400*
$

This smaller (160-room) motor hotel

looks like a Swiss chalet from the outside, yet on the inside offers all the modern amenities, including a swimming pool, whirlpool and sauna. Pets are allowed in rooms. Your room rate includes free parking. Some package deals are available. A dining room, coffee shop and bar/lounge are on-site.

SHERATON METRODOME
1330 Industrial Blvd.   *331-1900*
$$$

Don't let the name fool you. This hotel is a full 15 minutes by car from the Metrodome. If you don't mind the drive, you'll find this a pleasant hostelry with 254 rooms, an indoor pool, a whirlpool and a sauna. The hotel's Anchorage Restaurant is a very popular dining destination among locals. Weekend packages are available.

St. Paul and Suburbs

The hotel rates quoted below do not include the 13 percent hotel tax that is levied in St. Paul.

St. Paul Hotel

350 Market St.   292-9292

$$$$

The St. Paul, a highly acclaimed grand old hotel overlooking Rice Park, the historic Landmark Center and the Ordway Music Theatre, is *the* place to stay for that special occasion. This highly rated 254-room St. Paul hotel offers the traveling business executive modern amenities in a setting of Old World charm. The deluxe rooms and suites are all elegantly appointed with artwork and upholstered chairs and settees, and some contain big old armoires (just like Grandma's) and queen-size four-poster beds.

Why not pull out all the stops and conduct your next sales meeting in the Park Suite, furnished with a comfortable sitting area and a stunning walnut dining/meeting table for eight? The suite has a separate room for sleeping and terry bathrobes to make you feel right at home.

Though the hotel has no health club on premises, exercise equipment can be brought to your room. Just check with the concierge. The St. Paul also has seven large-function rooms that accommodate up to 260 people for meetings and 380 for banquets. The hotel's St. Paul Grill, with its clubby dark-wood atmosphere, walls lined with historic photos, gourmet cuisine and park views, is one of the best restaurants in the Twin Cities. The Cafe, on the lower level, is an upbeat eatery with a fun touch: a huge chalkboard wall detailing all the week's doings in the Saintly City. The hotel is linked, via above-ground skyways, to an extensive array of downtown restaurants, shops and museums. Ask about the weekend packages. Parking is available for a nominal daily rate.

The Radisson Hotel St. Paul

11 E. Kellogg Blvd.   292-1900

$$

Overlooking the Mississippi, the 22-story Radisson encompasses 475 elegantly appointed rooms, including luxurious suites and cabana rooms adjacent to the indoor garden court and Olympic-size pool. The popular top-floor Le Carousel Restaurant slowly revolves, affording an unforgettable panoramic view of the city

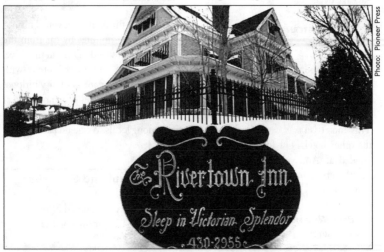

Photo: Pioneer Press

The Rivertown Inn in Stillwater.

Stay a Little Closer to Home

At the Hawthorn Suites Hotel-Edina your business is our pleasure. Our boardroom and meeting facilities can accommodate groups up to 50 people. They are perfect for interviews or small meetings.
Hawthorn Suites features:

- Two-room suites with living room and bedroom
- Fully equipped kitchen
- 2 TV's with video cassette player
- Complimentary hot breakfast buffet daily
- General Manager's reception (M-Th) with complimentary hors d'oeuvres, beer, wine & soft drinks
- Daily maid service
- Convenient in-house laundry facilities
- Complimentary airport shuttle

Best of all, we are connected to America's first indoor landscape park, with ice skating, pool, track, gym, amphitheater, children's playground and more.
Whether you stay for a few nights or a few months, we know you'll feel "at home" with us!
Conveniently located I-494 and France Ave.
3400 Edinborough Way • Edina, MN 55435

CALL FOR RESERVATIONS
(612) 893-9300 (800) 527-1133

HAWTHORN
SUITES
H O T E L
Edina
At Edinborough Park

and the Mighty Mississippi. Those booking a two-room executive suite receive a complimentary breakfast, newspaper and evening cocktails. A popular convention hotel, the Radisson offers flexible spaces for any type of business meeting or social gathering, including a simply grand ballroom with glittering chandeliers. The hotel is linked, via skyway, to the shops and cultural venues of downtown St. Paul.

BEST WESTERN KELLY INN
161 St. Anthony Blvd.   227-8711
$$

Politicians wheel and deal here in the dark and intimate Capitol Lounge or bustling Benjamin's restaurant. If only the walls could talk! This is a popular hostelry for government employees and lobbyists mainly because of its location almost in the front yard of the State Capitol. Over the past year, the Kelly Inn has remodeled its 125 rooms in pleasing shades of mauve and green. Other features include a large, pleasant indoor pool, whirlpool, sauna and children's pool. And it's easy to reach — just off the Marion Street exit of I-94.

CROWN STERLING SUITES
175 E. 10th St.   224-5400
$$$$

A Mediterranean villa transplanted to the snow country — that's the atmosphere at the Crown Sterling Suites of St. Paul. The interior is a huge atrium teeming with tropical plants, waterfalls, a gazebo and dining area. Eight floors of suites, adorned with tons of wrought iron and hanging plants, surround this tropical garden. You may feel like you're at a theme ride in Disney World. Actually, it all comes together to create a sunny, pleasant getaway.

The two-room suites, 210 in all, are contemporary in style and tastefully decorated in light woods and modern fabrics. Each has two TVs, two phones, separate sleeping and living quarters and a small kitchenette with microwave, coffeemaker and refrigerator. A made-to-order complimentary breakfast is included with the room. Work off breakfast with a dip in the indoor pool or nearby whirlpool and sauna. Fine dining is offered at Woolley's Restaurant and Lounge. Each floor has an executive conference suite for business meetings, and the large ballroom accommodates meetings and seminars.

DAYS INN CIVIC CENTER

175 W. Seventh St.   292-8929
$

A stone's throw from the St. Paul Civic Center and the Ordway Music Theatre, this serviceable, clean 205-room facility offers a double-occupancy room rate that's very affordable. Dining is available in Foster's lounge and cafe. Pets are accepted in rooms.

And coming soon . . .

A new 252-room Radisson Inn is slated to open in the spring of 1996 at the Town Square shopping/office complex in downtown St. Paul. The hotel will be on Minnesota Street between Seventh and Sixth streets. For more information, call the St. Paul Convention and Visitors Bureau, 297-6985.

Another new wrinkle in the St. Paul hospitality scene is the Covington Inn, slated to open in late 1995 or early '96. Housed in a 1946 towboat off Harriet Island (just across Old Miss from downtown), the Covington will be a floating bed and breakfast inn with three staterooms, a two-story suite and a restaurant called the No Wake Cafe. For more information, call 292-1411.

Other St. Paul Area Hotels

BEST WESTERN MAPLEWOOD INN

1780 E. County Rd. D
Maplewood   770-2811
$$

Shopaholics, take note! Maplewood Mall, a large suburban shopping center, is right across the street from this motel, which caters mostly to tourists and families. Kids will love splashing in the indoor pool. There's also a sauna, whirlpool, game room, Nickelby's restaurant and Nick's lounge. Nick's hosts the Totally Bonkers Comedy Club Thursdays through Saturdays, to which guests receive free tickets.

COUNTRY INN BY CARLSON-WOODBURY

6003 Hudson Rd.   739-7300
$$

True to its name, this new 158-room motel serves up country charm, from hardwood floors to quilted comforters. Features include the on-premises Green Mill restaurant-lounge, indoor pool, saunas, game room, free parking and free HBO.

HOLIDAY INN-EAST

2201 Burns Ave.   731-2220
$$

A favorite hostelry for traveling executives visiting nearby 3M headquarters, the Holiday Inn-East has 192 rooms and all the usual amenities, including an indoor pool, a sauna, whirlpool, exercise area, game room, restaurant, bar, gift shop and laundromat. This motor lodge is 10 minutes from downtown St. Paul. For a few bucks more, you can qualify for the executive level, which comes with a private lounge, refreshments, complimentary breakfast and newspaper, and speedy checkout.

HOLIDAY INN EXPRESS

1010 Bandana Blvd. W.   647-1637
$$

Built in an old railroad repair shop, this colorful 109-room motel has tracks running through the lobby and is connected via skyway to the Bandana Square shopping center. The hotel has an indoor pool, a wading pool, whirlpool and sauna.

Visiting the Twin Cities? Enjoy Eagan Hospitality!

Fun attractions, fine dining and excellent accommodations— call toll-free 1-800-EAGAN-20 for your free brochure and coupon book.

EAGAN
CONVENTION
AND VISITORS BUREAU

612-452-9872
1380 Corporate Center Curve
Suite 116
Eagan, MN 55121

Guests receive a complimentary continental breakfast.

SHERATON MIDWAY

400 Hamline Ave. N.   *642-1234*
$$$

Near I-94 and within minutes of both Twin Cities' downtowns, this 197-room motor hotel has an indoor pool, a whirlpool, sauna and exercise area, TV, complimentary coffee, Bigelow's restaurant and a bar. Ask about the "best-value" rate, based on availability.

ST. PAUL RAMADA HOTEL

1870 Old Hudson Rd.   *735-2330*
$

Just 10 minutes east of downtown St. Paul, off I-94, the St. Paul Ramada has an attractive sunlit indoor pool area and a casual ambiance. This is a refreshingly unpretentious, 200-room strip motel with meeting rooms for business conferences and social gatherings. A pleasant surprise is Summerfield's Restaurant and Lounge, where you can sip a drink next to a roaring open-hearth fireplace.

South Suburbs

BEST WESTERN SEVILLE PLAZA HOTEL

8151 Bridge Rd., Bloomington   *830-1300*
$

Situated on the intersection of Highway 100 and I-494, the Spanish-themed Seville has an indoor pool, a whirlpool and sauna, a restaurant and a lounge.

BEST WESTERN THUNDERBIRD HOTEL

2201 78th St. E., Bloomington   *854-3411*
$$

This hotel has 263 rooms and suites and an extensive collection of Native American handiwork and artifacts. Guests can use the indoor and outdoor pools, exercise facilities and a game room and restaurant and catch some live music in the Totem Pole restaurant and lounge. The Mall of America is right in the backyard.

BEST WESTERN YANKEE SQUARE INN

3450 Washington Dr., Eagan   *452-0100*
$

Convenient to the Minnesota Zoo and other south suburban attractions, this 108-

room motel offers a very reasonable room rate, whirlpool, sauna, exercise room, breakfast cafe and free shuttle service to the airport. Guests who are fitness buffs also receive a complimentary pass to a nearby health club.

BLOOMINGTON SUPER 8 MOTEL
7800 S. Second Ave.
Bloomington   888-8800
$

This basic motel offers a whirlpool and sauna, cable TV and complimentary coffee. There is no restaurant on premises, though several good ones are nearby.

BRADBURY SUITES BEST WESTERN
7770 Johnson Ave., Bloomington   893-9999
$$

This hotel, on the corner of I-494 and France Avenue, offers 126 corporate suites (large rooms with a divider between the sleeping and sitting areas). They also are equipped with refrigerators. Microwave ovens are available for guest use on the first and sixth floors. The hotel does not have a swimming pool.

COMFORT INN-AIRPORT
1321 E. 78th St., Bloomington   854-3400
$$

Minutes from the airport and Mall of America, the Comfort Inn is an attractive, moderately priced hotel offering free mall shuttle service, an indoor pool, exercise area, free HBO and a restaurant and lounge. In the special king-size rooms, you'll find a touch of home — a comfy recliner!

COUNTRY INN & SUITES
2221 Killebrew Dr., Bloomington   854-5555
$$$$

Taking a hint from the bed and breakfast inn movement, the Country Inn has incorporated such homey touches as

hardwood floors and floral wreaths in the decorating scheme for its 140 rooms and also offers a free continental-plus breakfast, local newspaper, local phone calls and a shuttle to the Mall of America, across the street. Some rooms also have whirlpools, microwaves and coffeemakers. A TGI Friday's is on the premises.

CROWN STERLING SUITES-AIRPORT
7901 34th Ave. S., Bloomington   854-1000
$$$$

The lobby of this all-suites hotel opens onto a skylit indoor courtyard accented with brick pillars, lush greenery and fountains. The hotel also has an indoor pool, a sauna, whirlpool, restaurant and bar. Each of the two-room suites contains a refrigerator, microwave, coffeemaker, two TVs and two phones. Guests receive a cooked-to-order complimentary breakfast.

DAYS INN AIRPORT
1901 Killebrew Dr., Bloomington   854-8400
$$$$

This motor lodge has an indoor pool and free shuttle to the airport and Mall of America, which is right across the street.

EMBASSY SUITES BLOOMINGTON
2800 W. 80th St., Bloomington   884-4811
$$$$

Like others in the chain, this all-suites hotel offers a lovely open atrium lobby/dining area, two-room suites with two phones, two TVs and a kitchenette with coffeemaker. Guests receive a free full breakfast and complimentary cocktails.

EXEL INN
2701 E. 78th St., Bloomington   854-7200
$ (800) 356-8013

So close to the Mall of America you can almost smell the bargains, this basic motel offers reasonable rates plus a free continental breakfast. Combination mi-

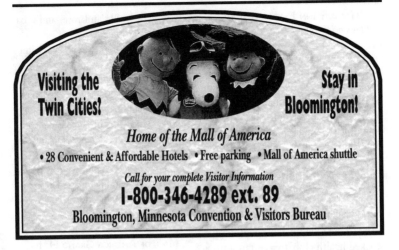

Visiting the Twin Cities?

Stay in Bloomington!

Home of the Mall of America

• 28 Convenient & Affordable Hotels • Free parking • Mall of America shuttle

Call for your complete Visitor Information

1-800-346-4289 ext. 89

Bloomington, Minnesota Convention & Visitors Bureau

crowave-refrigerators are available for a nominal charge.

FAIRFIELD INN

2401 E. 80th St., Bloomington   858-8475
$$

This new facility offers 134 comfortable rooms, free continental breakfast, swimming pool and whirlpool, plus free shuttle service to the Mall. There is no restaurant on premises.

FANTASUITE HOTEL

250 N. River Ridge Center   890-9550
Burnsville   (800) 666-7829
$-$$$$

Live out your wildest fantasies in theme rooms ranging from Arabian Nights, Sherwood Forest and Le Cave to Jungle Safari and Space Odyssey, among others. Conventional rooms and whirlpool suites are also available. The hotel has an indoor/outdoor pool complex and whirlpool.

HAMPTON INN-BLOOMINGTON

4201 W. 80th St., Bloomington   835-6643
$

This inn offers a very competitive rate, free deluxe continental breakfast, sports bar/grill and an adjacent Denny's restaurant. If you're here on business, meeting rooms are available. Some rooms have private balconies. It's 3.5 miles from the Mall of America.

HAWTHORN SUITES HOTEL

3400 Edinborough Way, Edina   893-9300
$$$

This hotel contains 142 one-bedroom suites with separate living rooms and complete kitchens. Guests enjoy a free hot buffet breakfast and have access to lovely indoor Edinborough Park and free use of its pool, track and ice rink. The Mall of America bus stops here.

HOLIDAY INN EXPRESS MPLS.-AIRPORT

814 E. 79th St., Bloomington   854-5558
$

Both standard rooms and suites with fridges are found at the Holiday Inn Express. This newly remodeled, limited-service hotel offers a free continental breakfast buffet and free shuttle service to Mall of America and the airport. There is no pool.

HOLIDAY INN EXPRESS-EAGAN
1940 Rahncliff Court, Eagan   681-9266
$$

Five minutes from the Minnesota Zoo and Mall of America, this moderately priced hotel offers 70 rooms (some with whirlpools) and 10 whirlpool suites, complimentary breakfast buffet and an indoor pool. For a nominal fee you can take a shuttle to the Mall of America.

HOLIDAY INN INTERNATIONAL
3 Appletree Sq., Bloomington   854-9000
$$$

This deluxe 431-room, 13-story hotel boasts an Olympic-size pool, a well-stocked health club, two restaurants, a lounge, gift shop and free shuttle service to the airport and Mall of America. The hotel also has extensive convention facilities. Come January, you'll appreciate the hotel's covered parking! To reach the hotel, take the 34th Avenue Exit south off Interstate 494 and watch for the sign.

HOLIDAY INN-MINNEAPOLIS AIRPORT
2700 Pilot Knob Rd., Eagan   454-3434
$$$

Here you'll find all the usual Holiday Inn amenities in 187 rooms and suites. The hotel has a full-service restaurant and lounge, not to mention an indoor pool, exercise room and shuttles to the airport and the Megamall.

HOTEL SOFITEL
5601 78th St. W., Bloomington   835-1900
$$$$

Vive le France! This elegant six-story French hotel, one of the classiest in Bloomington, has 287 lovely (recently remodeled) rooms and suites surrounding an atrium lobby filled with fresh flowers and elegant furniture. Other niceties include a pool and health spa, turndown service with truffle and rose, and a baguette as a parting gift.

This hotel is home to three acclaimed French restaurants: Chez Colette for hearty provincial fare; Le Cafe Royal for haute cuisine; and La Terrasse for casual dining (with some summertime outdoor seating). Not to be missed is the hotel's delightful gift shop for all that's French, fun and fanciful! The hotel's Executive Meeting Center offers spacious conference rooms with adjacent private dining rooms. The Grand Ballroom accommodates up to 500. Weekend packages are available.

MALL OF AMERICA GRAND HOTEL
7901 24th Ave. S., Bloomington   854-2244
$$$$ (800) 222-8733

After a long day of shopping, relax and put your feet up in a luxury room at the 15-story Mall of America Grand Hotel, formerly The Registry Hotel. Across the highway from America's largest mall, this deluxe hotel offers free mall and airport shuttle service. Its 322 rooms (including six suites) come equipped with alarm clocks and color TVs with Showtime, ESPN and in-room movies. The hotel has an indoor heated pool, whirlpool, sauna and full-service exercise room, as well as a lively lounge-bar for dancing. At the new Nine-Mile Grill, guests can enjoy a casual but classy dining experience.

If you really want to pamper yourself, spring for a room on the Concierge Floors (14 and 15), where you can relax in a private lounge that affords one of the best views of the Twin Cities' skyline and enjoy complimentary cocktails, hors d'oeuvres and a continental breakfast. The hotel also has a 5,568-square-foot ballroom, a 2,800-square-foot Grand Salon and seven small conference rooms for business meetings and conventions.

MINNEAPOLIS AIRPORT MARRIOTT

2020 E. 79th St., Bloomington   854-7441
$$$

This deluxe, full-service, 478-room hotel has an indoor pool, a health club, whirlpool, the Fairfield Inn restaurant, Pitchers sports bar and a gift shop. If you really want to live it up, stay in one of the suites or rooms on the luxurious concierge level, where you'll have a private lounge, complimentary breakfast and newspaper and evening hors d'oeuvres. Every guest enjoys complimentary shuttle service to the Mall of America and the airport.

MINNEAPOLIS/ST. PAUL AIRPORT HILTON

3800 80th St. E., Bloomington   854-2100
$$$

A business-oriented hotel offering state-of-the-art audio/visual support for meetings, the Airport Hilton also features an indoor pool and health club, casual and fine-dining restaurants and Flamingos nightclub.

RADISSON HOTEL SOUTH AND PLAZA TOWER

7800 Normandale Blvd.
Bloomington   835-7800
$$$$

Boasting 575 rooms, numerous conference suites and meeting rooms (including a 2,500-square-foot ballroom), this suburban hotel is a popular convention facility. Guest amenities include a full-size iron and ironing board in every room and coffeemakers in the oversized rooms of the hotel's Plaza Tower. For a special experience, stay on the Plaza Club level and receive complimentary breakfast, evening cocktails and hors d'oeuvres in your own private lounge. Poolside cabana rooms have private patios or balconies. The hotel has a large indoor pool, whirlpool, sauna, a bar-lounge and the Shipside restaurant, where fresh seafood is flown in daily. For less-formal dining, try the Scandinavian-themed Cafe Stuga.

SELECT INN

7851 Normandale Blvd.
Bloomington   835-7400
$ (800) 641-1000

This 140-room economy motel of-

Photo: Craig Brock, Pioneer Press

Nicollet Island Inn is located on an island in the Mississippi River in Minneapolis fers free continental breakfast, an indoor pool, satellite TV and an airport shuttle. While there is no on-premises restaurant, several good eateries are nearby.

SHERATON INN AIRPORT
2500 E. 79th St., Bloomington   854-1771
$$

A highly rated hostelry, the 235-room Sheraton has a snazzy health club with an indoor pool and extensive exercise equipment. After you've sweated off all those calories, add a few back at the Timbers restaurant and lounge. Large meeting facilities here can accommodate up to 400 people. The Mall of America is a stone's throw away. Special weekend packages are available.

Western Suburbs

BEST WESTERN AMERICAN INN
3924 Excelsior Blvd.
St. Louis Park
$ 927-7731
          (800) 528-1234

Newly remodeled and just a mile away from Minneapolis' Chain of Lakes, this 36-room motel offers complimentary continental breakfast, free parking and a very inviting room rate. There is no pool, but who needs a pool when you can walk to the lovely lakes?

BEST WESTERN KELLY INN
2705 Annapolis Ln. N.
Plymouth   553-1600
$

You can't help but have a good time here if you take advantage of the very popular in-house Plymouth Playhouse Theater and Green Mill restaurant. The theater is know for its boisterously fun musical-revue offerings, including *Pump Boys and Dinettes*. The Green Mill, part of a well-regarded local chain, consistently wins raves for its pizza and extensive beer

selection. The hotel also has an indoor pool, sauna and Jacuzzi, plus an exercise area with weights and Stairmasters. Kelly Inn has 141 recently remodeled rooms, plus several meeting rooms, the largest of which accommodates a group of 200.

DAYS INN-PLYMOUTH
2955 Empire Ln., Plymouth   559-2400
$

This motel, surrounded by several office parks and corporations, caters primarily to business travelers. Although it has no pool, the motel offers complimentary continental breakfast, satellite TV and free phone calls. The 113 rooms include some corporate suites with microwaves and refrigerators. For dining, follow your nose to the Perkins restaurant next door.

HAMPTON INN MINNETONKA
I-394 and U.S. Hwy. 169
Minnetonka   541-1094
$

Business executives like this limited-service hotel for its quiet atmosphere, reasonable rates and convenient location, just 10 minutes from downtown Minneapolis and near several west metro corporations. The hotel has no swimming pool or food service, except for the complimentary continental breakfast. The 127 guest rooms have free cable TV. Some suites are available. For business meetings, the Hampton Inn offers three conference rooms, the largest with a seating capacity of 75.

HOLIDAY INN EXPRESS WEST
6020 Wayzata Blvd.
Golden Valley   545-8300
$$

Rich hues of hunter green and burgundy, a fireplace and living room seating warm up the lobby of this new limited-service hotel with 83 rooms. Although there is no food service or lounge on premises, guests can take a dip in the indoor pool and hot tub, as well as have a free continental breakfast. The hotel is on Interstate 394 (Wayzata Boulevard), just 10 minutes west of downtown Minneapolis.

HOLIDAY INN WEST

9940 Wayzata Blvd.
St. Louis Park   593-1918
$$

You'll find an indoor pool, fitness center and spa here, plus cozy fireside dining in Martha's Vineyard restaurant. For business meetings and conventions, the hotel offers two large ballrooms that break down into several meeting rooms. The 196 guest rooms include a number of suites.

MINNEAPOLIS MARRIOTT SOUTHWEST

5801 Opus Pkwy., Minnetonka   935-5500
$$$$

Miles of landscaped running paths surround this well-respected 320-room hotel situated in a bustling business park. A restaurant, swimming pool and health club are on the premises.

RADISSON HOTEL AND CONFERENCE CENTER

3131 Campus Dr., Plymouth   559-6600
$$

Serious fitness buffs are attracted to this hotel's full-service fitness center, which features an extensive array of free weights and strength-training machines, as well as Stairmasters and other aerobic equipment, two racquetball courts and an indoor basketball court. The hotel's conference center includes 10 expansive meeting rooms and 21 smaller hospitality rooms for groups of six to eight. The 243 sleeping rooms were recently redecorated in dark green and burgundy hues. Views of the surrounding woods are especially nice from the Creekside Cafe restaurant and adjoining bar-lounge.

RAMADA HOTEL PLAZA MINNEAPOLIS WEST

12201 Ridgedale Dr., Minnetonka   593-0000
$$

Watch Canada geese soar overhead or catch a glimpse of deer running through the nearby woods from the windows of this four-story deluxe suburban hotel. Though it's across the street from bustling Ridgedale shopping center, the Ramada backs up to a scenic woodland and wetlands lush with migrating waterfowl. Amenities include an indoor pool, a whirlpool, exercise area, Christy's restaurant and Winners sports bar, an intimate setting for cocktail talk. Refreshments are also served in the large pleasant atrium lobby. A popular spot for traveling executives during the week, the hotel is also a favorite venue for weekend wedding receptions. Three ballrooms and several smaller meeting rooms accommodate special occasions. Guests may also use the nearby YMCA for a nominal fee.

Romance blooms at the very French — and very classy — L' Hotel Sofitel, a perfect destination for lovers. Guest freebies here include truffles and a rose.

Insiders' Tips

RESIDENCE INN-MINNEAPOLIS SOUTHWEST

7780 Flying Cloud Dr., Eden Prairie 829-0033
$$$$

A "home away from home," the Residence Inn caters to long-term guests, such as executives on extended business trips or new residents seeking transitional housing. The hotel has 126 suites with fully equipped kitchens; some also have fireplaces. Complimentary breakfasts are included in the room rate. And to fight homesickness, the inn offers catered dinners every Wednesday and evening socials with complimentary hors d'oeuvres.

SHERATON PARK PLACE HOTEL

5555 Wayzata Blvd.
St. Louis Park 542-8600
$$

This distinctive newer hotel, just 5 minutes west of downtown Minneapolis, has 268 rooms and 30 poolside suites. Special touches include a stunning skylit indoor pool and live music and gourmet fare served up at the hotel's Dover Restaurant. Eighteen banquet rooms meet the needs of business gatherings and conventions. The hotel offers package deals, and youths 18 and younger stay free in their parents' room.

North Suburbs

BEST WESTERN KELLY INN

5201 Central Ave. N.E., Fridley 571-9440
$

This attractive motel is newly remodeled with a pleasant tropical courtyard featuring an indoor pool, a whirlpool and game room. The inn has 96 rooms and an on-premises restaurant.

BEST WESTERN NORTHWEST INN

I-94 and County Rd. 81
Brooklyn Park 566-8855
$

Here you'll find 214 renovated rooms,

an indoor swimming pool, exercise room, whirlpool, coffee shop, dining room and cocktail lounge.

BUDGETEL INN

6415 James Circle N.
Brooklyn Center 561-8400
$ (800) 4-BUDGET

Stretch out in one of Budgetel's 99 "roomy" rooms furnished with easy chairs and extra-long double beds. Guests get a complimentary continental breakfast and free phone calls.

BUDGET HOST FRIDLEY

6881 U.S. Hwy. 65 N.E., Fridley 571-0420
$

Picturesque Rice Creek borders this 14-unit motel. The rooms are equipped with microwaves, TVs and refrigerators. Biking and hiking trails are nearby.

DAYS INN ROSEVILLE

2550 Cleveland Ave. N., Roseville 636-6730
$

The Days Inn offers clean and comfortable basic lodging with free continental breakfast in a location that's convenient to both cities.

HOLIDAY INN MINNEAPOLIS NORTH

2200 Freeway Blvd.
Brooklyn Center 566-8000
$$

You can jog off your stress on the nature trails next to this attractive hotel or take a dip in the indoor pool and whirlpool. Other amenities include free parking and free in-room movies, plus an on-premises nightclub and restaurant.

HOLIDAY INN ROSEVILLE

2540 Cleveland Ave., Roseville 636-4567
$$

This Holiday Inn offers 253 reasonably priced rooms, an indoor pool and a restaurant.

NORTHLAND INN
AND CONFERENCE CENTER

7101 Northland Center
Brooklyn Park   536-8300
$$$

This five-year-old luxury hotel and conference center offers 231 two-room suites, each furnished with double-wide whirlpool tubs, with the exception of 10 rooms with handicapped-accessible showers. A bustling conference center houses two ballrooms and 20 other meeting rooms. The hotel is handsomely furnished in warm woods, Minnesota granite and hues of burgundy and forest green. The complex has two restaurants, Wadsworth's and America's Harvest.

SUPER 8 MINNEAPOLIS NORTH

6445 James Cir., Brooklyn Center   566-9810
$

The 103-room Super 8 offers hard-to-beat rates, free continental breakfast and satellite TV. Restaurants and shopping are within easy access.

Bed and Breakfast Inns

These homey accommodations often lend a very special ambiance to one's travels. Here are a few of the bed and breakfasts found in the Twin Cities area. The list is by no means complete—consult friends or travel agents for their personal recommendations. And remember, in

most cases, breakfast is included in the prices listed below. Most bed and breakfasts are smoke-free.

St. Paul

CHATSWORTH BED & BREAKFAST

984 Ashland Ave.   227-4288
$$

This bed and breakfast inn, in the heart of St. Paul, near the Governor's Mansion, is a spacious Victorian home with five guest rooms, two with private whirlpool baths. Colorful Grand Avenue is within walking distance. Breakfast is served in a richly paneled dining room.

COMO VILLA BED & BREAKFAST

1371 W. Nebraska Ave.   647-0471
$$

This antiques-filled 1872 Victorian home is two blocks from lovely Como Park. The rooms are exquisitely decorated with period furniture. Lower rates apply during the week. Weekend breakfast guests are serenaded by music from the grand piano.

PRIOR'S ON DESOTO

1522 Desoto St.   774-2695
$$ *No credit cards*

Unlike many bed and breakfasts, Dick and Mary Prior's establishment is a relatively new (1991), handsome, modern structure boasting all the comforts of home and then some. Relax by the fire in a dramatic living room with vaulted ceiling and spectacular windows. You have

Don't be surprised if you spy a Broadway celebrity or two at the St. Paul Hotel. It's a favorite destination for entertainers, especially those who are appearing at the Ordway Music Theatre, across the park from the hotel.

Insiders' Tips

your choice of two sleeping areas. The Victorian Room offers landscape views through lace-curtained windows, a queen-size four-poster bed and an adjoining loft with a desk and phone. Overlooking the patio, the Paisley Room is equipped with twin beds (convertible to one king-size bed) furnished in blue and rose paisley fabric, and it too opens to a loft area. Each room has a private bath. An inviting communal sun deck and front porch are just right for bird-watching and quiet conversation. The inn is near I-35 and Larpenteur Avenue, just five minutes from downtown St. Paul.

Minneapolis

COE CARRIAGE HOUSE

1700 Third Ave. S.   *871-4249*
$$$$

Relax in this converted 1883 carriage house, one block from the Minneapolis Convention Center. A pleasant alternative to chain hotels, the Coe Carriage House is a recently renovated National Historic Register home. Inside this handsome brick and wood-paneled structure, you'll find a modern, gourmet kitchen and tastefully decorated large living room with overstuffed chairs and fine art. A spiral staircase leads to the three bedrooms, each furnished with period furniture. Bath amenities include a marble bathroom with a Jacuzzi, tub and spa and another half-bath. The living room and bedrooms have cable TV. Unlike most bed and breakfasts, the entire home is rented as a unit, with nightly rates based on the number of guests. From here, it's a healthy six-block walk to Orchestra Hall and Nicollet Mall.

ELMWOOD HOUSE

1 Elmwood Pl.   *822-4558*
$

Pluck out a tune on the baby grand in the parlor or just chew the fat 'round the living room fireplace. Whatever your mood, you're bound to feel at home in this gracious 1887 Norman chateau-style historic home. This South Minneapolis inn, just 15 minutes from downtown, offers three sleeping rooms and one suite with private bath. An added attraction is nearby nature trails.

LEBLANC HOUSE

302 University Ave. N.E.   *379-2570*
$$

An 1896 restored and elegantly furnished home, the LeBlanc House is just minutes away from Riverplace and downtown. It offers three rooms, one with a private bath. Zofi's Room is a floral fantasy with a walnut bed and marble-top dresser and private bath. Amelia's room looks out on the city skyline and is furnished in elegant white with a walnut bed, table and chairs. In Marissa's Room, the furnishings are oak with an antique brass bed topped with handmade quilts. Save room for the generous breakfast of rum-raisin French toast, filled crepes and pistachio quiche.

Minneapolis Suburbs

BLUFF CREEK INN

1161 Bluff Creek Dr., Chaska   *445-2735*
$$

Dating to 1864, this Minnesota River Valley inn encompasses five beautifully decorated, antique-filled rooms, each with a private bath. Some rooms also have balconies and whirlpools. Enjoy a gourmet three-course breakfast and evening hors d'oeuvres. With 20 miles of cross-country ski trails nearby, this is a perfect wintertime destination.

INN ON THE FARM
6150 Summit Dr. N.
Brooklyn Center   569-6330
$$$$ *(800) 428-8382*

Housed in a cluster of farm buildings on what was once a sprawling country estate, this large inn offers 11 exquisitely decorated period rooms, each with a double whirlpool, private bath and queen-size bed. Before turning in for the evening, enjoy a spot o' tea next to the cozy stone fireplace in the antiques-filled parlor. This is a very popular destination for honeymooners. Breakfast is served in the inn's dining room, and fine dining is available in Earle's restaurant on Friday and Saturday nights. Also on the grounds is the Earle Brown Heritage Center exhibition hall, which frequently hosts antique fairs and arts and crafts shows. Credit cards and checks are accepted.

THE MARSH
15000 Minnetonka Blvd.
Minnetonka   935-2202
$-$$$

The Marsh proclaims itself a center for "fitness and balance" and, according to loyal clients, the facility is succeeding at its mission. A fitness center/spa situated on a lovely wetlands area (of course!), The Marsh offers guests a choice of six warmly appointed guest rooms, continental breakfast and use of its fitness/spa (extra fees may apply for extra services). Each room is equipped with a TV and VCR.

You'll find a nice, health-conscious restaurant on premises.

THE NICHOLAS HOUSE
BED & BREAKFAST
134 Fourth Ave. E., Shakopee   496-2537
$$

Guests at this 1895 Queen Anne home can sip lemonade on a huge wraparound porch shaded by 100-year-old trees or relax in the formal parlor or living room, both filled with antiques, Oriental carpets and period wallpapers. There are three sleeping rooms, all located on the second floor. One has its own bath.

St. Croix River Area

AFTON HOUSE INN
3291 S. St. Croix Trail, Afton   436-8883
$-$$$$

Built in 1867, this historic inn is listed on the National Register of Historic Places. Here you'll find country-style hotel rooms with fireplaces and such modern amenities as Jacuzzis. The inn's restaurant is a popular destination for the aprés-ski crowd from nearby Afton Alps. This may feel like a bed and breakfast inn, but it's actually not — sorry, no free eats in the morning. Still, it's a fine choice for cozy accommodations.

ANN BEAN HOUSE
319 W. Pine St., Stillwater   430-0355
$$$$

A grand old (c. 1878) mansion built by a prosperous lumberman, the Ann Bean House boasts 11-foot ceilings and a

The Minnesota Department of Tourism publishes a very handy bed and breakfast guide. It's free and available by calling (800) 657-3700 or 296-5029.

Insiders' Tips

55-foot tower, original oak woodwork and antiques galore. The inn has five large sleeping rooms, some with double whirlpools and wood-burning fireplaces. All have private baths.

ASA PARKER HOUSE
17500 St. Croix Tr. N.
Marine on St. Croix   433-5248
$$$$

Nestled in this picturesque little burg overlooking the St. Croix River, the Asa Parker House, dating to 1856, features five antique-filled guest rooms with English wallcoverings and decor. One suite has a whirlpool. The breakfast here is legendary. Communal areas include a double parlor, wicker-filled porch, yard gazebo and tennis court. Canoes are available for river exploring.

THE BRUNSWICK INN
114 E. Chestnut St., Stillwater   430-2653
$$$$

One of the oldest structures in Stillwater, this 1848 Greek Revival inn nonetheless has such modern amenities as oversize double whirlpools in each of its three sleeping rooms, not to mention wood-burning fireplaces. For a real treat, call ahead and make reservations for the Victorian multicourse dinners Friday and Saturday evenings.

THE ELEPHANT WALK
801 Pine St., Stillwater   430-0359
$$$$

This Victorian home sends guests on "round-the-world" tours via uniquely themed bedrooms. Among them are the Rangoon Room, with a whirlpool and four-poster bed draped in mosquito netting; the Raffles Room, with a bamboo bed and fireplace; and the Spanish-style Cadiz Room, which has its own private sunroom. Long-term and midweek discounted rates are available.

JAMES A. MULVEY BED & BREAKFAST
622 W. Churchill St., Stillwater   430-8008
$$$

This Italianate Victorian home built by a lumber baron is filled with art, antiques and loads of charm. The inn has five sleeping rooms, some with fireplaces and whirlpools. All have private baths. During the summer, the four-course breakfast is served on the sun porch.

THE RIVERTOWN INN
306 W. Olive St., Stillwater   430-2955
$-$$$$

A sprawling three-story lumberman's mansion, this 1882 inn offers nine rooms elegantly decorated in period furnishings, some with whirlpools and fireplaces. Its hillside location affords breathtaking views of historic Stillwater and the St. Croix River Valley. Dinner packages are available.

WILLIAM SAUNTRY MANSION
626 N. Fourth St., Stillwater   430-2653
$$$$

Listed on the National Register, this Queen Anne-style 1890s home is decorated with historically correct wallpapers and room settings. Fantastic views are afforded through stained-glass windows. The inn has five guest rooms with fireplaces, private baths and whirlpools. Victorian dinners are offered on weekends.

Hastings

HEARTHWOOD BED & BREAKFAST
17650 200th St.   437-1133
$$

A multilevel Cape Cod log home built in 1986 is the setting for this bed and breakfast inn with five guest rooms, four of which have private whirlpools and fireplaces. Hearthwood's great room features a massive stone fireplace set amid an eclectic decor of traditional and antique furnishings. Guests greet the day with a candlelit full breakfast. The Hearthwood sits on 10 acres of land 5 miles south of Hastings and within easy reach of attractions along the Mississippi River and historic Red Wing.

THORWOOD INN
ROSEWOOD INN

Hastings   437-3297
$$$$

The Thorwood Inn, at 315 Pine Street, and the Rosewood Inn, at 620 Ramsey Street, are both listed on the National Register of Historic Sites. Filled with reading nooks, fireplaces and antiques, they provide a cozy retreat from the 20th century. Some suites have double whirlpools and fireplaces. All have private baths. The inns have 15 rooms in all.

Intimate in-house dinners are available upon request.

Convention
and Visitors Bureaus

For other lodging information as well as general information about Twin Cities destinations, the area convention and visitors bureaus can provide help.

• **Minneapolis Convention and Visitors Bureau**, 661-4700, 4000 Multifoods Tower, Minneapolis

• **St. Paul Convention and Visitors Bureau**, 297-6985, 55 E. Fifth Street, St. Paul

• **Bloomington Convention and Visitors Bureau**, 858-8500, 1550 E. 79th Street, Bloomington

• **Burnsville Convention and Visitors Bureau**, 435-6000, 101 W. Burnsville Parkway, Suite 150, Burnsville

• **Eagan Convention and Visitors Bureau**, 452-9872, (800) 324-2620, 1380 Corporate Center Curve, Eagan

Photo: Sully Doroshow, Pioneer Press

The Dakota, a jazz club and restaurant in St. Paul.

Inside
Restaurants

Here's the fattest chapter in the book — one that, consulted too often, may cause you to assume larger proportions. But, seriously, the size of this chapter testifies to the variety and quality of eating establishments in the Twin Cities. Old-timers can wax nostalgic about some of the region's now-vanished restaurants of repute, such as Charlie's Cafe Exceptionale in Minneapolis, but nobody with his or her palate on straight will deny that the eating is much better in these parts than it has ever been before.

Why? There are many answers, but recent immigrants are most responsible for the rising quality of Twin Cities dining. Twenty years ago, you would have been hard-pressed to locate many authentic African, Middle Eastern, Vietnamese, Thai or even Italian restaurants in the area. Since then, newcomers have arrived in Minneapolis and St. Paul from all over the globe, and you can see it in the menus. Asian food, in particular, is especially good and plentiful here, contributing to the Twin Cities' status as one of the Midwest's ethnic-eating capitals.

There's a venerable saying among restaurant hoppers: Those who have poor noses have unsatisfied appetites. In other words, if you want to be a fulfilled restaurant goer, you'll have to keep your nostrils always open to sniff out your own favorite haunts. Think of the restaurants listed here as just the starting steps on your path to eating nirvana. Hundreds of other fine, interesting and challenging restaurants in the Twin Cities are not included here, and they are for you to discover.

And several of our choices have more than one location, so if you see a restaurant that appeals to your appetite, check the write-up for a possible location near you.

The dollar sign code with each restaurant entry indicates the likely cost of dinner for two, excluding beverages, tips and taxes. Lunch at most restaurants costs less. Here's how the code works:

Less than $20	**$**
$21 to $40	**$$**
$41 to $60	**$$$**
More than $61	**$$$$**

Unless we note that an establishment does not accept credit cards, you can be fairly confident that the restaurant will take one of the cards you carry. Certainly ask before your meal if you want to make sure.

Grab your fork and let the eating begin!

African and Middle-Eastern Cuisine

THE BARBARY FIG
720 Grand Ave., St. Paul   290-2085
$$

The Barbary Fig is the Twin Cities' only couscous restaurant, with a small, enticing menu of gently spicy North African dishes and a smattering of foods from Provence. Recommended are the vegetarian couscous, fish and eggplant specials, and garlicky olives served with crusty bread. The restaurant is open for lunch and dinner Monday and Wednesday through Saturday, and dinner Sunday. Wine and beer are served.

CARAVAN SERAI

2175 Ford Pkwy., St. Paul   690-1935
$$

You can sit in a chair if you want, but it's much more fun to dine while reclining at this sumptuously appointed Middle Eastern restaurant. We recommend the soups, naan, tandoori chicken and sheer chai, a cardamom-scented tea with cream. Lunch is served Tuesday through Friday; dinner, daily. Reservations are recommended.

CASPIAN BISTRO

2418 University Ave. S.E.
Minneapolis   623-1113
$ No credit cards

Here you'll find Middle Eastern food bargains for cautious and adventurous diners alike. Recommended choices are the lemony chicken kebabs, shawirma and snowy buttered rice. Lunch and dinner are available Tuesday through Sunday. Reservations are recommended.

DUPSY'S AFRICAN CUISINE

474 W. University Ave., St. Paul   225-1525
$

The first of its kind in the area, this friendly West African cafe serves authentic dishes that range from comforting to challenging. Rice, beans, beef and fried plantains are easy to like; soups and fufu are satisfying, especially when eaten with fingers. It's open for lunch and dinner Tuesday through Saturday. Reservations are recommended.

EMILY'S LEBANESE DELI

641 University Ave. N.E.
Minneapolis   379-4069
$ No credit cards

Come here for the smooth, addictive hummos, the tabbouleh for parsley lovers and the big flat spinach pies that taste great even as leftovers. It's a good choice for take-out, but the crowded, ultra-casual dining room has a certain charm too. It's open every day but Tuesday, serving from midmorning to late evening.

JACOB'S

101 N.E. Broadway, Minneapolis   379-2508
$$

Experience the surprise of excellent Middle Eastern food in a northeast Minneapolis bar and restaurant. If you find it hard to decide what to order from the long, tempting menu, consider the appetizer sampler plate as a nice, light meal for two. Reservations are suggested. Jacob's is open for breakfast, lunch and dinner Monday through Saturday; breakfast and lunch Sunday.

JERUSALEM'S

1518 Nicollet Ave. S., Minneapolis   871-8883
$

Among the city's best Middle Eastern restaurants, this cozy den serves hearty food prepared with care. You'll discover smooth, garlicky hummos, a crunchy Jericho salad, lamb curry, combination plates and much more. On Friday and Saturday nights, dancers do their best to distract diners. It's open for lunch and dinner daily.

ODAA

408 Cedar Ave., Minneapolis   338-4459
$$

If you've never eaten with your fingers as an adult, this is the place to start. Odaa features a variety of West African

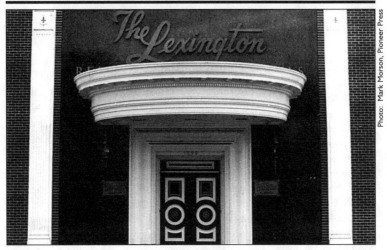

Photo: Mark Morson, Pioneer Press

The Lexington, St. Paul.

dishes in a comfortable, West Bank setting, marred only by sometimes lackadaisical service. Try lukuu waaddi gubaa (curried chicken with jalapeños) and a gingery beef stew called itto sa'a. Odaa is open for lunch and dinner Monday through Saturday (with later hours Friday and Saturday) and dinner Sunday.

OLD CITY CAFE

1571 Grand Ave., St. Paul   699-5347
$ No credit cards

Old City offers strictly kosher food prepared with care. The choices range from Middle Eastern specialties — hummos and eggplant — to a swell New York-style pizza. Yemenite rice and falafel Parmesan are also recommended. Take it out or eat in. It's open for lunch and dinner Sunday through Thursday, closes at 2 PM Friday and is closed on Saturday.

PORT OF BEIRUT

1385 S. Robert St., West St. Paul   457-4886
$$

Hearty seasonings are a trademark of this reliable West St. Paul cafe (garlic-lovers, dip into the creamy, pungent sauce accompanying many dishes). The Port Sampler for two offers a little of almost everything. Dancers undulate every Friday and Saturday night, beginning at 8 PM. Port of Beirut is open for lunch and dinner Monday through Saturday (later on Saturday). Reservations are recommended.

American Cuisine

APPLEBEE'S
NEIGHBORHOOD GRILL AND BAR

1600 W. University Ave., St. Paul   642-9757
$$

This consistent and competent chain offers a variety of appetizers, sandwiches, salads and entrees, with regular updates to follow seasons and trends. You'll find a visually busy atmosphere and a staff that's accommodating to children. Applebee's is open for lunch, dinner and late-night dining daily. The area has 15 other locations, including Town Center in Eagan and Ridgedale in Minnetonka.

BEAN COUNTER

World Trade Center, 30 E. Seventh St.
St. Paul   227-8283
$

The Bean Counter's warm, regular-folks service, good coffee and food make it a valuable find. In addition to the basics, the cafe offers its own hard-core creation, The Quad, four shots of espresso and steamed milk — perfect for groggy executives. The lunch chow is good to take out or eat in, including a satisfying cold club sandwich and food supplied by the Old City Cafe. It's open through the work week from early morning through dinner and opens later and closes earlier Saturday and Sunday.

THE BLUE POINT

739 E. Lake St., Wayzata   475-3636
$$$

There's more seafood here than you can shake a pole at, with a daily special sheet telling you the precise origin of your fish. It's open daily for dinner, with later hours on Friday and Saturday.

CALIFORNIA CAFE

Mall of America, Bloomington   854-2233
$$$

This is a tasteful San Francisco-based eatery serving satisfying, upscale California cuisine. Recommended menu items are the bruschetta trio, oak-fired pizza, farmers market salad, trout with red onion sauce and beets, crème brûlée and lemon-berry shortcake. The menu changes regularly. Lunch and dinner are served daily. It's best to call for reservations.

THE CAFE

St. Paul Hotel, 350 Market St.
St. Paul   292-9292
$$

The Cafe offers a sedate country atmosphere and a varied menu. Best bets are the cream of chicken soup with brie and artichokes and the spinach-strawberry salad. The Cafe is open for breakfast and lunch Sunday and Monday and breakfast, lunch and dinner Tuesday through Saturday. Reservations are recommended.

CAFE MINNESOTA

Minnesota History Center
345 W. Kellogg Blvd., St. Paul   297-4097
$ *No credit cards*

This better-than-basic cafeteria offers imaginative salads, great vegetarian chili, top-notch burgers and a full range of entrees. You can get a continental breakfast (juice, coffee, muffins, etc.) on weekday mornings. It's open for breakfast and lunch Monday through Friday, lunch only Saturday and Sunday.

CARIBOU COFFEE

2138 Ford Parkway, St. Paul   690-9934
$

This is a slick, upscale nook next to Bruegger's Bagel Bakery. It employs a legion of perky, well-trained workers who serve coffee, espresso drinks and a hefty selection of top-notch baked goods supplied by Goodfellow's. Caribou Coffee is open from early morning until late night daily. (There's another Caribou at 1055 Grand Avenue, St. Paul.)

CAROUSEL

Radisson Hotel, 11 E. Kellogg Blvd.
St. Paul   292-1900
$$

This revolving restaurant with a view boasts a full bar and a whole new look and menu, with lower prices and lighter fare. Specialties include coconut fried shrimp, sirloin steak and mushroom escargots. It's open daily from early morning until late night.

CHEROKEE SIRLOIN ROOM

886 S. Smith Ave., West St. Paul   *457-2729*
$$

This bustling steakhouse offers plenty for the chicken-eaters in the family too. While you're there, take a look at the mirrors, chandeliers and a mural that pays homage to the High Bridge. The Cherokee is a place where deals are sealed, both personal and professional. Lunch and dinner (through late-night) are served Monday through Saturday and brunch, lunch and dinner Sunday. A second Cherokee Sirloin Room is at 4625 Nichols Road in Eagan.

COGNAC MCCARTHY'S

162 N. Dale St., St. Paul   *224-4617*
$ *No credit cards*

Here's a friendly neighborhood bar with a staggering selection of spirits. It also offers bar food and beyond: little tortilla "pizzas," great burgers, meat loaf sandwiches, fried potatoes and Cuban chicken. The cozy booths are perfect for true confessions. Food is served daily from morning to late night (closing earlier on Sunday).

DARI-ETTE

1440 E. Minnehaha Ave., St. Paul   *776-3470*
$ *No credit cards*

In addition to burgers, malts and cherry Cokes, this drive-in — complete with carhops — serves pasta, meatball sandwiches and a nifty Italian soup. Make sure to allow time to do your drive-in duty: Tilt back the car seat and contemplate nothing in particular. You can pull in for lunch, dinner and late-night munching daily.

DAY BY DAY CAFE

477 W. Seventh St., St. Paul   *227-0654*
$ *No credit cards*

Looking for an atmosphere where you can get your life, not to mention your morning, together? Try the delish Red Earth breakfast, which mixes eggs with hashbrowns and tops it with cheese and salsa. Here you'll find nicely mismatched chairs and silverware, along with live entertainment on Friday night. It's open Monday through Friday for breakfast, lunch and dinner, and Saturday and Sunday for breakfast and lunch.

EXCELSIOR PARK RESTAURANT

685 Excelsior Blvd., Excelsior   *474-1113*
$$

You'll find few better places to munch a burger or pizza than on the outdoor deck of this casual Lake Minnetonka restaurant. During the summer, patrons, come by boat and car to enjoy the outdoor deck menu of hearty sandwiches, burgers and pizza. If you opt to dine indoors, you can choose from a more extensive menu ranging from pastas and salads to seafood and steaks. Excelsior Park has a full bar too. The Sunday brunch is tantalizing and hearty. It's open for lunch through late-night dining Monday through Saturday and brunch through late dining Sunday.

It's fun to people-watch from the outdoor tables at Figlio.

Insiders' Tips

FABULOUS FERN'S BAR AND GRILL

400 Selby Ave., St. Paul   225-9414
$$

The atmosphere may be a little predictable, but the food at this friendly and casual place is steps above the typical fern bar. Appetizers include spicy black bean dip with chips and fried salmon patties; recommended entrees are fettuccine with chicken and the Southwestern flank steak. For dessert, sink into the super-rich Jack Daniels chocolate and walnut pie. Lunch and dinner (through late night) are served Monday through Saturday and brunch, lunch and dinner Sunday. Reservations are recommended.

FIGLIO

Calhoun Square, 3001 Hennepin Ave.
Minneapolis   822-1688
$$

Cosmopolitan charm, luscious pasta and a sunny, upbeat waitstaff create a most pleasant dining ambiance at Figlio. This bustling eatery specializes in California-Italian fare at moderate prices. The people-watching is primo, especially in the big dining room overlooking Hennepin Avenue and Lake Street. Outdoor sidewalk dining is available in the summer. It opens for lunch and serves through the wee hours daily.

FOUR INNS

American National Bank Building Skyway
St. Paul   291-7939
$ No credit cards

This is an efficient, bustling skyway lunch spot offering traditional dinners and sandwiches. The pies are great — order early to avoid missing your favorite. Get breakfast and lunch here Monday through Friday.

GALLIVAN'S

354 N. Wabasha St., St. Paul   227-6688
$$

This is a woody, relaxing bar and restaurant, the ideal place to sink in and discuss the meaning of it all. For dinner, stick to basics like the steak sandwich. The happy hour hors d'oeuvres are generous and free. Lunch and dinner are available Monday through Saturday, dinner only Sunday. Reservations are recommended.

GOOD EARTH

Calhoun Square, 3001 Hennepin Ave.
Minneapolis   824-8533
$-$$

Wholesome food prepared with fresh, natural ingredients is the specialty of this pleasant, completely smoke-free restaurant chain. The baked goods here are exceptional. There's no bar, but wine and beer are served. Lunch and dinner (into late night) are served Monday through Saturday, brunch through late dinner Sunday. Other Good Earths are found in the Galleria shopping center in Edina and at 1901 W. Highway 36 in Roseville.

GOPHER BAR

241 E. Seventh St., St. Paul   291-9638
$ No credit cards

Here you'll find four-star Coneys with a buttery grilled bun; don't order fewer than two, or you'll just have to ask for seconds. There are burgers, gyros and tostadas too. The Gopher is open from morning to late night Monday through Saturday (closing earlier on Saturday) and for breakfast and lunch Sunday.

GRANDVIEW GRILL

1818 Grand Ave., St. Paul   698-2346
$ No credit cards

Great big burgers, nice fries and a neighborhoody feeling make this diner a good choice for lunch. It's open for breakfast and lunch daily.

GREEN MILL INN

57 S. Hamline Ave., St. Paul   698-0353
$$

Pizza's the point at this bustling cafe featuring delightful deep-dish specimens bursting with tomatoes alongside crisp, saucy thin-crust pies. You can order from a full menu of entrees, burgers, salads and kids' items. The restaurant is open daily. Other Green Mill locations include 2626 Hennepin Avenue, Minneapolis; 8266 Commonwealth Drive, Eden Prairie; 2705 Annapolis Lane, Plymouth; 6003 Hudson Road, Woodbury; 1595 W. Highway 36, Roseville and 14023 Aldrich Avenue S., Burnsville. Reservations are recommended.

HIGHLAND GRILL

771 Cleveland Ave. S., St. Paul   690-1173
$ *No credit cards*

A onetime ice-cream shop finally found its true identity in this friendly grill. The fare is fresh and surprisingly eclectic; in addition to burgers and pancakes, there's veggie hash, ratatouille, curried beef and black bean cakes. Breakfast is served all day. It's open for breakfast, lunch and dinner Monday through Saturday, breakfast and lunch Sunday.

IVORIES

Hwys. 55 and 169, Plymouth   591-6188
$$

Classic American fare of fresh seafood, steaks and chops, salads and appetizers is served in this elegant, modern restaurant. Cap off your dinner with a visit to the piano lounge. With its wall of windows and cozy candlelit tables, it's one of the most romantic spots in the Twin Cities. Talented co-owner Jimmy Martin tickles the ivories and sings his heart out. Lunch is served Monday through Friday, dinner Monday through Saturday and brunch Sunday.

JAX CAFE

1928 University Ave. N.E.
Minneapolis   789-7297
$$

Jax is an enduring favorite among locals, especially for its fresh lobster, rainbow trout (catch it yourself from Jax's brook) and steaks. A pianist performs Thursday through Sunday. Lunch through late-night dining is available Monday through Saturday, with brunch and dinner Sunday.

J.D. HOYT'S

301 Washington Ave. N.
Minneapolis   338-1560
$$$

Steaks, chops and Cajun are the specialties in this hopping warehouse-district bar. Try the stick-to-your-ribs breakfasts too. The restaurant is open from morning through late night daily. Reservations are recommended.

KEYS

767 Raymond Ave., St. Paul   646-5756
$

Keys specializes in big, buttery food in a well-worn atmosphere that lures you back. And they do come back — the regulars are legendary. Popular menu items are the weighty, spicy Italian hash, the thick homemade toast and the huge caramel rolls. Keys is open for breakfast and lunch daily (closing at noon Saturday and Sunday). Other Keys restaurants are in Minneapolis, Forest Lake, Brooklyn Park, Spring Lake Park, White Bear Lake, St. Paul, Roseville, New Brighton and Woodbury.

LAKE ELMO INN

3442 Lake Elmo Ave. N.
Lake Elmo   777-8495
$$$

Want fancy dining with a grandmotherly Minnesota touch? Here you'll discover a varied continental menu and the best salt and pepper shaker collection around. It's an appropriate dining choice for special occasions. Lunch and dinner are served daily. Reservations are recommended.

LAKE STREET GARAGE

3508 E. Lake St., Minneapolis   729-8820
$ No credit cards

This is a wholesome hangout in a former garage, adorned with signs for Quaker State and Prest-O-Lite. The menu includes superior burgers, malts and fries, a nice Italian salad and a sundae called the Wrecker. Enjoy free popcorn with your beer. The Garage is open daily for lunch through late night dining.

THE LEXINGTON

1096 Grand Ave., St. Paul   222-5878
$$

This venerable restaurant has an updated menu, but the comfortable, clubby atmosphere remains unchanged. Steaks are a reliable choice; among the newer offerings, try Shaw's crab cakes, the chicken fettuccine rosa, and The Beans, a spicy Oriental appetizer. It's open for lunch through late-night dining Monday through Saturday, and brunch through dinner Sunday. Reservations are recommended.

LINDEY'S PRIME STEAK HOUSE

3610 N. Snelling Ave., Arden Hills   633-9813
$ No credit cards

The choosing's easy — sirloin, sirloin or chopped sirloin. The tender meat arrives juicy and sizzling, along with plenty of potatoes and garlic bread. Here the ambiance is dark and North Woodsy. Lindey's is open every day except Sunday for dinner.

LOON CAFE

500 First Ave. N., Minneapolis   332-8342
$$

Chili reigns supreme at this bustling, sportsy bar and cafe, a block from Target Center. For a real kick in the pants, try the hot version of Pecos River Red. Food is served from lunch through late night daily; the bar is open until 1 AM.

LORD FLETCHER'S
ON LAKE MINNETONKA

3746 Sunset Dr., Spring Park   471-8513
$$

Diners come by boat and by car to this popular lakeside restaurant reminiscent of an old English tavern. Fare includes fresh fish and other seafood, prime rib and chicken. While the main restaurant is formal (or dressy casual), a lower-level cafe is strictly for the jeans and shorts crowd. Whether you're upstairs or down, the lake views are stunning. You can dine outdoors in the summer. Lunch and dinner are served Monday through Saturday, brunch on Sunday.

MAGNOLIA'S

1081 Payne Ave., St. Paul   774-3333
$ No credit cards

Magnolia's offers hearty Mom food served with friendly efficiency. Notable are the low prices, tender chicken, enormous dumplings and breakfast served all day. It's open daily from early morning until late at night (closing earlier on Sunday).

THE MALT SHOP

1554 Concordia Ave., St. Paul   645-4643
$

The old malt shop just ain't what it used to be: now ratatouille and spanakopita share menu space with burgers and fries. The food and service are uneven, but kids feel right at home, plied with crayons and live piano music. Other Malt Shops are at 50th Street and Bryant Avenue S., Minneapolis; and highways 7 and 10 in Minnetonka. You can get breakfast, lunch and dinner ('til late night) daily.

MANCINI'S CHAR HOUSE
531 W. Seventh St., St. Paul   224-7345
$$

This is a lively center of the St. Paul steak-and-potatoes universe. It's also a great place to unwind after a long week — but be prepared to wait during peak hours, for hordes are hooked on Mancini's no-nonsense charms. A bonus is the glitzy lounge with frequent live music. Dinner is served through the late evening hours daily.

MARKET BAR-B-QUE
1414 Nicollet Ave. S., Minneapolis   872-1111
$$

Choose from spare ribs, beef ribs, chicken and even barbecued sirloin, with a choice of sauces on every checkered tablecloth. Although relocated from its original downtown site, the Market still has the charm of the old place, with all the celebrity photos on the wall. Lunch through late-night munching is available daily. You'll find another Market at 15320 Wayzata Boulevard in Minnetonka.

MAYSLACK'S
1428 N.E. Fourth St., Minneapolis   789-9862
$$

Do you like garlic? Love beef? Then this old-time Nordeast bar is for you. The roast beef sandwiches are bigger than a wrestler's bicep, loaded with sliced onions and juice. It's open from lunch through late night daily.

MONTE CARLO
219 Third Ave. N., Minneapolis   333-5900
$$

Come for reliable, predictable sandwiches, burgers and wings in a cozy, bustling atmosphere. Take note of the gorgeous ceiling and huge selection of liquors; hang out for Sunday brunch and enjoy the hefty helpings. Monte Carlo is open for lunch through late-night dining Monday through Saturday and brunch through late dining Sunday. There's a full bar. Reservations are recommended.

NAPA VALLEY GRILLE
Mall of America, Bloomington   858-9934
$$$

Another winner from the proprietors of California Cafe, this elegant, smoke-free cafe offers a serious wine list, imaginative seasonal salads, fish and pasta, grilled steaks and chops. Even if you hate shopping, it's worth a trip to the mall to eat here. Lunch is served daily, dinner Monday through Sunday and brunch Sunday.

ON THE WAY CAFE
340 N. Wabasha St., St. Paul   222-5208
$ No credit cards

Here's an oasis of well-brewed coffees, spirited espresso drinks and real lunch food, including spicy chicken chili and

Minnesotans lead the nation in the per-capita consumption of popcorn.

Insiders' Tips

salads. You'll also find plenty of sweet pastries for breakfast. Proprietor Bookie Read hosts writers support groups Tuesday and Thursday evenings. Breakfast, lunch and early dinner are served Monday through Saturday; the cafe is closed Sunday.

PALOMINO
825 Hennepin Ave., Minneapolis   339-3800
$$

Minneapolis movers and shakers eat, drink and make merry at this sleek and sophisticated Euro-metro style bistro specializing in Mediterranean cuisine, including spit-roasted garlic chicken, Roma-style pizza, prime rib and seasonal game. Lunch is served Monday through Saturday, dinner daily.

PRACNA ON MAIN
117 S.E. Main St., Minneapolis   379-3200
$$

Billing itself as the "oldest restaurant-bar in Minneapolis," Pracna on Main is in the historic and charming St. Anthony Main buildings along the east bank of the Mississippi River, just across from downtown. The view is terrific, especially from the outdoor tables on a golden fall afternoon. Pranca serves a menu of American fare, from pasta and pork chops to spinach salad and burgers. It's open daily for lunch through late-night dining.

RAINFOREST CAFE
Mall of America, Bloomington   854-7500
$$

The food is almost an afterthought at this exotic eatery filled with tropical birds, splashing fish and lush foliage. A range of dishes from pasta to burgers is offered in this unusual setting. Lunch and dinner are served every day of the week.

ROSEN'S
430 First Ave. N., Minneapolis   338-1926
$$

Things are always hopping at this popular sports bar/cafe in the Warehouse District. Chomp on pasta, burgers or stir-fries while catching the latest Vikings game on one of Rosen's 10 giant TVs. Get lunch and dinner daily.

RUDOLPH'S BAR-B-QUE
1933 Lyndale Ave. S., Minneapolis   871-8969
$$

Rudolph's is a local landmark for delicious, sloppy, lip-smacking ribs and barbecued chicken. A full menu also includes steaks, chops and sandwiches. With walls smothered in autographed Hollywood photos and movie posters, Rudolph's is a popular after-movie or -theater meeting spot. Namesake Rudolph Valentino would be proud. It's open daily from midday to late night. The Twin Cities have three other Rudolph's restaurants: at Galtier Plaza in St. Paul; and 815 Hennepin Avenue E. in Minneapolis.

RUTH'S CHRIS STEAK HOUSE
Minneapolis Centre, 920 Second Ave. S.
Minneapolis   672-9000
$$$$

This national franchise is the latest addition to Minneapolis' upscale meat scene. Prime steaks and seafood abound, including Minnesota walleye and live Maine lobster. You can choose from eight kinds of potatoes, and the bourbon bread pudding is wonderful. Eye the elegant decor and extensive wine list. Dinner is served daily. Reservations are recommended.

SEBASTIAN JOE'S

1007 Franklin Ave. W.
Minneapolis   870-0065
$ No credit cards

Here's the home of arguably the best ice cream in town, in dozens of mind-bending flavors: raspberry chocolate chip, chocolate with cinnamon, and cayenne. They serve espresso drinks and muffins too. Another Sebastian Joe's is at 4321 Upton Avenue S., Minneapolis, and both locales have outdoor seating. It's open daily from early morning to late night.

SHANNON KELLY'S PUB

395 Wabasha St., St. Paul   292-0905
$

Here's a woody watering hole with burgers, chili, hot roast beef with mashed potatoes and plenty of bar snacks. You'll be impressed by the huge cheesy helpings of potato skins. The kitchen is open for lunch and dinner daily.

SHELLY'S WOODROAST

Hwy. 394 and Louisiana Ave.
St. Louis Park   593-5050
$$

This is the best-smelling restaurant in town, due to wood-burning ovens that cook fish, fowl and tender beef brisket. Check out the tart apple pie and bread pudding too, as well as a daily special of basic American fare, such as meat loaf sandwiches and corned-on-the-premises beef and cabbage. It's open for lunch and dinner daily, with later hours on Friday and Saturday. There's a full bar. Reservations are recommended; smoking is allowed in the bar only.

STONE'S FINE BAR-B-Q

1532 University Ave., St. Paul   646-3861
$$ No credit cards

This cheery, bustling cafe serves smoky, saucy and generously portioned food — the sort that makes you forget your manners and concentrate on how quick you're going to get the meat off that bone. The pork and beef ribs are tops. Lunch and dinner are served daily.

SUNSETS

700 E. Lake St., Wayzata   473-LAKE
$$

Overlooking picturesque Lake Minnetonka, this casual but classy restaurant serves up a feast for the eyes as well as the palate. The decor is one of clean lines, uncluttered spaces and generous windows. The menu offers a range of palate-pleasing entrees, from fresh seafood, ribs and pastas to sandwiches and soups. A full bar bustles on weekend nights, especially in the summer. Outside dining is available during balmy weather. It's open from morning to late night daily.

SWEENEY'S

96 N. Dale St., St. Paul   221-9157
$

This energetic bar makes you feel like you're on vacation. Burgers, sandwiches, salads and fries are just the thing with a glass of locally brewed Summit ale on tap. There's also $2.95 pasta on Sunday and Monday nights. Sweeney's is open Monday through Friday for lunch and dinner (into late night) and midmorning to late night Saturday and Sunday.

TIMBERLODGE STEAKHOUSE

1655 W. County Rd. B2, Roseville   628-0350
$$

This is a family-friendly restaurant boasting big portions and reasonable prices. Don't miss the deep-fried Paul Bunyan onion. It's open daily for dinner (later on Friday and Saturday). Other Timberlodge Steakhouse restaurants are at 13050 Aldrich Avenue S., Burnsville; at 16396 Wagner Way, Eden Prairie; and in St. Louis Park at Highway 100 and Excelsior Blvd.

TOBIE'S TAVERN

23 N. Sixth St., Minneapolis   376-9614
$$

Although this friendly establishment sits within shouting range of the Target Center, don't assume it serves sports-bar grub. In recent months, Chef Tobie Nidetz has won raves for his acclaimed chicken stir-fry as well as for a hearty offering of soups, salads, steaks and sandwiches. The atmosphere evokes a pub or tavern, which makes it a popular stop among downtown office workers. Lunch through late night munching is available daily.

TOBY'S ON THE LAKE

249 N. Geneva Ave., Oakdale   739-1600
$$

The lake in question is Tanner's Lake, and Toby's deck overlooking the water offers a lovely spot for summertime dining. Prime rib, barbecued ribs and fresh seafood are the specialties here, all served amidst a quaint and woody English atmosphere. Toby's also has banquet facilities and a full bar. Lunch and dinner are served daily, as well as a sit-down Sunday brunch.

TROTTER'S COUNTRY BAKERY

232 N. Cleveland Ave., St. Paul   645-8950
$ No credit cards

Visit for tasty muffins without the sugar rush, along with a bevy of other fine baked goods. The strong coffee is from Dunn Brothers; there are sandwiches, soups and salads too. It's a low-key, friendly spot to escape from the busy routine, good for take-out, as well. Closed Monday, you can get breakfast and lunch here the rest of the week.

TROUT HAUS

14536 W. Freeway Dr.
Columbus Township   464-2964
$$

You can just order off the menu, but it's more fun to work for your supper at the Trout Air fish farm, where the odds are always with you. Toss your line into a stocked pond (indoors during cold weather) and have the very fish you catch cooked up in the rustic, corny Trout Haus restaurant. This is a great place to take kids and out-of-town visitors who think they've seen it all. Reservations are recommended. It's open daily, with later hours on the weekend.

Asian Cuisine

AUGUST MOON

5340 Wayzata Blvd.
Golden Valley   544-7017
$$

Eat by the light of a lava lamp at this fun, casual cafe. Brother and sister owners Martin and Vivika Olander serve Vietnamese staples, as well as wild Asian hybrids. Try the spicy water buffalo chicken wings, stuffed Peking pancakes, stir-fries or goat-cheese stuffed tandoori chicken breast on curried potatoes. The coconut ice cream is wonderful, but the ginger and pepper frozen yogurt packs the greatest punch. Lunch and dinner are available Monday through Friday, dinner only on Saturday and Sunday. Wine and beer only are served.

CARAVELLE

799 W. University Ave., St. Paul   292-9324
$$

More than 100 Chinese and Vietnamese dishes fill the menu here. Recommended are the poached fish and the crisp spring rolls. Dine in the bamboo-and-

St. Paul Grill in the St. Paul Hotel.

beaded booths for optimum effect. Other Caravelle locations are at 783 Radio Drive, Woodbury; 1 E. Little Canada Road, Little Canada; 2529 Nicollet Avenue S., Minneapolis; and 2233 Energy Park Drive, St. Paul. Lunch and dinner are served Monday through Saturday. Reservations are recommended.

CHINATOWN
1533 W. Larpenteur Ave.
Falcon Heights   644-9194
$$ *No credit cards*
Every region of China is represented at this tasteful contemporary restaurant. Chinatown is noted for its soups and Peking duck. Lunch and dinner are served Monday through Saturday (with later hours Friday and Saturday) and dinner only Sunday. Reservations are recommended.

DELITES OF INDIA
1123 W. Lake St., Minneapolis   823-2866
$$
This cozy establishment is owned and operated by a Hindu couple who are strict about what they serve: no meat, seafood or dairy products. The variety is still astounding. The curries range from hot to explosive — watch out for "vindaloo." Don't miss the homemade pickles: mango, lemon, mixed vegetable. Lunch and dinner are served Tuesday through Sunday.

HOA BIEN
1129 W. University Ave., St. Paul   647-1011
$ *No credit cards*
You won't find a fancy restaurant setting here, just reliable, authentic Vietnamese food, including a mean ban xeo (crisp rice flour pancake). Hoa Bien is open daily from midmorning until late night.

KHAN'S MONGOLIAN BARBECUE
2720 N. Snelling Ave., Roseville   631-3398
$$
At this novelty restaurant, diners select raw meats, vegetables and noodles from a buffet, then watch as they are cooked by a chef at an enormous griddle. Try some curry, but go easy on the dragon sauce, or you'll be breathing fire. Another Khan's restaurant is at 500 E 78th St., Richfield. Lunch and dinner are served

• **57**

daily (dinner only Sunday in Minneapolis). Reservations are recommended.

KHYBER PASS CAFE

1399 St. Clair Ave., St. Paul   *698-5403*
$$ *No credit cards*

This is the place to go for delicious, carefully prepared Afghani specialties. Try the aushak (leek dumplings), lean lamb dishes, korma-e murgh (chicken stew) and excellent dal. Finish off with firni, a silken pudding flavored with cardamom and rosewater. Close Monday, the cafe serves lunch and dinner the rest of the week.

LEEANN CHIN

Union Depot Place, 214 E. Fourth St.
St. Paul   *224-8814*
$$

The Depot location of this mega-chain offers an attractive setting with a reliable buffet of stir-fried entrees, salads, dumplings and more. The efficient take-out outlets around the Twin Cities offer an even greater selection. You can get lunch and dinner daily. Reservations are recommended. Other Leeann Chin restaurants are at Har Mar Mall, Roseville; Highland Village Mall, St. Paul; Milton Mall, St. Paul; Norwest Skyway, St. Paul; Bonaventure Shopping Center, Minnetonka; Ninth Street and Second Avenue S., Minneapolis; and many other locations.

MIRROR OF KOREA

761 N. Snelling Ave., St. Paul   *647-9004*
$$

When this family restaurant changed locations, Minneapolis' loss was St. Paul's gain. The rich flavored, often peppery, dishes all come with delightful ban chan (small bowls of kimchee, sliced radishes and other tempting condiments). Recommended are the bulgogi (tender Korean barbecue), the dahk bokgeum (chicken stir-fry) and bibim bahp (rice with toppings to toss with pepper sauce). Closed Tuesday, you can get lunch and dinner here the rest of the week.

MY LE HOA

2900 Rice St., Little Canada   *484-5353*
$$

Chinese food came to Little Canada by way of Vancouver, where owner Alex Ha learned his trade. The food at this pretty mall restaurant is a wide-ranging culinary adventure. Recommended are the two-course Peking duck, singing chicken hot pot and the pork and salted cabbage soup. Lunch is a buffet, and dim sum is served every day, as is dinner. Reservations are recommended.

ORIGAMI

30 N. First St., Minneapolis   *333-8430*
$$$

Japanese cuisine's special affinity for the sea is shown to good advantage at this pleasant warehouse-district cafe and sushi bar. Recommended are the hamachi shioyaki, a simply grilled yellowtail, the miso soup and sashimi. Lunch is served Monday through Friday, dinner daily, with later hours on the weekend.

ROYAL ORCHID

1835 Nicollet Ave., Minneapolis   *872-1938*
$$

Looking for the Twin Cities' best Thai menu? Don't miss the mieng kham, a wrap-your-own appetizer in which coconut, ginger, dried shrimp, lime bits and other ingredients are rolled up in lettuce leaves. The Orchid's lavender decor won't win any awards, but the gai tom kha, a fragrant chicken and coconut soup, should. Lunch and dinner are served daily.

RUAM MIT THAI

544 St. Peter St., St. Paul   290-0067
$$ No credit cards

This cozy cafe is a perfect place to begin a culinary love affair with sensually pleasing Thai food. Roll your own mieng kham appetizer and try the lemony toam yum soup, roast duck curry and sticky rice with fresh mango. Lunch and dinner are served Monday through Saturday (later hours on the weekend) and dinner Sunday. Reservations are recommended.

SAJI-YA

695 Grand Ave., St. Paul   292-0444
$$

Perhaps the best way to dine at Saji-Ya is to order appetizers and sushi. The restaurant does swell things with fish (both cooked and raw), tofu and vegetables. Flashy tableside teppanyaki cooking is available too, but only certain nights. Don't be alarmed if shouting ensues when you first walk over the restaurant's wooden bridge — the host calls out the number in your party; when the rest of the staff responds, they are simply saying "Welcome." Lunch is served Monday through Friday, dinner daily. Reservations are recommended.

SAKURA

34 W. 6th St., St. Paul   224-0185
$$

A warm, friendly owner, carefully prepared food and a new location make this a fine spot to explore Japanese cuisine.

The serious sushi, filling bento box combination lunch, tasty teriyaki and tempura are all recommended, as is the ika shoga yaki (broiled cuttlefish) and goma ae (spinach and sesame) appetizers. Lunch and dinner are served Monday through Saturday, dinner only Sunday. Reservations are recommended.

SAPPHIRE DRAGON

Maplewood Square, 3035 White Bear Ave.
Maplewood   779-8623
$$

This is a friendly, family-operated restaurant offering a variety of fresh, expertly prepared Vietnamese foods with some concessions to Midwestern tastes. The egg rolls are tops, as are the shrimp stir-fry chow mein and curried mock duck. Lunch and dinner are served Monday through Saturday. Reservations are recommended.

SAWATDEE

118 N. Fourth St., Minneapolis   373-0840
$$

The restaurant-bar's raw brick, red ceiling and cobalt blue walls make an attractive setting for Supenn Harrison's spicy Thai food. Recommended are the fresh spring rolls, shrimp salad with lemongrass, chicken with cashews and, for a delightful dessert, sticky rice with fresh mango. Lunch through late-night dining are available Monday through Saturday, and dinner only through late night Sunday. Other Sawatdee locations are at 607 Washington Avenue S., Minneapolis; 8501 Lyndale Avenue S.,

Take advantage of the "Frequent Diner" cards that many Twin Cities bagel shops, espresso shops and fast food restaurants offer.

Insiders' Tips

Bloomington; and 289 E. Fifth Street, St. Paul.

SHILLA

694 N. Snelling Ave., St. Paul   645-0006
$$ No credit cards

The hot dishes here are tongue-tingling; the mild offerings are equally adventuresome. Shilla features delicious barbecued meats, noodle dishes and soups. It's open for lunch and dinner Tuesday through Sunday.

SUN SUN

854 W. University Ave., St. Paul   291-0212
$$ No credit cards

This pleasant, humble Chinese restaurant is good news for seafood lovers. Recommended are the lobster with five-spicy salt, the fresh walleye, duck with preserved vegetables, and the beef and mustard-greens soup for two. Lunch and dinner are served Monday through Friday, dinner only Saturday and Sunday. Reservations are recommended.

TASTE OF INDIA

1745 Cope Ave. E., Maplewood   773-5477
$$

Don't let the suburban strip architecture fool you at the Maplewood restaurant or the other Taste of India location at 5617 Wayzata Boulevard in St. Louis Park — there are spicy surprises in store inside. Try the scallop masala (melt-in-your-mouth shellfish, tomatoes, peppers and onions in a cumin sauce) or chicken vindaloo (potato-based sauce with a tamarind tang), dal, kheer and mango ice cream. The lunch buffet is a delicious bargain at $5.95. Wine and beer are served. Lunch and dinner are served daily.

TO CHAU

823 W. University Ave., St. Paul   291-2661
$$ No credit cards

The adventuresome Vietnamese menu offers everything from quail to eel, with plenty of noodle and stir-fry dishes too. To Chau boasts a pleasant setting and big portions. Lunch and dinner are served daily. Beer is served. Reservations are recommended.

VILLAGE WOK

610 Washington Ave. S.E.
Minneapolis   331-9041
$$

Skip the Americanized standbys and order off the wall — signs explain the seafood specials. Walleye is wonderful at this homey cafe, which is especially lively on weekend nights. It's open daily for lunch. Reservations are recommended.

VINA

756 S. Cleveland Ave., St. Paul   698-8408
$$ No credit cards

Vina features Vietnamese specialties, with a few Chinese standards thrown in. For a fun change of pace try the crisp, filling rice pancake, bites of which may be picked up with bits of lettuce and dipped in a sweet fish sauce. Around dinner time, the peach-colored restaurant is as sunny as the servers' dispositions. Lunch and dinner are served daily. Reservations are recommended.

WHITE LILY

758 Grand Ave., St. Paul   293-9124
$$

Here you'll find reliable, nonthreatening Vietnamese food in an airy, flowery setting. Lunch and dinner are served Monday through Saturday, dinner only Sunday. Reservations are recommended.

YIN YANG

2645 White Bear Ave.
Maplewood   777-1893
$$

Enjoy hot and mild Chinese food in a sleek, clean atmosphere. Cooks in white caps are visible behind a glass window, turning out some of the best fried dumplings in town. Yin Yang is open daily for lunch and dinner.

Eclectic Cuisine

ALEXANDER'S

714 Second Ave. S., Minneapolis   339-2893
$

Here's a pleasant, casual two-level eatery serving all the necessary burgers, sandwiches and salads with tasty ethnic daily specials such as Mediterranean chicken kebabs. The breakfasts are hearty too. Breakfast and lunch are served Monday through Friday.

AL'S BREAKFAST

413 Fourth Ave. S.E., Minneapolis   333-9991
$ No credit cards

Since 1950 this popular hole-in-the-wall has served breakfast near the U of M campus. The morning menu offers hash browns, omelets, eggs Benedict and blueberry and blackberry pancakes. It's a no-liquor, smoke-free environment. Breakfast and lunch are served daily.

BILLABONG AUSSIE GRILL & PUB

5001 W. 80th St., Bloomington   844-0655
$$

In the mood for Australian food? This Australian-themed restaurant serves sandwiches, steak, chops and pasta as well as a Sunday brunch. Specialities include ribs, lemon-artichoke chicken and raspberry salsa. Lunch and dinner are served Monday through Saturday and brunch, lunch and dinner Sunday. You can order appetizers until late night Monday through Saturday.

BREAD AND CHOCOLATE

867 Grand Ave., St. Paul   228-1017
$ No credit cards

Here you'll find special muffins flavored with espresso and pecans one day, cardamom and lemon the next. The rich caramel rolls are a delicate balance between crunch and tenderness, and the menu includes a selection of nice made-to-order sandwiches. It's open daily for breakfast and lunch through the late afternoon.

BRUEGGER'S BAGEL BAKERY

1 W. Seventh Pl., St. Paul   225-4363
$ No credit cards

Bruegger's fresh, chewy bagels will challenge your choppers; they're sold singly, by the dozen or as sandwiches. The garlic bagels, so fragrant they need their own bag, are especially good with Bruegger's olive-pimento cream-cheese spread or hummos and cucumber. It's open daily from early morning through early evening. Other Bruegger's restaurants are at 796 Grand Avenue, St. Paul; 2233 Energy Park Drive, St. Paul; 2136 Ford Parkway, St. Paul; 1100 Nicollet Mall, Minneapolis; 4953 Penn Avenue S., Minneapolis; 1808 S. Plymouth Road, Minnetonka; and many other locations.

BRYANT-LAKE BOWL

810 W. Lake St., Minneapolis   825-3737
$$

At this combination cafe, coffeehouse, bowling alley and experimental theater, the nifty menu offers plenty of vegetarian fare, including a swell burrito, potato salad and vegetarian chili. Also good is the Bryant-Lake Bowl plate and bete noir. The atmosphere is wholesome, in a funky sort of way. It's open daily from early morning to late night.

CAFE BRENDA

300 First Ave. N., Minneapolis   342-9230
$$

Vegetarians will go for the macrobiotic plate, open-faced black-bean enchiladas and soba noodles in ginger-tahini dressing. The menu offers plenty of temptations for seafood-lovers too, in this calm and airy restaurant. No dishes contain red meat or processed sugar. Lunch is served Monday through Friday, dinner Monday through Saturday. Reservations are recommended; smoking is not allowed.

CAFE CON AMORE

917 Grand Ave., St. Paul   222-6770
$ *No credit cards*

Here's an artsy nook featuring dandy coffee drinks and food that's above coffeehouse average — try the Michelangelo (a hot panino sandwich of turkey, provolone, sun-dried tomatoes and herbs) and the excellent heart-shaped scones. As a bonus the cafe has a private meeting room available for reservations. Breakfast, lunch and dinner (through late night) are served daily.

CAFE LATTE

850 Grand Ave., St. Paul   224-5687
$

This busy cafeteria is equally appropriate for a light healthy meal or a chocolate binge, offering a changing array of killer desserts and inventive salads and soups. There's a full selection of espresso drinks and heavenly scones (try the English currant variety). The cafe is open midmorning to late evening daily.

CAFE SFA

Saks Fifth Avenue, 655 Nicollet Mall
Minneapolis   333-7200
$

Models in expensive duds wander through this small cafe, while shoppers and downtown workers nibble on chicken Caesar salad and a sinful almond fudge pot (you can just bet those models don't indulge in this dessert very often). Lunch is served Monday through Saturday.

CARVERS

Minneapolis Hilton and Towers, 1001 Marquette Ave.
Minneapolis   376-1000
$$$

This formal, continental-American hybrid is perfectly situated for pre- or post-Orchestra Hall meals. Recommended are the crab cakes, steak salad and chestnut Charlotte. Lunch is served Monday through Friday, dinner Monday through Saturday. Reservations are recommended. Use the valet parking or hotel garage.

CECIL'S

651 S. Cleveland Ave., St. Paul   698-0334
$$

This homey family-owned and -operated deli has been serving comforting knishes and chicken soup for more than 20 years. Try the terrific chopped liver; take a dozen buttery hamantaschen home. It's open daily.

CHESAPEAKE BAGEL COMPANY

2112 Ford Pkwy.   690-0928
$ *No credit cards*

This bagel bakery makes its traditional and newer versions of chewy New York-style water bagels from fresh dough mixed on-site. Flavors include popular poppy and pumpernickel as well as tomato basil, sourdough and blueberry. Hot and cold bagel sandwiches and varieties of creme cheese are also available. Other locations are in Eden Prairie and Wayzata. Chesapeake Bagel is open morning through evening Monday through Saturday and morning through late afternoon on Sunday.

COSSETTA'S
211 W. Seventh St., St. Paul   222-3476
$ No credit cards

Here you'll get unsurpassed New York-style pizza with a thin, foldable crust. There's a cafeteria line for pastas, salads and sandwiches too. It's open for breakfast through late night daily (with shorter hours Sunday).

FRENCH MEADOW BAKERY & CAFE
2601 Lyndale Ave. S., Minneapolis   870-7855
$

This casual European-style cafe and bakery features breads, muffins, scones and sandwiches on a variety of fresh-baked breads. Selections from an espresso bar, vegetarian soups, salads, gourmet pizzas and all natural desserts can be enjoyed al fresco. It's open from early morning until later evening daily (with later hours Friday and Saturday).

GALLERY 8
Walker Art Center, 725 Vineland Pl.
Minneapolis   374-3701
$ No credit cards

Rest your eyes and exercise your palate at this tasteful top-of-the-museum restaurant. If only all cafeterias were this good: It has daily special entrees, straight-ahead sandwiches and salads, and artful desserts. It's open for lunch and dinner Tuesday through Sunday, but call ahead to verify dinner hours, since special events may close the restaurant some nights.

LORING CAFE AND BAR
1624 Harmon Pl., Minneapolis   332-1617
$$$

This hipper-than-hip cafe boasts a menu that's sensitive to the season. The appetizers shine: bucheron and sun-dried tomato pizza, and pretty composed salads. The sprawling bar, which offers a limited menu and nightly entertainment, is big on theatrical ambiance and attitude. The Bar has outdoor seating with a view of Loring Park; the cafe has a cozy courtyard. Lunch is served Monday through Friday, dinner daily. Food is served in the bar through midday Monday through Saturday and midafternoon to midnight daily; also Sunday brunch is served. Reservations are recommended.

LUCIA'S
1432 W. 31st St., Minneapolis   825-1572
$$$

Lucia's offers delicious, eclectic food, served in a room that hovers between casual and romantic. Though the selections are slim at the wine bar next door, it's a nice spot for a sip and a nibble of, say, bread with goat cheese, pesto and seasoned lentils. Lunch is served Tuesday through Friday, brunch Saturday and Sunday and dinner Tuesday through Sunday. Reservations are recommended. The wine bar is open until late night Tuesday to Sunday.

Blueberry is the flavor of the official Minnesota state muffin.

Insiders' Tips

MANHATTAN BAGELS

1672 Grand Ave., St. Paul   690-5138
$ No credit cards

This bagel shop offers not only freshly baked bagels with cream cheese or delish homemade chicken salad, but also a genuine New York accent, courtesy of the brothers from the Big Apple who run it. It's open daily from early morning to 6 PM.

MUD PIE

2549 Lyndale Ave. S., Minneapolis   872-9435
$$

A long, international list of vegetarian specialties is on the menu of this earthier-than-thou cafe, which is famous for its veggie burgers (also available in your grocer's freezer). Tamale pie, rotti, and peanut butter dandies are good too. Mud Pie is open for lunch, dinner and late-night munching daily, with opening in the morning on the weekend. No smoking is allowed.

THE NM CAFE

Neiman Marcus, 651 Nicollet Mall
Minneapolis   339-2600
$$

This cafe offers a high-quality lunch and snack menu of sandwiches, salads and skinny pizzas. The midafternoon tea, served Thursday through Saturday, is a classy pick-me-up, with tea sandwiches, scones, sweets and Ashby's tea. The cafe is open for lunch through late afternoon Monday through Saturday. Free parking is available in the Gaviidae Commons ramp; bring in your parking ticket for validation.

NEW RIVERSIDE CAFE

329 Cedar Ave., Minneapolis   333-4814
$ No credit cards

Food and politics mix in a gentle way at this worker-owned West Bank institution. The cafe offers reliable, inexpensive, healthful food, including Mexican dishes, rice and beans, salads, omelets and some awe-inspiring tofu specialties. The cafe hosts live music almost nightly, and there's always terrific people-watching. It's open from early morning to late at night daily except Sunday, when it's open from midmorning to midafternoon.

PLANET HOLLYWOOD

Mall of America, Bloomington   854-7827
$$

Owned in part by Demi Moore, Arnold Schwarzenegger, Sylvester Stallone and Bruce Willis, this movie museum/hype machine/restaurant is crammed with old and new memorabilia (check out the life-size cyborg from Terminator 2, Freddie Krueger's claw glove and outfits worn by Judy Garland and Prince). The menu — casual and eclectic — isn't really the point. But you might enjoy the Chicken Crunch appetizer, fajitas, turkey burger and ebony-and-ivory brownie. It's open daily until late night.

RISIMINI'S

1670 Grand Ave., St. Paul   699-0013
$ No credit cards

This counter-service eatery, popular among Macalester College students and staff, offers many choices of pizzas, pastas, salads and sandwiches. The calzone is impressive inside and out. Risimini's is open for lunch through late night Monday through Saturday and dinner only Sunday. No alcoholic beverages are available.

THE RIVER ROOM

Dayton's, Sixth and Cedar Sts.
St. Paul   292-5174
$$

This is a pink, relaxing place for ladies (and well-mannered men) who lunch, with a menu of trend-conscious staples and terrific popovers. Try the Moroccan salad. It is open for lunch through early evening dining Monday through Friday and serves lunch through midafternoon on the weekend. Reservations are recommended for lunch.

ROCK BOTTOM BREWERY
825 Hennepin Ave., Minneapolis   332-2739
$$

The made-on-the-premises ales are the main reason to visit this popular bar and restaurant; the food tends toward the heavy. Best bets are the salads and appetizers such as Asiago cheese dip, smoked Rocky Mountain trout and the glutton-size plate of maroon and gold nachos. Food is served daily until late night; the bar is open until 1 AM nightly, with live jazz 10 PM to midnight Wednesday through Saturday.

SANTORINI TAVERNA & GRILL
9920 Wayzata Blvd.
St. Louis Park   546-6722
$$

Mediterranean and Greek cuisine are the specialities here including fresh seafood pasta and phyllo specialty items. Appetizers run the gamut from a variety of spreads and dips to feta cheese, and eggplant and caviar. It's open daily until late night.

SCULLY'S BROILER AND BAR
1321 E. 78th St., Bloomington   854-0107
$$

Outstanding fresh fish and many creative pasta combinations head the eclectic menu at this pleasant airport-area bar and grill. It's open daily for breakfast, lunch, dinner and late-night dining.

SIDNEY'S PIZZA CAFE
2120 Hennepin Ave., Minneapolis   870-7000
$$

Here's a great place for unique pastas

and pizzas, beautiful salads and more, with an emphasis on fresh and delish. Try the Asian spicy chicken pizza, the Greek salad, fiesta chicken linguini and fettuccine with chicken and sun-dried tomatoes. The wine menu offers a fine variety by the glass and the half-glass "taste." There's a bustling atmosphere, with a view of the rotisserie and wood-burning oven. Breakfast is served Monday through Friday, brunch Saturday and Sunday and lunch/dinner daily. No smoking is allowed. Other Sidney's restaurants are at 15600 Highway 7, Minnetonka; and at the Galleria, 70th Street and France Avenue in Edina.

SOBAS
2558 Lyndale Ave. S., Minneapolis   871-6631
$$

More soba noodles than you can shake a chopstick at can be found in this casual neighborhood restaurant. Choose from pork tenderloin with garlic mashed potatoes, poached salmon and pasta. Breakfast, lunch and dinner are served daily (breakfast until midafternoon Saturday and Sunday).

SOFIA'S ITALIA
1420 Nicollet Ave. S., Minneapolis   872-4195
$$

Here's a delightful menu that features Italian cuisine and New York-style pizza, as well as garlic soup, veal chops, Caesar salad and risotto. Lunch and dinner (through late night) are served Monday through Friday, with midafternoon to late evening dining Saturday and Sunday.

SOPHIA
65 S.E. Main St., Minneapolis   379-1111
$$

This romantic continental restaurant in Riverplace specializes in Norwegian salmon, fresh fish, pasta, filet mignon and dry-aged beef. An afternoon Sunday brunch is served, and you can cap off an evening with live music and dancing after dinner. Lunch and dinner (through late night, earlier Sunday) are served daily.

TABLE OF CONTENTS
1648 Grand Ave., St. Paul   699-6595
$$

This consistently good restaurant, attached to a bookstore, offers a sophisticated array of fresh, creative food. Recommended are the fish specials, wafer-crust pizzas, the chicken salad and the sinful sauteed pound cake. Lunch is served Monday through Saturday, brunch Sunday and dinner daily. Reservations are recommended; smoking isn't allowed. A second location at 1310 Hennepin Avenue in Minneapolis features a similar menu, an expanded wine bar and a weekend brunch Saturday and Sunday.

THE TOUR CAFE
4924 France Ave. S., Edina   929-1010
$$$

Scott Kee's clever cookery thrives at this cafe, where you'll find heady, sophisticated flavors with many an international accent. Don't miss the polenta with prosciutto and spicy melon, smoked mozzarella risotto cakes, fettuccine with mushrooms, gorgonzola and cream, jerk chicken breast, and rhubarb crisp. Dinner is served daily, and reservations are recommended.

European Cuisine

BLACK FOREST INN
1 E. 26th St., Minneapolis   872-0812
$$

Here's all the German food you could want in a well-worn, utterly comfortable setting. Take note of the espresso drinks

and a hearty selection of beers. Don't miss the weighty ham and sauerkraut balls. The outdoor seating goes fast in good weather. Dine here any day of the week for lunch or dinner into the late night.

BRASSERIE
1400 Nicollet Ave., Minneapolis   874-7285
$$

The French fare plied by Brittany-born Paul Laubignat can be the model of uncomplicated clarity — it's cooking that showcases the quality of the food rather than the ego of the chef. Try the assiette de charcuterie, roast rack of pork, chicken and sun-dried tomato pasta, profiteroles, and chocolate ganache. You'll find a romantic ambiance and superior service here. Lunch and dinner are served daily (later hours Friday and Saturday) brunch Sunday and a limited menu from 2 to 5 PM Monday through Saturday. Reservations are recommended.

BRITS' PUB
1110 Nicollet Mall, Minneapolis   332-3908
$$

Steak and kidney pie, cock-a-leekie soup and other comforting aspects of British food are here aplenty, served in an attractive setting. Take some time to sit by the fire, below a portrait of the Queen Mum. Food is served from lunchtime through late night daily, with breakfast hours added on Saturday and Sunday.

BUCA
1204 Harmon Place, Minneapolis   638-2225
$$

Ideal for hungry groups, Buca offers southern Italian food served family-style in great quantity, in an ambiance of bustling *bonhomie*. Recommended dishes are the bruschetta, mixed green salad with gorgonzola and prosciutto, spaghetti marinara, chicken Marsala, green beans with lemon, and tiramisu. Dinner is served daily. Buca also has a St. Paul restaurant at 2728 Gannon Road and one in Eden Prairie at 7711 Mitchell Road.

CAFE DINAPOLI
816 Hennepin Ave., Minneapolis   333-4949
$

This popular old Italian cafe has the feel of yesteryear — cozy booths, scenic murals, a '40s-type bar lounge — that's a nice backdrop for a good traditional Italian meal at very reasonable prices.

CAFE UN DEUX TROIS
114 S. Ninth St., Minneapolis   673-0686
$$

This is Minneapolis' own version of the New York brasserie, serving French basics in a setting that looks fashionably crumbling due to trompe l'oeil paintings. Try the fish specials, the grilled steak, escargots, salads and the crème brûlée for dessert. Lunch is served Monday through Friday, dinner Monday through Saturday. Reservations are recommended; free valet parking is available in the evening.

CAFFE SOLO
123 N. Third St., Minneapolis   332-7108
$$

Goat cheese and sun-dried tomatoes are still in style at this contemporary Italian cafe. The menu contains a long list of gourmet pizzas, pastas and well-executed fish specials (look for sauteed snapper with leeks and scallions). Also good are the grilled eggplant appetizer, shrimp and scallop lasagna, galette and spumoni. The atmosphere is spacious and often noisy. It's open from early morning through late evening daily (until the wee small hours Friday and Saturday). Reservations are recommended.

CARMELO'S RISTORANTE
238 S. Snelling Ave., St. Paul   699-2448
$$

This family-owned and -operated cafe offers simple Italian fare, including a tasty chicken parmigiana, bracioletti (steak rolled around cheese and herbs) and salad with balsamic vinaigrette. All pasta is made on the premises; focaccia pizzas are a good choice for lunch. Lunch and dinner are available Monday through Friday, dinner only Saturday. Sundays are reserved for private parties. Carmelo's serves wine and beer. Reservations are recommended.

CHRISTOS
2632 Nicollet Ave. S., Minneapolis   871-2111
$$

Come here for a hearty helping of Greek cuisine; the long menu is good for experimenting. The appetizers are especially recommended: hearty hummos, light calamari, creamy taramosalata — and they even know how to do octopus right. Lunch and dinner are served Monday through Friday, dinner only Saturday and Sunday. Reservations are recommended.

D'AMICO CUCINA
100 N. Sixth St., Minneapolis   338-2401
$$$$

The food looks as good as it tastes at this elegant Italian restaurant. You'll find no heaps of pasta here, but delicate dishes that demand to be slowly savored — artful arrays of wild mushroom preparations, gnocchi that melts in your mouth, sumptuous roast birds and irresistible desserts. The waitstaff is always top-notch. Dinner is served daily. Call for reservations.

FRANCESCA'S BAKERY AND CAFE
W. Seventh Pl. and St. Peter St.
St. Paul   227-5775
$ No credit cards

Francesca's wholesome Italian-influenced fare is a delicious gift to hungry downtown workers. Recommended choices are the black bean soup, chicken and turkey salad sandwiches, wild rice salad, savory tarts and better-than-Mom-makes cookies. Francesca's serves wine and beer and also handles private parties and catering. Closed Sunday, Francesca's serves from early morning through early evening Monday through Saturday, with later hours Friday and Saturday.

GIORGIO'S

2451 Hennepin Ave., Minneapolis   374-5131
$$ No credit cards

Tasty Italian pastas, salads, meats and small courses, informal charm and the reasonable prices all recommend this small cafe. Lunch is served Tuesday through Friday, dinner and late-night dining daily and brunch Saturday and Sunday. Another location at 1601 W. Lake Street features an expanded wine bar.

IT'S GREEK TO ME

626 W. Lake St., Minneapolis   825-9922
$$

This is a casual, bustling, inexpensive eatery with some of the cities' best baklava. The spanakopita and lamb kebabs are also recommended. It's open daily for lunch and dinner.

ITALIAN PIE SHOPPE AND WINERY

777 Grand Ave., St. Paul   221-0093
$

For a richly sauced thin-crust pizza, and a deep dish that's memorably crisp, stop here. The casual atmosphere drips with nostalgia. It's open daily for lunch and dinner, with later hours on Friday and Saturday. There's a second location at 1438 Yankee Doodle Road in Eagan.

KRAMARCZUK SAUSAGE COMPANY

215 E. Hennepin Ave.
Minneapolis   379-3018
$ No credit cards

Belly up to the cafeteria line to order deep-fried piroshki, nalesnyky (meat-stuffed crepes covered with cheese), varenyky (soft folded dumplings stuffed with meat, potatoes or sauerkraut), cabbage rolls and sandwiches made with krakowska and other sausages. The prices are low and the lunchroom is sunny and spacious. Breakfast and lunch are served Monday through Saturday.

LINGUINI AND BOB

Butler Square Bldg., 100 N. Sixth St.
Minneapolis   332-1600
$$

This restaurant, popular before events at Target Center, features classy Italian food in a high-energy setting. Recommended are the spicy shrimp with angel hair cake, calamari, pizza with caramelized hot peppers and onions, linguini in parchment, and chicken breast with lemon mashed potatoes. Lunch and dinner are served Monday through Saturday, dinner Sunday.

LOWRY'S

1934 Hennepin Ave. S.
Minneapolis   871-0806
$$

Lowry's offers a fun menu concentrating on Italian preparations — pastas, polentas, risottos — often with a hearty twist. Try the polenta with mozzarella and black bean sauce. The kitchen also prepares many types of salads and some fish dishes. Check out the good wine and beer selection. Reservations are recommended. Lowry's is open daily, with early morning hours Monday through Friday.

MUFFULETTA CAFE

2260 Como Ave., St. Paul   644-9116
$$

Muffuletta's long menu with both French and Italian influences is strongest on pizzas, pastas and appetizers. The tortellini baronessa is especially good; so's the steak au poivre. During spring and summer, take advantage of outdoor dining on the deck. Lunch is served Monday through Saturday, dinner daily. A sumptuous brunch is served Sunday. Reservations are recommended.

NYE'S POLONAISE ROOM

112 Hennepin Ave. E.
Minneapolis   379-2021
$$

One of the few old-time restaurants with the sense to leave a good thing alone, Nye's features great 1960s decor and hearty Polish food. Recommended are the pierogi, kielbasa and sauerkraut — and plenty of time to let the weighty food and pleasant ambiance sink in. Cap off your evening with a visit to Nye's legendary piano bar. Lunch and dinner are served Monday through Saturday. Reservations are recommended.

OLD SPAGHETTI FACTORY

233 Park Ave., Minneapolis   341-0949
$

Italian gusto graces this recently opened family eatery. So does a life-size trolley car in the center of the dining room! Naturally, the specialty is pasta, smothered in a variety of sauces. Lunch is served Monday through Friday, dinner daily.

PANINO'S

2441 Rice St., Roseville   481-7009
$$

The best bets here are the unusual rolled sandwiches called paninos, which make an enormous meal. There are pizzas and pastas too. Another Panino's is at 857 Village Center Drive, North Oaks. Panino's is open daily for lunch and dinner.

PIZZAIOLA ROMA

704 S. Cleveland Ave., St. Paul   699-8321
$ *No credit cards*

This clean, pleasant cafe serves top-notch gourmet pizzas, including a delicious Thai chicken version, plus nice salads and hearty calzone. Order at the counter, then relax while you're served. Lunch and dinner are served daily.

RISTORANTE LUCI

470 S. Cleveland Ave., St. Paul   699-8258
$$

Olive oil, mushrooms and cheeses make beautiful music together at this cozy, family-owned cafe. The menu includes regional Italian pastas and entrees, plus lovely fruit tarts. The prices are moderate. Dinner is served daily, and reservations are highly recommended.

RUSSIAN TEA HOUSE

1758 W. University Ave., St. Paul   646-4144
$ *No credit cards*

This no-frills cafe serves great piroshki, which is mild ground beef and rice baked inside a chewy, leavened roll. Russian potato salad, cabbage rolls and borscht are also available. It's good for take-out. Go on a nice day, for the best seating is out front on a picnic table under a pine tree. It's open from midmorning to early evening.

STEPHANO'S

11849 Millpond Ave., Burnsville   895-1639
$$ *No credit cards*

This is the place for honest, home-cooked Italian food, served in a family-friendly atmosphere overflowing with knickknacks. Recommended are the ravioli, spaghettini alla Napolitana, pollo con carciofini (chicken with artichoke hearts), bistecci alla Italiana, pizza and the house salad. Lunch is served Monday through Friday, dinner daily.

TULIPS

452 Selby Ave., St. Paul   221-1061
$$

This cozy, reasonably priced Cathedral Hill cafe serves meats, poultry and seafood, personalized with French sauces. It's a popular spot for romancing. Lunch is served Monday to Friday, dinner daily. Reservations are recommended.

Four-star Cuisine

DAKOTA BAR AND GRILL

Bandana Square, 1021 E. Bandana Blvd.
St. Paul
$$ 642-1442

The town's classiest jazz club is also one of its best restaurants. A changing menu emphasizes seasonal ingredients and creative combinations. The fish is uniformly fine; garlic fans will worship the Dakota's Caesar, others will swoon over the brie and apple soup. Who says Midwestern cuisine is unsophisticated? Dinner is served daily (later hours Friday and Saturday) and brunch Sunday. The bar offers a food menu 4 PM to 1 AM daily. Sunday brunch is 10 AM to 2 PM. Reservations are recommended.

THE 510 RESTAURANT

510 Groveland Ave., Minneapolis   874-6440
$$$

The 510 has lowered prices and cut down on the formality, but still has charms, including its grand old dining room, an award-winning Caesar salad and a bargain-featured wine list, with prices just a buck over average retail. Rec-

ommended are the oven-roasted rack of New Zealand lamb and wild mushroom linguini. The 510 is open for dinner Monday through Saturday. Reservations are recommended.

FOREPAUGH'S

276 S. Exchange St., St. Paul   224-5606
$$$

Forepaugh's serves traditional continental favorites in the pretty, intimate rooms of a historic Victorian house. There's no question: This is a very popular special-occasion choice. Forepaugh's serves lunch Monday through Friday, brunch Sunday and dinner daily. Reservations are recommended.

GOODFELLOW'S

The Conservatory, 800 Nicollet Mall
Minneapolis   332-4800
$$$$

Allow yourself a big budget and a lot of time to enjoy this wonderful restaurant's creative food and classy, soothing ambiance. Goodfellow's also features a top-notch wine list and great artwork. Lunch is served Monday through Friday, dinner Monday through Saturday. Reservations are recommended.

KINCAID'S

8400 Normandale Lake Blvd.
Bloomington   921-2255
$$$

This is one of the Twin Cities' best-liked restaurants, a home for those who love Nebraska corn-fed beef as well as pasta, fresh fish and oysters. It's a popular dining stop for executives with food as well as business on their minds, plus couples and others wanting to create a good impression. Try the mesquite-grilled meats and homemade bread. You can dine here for lunch Monday through Saturday, brunch Sunday and dinner daily.

MANNY'S

Hyatt Regency Hotel, 1300 Nicollet Mall
Minneapolis   339-9900
$$$$

Waiters at this classy steakhouse wheel around a cart of raw dry-aged beef, pork and live lobsters, just in case you need help deciding. A winning menu boasts a fine Caesar salad and a whole section of potatoes and onions (try the hash browns). The food is excellent, and all of it is offered à la carte. Dinner is served daily. Reservations are recommended.

MORTON'S OF CHICAGO

555 Nicollet Mall, Minneapolis   673-9700
$$$$

The meals are enormous, and so are the prices. But if you have the dough to blow, Morton's is worth it for the simple, well-prepared food and pleasant, professional service. The steaks are superb, as is the grilled swordfish. The baked and Lyonnaise potatoes and beefsteak tomato salads are great. Don't forget your doggie bag. Lunch is served Monday through Friday, dinner daily. Reservations are recommended. Valet parking is offered at the Sixth Street entrance, just east of Nicollet.

MURRAY'S

26 S. Sixth St., Minneapolis   339-0909
$$$$

The sign on the outside proclaims that Murray's is "home of the silver butter-knife steak" — a characterization left by a traveling gourmand of the 1950s who found perfect steaks in precious few establishments throughout the United States. Forty years later, this restaurant is still preparing mouth-watering beef, as well as very good fish entrees (the salmon and walleye are particularly good). If for no other reason, come here

to see the professional, veteran waitstaff at work and to enjoy the violin and piano sounds Thursday through Saturday evenings. Lunch and dinner are served Monday through Friday (later on Friday) and dinner only Saturday and Sunday. There's also a weekday afternoon tea from 2 to 3:30 PM.

NEW FRENCH CAFE BAR AND BAKERY

128 N. Fourth St., Minneapolis   338-3790
$$$

This warehouse-district institution has been a popular destination for 17 years. Lively and inviting, it serves fresh interpretations of all manner of French food, such as a peppered tuna steak with shoe string potatoes in sherry wine vinegar shallot sauce. Adjacent to the cafe is the New French Bakery serving award-winning baguettes, arguably the best French bread in town, as well as sourdough hearth bread and European pastries. The place is hopping most all of the day, and in the evening the cafe is a perfect spot for dinner before the theater with a three-course fixed-price dinner at $17.95. It's open daily from early morning until late night.

NICOLLET ISLAND INN

95 Merriam St., Nicollet Island
Minneapolis   331-1800
$$$

This is a charming country inn serving sophisticated comfort food. The four-course Minnesota-made menu includes pan-fried chicken that is out of this world. Also recommended are the lamb chops, goat cheese with red-pepper compote, and walleye and scallop cakes. The Inn serves dinner daily, breakfast and lunch Monday through Saturday and a nice brunch Sunday. Reservations are recommended.

St. Paul Grill

St. Paul Hotel, 350 Market St.
St. Paul   224-7455
$$$

The woody, understated dining room looks as though it has been listening to business dealings and lovers' secrets for years. Here you'll find solid, uncomplicated American food, including steaks, tasty grilled chicken breast and fish. The smoked salmon appetizer is very good. Dinner is served daily, lunch Monday through Saturday and brunch Sunday. A bar menu is available until midnight daily. Reservations are recommended.

Whitney Grille

Whitney Hotel, 150 Portland Ave.
Minneapolis   339-9300
$$$

For fine dining, few places can compare with this elegant, hushed setting in the lower level of the Whitney Hotel. A feeling of intimacy is enhanced by the use of dark woods, plants and waist-high dividers that promote privacy without compromising the people-watching quotient. The Whitney serves contemporary American cuisine prepared with fresh, seasonal ingredients. Live entertainment is featured Wednesday through Saturday nights. Breakfast and lunch are served Monday through Saturday, brunch on Sunday and dinner daily.

Hispanic and Caribbean Cuisine

El Amanecer

194 Concord St., St. Paul   291-0758
$ *No credit cards*

Come here for a variety of filling Mexican basics, including tasty, chewy tacos al pastor. For $4.50 weekdays at lunchtime, you can choose from several hefty meat stews served with rice, beans and tortillas; you can order menudo and caldo specials Friday through Sunday. Breakfast is served daily, hence the name "the dawn." El Amanecer is open every day except Monday, and stays open until the wee small hours on Friday and Saturday.

Boca Chica

11 Concord St., St. Paul   222-8499
$$

This 26-year-old institution has added a snappy new bar for sipping those killer Margaritas and nibbling on nachos or chips with hot, hot sauce. Mexican-American basics are served, as well as lesser-known regional specialties, such as pork with nopales and enchiladas in a tangy green sauce. It's open daily for lunch, dinner. Reservations are recommended on weekends.

El Burrito

200 Concord St., St. Paul   227-2192
$ *No credit cards*

This neighborhood Mexican grocery includes a swell deli for take-out food. Try the chile chipotle or burrito filled with chili verde. El Burrito is open daily until early evening.

La Cazuela

197 Concord St., St. Paul   291-0498
$ *No credit cards*

This humble tortilla factory and cafeteria serves fresh corn torts smothered with spicy stews: chile verde, chipotle, nopales and much more. The borracho beans will set a happy little fire in your mouth. It's open from morning to early evening daily.

Chez Bananas

129 N. Fourth St., Minneapolis   340-0032
$$

This restaurant serves spicy, creative Caribbean specialties in a goofy atmosphere — rubber bats mingle with plastic

Godzillas. Where else can you eat expertly prepared fish, perfect cornbread and black beans while gazing at a picture of Pee Wee Herman or an inflatable version of Edvard Munch's *The Scream?* Dinner is served daily, lunch Tuesday through Friday.

LA CORVINA

1570 Selby Ave., St. Paul   645-5288
$$ *No credit cards*

This friendly family-operated cafe serves comforting, yet not always predictable, Mexican-Latin food. Recommended are the fajitas, burritos, garlic chicken and sopa de albondigas. Outdoor seating is available. La Corvina is open daily for lunch and dinner.

LA CUCARACHA

36 S. Dale St., St. Paul   221-9682
$

The food's zippy and so's the service. Order the nachos Azteca, the puerco guisado verde, and the pollo loco. There's also a new Minneapolis location at 315 First Avenue N. It's open for lunch and dinner daily, with later hours Friday and Saturday.

JUANITA'S

201 Concord St., St. Paul   290-2511
$ *No credit cards*

Juanita's offers a variety of inexpensive, authentic Mexican food: burritos, enchiladas and soft tacos with onions, fresh cilantro and sauces on the side. It's open for lunch and dinner daily, with earlier hours on the weekend. Juanita's does not serve alcoholic beverages.

EL MESON

3450 Lyndale Ave. S.
Minneapolis   822-8062
$$

Here's a rare taste of Spanish and other Latin-influenced eats marked by plenty of garlic, sweet peppers and often saffron. Call ahead for paella in this cozy, friendly nook. Lunch and dinner are served Tuesday through Sunday, dinner only Monday. There's another El Meson at 115 Vicksburg Lane, Plymouth. Reservations are recommended. Alcoholic beverages are limited to low-alcohol beer.

PASQUAL'S

2528 Hennepin Ave., Minneapolis   374-1415
$

This solid Southwestern deli has a full menu of enchiladas, tacos, burritos and the like; you can also buy fresh salsa, guacamole and foods to cook at home. Another Pasqual's is at 5057 France Avenue S., Minneapolis. Hours are 10 AM to 10 PM daily. You can eat in or take out.

Outside the Twin Cities, But Worth the Drive

THE CREAMERY

County Rd. C, east of Hwy. 25
Downsville, Wis.   (715) 664-8354
$$ *No credit cards*

A little over an hour's drive from St. Paul, this country getaway offers a relaxing atmosphere and simple, sometimes sophisticated food. The prices are good and the service friendly too. Dinner is served daily, lunch Tuesday through Saturday and brunch Sunday. A light menu is served in the lounge throughout the week as well.

DICK'S BAR

111 Walnut St.
Hudson, Wis.   (715) 386-5222
$$

When you order a Chicken in a Hubcap here, you really get a car part with your meal. Dick's cozy ambiance, cheerful staff and good fries make it a neat stop-off. The best bets are chicken, burgers and fresh pasta dishes, or order one of the nightly specials or cheap appetizers. You can eat here morning, noon and night seven days a week.

Dock Cafe

425 E. Nelson St., Stillwater   *430-3770*
$$

Grilled fish, meat and fowl, an eclectic appetizer list and plenty of salads appropriate to the season — they're all here in a tasteful, airy building that peers out onto the St. Croix River. The attractive, expansive deck on the riverfront beckons you when the weather's nice. Dock Cafe is open for lunch and dinner daily. Reservations are recommended.

Harbor View Cafe

First and Main Sts.
Pepin, Wis.   *(715) 442-3893*
$$ *No credit cards*

Lunch or dinner at this casual riverfront restaurant is worth the drive and the usually long wait for a table. The blackboard menu boasts a changing array of fresh fish, meats and much more. Try the magnificent coq au vin, the plump garlic prawns on pasta or the satisfying Caesar salad. Prices are moderate, to boot. Do go early; the fall color season creates a breathtaking dinner rush. It's open Thursday through Monday.

Inside
Nightlife

You can learn a great deal about a city from its bars.

Set yourself down on a stool, lean your elbows on the oak and order up your preferred libation. Then listen in on neighboring conversations or engage a new acquaintance in some friendly banter. Soon, you'll find yourself swept up in the homey warmth of pub culture, making new connections and gaining valuable insight into local culture.

Like any vibrant metropolitan area, the Twin Cities has a lively bar scene, with intimate, old-fashioned neighborhood joints and large commercial operations and nightclubs of varying sizes and styles.

When it comes to the latter, live music is where it's at in the twin towns. The area is internationally famous for its music scene — especially in the rock genre — and the cities' lively club scene has become an incubator for nationally acclaimed talent. In fact, the area has been nicknamed "The land of 10,000 bands."

But, like any dynamic urban area, you can have a good time on the town even without the music. What we've assembled here are a number of pub crawls that will take you through Twin Cities neighborhoods and let you glimpse some of the local color.

Within each walk, you'll find an interesting mix, from small watering holes to expansive music halls. In the case of the more lengthy crawls (for example, the bar-heavy Minneapolis Warehouse District), you're advised to pick and choose. Please don't try to hit 'em all, unless you're feeling restless and plan on ordering only iced tea or soda.

The crawls are, for the most part, in-

Gatlin Brothers Music City Restaurant at the Mall of America.

Photo: Buzz Magnuson, Pioneer Press

tended as walks. No driving should be necessary if you're drinking. A warning on that account: Unlike such bustling burgs as Chicago or New York, you're rarely able to step from the door of a Twin Cities restaurant, bar or theater and hail a taxi. Demand for taxis here is as meager as the supply. It may be a good idea to start the evening by looking up a cab company in the phone book and scrawling down the number. Then, when you feel you've had your fill of crawling, give them a call and they'll come get you. For those on a budget, MCTO buses are a reliable source of transportation to any area within the Twin Cities.

Although local liquor laws are a constant source of debate in the city halls of Minneapolis, St. Paul and surrounding suburbs, the standard closing time is 1 AM. Some pubs listed here will serve food, but no alcohol, after that time.

So, let's get started. We'll begin with what could be called Bar Central in the Twin Cities: Minneapolis' Warehouse District, on the northwest edge of downtown.

Pubs and Bars

Minneapolis

WAREHOUSE DISTRICT PUB CRAWL

The grand old brick buildings of the Warehouse District, once used primarily for storage, are now home to the Twin Cities' highest concentration of art galleries and feature some of Minneapolis' best restaurants within its loosely defined boundaries.

Like any center for artists (yes, many of them live and work in the neighborhood's renovated lofts), the attire and attitude are primarily Bohemian.

It's especially fun to take a crawl when the galleries are hosting opening receptions for new exhibits (on a Saturday night, roughly every six weeks) and the crowded sidewalks take on the ambiance of a street festival.

We'll start in the older section of the Warehouse District, with the **Acme Comedy Co.**, 338-6393, off by itself in the Itasca Building at 708 N. First Street. Situated amid a stretch of storefronts that also includes the rehearsal spaces for the Minnesota Opera and the Guthrie Theater's Laboratory offshoot, the Acme is regarded by many as the Twin Cities' best comedy club, thanks to its booking of national acts (five nights a week) and its unforced jovial atmosphere.

If you walk a few blocks southeast, you'll come upon **Nikki's**, 340-9098, 107 Third Avenue N., a friendly midsize pub with a thrown-together but inviting feel. Nikki's hosts music every night, with pianist Cornbread Harris (father of pop and R&B giant Jimmy "Jam" Harris) tickling the ivories every Wednesday, Friday and Saturday night. If you're in town during the summer months, the neighboring garden area is the nicest outdoor bar in the Warehouse District.

Bev's Wine Bar, 337-0102, 300 Third Avenue N., a few blocks down from Nikki's, offers a small, intimate setting for sipping a sunny Vouvray and sharing secrets over a loaf of crusty French bread. Grab an outdoor table or sit indoors and enjoy the sparse yet elegant setting of mottled rose-colored walls, candlelit wooden tables and soulful French accordion music on the stereo.

If Bev's is a study in subtlety, the **Tropix Beach Club**, 333-1006, 400 Third Avenue N., makes no pretense of being anything but a rowdy beach-party bar with beefy bartenders in muscle tees. For fun, enjoy a table in the sea cruiser boat near the dance floor. An adjoining game room offers pool and pinball.

The dividing line between the old and new Warehouse District is Washington Avenue, a major downtown thoroughfare. It has a far more commercial climate than any of the dimly lit side streets, and many of its bars have a raucous and rowdy atmosphere.

Exhibit A on that account is **Bunker's**, 338-8188, 761 Washington Avenue N., a boisterous, noisy live-music bar that specializes in blues and R&B of the old school (loads of horns, lengthy guitar solos and throaty vocals). The sightlines are limited, but the tunes are generally satisfying. Every Monday since the early '80s, Dr. Mambo's Combo has held forth with soulful funk, aided by guests from some of the area's most prominent bands (Prince's players, among them). Another regular is the blues-based big band, Mick Sterling and the Stud Brothers.

Head a few blocks southeast on Washington and you'll find **Mollie Malone's**, 333-1675, 119 Washington Avenue N. Unlike St. Paul, the Mill City is not known for its Irish-American community, but Mollie's is a charming little place to put away a pint or two and, on weekends, hear some folk music from the Emerald Isle.

Continue on to **Runyon's**, 332-7158, 107 Washington Avenue N. Once the hottest pub in the neighborhood, Runyon's has settled into its niche as a dark, chatty, checkered bar bursting with noise and energy. Now turn south on First Avenue and you'll be headed into the Warehouse District's more bustling environs, closer to the heart of downtown.

If you're in the mood for music, there are few better places to hear it than the **Fine Line Music Cafe**, 338-8100, 318 First Avenue N. The acoustics and sightlines are outstanding at this tiered den of pop, folk and rock, where you'll find a blend of emerging local bands and concerts by national acts with commensurate cover charges. Alas, the drink prices are steep, the kitchen's inconsistent and the waitstaff is notorious for its disappearing act. But if all you care about is listening to the music, it's a nice club.

Head west on Fourth Street and you'll encounter a couple of stops worth consideration. Duck in through the doorway of the New French Cafe (a first-rate restaurant) and follow the serpentine hallway to the **New French Bar**, 338-3790, 128 N. Fourth Street. Here you'll find a selection of outstanding wines of various vintages, best when imbibed at one of the bar's sidewalk tables in summer. But the inside is intimate and oak-laden, with a relaxing atmosphere that offers a sharp contrast to the neighboring **Urban Wildlife**, 339-4665, 331 Second Avenue N., a once-out-of-the-way watering hole that today has become a social hotbed for those in their 20s who clearly miss the frathouse parties.

Rosen's Bar & Grill, 338-1926, 439 First Avenue N., with its trendy California pastas, stylish wall art and no-smoking policy, is one of the classier sports bars around. Outdoor patio seating is available. A note of interest: Proprietor here is Mark Rosen, a popular local TV sportscaster.

No visit to the neighborhood would be complete without at least looking in the door and finding that you can't get a table at the **Loon Cafe**, 332-8342, 500 First Avenue N. There may be times when this institution isn't almost bursting out its big windows with people, but never in the evening. The chief attractions are the good chili, people-watching and pedestrian traffic patterns that are conducive to uninterrupted conversation.

There's room aplenty next door at the sprawling **Old Chicago**, 338-8686, 508 First Avenue N., a friendly, casual bar and grill that specializes in a dizzying array of beers and ales as well as Windy City pizza. You can grab a cozy booth upstairs or chalk your cue and enjoy a game of eight-ball in the huge downstairs pool room.

The Pickled Parrot, 332-0673, 26 N. Fifth Street, is a colorful, tropical-themed restaurant and bar that's always hopping with young professionals and families. Their ribs are among the best in the cities.

Now, a word about Prince (now known as a male/female symbol rather than by his name): Although some say the Minneapolis native's music has never climbed back to the level of popularity it achieved c. 1984 (thanks to his film and album, *Purple Rain*), he is still regarded as one of the Twin Cities' most prominent personalities. After years of surprise gigs at such nearby clubs as First Avenue and the Fine Line, he decided to set up a home base for these impromptu concerts and opened a nightspot named Glam Slam. In 1995, Glam Slam underwent a name change in an attempt to attract a broader range of clientele. It is now known as **The Quest Club**, 338-3383, 110 N. Fifth Street. The dance floor still throbs, but the club has traded in its urban/industrial decor for a warmer, more clubby atmosphere with conversation nooks and several diverse rooms, including a sports bar, jazz room and karaoke bar. Every night of the week is devoted to a specific type of music (mostly live), such as reggae, Latin salsa, Minnesota rock, alternative rock and rhythm and blues.

Cover charge ranges from $5 to $10 and there's a "no-jeans" policy.

On Sixth Street is an old favorite for many locals: **Gluek's**, 338-6621, 16 N. Sixth Street. The spacious woody interior is reminiscent of a German rathskeller, with towering ceilings and long tables down the center of the room, ideal for large parties. If relaxing is what you have in mind, the afternoon or early evening are your best times to stop. In the evening, a college-party spirit overwhelms the place, with all of the requisite rowdiness. But it's one of the only places you can still get Gluek's beer, an old Minneapolis label.

Heading back to First Avenue, you'll find a couple of interesting watering holes in the Butler Square building at the northwest corner of the First Avenue and Sixth Street. **Champps**, 335-5050, is a lively, noisy, sprawling upscale sports bar and grill, one of many branches in a popular local chain. Also in Butler Square is the more subdued and cosmopolitan **Linguini & Bob** restaurant, 332-1600, with its small, intimate window-lined bar area. You can sit right at the long, handsome wooden bar or sink into one of the cozy sofa groupings.

Depending upon your age and energy level, you may now be ready for the Twin Cities' premier music club, **First Avenue**, 338-8388, 701 First Avenue N. Don't expect anything clean or fancy, such as the Fine Line or Glam Slam: First Avenue is a concert club that delights in its grubbiness and laissez-faire ambiance. Music is what it's all about here, and the management is fiercely proud to have introduced local audiences to many acts that have since achieved international fame (the outside wall is emblazoned with a roster of them). Stain-resistant black is the color scheme here, and the music (either recorded or live) runs nonstop from your arrival to your departure. Check the Friday entertainment sections in the local papers or one of the weeklies for the schedule, for most nights are given over to touring acts, offering anything from grunge rock and reggae to R&B and African. If a table is a top priority, arrive early and don't expect wait service. The balcony is best for viewing, but the bustling dance floor is always a memorable experience.

First Avenue also has a smaller auxiliary room called the **Seventh Street Entry**, accessible through an unmarked entrance on, you guessed it, Seventh Street, as well as through First Avenue's main room. It's an intimate, grubby little club that makes its big brother next door look like the Waldorf Astoria by comparison. But, if alternative rock is your brew of choice, this is the best place to hear up-and-coming local bands or catch an emerging national act on its way through town. Just be prepared to stand or dance and don't lean on anything if you value your clothing.

RIVERPLACE AND ST. ANTHONY MAIN

From the Warehouse District, take the Hennepin Avenue suspension bridge just over the Mississippi to Riverplace and St. Anthony Main, two lovely old riverfront areas.

Sophia, 379-1111, 65 S.E. Main Street, is an elegant, continental restaurant with an attractive, romantic bar offering live jazz nightly. A few doors down

you'll encounter an enduring favorite, **Pracna on Main**, 379-3200, 117 S.E. Main Street. This casual, warm bar-restaurant has cozy booths indoors and a lovely outdoor eating area overlooking the Mississippi. Nearby is the infamous Nye's Polonaise Room (see the Northeast Minneapolis Pub Crawl section).

DOWNTOWN MINNEAPOLIS PUB CRAWL

Bars and restaurants are scattered throughout downtown Minneapolis, so many that you can choose any downtown street, start walking and duck into a number of interesting pubs. For our purposes here, we'll concentrate on downtown's two main north-south commercial streets: Hennepin Avenue and the Nicollet Mall. The former is the Main Street of downtown, home to theaters, restaurants, bars, crowds and, unfortunately, some accompanying crime. Nicollet Mall, on the other hand, is a retail district made for walking, with only city buses and bicycles allowed along its narrow center.

In the City Center shopping mall is the **Nankin**, 333-3303, 2 S. Seventh Street, best-known as one of the city's oldest Chinese restaurants. Its bar area offers hideaway booths where you can munch on fried wontons and sip one of the town's legendary concoctions, the Wanderer's Punch. We'd suggest you limit your intake to one: They're much stronger than they taste.

Back down on street level, you'll find a few interesting watering holes near the Historic State and Orpheum theaters.

You can't help but feel romantic listening to Jimmy Martin's piano mastery at Ivories in Plymouth.

Insiders' Tips

The Rock Bottom Brewery, 332-2739, 825 Hennepin Avenue, is a fairly new entry in the brew pub movement that's mushrooming nationally. They brew their own on the premises, but you can find tastier fare elsewhere, for example, at Mackenzie, 333-7268, 918 Hennepin Avenue, a bar that boasts of its Scottish heritage and backs it up with a nice selection of ales and scotches.

If you're interested in gay bars, check out the granddaddy of Twin Cities gay clubs, The Gay 90s, 333-7755, 408 Hennepin Avenue. The popularity of this multiroom nightclub never seems to flag, with crowds pouring in and out of its doors on most nights but especially on weekends. Among the rooms are a dance annex specializing in disco of the old school, a cabaret featuring flamboyant drag shows, a piano bar where standards and ballads are the tunes of choice and a quiet bar near the entrance if you need a break from all of the activity.

South on Hennepin off Ninth Street is a bar known as the Y'All Come Back Saloon, 332-0835, 830 Hennepin Avenue. While The Gay 90s may be the patriarch of local gay bars, The Saloon (as regulars call it) is considered the hipper hangout, with a more subdued, less theatrical clientele but an equally hopping dance floor.

If you continue on Hennepin a few blocks, you'll come upon one of downtown's nicest little bars, Eli's, 332-9997, 1225 Hennepin Avenue. Here, you can hold a quiet conversation unattainable at most of the noisy downtown hangouts while enjoying the wide variety of spirits and beers.

A couple of blocks farther, the hippest of the hip gather at the Loring Bar, 332-1616, 1624 Harmon Place, across the street from Loring Park. This self-described Bohemian pub, filled with mismatched overstuffed couches and chairs, exudes an attitude that may make some uncomfortable. But the waitstaff isn't nearly as rude as it used to be, and it's a nice place to hear music, which is delivered from one of the smallest stages in the city. It's especially pleasant on summer nights, when the large front windows are open and patrons can look out upon Loring Park. If you're lucky, you'll be there on a night when the rooftop sax player is in session.

Heading back into the center of downtown, you'll happen upon a few intriguing places near the end of Nicollet Mall that deserve mention. Each is within a block of Orchestra Hall and makes for a pleasant post-concert destination. The Times, 333-2762, 1036 Nicollet Mall, is a narrow little old-fashioned bar with good pub grub and nightly sessions by local musicians (no cover charge). The music is a mix of jazz and standards, with the emphasis on singers, but Thursday nights are given over to local blues legends Dave Ray and Tony Glover.

Speaking of music, you can find some of the area's best jazz musicians at Cafe Luxeford, 332-6800, 1101 LaSalle Avenue, in the lobby of the Luxeford Suites hotel down the block. Expect a mixture of traditional and straight-ahead, performed by trios and quartets.

Right across from Orchestra Hall is a friendly joint, Brit's Pub, 332-3908, 1110 Nicollet Mall, which does its best to recreate the ambiance of a bar in merry old England right down to the cuisine, such as it is, and an assortment of ales and single-malt scotches. And you can imbibe while sitting in a puffy chair beneath a portrait of the Queen Mum.

Not located along the Nicollet Mall, but just around the corner, are a couple of friendly dramshops. The Court Bar,

332-5589, 212 S. Seventh Street, used to be a quiet little neighborhood pub that attracted mostly newspaper and radio people, but now it's a popular stop for the college crowd, as well. And why not? It's an inoffensive old place with big tables that accommodate lively conversations among big groups.

Lyon's Pub, 333-6612, 16 S. Sixth Street, is similar in atmosphere and clientele and is at its most energetic and interesting right after work.

Step into **Kieran's Pub & Restaurant**, 339-4499, 330 Second Avenue S., and you'd swear you've been transported to the Emerald Isle. Co-owned by two Irishmen, Kieran's is a large, friendly, boisterous pub that serves traditional Irish pub grub and Guinness on tap. There's live Irish music, both traditional and modern, on weekends.

BEFORE OR AFTER A GAME AT THE METRODOME

If you plan on attending a Twins baseball game, Vikings or Gophers football game or other event at the Hubert H. Humphrey Metrodome , on the southeast end of downtown, you have a choice of a few nice bars nearby for meeting friends beforehand or catching a nightcap afterward. At one time there were more, but, in one of those classic urban tradeoffs, socializing was sacrificed to the automobile: Many bars were wiped out in an effort to provide more Metrodome parking.

The happiest beneficiary of that change is **Hubert's**, 332-6062, 601 Chicago Avenue, now the only watering hole within four blocks of the Dome. Its location is prime: right across the street from the principal entrance for Twins games, hence, it's always packed around game time. As food and drink go, it's pretty standard fare — burgers and Budweiser — but it's nice to gaze upon the walls of local sports memorabilia while you're waiting for your game date.

One of the more pleasant places to meet before a game is **Maxwell's**, 338-1980, 1201 Washington Avenue S., a small, narrow, wood-laden bar with elevated chairs and tables. The atmosphere is always friendly (even after a loss) and the burgers and the appetizers are pretty good. A few doors down is **The Roadhouse**, 340-9738, 1111 Washington Avenue S., a slightly larger venue that features the same menu and a few billiards tables.

If you prefer something a little more classy and expensive (and feel yourself suitably dressed), try the upscale bar at the **Whitney Hotel**, 339-9300, 150 Portland Avenue. Here you can be serenaded by a singing pianist while sipping top-shelf liquor or wine from the amply stocked cellar. In summer, the fountainside patio is a soothing place to sit and sip before taking a quiet walk along the nearby Mississippi.

If that sounds a little too rich for your blood, but you still like the idea of outdoor imbibing, you'll probably enjoy **Knickerbockers**, 375-1766, 1501 S. Sixth Street. This spot, on the other end of a walkway that connects the Metrodome with the Cedar-Riverside area, is a friendly, multilevel brick building with an intimate bar, a back dining room (again, burger and sandwich fare) and an upstairs pool room featuring a round table in a window-lined round tower. But the bar's best feature is a rooftop patio that's simply perfect for Twins fans who have just spent the better part of a beautiful summer evening trapped beneath the Metrodome's inflated roof. Lean back and stare at the stars — or at one of the best views of the Minneapolis skyline you'll find anywhere — and let that claustrophobic feeling float away.

WEST BANK PUB CRAWL

If you're in the mood for music, but you don't necessarily know what kind of music you're in the mood for, then, friend, welcome to the West Bank.

Here you'll find bars, cafes, coffeehouses and concert halls of many stripes, all located, roughly, along a 10-block stretch of Cedar Avenue from Seven Corners (Cedar and Washington Avenue) to the railroad yards down around Franklin Avenue.

We'll begin at the north end of the area, at the bustling Seven Corners. Actually, construction has limited the intersection to a more manageable four corners, and that's where you'll find a few of the bars. If you want to make the transition from University culture to Cedar-Riverside counterculture, these bars will ease the shift.

Bullwinkle's, 338-8520, 1429 Washington Avenue S., has all the ambiance of a typical college bar, but it's considerably cozier, especially in the loft section that overlooks the intersection. The **Up North Bar & Deli**, 375-1718, 1501 Washington Avenue S., is a new, cozy nightspot featuring native game dishes and a full bar in an atmosphere reminiscent of a northern Minnesota cabin. A guitarist performs on Tuesday evenings.

Sgt. Preston's, 338-6145, 221 Cedar Avenue S., is a narrow, intimate, mahogany-hued pub with a cafeteria line for sandwiches in the back, while **Grandma's**, 340-0516, 1810 Washington Avenue S., is the neighborhood "meat market," designed for making fresh acquaintances and sustaining a more refined version of the University house party.

Once you've crossed the bridge over Third Street, you've entered the music center of Minneapolis. On your right you'll come upon the **Red Sea**, 333-1644, 316 Cedar Avenue S., the Twin Cities' foremost world-music bar, presenting the sounds of the Caribbean, South America and Africa on weekends but leaning upon the area's populous alternative-rock milieu on weeknights.

Now you've reached the legendary intersection of Cedar and Riverside, the hub of Twin Cities radicalism, where aging hippies mingle with mellowing anarchists and holistic healers. This is also the most warmly multicultural neighborhood in the Twin Cities, a place where immigrants and exchange students from around the world are made to feel welcome.

This warmth is nowhere more palpable than at the **New Riverside Cafe**, 333-4814, 329 Cedar Avenue S., one of the Twin Cities' best vegetarian restaurants. Here, you can grab a cup of herbal tea, served cafeteria style, and listen to the tunes of local folk artists five nights a week, with early shows Tuesday through Thursday. Across the street is a musical landmark, the **400 Bar**, 400 Cedar Avenue S., where local bands hold forth nightly, mostly playing the kind of alternative rock descended from the late '70s punk movement and early '80s new wave.

A couple of doors down is the **Cedar Cultural Centre**, 338-2674, 416 Cedar Avenue S., the Twin Cities' premier folk music venue, which hosts two or three concerts a week by nationally and internationally known acts. Passing through the Cedar once or twice a year are such performers as wry singer-songwriter Loudon Wainwright III, Iowa troubadour Greg Brown and some of the top traditional music acts from Africa, South

America, China, India, Ireland and elsewhere. Basically, the inside of the Cedar looks like a movie theater, which it was at one time, but the sightlines are good and the acoustics fine for a night of folk (see The Arts chapter).

Now you're getting into blues territory. The Cedar-Riverside area is home to some of the Twin Cities' top blues musicians, with such local legends as Koerner, Ray and Glover and Willie Murphy regularly playing in the area, along with bands led by any of the local "big" men: Big Walter Smith, Big John Dickerson and Big George Jackson. On Riverside, just off Cedar, you'll find the **Viking Bar**, 332-4259, 1829 Riverside Avenue, a corner pub that is given over to the blues a few nights a week, including regular gigs by Willie Murphy and Joel Johnson.

But the place to find blues, reggae or jams in the Grateful Dead vein seven nights a week is the **Five Corners Saloon**, 338-6425, 501 Cedar Avenue S. It's an intimate, casual place where dancing is encouraged, with a fairly regular clientele that gladly accepts new faces. And there's rarely a cover charge. If you want to rest your ringing ears from all of this music, **Palmer's**, 333-7625, 500 Cedar Avenue S., is another friendly neighborhood pub where you can have a quiet conversation. Similar in style is **Blondie's on the Avenue**, 333-0105, 629 Cedar Avenue S., drawing heavily on students from nearby Augsburg College.

Pass under I-94 and keep on straight ahead and you'll hit a couple more reliable music bars. **Whiskey Junction**, 338-9550, 901 Cedar Avenue S., has music seven nights a week at no cover, with an almost permanent roster of local blues jams and favorites of the local bikers. Next door is one of the Twin Cities' main music venues: **The Cabooze**, 338-6425, 917 Cedar Avenue S. Its odd shape makes for difficult viewing sometimes, as it's constructed like a big, wide train car, with the band in one corner. However, the Cabooze books national acts every week or two (ranging from surf guitar idol Dick Dale to funk icon George Clinton) and is respected as one of the granddaddies of area clubs. But a hint: If there's a band you really want to catch here, arrive early and get one of the only seats available opposite the stage on the tiered balcony.

UPTOWN PUB CRAWL

Even though it has been discovered by suburbanites, the Uptown area of South Minneapolis hasn't shaken its Bohemian roots. Today, teenage punks share the sidewalks with gray-bearded professional types, artists and the ultra-hip. Naturally, this mix lends itself to a fantastic bar/cafe scene.

The Uptown area, roughly speaking, consists of the thoroughfares that form The Wedge, a densely populated community shaped like an isosceles triangle. These streets are Lyndale Avenue on the east, W. Lake Street on the south end and the curving South Hennepin Avenue on the western border.

Warning: This crawl is not a short one, so if you're on foot, you might want to think about alternative transportation between some of the stops.

We'll start at **Lyle's**, 870-8183, 2021 Hennepin Avenue S., or Liquor Lyle's, as it's known to many a local, thanks to the frenetic chaser lights that spell "liquor" above the front door. That should give you an idea of the ambiance: Drinking is unabashedly the first order of business here, as the plaster walls are lined with those uniquely American hand-printed signs advertising nightly drink and beer specials. The decor, service and menu are no great shakes, and the place is crowded, noisy and smoky, but still everybody comes here! Perhaps it's because it's the only old-fashioned neighborhood bar on South Hennepin for miles, refreshingly unencumbered by a modern marketing strategy.

Now you're approaching Hennepin and Lake, the hub of the Uptown area (sometimes called Yuptown for its high concentration of young urban professionals). The most popular bar near the intersection is also the area's oldest, **William's Pub**, 823-6271, 2911 Hennepin Avenue S. There's a restaurant on street level, but the most pleasant part of the pub is its basement, which houses the peanut bar. Here, you'll find groups of various sizes engaged in earnest conversation while leaning on checkered tablecloths and mulling over their choices from one of the Twin Cities' legendary beer lists. A fun activity for a large group is making your way around the world with beers, forming a human chain across the continents, country by country. As we said, it's best for large groups.

The trendy **Figlio**, 822-1688, 3001 Hennepin Avenue S., always attracts a large post-work contingent and is great for people-watching. While Italian cuisine is Figlio's specialty, drinking is the chief objective at its upstairs neighbor, the **Smiling Moose**, 822-5988, 3001 Hennepin Avenue S. This Colorado-based chain specializes in a variety of potent concoctions and one of the area's most impressive tap-beer selections (yes, the neighborhood is a brew fan's dream). Say what you will about the bland shopping-mall decor; you can ignore it and enjoy the people-watching out the big windows.

If you're intrigued by alternative rock performed by up-and-coming Twin Cities ensembles, spiced with the occasional national act, then the **Uptown Bar**, 823-4719, 3018 Hennepin Avenue S., is a must. Yes, the decor is reminiscent of a VFW hall that's fallen into disrepair, but the music's often worthwhile and, if the volume gets to be too much, you can retreat to a much quieter section of the bar.

Lucia's Wine Bar, 825-1572, 1432 W. 31st Street, could be described as the Uptown Bar's antithesis. Here, patrons sip chardonnays and pinot noirs in a subdued atmosphere with low lighting, perhaps partaking of the appetizers from the restaurant section, which specializes in the culinary arts of northern Italy.

Follow Lake Street eastward and you'll see one of the most interesting places to emerge in recent years on the local pub scene: **Bryant-Lake Bowl**, 825-3737, 810 W. Lake Street. Now, granted, the bowling alley has existed for years, but it's only recently become a gathering place for the Twin Cities' copious number of progressive and experimental theater artists. It's a friendly place, where stereotypes are broken by creatively coiffed social rebels who like to toss a ball or two. A theater with cabaret tables is also on the premises, and small troupes perform here along with alternative rockers and modern dancers, or you can catch an occasional film.

A few blocks down Lyndale is a bar that could be described as the eastern Wedge's version of Lyle's: the **C.C. Club**, 874-7226, 2600 Lyndale Avenue S. It's an unassuming neighborhood bar, best for darts and pitchers of beer. It has a lived-in atmosphere that not even Lyle's can match, and you always get the feeling that the majority of your fellow patrons are from the neighborhood. In the early to mid-'80s, the C.C. became best-known as the favored watering hole of the Replacements, one of the most critically acclaimed bands to ever come out of the Twin Cities. Sitting at the bar and watching the locals come and go, you can see where the band's chief songsmith, Paul Westerberg, found the inspiration for "Here Comes a Regular."

If the Bryant-Lake Bowl is the main haunt of the Twin Cities' many theater people, it has stolen the title from **Oliver's**, 871-5591, 2007 Lyndale Avenue S., for this is where actors and techies have gathered for years after the show, flamboyantly recounting the peaks and valleys of the evening's performance while relaxing in a woody, tiered bar. True, Bryant-Lake may get the more adventurous performance artists, but Oliver's is still where the casts from such nearby theaters as the Guthrie, Children's Theater, the Minneapolis Theatre Garage and the innumerable small companies gather for a post-show drink.

Want to cap your evening with a chess match or a hot game of Yahtzee? Then make tracks to a colorful little coffeehouse called **Muddy Waters**, 872-2232, 24th Street and Lyndale Avenue S., where the games-playing is exceeded only by the primo people-watching. Seriously, it's a fun, comfortable little java spot with a limited food menu that's open 'til 1 AM seven days a week.

South Minneapolis

South Minneapolis' primary east-west artery is Lake Street, and it's best navigated by wheels rather than feet. Apart from the usual shot-and-a-beer joints, the thoroughfare is home to a decent sports bar, **Champions**, 827-4765, 105 W. Lake Street, and a grungy little rock bar, **Fernando's**, 721-2107, 1501 E. Lake Street, that offers new local bands their first gig. Speaking of music, **Dulono's Pizza**, 827-1726, 607 W. Lake Street, is the unlikely venue for live bluegrass performed by local and national acts every Friday and Saturday night. The staff sometimes asks the band to tone it down when the phone rings so they can take delivery orders.

In the neighborhood of the Minneapolis Institute of Arts lies a well-worn, well-loved drinking/eating establishment known as the **Black Forest Inn**, 872-0812, 1 E. 26th Street. The restaurant serves generous portions of German fare in a comfy setting, and the always-crowded bar pours an impressive array of beers and ales. Clientele is a hodgepodge of artists, Bohemian types and blue-collar regulars who relax under the wall-size, legendary Avedon photograph of the Daughters of the American Revolution that over the years has been adorned by two bullet holes. The outdoor patio seating is very popular and romantic.

The bars in the area of 26th Avenue and 26th Street are patronized by a mix of area factory workers and the left-wing Bohemians from around Franklin Avenue and the Cedar-Riverside area. Their haunts include one of the Twin Cities' most popular old-fashioned bowling alleys, **Stardust Lanes**, 721-6211, 2520 26th Avenue S., as well as a friendly shot-and-beer joint, the **Hexagon Bar**, 722-3454, 2600 27th Avenue S.

One of the Twin Cities' more unusual music venues is around the corner: **Mirage**, 729-2387, 2609 26th Avenue S. This large nightclub seems to have everything going for it: a large stage, high-tech lighting and sound systems and plenty of seating. Unfortunately, Mirage limits its bookings to heavy-metal and hard-rock bands, and — unless hosting a concert by a well-known national act — it just doesn't draw the crowds.

Also in the area, you'll find a local favorite, **Matt's**, 722-7072, 3500 Cedar Avenue S., where they serve the legendary Juicy Lucy, a popular cheese-filled hamburger that bursts at first bite.

As mentioned, there are dozens of little grogshops throughout South Minneapolis that offer the minimum necessities and few frills. But most of them will probably remind you of Nick's, the place in *It's a Wonderful Life*, where, as bartender Sheldon Leonard rasped, "Men come to drink and get drunk. And we don't need any characters around to lend the place atmosphere, know what I mean?"

NORTH MINNEAPOLIS

The pubs of the North side are similar in style to those of the South side: mostly working-class places with little flair, some of them in neighborhoods you might want to avoid after dark unless you have a specific destination. Yes, the Twin Cities area has one of the lowest per capita crime rates of any American metropolis, but a city's a city, and the working-class neighborhoods are usually the first to feel the sting of crime. Hence, the North and South sides both have rough pockets (as do some sections of St. Paul, but we'll get to that).

The hub of activity for pub crawlers is an area on the east end of the North side: the intersection of Washington and Broadway (or I-94). Here, you'll find such bustling gin mills as **Standup Frank's**, no phone, N. Second Street and 21st Avenue N., so named for its lack of seating, where the drinks are powerful and cheap. It's a point of pilgrimage for University of Minnesota students of legal age, and the atmosphere is predictably rowdy.

A much more subdued stop is the **Broadway Bar**, 529-7666, 2025 N. West River Road, an unassuming caboose-shaped saloon specializing in beer and pizza. Nearby is the **Riverview Supper Club**, 521-7676, 2319 N. West River Road, one of the only upscale cocktail lounges in the neighborhood, which offers jazz and rhythm-and-blues, sometimes by internationally known artists like Bobby "Blue" Bland and Evelyn "Champagne" King. But the east end of the North side isn't the only place you can find a friendly dramshop: **DeLisi's**, 529-9265, 2119 W. Broadway, is toward the west end of the neighborhood and serves up good pizza and Italian food, along with the occasional rock band or theatrical venture in the upstairs hall.

NORTHEAST MINNEAPOLIS PUB CRAWL

This fiercely ethnic area (often called Nordeast by locals) is home to a high concentration of families who have lived in the area for generations, and they all seem to be proud of their cultural heritage, whether it be Polish, Slavic, Italian, Norwegian, Swedish, German or Lebanese. Just about every bar in the area has an ethnic affiliation of some sort, and most of them are very colorful places, rich in the kind of character you'll find missing in the newer, prefab places on the other side of town.

For Northeasters, a pub acts as a community gathering place where generations — and perhaps social classes — come together.

For this pub crawl, we'll give you some interesting taprooms that not only act as social hubs for their neighborhoods but also embrace visitors and offer a glimpse into the rich history of the area. Of all of the pub crawls in this chapter, you may find this the cheapest, as prices for both

Ordway Music Theatre in downtown St.Paul.

Photo: Joe Rossi, Pioneer Press

drinks and food in Northeast are refreshingly low.

If you're feeling like a little exercise, this crawl is possible on foot. We'll start at a typically intimate rathskeller, **Dusty's**, 378-9831, 1319 N.E. Marshall Street. Although its Italian influences don't show through as much as they used to, Dusty's still serves a variety of cheap sandwiches and a couple of tap beers while locals sit and smoke in a jovial atmosphere. It lies in the shadow of the old Grain Belt Brewery (since closed), which kept it bustling for decades.

Although Grain Belt was the largest brewery in Northeast, it certainly wasn't the only one. A few blocks down Marshall, you'll find Gluek Park, site of the now-defunct Gluek Brewery. That's right, the same Gluek mentioned earlier as lending its name (and limited supply of beer) to a Warehouse District bar. You can't get Gluek's at the **Polish Palace**, 789-

6626, 2124 N.E. Marshall Street, but it used to be the after-work stop for the brewery crew. And the tiny tavern still hops almost every night, serving Polish beers and specialty sandwiches to a youngish crowd.

Tony Jaros' River Garden (referred to as Jaros' by most locals), 789-9728, 2500 N.E. Marshall Street, bears the name of a player for the old Minneapolis Lakers, a team that took five NBA titles in the '40s and '50s before flying off to Los Angeles. Jaros' is best known for the Greenie, a vodka-based concoction both sweet and potent. It could be that a lot of the young crowd at the Polish Palace is merely overflow from Jaros', as some nights it's difficult to even get in the door, much less find a seat.

Go east on Lowry and you'll discover another popular community haunt. **Stasiu's**, 788-2529, 2500 University Avenue N.E., serves cheap sandwiches to a crowd often dominated by softball players and billiard aces. The tables seem to always be covered with pitchers of beer here. A block down the road is the **Chance Bar**, no phone, Lowry Avenue N.E. and N.E. Fourth Street, similar in atmosphere to Stasiu's. The reason is simple: As you approach from the west, its sign reads "Last Chance Bar"; if you're coming from the east, it says "First Chance Bar." And they're right. It's the only bar for miles if you're traveling eastward on Lowry Avenue. So, if you live east of the Chance, it's your corner bar.

Now head back south toward downtown and you'll come upon the **Sun**, 781-4405, 1528 University Avenue N.E. Don't be intimidated by the motorcycles out front. It's an amiable enough place, not rough at all. It's just that many bikers like the blues, and that's what the Sun often features on weekends.

A block or so away is a Northeast institution (although just about any of these bars could claim that title): **Mayslack's Polka Lounge**, 789-9862, 1428 N.E. Fourth Street. Its colorful owner, Stan Mayslack, passed away, but the lounge still specializes in the kind of heaping garlic-laced roast beef sandwiches that Stan himself used to build while manning a buffet line. And the kitchen stays open late.

We'll conclude this crawl at another Northeast landmark, **Nye's Polonaise Room**, 379-2021, 112 Hennepin Avenue E., just a stone's throw from downtown Minneapolis. Although visitors flock from all over to this multiroom temple to the traditional, it's still a personal favorite of Northeasters. The attraction here is the piano bar, which draws singers (and those who attempt it) for the warm encouragement they get from the pianists. It's the Twin Cities' best stop if you're interested in a full-bar sing-along. And if you've got dancin' feet, duck into the adjoining polka room, where you'll find people of all ages bouncing to the beat of the "World's Most Dangerous Polka Band." This joint is always hopping!

St. Paul

DOWNTOWN ST. PAUL PUB CRAWL

If you're looking for a vibrant hotbed of activity, where crowds mingle in the streets after dark, traversing from one rowdy bar to the next, each bursting with noise and music, then downtown St. Paul is definitely not the place to go.

But bustle isn't everything. If what you want is a nice, quiet place to walk around and visit interesting bars and restaurants, downtown St. Paul is the perfect destination.

Locals in the know will tell you that downtown St. Paul is actually more like two downtowns, each centered around a tree-filled urban park. On the west end of downtown, near Rice Park, is an area of beautiful restored buildings and new ones with old-fashioned elegance. On the east end is Lowertown, an area dominated by residential buildings and artists' lofts. The center of this neighborhood is Mears Park.

We'll start off by hitting a few pubs near Rice Park, considered the crown jewel of downtown St. Paul. Each of the four sides of Rice Park is graced with a lovely piece of architecture. The major attraction here is the newest, the lovely Ordway Music Theatre, which hosts touring Broadway shows, concerts by the Saint Paul Chamber Orchestra and esteemed soloists who offer Schubert Club recitals. It's also the chief venue for the Minnesota Opera and presents an eclectic mix of ballet, modern dance, jazz and world music.

Before or after the concert or show, you'll find crowds gathering at the **St. Paul Grill**, 224-7455, 350 Market Street. Located in the St. Paul Hotel, the Grill not only offers one of the best dinners downtown, but also features its most endearing bar. The rich history of the capital is displayed all over the walls, but in a classy, clubby manner that makes you feel as if F. Scott Fitzgerald and Charles Lindbergh were just faces in the colorful crowd here. This dimly lit dark-oak bar mixes first-class drinks with a healthy wine list and an ample collection of single-malt scotches and small-batch bourbons. There's also an economical and excellent bar menu. It's one of the only places in downtown St. Paul where you really feel like you've walked into history.

After pausing at Rice Park to admire the beauty of Landmark Center and the St. Paul Public Library, you're ready to move on.

One of downtown St. Paul's oldest bars is **Gallivan's**, 227-6688, 354 N. Wabasha Street. Although, like the St. Paul Grill, it's dominated by a restaurant that specializes in traditional fare such as steaks and seafood, Gallivan's differs from its art deco compatriot by exuding the ambiance of an elegant old library. It's the principal post-work hangout for those in the judicial or bureaucratic professions, a place where deals are struck and differences set aside. But, on St. Patrick's Day, all of this grace and dignity takes a holiday, as Gallivan's becomes the raucous post-parade hangout for St. Paul's large Irish-American population. Then, it's more like a beer hall with a bacchanalian electricity in the air.

An apt transition between the old establishments and the modern joints might be **Shannon Kelly's**, 292-0905, 395 N. Wabasha Street, a woody dramshop with an intimate air. It looks and feels incongruous amidst the rows of concrete and brushed-steel shops on Wabasha Street, presenting a relaxed retreat from its commercial surroundings.

Speaking of commercial, much of this section of Wabasha is dominated by two monumental paeans to shopping, Dayton's Department Store and the World Trade Center. The latter houses a couple of prefab watering holes, the most popular being the **Heartthrob Cafe**, 224-2783, 30 E. Eighth Street. The theme is an early-'60s malt shop, with roller-skating waiters and early rock tunes pouring from the stereo speakers. But it's one of downtown's most popular bars. Upstairs on the third floor you'll find the **Pig's Eye Grille and Brew Annex**, 298-9899, another favorite watering hole for downtowners.

Now, let's head to Lowertown. As mentioned earlier, this neighborhood is more residential than commercial, but it's also a smaller variation on Minneapolis' Warehouse District, filled with lofts, galleries, artists' housing and, of course, actual warehouses. The area's primary bow to the retail sector is Galtier Plaza, a combination high-rise/shopping mall that features a few decent restaurants and some pleasant pubs, as well.

Over on the eastern side of the building, you'll find three levels of pubs overlooking Mears Park. On street level is **O.J.'s**, 225-8105, 175 E. Fifth Street, a friendly sports bar with dark windows, a late-night menu and a balcony that looks out upon the park. Upstairs is **Amelia's**, 291-1590, which really bustles on weekends, especially when the music is provided by some of the top-notch Latin jazz bands from points west. Otherwise, it's still downtown's best place for dancing to live music and mingling with a diverse clientele. On the third floor is **Plaza Billiards**, 291-1779, which might answer a commonly asked question from first-time visitors to downtown St. Paul: "Where is everybody?" Well, they're chalking up their cues at the Plaza tables.

Sharing the third floor is **Scott Hansen's Comedy Gallery St. Paul**, 331-5653, which offers standup comedy by national and local acts.

Galtier Plaza is also the home of the new **Great Northern Supper Club**, 224-2720, a very good, non-gimmicky restaurant with a spacious, airy bar where you'll hear great live jazz on Friday and Saturday evenings. It's on the second floor of Galtier. If you want to impress someone — a date or a client — the Great Northern is the place to go.

Next-door to Galtier you'll find a cozy little basement jazz club called the **Artist's Quarter**, 292-1359, 366 Jackson Street, which hosts nationally known acts as well as local jazz musicians.

For a late-night jolt of java, head farther east into Lowertown to **Kuppernicus**, 290-2718, 308 Prince Street, St. Paul, a coffeehouse oozing artsy character and comfort. Housed in an old warehouse, Kuppernicus offers high beamed ceilings, wooden floors, striking original art, living-room seating and occasional live music on weekends.

As you move northward toward the State Capitol area, the nightlife becomes fairly sparse, but there are a couple of haunts here. **The Gopher Bar**, 291-9638, 241 E. Seventh Street, has thrown off its ancient image as a bowery dive and become a favorite stop for Lowertown residents and after-work downtowners. The specialty of the house is the Coney Island, arguably the Twin Cities' best.

Toward the confluence of freeways known to locals as Spaghetti Junction, you'll find a couple of places. **Rumours**, 224-0703, 490 N. Robert Street, is one of St. Paul's most popular gay bars, although it doesn't pack them in as it once did. **Woolley's**, 224-5111, 175 E. 10th Street, is a chain bar, albeit a pleasant one, in the Crown Sterling Suites hotel.

SUMMIT HILL-GRAND AVENUE PUB CRAWL

Lest you think St. Paul is a lifeless backwater burg where they roll up the sidewalks after dark, be advised there are some parts of town where nightlife is the chief attraction.

Perhaps one of the reasons that downtown doesn't seem to catch on as a social center is the proximity of Summit Hill and Grand Avenue, where the bars are always hopping on weekends and often on other nights, as well.

Here's a pub crawl that can be done in one night or two. It will take you in an uncomplicated "Z" pattern down the main streets of the two neighborhoods, Summit Hill and Grand Avenue. We'll start off on the eastern end, near the lovely, green-domed Cathedral of St. Paul. This neighborhood is often referred to as Cathedral Hill, and our first stop is at its most popular restaurant and bar, **W.A. Frost**, 224-5715, 374 Selby Avenue. This historic brick building houses not only an elegant restaurant but the nicest bar in the neighborhood. Like the St. Paul Grill, this is old St. Paul, with a subdued, high-class feel that seems to cry out for cognac in large snifters. But the chief attraction at Frost is the large, tiered outdoor patio, where Chinese lanterns burn into the night and tree boughs loom above you. This is the Summit Hill that inspired F. Scott Fitzgerald, a neighborhood of great mansions and a little smart-set stuffiness.

Speaking of literary figures, a few doors down is **Fabulous Fern's**, 225-9414, 400 Selby Avenue, which, under previous management, used to be a daily stop for playwright August Wilson, winner of the Pulitzer Prize for his gripping dramas *Fences* and *The Piano Lesson*. Wilson used to live upstairs in the Blair Arcade building, but he was well-known for doing much of his writing in St. Paul bars, sometimes catalyzed by the conversations at neighboring tables. Wilson has since left the Twin Cities, but his spirit lives on in this friendly establishment.

A few blocks up in a historic old building is another pleasant pub, **Chang O'Hara's**, 290-2338, 498 Selby Avenue. What was once an old fire station is now a bar with three distinctly different sections: a window-lined bar with elevated booths, a white-linen restaurant that sometimes hosts jazz bands and a multilevel outdoor deck that offers a cozier variation on the garden at W.A. Frost.

Travel west on Selby Avenue, then turn left at Dale and you'll come upon the neighborhood's most pleasant pub, **Cognac McCarthy's**, 224-4617, 162 N. Dale Street. It's a homey little place with scratched-up wood booths and a small dining room where they serve consistently fine home-style meals such as pot roast and turkey with all the trimmings. It's easily the friendliest bar in the neighborhood, and its regulars come from near and far.

A couple of blocks farther down Dale is **Sweeney's**, 221-9157, 96 N. Dale Street, which shares some of the same ownership as Chang O'Hara's and Cognac McCarthy's but is clearly the flagship of the fleet. It seems that Sweeney's has been bustling every night since it opened in the late '70s, constantly awash in conversation and taped music. The library area is especially conducive to group discussions, and, of course, the bar has a patio.

You can stop now and say that you've conquered Summit Hill, but if you still crave some social interaction, you can continue on to Grand Avenue. Sometime in the '70s Grand changed from a conventional commercial strip to a hip hangout, both for living and for socializing. It's now lined with trendy boutiques that dispense such commodities as spices and socks. Some might call it "yuppified," but it's still an amiable place to stroll on a summer night.

Take a right when you reach Grand and, on the first block, you'll see **Tavern on Grand**, 228-9030, 656 Grand Avenue. Some locals call this "the last real bar left on Grand," inferring that others lack the neighborhood watering-hole ambiance that rules at the Tavern. The decor is reminiscent of a northern Minnesota fishing lodge, and that's the kitchen's metier: the fish indigenous to Minnesota lakes, most notably the walleye pike. All of the bars on this crawl have celebrity stories, but the Tavern tops them all: Mikhail Gorbachev once dropped in for some walleye while visiting St. Paul. He reportedly pronounced it delicious.

Up the block is **Dixie's**, 222-7345, 695 Grand Avenue, which serves up a mildly seasoned menu of Southern dishes. It's an expansive place by Grand Avenue's intimate standards, but that's fine, for it's also one of the street's most popular bars. Model trains chug by above your head as you sample from the lengthy beer list or sip one of their Southern variations on the martini or Bloody Mary.

One block west stands **Lyons' Pub**, 224-1787, 788 Grand Avenue, which caters to the college crowd with pitchers of beer and tables designed for large groups. If you're over a certain age, this is the one bar on the crawl that can really make you feel it: Virtually half of the pub is given over to video games, and the constant cacophony of crashes may be the idea of Hell's soundtrack, for some.

Downright tasteful and restrained by comparison is **Billy's**, 292-9140, 857 Grand Avenue, a meandering, multiple-room bar and restaurant offering a few options, depending upon your mood. The summer patio is a pleasant meeting place for a summer night, you can hedge your bets on the weather and retreat to the window-lined area just off the garden or you can catch the constant activity in the bustling bar section.

Once you make it through the crowd, you'll be right next to **Music City Cafe**, 857 Grand Avenue, one of the Twin Cities' nicest little places to sit and listen to acoustic folk, blues or jazz. It's a candlelit L-shaped tavern that might remind you of a Greenwich Village coffeehouse. The conversation is always quiet, and the music is almost invariably as laid back as the atmosphere. It provides a wonderful wind-down after a lengthy crawl.

WEST SEVENTH STREET

Every major city in America (with the possible exception of Salt Lake City) has a main drag or two lined with working-class bars that specialize in mainstream tap beers and an occasional shot of the hard stuff. As a city with large parcels of land devoted exclusively to industry, St. Paul is, of course, no exception. And the city's longest street is the one that provides a bumper crop of these alehouses: West Seventh Street (also known as Old Fort Road).

For the sake of convenience and stamina, we won't view this as a pub crawl — the street is several miles long. Instead, we'll just tell you about some of the typical watering holes on the avenue and let you choose one that fits your style. Starting at the St. Paul Civic Center, which acts as the gateway to (or exit from) downtown St. Paul, you can head down a block and come upon **Patrick McGovern's**, 224-5821, 225 W. Seventh Street. This is one of the nicest pubs on West Seventh, with a relaxed atmosphere inspired by old wood booths and a long bar with an old-fashioned brass rail. It's a popular after-work stop for those with offices toward the west end of downtown, and it serves as the corner bar for those who live in the Irvine Park area, one of St. Paul's oldest neighborhoods.

Perhaps the most popular establishment on all of West Seventh is **Mancini's**, 224-7345, 531 W. Seventh Street, one of the Twin Cities' favorite steak houses and a hotbed of local color. The current mayor was wise to headquarter all of his campaign parties here, for it has the kind of "all things to all people" reputation that politicians desire. The bar area plays host to a crowd of many ages and social classes, and they all get up to polka when the band strikes up. But beware of bad Elvis impersonators.

Farther down West Seventh, you'll find **Champps**, 698-5050, 2431 W. Seventh Street, the original sports bar that inspired the popular Twin Cities chain. It's a wide-open place, with TVs galore and some of the best burgers in the Twin Cities. Nearby is a popular supper club, the **Manor**, 690-1771, 2550 W. Seventh Street, with both a piano bar and a lounge that hosts an old-fashioned show band every weekend.

HIGHLAND PARK AND
MACALESTER-GROVELAND

Looking to take a pub crawl through these two nicely appointed St. Paul residential neighborhoods? Good luck. Believe it or not, ancient city liquor laws have made it darn near impossible to open an alehouse in these large and densely populated neighborhoods. The word we've heard (and we're not making this up) is that the dramshop laws are based upon the police department's complaint that their horses couldn't make it all the way from downtown to Highland Park in order to deal with disturbances in bars. That's right, it's a holdover from the 19th century.

Hence, one of St. Paul's largest geographical areas, Highland Park, only has three — count 'em, three — bars. **The Tiffany Bar**, 690-4747, 2051 Ford Parkway, is a slightly cleaner version of the corner shot-and-beer joint, with Tiffany lamps above the tables and plenty of pool tables. It's long been a popular hangout with students from the College of St. Catherine and the University of St. Thomas, but business has become more scarce from such quarters since the drinking age was raised to 21.

The other two Highland Park bars are virtually next door to one another. **Plums**, 699-2227, 480 S. Snelling Avenue, used to fancy itself a yuppie fern bar with a lively singles scene until someone decided it was better for business to be all-embracing than exclusive. So it's now more

like an even-nicer version of the neighborhood beer joint. A few doors down is **Goby's Grille & Pub**, 690-5731, 472 S. Snelling Avenue, a dimly lit but airy bar that's built for talk, not a party atmosphere.

The Macalester-Groveland area is indeed St. Paul's most densely populated neighborhood, but it has the distinction of having virtually no bars in the area. If locals feel like having a drink, the stop of choice is generally **O'Gara's Bar & Grill**, 644-3333, 164 N. Snelling Avenue, an old family-owned establishment that's been around for many a generation. Over the past 15 years, O'Gara's has grown from a small corner pub with wholesome home-style cooking into a popular hangout that has expanded into almost all of the stores next door. O'Gara's has five distinct sections: the humble old restaurant; the intimate old bar; a newer central bar area; the Shamrock Room, which features jazz and a piano bar on most nights; and the Garage, a large room where local rock bands hold forth on weekends.

UNIVERSITY AVENUE,
MIDWAY AND FROGTOWN

The closest thing you can find in the Twin Cities to a main street that runs all the way through the metropolitan area is University Avenue. It begins at the northwest end of Northeast Minneapolis and ends just east of the State Capitol in St. Paul. The nature of the street takes on different styles as you travel its length. It's residential in Northeast, lined with

Hot local acts are Debbie Duncan, who appears all over town, and the Wolverines, whom you can catch regularly at The Times Bar.

Insiders' Tips

houses and corner pubs before hitting one of its many industrial sections, then gives way to the University of Minnesota campus and the towering trees of Prospect Park. But, in St. Paul, it's almost unrelentingly industrial and commercial, dominated by small businesses in the service and retail sectors.

The bars of University Avenue are primarily working-class joints frequented by blue-collar workers after a hard day at the plant. But there are exceptions. Traveling eastward from the St. Paul-Minneapolis border, we'll try to fill you in on some of the highlights. The first bar you'll hit is the **Cromwell**, 646-1243, 2511 W. University Avenue, a shot-and-beer joint disguised as a supper club serving steaks and seafood. The atmosphere is usually rowdy on a weekend, exacerbated by the occasional country band. The Cromwell is in one of St. Paul's most intensely industrial areas, near the intersection of University Avenue and Minn. Highway 280, but much of its clientele seems to come from elsewhere.

The city of St. Paul has done an admirable job of converting many of the empty warehouses in the area into studio and office space for artists. Writers, painters, sculptors, dancers, filmmakers — the intersection of University and Raymond Avenue is teeming with them. Where do they go to wind down after a creative endeavor? None other than **Johnny's Bar**, 645-4116, 2251 W. University Avenue. And they aren't the only ones. Johnny's is a favorite of beer-lovers from throughout the Twin Cities area. The bland interior is nothing to look at, but the ever-changing tap-beer menu on the wall certainly is. The choices always include a few obscure European draught ales or pilsners, but the specialty of the house is

whatever the neighboring microbrewery, Summit, is currently trying out.

University and Snelling is the Twin Cities' busiest intersection, and most of the bars here are of the no-frills, working-class variety. **The Turf Club**, 647-0486, 1601 W. University Avenue, has the most character of the bunch, as it specializes in country music and lively two-stepping. Nearby is a pleasant, albeit rather bland, chain bar, **Applebee's**, 642-9757, Spruce Tree Centre, W. University and N. Snelling avenues.

One of the Twin Cities' oldest gay bars, the **Town House**, 646-7087, 1415 W. University Avenue, is along this stretch, but, in the tradition of old gay bars, it's unmarked. Just look for a gray freestanding building west of Hamline Avenue on the north side of the street. The clientele is a mix of younger folks and others who have been regulars for decades. A couple of blocks away is **Arnellia's**, 642-5975, 1183 W. University Avenue, a nightclub that offers a live mix of jazz and old-fashioned R&B under swirling lights.

Before we leave the Midway area, we'd be remiss not to mention some of the other appealing nightspots of the area. **Ginkgo**, 645-2647, 721 N. Snelling Avenue, is a coffeehouse that offers concerts once a week by local and national folk acts.

In a neglected shopping center called Bandana Square stands the Twin Cities' top stop for jazz, the **Dakota Bar & Grill**, 642-1442, 1021 E. Bandana Boulevard. Not only is this clean, classy club a first-rate restaurant (one of the Twin Cities' best, in the opinion of many), but it also hosts jazz combos of various sizes and styles every night. Most often it's a local group — there are many very good ones — but it's also the prime place for concerts by such legendary luminaries as Elvin Jones and Max Roach, as well as "young lions" Marcus Roberts, Terrence Blanchard and others. It's sometimes traditional, sometimes contemporary, but always worth a listen.

A couple of blocks east is **Gabe's by the Park**, 646-3066, 991 N. Lexington Parkway, which would be a fairly typical sports bar were it not for its position as official pre- and post-game hangout for fans of the St. Paul Saints, an independent minor league baseball team that packs them in for every game. Although the outdoor deck sits beside busy Lexington Parkway, it's a pleasant place to spend a summer evening.

Continue east and you'll come upon the **Half Time Rec**, 488-8245, 1013 Front Avenue, the Twin Cities' most popular pub for listening (and perhaps dancing) to traditional Irish music. Most of the bands are local, although usually born and bred across the pond, and it's a marvelous place to acquaint yourself with St. Paul's rich Irish music scene. Half of the Half Time seems like a concert hall in miniature, while the other half is more like a typical shot-and-beer joint. But not many bars can boast of having bocce ball in the basement.

About a mile southeast, you'll find yourself in the middle of Frogtown, a working-class St. Paul neighborhood that's run into some problems with crime in recent years, but nonetheless has some worthwhile places to visit. The most famous is the **Blues Saloon**, 228-9959, 601 N. Western Avenue, the Twin Cities' premier venue for the blues. Music is offered Thursday through Monday, usually with a nominal cover charge. More often than not, Friday and Saturday nights are given over to respected blues artists from around the country, and the club seems to have a pipeline for players from the rich Chicago scene that never seems to run dry.

Frogtown is the unlikely home of St. Paul's most popular gay and lesbian bar, **Club Metro**, 489-0002, 733 Pierce Butler Route. Actually, it sits off by itself on an expressway alongside the Burlington Northern railyards. Club Metro is packed on many nights and is known for being a lively, sprawling place that offers a warm reception to new faces. The club is also host to Unicorn Theater Company, which specializes in plays about gay issues.

THE EAST SIDE

St. Paul's East Side is, geographically, the city's largest neighborhood (although longtime residents might argue that it comprises several neighborhoods). Roots run deep in this working-class community. Many families have lived here for generations, since their European-immigrant ancestors first settled these streets. Italian names stand out most prominently on local business signs. But many new faces have moved into the area within the past decade, as well.

The bars of the East Side reflect the area's blue-collar population. The majority of the bars along the area's main drags — Payne Avenue, E. Seventh Street, Arcade Street and White Bear Avenue — are the kind of shot-and-a-beer joints we've detailed above: pressed wood paneling, a lot of beer lights and billiard tables. The ones we list here have exceptional characteristics that make them among the most popular haunts of Eastsiders, many of whom also enjoy the nightlife in the neighboring suburb of Maplewood. Due to the enormity of the East Side, this pub crawl is only possible by car.

Peppercorns, 776-2314, 1178 Arcade Street, is a hard-rock bar that provides young and 30ish Eastsiders with their music of choice. It's a clean, neon-infused pub with decor reminiscent of a '50s malt shop, but it has everything an Eastside bar needs (pool tables, dart boards, all of the usual suspects on tap).

Off Minn. Highway 36 you'll find a paean to kitsch that's remained popular for decades. **Bali Hai**, 777-5500, 2305 White Bear Avenue, Maplewood, is a Polynesian restaurant that presents not only the cuisine of the South Pacific islands but the traditional music, dancing and drama as well. Depending upon your tastes, it's either wildly entertaining or just plain too much. But the umbrella-adorned tropical drinks are potent and tasty, and the dimly lit bar has an infectious party atmosphere.

Maplewood Mall is the area's temple to shopping, and it's surrounded by many national-chain bars that look as if they've been manufactured elsewhere for assembly on the suburban plains. But there are a couple of interesting bars nearby that have been serving Eastsiders and suburbanites for a number of years. **T-Bird's**, 779-2265, Maplewood Square, White Bear and Woodlynn avenues, Maplewood, has the open, tiered look of a sports bar, but it's really an old-fashioned watering hole that offers dancing most nights.

Nearby is the **Red Rooster**, 770-7822, 2029 Woodlynn Avenue, Maplewood. From the outside it looks like a little motel bar, but the interior is reminiscent of a country roadhouse, with rustic walls and an arched, beamed ceiling. You can always tell a place that draws regulars from the bartender's familiar manner with the customers and signs that list the birthdays of patrons. There's karaoke, darts and a genuine small-town feel in the place.

Our final stop is a bit distant from the rest. Off Century Avenue near I-94 stands **Blackie's**, 738-3333, 271 N. Geneva Avenue, Oakdale, a barbecue restaurant with a popular bar area. Another place with Old World decor, Blackie's is a brick-lined hangout for those in their 20s who like to dance to pop and funk heavy on the backbeat (the place positively throbs sometimes). But those uninterested in the music can retire to the deck overlooking Tanner's Lake and sip one in relative quiet.

The Suburbs

Bloomington Pub Crawl

Bloomington is a prototypical American suburb. You know, the kind that started out as a provincial little extension of its neighboring metropolitan area and eventually turned into one of the largest communities in the state. Population-wise, Bloomington is now the third-largest city in Minnesota behind Minneapolis and St. Paul.

But, as far as nightlife goes, Bloomington has undergone major changes in recent years. When Metropolitan Stadium was home to the Twins and Vikings, and the neighboring Met Center hosted North Stars hockey games and most of the national concert tours that came to town, Bloomington had an energetic after-dark atmosphere. But then the Twins and Vikings set up shop at the Metrodome in downtown Minneapolis in 1982, the North Stars left town in 1993, and the face of Bloomington changed. It ceased to be a fashionable place to party.

Along came the Mall of America, the temple to American consumerism that has put Bloomington back on the national map. Transcending all that came before it in the way of retail clusters, the "megamall" not only houses department stores and boutiques by the hundreds, but bars and restaurants as well. And you'll find these pubs hopping almost any night of the week.

However, the Mall's effect upon the legendary I-494 strip has evidently not been particularly favorable. Popular old haunts have closed, and most of the clubs left standing are part of national chains. Unfortunately, these places aren't usually rich in character. Like your average fast-food restaurant, they seem to have come out of the same factory, ready for assembly in any American suburb. **Bennigan's**, 881-0013, 1800 W. 80th Street, is a classic example of this style, although it's still one of the more popular pubs among what's left of the Bloomington singles scene.

A local minichain that packs them in most nights is **Joe Senser's**, 835-1191, 4217 W. 80th Street. Bearing the name of a former Vikings tight end and broadcaster, the bars are of the classic sports-bar variety, expansive and multilevel, with TVs galore. On the same stretch, there's a more intriguing stop, the Australian-themed **Billabong**, 844-0655, 5001 W. 80th Street. Yes, it's just a gimmick, and neither the food nor drink is particularly Aussie, unless you count Foster's on tap. But the tropical decor is pleasant, as is the waitstaff, and the food is consistently good, for pub grub.

As nightlife goes, much of the fun is found at **Steak and Ale**, 884-0124, 2801 Southtown Drive. Granted, the restaurant section is standard franchise, but the nightclub area hops on weekends to the sounds of tight, professional R&B bands. (A caveat: For some strange reason, there's no live music in the summer. The bands reappear in September and play through May.)

Well, now it's off to the Mall of America, and we'll warn you in advance: You're either going to love it or hate it.

If you think suburban shopping malls are either a lot of fun or, at worst, unobjectionable, then you'll have no problem with the mother of all malls. In fact, you'll be in shopping nirvana. But, if there's something about excessive commercialism and large, enclosed courtyards that makes you feel a little queasy, do yourself a favor and stay away.

That said, there are some bars in the Mall that are among the Twin Cities' best for their type. For example, **Gatlin Brothers Music City Grille**, 858-8000, is the Twin Cities' No. 1 club for booking national country acts that aren't quite big enough to fill an arena — people such as Carlene Carter and John Michael Montgomery before his explosion of popularity. Most nights, it's a pretty hopping club for the country set, with all of the requisite hats, boots and a huge dance floor for line dancing or two-steppin'.

If comedy is your favorite form of entertainment, **Knuckleheads**, 854-5233, is one of the nicer laugh emporiums in the Twin Cities area. Unlike some places that stack the audience a tad too tightly, Knuckleheads is comfortable and intimate. Its headliners are always national acts, usually visiting from New York, Chicago or Los Angeles.

The Mall's version of a college bar, **Gator's**, 858-8888, attempts to recreate the atmosphere of a frat party — that is, if you attended keggers beside a tropical swamp.

A few doors down, you'll find a cluster of bars. The biggest is **America's Original Sports Bar**, 854-5483. Remember what we said about the layout of your average sports bar? Multiply its acreage by 10 and you'll have this stadium-sized shrine to all things athletic. Despite its roominess, the place is inevitably crowded and, unfortunately at times, its inebriated clientele lacks Minnesota-nice social manners.

To escape this unruly mob scene, slip through the door of **Lil' Ditty's**, 854-5483, a quiet piano bar with dueling ivory-ticklers and jovial sing-alongs. Another laid-back oasis is **Players**, 854-3110, the Mall's fairly good imitation of a friendly corner bar. It certainly offers a more pleasant atmosphere than **Hooters**, 854-3110, a national chain that's fine if you don't mind mediocre food and a sexist atmosphere. Minnesota nice, it ain't.

LAKE MINNETONKA PUB CRAWL

Most of the suburbs that surround Minneapolis and St. Paul have more similarities than differences. Some are more commercial; others more distinctly rural; some downright small-townish. But the many small suburbs that surround Lake Minnetonka, west of Minneapolis, have a culture quite different from anything else in the Twin Cities area.

Perhaps the best environment to use for comparison would be the blue-blooded leisure ports of Newport, Rhode Island, or Cape Cod. But, while those bastions of boating and old-money families are set against the majestic Atlantic, these communities are wrapped around the labyrinthine bays and satellite lakes of the Minnetonka chain. These small suburban areas (Navarre, Greenwood, Tonka Bay) are set away on islands, peninsulas and isthmuses, sheltered by forests and often easier to reach by boat than car.

Two things that you should know before undertaking a Minnetonka pub crawl. One, there's a maritime feel to just about everything. Boating is a central activity for people of all ages, and many of the bars and restaurants are accessible by

boat, with slips available out back. And two, it shares with the aforementioned Newport a clear stratification of economic classes. This makes for a not-necessarily-friendly atmosphere at some places (at least by Minnesota standards), but there's still plenty of character to be found at the local watering holes.

If you're traveling westward on Minn. Highway 7 toward the Lake Minnetonka area, keep your eyes open for a joint called the **Will Hop Inn**, 938-9892, 14824 Minn. Highway 7, Minnetonka. Typical of old Minnetonka before the postwar suburban sprawl struck, the Will Hop Inn is like a big, friendly fishing shack.

One of the more popular places in Minnetonka is **T. Wright's**, 475-2215, 3310 Minn. Highway 101 S., Wayzata, which looks like an airplane hangar from the outside but is more like a suburban supper club on the inside, filled with curved-back wooden captain's chairs (naturally) and red leather booths. On weekends it has the reputation of being a meat market, but also draws locals to its lively game room for pool and darts.

One of the most monied of Twin Cities suburbs is Wayzata, and it features a main drag that runs alongside the shore of a large open section of Lake Minnetonka. Along this stretch, you'll find **Sunsets**, 473-5253, 700 E. Lake Street, Wayzata, a window-lined pub that seems to be crowded every night. It has a touch of class that some of the other bars on this crawl lack, but it's also more casual than many (Docksiders and polo shirts allowed).

The Minnetonka Mist, 471-8471, 4050 Shoreline Drive, Spring Park, is an artificially weather-beaten building constructed in the style of a New England Colonial home. The Mist is permeated with the maritime motif that dominates the bars of the area, and the upstairs deck overlooks a public boat landing where there is a fairly constant stream of activity.

Although **Al and Alma's**, 472-3098, 5201 Piper Road, Mound, is best-known as a popular family restaurant and bar, the old establishment also owns a fleet of yachts with well-stocked bars. Some of their on-board bacchanals are the stuff of legend.

The centerpiece of the Lake Minnetonka social circle is **Lord Fletcher's on the Lake**, 471-8513, 3746 Sunset Drive, Spring Park, a virtual Disneyland of a bar/restaurant complex, set on what was once the edge of a swamp. But the founders discovered paydirt by dredging up a canal, installing some slips for passing boats and building a sprawling wooden deck referred to as "the wharf." Inside are three other bars and a couple of restaurants. Lord Fletcher's offers a somewhat incongruous combination of decor, blending nautical New England with the mutton-and-ale ambiance of Old England. And, outside, the volleyball sandpits stretch on for acres and are crowded throughout the summer.

If all of the suburbs leave you longing for something a bit more urban than urbane, the closest thing you'll find is the town of Excelsior. The town once had a popular amusement park, and you can see some architecture here that's actually pre-World War II. The most popular bar in town is **Haskell's Port of Excelsior**, 474-0935, 1 Water Street, Excelsior, a small pub that's almost bursting out its few windows with youngish drinkers every night. The socializing is loud and raucous, but don't expect mingling if you're not from the area.

The overflow crowd heads to **The Ex-celsior Park**, 474-1113, 685 Excelsior Boulevard, Excelsior, where things are considerably quieter. The restaurant's bay windows and sprawling deck look out upon, appropriately enough, a bay. The dock here has abundant slips for the boating crowd, and the Excelsior Park tries to grab some of the Lord Fletcher's overflow as well by offering volleyball on the beach.

A little restaurant and bar with a German flavor, **The Copper Stein**, 474-5805, 5635 Manitou Road, Excelsior, sits just outside of town, and it's a nice place to stop for a brew. On the wall inside the door is a large portrait of Excelsior Jimmy, a legendary local eccentric. Just a little celebrity story here: In the early years of their career, the Rolling Stones performed at the Excelsior Amusement Park. During their stay, Mick Jagger had a prescription filled at a town pharmacy, where he was said to have fallen into conversation with the town's chief character, Excelsior Jimmy. There are those who claim that this exchange provided the inspiration for a story in the Stones song "You Can't Always Get What You Want" and that the name was changed from "Excelsior" to "Chelsea" for rhythmic purposes.

A little farther from the lake area, but still within the Minnetonka border, is **Sherlock's Home**, 931-0203, 11000 Red Circle Drive, Minnetonka, which was the Twin Cities area's first brew pub, meaning that most of its beer is created on premises from original recipes. It's a homey place designed to look considerably older than its years, with the decor feigning that of an Old English pub. Across the way is **Konrad's**, 938-9100, 6001 Shady Oak Road, Minnetonka, a restaurant-bar featuring German-Austrian fare and live jazz on weekend evenings.

STILLWATER PUB CRAWL

Out on the eastern edge of the Twin Cities area is the quaint little town of Stillwater, which refers to itself as The Birthplace of Minnesota. The devoted preservation of its historic feel is one of the charms of this little St. Croix River Valley village.

Stillwater is close enough to St. Paul that workers in the capital city often commute. There are few more pleasant places east of the Mississippi River that can still be considered part of the Twin Cities metropolitan area, and few better for a pub crawl.

All of the bars near the Main Street area of Stillwater have some historic ties. We'll begin our journey at **Cat Ballou's**, 439-4567, 112 N. Main Street, which affects the decor of a 19th-century bordello, including gaudy, bawdy life-size paintings and ornate etchings on the windows. But it's just a brightly lit fern bar without the ferns. However, it has music on weekends (mostly blues and alternative rock) and a separate entrance for the upstairs pool hall. A block down, you'll find a much more appealing (and lively) watering hole, **The Mad Capper**, 430-3710, 224 S. Main Street. Beer is the specialty of the house here, with a list of 20-odd imports and a tap-beer selection that includes the wares of obscure micro-breweries and such delights as the Czech beer Pilsner Urquell. Decor is a hodgepodge of stuffed armadillos, antique clocks, beer signs and Grandma Moses-style sports paintings, if you can imagine that.

Brine's, 439-7556, 219 S. Main Street, is a trilevel bar and restaurant with three distinctly different atmospheres. The main floor is given over to the brick-lined bar, which offers a copious selection of tap beers and the same etched-mirror decor you'll find in most Stillwater bars. The second floor is the restaurant section, decked out like an old-fashioned malt shop, while the third floor has the best view of any pool hall in the Twin Cities area, looking out upon the lovely St. Croix River. A few doors down is **Trumps**, 439-0024, 317 S. Main Street, occupying the top floor of a small mall loaded with boutiques and the kind of specialty stores that line the streets of Stillwater. The view of the river out the back windows is the main attraction here, although there's something to be said for the clean, woody, well-lit interior and the erratic but intriguing music schedule (blues and reggae seem to be the genres of choice).

Now let's go down to the riverfront. Stillwater's social centerpiece is the **Freighthouse**, 439-5718, 305 S. Water Street, an 1883 railroad warehouse that's listed on the National Register of Historic Places (much of the town could qualify for the honor). The Freighthouse has restaurant and bar sections both inside and out, depending on what time of year you visit. The gazebo bar is pleasant on a summer evening, but the area that really hops is the nightclub, a big split-level room with a large dance floor. Continue north along the river's edge and you'll find **P.D. Pappy's**, 430-1147, 422 E. Mulberry Street. Upon arrival, it shouldn't take you long to figure out that this was once the social center of the Stillwater Yacht Club. It's an open, airy place with a sparse maritime decor and a big deck outside that overlooks the crowded slips of local boaters. It's clearly the favored dramshop of those who cruise the river, but it also draws urbanites who like the full and varied music schedule (Wednesday through Sunday). And, if all of this hanging out by the river makes you feel too much like a landlubber, give the folks at **Andiamo Showboat** a call at 430-1236. They operate a nightclub on wheels — paddlewheels, that is — on Saturday from spring to fall, hosting parties that cruise up and down the St. Croix with local bands on deck.

OTHER SUBURBS

Every local suburb has its own little subculture, and the bars in each run the gamut from friendly corner pubs to glitzy national chains.

One of the fastest-growing sections of the Twin Cities metropolitan area is Dakota County, and although housing starts have skyrocketed in recent years, the development of nightlife hasn't kept pace. Most of the bars in Dakota County are either old roadhouses (some pretty colorful) or franchise places in search of a mall. Among the more interesting places in the area are the **Chart House**, 435-7156, 11287 Klamath Trail, Lakeville; **Russ' Pub**, 890-5710, 3080 Minn. Highway 13 W., Burnsville; and **J. Doolittle's**, 542-6627, 2140 Cliff Road, Eagan.

There's also a St. Paul export, the **Cherokee Sirloin Room**, 454-6744, 4625 Nicols Road, Eagan, which, in addition to great steaks, offers music and dancing on weekends. A little closer to St. Paul, within the usually sleepy old town of Mendota, you'll find the **Ragin' Cajun**, 452-1830, 1351 Sibley Memorial Highway, Mendota, offering blues and boogie a few nights a week. Across the road is the **Mendota Saloon**, 452-9582, 1352 Sibley Memorial Highway, serving up country and old-fashioned rock 'n' roll in a roadhouse atmosphere.

Speaking of roadhouses, you'll find a number of cavernous honky-tonks along Minn. Highway 61 south of St. Paul as it runs parallel to the Mississippi River. Highway 61 is good for that kind of thing, no matter what part of the Twin Cities area you're in. There are some nice bars in the town of White Bear Lake, along Minn. Highway 61 north of St. Paul, and a string of working-class places with cold beer and dancing stretching down south to the river town of Hastings.

A center of nightlife in the near-north suburb of Arden Hills is **McGuire's Manhattan Grille**, 636-4123, in the Holiday Inn, 1201 W. County Road E. It features music, mostly pop and R&B, a few nights a week and has several rooms full of activity.

One of the prime gathering places in Blaine is the **Blainbrook Entertainment Center**, 755-8686, 12000 Central Avenue N.E., offering music on weekends in a room as sprawling as the suburb that houses it.

The Mounds View area has a few interesting places. **The Mermaid**, 784-7350, 2200 E. Highway 10, has been through several incarnations but has always seemed to find its greatest success with hard-rock fans who like the smoky, rough-hewn atmosphere.

But most of the nightlife in the northern suburbs can be found at such chains as the **Bombay Bicycle Club**, 786-0380, 199 Northtown Drive N.E., Blaine, and **Tequilaberry's**, 780-1850, 133 N.W. Coon Rapids Boulevard, Coon Rapids. They pack 'em in even though the ambiance is a bit contrived and sterile.

So, let's finish up with the western suburbs. Yes, you can find the same kind of chain bars mentioned above (add T.G.I. Friday's and Chili's, as well as the Champps local sports bar chain), but you can also choose from some friendly places with good music by local bands.

Dover, 542-1060, 5555 Wayzata Boulevard, St. Louis Park, inside the Sheraton Park Place Hotel, is an intimate bar that offers up bands specializing in pop and jazz tunes. Out in Crystal is the **Iron Horse**, 533-2503, Hennepin County Road 81 and Bass Lake Road, one of the Twin Cities' old standbys for heavy metal and hard rock by local and national acts.

Ivories, 591-6188, 605 Minn. Highway 169, Plymouth, is one of the classiest piano bars in the Twin Cities, featuring talented Jimmy Martin tickling the keys. It's on the northwest corner of the intersection of Minn. Highway 55 and Highway 169. If you're traveling farther west on Highway 55, you have the choice of a couple of stops worth making. **J.P. Mulligan's**, 559-1595, 3005 N. Harbor Lane, Plymouth, is a friendly bar and restaurant that occasionally offers music. **The Country House**, 546-4655, 10715 South Shore Drive, Medicine Lake, is tucked away alongside Medicine Lake and prides itself on being an old-fashioned roadhouse with a country clientele in the midst of the ever-developing western suburbs.

Speaking of country, the Twin Cities' foremost venue for national country acts has long been the **Medina Entertainment Center**, 478-6661, 500 Minn. Highway 55, Medina. Whether the music is provided by Waylon Jennings or such hot down-home locals as the Killer Hayseeds, you'll find a friendly atmosphere and a large dance floor designed for two-stepping. But if your musical tastes veer more toward Big Band standards, '50s and '60s oldies or progressive rock, Medina may have something for you. The sprawling facility has a second, smaller concert/dance area with live music, a large bowling alley and a full-service restaurant.

Movies

From arty foreign-film houses to sub-

urban multiscreen complexes, you can find a movie theater to fit every taste and budget in the Twin Cities. Here's a look at the variety of it all. For complete listings, check either daily newspaper, the *St. Paul Pioneer Press* or the *Star Tribune*. For capsule reviews, call the *Pioneer Press* audiotext service, The Line, at 222-1000.

Foreign and Art Film Houses

The Uptown Theatre, 825-4644, 2906 Hennepin Avenue, Minneapolis, specializes in first-run foreign and art films, plus revivals of great vintage flicks such as *Casablanca* and *Lawrence of Arabia*. Nearby, the new **Lagoon Theater**, 825-6006, 1320 Lagoon Avenue (just east of Hennepin), offers similar fare on six screens.

Serious film buffs also flock to the **U Film Society**, 627-4430, housed in the Bell Auditorium at 17th and University avenues, Minneapolis, on the University of Minnesota campus. The society also sponsors a terrific annual film festival of new works from around the world.

Another interesting independent theater near the university campus is the **Oak Street Cinema**, 331-3134, 309 Oak Street S.E., which specializes in a merry mix, everything from Buster Keaton silent flicks and Sam Peckinpah (*Straw Dogs*) retrospectives to recent Sundance Film Festival winners.

The **Walker Art Center**, 375-7622, Vineland Place, Minneapolis, frequently shows new and old controversial works, sometimes pairing them with live music performances. In the summer, the Walker sponsors a popular Movies and Music in the Park series, presenting free flicks on an outdoor screen in Loring Park, preceded by live music.

The Parkway, 822-3030, 4814 Chicago Avenue, Minneapolis, is a second-run theater that shows foreign and off-beat fare at reduced prices.

Bigger than Life

The Omnitheater 221-9444, at the Science Museum, Wabasha and Exchange streets, St. Paul, shows nature films on a gigantic "you are there" Omni screen. A word of caution: Arrive early and purchase your tickets hours in advance, because this is a very popular attraction, especially during the summer months. Also during the summer you'll find a similar Omni theater at Valleyfair amusement park, 445-6500, in Shakopee.

Some Great Mainstream Houses

Centennial Lakes Cinema, 920-3334, 87311 France Avenue S., Edina, is a modern multiplex offering state-of-the-art projection and booming stereo acoustics in eight screening rooms. And not content to just serve the old popcorn-and-Milk Duds menu, Centennial Lakes also sells tacos at its refreshment stand!

For the indecisive types, we have the perfect spot. The General Cinema, 546-5700, at Mall of America, I-494 and 24th Avenue, Bloomington, lets you choose from 14 screens of new releases — something for everyone and every mood. It's on the fourth floor of the Mall's south side.

Bargain Venues

The following are second-run houses, showing features just months after their first run at bargain prices, around $1.50. Considering some of Hollywood's dubious "hits," it's definitely worth the wait.

In Minneapolis, Riverview Theatre, 729-7369, 3800 42nd Avenue S., is loaded with kitsch and character. Its decor is a happy blend of '40s and '50s — comfy lobby couches, coffee tables and gold cylinder lamps, plus a lot of turquoise. It's an enjoyable trip down memory lane.

Looking for comfort? Roseville 4 Theatres, 488-4242, 1211 Larpenteur Avenue, Roseville, is reputed to have the cushiest seats in town: plush, neck-supporting rockers.

Here's a quick list of other second-run houses: Ridge Square, 546-1404, Minn. Highway 394 and Plymouth Road, Minnetonka; Excelsior Dock, 474-6725, 26 Water Street, Excelsior; Spring Brook, 780-3706, 4 Theatre 141 N. 85th Avenue, Coon Rapids; Plaza Maplewood Theater, 770-7969, 1847 Larpenteur Avenue E., Maplewood.

For something a little different, try Cinema Cafe, 546-6305, 2749 Winnetka Avenue N., New Hope. Order a pizza, glass of wine or mug of beer and munch away to your heart's content while you watch a second-run movie on one of six screens in this comfortable blend of restaurant and movie house. All seats are $2.50.

Come For A Visit.

You'll Never Want To Leave.

©1994 Mall of America SNOOPY: ©1958, United Feature Syndicate, Inc.

Shop over 400 stores, including Bloomingdale's, Macy's, Nordstrom, and Sears. Thrill to Knott's® Camp Snoopy® indoor amusement park. Unwind in restaurants and nightclubs. "One Call For The Mall," (612) 883-8800, answers any question.

Bring in this coupon to any Mall of America Logo Merchandise Store and receive $2.00 off a Super Savings Coupon Book, which contains hundreds of dollars in savings at retail stores, restaurants and entertainment.

MALL OF AMERICA®
Bloomington, MN

Inside
Shopping

Once upon a time, sophisticated Twin Citians eschewed our stodgy Midwestern retail emporiums and flew to Chicago or New York to shop for the latest designer fashions or furnishings.

Well, baby, times have changed.

Today, local trendsetters can find their hearts' desires in fashions, furnishings and bric-a-brac right here in their own back yard, thanks in large part to the Twin Cities' new temple to consumerism, the Mall of America, not to mention numerous other unique retail complexes and shopping centers that have sprouted here in the past decade.

Minneapolis and St. Paul have developed into a shopping mecca for the Upper Midwest. Now, Chicagoans — heck, even the French, Japanese and Swedes — are coming here to shop 'til they drop.

In reality, the twin towns have a long tradition of innovative retailing. After all, the country's first enclosed shopping mall, Southdale, was built here in suburban Edina in the late '50s. The concept proved so successful that other 'Dales soon graced other suburbs. Not to be outdone, the downtowns fought back with attractive, upscale stores linked by enclosed skyways to draw shoppers year round, even in blustery January.

In the '60s, Minneapolis turned its retail center, Nicollet Avenue, into a pedestrian (plus buses) boulevard, named it Nicollet Mall, and adorned it with benches, shade trees and unique sculptures and water fountains. The '80s saw such tony shopping centers as The Conservatory and Gaviidae Common join the pedestrian but ever-popular City Center complex on this retail avenue.

St. Paul has created attractive shopping centers in the stunning World Trade Center and Town Square, the latter encompassing an indoor park with waterfalls and greenery. The Saintly City also is home to Galtier Plaza, a complex of shops, restaurants and movie theaters in historic Lowertown, located on the eastern edge of downtown. For those who prefer to shop on a more intimate scale, numerous old-fashioned neighborhood retail clusters, typically hardware stores, bakeries and quaint gift shops, are sprinkled throughout both cities and the suburbs.

A new wrinkle on the local shopping scene is the large discount outlet centers offering famous-label fashions and furnishings at discount prices.

But then, shopping has always been economical in Minnesota, because there's no sales tax on clothing.

The following shopping tour highlights major retail centers as well as one-of-a-kind shops in the Twin Cities. Be forewarned: In the topsy-turvy world of retail, favorite old stores can close with little notice, while new shops seem to open overnight. We've tried to be up-to-date, but inevitably, changes might have occurred since press time.

Let's begin with the obvious.

Bloomington

Mall of America

This shopper's paradise, the largest enclosed retail/entertainment complex in the United States, is fast becoming one of the top tourist attractions in the country. And it's easy to see why. The Mall of America literally offers something for everyone — amusement rides, movies, even wild animals. Oh, yes, and then there's the shopping!

In addition to its four anchor stores — **Bloomingdale's**, **Macy's**, **Nordstrom** and **Sears** — the megamall houses nearly 400 specialty stores, loads of freestanding shopping kiosks and carts, a 7-acre indoor **Camp Snoopy** amusement park with 24 rides, a dinner theater, a 14-screen movie theater, a huge Lego play center, a miniature golf course and 25 restaurants (including **Planet Hollywood**), in addition to 27 fast-food outlets, plus nightclubs, sports bars and comedy clubs. Whew! Still not impressed? Did we fail to mention the **Starbase Omega** attraction, where you can dress up in sci-fi gear and play laser shoot-'em-up? (Yes, adults can play too.)

As if that weren't enough, slated to open in early 1996 is **Underwater World**, a two-level, 70,000 square-foot aquarium that will take visitors on an deep-sea journey via a 400-foot-long tunnel.

But the heart and soul of the Mall of America is its many and varied shopping venues. The Mall is laid out along four "avenues" surrounding Camp Snoopy. These avenues are three or four levels high with an anchor store at each corner.

In addition to the nationally known large anchor stores, Mall retailers include the upper-crusty **Brooks Brothers**, Ba-

nana Republic, **Filene's Basement**, **Abercrombie & Fitch**, **The Gap** and **Guess**, **Chico's** women's apparel, plus specialty stores such as **Linens 'N' Things**, **Lechter's Home Store**, **Warner Bros. Studio Store**, **Williams-Sonoma** and oodles more. Not to be missed is the innovative **Oshman's Super Sports USA** store, with basketball courts and batting cages for an interactive shopping experience.

One can literally spend days in MOA, visiting a mind-boggling array of shops. Here are a few of the more unusual ones: **BareBones**, offering skeleton-themed games, gifts and science kits; **Butterflies by Nancy**, where butterflies aren't free; **Callido Chile Traders**, a hot-sauce emporium; **Love From Minnesota**, selling North Star State mementoes; **Enchanted Tales**, where kids (and, be honest, even adults) love the specialty stuffed animals; **Snoopy Boutique**, where you can find Charles Schulz's favorite pup on everything from ties to bookmarks; and **The Lost Forest**, an enchanting collection of stuffed species in a tropical-forest setting.

The Mall can literally fill your every need — even those needs you didn't think you needed! At the Mall, it's possible to:

• Buy a home security system (**Security Store**)

• Dress up in a Victorian gown and have your photo taken (**Old Time Photography** or the **Victorian Photographer**)

• Buy intriguing 3D holographic items (**Hologram Fantastic**)

• Dress up in satin and sequins and have your photo taken (**Glamour Shots**)

• Book a cruise (**Cruise Holidays**)

• Get your teeth cleaned (**Group Health Dental Clinic**)

• Build a LEGO dinosaur with your kids (**LEGO Imagination Center**)

• Go to the same movie theater every

MORE CHOICE**S**

OVER 1200 COMBINATIONS	**QUIET, QUALITY FANS**
BETTER PRICES	3-speed reversing, summer/winter comfort, 14 finishes, quiet, dependable Limited Lifetime
FOR THE NEAREST LOCATION CALL 644-1203	Warranty. Remote controllable, easy installation features.

DAN'S FAN CITY

day of the week and never see the same film twice (**General Cinema 14**)

• Attend a dinner theater (**Ford Playhouse**)

• Buy a snazzy-looking bird feeder (**Natural Wonders**)

• Get a foot massage (via machine, in **Nordstrom's** women's lounge)

• Find a job (**Hennepin Employment Brokerage**)

• Buy a dreamcatcher (**Painted Tipi** or **Pueblo Spirit**)

• Complete your cow collection (**Cowabuddies**)

• Find lip-smackin' boysenberry jam (**Knott's Berry Market**)

• Get that just-right Minnesota-type gift or card (**Minnesot-ah**)

• Buy mulch for your garden (**Gardener's Paradise**)

• Join the **American Association of Retired Persons** (AARP office)

• Delight a duffer (**Mac Birdie Golf Gifts**)

• Delight your spouse (**Victoria's Secret**)

• Find automobile paraphernalia (**Runkel Bros. American Garage**)

• Add to your music box collection (**San Francisco Music Box Co.**)

• Get married! (**Chapel of Love**)

Some of the Mall's retail outlets are actually playhouses disguised as stores. At **Tempus Expeditions**, you can "ride" an action-packed motion simulator and, then, if you're not too woozy, browse among interesting artifacts, models, toys and apparel.

Book-lovers need not go home empty-handed. The mall has three bookstores to feed your hunger for the written word. **B. Dalton**, of course, is part of popular national chain. You'll also find **P.B. Pages**, an intimate shop with an extensive collection, and **Readwell's**, a friendly, service-oriented bookstore.

A great place to shop with children without denting the pocketbook is the **All for One** store, where everything is priced at $1 or less. Give the kids $1 each and let them loose!

Restaurants include **Wolfgang Puck's Pizzeria**, the **California Grill** in Macy's, the wildly popular **Planet Hollywood**, **Tony Roma's**, **Tucci Benucch** and many more. Perhaps the most imaginative is the expansive, exotic **Rainforest Cafe**, which has a jungle decor, aquariums, sounds of the wild and even spooky mists. In addition, Mall of America houses two large food courts offering an array of fast food.

One of the more pleasant surprises about the Mall of America is its incredibly convenient, free parking. Even though there are more than 12,700 spaces on two parking decks and four ground-level parking lots, no parking space is more than 300 feet from a mall entrance. And you run little risk of experiencing the shopper's nightmare — forgetting where you've parked the car. Each parking section is labeled with the name of a state. We find it easier to park at the Mall of America than at any suburban mall in the Twin Cities.

But if you'd rather leave the car at home, the Twin Cities' Metropolitan Council Transit Operations offers daily express bus service to the Mall from both downtown Minneapolis and St. Paul every half-hour. And an airport shuttle leaves the Minneapolis/St. Paul Airport for the Mall every half-hour.

Visiting this gigantic complex can be a daunting experience. But it needn't be that way, if you keep things in perspective. Here are a few guidelines on how to make your Mall of America experience one you will remember:

1) Get there early and, if you can, go on a weekday when the crowds are thinner.

2) Wear comfortable shoes and clothes! This is a must, as you will be walking, walking, walking.

3) Make use of the Mall's Guest Service Centers, at each main entrance. Services include foreign language interpretation, messaging, strollers, wheelchairs, lockers, electronic convenience vehicles, lost and found, automatic teller machines, telephones (including devices for the deaf), directories and shopping bags. Also, restrooms are located near these centers.

4) Don't try to see it all in one visit. Take your time, breathe deeply and keep your sense of perspective.

5) When things get a bit overwhelming, head for Nordstrom or Macy's, where the restroom-lounges are terrific.

6) If you're planning to eat in one of the fast-food courts, go during a non-peak time to avoid the crowds and noise. These expansive courtyards can be stressful and noisy. The food courts in Camp Snoopy seem to be less crowded. A pleasant alternative is to choose one of the Mall's many nice, sit-down restaurants.

7) If you're planning to ride Paul Bunyan's Log Chute in Camp Snoopy, make it the last stop before going home, because you'll get drenched!

Mall of America stores are open from 10 AM to 9:30 PM Monday through Friday, 9:30 AM to 9:30 PM Saturday and 11 AM to 7 PM Sunday. Some of the restaurants and Camp Snoopy open earlier and remain open later; call the mall office at 883-8800 for information.

To get to the Mall from the airport, take I-494 toward 24th Avenue. Watch for the Mall signs and turn south. From the west, take I-494 until you approach Cedar Avenue. Watch for the signs. Technically, the Mall is sits at the intersection of I-494 and Minn. Highway 77 (Cedar Avenue). You can't miss it!

Minneapolis

Downtown

Despite the numerous malls that dot the suburbs, many Twin Citians still prefer to shop downtown Minneapolis and St. Paul, where they can enjoy traditional department stores and specialty shops, terrific restaurants and nightlife in a cosmopolitan ambiance you just can't find in suburbia.

In downtown Minneapolis most shopping centers on the Nicollet Mall. In addition to the many indoor shopping areas detailed below, there are many boutiques, gift shops and specialty stores located at the south end of the mall and on streets to the east and west of the mall.

Here's an overview of downtown Minneapolis shopping.

City Center, 372-1234, 33 S. Sixth Street, is a multilevel indoor shopping center with 65 stores, including **Montgomery Ward, Marshalls** (outlet shopping), **The Limited, Sam Goody, The Gap, Victoria's Secret** and **B. Dalton** bookstore. The Center also has restaurants including the **Nankin** (Chinese) and, for the casual crowd, **TGI Friday's** and **Mick's**, plus a fast-food court. In the center of downtown, City Center is linked via skyways to Dayton's and Gaviidae Common shopping center. This is a very popular mainstream center, offering the right mix of stores for Mr. or Ms. Middle America.

The Conservatory, 332-4649, 800 Nicollet Mall, offers 20 attractive, high-calibre shops such as **Mark Shale** (menswear), **Ann Taylor** (women's clothing), **The Nature Company** and **Sharper Image** (yuppie gadgets) in a classy atrium setting of winding stairways and lush plantings. The award-winning **Goodfellow's** restaurant is also in The Conservatory, which is linked via skyway and tunnel to Dayton's.

Gaviidae Common, 372-1222, 651 Nicollet Mall, is named for the Minnesota state bird, the common loon (*Gavia* in Latin), which is memorialized here in a handsome bronze sculpture. But there's

HunterDouglas
DUETTE®

WINDOW FASHIONS

Regardless of your style of window, it can be made more beautiful with custom made DUETTE® SHADES.

DO
check us out!

DON'T
fall for 40% to 80% savings claims!

The LITTLE BLIND SPOT

HOPKINS 935-4353
ST. CLOUD 253-3067
BLOOMINGTON 884-7748

WOOD SHUTTERS
Plantation Style

• Painted or stained finish

• Available in louver, 2 1/2, 3 1/2 and 4 1/2

• Fabric insert panels also available

• Inside mount or framed available

SHUTTERS 'N SHADES

811 MAINSTREET
HOPKINS, MN
931-0410

"Specialists in Shutters and Sun Control Devices"

Farmers Market in downtown St. Paul.

Photo: Chris Polydoroff, Pioneer Press

nothing loony about this upscale shopping emporium housed in two large complexes linked by skyway over Sixth Street. In addition to **Saks Fifth Avenue** and **Neiman Marcus, Gaviidae** is home to more than 60 specialty shops and restaurants. Among them is **Room & Board**, a locally based home furnishings store that specializes in high-quality contemporary and classical (i.e. Shaker, Mission) styles of furniture, upholstery and kitchenware.

Other well-known stores include: **Burberrys, Eddie Bauer, Jessica McClintock, Lillie Rubin, Pendleton, Cole-Haan** (shoes), **Joan Vass, The Museum Company, Talbots** and **Brentano's Bookstore**.

Hints for bargain-hunters: Neiman Marcus' **Last Call on 4** (on the fourth floor, obviously) is an entire department of greatly reduced merchandise. Saks also has a similar department, called the **Clearinghouse**, also on its fourth floor. Great buys for serious shoppers!

On Gaviidae's concourse level is **Morton's of Chicago Steakhouse**, 555 Nicollet Mall, purveyors of huge steaks and fresh lobster. For lighter fare, enjoy a spot o' tea at **Bronte's English Tea Room and Gifts** on the second level.

Parking, available in ramps off Fifth and Sixth streets, is free for up to three hours with a minimum $20 same-day purchase at Gaviidae.

Dayton's, 700 Nicollet Mall, the flagship store of the locally based department-store chain, offers quality merchandise and great customer service. The gigantic store has eight floors of appliances, home furnishings, gourmet food, men's, women's and children's apparel and much more. Dayton's lower level Marketplace area is especially fun with its gourmet foods, trendy furnishings and kitchenware. In fact, Dayton's has a popular wedding registry service. This emporium is a local favorite of Twin Citians, who come here to shop, socialize or meet for lunch at the **Oak Grill** or **Sky Room**.

In addition to its retail offerings, Dayton's also sponsors many annual special events in its eighth-floor auditorium. These include annual wintertime displays with animated figures, which have become a popular holiday tradition, and spring flower show extravaganzas.

Adjacent to Dayton's is **J.B. Hudson Jewelers**, a must-see for fine jewelry, crystal and collectibles, such as Limoges pill boxes, Lladro and Beatrix Potter figurines. An elegant old store, Hudson's is a delightful feast for the eyes.

Across the street, a two-story **Barnes & Noble** tempts you with thousands of titles. The **Polo/Ralph Lauren** store at Ninth Street and Nicollet Mall is remarkable not only for its internationally famous fashions for men, women and children, not to mention home furnishings, but also for the elegant, old Young-Quinlan building it inhabits. This is, in fact, the third-largest Polo shop in the world. Step inside and enjoy the history.

Also on this block is **Crate & Barrel**, 915 Nicollet Mall, packed with contemporary home furnishings and kitchenware. This store also has a popular bridal registry service.

The **IDS Crystal Court**, 80 S. Eighth Street, was made famous in the opening scenes of "The Mary Tyler Moore Show." The famous shot pictured Mary riding one of the Crystal Court escalators and eating lunch here. The expansive courtyard has also been the setting for President Clinton's speeches here in the summer of 1994. The Crystal Court is a smaller retail center offering several boutiques, plus local branches of **The Gap, Gap Kids, TJ Maxx, Godiva Chocolatiers, Adidas** and **Banana Republic**. New to the complex is a **Williams-Sonoma** cookware shop. Oh, by the way, it's housed in the tallest building in Minneapolis and is worth a visit, whether you're shopping or not. As for Mary's table, it's now in **Basil's Restaurant** overlooking the courtyard. Don't be embarrassed. Everyone asks about it.

The **Dublin Walk**, 1200 Nicollet Mall, offers a little bit o' the old sod — Irish sweaters and Claddagh jewelry, plus Waterford crystal and Belleek china. Even though it has changed its downtown address over the years, this tasteful shop is an enduring favorite of Twin Citians. Also on the mall, you'll find a lot of bridal shops, art galleries and import gift shops, including **Mhiripiri Gallery**, 1020 Nicollet Mall, (African art) and **Esperanto**, 910 Nicollet Mall, for home furnishings. And don't forget about the second floor shopping arcade of the **Hyatt Regency Hotel**, 1300 Nicollet Mall.

For collectors of fine and rare books, **James & Mary Laurie Booksellers**, at 921 Nicollet Mall, and **Lien's Book Shop**, at 57 S. Ninth Street, are must stops for their extensive and unusual collections.

Don't make the mistake of limiting your shopping only to the Nicollet Mall. Other surprises are just blocks away.

Columnist Molly Ivins on her visit to Mall of America: "Great Caesar's armpit! Sweet suffering catfish! Holy gamoly! I have been to the pyramids of America. I have seen the cathedral of commerce. Our Parthenon, our Coliseum, our Chartres. I have been to the Mall of America, the world's largest shopping mall."

Insiders' Tips

Baxter's Books, 608 Second Avenue S., is an inviting emporium of volumes on every subject, specializing in business, travel and children's books. The large wooden bookcases create intimate nooks for browsing and reading on a world of subjects. This independent book shop specializes in personalized service and special events and clubs for readers and writers.

For the latest in traditional and contemporary furnishings, **Design Studio 1200**, 1200 Second Avenue S., offers personalized design services.

Also worth a visit is **Hubert W. White**, 611 Marquette Avenue, a classy shop for the latest in men's fashions.

Haskell's, 81 S. Ninth Street, is the flagship store of a local chain of liquor stores known for its extensive wine selection and friendly, helpful staff.

Sports buffs will find their favorite team logos at **Nick's Sports World**, Seventh Street and Second Avenue S.

For the new and unusual in gifts, books and wearable art, check out the gift shops at **Walker Art Center** and the **Guthrie Theater**, Vineland Place. Both have great one-of-a-kind baubles, books, sarcastic T-shirts and mementoes you just won't find in a department store or mall. Both are just southwest of downtown, across Loring Park.

Warehouse District

The Warehouse District, west of Hennepin Avenue between Ninth Street and Washington Avenue, is home to several antique shops, art galleries, nightclubs and restaurants in historic buildings. The Wyman Building, at Sixth Street and First Avenue N., contains several first-rate art galleries, such as **MC Gallery** and **Carolyn Ruff Gallery**. It is also the address of **Parmees**, an elegant,

airy fashion salon specializing in strictly haute couture for men and women — a new and exciting addition to the local fashion scene.

Architectural Antiques, 801 Washington Avenue N., is a unique source of marble table tops, stained-glass windows, plaster columns and other architectural remnants salvaged from old buildings, homes and churches.

Just for the fun of it, check out **Sister Fun**, 121 N. Fourth Street, where you can buy an Elvis lamp, squeeze toys, zany T-shirts and assorted whimsies for the person who has everything.

Nate's Clothing Co., 27 N. Fourth Street, is a local institution offering a wide selection of discounted men's clothing.

Off on the western side of the Warehouse District is **International Market Square**, at 275 Market Street, a first-class showplace of home furnishings housed in, of all places, a converted underwear factory. The public is invited to come in and browse, but purchases must be made through a trade professional.

Riverwalk Antiques, 212 Third Avenue N., is a treasure trove of great finds, from furniture to china and old artwork. More than 20 dealers are represented in this rambling old marketplace.

Northeast

Check out **Surdyk's** liquor store, East Hennepin and University Avenue N.E., for its wide selection of beer, wine and cheese. (They have great sales.)

International Gallery and Gifts, 207 E. Hennepin Avenue, sells Ukrainian Easter eggs and other decorated eggs from Poland and other Eastern European countries.

Also in this ethnic enclave, stop in at

At Oshman's Superstore in the Mall of America customers can test sporting goods before buying them.

Kramarczuk Sausage Co., 215 Hennepin Avenue E., for tasty Polish sausages and old-fashioned franks, and **Emily's Lebanese Deli**, 641 University Avenue N.E., for to-die-for takeout tabbouleh.

Nearby are **Riverplace** and **St. Anthony Main**, lovely riverfront shopping/entertainment/office complexes in historic buildings housing a few interesting gift shops; the fascinating **Museum of Questionable Medical Devices**; and restaurants such as **Pracna on Main** (American bistro fare with summertime outdoor seating), **Sophia** (continental fare in an elegant setting), **Kikugawa** (Japanese food) and **Tuggs Saloon** (pub fare).

Uptown

The Uptown area is a vibrant community southwest of downtown and roughly bordered by Hennepin Avenue to the west, Lyndale Avenue to the east and 32nd Street to the south. Mirroring the tastes of its youthful, cosmopolitan residents, this area offers many unusual shops, from antiques and alternative

bookstores to counterculture grunge venues.

Calhoun Square, an indoor shopping center at Hennepin and Lake, houses many specialty shops, with an emphasis on contemporary/global apparel and gifts. Stores include **Kitchen Window, Main Street Outfitters, Borders Book Shop, Urban Traveler, Uptown Art, Games People Play** and **The Limited Express**. When you're tired of browsing, grab an outdoor table at **Figlio** (continental cuisine) and enjoy the people-watching. Or dine indoors at the **Smiling Moose** (casual fare) or the **Good Earth** (sprouts). Just across Hennepin from Calhoun Square are a large branch of **The Gap**, 3000 Hennepin Avenue, and **Urban Outfitters**, 3006 Hennepin Avenue S., specializing in the latest trends. **Fleetham Furnishings and Design**, 2910 Hennepin Avenue, is a longstanding Twin Cities favorite for home furnishings.

Across Lake Street from Calhoun Square is the **New Power Generation** boutique, 1408 W. Lake Street, owned by the rock star formerly known as Prince, and, to the east, several antiques shops. Up and down Hennepin you'll find mountaineering stores, futon outlets, espresso shops and interesting little nooks and crannies, including a very good bakery, **Gelpe's Napoleon Bakery and Cafe**, 2447 Hennepin Avenue.

Of special note, at 3505 Hennepin Avenue S., is **Play It Again Sports**, a secondhand sports equipment store that's a favorite among parents of Little Leaguers and budding sports stars. The store buys used equipment for cash or as a trade-in on other equipment. Fourteen Play It Again Sports outlets are scattered throughout the Twin Cities metro area.

Lunds Food Store, 1450 W. Lake Street, is part of a local grocery chain characterized by an appealing ambiance, a wide variety of specialty and import foods, quality produce and meats and customer service. This food store also is a nonthreatening place for Uptown's many young and beautiful singles to meet ("Our eyes locked over the cantaloupe display"). The Twins Cities have nine Lunds stores, and, best of all, they're open 24 hours a day.

Veering eastward, follow the scent of strong java and fresh, yeasty bread to a favorite neighborhood eatery, the **French Meadow Bakery**, at 2610 Lyndale Avenue S. A charming egalitarian attitude infuses this funky, unpretentious cafe/bakery, known for its delicious loaves (of course), unusual salads and an arty, casual atmosphere that makes everyone — especially solo diners — feel at home. In the summertime, the outdoor tables are at a premium.

The **Wedge Co-op**, at 2105 Lyndale Avenue South, is one of the most successful natural food co-ops in the Twin Cities, offering an extensive range of products beyond the traditional sprouts and nuts.

Farther south, **Art Materials Inc.**, 3018 Lyndale Ave. S., is a good resource for art supplies and instruction, offering classes in everything from Watercolor Basics to Intermediate Airbrushing.

South

Check out **Ingrebretsen's Scandinavian Gifts**, 1601 E. Lake Street, for specialty foods, cookware, albums and other Scandinavian imports. Another great source of Scandinavian goods is the gift shop at the **American Swedish Institute**, 2600 Park Avenue.

The gift shop of the **Minneapolis Institute of Arts**, 2400 Third Avenue S., sells wonderful art books, cards, posters and unique gifts.

For those hooked on whodunits, **Uncle Edgar's Mystery Bookstore**, 2864 Chicago Avenue, in south Minneapolis, is just the place. Then, leave the mysteries and head next door for the outer limits at **Uncle Hugo's Science Fiction Bookstore**.

Hungry? **Broder's Cucina Italiana**, 50th Street and Penn Avenue S., serves up all types of Italian specialties and groceries for in-store dining or takeout. **Judith McGrann & Friends**, 3016 W. 50th Street, has a fun and unusual collection of fashions, home furnishings and gifts.

Wild Rumpus Bookstore, 2720 W. 43rd Street, is an enchanting children's bookstore filled with fun surprises and an array of animals (see the Kidstuff chapter). Plan your visit around lunchtime and make tracks next door (at 2724 W. 43rd Street) to **D'Amico & Sons**, a superb Italian deli and market.

Wild Rumpus and D'Amico are part of a modest but inviting shopping district centered on 43rd Street and Upton Avenue. A wonderful antidote for megamallitis, this area is a fun collection of yarn shops, bakeries, gift shops (including one of the very popular **Bibelot** shops) and the great Sebastian Joe's ice cream parlor, all just a stone's throw from the western shore of Lake Harriet.

If you venture a few blocks farther west on 44th Street, you'll discover a wonderful little bakery, the **Turtle Bread Company**, at 3415 W. 44th Street, which specializes in big, rustic loaves made from organic flour.

St. Paul

Downtown

Over the past decade, St. Paul's retail offerings have expanded, thanks to the relatively new World Trade Center and Galtier Plaza. Here's an overview of shopping in the Saintly City's downtown core.

Town Square, 298-0900, 445 Minnesota Street, offers 40 stores, including **Brauns, Casual Corner, Executive Coffee and Tea, Accent Minnesota** (for Minnesota-themed gifts), **Twin Cities Poster, Billy's Deals** (shoes), **B. Dalton** bookstore and many others in a picturesque setting that includes an indoor park. If all the great shopping has left you with a growling stomach, check out the lower level fastfood court, where you'll dine amid gurgling water fountains.

Just across the street (or skyway), the **World Trade Center**, 291-1715, 30 E. Seventh Street, is home to such retail establishments as **Eddie Bauer Outlet, Lane Bryant, Caren Charles, Victoria's Secret, Sam Goody** (CDs and tapes), **The Map Store** and other specialty stores, plus a food court, all in an attractive multilevel setting, the centerpiece of which is a 52-foot fountain. Restaurants include **Pig's Eye Grille and Brew Annex**, offering the popular local brew and pub fare, and the **Heartthrob Cafe** on the first floor, where your burger and fries are delivered by in-line skating waiters. If you're in a hurry, check out **Au Bon Pain** for fresh sandwiches and soups that you can eat in or take out.

Next door to the World Trade Center and across the street from Town Square is **Dayton's**, 411 Cedar Street, offering the same amenities as the Minneapolis version in a setting that's a bit more friendly and a lot less crowded. Dayton's has two popular restaurants: the intimate **Iron Horse** on the lower level and the larger, elegant **River Room** on the main floor.

Located in Lowertown, **Galtier Plaza**, 175 E. Fifth Street, is a shopping/entertainment complex with a few one-of-a-kind shops, such as **Inside Africa** (African arts and crafts such as stone carvings and batiks), **Native Wings** (American Indian gifts), **Milbern Clothing Company** and **Lee's Outlet Books** for fantastic overstock bargains. Galtier is also home to the very popular and elegant **Great Northern Supper Club**, several nightclubs, a four-screen movie theater, the **Comedy Gallery** comedy club, plus a main-floor food courtyard that overlooks attractive Mears Park.

The *New York Times* on the Mall of America: "It's like the difference between a space station and a bus station."

St. Paul has several individual downtown stores worth noting. **David Edwins/Frank Murphy**, St. Peter and Fifth streets, is a landmark offering a range of women's fashions from moderately priced career wear to designer names. Since 1906, **Nakashian-O'Neil**, Sixth and St. Peter streets, has been selling incomparable antiques, including French, Chinese and English porcelain, oil paintings and fine, unique gifts.

The **Science Museum of Minnesota**, 30 E. 10th Street, the **Minnesota History Center**, 345 W. Kellogg Boulevard, and the **Minnesota Children's Museum**, 10 W. Seventh Street, have delightful shops brimming with books, educational toys and rare finds.

Along W. Seventh Street in St. Paul you'll find interesting shops and antiques stores, not to mention one of the best hardware stores in St. Paul, **Seven Corners Ace Hardware**, 216 W. Seventh Street. Across the street is an authentic Italian restaurant/deli, **Cossetta's Market and Pizzeria**, 211 W. Seventh Street.

Grand Avenue

Eclectic, homespun Grand Avenue, just west of downtown St. Paul, offers a refreshing change of pace from the modern, hermetically sealed suburban malls.

This bustling thoroughfare lined with elegant old apartment buildings and homes also boasts specialty and gift shops selling everything from world crafts to kitchenware, books, clothing and home furnishings.

Irish on Grand, 790 Grand Avenue, specializes in blarney, Belleek china, Celtic jewelry and apparel; **Trade Winds International** in Victoria Crossing shopping complex, 857 Grand Avenue, features world crafts; and **The Gathering**, 850 Grand Avenue, offers contemporary gifts and jewelry.

Book-lovers, take note: The avenue is home to some great independents, including **Odegard Books**, a book-lover's bookstore in Victoria Crossing, 857 Grand Avenue; and the **Red Balloon Bookshop**, 891 Grand Avenue, a delightful children's bookstore. Also at and near Victoria Crossing are **Books for Travel** and **Odegard Encore Books**, offering a selection of remaindered books and publishers' overstocks.

Last but certainly not least is the wonderful **Hungry Mind Bookstore**, 1648 Grand Avenue, housing an extensive, diverse collection of old and new titles in a rambling old building that simply begs you to linger awhile. An adjacent cafe/coffeeshop lends a gustatory dimension to your literary pursuits. The Hungry Mind also hosts numerous readings and literary discussions.

Be sure to make a stop at the **Jubilee Shop**, 1051 Grand Avenue, a nonprofit store that sells handmade crafts from around the world. Profits are returned to the village artisans.

Also worth a visit are **Chico's**, 1068 Grand Avenue, selling cotton casual apparel with ethnic touches; **The Bibelot Shop**, 1082 Grand Avenue, selling one-of-a-kind gifts and clothes; **Silver Creek Traders**, 1144 Grand Avenue, simply ooz-

Insiders' Tips

Antique-hunters flock to St. Paul's Payne Avenue (north of E. Seventh Street) and W. Seventh Street (west of Kellogg Boulevard).

It's a Mall World After All

Photo: Pioneer Press

The Mall of America is America's largest shopping and entertainment complex.

Here are a few fun and fascinating facts about the Mall of America, the nation's largest retail and entertainment center:

- Total square footage: 4.2 million square feet
- Number of Yankee Stadiums that would fit inside Mall of America: 7
- Cost to build: more than $650 million
- Number of stores: more than 400
- Number of sit-down restaurants: 25
- Number of fast-food restaurants: 27
- Number of specialty food stores: 36
- Number of nightclubs: 9
- Number of theater screens: 14
- Weekly tally of visitors: from 600,000 to 900,000 (depending on the season)
- Number of LEGO plastic blocks used to construct the blimp that hangs over LEGO Imagination Center: 138,240
- Number of people employed at Mall of America: 12,000
- Number of parking spaces: 12,750 on-site, 2,200 off-site
- Number of plants growing in Knott's Camp Snoopy: 30,000 plants and 400 trees
- Percent of visitors from outside the Mall's 150-mile radius: 30 percent
- Opening in 1996: A 1.2 million gallon walk-through aquarium.

ing North Woods charm, with its rustic birch, pine, willow and cedar furniture, animal carvings and metal sculptures.

Celebration Designs, 1457 Grand Avenue, offers tasteful religious banners and one-of-a-kind, handcrafted inspirational gifts.

You should know that parking can be a challenge along Grand Avenue. Check the Victoria Crossing lot for space.

Bandana Square

Bandana Square, 642-9676, 1021 E. Bandana Boulevard, is a shopping/entertainment complex housed in a former railroad-car repair warehouse. While it's not as popular as other venues, it nonetheless has fine specialty shops including **Europa European Imports** and **Miniature Merchant**, featuring dollhouse furnishings and military miniatures. The complex also has a huge room-size model railroad display, sponsored by the Twin City Model Railroad Club, and the **Dakota Bar & Grill**, one of the best jazz clubs in the Twin Cities.

St. Anthony Park

Milton Square is a charming neighborhood shopping area at the intersection of Como and Carter avenues in St. Anthony Park, in the northwest corner of St. Paul. In or near this cozy, flower-lined commercial courtyard you'll find such interesting little shops as **Taste of Scandinavia Bakery** and **L'Europa Deli**, **Micawber's Books**, **Country Peddler Quilt Shop**, **Oriental Gift Shoppe**, **Emil Gustafson Jewelers**, the **Bibelot Shop**, plus a couple of fun little restaurants: **Muffuletta**, where you can munch outdoors, and **Manning's in the Park**.

Suburban Specialties

West Metro Suburbs

Excelsior, a picturesque town on the southeast shore of Lake Minnetonka, is blessed with a thriving old-fashioned downtown centered on Water Street, its main thoroughfare. Here you'll find boutiques, gift shops and antiques stores mixed in with unpretentious cafes, a genuine hardware store, a few hair salons and other businesses.

Recent citywide gussying-up has transformed an old lumber yard into a new jewel-like city park bordered by a lovely Impressionist-style mural (à la Monet), introduced some truly extraordinary new retail establishments and revived an old waterfront park with a new children's playground.

Lining Water Street, north to south, are: **Bay Tree**, offering a high-quality array of nature-themed gifts, gourmet foods, soothing musical tapes and home accessories; **Affaire De Coeur**, selling handmade gifts, artwork, furniture and home accessories created by local artisans; **Into the Mystic**, specializing in unique handcrafted jewelry; **Frog Island Bookstore**, a cozy refuge for bibliophiles of all ages; **Leipolds**, a gift/antiques/whatever! shop; **A Country Look**, home furnishings; **Capers**, cards, gags and unique gifts; **Water Street Clothing**, women's fashions; **Tonka Bay Tots** children's wear shop; **D.B. & Co.**, unusual gifts; and, last but not least, **Goosebumps**, a groovy little antiques and gourmet gift shop.

Just off Water Street is an authentic white-glove, old-fashioned ladies' tea room called **Antiquity Rose**. It's a must see!

Need a break from all the shopping? **Excelsior Park** restaurant (with a lakeside deck), **Cafe Excelsior/Tom's Breakfast Bar** (a real soda fountain) and the **Waterfront Eatery** are all good bets.

A leisurely day in Excelsior is all the elixir you need in this workaday world.

On the way to Excelsior, you'll undoubtedly pass the **General Store**, less than a half-mile west of I-494 on Minn. Highway 7 (14401 Minn. Highway 7, Minnetonka). Set in a huge, rustic building, the General Store is crammed with homemade crafts, Victoriana, folk-art primitives and Minnesota mementoes, plus a great selection of kids' toys.

Wayzata is another picturesque Lake Minnetonka community where the main street is lined with fun, exclusive boutiques, galleries and restaurants. Especially worth visiting are several interesting fashion boutiques, including **Jan's** and **Bumber Shute**; **Blanc de Blanc, Ltd.**, selling everything white from clothing to home accessories; **Frost & Budd** for ahhsome home and garden accessories; **Silver Creek Design Studio**, home accessories; **The Bookcase**, a great little independent bookstore; **Overland Gallery**, specializing in Russian Impressionist art; **Decoratique**, a very romantic home-furnishings boutique; **Wuollet Bakery**, for tasty tidbits; and, last but not least, **The Quilted Bear**, a huge emporium of locally handcrafted country-style bric-a-brac, home furnishings and apparel.

The up-and-coming southwestern suburb of Eden Prairie is home to **Eden Prairie Center**, 941-7650, at Prairie Center Drive near I-494. This modern shopping mall has many clothing and gift stores, including **The Limited**, **Gigi Fashions** and **Lane Bryant**. There's also **Mervyn's of California** and **Kohl's** department stores here.

In Minnetonka, you'll find **Ridgedale Shopping Center**, 541-4864, at 12301 Wayzata Boulevard (or I-394). This attractive enclosed mall has nearly 100 stores, including anchors **Sears**, **Dayton's** and **JCPenney**. Other stores include **Ann Taylor**, **Victoria's Secret**, **Eddie Bauer**, **The Gap**, **The Limited**, **The Museum Store**, **Natural Wonders** and **Lechter's** kitchenware, plus **Applebee's** and **Uno Pizzaria** restaurants.

West of Ridgedale — across the parking lot, actually — is a small shopping complex housing **Borders Book Shop and Espresso Bar**, a huge, inviting book emporium that also sponsors readings and lectures. Also in this complex are **Joanne Fabrics**, **Champps** sports bar and **Leeann Chin** restaurants.

Across Plymouth Road from Ridgedale and is another small complex housing an ever-popular **Target** discount store and **Byerly's**, part of a local upscale grocery-store chain that emphasizes a luxurious shopping atmosphere (i.e. carpeting and chandeliers), fine imported foods, freshness and customer service. A huge **Barnes & Noble** bookstore here caters to your lust for literature.

Suburban St. Louis Park is home to the flagship **Byerly's** store, at 36th Street S. and

Watch for these Dayton's sales: Anniversary Sale in March, Daisy Sale in June and Jubilee Sale in October. Also legendary are the sales in Dayton's ritzy Oval Room.

Insiders' Tips

Minn. Highway 100, where, in addition to groceries, you'll find an in-store gift gallery, candy store and liquor shop, as well as a popular cafe.

Two smaller, older shopping centers, **Knollwood** and **Miracle Mile**, cater to the needs of St. Louis Park residents. Knollwood, at 8332 Minn. Highway 7, houses many clothing and specialty shops, including a new **Kohl's**, **Montgomery Ward**, **Everyday Hero**, **Casual Corner** women's store and many other shops, as well as a fast-food court.

A block west of Knollwood, in the Firstar Bank building at 8800 Minn. Highway 7, you'll find a truly extraordinary art boutique aptly named **Out of the Ordinary**, selling art glass, ceramics, whimsical kitchenware and gifts that will bring a smile to your lips.

Miracle Mile, 5009 Excelsior Boulevard, is noteworthy as the home of **Half-Price Books**, offering used and new books, records and CDs at a 50 percent discount (other locations are in St. Paul and Maplewood); **Once Upon a Child**, featuring high-quality used children's clothing (several other suburbs also have shops); **Mike Lynne's Tennis Shop**; **Cafe Sorella**, dishing up scrumptious brownies and strong java; **B. Dalton Bookseller**; and many other small and interesting shops.

We would be remiss if we left St. Louis Park without mentioning the best bagel bakery in the Twin Cities: **New York Bakery & Bagels Inc.**, in the small Texatonka strip mall at 8128 Minnetonka Boulevard.

Take Excelsior Boulevard a few miles west of Miracle Mile and you'll come to Hopkins, a small town with an old-fashioned main street that's nice for strolling and leisurely shopping. Here you'll find a strange, but interesting range of shops

that includes: **La-La-Land Store** (toys), **Steve's Train City** (model trains), **Windmill Imports** (Dutch-themed gifts), **Red Wing Shoes** (work shoes), **Books on Main** (unusual books), the **Antique Mall**, the **United Store** (outdoor clothing and camping gear) and, in the home furnishings realm, **Little Blind Spot** and **Shutters 'N' Shades**, featuring custom shades and wood shutters.

The town also has a generous number of downhome cafes, a few bars and even a tattoo parlor for the total shopping experience.

South Suburbs

The intersection of 50th Street and France Avenue S. in the tony suburb of Edina is just teeming with trendy shops and boutiques such as **White Oak Gallery** and **Doncaster**, **Talbots**, **Tonya's** (owned by baseball player Kirby Puckett's wife) and **Spirit** (women's fashions), plus **Lunds** grocery store, **Clancy's** drugstore (check out their basement gift and toy departments), **Pearson's** family restaurant, **Edina Five-O Florist**, **Kids' Hair** (with another location in Eden Prairie) and **Wuollet Bakery**.

Other standouts include **Chico's** women's clothing, **R.F. Moeller, Jeweler**, **Periwinkles** and **RSVP** for unusual gifts, the **Southwest Connection**, featuring fine Southwestern-themed gifts and bric-a-brac, and **Stay Tooned**, an animated gallery. **B. Dalton** bookstore, right on the corner, offers all the latest titles. Free parking for the area is available in the ramp behind the Edina Theater.

Did you shop 'til you dropped? Grab a little R&R at **Tejas**, an award-winning casual, Southwestern-flavored restaurant at 3910 W. 50th St.

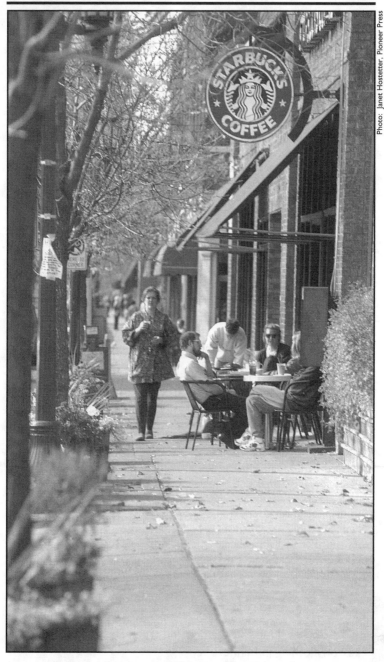

Photo: Janet Hostetter, Pioneer Press

Shoppers take a respite on Grand Avenue at Victoria Crossing.

Just a few blocks north, at 44th and France, check out the heavenly **Presents of Angels** gift shop and the **Chameleon** clothing shop, which sells its own brand of locally made colorful, casual women's knits and jewelry.

Southdale, 925-7885, at 66th Street and France Avenue S. in Edina, was the country's first enclosed shopping mall, built in 1958. Its original 800,000 square feet has grown into 1.6 million square feet, thanks to recent remodeling. The mall has more than 150 retail stores, including **Dayton's** and **JCPenney**. Other popular shops include **Ann Taylor, Banana Republic, Casual Corner** and **The Limited Express**. Go ahead and indulge! Stock up on fine soaps at **Crabtree & Evelyn**, a skimpy teddy at **Frederick's** or a lovely piece of wildlife art at the **Wooden Bird**.

Just south of Southdale, at 69th and France, is **The Galleria**, 925-9534, an upscale collection of 75 boutiques and shops, anchored by the large **Gabberts Furniture and Design Studio**, one of the premier furniture stores in the area. The Galleria also houses more than 25 designer fashion stores plus gift shops and galleries galore, offering one-of-a-kind wares. **The Good Earth, Ciatti's Italian Restaurant** and **Sidney's Pizza Cafe** here are popular eateries among locals. Hours of great shopping await at such venues as **Bellini** (kids' furniture), **C.G. Rein Galleries** (art), **Pottery Barn** (ceramic art), **Sticks & Stones** (home furnishings) and such tony clothing shops as **Timbuktu,**

Epitome, Polly Berg, Laura Ashley, Jonci Petites, Cedrics, Len Druskin, Liemandt's, Mondi and **Pendleton**, to mention a few. You'll also discover a large **Barnes & Noble** bookstore, **Strouds** (linens), **Williams-Sonoma** (upscale housewares), a large **Schmitt Music** store, **Games by James** and **T.R. Christian** (crystal and unique gifts).

Southtown, 375-1077, an older shopping center at I-494 and Penn Avenue S. in Bloomington, has undergone extensive renovation in the past year. Here you'll find such standards as **Montgomery Ward, Linens 'N' Things, Toys R Us, B. Dalton** bookstore, **TJ Maxx** and **Brauns**, as well as unconventional stores, such as **Audiobook Express** and the **Alleluia Shop**. A recent addition is a new **Media Play** store, selling books, videos and CDs.

Burnsville Center, 435-8182, in the suburb of the same name, is a large, modern shopping mall housing 160 retailers including **Dayton's, JCPenney, Sears, Mervyn's, Kohl's, The Limited, The Gap** and **B. Dalton** bookstore.

Northern Suburbs

Brookdale, 566-6672, Minn. Highway 100 and Brooklyn Boulevard in Brooklyn Center, features four anchor stores, **Dayton's, Mervyn's, Sears** and **JCPenney**, in addition to 70-plus specialty and clothing stores, including **Lane Bryant, The Limited, Brauns** and **Casual Corner** for

Insiders' Tips

It's a clothes hound's dream-come-true: There's no sales tax on clothing in Minnesota!

women's apparel, **Northern Getaway** for North Woods kids' clothes and **Minnesota Moments** for local souvenirs. For the gourmet, there's the pungent and inviting **Gloria Jean's Coffee Bean** shop selling great grinds and a captivating assortment of teapots and mugs. Strollers and wheelchairs are available at the mall's Customer Service Counter.

Farther north in Blaine is **Northtown Mall**, 786-9704, University Avenue and Minn. Highway 10, a large complex catering to the down-to-earth, practical shopper with such moderately priced stores as **Kohl's, Montgomery Ward, Best Buys** and **Mervyn's**. The place is usually packed with young families and teens leisurely browsing or madly power-shopping the 105 stores. The selection includes: **Petite Sophisticates, Casual Corner, The Limited, The Limited Express** and **Structure** clothing stores; **The Gallery**, for Lladro, Hummel and Waterford giftware; **Easy Spirit** shoe store; and others.

If you're looking for high-quality, environmentally-sensitive beauty products, scents and musical tapes, head on north to the **Aveda Headquarters**, 783-4000, 4000 Pheasant Ridge Drive N.E., Blaine. This is the headquarters of the beauty empire created by Horst Rechelbacher, whose products are based on "the art and science of pure flower and plant essences." The complex has a large on-site store selling an extensive range of Aveda products and other nature-themed beauty gifts. To reach Aveda from the Twin Cities, take I-35W north to Lexington Avenue (Exit No. 35) in Blaine; take a left at Lexington and another left at the first stoplight.

Rosedale, 633-0872, Minn. Highway 36 and Snelling Avenue in Roseville, is one of the classiest of the suburban malls. On our recent visit, we were serenaded by a harpist in **JCPenney's** fine jewelry and a tuxedo-clad pianist in **Dayton's** cosmetics. All that was missing were the ballroom dancers!

Flowers, foliage and benches galore enhance this clean, attractive, modern complex that boasts 160 stores. In addition to the usual fare — **Montgomery Ward, Dayton's, Mervyn's, JCPenney, Eddie Bauer, The Gap** — Rosedale is home to **American Eagle Outfitters** (men's and women's casual), **Northern Reflections** (casual women's with a North Woods theme), **The Museum Company** and **Natural Wonders** (both offering tasteful, high-quality gifts and collectibles), **The Bombay Company** (traditional home furnishings in dark woods and brass), **Franklin Quest** (specializing in calendars and daily planners) and **Air Traffic** (windsocks and kites). Restaurants include the **Green Mill**, a popular local chain that touts the best pizza in town, and **Ruby Tuesday** for everything from chops to fajitas in a fun atmosphere.

Har-Mar Mall, also at the Highway 36 and Snelling intersection, is home to **Barnes & Noble, TJ Maxx, Michael's** arts and crafts and a **Homeplace** home-furnishings store.

Farther east, at the busy intersection of White Bear Avenue and I-694, lies another shopping mecca, **Maplewood Mall**, 770-5020, with approximately 100 stores. In addition to **Mervyn's of California** (opening spring '96), **Sears** and **Kohl's**, this pleasant suburban complex boasts such familiar names as the **Body Shop, Frederick's of Hollywood, Victoria's Secret, Brauns** and **Gigi's, Goodman's Jewelers** and **Footlocker**, as well as one-of-a-kind shops such as **Evening Moon**, a gallery of original art and home furnishings. Maplewood Mall also has an

Applebee's restaurant; a multi-screen movie theater is right next door.

If you venture north a bit — and you really should — you'll find yourself in White Bear Lake. Veer off the busy Minn. Highway 96 and Highway 61 into the old downtown near the intersection of Washington and Fourth streets to discover a charming commercial area of tree-shaded streets, old-fashioned storefronts and even a barbershop or two. Each store is distinctive. Here's a sampling: **Heritage II** (Scandinavian and British Isles wares), **White Bear Lake Pottery**, **Sassafras Whole Foods Market**, **White Bear Lake Children's Shop**, **Country Goose** (handmade gifts), **Conrad's** women's boutique, the **Cupping Room** for a sip of espresso and finally **White Bear Variety**, where you can still buy penny candy. During the summer, the town offers street entertainment on Thursday nights and a farmers market every Friday.

Eastern Suburbs

South and east of St. Paul in the rolling green hills of suburban Woodbury, you'll find plentiful shopping at **Woodbury Village**, just east of I-494 on Valley Creek Plaza Road. In addition to the ubiquitous **Barnes & Noble** bookstore, this large shopping complex contains **Creative Kidstuff** (part of a chain selling high-quality arts, crafts, books and toys for children); **Casual Corner** and **Sonnie's** (women's apparel), **Kohl's**, **Target**, **Famous Footwear** (shoes), **Linens 'N' Things** (home furnishings), **Men's Wearhouse** (menswear), **Burger Brothers** (outdoor wear and gear), **Best Buy** (electronics) and **Rainbow** grocery store.

Directly east of downtown St. Paul on I-94, the **Sun Ray Shopping Center** offers an array of retail establishments, including **JCPenney**, **TJ Maxx**, **Dana's** (women's fashions), **Minnesota Fabrics**, **Michael's** (crafts and clothing) and **Kowalski's** grocery store, among others.

Just 20 minutes northeast of St. Paul, the little city of Stillwater offers tons of antiques shops, a phenomenal number of bookstores (antiquarian and contemporary), gift shops and art galleries in a picturesque setting along the St. Croix River.

The tiny New England-flavored town of Afton, just 20 minutes southeast of St. Paul, is set like a jewel between rolling, forested hills and the shimmering St. Croix River. It's a favorite destination for summertime boaters, wintertime skiers, casual shoppers and Sunday drivers who seek to escape urban madness for a few brief hours. Here you'll find such one-of-a-kind shops as **The Afton Toy Shop** (quality, old-fashioned toys and dolls), **Cream of the Crop** (unique home accessories, including miniature tea sets, handmade jewelry, baskets, pottery), **Squire House Gardens** (gardening gifts and home accessories), **The Little Red House** (kitchenware, gourmet foods, candles, jewelry), **The Afton Merchant** (baskets, exclusive gifts) and **Baglio's of Afton** (a choice collection of smart and comfy designer fashions and accessories).

Dawdle and enjoy the rivertown ambiance at **The Historic Afton House Inn** (circa 1867), where you can eat indoors in the historic dining room, the adjacent **Catfish Saloon**, outdoors on the veranda or on the water in one of the Afton House's dinner-excursion boats.

Top off your meal with a scrumptious double-dip cone at **Selma's Ice Cream Parlour** and tree farm (don't ask!).

Outlet and Bargain Shopping

Horizon Outlet Center, 728-5170, located off I-94 and County Road 19 (Exit 251), in the St. Paul suburb of Woodbury, offers more than 40 outlet stores, from **American Eagle**, **Eddie Bauer**, **Van Heusen** and **Geoffrey Beene** to **Leslie Fay**, **Corning/Revere** cookware and **Spiegel** and everything in between.

Tanger Factory Outlet in North Branch, 40 miles north of the Twin Cities, features brand names such as **Liz Claiborne**, **Woolrich**, **Nine West**, **Van Heusen**, **Capezio**, **Kitchen Collection** and **Carter's Childrenswear**. To reach Tanger, take Exit 147 off I-35 and follow the signs. For more information, call (612) 674-5885 or (800) 727-6885.

About 50 miles south of the Twin Cities, but well worth the trip, is the **Medford Outlet Center** in Medford. This center offers 30 shops, from **Bass Shoe**, **Liz Claiborne**, **The North Face** (sportswear and outdoor equipment) and **Adolfo II** to **Jordache**, **Guess?**, **Nike** and **Mikasa** china. To reach the Medford Outlet Center, take I-35 south to Exit 48 and follow the signs.

On a smaller scale, you can find high-quality department-store merchandise at discounted prices at such Twin Cities stores as **TJ Maxx** and **Marshalls**, each with several locations in the Twin Cities.

Last but not least, there's a store for people who spurn copycat fashion. It's **Ragstock**, a funky shop selling second-hand — or shall we say "vintage" — clothing. Ragstock stores can be found in Uptown, Dinkytown (near the University of Minnesota East Bank campus) and in St. Paul at 1515 University Avenue W.

Knott's Camp Snoopy inside the Mall of America.

Photo: Associated Press

Inside
Kidstuff

The Twin Cities abound in delightful adventures for the young and the young at heart. In true Midwestern spirit, Minnesotans genuinely adore children and the pleasures of family life. Indeed, much of that ballyhooed Minnesota quality of life centers on the easy availability of wholesome recreational and cultural offerings for all ages.

First and foremost, Minneapolis and St. Paul's many lakes and parks serve as Mother Nature's own playground for the younger set. In Minneapolis, Thomas Beach on the south shore of Lake Calhoun and the beaches at Lake Harriet, Cedar Lake and Lake Nokomis are ideal spots to laze away a summer day. Cap off your summer evening with a free concert at the Lake Harriet Pavilion, where dancing in the aisles is encouraged — and sometimes even applauded!

When the weather turns frosty, families lace up the skates and cut figure 8s on those same crystalline waterways. Minneapolis' Minnehaha Park, with its roaring Minnehaha Falls and rolling lawns, is another fun-filled year-round destination for families. In St. Paul, Lake Phalen sports a sandy beach and jogging/walking paths aplenty. Another popular destination, Lake Como, has paddleboats, picnic areas, a restored concert pavilion, not to mention a Japanese garden, conservatory, zoo and amusement park — all just 3 miles north of downtown St. Paul.

In St. Paul itself, Rice and Mears parks are quiet, green refuges from bustling urban life. In winter, Rice Park becomes a frozen fairyland with a jewel-box skating rink, bordered by thousands of twinkling lights and ice sculptures.

The Twin Cities suburbs also offer countless parks, fanciful outdoor playgrounds and beaches. For further details, consult the chapters entitled In, On and Around the Water and Recreation and Parks.

Minneapolis and St. Paul also have many man-made attractions for children, from unstuffy museums to tummy-churning amusement parks, as well as a nationally acclaimed Children's Theatre Company and other cultural offerings (see The Arts chapter). The following are capsules of the best and brightest childhood delights.

By the way, while you're driving to these fun spots, entertain the kids by turning your radio dial to Radio Aahs (1280 AM), the Twin Cities' own children's radio station (now nationally syndicated). Its lively tunes and soothing stories are sure to transform the most restless critters into happy campers. (The radio station, housed at 5501 Excelsior Boulevard, St. Louis Park, also offers tours every Tuesday, Thursday and Saturday. Call ahead for a reservation at 926-1280.) •

Major Kids' Attractions

MINNESOTA CHILDREN'S MUSEUM
10 W. Seventh St., St. Paul   225-6000

In this hands-on, giant playhouse, children learn about themselves and the world around them through interactive play and exploration. Formerly housed in an old railroad building, the popular Minnesota Children's Museum moved into a new 65,000-square-foot facility in downtown St. Paul in September 1995. Here, four permanent galleries and two changing exhibit spaces engage and enthrall youngsters. The World Works gallery celebrates invention and encourages children to take up the tools of scientist, tinkerer or artist. A popular attraction here is the construction crane, where eager youngsters climb into the driver's seat and pull levers and push buttons to move magnetized building blocks from one area to another. In the One World exhibit area, children learn about their own and other cultures by visiting an international marketplace, "eating" in a Korean restaurant and casting a vote in a national election. The Earth World display invites wee ones to crawl into a muskrat lodge for an underwater view of nature, tunnel through a giant ant hill or create a thunderstorm or rays of sunshine in a unique weather station.

There's also an adventure maze of tunnels and secret passages that no kid can resist. Even infants and tots (ages 6 months to 4 years) have their own tunnel-like play space called Habitot.

The facility, ranked among the top-10 children's museums in the country, also hosts ever-changing exhibitions on various scientific and cultural subjects throughout the year.

Hours are 9 AM to 5 PM daily Memorial Day through Labor Day and 9 AM to 5 PM Tuesday through Sunday the remainder of the year. Admission is $5.95 for ages 3 to 60 and $3.95 for toddlers and seniors. Parking is available ($1 for three hours) at the Seventh Street Ramp, diagonally across Seventh Street from the museum.

SCIENCE MUSEUM OF MINNESOTA AND THE WILLIAM L. McKNIGHT -3M OMNITHEATER
30 E. 10th St., St. Paul   221-9488

Iggy, a whimsical 40-foot metal iguana sculpture, greets visitors at the entrance to this science showcase. The kid-tested scaly critter symbolizes the museum's fun-filled, please-touch approach to the sciences.

The museum features permanent exhibits in biology, paleontology, technology and geography. In the East Building, visitors learn about the geology and natural history of the North Star State in a colorful "Our Minnesota" permanent exhibit. There's also a Hall of Paleontology featuring huge re-creations of dinosaurs and a lab where fossils are cleaned and categorized.

The West Building boasts three floors of neat stuff, all connected by a musical stairway — as they say, getting there is half the fun! The first floor features traveling exhibits and an auditorium for experiments and lectures. On the second floor is the Hall of Anthropology, where the most popular exhibit is a mummy in a rather alarming state of undress. Also showcased here are intricate Native American and Southeast Asian weavings (plus a loom where kids try their hand at weaving), Egyptian hieroglyphics, a model of a Southeast Asian farm home and much more.

Undoubtedly, the most popular exhibits for children are found on the third

"Alice in Wonderland" performed by The Children's Theatre Company in Minneapolis.

floor, which houses the Experiment Gallery, a collection of participatory, hands-on experiments in weather, electronics, robotics, energy, chemistry and physics. Kids can pedal a stationary bicycle to power a light bulb, radio and fan. They can try their hands at lifting a compressed auto using air pressure or witness the formation of a tornado in a wind tunnel. Adults find themselves elbowing out the youngsters for a turn at these fun and fascinating science lessons.

Nature in all its glory comes alive on the "aahh-some" 76-foot-diameter dome screen of the Omnitheater, in the Science Museum. The Omni nature films feature spectacular you-are-there footage, accompanied by stereo sound. The Omni is so popular that reservations are strongly recommended. Showtimes are Monday through Friday at 1, 3, 7 and 8 PM (also 9 PM Friday only); Saturday and Sunday, 11 AM, noon, 1, 2, 3, 4, 7 and 8 PM (plus 10 AM and 9 PM Saturday only).

The Science Museum is open Monday through Friday from 9:30 AM to 9 PM; Saturday 9 AM to 9 PM; and Sunday 10 AM to 9 PM. Admission is $5 for exhibits only; $6 for Omnitheater only; $7 for both exhibits and Omni. For children 12 and younger, admission is $1 less in all categories. Gift shops and food concessions are located on premises.

JAMES FORD BELL
MUSEUM OF NATURAL HISTORY
17th Ave. and University Ave. S.E.
(On the University of Minnesota
East Bank campus)
Minneapolis   624-7083

While this museum houses an impressive collection of more than 100 works of wildlife art, visiting kids make a beeline to the Touch and See Room, where everything is displayed at child height and the motto is "please DO touch." There are animal skins, skeletons and bones and even live snakes. In addition to this fun exhibit, children will enjoy the museum's lifelike displays of animals in their natural habitat.

Hours are 9 AM to 5 PM Tuesday through Friday, 10 AM to 5 PM Saturday

Photo: Pioneer Press

and noon to 5 PM Sunday. The Touch and See room closes at 2 PM Tuesday through Friday. Admission is $3 for adults, $2 for youths (3 to 16) and seniors, and free for children younger than 3. Admission is free on Thursday.

MINNEAPOLIS PLANETARIUM

300 Nicollet Mall, Minneapolis   372-6644

Built within the Minneapolis Public Library in 1961, the Minneapolis Planetarium offers dazzling simulated tours of the night sky under a domed 40-foot ceiling. The astronomy shows are multimedia presentations with laser lights, soundtracks and stunning visual effects. Shows change frequently to highlight seasonal sky changes and various astronomical themes. Call for a schedule of shows. Admission is $3.50 for adults and $2 for children 12 and younger.

MINNEAPOLIS SCULPTURE GARDEN

Vineland Place, Minneapolis   375-7622

This 11-acre urban garden, across the street from the renowned Walker Art Center, is dappled with more than 40 sculptures — ranging from "Spoonbridge and Cherry," a gigantic spoon and cherry creation by Claes Oldenburg and Coosje van Bruggen, to a fanciful leaping acrylic fish by Frank Gehry (see our chapter, The Arts).

Kids love skipping over the expansive rolling greenery while their parents ponder the weighty meaning of these provocative pieces. The Cowles Conservatory, which houses the Gehry fish and indoor tropical plants, is a special treat. Hours are 6 AM to midnight daily; Conservatory hours are 10 AM to 8 PM Tuesday through Saturday; 10 AM to 5 PM Sunday; closed Monday. Admission is free.

While you're here, check out the internationally acclaimed Walker Art Center and Guthrie Theater, both of which are described in detail in The Arts chapter. (Hungry? The Walker's Gallery 8 Restaurant offers cafeteria-style lunch Tuesday through Sunday.)

GIBBS FARM MUSEUM

2097 W. Larpenteur Ave.
Falcon Heights   646-8629

The 7-acre garden farm, an actual pioneer's homesite for more than 100 years, now is a living history museum with costumed guides re-enacting turn-of-the-century daily life. Visitors may wander through the antique-filled farmhouse, the barns cluttered with oldtime farm implements, a furnished one-room schoolhouse and farm fields grazed by amiable livestock.

The museum is open April 30 through October 31. Hours are 10 AM to 4 PM Tuesday through Friday, noon to 4 PM Saturday, Sunday and holiday Mondays. Admission is $2.50 for adults, $2 for senior citizens and $1 for children. Gibbs Farm is on the corner of Cleveland and Larpenteur avenues in Falcon Heights, just northwest of St. Paul city limits.

And If You Have The Time — Small Treasures

Sometimes the best gifts come in the smallest packages. The following are a few less-publicized, off-the-beaten track destinations that are nonetheless worth a visit.

NATIONAL FIREFIGHTERS MEMORIAL MUSEUM

Broadway and Central Ave. N.E.
Minneapolis   623-3817

This is the place for every kid who's ever dreamed of climbing aboard a gleaming red fire truck and blowing the sirens. Children are encouraged to live out the fantasy in this engaging museum that also spotlights many other historic and modern pieces of firefighting equipment. Hours are 9 AM to 3 PM Saturday and 6 to 9 PM Thursday. Admission is $4 for adults and $2 for children.

TRAINS AT BANDANA SQUARE

Bandana Square in Energy Park
1021 Bandana Blvd. E. , St. Paul   647-9628

Even in the jet age, trains continue to fascinate children. This small railroad "museum," with its extensive operating model railroad — one of the largest in the country — brings alive the romance and adventure of riding the rails.

Great care was taken in creating these exact reproductions of locomotives, passenger and freight cars, even down to the replica mini-spikes in the railroad ties. The model trains are on the O-gauge scale of ¼-inch-to-the-foot. Several pieces of artwork depicting the mighty ironhorses also line the walls. Appropriately, the exhibit, run by the Twin City Model Railroad Club, is located at Bandana Square, a renovated complex of turn-of-the-century Northern Pacific railway shop buildings, where passenger cars were once constructed. Today, the cavernous buildings house retail shops, restaurants and offices, so plan in a little time for browsing. There's plenty to see.

Hours are Monday through Friday, 10 AM to 8 PM; Saturday, 10 AM to 6 PM; and Sunday, noon to 5 PM. Admission to the train exhibit is on a donation-only basis. Free parking is plentiful in the shopping center lot.

DOME SOUVENIRS PLUS AND THE ORIGINAL BASEBALL HALL OF FAME OF MINNESOTA

910 Third St. , Minneapolis   375-9707

Former Minnesota Twins equipment manager Ray Crump has compiled a baseball-lover's dream-come-true collection of memorabilia in a hole-in-the-wall setting. In a couple of the meandering rooms in a tattered old building, there are 10,000 autographed baseballs and World Series bats, plus informative exhibits on how bats, baseballs and gloves are made. This little gem is in the shadow of the Hubert H. Humphrey Metrodome, home of the Minnesota Twins.

Hours are 9 AM to 5 PM Monday through Friday, 11 AM to 3 PM Saturday and before and after all Metrodome events. Admission is free.

COMO-HARRIET STREETCAR LINE

Linden Hills Depot (at Lake Harriet)
Queen Ave. S. at W. 42nd St.
Minneapolis   291-7588

Treat the children to a ride on a genuine antique streetcar, that colorful, clangy and very efficient precursor to the Twin Cities' current mass-transit bus system. Until their demise in the 1950s, the bright yellow streetcars crisscrossed the entire Twin Cities. At one time, more than 1,000 streetcars ran on 523 miles of track stretching from Stillwater to Excelsior. Today, the streetcar only traverses the rolling parkland between lakes Harriet and Calhoun in a 2-mile round-trip jog. Passengers may board at Linden Hills De-

---

Make a kid smile when you buy a cup of raw fish for a quarter at Como Zoo and feed the barking sea lions.

Insiders' Tips

• 131

pot on the northwest shore of Lake Harriet or at the Lake Calhoun Platform on E. Lake Calhoun Parkway, south of W. 36th Street. Short but sweet, the ride is a refreshing change of pace.

From Memorial Day weekend through Labor Day, the streetcar runs from 6:30 PM to dusk Monday through Friday, from 1 PM 'til dusk Saturday and from 12:30 PM to dusk Sundays. In September (after Labor Day), it operates only on weekends during the hours listed above. Hours are shortened in October to 1 to 5 PM Saturday and 12:30 to 5 PM Sunday. The streetcar closes after October. Fare is 75¢; ages 4 and younger ride free.

BEAR-HAWK
INDIAN STORE & MUSEUM

1207 E. Franklin Ave. Minneapolis   872-9166

A giant stuffed polar bear, more than 30 mannequins displaying authentic American Indian clothing and even a jackaloupe await visitors to this interesting facility. On Franklin Avenue in the heart of Minneapolis' American Indian community, this little jewel of a store/ museum also sells beads, beadwork equipment and attractive Indian pottery, as well as beaded earrings and silver jewelry. The in-store museum charges an admission of $2 for adults and $1 for children.

HENNEPIN HISTORY MUSEUM

2303 Third Ave. S., Minneapolis   870-1329

In 1995 this modest museum opened the small but engaging "City Kids" exhibit in the upstairs Roseblatt Gallery, offering visitors an enchanting look at what it was like to be a child in the Twin Cities nearly 100 years ago. A bright, splashy mural painted by local schoolchildren decorates the walls of this tiny, fun-filled

space. The hands-on display allows children to touch such oldtime tools as a laundry wringer and coffee grinder, sit in an antique school desk and attempt to answer 19th-century word problems — not as easy as it would seem. Cabinet drawers open to reveal collections of marbles and "antique" Barbie clothes. Peek around the corner and discover a kid-size carpeted hiding spot with pillows and games and plenty of books. The museum, kitty-corner from the renowned Minneapolis Institute of Arts, also harbors other exhibit areas highlighting Hennepin County history, American Indian artifacts and traditional crafts. It is open from noon to 5 PM Tuesday through Sunday. Admission is free.

WILD RUMPUS
CHILDREN'S BOOKSTORE

2720 W. 43rd St., Minneapolis   920-5005

In most cases, children and shopping don't mix. But Wild Rumpus is a delightful exception to the rule. This magical store is a child's pet-filled playhouse. Kids can peer through a plexiglass floorboard to view the shop's pet rat, enjoy the pleasant "coo" of the resident mourning dove and pet two very spoiled house cats. Oh, yes, and there are the books, all enchanting and within easy reach of little fingers. Store hours are 10 AM to 8 PM Monday through Friday; 10 AM to 5 PM Saturday; and noon to 5 PM Sunday.

INDIAN GOD OF PEACE

St. Paul City Hall, Fourth and
Wabasha Sts., St. Paul

This enormous 36-foot-tall statue sculpted of white onyx towers over the city hall lobby, striking awe in the hearts of little viewers. From an adult's vantage point, the statue is impressive; from a tyke's perspective, it's magnificent! The statue was carved by artist Carl Milles. The St. Paul City Hall is open from 8 AM to 4:30 PM Monday through Friday.

Zoos and Aquariums

MINNESOTA ZOO
13000 Zoo Blvd., Apple Valley   432-9000

This 500-acre zoological garden, in the southern suburb of Apple Valley, is home to more than 2,700 mammals, birds, fish, reptiles and amphibians living in natural-habitat settings. A series of winding trails brings visitors nose-to-snout with the Earth's creatures.

The Ocean Trail offers dolphin performances and underwater views of sea creatures from around the world. The Tropics Trail takes visitors through an indoor oasis of lush greenery, exotic birds and gibbons. A new coral reef exhibit showcases sharks and brilliantly colored tropical fish.

The Minnesota Trail spotlights regional wildlife such as puma, beavers and otters in indoor and outdoor habitats. The Northern Trail offers glimpses of timber wolves, moose, Asian wild horses and camels. And, finally, the Discovery Trail features a Children's Zoo and a "please touch" Zoolab tank of interesting critters.

If the trails prove too daunting, hop aboard the Skytrail monorail ($2) for a treetop look at the animals. A new amphitheater features the World of Birds show, plus evening concerts by well-known musical groups. And don't leave without dropping in on the new, very exotic Komodo Dragon. In the winter, Nordic skiing trails crisscross the zoo grounds.

The zoo offers extensive educational outreach programs for people of all ages. Summer zoo hours are 9 AM to 6 PM Monday through Saturday and 9 AM to 8 PM Sunday. Winter hours are 9 AM to 4 PM daily. Admission is $8 for adults; $4 for children 12 and younger; $5 for seniors 65 and older; and free for kids 2 and younger. The Skytrail fee is $2 (ages 2 and younger, free).

COMO PARK ZOO, CONSERVATORY AND AMUSEMENT PARK
Midway Pkwy. and Kaufman Dr.
St. Paul   488-5571

Como Zoo is an enduring old favorite for Twin Cities children and their parents, many of whom spent their own childhood days at Como feeding the seals, grunting at the gorillas and soaring on amusement park rides.

The zoo's collection of 400 animals is impressive, ranging from snow leopards and Siberian tigers to Alaskan timber wolves, gorillas and polar bears. Don't miss the popular daily performances by Sparky the sea lion. Shows are presented at 11 AM and 2 and 4 PM daily May 15 through August (except Monday), with an extra 5 PM show on weekends. Shows are at 2 and 4 PM weekends only in September.

The Como Park Conservatory, on zoo grounds, features seasonal blooming plants and tropical and semitropical vegetation year round. And a formal Japanese tea garden is open on a limited basis from May through August. The zoo has an adjoining amusement park and picnic area.

Como Zoo is, by no means, as expansive or modern as the Minnesota Zoo in suburban Apple Valley, but even so, it has definite advantages: It's more centrally located than the Minnesota Zoo and, best of all, it's free. You'll pay fees for the amusement park rides, however, and the Conservatory charges 50¢ for adults and 25¢ for children ages 11 to 16 (kids 10 and younger get in free).

Also on the expansive Como Park grounds are an 18-hole golf course, swimming pool and lake-side walking and biking trails. Zoo hours, from April through September, are 8 AM to 8 PM (buildings are open from 10 AM to 6 PM). In winter, the zoo is open from 8 AM to 5 PM (buildings from 10 AM to 4 PM). Parking is free.

UNDERWATER WORLD

Mall of America, I-494 and Minn. Hwy. 77
Bloomington 883-8846

Slated to open in early 1996, Underwater World is a 1.2 million-gallon walk-through aquarium at Mall of America in suburban Bloomington. This two-level, 70,000-square-foot attraction will differ from conventional aquariums by simulating a deep-sea dive. Visitors will be "submerged" through a 7-foot acrylic tunnel that brings them within inches of fish, reptiles, stingrays, sharks and other creatures of the deep blue. The waters will contain almost 5,000 fish, reptiles, amphibians and invertebrates representing approximately 60 species of plant and animal life.

Amusement Parks

VALLEYFAIR FAMILY AMUSEMENT PARK

I Valleyfair Dr., Shakopee 445-6500

Valleyfair, in the southwest suburb of Shakopee, is Minnesota's answer to Disneyland with more than 50 thrilling rides, a terrific water park, concert stages and an Imax giant-screen theater — all laid out on immaculately maintained, landscaped grounds. A single admission fee covers the cost of all rides.

The park is staffed by perky, wholesome teenagers, and the rides range from the pleasant Tilt-O-Whirl to the stomach-flipping Corkscrew and gravity-defying Excalibur roller coaster. Not for the fainthearted!

A new attraction at Valleyfair is Berenstain Bear Country, based on the popular children's book series. Children can tour the bears' family treehouse, visit Dr. Grizzley's office, dig for fossils in the dinosaur pit and view the Bears' daily show. Also included are an Actual Factual Museum and a variety of hands-on activities.

Admission to Valleyfair includes entry into the adjacent Whitewater Country Waterpark. Fun-lovers can choose among many slippery attractions, including the Raging Rapids inner-tube slide and — for the daring — the Speed Slide, a very vertical 50-foot fall. New this year is the Hydroblaster, which sends unsuspecting raft-riders twisting and turning down a fully enclosed (that means, totally dark!) chute. Live entertainment is featured nightly at the Amphitheater.

Valleyfair is open May through mid-September from 10 AM to late evening (closing hours vary). Admission is $19.95 for adults; children age 4 and up to 48 inches tall pay $4.95; children 3 and younger get in free; and adults 62 and older pay $11.95. A two-day pass is $25.95. Starlight admission after 5 PM is $11.95. Season passes are $56 per person. An adjacent campground is available for those who wish to extend their stay.

In addition to the amusement and water park, Valleyfair also operates Challenge Park, a go-cart track and miniature-golf course. There is no entry charge for Challenge Park, but a fee (generally in the $3 to $5 range) is charged for each ride or round of golf.

MALL OF AMERICA AND CAMP SNOOPY
South of I-494 and Minn. Hwy. 77 intersection
Bloomington   883-8600

America's largest enclosed shopping mall is described in detail in the Shopping chapter, but it's worth noting here that the huge facility offers activities beyond marathon shopping at more than 400 specialty stores. No. 1, of course, is Knott's Camp Snoopy, a seven-acre landscaped indoor amusement park with 24 rides and attractions, nine eating places and four entertainment stages. Attractions include the overhead Ripsaw roller coaster and a wet and wild ride called Paul Bunyan's Log Chute, which splashes down a 40-foot waterfall.

Three new rides were added in 1995: Skyscraper, a towering 63-foot Ferris wheel; Camp Bus, described as a "wacky and whirling adventure ride" for all ages; and the Li'l Shaver pint-sized roller coaster. The Mystery Mine Ride is a "fly by the seat of your pants" 3-D movie theater that places viewers in the middle of the action.

Camp Snoopy hours are 9:30 AM to 9:30 PM Saturday; 10 AM to 7:30 PM Sunday; and 10 AM to 9:30 PM Monday through Friday. There's no admission fee to the park, but each attraction has a point value. Visitors purchase point passes in varying amounts. To enter each ride, a visitor merely runs the point pass under a scanner, which reads a bar code, à la the modern grocery store.

Also of interest for kids is the free Lego Imagination Center, a shrine to those little interlocking plastic blocks. It houses more than 30 giant Lego creations and a Lego play area for kids.

Aspiring golfers can try out Golf Mountain, an 18-hole miniature golf challenge overlooking Camp Snoopy. For movie buffs, the Mall's General Cinema

Valleyfair amusement park in Shakopee.

Photo: Pioneer Press

has 14 screens showcasing the latest from Hollywood. At Starbase Omega, another mall attraction, kids and grownups can play laser tag with Star Trekky gear and costumes.

Water Parks — Indoor and Outdoor

EDINA AQUATIC CENTER
Valley View Rd. and W. 66th St.
Edina   927-9829

The water slide at this outdoor water park is rather tame, but the place has other fun attractions, including a kiddie pool with an underwater tire swing, spouting fountains and squirting hoses. Admission is $5 per person ($2 after 6 PM).

RICHFIELD POOL
630 E. 66th St., Richfield   861-9355

This centrally located pool has three thrilling water slides, two of which spill into the shallow end and the third into the deep end. Admission charge varies from $3 to $5 and includes use of the pool and slides.

WHITEWATER COUNTRY
Waterpark at Valleyfair

See details in the earlier section on "Amusement Parks."

EKO BACKEN
22570 Manning Tr., Scandia   433-2422

This outdoor park, situated in the midst of rolling farmland in the northern suburb of Scandia, has two huge (350-foot-high) slides for water-whooshing in the summer and plentiful hills with tows for snow-tubing in the winter. There's also a brand-new miniature golf course, picnic area, volleyball courts and concession stand.

Hours are 10 AM to 7 PM daily in summer (June 1 through Labor Day). Winter hours are 11 AM to 10:30 PM weekends and holidays and 6:30 to 10 PM Monday through Friday. Admission fee is $7.50 ($6.50 for those 12 and younger). Directions: From St. Paul, take I-35E north to Minn. Highway 97; go east on Highway 97 to Manning Trail (County Road 15). Go north on Manning Trail 1.5 miles to Eko Backen.

BEAVER MOUNTAIN WATER SLIDE
15100 Buckhill Rd., Burnsville   435-1700

This south suburban water park has six slides, ranging from "kiddie" to "black hole." It's open during daylight hours all summer. Admission is $12 for all day; other packages available.

BUNKER HILLS WAVE POOL
Foley Blvd. and Hwy. 242
Coon Rapids   767-2895

This is as close to California surf as you get in landlocked Minnesota. Patrons rent inner tubes and "surf" over machine-generated waves in this popular outdoor pool in the northwestern suburb of Coon Rapids. Admission is $4 for all day; $3 for kids younger than 12. Tube rental is $1 per hour.

WILD MOUNTAIN WATER SLIDE
37350 Wild Mountain Rd.
Taylors Falls   1-462-7550

This wintertime downhill ski area northeast of the Twin Cities transforms itself into a water park during the summer months, offering water slides, alpine slides, a go-cart track and canoe rentals. The park also operates riverboat cruises on the scenic St. Croix river. Summer hours are 10 AM to 8 PM seven days a week, beginning Memorial Day weekend. Fees: Superday pass (unlimited water and dry rides), $18.80 plus tax for ages 6 and older; unlimited water rides and three dry-ride tickets, $14.95 plus tax; unlimited water rides, $10.95 plus tax. For ages 3 to 5, the fee for unlimited water rides is $5.95 plus tax. The park also offers several riverboat cruises at varying fee levels.

SHOREVIEW COMMUNITY CENTER
4600 N. Victoria St., Shoreview   490-4700

This modern city-owned indoor recreation center in the northern suburb of Shoreview is a wet 'n' wild place for the whole family, with a huge water slide and swimming pools equipped with rope swings and fountains, a hot tub, two basketball courts, a weight room and running track. Hours are noon to 7:45 PM on weekends and noon to 9:45 PM on weekdays. Admission is $5.75 for adults and $3.75 for children (add $1 for the waterslide). Shoreview residents receive discounts.

CHASKA COMMUNITY CENTER
1661 Parkridge Dr., two blocks east of
Minn. Hwy. 41 and Anchor Blvd. intersection
Chaska   448-5633

This facility was modeled after the Shoreview Community Center and offers basically the same attractions in a clean, modern indoor setting in the southwest suburb of Chaska. Hours are 1 to 5

PM and 7 to 8:30 PM Monday through Thursday, and 1 to 5 PM and 6 to 9 PM Friday through Sunday. Admission is $3.75 for adults (17 and older) and $3.25 for children. Discounts are offered for residents of Chaska.

MAPLEWOOD COMMUNITY CENTER

2100 White Bear Ave., Maplewood   779-3555

This handsome, new indoor center offers the mandatory water slide, hot spa, water toys and zero-depth "beach," plus a health club for adults. Hours are 3:30 to 10 PM Monday through Friday and noon to 9 PM Sunday. Admission ranges from $2.25 to $4.

Indoor Play Centers

DISCOVERY ZONE

In the Minneapolis suburbs:
Springbrook Mall, 8601 Springbrook Dr.
Coon Rapids   785-8910
Yorktown Mall, 3441 Hazelton Rd.
Edina   893-9950
In the St. Paul suburbs:
Woodbury Village, 1505 Queens Dr.
Woodbury   735-4386

These playlands offer tunnels, ball pools, rope climbing and lots of physical fun. Hours are 10 AM to 8 PM Sunday through Thursday; 10 AM to 10 PM Friday and Saturday. Admission is $5.99 for ages 2 through 12 and $2.99 for ages 24 months and younger.

EDINBOROUGH PARK

7700 York Ave. S. , Edina   893-9890

This lushly landscaped indoor park features a skating rink, playgrounds, picnic area, swimming pool and an amphitheater with free entertainment, all enclosed in an attractive high-rise setting. Admission is free except for a pool charge of $3 per person. Call for the pool hours.

JUMPIN' JAX

Burnsville Center, I-35E and County Rd. 42
Burnsville   898-9798
Maplewood Mall, 3001 White Bear Ave.
Maplewood   770-9860

These new family fun centers try their darnedest to meet your entertainment needs with everything from virtual-reality video games and laser-tag systems to a Dynamaze fitness course and a family restaurant. The 12,000-square-foot facilities also house extensive play areas for children 4 and younger. Parents may join in the fun or take advantage of Jumpin' Jax' child-care services for up to three hours. Jumpin' Jax is open from 9 AM to 9 PM Monday through Thursday, from 9 AM to 10 PM Saturday and from 10 AM to 8 PM Sunday. Additional child-care hours are available. Admission is $3.99 for children 4 and older and $2.99 for those younger than 4.

NEW HORIZON KIDS QUEST

2228 Eden Prairie Center
Eden Prairie   941-1007

This is a top-of-the-line play center that offers such extras as free, nonviolent video games and an obstacle course with rope swings, karaoke room, computer art and a Barbie corner. This facility offers drop-off day care only, with no time restrictions. Hours are 9 AM to 10 PM Monday through Thursday; 9 AM to midnight Friday and Saturday; and 11 AM to 8 PM Sunday. The fee is $5 per hour.

Outdoor Playgrounds

The Twin Cities boast many state-of-the-art outdoor playgrounds where children can run and jump in the fresh air and sunshine. (Please note that French Regional Park and Baker, Hyland Lake, Elm Creek and Lake Rebecca park reserves are part of the Hennepin County park system, and therefore, charge a $4 daily parking fee.)

BAKER PARK RESERVE
3800 County Rd. 19, Maple Plain   476-4666

This park, part of the Hennepin County park system, has a wonderful playground filled with wooden climbing structures, slides and tire swings. It's adjacent to rolling picnic grounds on the shores of Lake Independence. County Road 19 is between U.S. Highway 12 and Minn. Highway 55.

FRENCH REGIONAL PARK
12605 County Rd. 9, Plymouth   559-8891

Also part of the Hennepin County system, this park's exceptional wooden playground is a kid's dream come true with tire swings, extensive jungle-gym ropes and cargo nets, plus winding slides and great hide 'n' seek areas.

CHUTES AND LADDERS
Hyland Lake Park Reserve
8737 E. Bush Lake Rd.
Bloomington   941-4362

The "chutes" are several 40- to 50-foot enclosed slides that offer thrills aplenty. Also available at this Hennepin County park is the usual complement of traditional playground equipment for all ages.

ELM CREEK PARK RESERVE
13080 Territorial Rd.
Maple Grove   424-5511

Located in yet another Hennepin County park, this playground offers popular pulley rides, extensive tunnels, slides and swings.

LAKE REBECCA PARK RESERVE
8600 Rebecca Park Tr., Rockford   972-3407

This lovely Hennepin park sports a fanciful playground with a climbing tower, swings and curving slides.

LONG LAKE REGIONAL PARK
New Brighton   777-1707

This Ramsey County park has a new playground with climbing areas, swings and slides. The park is off County Road 77 near the intersection of I-35W and I-694.

OTHER PLAYGROUNDS

Here are several fun spots worth visiting:

* Linden Hills Park, 34th Street and Xerxes Avenue S., Minneapolis
* Powderhorn Park, 33rd Street and 10th Avenue S., Minneapolis
* Harriet Bishop Playground, Harriet Island, St. Paul
* Central Park, Victoria Avenue between county roads B and C, Roseville
* Skyland Park, Cliff Road (.35 mile east of I-35W), Burnsville.

Inside
Recreation and Parks

The real joys of Twin Cities living are found in the area's many outdoor pleasures.

The greater metro region offers a dizzying array of outdoor pursuits. You can swim, canoe or drop a fishing line in a sparkling urban lake, hike the St. Croix riverbanks, listen to the call of a trumpeter swan in a peaceful park reserve, camp out under the stars or sprint the Mississippi River roads on a blazing autumn day.

Tree-shaded parks and shimmering lakes are the crowning glories of the Twin Cities, home of one of the most extensive park systems in the country.

Within the seven-county metropolitan area are four state parks, 19 wildlife management/refuge areas, 43 regional parks and approximately 1,000 municipally owned parks. This is truly the land of lakes: 31 large lakes in the Twin Cities proper and hundreds in the greater metro area. Let's not forget Old Man River, the Mighty Mississippi; the lesser-known Minnesota River; the nearby scenic St. Croix River; or lovely Minnehaha Creek, a ribbon of water that meanders willy-nilly through South Minneapolis to a crashing finale at the legendary Minnehaha Falls (see our In, On and Around the Water chapter).

In this chapter, we provide an overview of the parks and recreation scene in the Twin Cities and suburbs, including city, state and county parks, golf courses, swimming pools, health and fitness clubs and much more (see the Winter's Won-

Photo: Joe Rossi, Pioneer Press

Dog sledding in Como Park, St. Paul.

derland chapter for information on wintertime recreation).

Let's begin with a look at city parks.

City Parks

Minneapolis

Minneapolis has approximately 170 city parks and 18 lakes, not to mention 38 miles of designated walking trails and 36 miles of biking trails. For detailed information on specific parks, call 673-4817.

Here are a few of our local favorites.

MINNEHAHA PARK
Minnehaha Ave. and Godfrey Rd.

Steeped in history, legend and natural beauty, Minnehaha Park consists of 142 acres of rolling lawns and thick woods, crowned by the lovely Minnehaha Falls, a breathtaking 40-foot waterfall that cascades ·through a wooded glen. The cataract has inspired artists, poets, composers and photographers, not to mention sweethearts, their passions presumably stirred by the roaring waters.

Henry Wadsworth Longfellow was so taken by a picture of the falls that he used it as the setting for his narrative poem "Song of Hiawatha," even though he never actually visited the falls. The epic's lovers, Hiawatha and Minnehaha, are memorialized here in a statue by Jacob Fjelde that was purchased in 1893 with pennies collected by Minnesota schoolchildren.

Another historical note: While visiting the falls, an inspired Antonin Dvorak scribbled down the musical notes that eventually became his Opus 100, the "Indian Maiden."

The falls are created by Minnehaha Creek, a stream that begins in Lake Minnetonka, winds through southwestern suburbs and South Minneapolis and bisects the park before joining the Mississippi to the east. During dry spells, the creek water is augmented by water piped in from wells. The falls are in their fullest glory in late spring.

Many a Twin Citian recalls childhood jaunts to Minnehaha Park: climbing down the long stone stairway to the lower lookout bridge, leaping from boulder to boulder across the creekbed (more often than not, getting soaked in the process) and playing hide 'n' seek on the park's many wooded paths. For your convenience, the park pavilion has a souvenir shop, sheltered tables, restrooms and a canteen.

Minnehaha Park is also the site of the historic Stevens House, the first framed dwelling on the Mississippi's western banks in Minneapolis. Originally located near St. Anthony Falls, the house was moved to its present locale around the turn of the century. For Stevens House tour information, call 722-2220.

This venerable park is undergoing an extensive restoration to be completed in 1997.

A pleasant way to cap your visit to the falls is a drive along gorgeous, tree-lined Minnehaha Parkway, just west of Minnehaha Park. On a sunny day, you'll see an endless parade of bikers and walkers strolling and rolling past the elegant homes in this stable, old Minneapolis neighborhood.

LYNDALE PARK GARDENS AND ROBERTS BIRD SANCTUARY
Lake Harriet Pkwy. N.

Two precious parkland gems — the Lyndale Park Rose and Rock Garden and the Thomas Sadler Roberts Bird Sanctuary — adorn the north shore of lovely

Lake Harriet in Minneapolis. For more on the lake itself, see the In, On and Around the Water chapter.

The Lyndale Park Rose and Rock Garden is a beckoning expanse of greenery and lush color. It's also the second-oldest public rose garden in the United States. In their full summer glory, the gardens are a heady, sensual feast with the centerpiece roses flanked by a dazzling array of perennials. Horticulturists may be interested in seeing the All American rose test selections.

The Japanese-style rock garden is graced by a bridge containing peace stones found near the site of the atomic bomb explosion at Hiroshima and Nagasaki.

Heed the call of the wild in the bogs and woods of the nearby Thomas Sadler Roberts Bird Sanctuary, home to numerous common and rare species — a birder's delight.

Continue north on William Berry Parkway, if you wish, and converge with Lake Calhoun Boulevard for a scenic drive around Lake Calhoun and, north of that, Lake of the Isles (see our In, On and Around the Water chapter).

LORING PARK
Harmon Place and Willow St.

Just northeast of Lake of the Isles and in the shadow of downtown, this jewel of a park is our version of New York's Washington Square, attracting a mix of urban professionals and office-workers, young artistic types, ne'er-do-wells, hipsters and hoops-playing kids.

In addition to the basketball courts, the park has shuffleboard courts, horseshoe pits, tennis courts and a children's playground — all surrounding the seven-acre, man-made Loring Lake.

One of the Twin Cities' loveliest water fountains, the Berger Fountain, is found here at 14th and Willow streets. Rising like a large dandelion puff, the fountain spews water from 250 copper tubes in a spherelike configuration. It's a glistening sight on a sunny summer day.

Loring Park is hip and happening. On the northwest side of the park, at 1624 Harmon Place, is the Loring Cafe, a trendy salon filled with artists, sneering waiters and black-clad sax players. To the east is an interesting neighborhood of theaters, bars and ethnic restaurants adjoining downtown. And to the west is . . .

MINNEAPOLIS SCULPTURE GARDEN
Hennepin Ave. and Vineland Pl.

A whimsical pedestrian bridge designed by Siah Armajani is just one of the gateways to the Minneapolis Sculpture Garden, an 11-acre park filled with 40-plus works by renowned sculptors. The park is a collaborative project of the Minneapolis Park and Recreation Board and Walker Art Center, on the south edge of the park.

The landmark piece is the huge, delightful "Spoonbridge and Cherry" sculpture by Claes Oldenburg and Coosje van Bruggen. One can't help but smile at the sight of this monstrous spoon measuring 52 feet and topped by a 9½-foot cherry.

Other artists whose works are found in the garden include Henry Moore, George Segal and Jackie Ferrara. The grounds also feature the glassed-in Cowles Conservatory, housing the vibrant "Standing Glass Fish" plexiglass sculpture designed by Frank Gehry, as well as seasonal floral displays.

The sculpture garden is an attraction for all ages. Open year round, it makes a pleasant stop in conjunction with a visit to the nearby Guthrie Theater or Walker Art Center. The park is open from 6 AM to midnight. The conservatory is open 10

AM to 8 PM Tuesday through Saturday and 10 AM to 5 PM Sunday; it is closed Monday.

POWDERHORN PARK
14th Ave. S. and 35th St.

Smack-dab in the middle of a lively, culturally diverse urban neighborhood is this 65-acre patch of green known as Powderhorn Park, a historic magnet for family gatherings and the site of a colorful Mayday parade and summertime arts fair. At the park's center is Powderhorn Lake, deriving its name from its unique shape.

The park also boasts four fanciful children's playgrounds — one for each season — and, in the winter, the only speed-skating ice oval in Minneapolis.

THEODORE WIRTH PARK
Wirth Pkwy. and Glenwood Ave. N.   *521-9731*

This sprawling 957-acre wooded park, the largest in the Minneapolis parks system, offers something for everyone.

For gardeners and nature lovers, the spectacular 14-acre Eloise Butler Wildflower Garden and Bird Sanctuary features plant species and wildlife native to woodland, bog and prairie habitats. A world away from the urban madness, the Butler garden is open from 7:30 AM to dusk daily April 1 to October 31. Naturalists are at hand to offer tours and programs. Nearby is a large pavilion with picnic tables.

Also of interest to green-thumbers are the J.D. Rivers' 4-H Children's Garden and a daylily-perennial garden.

Theodore Wirth Park also contains extensive evergreen groves, a five-acre tamarack bog and several natural springs.

Wirth Lake attracts swimmers with its sandy beach and adjacent picnicking and play areas. The lake is also a popular fishing spot.

This is a year-round park. Its 18-hole golf course is transformed into a Nordic sports playground in winter, offering downhill and cross-country skiing, snowshoeing, skating, snow-tubing and sledding — not to mention hot cocoa in the Swiss chalet clubhouse. Call ahead for complete program information.

To get to Wirth Park, take I-394 W. from downtown Minneapolis to Wirth Parkway. From there, go north to the park.

St. Paul

St. Paul's parks are as varied and charming as the city itself: expansive Como Park with its gently rolling lawns; the sedate and Victorian Irvine Park; the urban and urbane Rice Park; and scenic Mounds Park with its mysterious Indian burial mounds and magnificent river views. More than 50 recreational sites cover 2,000 acres in the St. Paul park system, not to mention several lakes and 29 miles of Mississippi River shoreline. For more information on St. Paul parks, call 488-7291.

Here is a listing of St. Paul's most popular parks.

COMO PARK AND LAKE
1431 N. Lexington Pkwy.

Conservatory	489-1740
Zoo	488-5571
Golf course	488-9673

The 450-acre Como Park is a delightful family destination that features a free public zoo (with nearly 400 animals) and adjacent amusement park, a Victorian-style conservatory bursting with flowers and fountains, Japanese gardens, swimming pools, picnic areas, athletic fields, a lake for fishing, an 18-hole golf course and paddleboating, biking and jogging trails. The park's recently restored Lakeside Pavilion offers food and free evening concerts during the summer months. The pavilion is also the place to rent bicycles, paddleboats and canoes (see the Kidstuff chapter for more information on the zoo).

It's easy to see why this handsome park is an enduring favorite of Twin Citians young and old.

Como Park is about 2.5 miles north of I-94.

PHALEN PARK AND LAKE
Wheelock Pkwy. and Arcade St.

A popular St. Paul destination, this park is centered on Lake Phalen, with its sandy swimming beach, volleyball courts and 3 miles of shoreline jogging and biking paths. At the park activity center, you can rent paddleboats, canoes, rowboats, sailboards and sailboats.

You'll also find an 18-hole golf course (used as a downhill and cross-country ski area in the winter), tennis courts, an indoor recreation center, picnic pavilion and an amphitheater offering free summer concerts.

MOUNDS PARK
Mounds Blvd. and Burns Ave.

Mounds Park, laid out on the scenic Mississippi River bluffs east of downtown St. Paul, is the site of 2,000-year-old burial mounds of the Hopewell Indians, ancestors of the Dakota tribe.

This 77-acre park offers a not-to-be-missed panoramic view of downtown St. Paul, its bustling river barges, Holman airfield and surrounding areas.

IRVINE PARK
Walnut St. and Ryan Ave.

Escaping to Irvine Park is like stepping back in time to the Victorian era of elegance and grace. In an age of artificial noise and mayhem, Irvine gives us water dancing in a graceful old fountain, acorns crunching underfoot, mothers quietly chatting over strollers. Created in the mid-1800s in one of St. Paul's first neighborhoods, the park and surrounding area experienced years of neglect before being lovingly restored in the 1970s. Today, this urban jewel, just southwest of downtown St. Paul, is surrounded by many well-tended Victorian homes, including one that houses Forepaugh's, a popular restaurant. A block away is the Alexander Ramsey House, home of the first governor of Minnesota (see the Architecture and Historic Sites chapter).

RICE PARK
Washington and Fourth Sts.

New York may have Rockefeller Plaza, but St. Paul has charming little Rice Park, a peaceful urban escape complete with gurgling fountains, hot-dog vendors, flower gardens and plenty of stone benches for people-watching. This is where downtown workers go to loosen their collars, kick off their shoes and shake off their cares.

During the annual Winter Carnival, Rice Park is illuminated by thousands of sparkling lights, enchanting ice sculptures and a small ice rink.

Rice Park is surrounded by four St. Paul landmarks: the elegant St. Paul Hotel, the Ordway Music Theatre, Landmark Center and the historic St. Paul Public Library.

MEARS PARK
Wacouta and Sixth Sts.

Another spot of urban greenery, Mears Park in St. Paul's Lowertown district is across Sibley Street from Galtier Plaza. This recently renovated city park boasts a trickling stream, Norway pines, Japanese birch, maples and lindens, plus a perennial garden and abundant benches and paths. There's also a bandstand for concerts.

HIGHLAND PARK
Montreal Ave. and Edgcumbe Rd.

So ya think you got us Minnesotans pegged, huh? You think we're just a bunch of cribbage-playing Lutherans? Well, head on over to Highland Park for a dose of reality. That's where we indulge our secret passion for Frisbee golf — on a regulation 12-hole course, no less. Top it off with a dip in one of St. Paul's best swimming pools, followed by a heaping bowl of booya, if you're lucky enough to happen upon a Belgian picnic! (Editor's note: Booya, a tantalizing stew, is prime picnic fare in St. Paul.) The park's rolling acres also harbor a golf course and large pavilion.

HIDDEN FALLS/CROSBY PARK NATURE CENTER
2450 Crosby Farm Rd.   292-6548

This Mississippi River-hugging, meandering park has 8 miles of scenic paved hiking trails (popular among urban joggers), a marina, several picnic areas and a nature center, not to mention the namesake waterfalls. It stretches along Shepard Road and Mississippi River Boulevard, just across the river from Minneapolis' Minnehaha Park.

The Suburbs

Here are a few green treasures tucked away in the suburbs.

CAPONI PARK
1215 Diffley Rd., Eagan   454-4338

Art and nature come together in the 60-acre Caponi Park, where sculptures are conceived and built on site as an outgrowth of their natural surroundings. Tours are by appointment only.

NORMANDALE JAPANESE GARDEN
9400 France Ave. S., Bloomington   881-8137

This two-acre Japanese garden on the grounds of Normandale Community College is a tranquil retreat in the bustling suburb of Bloomington. The traditional Japanese garden features footpaths and carved bridges that span pools and provide vantage points for viewing this contemplative setting. There is no admission charge.

MINNESOTA VALLEY NATIONAL WILDLIFE REFUGE VISITOR CENTER
3815 E. 80th St., Bloomington   854-5900

Enjoy an exhilarating view of the Minnesota River Valley from the observation deck of this handsome nature center set in the midst of the Minnesota Valley National Wildlife Refuge (see In, On and Around the Water for more on the refuge). The facility houses numerous exhibits and a free slide show on four levels. The refuge, which follows the Minnesota River for 34 miles from Fort Snelling to Jordan, is a birdwatcher's paradise.

WESTWOOD HILLS ENVIRONMENTAL EDUCATION CENTER
8300 Franklin Ave. W.
St. Louis Park   924-2544

Tucked between the hilly neighborhoods of northern St. Louis Park and I-394 is this natural retreat filled with thick woods and a wetlands rich with waterfowl. Owned by the city of St. Louis Park, Westwood Hills sponsors many educational programs for children and families. Numerous paths wind through the woods and a boardwalk circles the wetlands. There is no admission charge.

WOOD LAKE NATURE CENTER
735 Lake Shore Dr., Richfield   861-9365

This Richfield nature area totals 150 acres, 70 acres of which is the Wood Lake wetlands, filled with wildlife galore. The park has 3 miles of walking paths and a floating boardwalk. The nature center offers a working weather station, a marsh exhibit and a diroama featuring Wood Lake animals and their habitats. The park is popular among local bird-watchers. There are no entry fees.

SPRINGBROOK NATURE CENTER
100 85th Ave. N.E., Fridley   784-3854

This 127-acre refuge of woods and wetlands also boasts a visitors center filled with natural-history displays, live snakes, fish and much more. There are 3 miles of hiking trails through prime bird-watching areas. The center is open to the public free of charge.

STARING LAKE OUTDOOR CENTER
13765 Staring Lake Pkwy.
Eden Prairie   949-8479

This nature park encompasses 159 acres dotted with lakes, ponds and woods, plus a genuine log cabin. There is no admission fee to this refuge.

THOMAS IRVINE DODGE NATURE CENTER
1795 Charlton St. W., St. Paul   455-4531

This private natural refuge consists of 300 acres of marshes, ponds, meadows, woodlands and restored prairie. There are also such educational facilities as a model farm, apiary, live animal displays, maple-syruping room, boardwalk, greenhouse and classrooms. Weekdays, the refuge is reserved for school groups and educational programs. Its trails are open to the general public for hiking from 10 AM to 4 PM Saturdays.

County Parks

Hennepin County

Encompassing Minneapolis and many of its western suburbs, Hennepin County offers more than 24,000 acres of park reserves and regional parks in a variety of woodland settings.

These well-maintained natural areas offer something for the whole family — from state-of-the-art playgrounds and cross-country ski trails to environmental programs led by park naturalists.

Hennepin Parks charge a daily parking fee of $4. Frequent users may be interested in the annual $20 pass, permitting unlimited use from the date of purchase. The Hennepin Parks' annual pass is reciprocal with Carver, Washington and Anoka counties, allowing free admission to their county parks. The first Tuesday of every month is a free-admittance day at Hennepin parks.

In this section, we describe several of the most popular Hennepin Parks and their offerings. Other Hennepin parks worth visiting are Carver Park Reserve in Victoria, Cleary Lake Regional Park and Murphy-Hanrehan Park in Prior Lake, Coon Rapids Dam Park, Crow-Hassan Park Reserve in Hassan Township, Elm Creek Park Reserve in Osseo, Fish Lake Regional Park in Maple Grove and Lake Rebecca Park Reserve near Rockford.

For complete information on all Hennepin parks, call 559-9000.

BAKER PARK RESERVE
County Rd. 19, Medina

This park, just 20 minutes west of the metropolitan area on Lake Independence, offers a diversity of recreational activities in addition to its popular campground.

Attractions include an imaginative children's play area, well-groomed swimming beaches, a golf course, 6 miles of paved biking/hiking trails with bike rentals, 8 miles of cross-country ski trails and 9 miles of snowmobile trails.

To get to Baker Park, go west on I-394 about 20 miles to Maple Plain. Then take county roads 24 and 19 north to the park.

BRYANT LAKE REGIONAL PARK
Rowland Rd., Eden Prairie   *941-4518*

This 170-acre park underwent extensive redevelopment and reopened in 1995 with a new paved boat launch, 1-mile biking/hiking trail, general picnic area, concession stand, three-season pavilion and swimming beach. A new playground will be added in 1996. Visitors may also rent boats here.

FRENCH REGIONAL PARK
Rockford Rd., Plymouth

Within view of the Minneapolis skyline, this park on Medicine Lake in the western suburbs offers many lake-oriented activities, from swimming in the summer to skating in the winter. There's also a great multilevel maze of cargo climbing nets and slides for the younger set. Cross-country skiers enjoy the 9 miles of trails, some of which are lighted for night skiing.

French Park is off Minn. Highway 9 (Rockford Road) between U.S. Highway 169 and I-494.

HYLAND LAKE PARK RESERVE
County Rd. 28, Bloomington

The 12,000-acre Hyland Lake Park is a quiet, green refuge for deer, pheasants and wild songbirds. A newly renovated nature center offers year-round programs, and you'll enjoy the lake for fishing and canoeing (no swimming). Other features include 8 miles of hiking trails, 5 miles of

biking trails, 7 miles of cross-country ski trails and a downhill skiing area with a chalet and 14 runs.

The park's Chutes 'n' Ladders play area, including a 60-foot enclosed slide, is wildly popular with kids.

To reach Hyland, take U.S. 169 S. Continue south of I-494 where Highway 169 turns into County Road 18. Take a left at County Road 1 and another left at County Road 28. Continue to the park entrance.

NOERENBERG
MEMORIAL PARK GARDENS
2840 North Shore Dr., Wayzata

These pristine formal flower gardens on the shores of Lake Minnetonka attract many people for tours, informal viewing and weddings. Flowers include unusual annuals and perennials, ornamental grasses and daylilies. No food or recreation is allowed, however. The gardens' Oriental boathouse provides an expansive view of the famous lake. The gardens are open from 7 AM to 8 PM weekdays and 8 AM to 8 PM weekends.

Dakota County

We have provided information about some of the larger parks in Dakota County. Two others that you may want to visit are Spring Lake Park Reserve on the Mississippi River, just northwest of Hastings, and Thompson County Park in South St. Paul. For more information on Dakota parks, call 437-6608.

LEBANON HILLS REGIONAL PARK
Cliff Rd., Eagan   *454-9211*

This pine- and birch-filled 2,000-acre park is dotted with a dozen woodland lakes and ponds and includes two major picnic areas, 7 miles of hiking trails, 10

A youngster laces up a loose skate while his friends wait for him at Wakefield Park rink in Maplewood.

miles of horseback trails and 2 miles of canoe trails and portages. Horses are available at nearby stables. Schultz Lake boasts a nice swimming beach. There's also a good-sized campground with 53 full-service RV sites, 10 tent sites, hot showers, tables and grills.

Lebanon Hills Park is off Cliff Road, between Pilot Knob Road and Minn. Highway 3.

LAKE BYLLESBY REGIONAL PARK
County Rd. 88, east of Randolph

This Dakota County park is situated on a deep fishing lake formed by a dam on the Cannon River. It has a swimming beach, picnic area, camping facilities and a boat launch. This 1,490-acre reservoir is the largest body of water in the metropolitan area south of the Mississippi and Minnesota rivers.

To get there, take Minn. Highway 52 S. from the St. Paul area to County Road 86. Take a right, then exit on Harry Avenue and continue south to the park.

Ramsey County

Ramsey County, encompassing St. Paul and east metro suburbs, has set aside 25 percent of its land for use as public parks. Here's a listing of a few Ramsey parks. Others are at Long Lake, Snail Lake, Beaver Lake, Island Lake, Lake Johanna, Lake Josephine, Silver Lake, McCarron's Lake, Lake Owasso, Turtle Lake and White Bear Lake in St. Paul and suburbs. Admission is free to these parks.

For information on Ramsey County Parks, call 777-1707.

BALD EAGLE-OTTER LAKES REGIONAL PARK
Near County Rds. 149 and 60
White Bear Township
TAMARACK NATURE CENTER
5287 Otter Lake Rd.   429-7787

This 862-acre park encompasses the northeast side of Bald Eagle Lake, as well as land between Bald Eagle and Otter lakes in White Bear Township. The entrance is

Photo: Richard Marshall, Pioneer Press

off Hugo Road. Amenities include picnic facilities, a swimming beach, shoreline fishing and a playground. The nearby Tamarack Nature Center offers cross-country skiing, hiking, a scenic dock overlooking Tamarack Lake and year-round educational programs. The interpretive center has educational exhibits and displays.

BATTLE CREEK REGIONAL PARK
Upper Afton Rd. in Maplewood and St. Paul

This 805-acre park affords sweeping views of the Mississippi while offering 5 miles of cross-country ski trails, 4 miles of hiking trails, great sledding hills, picnic areas and playgrounds.

KELLER REGIONAL PARK
Phalen and Maplewood Drs.

This 103-acre park offers access to Keller, Gervais, Kohlman, Phalen and Round lakes in St. Paul and Maplewood, with picnic areas, hiking trails and other amenities.

Washington County

Washington County, east of St. Paul, has five county parks. We've described the largest, Lake Elmo Park Reserve; others are Point Douglas, Square Lake, Pine Point and Cottage Grove Ravine parks. For additional information, call 731-3851.

LAKE ELMO PARK RESERVE
Between Inwood and Lake Elmo Aves. N. Lake Elmo

Encompassing 2,165 acres of rolling hills, wetlands, lakes, prairies and forests, the park offers 80 camping sites (either tent or RV), 20 miles of hiking trails, 12 miles of cross-country ski trails and 5 miles of biking trails, swimming beach, fishing pier and playground. The entrance is north of I-94 on County Road 19.

State Parks

Want a quick getaway from the city's hustle and bustle? Pack the cooler, throw the tent in the trunk and head out to one of the three Minnesota state parks within the Twin Cities greater metropolitan area.

Entrance fees may be paid on a daily basis or with an annual pass. Parks are open to the public year round from 8 AM to 10 PM. For more information, call 296-6157 or (800) 766-6000. The TDD number for the hearing impaired is (800) 657-3929. To reserve a campsite or cabin, call (800) 765-CAMP. Campsites can be reserved from three to 120 days in advance for a nonrefundable fee.

AFTON STATE PARK
County Rd. 20, Afton   *436-5391*

This is a great hiking park filled with rugged hills and St. Croix River overlooks, where one can view migrating hawks, bald eagles and other birds of prey. The park has 18 miles of trails for hiking and cross-country skiing, plus 24 hike-in backpack camping sites. The park also features 5 miles of horse trails and 4 miles of biking trails.

From St. Paul, go 8 miles east on I-94, 7 miles south on County Road 15, then 3 miles east on County Road 20.

MINNESOTA VALLEY STATE PARK
U.S. 169, Jordan   *492-6400*

Just west of Jordan lies one of Minnesota's best-kept secrets. Only minutes from the Twin Cities, this attractive wooded park offers outstanding recreational opportunities, including Minnesota River trails, historic farmsteads, lakes and abundant wildlife.

Minnesota Valley has 25 drive-in camping sites, plus eight hike-in backpack camping sites. The park also offers 47 miles of hiking trails, 35 miles of snowmobile/horse trails and 5 miles of cross-country ski trails.

WILLIAM O'BRIEN STATE PARK
Minn. Hwy. 95, Marine on St. Croix   433-0500

This very popular park on the St. Croix River features rolling wooded hills and flood-plain forests. Recreational activities include camping, canoeing, hiking, swimming, interpretive programs, picnicking and cross-country skiing. The park has 127 drive-in campsites.

To reach William O'Brien, take Minn. Highway 95 2 miles north of Marine on St. Croix.

FORT SNELLING STATE PARK
Post Rd.   725-2390

This park, below and separate from Historic Fort Snelling, has 18 miles of hiking trails and 5 miles of biking trails in a stunning setting at the confluence of the Mississippi and Minnesota rivers. The park also has canoe and paddleboat rentals, as well as a popular beach on Snelling Lake. There is no overnight camping.

To get to Fort Snelling State Park, take Minn. Highway 5 to Post Road and look for the entrance.

Not to Be Missed

MINNESOTA LANDSCAPE ARBORETUM
3675 Arboretum Dr., Chanhassen   443-2460

This 905-acre showcase harbors woods, gently rolling hills, native prairies and formal display gardens ranging from serene Japanese rock gardens to colorful English formal gardens. Thousands of varieties of flowers, trees and shrubs are visible from 6 miles of hiking trails, paved paths and a 3-mile drive. You can take a tram ride, offered several times daily, through the grounds. Open year round is the arboretum's Tearoom restaurant and

Linden Tree Gift Shop, as well as the Andersen Horticulture Library.

From May through October, free walking tours are offered at 10 AM Tuesday and Wednesday and the first Saturday of the month. Admission is $4 for adults 16 and older and $1 for children younger than 16 (free with a parent). The arboretum grounds are open 8 AM to sunset daily. The buildings are open from 8 AM to 4:30 PM Monday through Friday and from 11 AM to 4:30 PM Saturday and Sunday.

Golf

Minnesotans love the links!

Although the seasonal sport can be played here only six months a year (if it's a good year), golf has an enthusiastic following in the North Star State. Minnesota has about 720,000 golfers, comprising about 20 percent of the state's population! That's the highest number of golfers per capita of any state in the union. In fact, Minnesota has hosted several important golf tournaments — the 1991 U.S. Open at Hazeltine National Golf Club in Chaska is one — precisely because of the sport's popularity here.

More than 100 golf courses, public and private, dot the greater Twin Cities area — more than in any other urban area in the country. Among the private courses are the upper-bracket, nationally known Hazeltine and Interlachen clubs, which have equally upper-bracket membership fees.

For us common folk, we'll start with a look at some of the most challenging and popular public courses in the Twin Cities. (Please note: The greens fees are 1995 figures, so expect an increase in 1996.)

By the way, a storehouse of information on local golf events and tournaments is the Minnesota Golf Association at 927-4643.

Public Courses

THE WILDS
14365 N.W. Wilds Pkwy., Prior Lake 445-4455

If you're looking for a "private club" experience on a public course — and you're willing to spend $80 for the experience — The Wilds is your spot. Designed by Tom Weiskopf and completed in 1995, this luxurious course hugging Mystic Lake offers 18 holes of handsomely sculpted landscape, natural water hazards and scenic bluffs that will test every club in your bag. The 180-acre course, the centerpiece in a new exclusive housing development, is just off County Road 83 and adjacent to Mystic Lake Casino. The $80 greens fee includes a cart.

BROOKVIEW GOLF COURSE
200 Brookview Pkwy., Golden Valley   544-8446

Just north of I-394 (and east of General Mills headquarters) in Golden Valley, this older public course offers lots of character in the form of tree-shaded rolling hills interspersed by plentiful water hazards. Fees are $20 for 18 holes, $12 for nine and $6.75 for the par 3 nine-hole course. Other features include a driving range, lessons and a restaurant/grill.

BAKER NATIONAL GOLF COURSE
2935 Parkview Dr., Medina   473-0800

Hennepin Parks operates this 18-hole regulation course, nine-hole executive course, driving range and new clubhouse. Greens fees are $22 for 18 holes, $13 for nine and $7 for the executive course. Reservations may be made up to three days in advance.

BLUFF CREEK GOLF COURSE
1025 Creekwood, Chanhassen   445-5685

Bluff Creek offers 18 holes in a quiet, rolling terrain overlooking the Minnesota River Valley. A variety of challenges awaits, from sandtraps to water hazards. The course is 3 miles south of Chanhassen off Minn. Highway 101. Greens fees for 18 holes are $24 weekends and $19 weekdays.

BRAEMAR GOLF COURSE
6364 Dewey Hill Rd., Edina   941-2072

This tree-filled, rolling course is owned and operated by the city of Edina. Edina residents may reserve tee times; the general public may golf on a walk-on, space-available basis. Greens fees are $20 for 18 holes and $11 for nine.

BUNKER HILLS GOLF COURSE
Minn. Hwy. 242 and Foley Blvd.
Coon Rapids   755-4141

Bunker Hills, with its abundant woods and bunkers, is reputed to be the toughest public course in the metropolitan Twin Cities. Greens fees for 18 holes are $24 weekends and $22 weekdays; for nine holes, $12. Reservations are accepted.

COLUMBIA GOLF COURSE
St. Anthony Pkwy. and Central Ave.
Minneapolis   789-2627

The focus at this municipal golf course, one of five operated by the city, is a state-of-the-art learning center. Fees are $18 for 18 holes and $13 for nine. Reservations may be made for weekends and holidays only.

COMO PARK GOLF COURSE
1431 N. Lexington Pkwy.
St. Paul   488-9673

Reopened in 1988, this picturesque course is riddled with traps, trees and several ponds. It is owned and operated by the city of St. Paul. Greens fees are $18.50 for 18 holes and $13 for nine. Reservations are accepted.

EDINBURGH USA GOLF COURSE
8700 Edinbrook Crossing
Brooklyn Park   424-7060

Robert Trent Jones designed this new golf course, which is handsome yet hazardous to your golf score. Watch out for the treacherous third and 17th holes; those water hazards will get you every time! Greens fees are $31 for 18 holes and $15 for nine (after 6 PM only). Reservations are accepted four days in advance. This course, owned by the city of Brooklyn Park, also features a stately clubhouse and an elegant restaurant.

GOODRICH GOLF COURSE
1820 N. Van Dyke Rd., St. Paul   777-7355

Owned by Ramsey County, this course charges $18 for 18 holes and $12.50 for nine. Reservations are accepted four days in advance.

FRANCIS GROSS GOLF COURSE
St. Anthony Pkwy. and 27th Ave. N.E.
Minneapolis   789-2542

Serious golfers like the distinctive topography at this municipal course. Greens fees are $18 for 18 holes and $13 for nine. Reservations are accepted. Holes three and 12 can be especially challenging.

HIAWATHA GOLF COURSE
4553 Longfellow Ave. S.
Minneapolis   724-7715

Another municipal course, this one skirts lakes Hiawatha and Nokomis in South Minneapolis and is a longtime favorite for its easy accessibility and attractive layout. Minnehaha Creek winds through the links. Greens fees are $18 for 18 holes and $13 for nine. Reservations are accepted for weekend use only.

HIGHLAND PARK GOLF COURSE
1403 Montreal Ave., St. Paul   699-0193

A par 72, city-owned course, Highland Park is well-trapped and challenging and offers scenic views of gently rolling hills and a meandering creek. Greens fees are $18.50 for 18 holes and $13 for nine. Reservations are accepted.

HOLLYDALE GOLF CLUB
4710 Holly Lane N., Plymouth   559-9847

This suburban course tests every skill level. Greens fees weekdays are $17 for 18 holes and $12 for nine; weekends, $19 for 18 holes, $13 for nine. Reservations are accepted.

KELLER GOLF COURSE
2166 Maplewood Dr., St. Paul   484-3011

Challenges aplenty await duffers at this handsome public course, the site of LPGA and PGA tournaments. Greens fees are $20 for 18 holes.

THE LINKS AT NORTHFORK
9333 153rd Ave. N.W., Ramsey   241-0506

The only Scottish links-style course in Minnesota, Northfork is characterized by large areas of roughs and nearly constant winds. Greens fees (18 holes only) are $26 for weekdays and $29 for weekends. Lower twilight fees are available.

MAJESTIC OAKS GOLF COURSE
Minn. Hwy. 65 N. and Bunker Lake Rd.
Ham Lake   755-2142

Play here is characterized by deep, unforgiving bunkers on a handsome course that is the site of many corporate and local tourneys. The facility has two 18-hole courses — Platinum and Gold. Hole seven on the Platinum Course is particularly tough. The greens fees for the Platinum course are $22 on weekends and $18 weekdays; Gold, $20 weekends and $16 weekdays. You can play an executive nine-hole course for $7.50.

MANITOU RIDGE

3200 N. McKnight Rd.
White Bear Lake   *777-2987*

This Ramsey County course sports a newly constructed clubhouse with a pro shop, bar and grill. Watch out for Hole 10 with its devilish water hazard. Greens fees are $18 for 18 holes, $12.50 for nine.

MEADOWBROOK GOLF COURSE

300 Meadowbrook Rd., Hopkins   *929-2077*

The fifth hole here can give you gray hair! A well-maintained course, it's easy to get to, just off Excelsior Boulevard in suburban Hopkins. Greens fees are $18 for 18 holes and $13 for nine. Reservations are accepted.

PHALEN PARK GOLF COURSE

1615 Phalen Dr., St. Paul   *778-0413*

An 18-hole, city-owned course, this one stretches along the west shore of Phalen Lake, presenting enough doglegs, water hazards and sand bunkers to test all ability levels. Greens fees are $18.50 for 18 holes; $13 for nine.

STONEBROOKE GOLF CLUB

2693 S. County Rd. 79, Shakopee   *496-3171*

This 18-hole course encompasses part of Lake O'Dowd, which poses a special challenge on the par 4 eighth hole, where a carry of at least 175 yards is required to clear the watery expanse. A leisurely ferryboat ride takes you to the fairway where more challenges await. Fees are $30 on weekends and $24, weekdays.

SUNDANCE GOLF AND BOWL

15240 113th Ave., Maple Grove   *420-4700*

The rolling landscape here is deceptively challenging. Greens fees are $22

for 18 holes and $12 for nine. Reservations are accepted.

THEODORE WIRTH GOLF COURSE

Wirth Pkwy. and Plymouth Ave.
Minneapolis   *522-4584*

Just minutes from downtown Minneapolis, Wirth offers a beautiful wooded setting for golf enthusiasts. Greens fees are $18 for 18 holes, $13 for nine. Reservations are accepted.

UNIVERSITY OF MINNESOTA GOLF CLUB

2275 Larpenteur Ave. W., St. Paul   *627-4000*

This is an 18-hole course filled with delightfully difficult holes. Greens fees are $17.75 weekdays and $20.75 weekends. Lower fees area available for U of M students, faculty and alumni association members.

ELMDALE HILLS GOLF COURSE

Miesville   *(507) 263-2507*

For a wild and woolly golf game, this new course in the extreme southeast corner of Dakota County earns points for ingenuity, if nothing else. On certain nights of the week, golfers can rent llamas — yes, llamas — to caddy their bags from hole to hole! The animals are hardy and efficient, and best of all, they don't talk back or give you annoying advice on which club to use. Fees are $9 for nine holes, $11 for a cart and $25 for a llama.

Indoor Driving Ranges

For those golfers who just can't let go of the game when the mercury dips, here are four places to swing your clubs without hitting a snowdrift.

• Airena Golf Center, 780-3663, 7833 N.E. Highway 65, Spring Lake Park.

• Braemar Golf Dome, 944-9490, 7420 Braemar Boulevard, Edina.

Photo: Pioneer Press

Itasca State Park, headwaters of the Mississippi River, north of the Twin Cities.

• Fore Seasons Golf Inc., 473-4813, 2465 W. Industrial Boulevard, Long Lake.

• Tony's Clubhouse, 647-0233, 1526 Larpenteur Avenue W., Falcon Heights.

Outdoor Miniature Golf

A round of miniature golf and a hot summer's day are a perfect match for all ages. Here are a few fun minigolf courses in the Twin Cities.

BIRDIE'S SPORTS PARK
8595 Columbine Rd., Eden Prairie   828-1928
This hot new 18-hole course, near the intersection of Anderson Lakes Parkway and U.S. Highway 169, also sports seven batting cages and a refreshment stand.

NORA'S
3118 W. Lake St., Minneapolis   927-5781
Work off one of Nora's home-cooked meals at the restaurant's very own 18-hole miniature golf course. It's a quaint course with a popular target hole and windmill obstruction.

GASOLINE ALLEY
10300 Central Ave. N.E., Blaine   784-7223
A super-dooper course, Gasoline Alley features fast fairways and challenges aplenty. It's part of a popular entertainment complex that also has a go-cart track and video game center.

CHALLENGE PARK AT VALLEYFAIR
1 Valleyfair Dr., Shakopee   445-7600
This park is adjacent to Valleyfair and offers miniature golf, bumper boats and go-carts, all with separate fees.

SPRING LAKE AMUSEMENT PARK
1066 N.E. Minn. Hwy. 10
Spring Lake Park   786-4994
Choose from two 18-hole miniature golf courses and two water slides. The park also has battery-powered cars for tots and a water-balloon tossing area.

FORE SEASONS GOLF
2465 W. Industrial Blvd.
Long Lake   473-4813
This large complex has an outdoor mini-golf course in addition to an indoor driving range.

FAMILY FUNWAYS
GO-CARTS & MINI GOLF

2100 N. Frontage Rd., Burnsville 894-9782

This outdoor amusement complex features 18 holes of mini-golf fun. The facility also has go-carting, carnival rides and outdoor batting cages.

Indoor Miniature Golf

GOLF MOUNTAIN

Mall of America, Bloomington 883-8899

Overlooking Camp Snoopy, this 18-hole course is great for people-watching.

GRAND SLAM SPORTS & ENTERTAINMENT CENTER

3984 Sibley Memorial Hwy., Eagan 452-6569

Miniature golf is just one part of this state-of-the-art sports center. There are also batting cages, a video arcade, basketball courts and much more.

Swimming Pools

Even in the land of lakes, some prefer swimming in pools. Here's information on popular public pools in the Twin Cities area.

Minneapolis

Minneapolis has three public, outdoor 50-meter swimming pools. Daily fees are $1.50 per person. Season passes for families and individuals are also available at prices ranging from $27.50 for resident families to $14.50 for resident individuals. For nonresidents, season passes range from $41.25 for families to $21.50 for individuals. Note that the prices quoted are for 1995 and are subject to change.

Minneapolis outdoor public pools are:

• **Rosacker Pool**, 348-8840, 1520 N.E. Johnson Street
• **North Commons Pool**, 348-2266, 1701 Golden Valley Road
• **Webber Pool**, 348-6412, 4400 Dupont Avenue N.

There also is public indoor swimming at:

• **Franklin Junior High**, 348-2226, 1501 Aldrich Avenue N.
• **Phillips Community Center**, 348-2373, 2323 11th Avenue S.

St. Paul

St. Paul has two outdoor public pools. Admission is $2.50 for adults and $1.50 for kids 17 and younger.

• **Como Pool**, 489-2811, Horton and Lexington avenues
• **Highland Pool**, 699-7968, 1840 Edgcumbe Road.

The city also operates an indoor pool, open daily except Sunday.

• **Oxford Pool**, 647-9925, 1079 Iglehart Avenue

The Suburbs

The suburbs have a number of swimming pools that cater to the public.

WESTERN SUBURBS
• **St. Louis Park Recreation Center**, 924-2545, 5005 W. 36th Street, St. Louis Park

NORTHWESTERN SUBURBS
• **Crystal Public Swimming Pool**, 531-0950, 4800 N. Douglas Drive, Crystal
• **Honsey Outdoor Pool**, 531-5177, 4301 Xylon Avenue N., New Hope

SOUTHWESTERN SUBURBS

• **Eden Prairie Community Center,** 949-8470, 16700 Valley View Rd.

• **Edina Aquatic Center,** 927-9829, Valley View Road and W. 66th Street, Edina

SOUTH SUBURBS

• **Richfield Municipal Outdoor Pool,** 861-9355, 630 E. 66th Street, Richfield

• **Redwood Community Building and Outdoor Pool,** 431-8850, 311 County Road 42, Apple Valley

• **Valley View Pool,** 881-4937, 201 E. 90th Street, Bloomington

NORTHERN SUBURBS

• **Edgewood Pool,** 784-0618, 5100 Edgewood Drive, Mounds View

EASTERN SUBURBS

• **Woodbury Junior High School,** 458-4300, 425 School Drive, Woodbury

• **Woodbury Senior High School,** 458-4320, 2665 Woodlane Drive, Woodbury

SOUTHEASTERN SUBURBS AND COMMUNITIES

• **Cottage Grove Pool,** 458-2834, 6541 85th Street, Cottage Grove

• **Hastings Outdoor Pool,** 437-6111, Highway 55 and Maple Street, Hastings

• **Northview Pool,** 450-8744, 19th Avenue N. and Thompson Avenue, South St. Paul

• **McClain Pool,** 450-8744, Third Avenue and Seventh Street N., South St. Paul

• **West St. Paul Pool,** 552-4150, 92 W. Orme Street, West St. Paul

Water Parks

You can splish and splash at numerous water parks in the Twin Cities area.

They include the indoor water parks at Shoreview Recreation Center, Chaska Community Center, Edinborough Park and Maplewood Recreation Center. Turn to our Kidstuff chapter for complete information on these.

Bowling

This traditionally blue-collar sport is an enduring favorite in the Twin Cities, perhaps because it provides an easy and affordable recreational outlet during our long winters. Many families are taking up the sport, and alleys are encouraging this new trend by offering other attractions for children and smoke-free bowling times.

The Twin Cities boast many modern, attractive family-oriented bowling centers, as well as a smattering of old-time, smoke-filled "alleys." There isn't space to list them all. Here we've selected a few that stand out from the rest.

BRYANT-LAKE BOWL

810 W. Lake St., Minneapolis   825-3737

This is '90s-style bowling! The oh-so-trendy Bryant-Lake serves up espresso, designer beer and brie to black-ball enthusiasts, who, after hurling a few strikes, can catch the latest live performance at the in-house cabaret theater.

BRUNSWICK EDEN PRAIRIE LANES AND FAMILY FUN WORLD

12200 Singletree Ln., Eden Prairie   941-0445

This new, high-tech bowling alley/entertainment center has 40 lanes and 45,000 square feet of space. Also on the grounds are a pro shop, a fun pizza parlor, a three-level children's indoor playground/day-care center and bar. Scoring is done by computer.

Snowboarding at Wild Mountain, a ski area north of the Twin Cities.

Photo: Joe Rossi, Pioneer Press

NICOLLET BOWLING LANES
3813 Nicollet Ave., Minneapolis   822-4112

This old neighborhood alley has a humble eight lanes, but that's part of its appeal. We're talking cozy and quaint here. Built in the '40s, Nicollet Lanes' alleys feature the old-fashioned above-the-floor ball returns. The beer bar has great burgers at rock-bottom prices. You can also play table tennis, pool and steel and electric darts.

STARDUST LANES
2520 26th Ave. S., Minneapolis   721-6211

A 20-year-old alley with 30 bowling lanes, video games and a bar, the Stardust is an enduring favorite of Twin Citians. It's open 24 hours.

MAPLEWOOD BOWL & FUN MALL
1955 English St., Maplewood   774-8787

This bowling entertainment center features 40 lanes and also has billiards, darts, foosball and a sports bar with live entertainment and karaoke. Wouldn't Norton and the guys be impressed!

Martial Arts

People study the martial arts for a variety of reasons: to develop muscular strength and self control, for self defense, to meet new people or just for the fun of it.

The Twin Cities have many schools teaching a variety of martial-arts forms, everything from tae kwon do and Okinawa shirite karate to judo. For information on specific studios or schools, consult the Yellow Pages under "Karate." A word to the wise: Many so-called associations or organizations are simply fronts for specific schools or studios and are unreliable sources of objective information.

The best introduction to the martial arts may be through a low-cost community education class offered through local school districts. Many martial arts centers also offer a free introductory lesson.

Running

Every October, 6,000 runners come from all over the world to race in the Twin Cities Marathon. Acclaimed as "the most beautiful urban marathon in America," this 26-mile course encompasses stately tree-shaded neighborhoods, Mississippi River boulevards and even the State Capitol lawns in St. Paul.

For information on running in or working as a volunteer for the **Twin Cities Marathon**, call its headquarters at (612) 673-0778.

Minneapolis and St. Paul are swarming with running and jogging enthusiasts who pursue the sport year round. That's right, year round! In the dead of winter, you'll see these daring — some might say foolhardy — runners, clad in sweats and earmuffs, leap over snowbanks and stride through slush to log their daily 5-miler. Racing events are held virtually every weekend of the year, including a half-marathon during the St. Paul Winter Carnival in late January and early February.

Favorite running spots in the Twin Cities are at any of the major lakes, most notably Lake of the Isles, Lake Calhoun and Lake Harriet in Minneapolis and lakes Phalen and Como in St. Paul; Minneapolis' Minnehaha and Theodore Wirth parkways; St. Paul's mansion-lined Summit Avenue; and Hyland Lake Park Reserve in Bloomington.

Along the Mississippi River, popular runs include the loop between Franklin and Washington avenues; S. River Boulevard south of the Lake Street Bridge and through Hidden Falls Park in St. Paul; and Minneapolis' Minnehaha Park.

The Twin Cities have several running clubs. One of the largest is the **Minnesota Distance Running Association**, 927-0983, which meets at the Edina Community Center, 5701 Normandale Road. You can also call the association's race-information line, 925-4749, for updates on Twin Cities running events. Another is the **American Lung Association Running Club**, 227-8014. One caveat: This club is only for runners who have completed a marathon.

Several health and fitness clubs also have running clubs, such as the 500-member **Northwest Club Run**, 673-1282, sponsored by Northwest Racquet, Swim and Health Clubs. The club meets for runs every Monday and Wednesday evening, offers guidance from professional trainers and sponsors several racing and social events. Northwest membership is required.

Rock Climbing

The bluffs at Taylors Falls along the St. Croix River and the craggy cliffs along the North Shore of Lake Superior attract many rock-climbing enthusiasts.

Two indoor climbing facilities in the Twin Cities offer rock climbers a place to hone their skills by literally scaling the walls!

•**Peak Adventure**, 884-7996, 9208 James Avenue S., Bloomington

•**Vertical Endeavors**, 776-1430, 844 Arcade Street, St. Paul

Another organization, **Footprints**, 788-1414, teaches rock climbing at various sites in Minnesota and Wisconsin.

Walking and Hiking

To discourage wintertime sloth and dissipation among the citizenry of these cold climes, several enclosed shopping malls in the Twin Cities suburbs have started walking clubs. Members meet early in the morning, before the stores open, to walk from the halls and byways of these modern indoor shopping centers.

The Mall of America's walking club is called the Mall Stars, 885-8500.

For information on walking clubs in other malls, such as Southdale, Ridgedale or Rosedale, call each mall's management office.

While great hiking areas abound in the Twin Cities area — the Chain of Lakes, river roads and the Minnesota Landscape Arboretum come to mind — two trails in particular are worth noting.

•**Luce Line Trail**. Beginning at Vicksburg Lane in Plymouth, this DNR-maintained trail continues west for 30 miles to Winsted. You'll find a rest area and picnic table at mile 6.

•**Gateway Trail**. This trail begins on

Arlington Avenue, just west of Westminster Street in St. Paul, and continues through 17 miles of woods and wetlands to Stillwater.

Here are other resources for walking and hiking enthusiasts.

- **Minneapolis Municipal Hiking Club**, 661-4875
- **City of St. Paul Seniors Hiking Club**, 266-6370 or 266-6377
- **Meandering Minnesotans Volksmarch**, 890-7560 or 894-3213
- **Twin Cities Volksmarch Club**, 699-9026 or 348-7896
- **Minnesota State Parks Hiking Club**, 296-6157
- **Hennepin Parks Hiking Program**, 559-9000
- **Summit Avenue Walking Tours**, 297-2555
- **St. Anthony Falls Walking Tours**, 627-5433

In-line Skating

Every park in the cities is filled with these zanies on wheels. After all, this is the home of Rollerblade Inc. The areas surrounding the lakes of Minneapolis, especially Calhoun and Lake of the Isles, are favorite spots for 'bladers, and in-line skate rental outlets nearby along Lake Street can fit you with the right gear..

The **Hubert H. Humphrey Metrodome**, 335-3370, opens its doors for in-line skating through its circular lobby on certain days during the winter months. Call 825-DOME for information. In the St. Paul suburb of Roseville, the **John Rose Minnesota Oval**, 484-0268, outdoor skating rink at 1200 Woodhill Drive, draws in-line skaters during the summer months. Many of the county parks also sponsor in-line skating clinics and rent all the necessary equipment, including helmets and knee and elbow pads, which are necessities for this free-wheeling sport.

Both Minneapolis and St. Paul discourage in-line skating and skateboarding on downtown sidewalks. In-line skaters are welcome to use the bike paths around the lakes.

League Events

Kids

A myriad of leagues offer youth baseball, basketball, soccer, gymnastics, tennis, swimming and other sports. Your best source of information on a specific youth league is the local parks and recreation department. Minneapolis and St. Paul and virtually all suburbs have such departments. Local schools are also important resources for youth sports.

Adults

Don't let the kids have all the fun! Active adults are faced with an array of sports choices, from women's hockey leagues to coed volleyball and softball to tennis ladders. Call the park and recreation department of your local city or suburban offices for complete information. In Minneapolis, call 661-4875 or TDD 661-4788, or the "Leisure Line," 673-2489 Ext. 22, for a weekly recorded message. In St. Paul call 266-6400.

Tennis, Health and Fitness Clubs

The Twin Cities area is a competitive market for health clubs, and, for that reason, many facilities frequently offer membership specials and discounts. Keep your eyes open; it could save you some bucks!

By all means, visit and try out any club before you commit yourself to a membership plan. Here's a quick survey of some of the Twin Cities' most popular facilities.

BALLY'S U.S. SWIM AND FITNESS
1166 University Ave., St. Paul   644-2444

This national fitness chain offers a full range of options in a bright, modern setting. Amenities include strength and cardiovascular machines, aerobics classes, a pool, gym and jogging track, plus racquetball courts in some locations. Bally's also has facilities in Bloomington, Little Canada, Eagan, St. Louis Park, Richfield, New Hope and Fridley.

CALHOUN BEACH CLUB
2925 Dean Pkwy., Minneapolis   927-9951

On the northern shore of Lake Calhoun, this recently renovated, attractive club has swimming pools, strength and cardiovascular machines, a members' dining room, a full range of social activities and courts for tennis, racquetball and squash. The Calhoun Beach Club, Regency Athletic Club and University Club of St. Paul have reciprocal membership agreements.

CATHEDRAL HILL YWCA
198 Western Ave. N., St. Paul   225-YWCA

This is a small but appealing coed facility where you can take advantage of strength-training and cardiovascular machines, aerobics classes, an Olympic-size pool and other amenities. Child care is available.

EAGAN ATHLETIC CLUB
3330 Pilot Knob Rd., Eagan   454-8790

Smaller than the chains, this club has a cozy, neighborhood feel. Amenities include strength and cardiovascular machines, four indoor tennis courts, racquet-

ball, volleyball, indoor and outdoor swimming pools, aerobics classes and children's programming.

FLAGSHIP ATHLETIC CLUB
755 Prairie Center Dr., Eden Prairie   941-2000

The first thing you see when you walk through this club's front door is a grand piano and an elegant restaurant, indications this is as much a social scene as it is a health club.

Flagship has a full range of fitness services, including 11 outdoor and seven indoor tennis courts, four racquetball courts, cardiovascular and strength machines, an indoor jogging track, indoor and outdoor pools and a hair salon, plus the aforementioned formal restaurant with bar.

LIFETIME FITNESS CLUB
7970 Brooklyn Blvd., Brooklyn Park   493-9393

The 4-year-old Brooklyn Park club and new branches in Woodbury, Eagan, Highland Park, Roseville and Coon Rapids are modern, attractive facilities loaded with cutting-edge cardio and weight machines, pools, aerobics studios and health-food cafes. The Eagan facility also has a climbing wall and a children's play center/day care. The Roseville branch is for women only. Call the above number for information on all the area LifeTime clubs.

THE MARSH
15000 Minnetonka Blvd.
Minnetonka   935-2202

Describing itself as "a center for balance and fitness," this club adds a hearty dose of Eastern philosophy to Western concepts of physical fitness. Features include exercise classes, a sauna/whirlpool, 75-foot indoor pool, running tracks, a rock-climbing simulator, weight room, range of aerobic equipment and massage and spa services as well as a restaurant and meditation tower.

SHOREVIEW RECREATION CENTER
4600 Victoria St., Shoreview   490-4700

CHASKA COMMUNITY CENTER
1661 Parkridge Dr., Chaska   448-5633

These two facilities are state-of-the-art indoor water parks/fitness centers (see the Kidstuff chapter for more about each park).

EDINBOROUGH PARK
7700 York Ave. S., Edina   893-9890

This attractive indoor park has a pool, ice rink and fully equipped health club on premises.

LILYDALE CLUB
Minn. Hwy. 13 and I-35E, Lilydale 457-4954

This is a well-maintained older facility with a serious tennis program. The club has nine indoor tennis courts, four racquetball courts, an aerobics studio, an outdoor swimming pool and indoor jogging track, plus a limited number of strength and cardiovascular machines.

MAPLEWOOD RECREATION CENTER
2100 White Bear Ave., Maplewood   770-4570

This new city-owned facility, completed in fall 1994, features pools, water slides, banquet facilities and an athletic club equipped with strength and cardiovascular machines.

NORTHWEST RACQUET,
SWIM & HEALTH CLUBS
5525 Cedar Lake Rd., St. Louis Park   546-5474

This is the premier local chain of athletic clubs, with heavy emphasis on tennis. With 13 locations in Minneapolis and the western suburbs, Northwest clubs are well-run, top-notch facilities. While some of the branches are strictly tennis clubs, others, including the flagship St. Louis Park

club, offer a full range of services, including strength and cardiovascular machines, swimming pools, jogging tracks, racquetball and classes in aerobics, self defense and dance. Squash courts are available at some locales.

Northwest's Arena Club, in the Target Center in downtown Minneapolis, is especially popular for young, single professionals. The suburban clubs are more family-oriented.

For tennis buffs, Northwest is the place to be for year-round play. The Northwest system offers more than 100 indoor courts and 46 outdoor courts in addition to a staff of nearly 50 tennis pros who coach group lessons, women's daytime leagues, club leagues and youth lessons and drills. All staff are U.S. Professional Tennis Association members.

A new addition at Northwest is an indoor driving range for golfers.

REGENCY ATHLETIC CLUB
Hyatt Regency Hotel, 1300 Nicollet Mall
Minneapolis   343-3131

This deluxe club, housed in the posh Hyatt Regency, offers strength and cardiovascular machines, aerobics classes, indoor pool, six racquetball courts, two squash courts and four indoor tennis courts and a basketball gym, plus a restaurant, spa and hair salon. Hotel guests may use the club for a nominal daily fee.

SWEATSHOP
171 Snelling Ave. N., St. Paul   646-8418

This is a small but friendly workout spot specializing in aerobics classes. The Sweatshop also offers strength-training machines and free weights, cardiovascular machines, child care, personal trainers and counseling.

UNIVERSITY CLUB

420 Summit Ave., St. Paul   222-1751

This stately old club has the usual complement of machines, aerobics classes, an outdoor pool and tennis courts, plus lovely Summit Avenue for jogging.

UPTOWN YWCA

2808 Hennepin Ave. S., Minneapolis   874-3171

This relatively new YWCA branch offers weight-training and cardiovascular machines, a gym, swimming pool and aerobics classes in a modern, attractive setting. Membership is transferable to other Ys in the area that feature tennis and racquetball courts.

WHITE BEAR LAKE RACQUET & SWIM

4800 White Bear Pkwy.
White Bear Lake   426-1308

This handsome, modern facility exudes a private-club atmosphere. Amenities include strength and cardiovascular machines, a children's wading pool, indoor and outdoor pools, 10 tennis and four racquetball courts, squash courts, a basketball gym and an aerobics studio with a cushioned wood floor. There's also an extensive tennis program of leagues and classes. This club doubles as a social center with a restaurant and bar on premises and a full calendar of social events.

YMCA

1130 Nicollet Mall, Minneapolis   332-0501

This clean and spacious facility includes a weight-training center, basketball and racquetball courts, and a swimming pool, plus educational programs on a variety of subjects.

YMCA OF GREATER ST. PAUL

194 Sixth St. E., St. Paul   292-4130

The Y offers full-service clubs with strength training and cardiovascular machines, swimming pools, jogging tracks, racquetball courts and a range of fitness classes for all ages. In addition to the downtown St. Paul club, the Y has five other facilities sprinkled throughout St. Paul and its suburbs. The Northeast Y, in White Bear Lake, has a popular water slide.

Where the Champs Compete

NATIONAL SPORTS CENTER AND BLAINE SOCCER COMPLEX

1700 105 Ave. N.E., Blaine   785-5600

No discussion of Twin Cities amateur sports and recreation is complete without mention of the National Sports Center in Blaine. This state-of-the-art complex is one of the nation's finest sports training and competition centers, having hosted the likes of Carl Lewis, Jackie Joyner-Kersee, Greg LeMond, the U.S. National Men's and Women's Soccer Teams, the National Weightlifting Championships, the 1991 International Special Olympics and the 1992 U.S. Olympic Cycling Trials, to mention just a few.

The NSC's velodrome, seating up to 2,500 spectators, is the only all-wood, all-weather cycling track in the United States.

Outdoor arenas and fields include 32 soccer fields and a 400-meter performance track. The indoor arena offers basketball courts, indoor soccer fields, tennis courts and track and field space.

Many local and national amateur sporting events take place at the Blaine facility, located just 20 minutes north of the Twin Cities. It's definitely worth the trip just to see the facility!

Finally... If You Have Any Energy Left

The possibilities for a variety of recreational activities continue with these popular pastimes.

Biking

Biking is becoming increasingly popular in the Twin Cities, so much so that Minneapolis, for example, has greatly expanded its number of streets with designated bicycle lanes (see the Getting Around chapter).

• **Minnesota Coalition of Bicyclists**, 452-9736

• **Twin Cities Bicycling Club**, activity hotline, 924-2443

• **Minnesota Cycling Federation**, 729-0702

Bird-watching

Bird-watchers have much to gaze upon in Twin Cities skies. For that, you can thank our strategic location on the great Mississippi flyway migration route. Because we're so centrally located, we also are visited by migrating eastern and western birds. The Minneapolis Audubon Society, 926-6338, sponsors bird walks in the Thomas Sadler Roberts Bird Sanctuary every Tuesday at 9 AM in April and May. You can also contact the St. Paul Audubon Society at 291-2596.

Bocce Ball

Bocce ball is a cross between bowling and curling — without the kilts and ice! This is an especially popular sport on the east side of St. Paul, home to a large Italian enclave. The Minnesota Bocce Ball Association, 772-2357, counts about 600 members and competes on courts at 615 Lafayette Road, St. Paul.

Frisbee

The Minnesota Frisbee Association, (612) 255-0966, with a membership of around 300, sponsors tournaments in disc golf and other Frisbee activities. Popular Frisbee-tossing areas in the Twin Cities are at Minneapolis' Lake Calhoun (south shore), Highland Park in St. Paul, North Valley Park in Inver Grove Heights and Kaposia Park in South St. Paul. There's also a coed Ultimate Frisbee league that meets at Fort Snelling State Park.

Horseback Riding

The Twin Cities metro area has a lively horse community. The **Minnesota Horse Council**, 755-7729, is an advocacy organization for the promotion of horseback riding and trails. Here are a few popular stables.

BRASS RING STABLES
9105 Norris Lake Rd., Elk River   441-7987
This facility offers guided trail rides and riding lessons.

BUNKER HILLS STABLES
Minn. Hwy. 242 and Foley Blvd.
Coon Rapids   757-7010
This stable leads rides through scenic Bunker Hills Park.

EAGLE CREEK STABLES
7301 Eagle Creek Blvd., Shakopee   445-7222
Eagle Creek offers horse rentals, riding instruction and hay and sleigh rides.

HANSON'S RANCH
1401 County Rd. 18, Shakopee   445-9970
You can rent horses or go on a sleigh or hay ride here through 650 wooded acres.

DIAMOND T RIDING STABLES

4889 Pilot Knob Rd., Eagan   454-1464

In this pretty wooded spread, you can rent a horse or lean back on a hay wagon and just enjoy the view.

Outdoor Adventure Club

Founded at the University of Minnesota decades ago, the **Minnesota Rovers Outing Club**, 522-2461, is now community-based and offers countless outdoors activities and social events for active individuals of all ages. Recent excursions have included Boundary Waters canoeing, apple-picking and St. Croix River hiking trips.

Outdoor Adventures for Women Only

Woodswomen Inc., 822-3809, leads rather challenging excursions into nature, everything from dog sledding to canoe trips.

Skydiving

For instruction in this daredevil sport, contact the **Minnesota Skydivers Club**, 431-1960.

Adult Softball

Several adult softball leagues serve players in the Twin Cities area. These include the **Riverview League** (western suburbs), 895-5026; **St. Paul Amateur Baseball League**, 266-6406; **Park National League** (Minneapolis), 661-4893; and the **Carver Central League** (Chaska, Shakopee), 492-2734.

Inside
Winter's Wonderland

Minnesota is a meteorologist's dream.

From winter's Arctic blasts to summer's sweltering haze, the weather here is never boring.

Due to our location, near the geographic center of North America and far removed from the tempering oceans, we are blessed with a hardy climate of extremes. On occasion, temperatures have been known to range from 30 degrees below zero to 100 above within the same calendar year. Typically, the average high in January is 19 degrees, while in July, readings of 83 are common.

Making life even more interesting are the blizzards, impulsive tornadoes and nasty wind and hail storms that regularly cross our borders.

While each season has its unique charms, it is winter that stirs our deepest emotions. And it's easy to see why. Total seasonal snowfall is more than 40 inches. Days are grayer and shorter, with darkness setting in around 5 PM during bleakest January. And, worst of all, it can be so doggone, unrelentingly cold.

But, you know what? Real, true-blue (and we mean blue) Minnesotans love winter. We can't get enough of it! Maybe our brains are permanently frostbitten, or maybe we're just plain loopy, but our hearts tremble with excitement at the mere mention of "black ice," "wind-chill factor" and "goose down."

For us, there aren't words to describe the peace and contentment that come when the first giant flakes fall from the heavens, blanketing the world in white . . . the sensual pleasure of coming in from the cold to dinner in a warm, fragrant kitchen . . . the joy of strapping on a pair of cross-country skis and gliding silently through a pristine frozen forest . . . the grace of steel blades on glassy ice . . . the fun of pushing a kid's sled down a billowy slope.

Some of us — admittedly, the more perverse ones — even get a kick out of winter's minor highway mishaps. There's a special "misery loves company" camaraderie in going shoulder-to-shoulder with total strangers to free cars from snowbanks and sharing a few jokes while hunched over crackling jumper cables. These are bonafide social events in January.

Some consider winter their favorite season even though they rarely step outdoors. For them, it's a wonderful excuse for cocooning and recharging emotional batteries: reading a good book by a roaring fire or watching videos 'til the eyes glaze over. It's no small coincidence that the Twin Cities are filled with voracious readers, countless book clubs and busy libraries, not to mention a thriving community of writers. You can, in part, thank the long winter months for that.

Alas, despite all these wonderful arguments, some Minnesotans succumb. They give up the good fight and head south at the first tinkle of a snowflake.

To those wimps, we say, "Good riddance!" Their loss is our gain.

Truth be told, perhaps the best thing about Northern winters is that they help you truly appreciate the arrival of spring. When the first warm breezes of April roll in, we're out the door, strolling, biking, jogging — one mass of humanity pouring onto lake shores and walking paths. You can almost hear a collective sigh of relief.

In this chapter, we offer a winter survival guide filled with practical pointers on adapting to the elements, plus fun things to do.

The Basics

Clothing

The layered look is "Minnesota chic." Dress in layers that can be easily discarded as the temperatures warm during the day, and top it all off with a sturdy wool or down-filled jacket. Gloves, scarves, hats and waterproof boots are all winter necessities. You might even want to throw in a set of silk long underwear if you're planning to spend a lot of time outdoors.

Don't forego comfort for the sake of fashion. During wintry cold spells, you'll see Guthrie or symphony audiences all snugly outfitted in sweaters, wool shirts and down vests. Nobody thinks twice about it.

Your Home

Here are a few tips for maintaining your home in winter:

• Make sure the exterior of your home is well-caulked, especially around vents and windows.

• Install a CO (carbon monoxide) monitor, and check it routinely.

• Have your gas furnace professionally examined once a year, as well as cleaned regularly.

• Change your furnace filters regularly.

Vehicles

Be kind to your car, and it will serve you well all winter. In fall, take time for that winter tune-up, oil change and battery check. It's well worth it. And don't forget windshield washer fluid! It's also a good idea to keep your gas tank at least half full during cold weather.

Slow down during snowy conditions and allow extra space between your car and the vehicle in front of you. Remember, under Minnesota law, you must drive with your lights on during any form of precipitation — and that includes snow flurries!

Weather Reports

It's important to heed storm warnings and road reports, because driving can be difficult during wintry weather. While many radio and TV stations provide adequate service, WCCO Radio (830 AM) has developed weather reporting to a fine art. It is nationally known for its up-to-the-minute weather coverage, even to the point of being excessive about it. WCCO is also the station to turn to for information about weather-related school or business closings.

Speaking of weather reporting, you'll undoubtedly hear the phrase "wind-chill factor." This is a number that expresses the combined effect of low temperatures and high winds on exposed skin. Ouch!

If you're planning an outstate trip and wondering about road and weather conditions throughout Minnesota, call the state Department of Transportation hotline at 296-3076 for detailed information.

Winter Recreation

Cross-country Skiing

Cross-country skiing (also known as Nordic skiing) gained widespread appeal in Minnesota during the 1970s, and it remains a very popular sport. There are hundreds of miles of cross-country ski trails in the Twin Cities and environs, in city, county and state parks. Most facilities require skiers to purchase and wear a Great Minnesota Ski Pass, which helps pay for trail upkeep. The season pass costs $5 for individuals and $7.50 for husband and wife. The pass also may be purchased on a daily basis for $1. For more information on the ski pass, call 296-4506. Some county and state parks also charge daily or seasonal vehicle parking fees. Several parks also offer rental equipment and lessons.

Here's a listing — by no means complete — of parks offering cross-country skiing.

CITY PARKS — ST. PAUL

For information on city trails, call 266-6445.

Como Park Golf Course, Kaufman Drive and Lexington Avenue, 4.5 miles of trails in an easily accessible location

Phelan Golf Course, 1615 Phalen Drive, 6 miles of trails

CITY PARKS — MINNEAPOLIS

For details on these trails, call 661-4800.

Theodore Wirth Park, 1301 Wirth Parkway, 8.5 miles of hilly trails.

Columbia Golf Course, St. Anthony Parkway and Central Avenue, 3 miles of trails.

Hiawatha Golf Course, 46th Street and Longfellow Avenue, 3 miles of trails.

Francis Gross Golf Course, St. Anthony Parkway and Fillmore Street N.E., 3 miles of trails.

RAMSEY COUNTY PARKS

The following Ramsey County parks have cross-country ski trails and no parking fees but do require a Great Minnesota Ski Pass. For more information, call 777-1707.

Battle Creek Regional Park, Winthrop Street and Lower Afton Road, St. Paul, 6.5 miles of trails through rollings hills.

Tamarack Nature Center, 5287 Otter Lake Road, White Bear Township, 4.5 miles of trails in a secluded setting.

Keller Golf Course, 2166 Maplewood Drive, Maplewood, 4.75 miles of intermediate trails.

Manitou Ridge Golf Course, 3200 N. McKnight Road, White Bear Lake, 3-mile intermediate/advanced trail.

HENNEPIN PARKS

These parks require a daily parking fee of $4, plus the Great Minnesota Ski Pass. For more information, call the Hennepin Parks Ski Hotline at 559-6778.

Crow-Hassan Park Reserve, 11629 Crow-Hassan Park Road, Rogers, 10.9 miles of trails in a remote prairie park.

French Lake Regional Park, Medicine Lake, Plymouth, 5.4 miles of easy trails. Some are lit for night skiing.

What Every Minnesotan Needs to Know

Black Ice: This is a very slick road surface created when car exhaust meets frigid temperatures. It commonly happens during rush hour when there's more idling (and exhaust) than real movement. Because you can't see black ice, it's a good idea to drive cautiously during heavy-traffic conditions.

This woman is using a phone booth in St. Paul in November, 1991, a month that shattered records for snowfall in Minnesota.

Skids: If you don't heed the above advice, you*will* need to know how to maneuver through a skid. The best rule of thumb is to ease up on the brakes, steer in the direction of the skid and hope against all hope that no one's in your way. Gradually, gently accelerate and try to regain control of your steering. A skid can be a terrifying experience no matter how many times you've experienced it. This is one time when landing in a snowbank is a definite blessing, considering the alternatives. Cars are especially skid-prone on icy bridges and highway ramps.

Lock Freeze-up: Now, you know it's cold when you can't even get a key in your car door because the locks are frozen. What to do? Do *not* pour hot, boiling water into your locks. They'll only freeze up again. Do *not* kneel down and breathe into the keyhole. One misstep and you'll find yourself in a liplock with your Buick — which can be very difficult to explain to onlookers, not to mention painful!

Here's what may work. If you have time, just wait a few hours and let the sunlight thaw the locks. If you're in a hurry, use one of those aerosol-spray de-icers. Short of that, try the good, old-fashioned hair dryer.

Helpful Telephone Numbers

DEPARTMENT OF TRANSPORTATION

Road condition hotline	296-3076

AMERICAN AUTOMOBILE ASSOCIATION (AAA) ROAD SERVICE

In Minneapolis and western suburbs	927-2727
In St. Paul Ramsey County and other metro areas	891-8000
For membership information	927-2567

Ice sculpture at the St. Paul Winter Carnival.

Hyland Lake Park Reserve, 10145 E. Bush Lake Road, Bloomington, 6.7 miles of trails on varied terrain, plus a visitors center with a fireplace.

Baker Park Reserve, County Road 19, Medina, 8 miles of trails on rolling hills.

Cleary Lake Regional Park, 18106 Texas Avenue, S. Prior Lake, 9.7 miles of trails.

Murphy-Hanrehan Park Reserve, County Road 74 and 164th Street, Prior Lake, 17 miles of trails on challenging terrain for experienced skiers.

STATE PARKS

For more information on state parks, call 772-7999.

Afton State Park, County Road 20, Afton, 18 miles of trails in hilly, scenic terrain along the St. Croix River.

Fort Snelling State Park, Post Road and Minn. Highway 5, St. Paul, 17 miles of trails running along the riverfront.

William O'Brien State Park, Minn. Highway 95, Marine on St. Croix, 15.5 miles of trails in a varied mix of prairie and woods.

FOR SOMETHING A LITTLE DIFFERENT

Ski past elk, buffalo and a Siberian tiger or two on the Minnesota Zoo's unusual trails. Admission is $8 for adults, $4 for children. The zoo is at 13000 Zoo Boulevard, Apple Valley; call 432-9000.

Downhill Skiing

Several downhill skiing slopes have sprouted in the Minnesota prairie. Here are a few of the most popular in the Twin Cities and nearby communities. Most also have areas for snowboarding, a cold-weather marriage between skateboarding and surfing. Call the **Minnesota Ski Council** at 673-0828 for information on local ski clubs, equipment swaps, tours and clinics.

AFTON ALPS

Cty. Rd. 20, Afton　　　　　　*436-5245*

This picturesque ski area boasts a 350-foot vertical drop, night skiing, 36 runs plus a snowboard half-pipe, 18 chairlifts, one T-bar and two rope tows.

Photo: Chris Polydoroff, Pioneer Press

BUCK HILL
15400 Buck Hill Rd., Burnsville   435-7187

Buck Hill has a 306-foot vertical drop, 10 runs, four chairlifts, one T-bar and three rope tows.

COMO PARK
1431 N. Lexington Pkwy.
St. Paul   488-9673

This small course has two runs, two tow ropes and night skiing.

HYLAND HILLS
8800 Chalet Rd., Bloomington   835-4604

Hyland Hills offers a 175-foot vertical drop, night skiing, 14 runs, plus a snowboard half-pipe, three chairlifts and three rope tows.

MOUNT FRONTENAC
U.S. Hwy. 61, Frontenac   (612) 388-5826

Mount Frontenac offers a 420-foot vertical drop, two chairlifts, one T-bar and two rope tows. Mount Frontenac ski area is 9 miles south of Red Wing.

POWDER RIDGE SKI AREA
Minn. Hwy. 15, St. Cloud   398-7200
*   (800) 348-7734*

Powder Ridge, 16 miles south of St. Cloud, Powder Ridge offers three chairlifts, a J-bar and two rope tows. There's also an on-site cafeteria and bar.

THEODORE WIRTH REGIONAL PARK
1301 Wirth Pkwy., Golden Valley   661-4867

This small city ski area has two runs, a tow rope, snow tubing and night skiing.

WILD MOUNTAIN SKI AREA
County Rd. 16, Taylors Falls   462-7550

Wild Mountain has a 300-foot vertical drop, 21 ski runs, night skiing, four chair lifts and one rope tow.

WELCH VILLAGE
County Rd. 7, Welch   258-4651
*   (800) 421-6099*

Welch Village offers a 350-foot vertical drop, 36 runs, eight chairlifts and one T-bar.

Sledding

As soon as the first snowflakes fall from the skies, Twin Cities children grab sleds, snowboards and cardboard slabs and head to their favorite neighborhood hills. On special occasions, the entire family might jump in the van and visit any of the following super sledding slopes in the metro area.

ST. PAUL SLEDDING SPOTS
Highland Park Golf Course, 1403 Montreal Ave.
Como Park Golf Course, 1431 N. Lexington Pkwy.
Town and Country Club, 2279 Marshall Ave.

MINNEAPOLIS SLEDDING
Theodore Wirth Park, 1325 Wirth Pkwy. N.
Powderhorn Park, 32nd St. and 10th Ave. S.
Minnehaha Pkwy. at Cedar Ave. S.
Columbia Golf Course, 3300 Central Ave. N.E.

Smart Minnesotans always carry extra winter clothing and emergency equipment in their car trunks during the winter months.

Insiders' Tips

SUBURBAN SLEDDING

Ingerson Park, 3255 N. Lexington Ave., Arden Hills.
Lakewood Hills Park, 2110 Orchard Ln.
White Bear Lake
Oak Hill Park, 34th St. and Quebec Ave. S.
St. Louis Park.
Brookside Park, 10001 Xerxes Ave., Bloomington

Snowmobiling

Snowmobiles — mobile, fast and loud — are the Harley-Davidsons of the Great North. The recreational machines were invented in northern Minnesota in 1953. The Polaris snowmobile company was founded in the northern Minnesota town of Roseau. And nearby Thief River Falls is the original home of Arctic Cat, now called Artco. Today, one in 20 Minnesotans owns a snowmobile.

Minnesota has more than 2,000 miles of state-groomed trails, plus another 10,200 miles of locally maintained trails.

In the Twin Cities area, snowmobile trails traverse several Hennepin County parks, such as Baker Park Reserve (9 miles), Carver Park Reserve (5 miles), Cleary Lake Regional Park (1 mile), Crow-Hassan Park Reserve (5 miles), Lake Rebecca (5.5 miles) and Elm Creek Park Reserve (11 miles), plus the North Hennepin Trail Corridor (7 miles) linking Coon Rapids Dam Regional Park to Elm Creek Park Reserve.

In Dakota County, Lebanon Hills Regional Park affords 5 miles of trails. In Ramsey County, snowmobiling is permitted on many lake surfaces and prohibited on all other park land except for designated trails along Keller Creek (connecting Keller Lake and Phalen Lake) and between Otter Lake and Bald Eagle Lake.

As for local state parks, Minnesota Valley State Park has 34 miles of snowmobile trails, and William O'Brien State Park has a 1-mile trail.

The Luce Line State Trail, west of Stubbs Bay Road in Orono to Thompson Lake near Cosmos, offers a 50-mile trail with connections to other state trails.

The Rice Creek Trail, based at the Rice Creek Chain of Lakes in Lino Lakes, affords 70 miles of snowmobile trails.

Outstate Minnesota is riddled with snowmobile trails. For information on them, check with local snowmobile dealers. The state also is home to many snowmobiling races, including the I-500, a grueling three-day competition from White Bear Lake to Thunder Bay, Ontario.

Call the Minnesota United Snowmobile Association at 577-0185 for more information on trails and regulations.

Ice-skating and Hockey

In the state of 10,000 frozen lake surfaces, ice-skating and hockey are understandably popular sports.

In fact, hockey enthusiasm reaches manic proportions every March when the entire state is mesmerized by the State High School Hockey Tournament in St. Paul. That's the culmination of a dream for every Minnesota kid who has donned 50 pounds of padding and chased a wily puck through the ranks of mini-mites to peewee to bantam leagues and then on to the big time in high school teams and state competition. In fact, many successful players in the National Hockey League had their beginnings on Minnesota rinks. Minnesotan Herb Brooks coached the 1980 Miracle on Ice Olympic team that won the gold medal. Twelve members of that team were from Minnesota.

Photo: Joe Oden, Pioneer Press

Blizzards can seriously affect modes of transportation in Minnesota.

Incidentally, hockey isn't just for the guys anymore. Girls hockey is now officially sanctioned in the state and many high schools now have girls' hockey teams.

Those who prefer the more genteel sport of figure skating or the thrill of speed skating will find ample opportunity to do both on Twin Cities frozen lakes, such as Lake of the Isles in Minneapolis and Como Lake in St. Paul, and other local rinks. In downtown St. Paul during the Winter Carnival, a small but picturesque ice rink ringed with ice sculptures is usually set up in the middle of Rice Park.

St. Paul Area Rinks

St. Paul has around 30 outdoor rinks for pleasure skating and another 30 specifically for hockey. Some of the more

popular pleasure-skating rinks are on Como Lake and at Langford Park, Edgecumbe, Battle Creek, Hazel Park, Phelan, North Dale and Palace recreation centers. Here's a listing of some favorite public indoor ice arenas in the St. Paul area. Because many of these facilities reserve ice time for hockey practice and figure-skating lessons, it's important to call ahead for open-skating hours and admission fees. For information on other rinks, call 777-1707.

Aldrich Arena
1850 N. White Bear Ave.
White Bear Lake   *777-2233*

A huge facility, Aldrich has been the site of some wild and woolly high-school hockey action over the years. It is a very popular, multi-use arena.

During a Minnesota cold snap, you have to run backward in order to spit.

Insiders' Tips

GUSTAFSON-PHALEN ARENA
1320 Walsh St., St. Paul   776-2554

This arena is open year-round for open skating, lessons and team play.

ROSEVILLE ICE ARENA
AND JOHN ROSE MINNESOTA OVAL
1200 Woodhill Dr., Roseville   484-0268

Skating is year-round at this new sports complex featuring a large, attractive indoor ice rink, plus an outdoor hockey rink and a 110,000-square-foot outdoor sped-skating oval. The oval is used for in-line skating in the summer. The complex is near the intersection of Lexington Avenue and County Road C.

FAIRGROUNDS COLISEUM
Minnesota State Fairgrounds
Snelling and Larpenteur Aves.
Falcon Heights   642-2200

Used for horse shows during the state fair, the Coliseum is transformed into a skating paradise during the winter months.

MINNEAPOLIS AREA RINKS

The city of Minneapolis boasts about 50 outdoor public skating rinks in parks and on lake surfaces. The most popular of these are at Lake of the Isles and Lake Harriet, Folwell Park in North Minneapolis, Theodore Wirth Park on the western edge of the city, Logan and Van Cleve parks in Northeast Minneapolis and Lynnhurst Park, Keewaydin Park, Lake Nokomis and Powderhorn Park in South Minneapolis, which has the city's only outdoor speed-skating oval.

For a unique skating experience à la New York's Rockefeller Center, strap on your skates and go for a spin on the ice at **Peavey Plaza**, in the heart of downtown. It's near Orchestra Hall on Nicollet Mall between 11th and 12th streets, with plentiful parking nearby.

Minneapolis also has a large public indoor skating arena, **Parade Ice Garden**, 348-5724, 800 Kenwood Parkway, on the western edge near the Guthrie Theater. Open skating hours are 11:30 AM to 1 PM Monday through Friday, 6:30 to 8:15 PM Monday and 4 to 5:45 PM Tuesday, Thursday, Saturday and Sunday. It's adults only from 7:45 to 9:30 PM Friday. Admission is $2.50 for adults and $2.25 for juniors and seniors.

Here's a partial listing of indoor skating arenas in Minneapolis and surrounding suburbs. Other options include outdoor ice-skating rinks at several Hennepin County parks, including **Carver Park Reserve**, **Fish Lake Regional Park** and **French Regional Park**. Also, because of the popularity of hockey, many area high schools open their own indoor or outdoor rinks for public open skating at specific times. Check with individual school districts for more information.

BLOOMINGTON
COMMUNITY ICE GARDEN
3600 W. 98th St., Bloomington   948-8842

Only a few years old, this showcase arena boasts three indoor rinks, one of which is Olympic-size. Refreshments and rentals are available.

BRAEMAR ARENA
7501 U.S. Hwy. 169, Edina   484-0268

Two indoor rinks offer year-round skating.

BROOKLYN PARK
COMMUNITY ACTIVITY CENTER
5600 85th Ave., Brooklyn Park   493-8363

Brooklyn Park is another excellent family skating facility.

EDEN PRAIRIE COMMUNITY CENTER
16700 Valley View Rd.
Eden Prairie   949-8470

Skaters have a choice of two rinks, one Olympic-size. The complex also has an indoor pool and three racquetball courts.

EDINBOROUGH PARK
7700 York Ave. S., Edina   893-9890

Cut figure 8s in an attractive indoor park setting, which also includes a pool and fitness center.

HOPKINS PAVILION
1515 County Rd. 3, Hopkins   939-1410

This new facility has large indoor rinks and an indoor soccer field.

MINNETONKA ICE ARENA
3401 Williston Rd., Minnetonka   939-8310

Lots of character here, that is, for an ice arena. A wood-beamed ceiling tops two large rinks that are open year-round for skating.

ST. LOUIS PARK RECREATION CENTER
5005 W. 36th St., St. Louis Park   924-2545

An attractive year-round facility, this center has a full skating program.

Curling

This quirky ice sport involving "stones" and brooms originated in Scotland and has an enthusiastic following in the Twin Cities. In fact, the **St. Paul Curling Club**, with 650 members, is the largest curling club in the United States.

The game is played in this way: One player slides a big, rounded 42-pound curling stone down a lane of ice toward a target; other teammates then rush ahead of the stone and sweep the ice to alter the stone's speed and direction. The goal is to land your team's stones closer to the center of the house, or target, than the opposing team's stones.

In the 1880s curlers played the game on the Mississippi River at St. Paul. The St. Paul Curling Club was established on Christmas Day 1885, and in 1912 it built its present clubhouse at 470 Selby Avenue, St. Paul. The facility was significantly renovated, including a new ice surface, in 1995 and is still going strong.

Curling is a game long on tradition and camaraderie. For more information on the sport, call the St. Paul Curling Club at 224-7408. The club welcomes new members and hosts an annual newcomers bonspiel (tournament) as an introduction to the sport.

Ice Fishing

No discussion of Minnesota winter recreation is complete without mentioning the infamous sport of ice fishing, wherein otherwise sane individuals drive their vehicles out onto frozen lake surfaces in 30-below weather, saw holes in the ice, drop in a fishing line, pop open a brewski and wait eternally in the wind and cold for the big one to bite.

Serious ice-fishing enthusiasts haul little fishing houses — complete with heaters — onto the ice and keep them there the entire winter. In fact, many of the larger

Locals know to leave that infamous Scandinavian delicacy, lutefisk, well enough alone.

Insiders' Tips

lakes have fish-house communities. One fish-house "town" even elects a mayor!

The 1993 filmed-in-Minnesota movie *Grumpy Old Men*, starring Walter Matthau, Jack Lemmon and Ann-Margret, depicted this loony sport in all its glory.

Winter Festivals

Several winter celebrations and events are testimony to our Nordic fortitude. Here's a glimpse at a few.

ST. PAUL WINTER CARNIVAL
Various St. Paul locations   223-4700

This annual celebration melts winter's gloom with a dazzling array of events and attractions. One of the oldest winter celebrations in the United States, the Winter Carnival was founded in 1886 in reaction to a New York reporter's comment that St. Paul was so cold it was worse than Siberia. A group of St. Paul businessmen decided to hold a celebration to prove how much fun winter can be.

And fun it is! The carnival boasts a parade, parties, ice sculpting, wintersports competitions, ice slides, a King Boreas Medallion Hunt and the coronation of mythical figures. Ruling the carnival are King Boreas and the Queen of the Snows. And to provide mischief and drama, the carnival also selects a Vulcanus Rex and Krewe, evil forces that try to drive out winter and spoil the festival. They wreak all kinds of mischief on city streets, including smudging the faces of innocent folks with black ash marks.

In some years, an ice palace is constructed using frozen blocks from Minnesota lakes. Its size varies, depending on the carnival's budget. In 1992 a grand ice palace measuring 150 feet high and costing nearly $1 million captured international attention. The Super Bowl was held in Minneapolis that year, increasing the exposure of the palace.

The Winter Carnival is traditionally held in late January and early February.

HOLIDAZZLE PARADES
Minneapolis

To light up the wintry skies — and attract holiday shoppers away from suburban malls — downtown Minneapolis offers enchanting lighted parades down Nicollet Mall virtually every night during the holiday shopping season, from late November to New Year's Day.

HOLIDAY IN LIGHTS
13000 Zoo Blvd., Apple Valley   432-9000

The Minnesota Zoo also offers a dazzling display of holiday lights during the same time period.

CHILLY OPEN
Lake St., downtown Wayzata   473-9595

Those crazy folks in Wayzata shake off their winter woes at the annual Chilly Open, a golf tournament on the frozen surface of Lake Minnetonka. It's usually slated for early February.

FESTIVAL OF TREES
Minnesota Landscape Arboretum
3675 Arboretum Dr., Chanhassen 443-2460

The Minnesota Landscape Arboretum dresses up its greenery and displays creatively decorated Christmas trees in this lovely festival usually held throughout the month of December. The Arboretum is off Minn. Highway 5, just west of where it crosses Minn. Highway 41.

OTHER CELEBRATIONS

Other can't-miss events during the winter months include the annual staging of Dickens' *A Christmas Carol* at the Guthrie

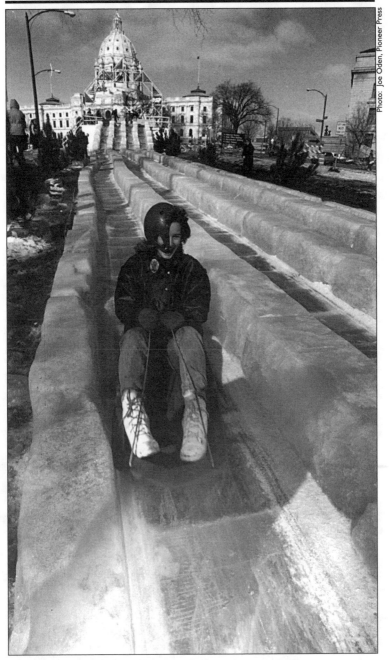

Photo: Joe Oden, Pioneer Press

A giant ice slide at the St. Paul Winter Carnival.

Theater, plus several other holiday productions by local troupes; an exhibit, "Christmas in the Period Rooms," at the Minneapolis Institute of Arts; a holiday bazaar at the Landmark Center in St. Paul; the American Swedish Institute's St. Lucia Day celebration; and the Minnesota Zoo's annual Tropical Beach Party in February, not to mention several local observances of Black History Month (February).

Inside Escapes

It's mid-January. Outside, the snowbanks are dirty, the sky is gray and your discarded Christmas tree sits forlornly on the curbside waiting for the garbage truck.

Inside your home sweet home, you're surrounded by cranky, sniffling loved ones, a droning TV set and petrified fruitcake. You're so restless you could climb the walls. It's a classic case of the wintertime blues. Even the hardiest Minnesotan eventually catches this malady sometime during our long, long winter. Short of a charter to Cancun, what's a Minnesotan to do?

Here are a few great Twin Cities "escape" destinations to help cool that cabin fever.

• **The Minneapolis and St. Paul skyway systems.** You can escape the elements and stroll forever in these glass-enclosed, above-street walkways without retracing your steps. Go to lunch, take in a movie, browse in the shops or just indulge in some fantastic people-watching. In Minneapolis, stop by the Crystal Court and check out Mary Tyler Moore's famous lunch spot and do some power-shopping at the Conservatory or Gaviidae Common. In St. Paul, head for Town Square Park and take in the greenery and fountains (see the Getting Around chapter for more information on skyway routes).

• **The Mall of America.** Go for shopping, lunch and a visit to Camp Snoopy, the fantastic indoor amusement park. The megamall also has 14 movie theaters, a walk-through aquarium and a miniature golf course, not to mention one-of-a-kind shops.

• **Museums.** Now's the time to absorb some of the great culture in the Twin Cities. Visit the always provocative Walker Art Center, check out the sunsplashed landscapes of Van Gogh and Gauguin at the Minneapolis Institute of Arts or drop by the stunning Weisman Art Museum. In St. Paul, let the kids run out their ya-yas at the Children's Museum or the Science Museum. Nearby are the new Minnesota History Center and the Minnesota Museum of American Art.

• **Indoor parks.** Edinborough Park in Edina is a lush indoor refuge with vegetation, playgrounds, a picnic area, a swimming pool and an indoor skating rink. Or take a plunge at the great city-owned indoor water parks in Chaska, Shoreview and Maplewood.

• **Tropical restaurants.** Take a gastronomic vacation to the southern climes. Try the Pickled Parrot, Dixie's and Chez Bananas for some Southern and/or tropical fare or any of a number of Indian, Ethiopian or Southeast Asian eateries.

• **Casinos.** It may be cold outside, but the action's hot inside these Las Vegas-style gaming emporiums featuring blackjack, slots, bingo, food and entertainment. Within a few hours' drive of the Twin Cities are Mystic Lake Casino in Prior Lake, Treasure Island Casino near Red Wing and Grand Casino at Hinckley.

• **Minnesota Zoo.** Head for the zoo's Tropics Trail, an indoor oasis of lush

Photo: Chris Polydoroff, Pioneer Press

These citizens give a stuck fellow motorist a helping hand.

greenery, colorful birds, gibbons and other tropical animals. Don't miss the coral reef exhibit of sharks and brilliantly colored tropical fish.

• **Como Park Conservatory**. Escape the frozen north in this lovely showcase of tropical plants and flowers.

•**Hotel getaways**. Many Minnesota families take weekend minivacations in lo-cal resort hotels, where they soak in the pool or hot tub to recharge their batteries.

If all else fails, take heart. Coming just around the corner in late winter are the annual boat and vacation, camping and RV shows at the Minneapolis Convention Center. Featuring the latest models of rec-reational equipment, they bring a splash of summer into the darkest winter.

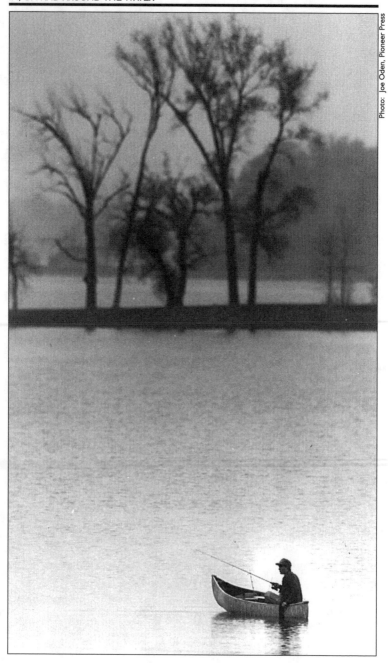

Photo: Joe Oden, Pioneer Press

Fishing in Chicago Lake.

Inside
In, On and Around the Water

Ever wonder why people in the Twin Cities love their water so much? The answer is simple: If you can see water flowing, lapping, dripping, falling or simply accumulating in a pool, that means it's warm enough *not* to be winter. And for most folks, that's real good news.

It is lucky, then, that we're blessed with so many lakes, rivers, creeks and ponds, not to mention the abundant opportunities for fishing, boating and swimming that go with them. All told, Minnesota has 6,564 rivers and streams totalling 92,000 linear miles and 11,842 lakes with more than 10 acres each of surface area adding up to 4,967,510 acres of lake water. The state also has one boat for every six residents — more than for any other state — and 2.3 million people who like to go fishing. Obviously, counting all the lures, oars, life jackets and flippers would be an impossible task.

A newcomer might assume that all this water activity must take place in northern and central Minnesota, where most of the lakes lie. Not so! Dozens of large lakes dot the Twin Cities metropolitan area, and we have creeks, marinas and the mighty Mississippi and Minnesota rivers as well. Not too far to the east, straddling the Wisconsin border, flows the St. Croix River, one of the Mississippi's major tributaries.

Visitors often express surprise at all the lakes in Minneapolis, whose name, after all, is an Indian-Greek hybrid meaning "city of water." Minneapolis even has its own annual festival devoted to water, Aquatennial (see our Annual Events chapter). Amazingly, nearly 7 percent — 2,324 acres — of Minneapolis' total area is water. St. Paul has its lakes as well, and, together with Minneapolis, forms the northernmost major metropolis on the Mississippi River.

So there's no excuse for remaining a landlubber. Dip your toe into the water activities of the Twin Cities, and you'll soak up plenty of fun and exercise, along with an enhanced appreciation for the element that, more than any other, makes this urban area physically distinctive.

Boating

It must be human nature: Where there's water, there's someone who wants to travel on it. Minnesota, it sometimes seems, has almost as many boats as people. A Twin

The name Minnesota is a combination of Native American words meaning "sky-tinted water."

Insiders' Tips

Cities boat census would include sailboats, canoes, kayaks, motorboats of all sizes, dinghies, inflatable rafts, houseboats, floating restaurants, tugs, barges and sternwheelers. You can buy them, rent them, borrow them or build them. Most boats are not exactly status symbols, but they do identify their owners as members of the water/fishing/outdoorsy urban culture.

Canoeists can have a great time in the Twin Cities. In addition to all kinds of opportunities on area lakes, they can take advantage of 57 miles of scenic canoeing on the Mississippi River, between Anoka and Hastings. From the canoe's unique vantage point in the river, you can see dramatic wooded bluffs, wildlife, water traffic and a side of the Twin Cities normally not viewed. You do, though, need to deal with river locks in Minneapolis and farther south, but usually even novice canoeists can handle them. Other popular canoeing rivers are the Crow River west of the Twin Cities, the St. Croix River to the east, and the Cannon River to the south.

All canoes need to be licensed. In the Twin Cities, you can rent canoes from **Ketter Canoeing**, 560-3840; **Midwest Mountaineering**, 339-3433; or at several area lakes. For general information on canoeing in Minnesota, contact the Minnesota Department of Natural Resources, 296-6157.

Users of sailboats and windsurfers abound. The area is lucky to have several lakes that provide public landings for sailboats. Lake Calhoun in Minneapolis appears to be the center of windsurfing activity in the Twin Cities.

Boat enthusiasts who want someone else to do the piloting should check out some of the many boat excursion businesses whose crafts ply the Twin Cities' waters. Most of the firms are in operation

Memorial Day through Labor Day. Here are a few of them.

ANSON NORTHRUP RIVERBOATS
Boom Island Park, Minneapolis   227-1100

This company offers Mississippi River cruises in Minneapolis aboard the *Anson Northrup* or the *Betsy Northrup*. Cruise highlights include views of the Falls of St. Anthony, the Stone Arch Bridge and downtown and a trip through the river's upper lock. Meals are served in some cases.

CREATIVE RIVER TOURS
Shakopee   445-7491

This firm's excursion boat, the *Emma Lee*, gives history and wildlife tours of the Minnesota River.

EXCELSIOR PARK CHARTERS
701 Minnetonka Blvd.
Excelsior   474-4772

Lake Minnetonka is the cruising territory of the Excelsior Park, which offers Sunday and holiday brunch trips, as well as scenic and historic excursions to such spots as Big Island.

PADELFORD PACKET BOAT COMPANY
Harriet Island, St. Paul   227-1100

Two of the Twin Cities' best-known cruisers, the *Jonathan Padelford* and the *Josiah Snelling*, churn water on the section of the Mississippi between St. Paul and Fort Snelling. During the past 25 years, more than 3 million people — about 150,000 a year— have cruised the river on these boats.

QUEEN OF EXCELSIOR
10 Water St., Excelsior   474-2502

From May through September, the *Queen of Excelsior* offers brunch, dinner and cocktail cruises that explore Lake Minnetonka's coves, islands and bays.

Fishing in City Lakes

Currently swimming in city lakes:

Photo: Buzz Magnuson, Pioneer Press

- **Walleye.** The state fish, walleye, is prized for its flaky, white fillets.
- **Northern Pike.** This fish is distinguished by its light markings on a dark green background.
- **Muskie.** A cousin of the northern pike, the muskie is revered as one of the state's great game fish.
- **Largemouth Bass.** Rising in popularity with local anglers, largemouth bass are dark green on top with a cream belly and a dark side stripe.
- **Crappie.** Minnesota's mainstay offers fine sport and fine eating.
- **Bluegill.** The brightly colored bluegill is the most popular sunfish and provides easy fishing for any age.
- **Bullheads.** These come in three varieties, are easy to catch and inhabit lakes, creeks and ponds.

A young angler tries Lake Owasso in Shoreview.

Fishing

From the shore, in a boat, on a bridge or off a dock, fishing in the Twin Cities is good. The fish are generally plentiful, can sometimes tip the scales (anglers have pulled record-big crappies, sunfish, bass and catfish out of Twin Cities lakes and rivers) and include such prized gamefish as northern pike, walleye and trout. And for city fish, these are reasonably clean critters. However, women who are or plan to become pregnant, nursing mothers and children should be especially careful not to eat fish that are high in contaminants. Call the Minnesota Department of Health at 627-5146 for a booklet of advisories and updates about eating fish.

Step one in going fishing in the Twin Cities, if you're 16 or older, is to get a Minnesota fishing license, available at bait shops, sporting goods stores and county license offices all over town. Special licenses are available for nonresidents, seniors and trout anglers.

The next step is to know the seasons for different fish species and the limits on your catch, both set by the Minnesota Department of Natural Resources, 772-7950. In addition to these restrictions, municipalities and individual lakes may have their own rules on what fish you can catch, how you catch them and what kind of boat you can use. Regulations are usually posted at public landings or near public docks. If you're fishing from a boat (rental boats are available at most of the larger lakes), you must wear a life jacket.

Fishing, of course, is a great kids' activity, and the Department of Natural Resources annually stocks 24 Twin Cities area ponds with crappie, bluegill and other species ideal for younger anglers. For a tape-recorded update on this kids' fishing program, call 296-9131. Children younger than 16 do not need a license to fish.

Several books give the ins and outs of fishing in the Twin Cities, some complete with lake charts giving depths and favorite biting grounds for different species. One of the most popular and readable is Ron Schara's *Twin Cities Fishing Guide*, available at many area bookstores.

Lakes

More than just places to swim, boat or fish, the Twin Cities lakes, in many cases, are recreational focal points, offering opportunities to skate or bike along their shorelines on dedicated bikeways, stroll on pedestrian pathways or simply hang out and get an eyeful of the passing fauna. (In addition to humans, you can admire the dogs, part-wolves, cats, ferrets, potbellied pigs, gerbils and lizards they take on their walks for company.) Some of our urban lakes are for dedicated anglers, some attract yuppies and their families, some lure bathers and others bring out the boats. There's a lake in the Twin Cities for every personality, activity and persuasion.

BROWNIE LAKE
Cedar Lake Pkwy., Minneapolis
Brownie, at the head of Minneapolis'

chain of lakes, is a little piece of water, just 18 acres, situated at Cedar Lake Parkway south of U.S. 394. The anglers who visit it find crappies and bluegills aplenty.

CEDAR LAKE
Minneapolis
Less visible from main roads than many of Minneapolis' other lakes, Cedar Lake, south of U.S. 394 along Cedar Lake Parkway, is snuggled on the west end of the city, near the border with St. Louis Park. On its 168 acres of weedy and lily-padded water, you can canoe (and also take in Lake of the Isles via a canal; call 348-5364 for rental information); swim at lifeguard-staffed beaches at Southeast Point and Cedar Point; and take a dip at an unguarded area on the northeast shore that has long served as an unofficial (and technically illegal) nude beach. The area surrounding the lake also has numerous trails. Cedar Lake is the only Minneapolis lake with private access to some of its 2.9 miles of shoreline, so don't trespass.

On the lake's north shore are rare remnants of the prairie that once covered much of the Twin Cities. The red cedar evergreens for which the lake is named can still be seen on the west side.

For anglers, Cedar offers bass, muskie and northern pike, along with the smaller bluegill and crappie that live in most of the city's other lakes. Like lakes Harriet, Calhoun and Nokomis, it has a public fishing dock.

Insiders' Tips

The official state fish is the walleye, which gained that status by a legislative vote of 128-1 in 1965.

Photo: Joe Rossi, Pioneer Press

Sails catch the breeze on a sultry July morning as sailboats participate in a regatta on White Bear Lake.

COMO LAKE

St. Paul

This lake in St. Paul's delightful Como Park holds a peculiar distinction in Minnesota's angling history. In 1882 it became one of the first lakes in the state in which carp (*Cyprinus carpio*) swam. With the mistaken idea that people would line up to catch and eat the imported Asian fish, the Minnesota Fish Commission stocked Como Lake with the big fat minnows and waited to see what would happen. What has happened, of course, is that carp have joined suckers, dogfish, buffalofish and other unsavory, nongame species in the "rough fish" category and have spread throughout much of the state.

In addition to carp, Como's waters have crappies and bluegills, and many fishers take advantage of the public fishing dock to catch them.

Another popular activity at the lake is renting a foot-operated paddleboat for a spin in the sun.

DIAMOND LAKE

Minneapolis

This small wetland lake in a south Minneapolis residential neighborhood near the southern border of Minneapolis attracts waterfowl and other wildlife. On the lake's east shore is a walking path that, if you're lucky, can allow you a view of the wild birds.

LAKE CALHOUN

Minneapolis

Calhoun, at 518 acres the largest of Minneapolis' lakes, is one of the city's best places to go for sailing, windsurfing, fishing, swimming and strolling. In its waters idle bass, northern pike, and crappie, and at its shore idles a fairly young crowd of sun-worshipers, wind surfers, walkers and swimmers. Its location near the busy Uptown district and in a heavily residential area attracts plenty of people and keeps them there. Its waters are by no means ignored during the winter; you'll undoubtedly spot ice-fishing houses during the chilly season.

Named after U.S. Vice President John Calhoun, who was instrumental in the establishment of Fort Snelling, the lake long served as home ground for Dakota Indians and was once surrounded by deer-filled woods. In 1834 the city's first dwelling built by whites was a cabin that the Pond brothers raised on its shores.

Nowadays, a walk around the lake is 3.4 miles. Your stroll will take you past a food concession stand (we recommend the buttered popcorn), a canoe rental area and the canal leading to Lake of the Isles, all on the north end. At times of peak use, driving around the lake can be an arduous process. You'll find parking lots on the north and south ends.

LAKE HARRIET
Minneapolis

Who was Harriet, anyway? Her full name was Harriet Lovejoy Leavenworth, and she was the wife of a U.S. Army colonel at the time the region was surveyed.

Lake Harriet lies near the chain formed by Cedar Lake, Lake of the Isles and Lake Calhoun in southwest Minneapolis, but it is not connected to the other lakes. Covering 337 acres and reaching a depth of up to 70 feet, it bears muskie, crappie and the occasional largemouth bass. Even better, it is a rare urban source of walleye, the Minnesota state fish and a highly sought-after main course. The public-access boat landing is at the lake's northwestern corner, just off William Berry Drive and W. Lake Harriet Parkway.

Perhaps the visual highlight of the shoreline is the Lake Harriet Bandshell, near W. 42nd Street, a splendid venue for outdoor concerts that take place throughout the summer. It's the fifth bandshell to stand on that site since 1888. Nearby are restrooms, a refreshment stand and the dock used by the sternwheeler *Queen of the Lakes*, which plies the Lake Harriet waters for paying passengers. Another stone's throw away, along Queen Avenue S., is the boarding area of the Harriet-Como Streetcar (see Attractions) and a hand-operated water

pump providing liquid refreshment that many people swear by.

Lake Harriet is undeniably pretty, the haunt of families with kids and older walkers. It carries a tamed beauty, however, and the only whiff of wilderness here is at the magical grounds of the Thomas Sadler Roberts Bird Sanctuary, just to the north. Here, with a sharp eye, you can see wild birds and forget that you're right in the middle of a city. Adjacent to the bird sanctuary is the Lyndale Park Rose and Rock Gardens (see the Recreation and Parks chapter).

LAKE MINNETONKA
Minnetonka, Wayzata, Orono, Deephaven, Excelsior, Shorewood and Mound

If you claim to know Lake Minnetonka like the back of your hand, you're either a liar, a real old-timer or a fishing fanatic. It is huge, easily the largest lake in the metropolitan area, with more than 100 miles of shoreline and covering 14,528 acres. Much of the water laps in chains of cozy bays.

Like most of the bodies of water in the Twin Cities, Lake Minnetonka has many identities. To anglers, it offers a compendium, of sorts, of virtually every kind of fish available in the area: walleye, northern pike, largemouth bass and different varieties of panfish. Boaters appreciate it as a lake where they can sail or motor in a straight line for a goodly distance, provided nobody else is in the way (Lake Minnetonka's waters can get quite congested at peak times). Others like to view the water from the vantage point of a cafe window or, even better, their own picture window.

Back when Lake Minnetonka was still well beyond the boundaries of the metropolitan area, it had yet another identity: summer resort. For most of the 19th century, the lake was the playground of the wealthy, many of them visitors from the southern states, who stayed in lavish shoreline hotels. One of the most famous of the ritzy hostelries was the Hotel Lafayette, constructed by railroad magnate James J. Hill in 1882 on a hill between Crystal and Holmes bays. The 300-room hotel rose in only 100 days, gobbling up 3 million feet of lumber, three carloads of nails and nearly a mile of shingles. Its visitors included U.S. presidents Ulysses Grant and Chester Arthur. The Lafayette burned to the ground in 1897 despite the efforts of the Minneapolis Fire Department, which made a then-record 50-minute run to Lake Minnetonka to battle the blaze.

After the turn of the century, year-round lake living became more common, and folks of more modest means began to frequent the lake. Streetcars carried in people from Minneapolis and St. Paul, sternwheelers plied the waters with more than 1,000 passengers each, and several amusement parks offered roller coasters and other thrills. Popular songs such as "By the Waters of Minnetonka" and "Land of the Sky Blue Water" praised the lake.

Today boating remains one of Lake Minnetonka's biggest attractions. Nine public boat landings are scattered among the bays, and several area businesses rent boats to the public.

LAKE NOKOMIS
Minneapolis

Removed from the other lakes in Minneapolis, Nokomis has its own nontrendy, slower-paced atmosphere. Its shores are a popular picnic choice, and its 2.7 miles of paths for biking, skating or walking do get their share of users. Its waters are a reliable source of panfish, or you can eat at the public concessions stand if you'd prefer to let someone else catch your food.

Lake Nokomis, along with lakes Harriet and Calhoun in Minneapolis, offers sailing opportunities almost unheard of in other large cities. The lake has public-use sailboat buoys and launches, along with frequent sailboat races. Restrooms are available, and parking is usually no problem.

LAKE OF THE ISLES
Minneapolis

Lake of the Isles, in the heart of Kenwood, is far busier at its edges than on the water. On summer days and weekends, it boasts one of the area's most trodden strips of asphalt along the shoreline, and an outer path whizzes with bikers and in-line skaters. Eavesdroppers can hear deep discussions about relationships, the birthing of business deals, astute restaurant reviews and even an occasional marriage proposal. One circumnavigation is about 3 miles.

Due to the lake's shallows (Isles was originally a marsh; the city transformed it into a lake by dredging it at the turn of the century, and the deepest point is only 31 feet), canoers rarely stray beyond the southern end, and the lake has no access for larger boats. During the winter, one of the northern arms becomes a popular skating rink. Two islands, both designated as wildlife refuges, do not welcome people.

The area definitely has no shortage of wildlife. Sharp eyes can spot black-crowned night herons and great egrets. Canada geese and ducks are notoriously numerous spring through fall, and their presence sometimes transforms the walking path into a guano-streaked obstacle course. The lake also harbors bass and northern pike. Several years ago, high water filled offshore depressions with carp of legendary proportions.

Canals connect Lake of the Isles with Lake Calhoun and Cedar Lake. Its total area is 109 acres.

LAKE PHALEN
St. Paul

Covering 198 acres in St. Paul's northeast corner, Lake Phalen is one of the Twin Cities' most dependable sources of walleye, bass and northern pike. You have access to walking and biking paths, rental canoes (call 774-9759) and ample sites for picnics and play.

LORING LAKE
Minneapolis

The geese, ducks and carp have the run of this little man-made pond, which covers only seven acres and surrounds a very small island. The fishing is poor, and the shallows preclude any boating. However, it's a prominent feature of downtown Minneapolis' Loring Park.

MEDICINE LAKE
Plymouth

Medicine Lake is a medium-size body of water (885 acres) planted smack dab in the middle of Hennepin County, north of Minn. 55 and east of County Road 61. The angling here is considered very good, even during the winter, and the most common catches are largemouth bass, northern pike and various panfish. A public fishing dock and a public boat landing are at the north end, which is also the site of French Regional Park (see the Recreation and Parks chapter).

POWDERHORN LAKE
Minneapolis

Powderhorn Lake is the jewel of Powderhorn Park in south Minneapolis.

It's really not much more than a wedge-shaped pond, but people (mostly kids) do fish there and catch the bluegills and crappies with which it is stocked.

WHITE BEAR LAKE
Dellwood, Mahtomedi and city of White Bear Lake

A Native American legend tells of a magnificent white bear slain by an Indian brave just as it was about to attack a family near the lake. From that point on, the story relates, the spirit of the bear has haunted the place. Nowadays, the lake is haunted by anglers, recreational walkers and thrill-seeking in-line skaters.

This is one of the larger lakes in the Twin Cities, with 2,416 acres of unusually clear water. A Ramsey County beach offers a good spot for swimming, and paths for walkers, bikers and skaters line the west end. Boaters use two public-access landings on the northwest side. Boat rental is available from Nelson Marine, 429-4388.

Anglers like White Bear Lake for its walleyes, smallmouth and largemouth bass, muskies, northern pike and panfish.

Manitou Island, which is quite large, was known as Spirit Island in the old days and provided an annual bounty of maple syrup to Native Americans.

Rivers and Creeks

Minnehaha Creek

Passing through many Hennepin County communities, Minnehaha Creek runs 22 miles from Lake Minnetonka to the Mississippi River. It never gets very wide, allowing kids to wade in it and ride its surface in inner tubes for much of its length.

Not long before it reaches the Mississippi in Minneapolis, the creek makes a dramatic 40-foot drop at **Minnehaha Falls**, which has always drawn all kinds of visitors. The 19th-century Bohemian composer Antonin Dvorak paid a visit there, and Henry Wadsworth Longfellow's famous poem "Song of Hiawatha" pays tribute to the falls, although he never set foot there.

Visitors to Minnehaha Falls can get drastically different views, depending on the season and state of drought. But regardless of whether the water is dropping at a trickle or in a torrent, the falls is one of the most charming spots in the Twin Cities.

Mississippi River

It all begins more than 200 miles north of the Twin Cities at Lake Itasca, where the trickling source of one of the world's great rivers eluded European searchers for more than a century. Now, at the Mississippi headwaters in Itasca State Park, you can pick your way across the water on stones rubbed smooth by the soles of countless other visitors who wanted to walk across Old Man River.

By the time the Mississippi rolls into the Twin Cities area as part of its 2,552-mile journey to the Gulf of Mexico, it's already a great big highway of water. In years past, people in this region tapped that force to move forests of logs, power mills that for many years made Minneapolis the world's largest flour producer and turn the turbine of the Western Hemisphere's first hydroelectric power generator. The Mississippi River is the main reason both Minneapolis and St. Paul exist at all, and it is a bit puzzling that both cities in the past turned their backs on the river.

Nowadays, however, the river is a focus of attention in the Twin Cities. In downtown Minneapolis, where the **Mississippi River Regional Park** stretches for 150 acres, a project to create bikeways and walking paths along the river, connected to the trails of other city parks, has reached completion. For a few years now, one of the most wondrous spots in the city has been the area along the west bank of the river just north of the Hennepin Avenue bridge, a place heavy with past significance and contemporary beauty. It was here that the first bridge across the Mississippi was erected; it has since had two successors. It's here that you can see runners, bikers and walkers passing at a steady clip on the trails, as President Bill Clinton did on a recent jog. And it's here that you can look across the river at Nicollet Island, downriver at the Falls of St. Anthony and, with some neck craning, farther downriver at the historic Stone Arch Bridge. No one knows what things will look like when the Federal Reserve Bank, which forced its way onto this historic real estate at the old bridgehead and leveled several important old buildings in the process, raises its new facility, in which checks will be processed.

In Minneapolis, the Mississippi River is just as important for what has floated down it as for what is permanently fixed in its course. **Nicollet Island**, a residential and commercial hybrid community that falls under the shadow of the Hennepin Avenue Bridge, is one of those oft-fantasized areas right in the middle of things that seems way out of things. First settled in the mid-1800s, the northern half still boasts 19th-century rowhouses, duplexes and single-family dwellings that are among Minneapolis' oldest and most architecturally interesting. The homes are arranged along narrow streets that suggest a small town, and an old one at that. Until a few years ago, a donkey grazed this piece of land within view of the downtown skyscrapers. In the center of

Nicollet Island are a few businesses and De La Salle High School. At the south end is the lovely **Nicollet Island Inn** for dining and sleeping, in addition to an amphitheater that hosts frequent summer concerts and plays, a deck allowing a splendid view of downtown, and the William Brothers Boiler Works building, now a public pavilion.

Downriver from Nicollet Island is the site of the **Falls of St. Anthony**, the only falls anywhere on the Mississippi. What we see now — a concrete apron supporting a modest rush of water — is just a shadow of what this waterfall used to be. For 200 years it was the region's best-known physical feature, a natural marvel that early European explorers compared favorably against Niagara Falls and that inspired countless paintings, drawings and poems. At the end of the 19th century, though, the development of log and flour mills along the river, along with poorly planned efforts to divert Mississippi water to power them, had reached a feverish pitch, eventually causing a nearly catastrophic fracture of the river's channel that threatened to flood everything. The river obviously had to be tamed, and the falls were mastered in the process.

Also subdued was **Spirit Island**, a small, rocky outpost below the falls and practically in its froth. A Dakota legend held that a woman paddled over the falls with her children when her husband introduced a second wife into the household and that her spirit haunted the island. Starting at the end of the 1800s, Spirit Island shrank with each mining of gravel from its shores, and an effort to make the river more navigable in the early 1960s finally did it in.

From downtown Minneapolis, the Mississippi flows under the historic **Stone Arch Bridge** (see our Architecture and Historic Sites chapter), past the sites of the old flour mills on both banks and between the halves of the **University of Minnesota's** Minneapolis campus, spanned by the **Washington Avenue Bridge**, from which poet John Berryman jumped to take his own life. One more bridge crosses it at Franklin Avenue and another at Lake Street. Near this stretch is the **Great River Road**, a system of walking trails, bike paths and scenic overlooks. At this point the river glides along residential St. Paul on its eastern bank.

On the way to downtown St. Paul, it passes **Fort Snelling** at a confluence with the Minnesota River. A sojourner through much of the southern part of the state, the Minnesota is the main waterway of that region. Most Twin Citians see little of this river except at crossings, which is too bad. Running for 34 miles along its banks from Fort Snelling to Jordan is the **Minnesota Valley National Wildlife Refuge**, an 8,000-acre oasis for wildlife in the heart of the metropolitan area. Several trails in the refuge offer great birdwatching and the chance to escape from the pressures of the city; one of the trails is accessible to people with disabilities. The Refuge also hosts wildlife programs and exhibits; call 854-5900.

When it nears downtown St. Paul, the Mississippi bends, actually running northeast for a while and causing some directional confusion. West St. Paul is actually south of St. Paul, but it is so named because it lies on the former west side of the river. Here the channel is wider and deeper, allowing the passage of barges gliding low in the water, seemingly without end. **Swede Hollow**, a St. Paul riverfront neighborhood that housed waves of Scandinavian, Italian, Jewish, Hispanic and other immigrants for nearly 100 years, was regularly flooded by the

Mississippi until its residents vacated for good in the 1960s.

Many people fish the Mississippi (as well as the Minnesota River) in all manners possible, and they catch catfish, muskies, walleyes — you name it. Carp aficionados should head straight to part of the river near **Coon Rapids Dam** (upriver of Minneapolis); this area has such a good reputation for carp angling that the dam is the site of an annual carp festival each June.

River fish should not be eaten without first consulting the fish advisories of the Minnesota Department of Natural Resources. The Mississippi, after all, has always been the Twin Cities' main liquid dump. It's lovely in spots, historic and dignified, but nobody would call Old Muddy Waters pristine.

Photo: Pioneer Press

The Minnesota Twins won both the 1987 and 1991 World Series.

Inside
Spectator Sports

When it comes to spectator sports, the Twin Cities has been a big-league town far longer than most people realize. In 1884 St. Paul fielded a team in the Union Association, one of that era's major baseball leagues, although a financially unstable one. The local nine went on to lose six of eight games before ignobly disbanding. That brief existence still stands as the record for the shortest life of any American major-league baseball team.

Though it wasn't a success, the St. Paul baseball team at least got out the gate and paved the way for a long procession of professional teams that would follow. Right now the Twin Cities is the home of major-league teams in baseball, basketball and football, with some local minor-league activity in other sports, along with a wealth of intercollegiate and high school competition. To contain all the flying balls and whizzing pucks, the area has a good assortment of stadiums and arenas, most of them recently built.

You can judge sports teams not only by their win-loss records, but also by the amount of entertainment and civic pride they generate. We've had World Series championships, Super Bowl appearances (no victories yet), All Star games on the

home fields and great players who have become important members of the community — Kirby Puckett immediately comes to mind. And don't forget the recently concluded drama of who would own the Minnesota Timberwolves and where that team was going to play in the future. That was rich entertainment in itself, and nobody knew how it would play out until the final seconds.

The phone numbers listed for all sports teams will connect you with ticket sales and information.

Professional Sports

Baseball

MINNESOTA TWINS
338-9467

Until recently, the players of the Minnesota Twins wore little "TCs" on their caps, now supplanted by an "M" that is undoubtedly easier for the opposing team's fans to figure out. The Twins arrived here in 1961 from out East, where they were once known as the Washington Senators. They started out playing in Metropolitan Stadium in Bloomington, a classic open-air field built five years ear-

LeRoy Neiman, creator of internationally famous sports paintings, is a native of St. Paul.

Out of the Race

Besides the big three — the Twins, Vikings and Timberwolves — the Twin Cities have been hometown to a handful of other professional clubs. They've since folded or moved, but do you remember them?

Minneapolis Bruins (ice hockey)
Minneapolis Lakers (basketball)
Minneapolis Millerettes (women's baseball)
Minnesota Fighting Saints (ice hockey)
Minnesota Fillies (women's basketball)
Minnesota Kicks (soccer)
Minnesota Muskies (basketball)
Minnesota North Stars (ice hockey)
Minnesota Pipers (basketball)
Minnesota Strikers (soccer)

lier precisely to attract a big-league team. The Twins had many good seasons at Met Stadium, winning an American League championship in 1965 and division championships in 1969 and 1970. Some of their best players during these years were Harmon Killebrew, Tony Oliva, Rod Carew, Jim Kaat, Jim Perry, Dean Chance, Zoilo Versailles and Earl Battey.

In 1982 the Hubert H. Humphrey Metrodome opened at the edge of downtown Minneapolis. The Twins moved to this new home field and old Met Stadium — along with its 4,300 tons of steel, 2.1 million bricks, 9 miles of pipe rails, 71 turnstiles, 460 doors, 5,200 light fixtures and more than 40,000 seats — fell to the bulldozers. The site is now occupied by the Mall of America, and a marker shows the old location of home plate on the floor of the shopping and entertainment complex.

Some losing years followed for the Twins, and it took the team several seasons to adjust to these new surroundings. In 1987, however, the team won the World Series, an effort duplicated in 1991.

Since the move to the Metrodome, some of the team's most outstanding players have been Kirby Puckett, Kent Hrbek, Frank Viola, Gary Gaetti, Greg Gagne, Jack Morris, Brian Harper, Jeff Reardon, Chuck Knoblauch and Rick Aguilera.

Unless you're undyingly attached to sunlight, the Metrodome is a good place to watch a baseball game. Most of the lower-deck seats surrounding the infield go to season-ticket holders, however. For occasional attendees, that means some of the best seats are on the lower deck, running from first and third bases to the outfield. For the thrill of sitting next to the more expensive season-ticket sections, order early to get sections 118 or 132. If you're more economically minded and like the view from left field, try the lower left-field bleachers. Upper-deck seats behind home plate (sections 222 through 226) are a good deal and offer an excellent view of the action. The upper-deck outfield seats are cheap, but they place you far away (sometimes pitched and batted balls are invisible), and at the Dome you don't have the benefit of catching rays.

A stadium-wide bonus for some fans and a drawback for others is one hard and fast rule, expressed with gusto at the start of each game by the Metrodome's announcer: "There is noooooooooooo smoking in the Metrodome! No smoking!"

Of the food at the Metrodome, the less said, the better. (If it does to the inside of you what it does to the bottom of your shoe, that's genuine cause for alarm.) But, hey, they've started serving espresso and gourmet coffees, so who needs to eat anyway?

Many independently operated parking lots scattered throughout the area serve Dome fans. Street parking is also available, but most of the nearby meters are in force until 10 PM. If you're willing to make a 10-minute walk, you might be able to find free on-street parking in downtown Minneapolis.

Purchase tickets by phone, mail or in person at the Metrodome, which is at the downtown Minneapolis intersection of Chicago Avenue S. and S. Fifth Street (just look for the white hump).

St. Paul Saints
644-6659

In 1993 outdoor professional baseball made a big comeback in the Twin Cities with the arrival of the St. Paul Saints, competitors in the independent Northern League. (Other teams in the league represent Sioux Falls, Thunder Bay, Sioux City, Winnipeg and Duluth-Superior.) With a roster made up of major-league wannabes, couldbes and never-willbes, the Saints from the start displayed plenty of marketing savvy and the kind of on-the-field irreverence that made fans happy. For instance, a young pig, Saint III, the team's mascot, delivers balls to the umpire, and a nun is sometimes on

hand in the stands to give massages during the game. Need an in-stadium haircut? A Saints barber is ready to serve you. The Saints have also sponsored a baseball film festival, Wizard of Oz Night and several tributes to the Negro League.

The team's home field, the 6,305-seat Midway Stadium in St. Paul, at 1771 Energy Park Drive, just off N. Snelling Avenue, is unabashedly nostalgic. Part of the zaniness of this team's on-the-field antics could be because movie star Bill Murray is one of the owners (another is Mike Veeck, son of the former White Sox owner Bill Veeck).

Football

Minnesota Vikings
333-8828

The same year the Twins started up in business in the Twin Cities, the Minnesota Vikings also came to town. Wearing their distinctive purple, white and gold uniforms, along with those horned helmets, the Vikings quickly won a dedicated following. During their time at Metropolitan Stadium in Bloomington, they posted several remarkable seasons — particularly the golden years of 1969 through '77 — going four times to the Super Bowl. For some Twin Citians, that quartet of appearances on Super Sunday, all losses, evokes deep humiliation and frustration, but the fans of few other teams received as many football thrills during those years as did Vikings followers.

The Vikes moved out of the Met in favor of the Metrodome in 1982, with mixed results in the new stadium. The 1984 season under the coaching of Les Steckel was a notable low point (3-13), but in recent years the team has reached the playoffs with some consistency. Many great players have filled the Vikings roster over the years, including Alan Page (now a Minnesota Supreme Court justice), Carl Eller, Fran Tarkenton, Chris Doleman, Keith Millard, Ahmad Rashad, Anthony Carter, Matt Blair, Chuck Foreman and Sammy White.

As configured for football, the Metrodome's seating is dominated by season-ticket holders. Often they take up virtually the entire 30,000-seat lower deck. Although many people think the best seats for football are those closest to the 50-yard line, the seats near the end zones and the corners of the field will spare you much cranking of the head. In fact, the seats that are physically closest to the field are behind the end zones in the first rows of lower-deck sections 100, 101, 117, 118 and 141. On the other hand, plenty of fans prefer the panoramic view afforded by upper-deck seats.

Basketball

MINNESOTA TIMBERWOLVES
337-3865

Although the Minnesota Timberwolves have made plenty of headlines the past couple of years, this attention has nothing to do with the team's dismal efforts on the court. Instead, everyone was clamoring about the attempts of former team owners Marvin Wolfenson and Harvey Ratner (universally referred to as "MarvandHarv") to sell the franchise. During the spring of 1994, they entered into an agreement to sell the Wolves to a group who wanted to move the team to New Orleans, but the NBA blocked the deal. Eventually, Glen Taylor, a former state senator from Mankato, Minnesota, and a wealthy printing mogul, agreed to plunk down $90 million for the team and keep it here for the next 30 years. Kevin McHale, a native of Hibbing, Minnesota, and former Boston Celtic for 13 years, was named vice president of basketball operations.

The Timberwolves, which began as an expansion team in the 1989-90 season, had big shoes to fill. From the late 1940s through the mid-'50s, the Minneapolis Lakers were the dominant team in the NBA. Led by superstar center George Mikan, the Lakers won a string of championships that ended only with the big man's retirement. After several more seasons in small-capacity arenas, the Lakers moved to Los Angeles (thus creating the curiosity of a Lakers team in semi-desert Southern California).

The Wolves, kept going in past seasons by such players as Doug West, Tony Campbell, Pooh Richardson, Randy Breuer, Christian Laettner, Felton Spencer and Thurl Bailey, are still looking for their first winning year after experiencing five consecutive seasons of 60 losses — the most ever by an NBA team. Nobody can fault lack of support from the fans, who crowd the Target Center arena for each home game. In this facility, built for the Wolves at 600 First Avenue N., downtown Minneapolis, seats on the lower level near midcourt are virtually sold out to season-ticket holders, but that

Insiders' Tips

Three players — Harmon Killebrew, Tony Oliva, Kent Hrbek and Rod Carew — have had their numbers retired by the Minnesota Twins.

Hubert H. Humphrey Metrodome in downtown Minneapolis is home to the Minnesota Twins and the Minnesota Vikings.

Photo: Joe Oden, Pioneer Press

still leaves good seats in the corners — sections 109, 113, 129 and 133 — where you can watch without swiveling your head. Seats behind the baskets also can provide exciting views. Up on the second level, however, the behind-the-basket seats are significantly farther from the action than those on the sides, and the side seats opposite the team benches allow you to watch the coaches scream and whine. If you're in a particularly expansive mood, reserve one of the 12-seat suites, running more than $2,000 a game, that come with leather sofas, a private bathroom, a TV, some fleeting prestige and, for a little more money, a well-stocked refrigerator and bar.

Ice Hockey

MINNESOTA MOOSE
26-MOOSE

After the Minnesota North Stars of the National Hockey League abandoned the Twin Cities in favor of Dallas in 1993, Minneapolis-St. Paul was, quite amaz-ingly, without a professional hockey team. But that situation changed in the fall of 1994 when the Minnesota Moose, a new franchise in the 50-year-old International Hockey League, came to town. They play their home games at the St. Paul Civic Center, 143 W. Fourth Street, marking the first time this facility has regularly hosted pro hockey since the old Minnesota Fighting Saints folded midway through the 1977 World Hockey Association season. The Moose have an 81-game season that lasts from late September through mid-April. Their competitors in the IHL's Midwest Division are teams representing Atlanta, Houston, Kansas City and Milwaukee. All told, the IHL has nearly 20 teams.

The Moose are by no means the first Minnesota team to skate into IHL action. Two Twin Cities franchises, the St. Paul Saints and the Minneapolis Millers (adopting the names of the area's minor-league baseball teams), joined the IHL in 1959, and the Saints went on to win the league championship in 1960 and

1961 before both teams went out of business in 1962.

Attendance for the first season of the Minnesota Moose came in at 281,912 with a record of 24 wins and 35 losses.

Rollerblade Hockey

MINNESOTA ARCTIC BLAST
3800 First Bank Pl., Minneapolis   376-PUCK

If the arrival of summer leaves you still longing for hockey action, check out the Arctic Blast, a team that plays on Rollerblades. The Blast compete in a 24-team league of American and Canadian clubs, and games take place at Target Center in Minneapolis. Tickets are available through Ticketmaster, 989-5151, or in person at Target Center's box office.

Another Rollerblade hockey team, Minnesota Blue Ox, plays in Aldrich Arena. Its premiere season was 1995-96.

Soccer

MINNESOTA THUNDER
893-1442

Minnesota's earlier pro soccer clubs, the Kicks and the Strikers, were able to gain a certain measure of popularity, but neither ever put together the astounding win-loss record that the Thunder, a member of the U.S. Interregional Soccer League, has amassed. Since the team began in 1990, it has built a strong tradition of winning, finishing with a perfect 20-0 record in 1994 and perfect 11-0 record at midseason 1995. Goalie John Swaller ranks among the nation's best. Other teams in the league represent such places as Milwaukee, Long Island, Los Angeles, Charleston (South Carolina) and Greensboro, North Carolina. Most home matches are played at the National Sports Center in Blaine (see the Recreation and Parks chapter).

Intercollegiate Sports

Just about every college and university in town fields a varsity team of some kind, and many have very full intercollegiate schedules for men and women. The most closely followed teams, however, are those of the University of Minnesota, whose Golden Gophers compete in the Big Ten conference. The teams' archrivals, of course, are the Wisconsin Badgers and Iowa Buckeyes. To order tickets for men's or women's Gopher events, call the Gopher Ticket Hotline at 624-8080. Here's a roundup of U of M sports.

Men's Athletics

BASEBALL

The Gophers baseball team plays at Siebert Field on the East Bank Minneapolis campus, at Ninth Street S.E. and 15th Avenue S.E., a fine no-beer stadium. The squad has a great winning tradition, with 80 winning seasons over the past 111 years. In 1995 the team came in second in regular season play and second in Big Ten Tournament Competition.

The team has a lot of young talent and should do well in the coming seasons.

BASKETBALL

The basketball team, playing its home games at the recently renovated Williams Arena, at Fourth Street S.E. and 18th Avenue S.E. in Minneapolis, last year advanced to the first round of the NCAA Division I Tournament. It was the sixth time in the past seven years that the dribblers qualified for post-season play. Coach Clem Haskins has been popular and successful.

FOOTBALL

It's been a loooooooong time since the Gophers won the Big Ten and went on to the Rose Bowl — more than 30 years. The last three seasons, in fact, have been losing ones. Part of the problem, some fans would argue, is the team's move several years ago to play its home games at the Metrodome, where the stadium's downtown location and scattered parking have effectively ended the tradition of pre-game tailgating.

ICE HOCKEY

Three-year-old Mariucci Arena, on the East Bank of the Minneapolis campus, at Fourth Street S.E. and 19th Avenue S.E., is the home for the men on ice, who in 1995 became one of the NCAA Final Four for the sixth time in the past 10 years, the only team to make that many appearances. In the NCAA final game against Colorado, Coach Doug Woog gained his 300th win as the University's head hockey coach.

TENNIS

The Gopher Men's tennis team is one of the biggest success stories in U of M athletics. Playing on the courts next to Mariucci Arena, the team recently won its fourth consecutive Big Ten title and has put together a record of 40 consecutive Big Ten victories against conference opponents.

OTHER MEN'S SPORTS

The Gophers also field teams in swimming and diving, track and field/cross country, wrestling, golf and gymnastics. Call the Gopher Ticket Hotline, 624-8080, for more information on these teams.

Women's Athletics

BASKETBALL

Minnesota basketball and women's athletics hosted the 1995 NCAA women's Final Four at Target Center. The Gopher women's basketball team, which plays in the spiffed up Sports Pavilion (old Mariucci Arena), on the East Bank, ended the season with a 12-15 record and 7-9 in the Big Ten. During tournament play the Gophers upset No. 7 Penn State and No. 19 Purdue in consecutive games in what Coach Linda Hill-MacDonald termed the "greatest weekend in the history of Minnesota women's basketball."

SOCCER

In 1994, their second year of intercollegiate soccer play, the Gopher women ran up a 10-6 overall record, playing home games at Bierman Field, on the East Bank Minneapolis campus. 1994 marked the first year in which the Big Ten recognized women's soccer as a conference sport. The Gophers placed 12th and finished the year ranked ninth in the NCAA Central Region, its first top-10 regional ranking in the history of the program.

OTHER WOMEN'S SPORTS

The Gopher women also have teams in cross country, softball, gymnastics, swimming and diving, tennis, track and field, and golf. Call the Gopher Ticket Hotline, 624-8080, for more information.

Photo: Pioneer Press

A fireworks display over the Ice Palace at the Winter Carnival.

Inside
Attractions

There are so many things to do and see in Minneapolis and St. Paul that it's a wonder Twin Citians ever manage to spend a night at home. From history museums to honkytonks, from art galleries to amusement parks, from sculpture gardens to skywatches, Minneapolis and St. Paul have something for everyone.

In this chapter, we describe major attractions that aren't already written about in other chapters. For example, the Twin Cities' vibrant cultural offerings, such as art museums, theaters and concert series, are outlined in The Arts chapter; most historic locales are enumerated in the Historic Sites chapter; sporting events are in the Spectator Sports chapter.

Whatever's left is included here. It's an admittedly eclectic mix. We've also included offbeat — but fascinating — specialty attractions. Enjoy! A note of caution: Although our information on these attractions, including their hours of operation and fees, was current at press time, things can change at a moment's notice.

Tourist Information

It's best to call ahead to confirm details or check in at the following tourist information outlets for any last-minute changes.

MINNESOTA OFFICE OF TOURISM
100 Metro Square, 121 Seventh Pl. E.
St. Paul, Minn. 55101   *296-5029*
                         (800) 657-3700

The friendly folks at this tourism office offer reams of information on every-

thing from art galleries to zoos. Call their travel counselors even before you step on Minnesota soil. They'll happily help customize a trip that fits both your interests and pocketbook, providing lists on hotels, campgrounds and cultural offerings. The tourism office also publishes the *Minnesota Explorer*, a seasonal tabloid highlighting attractions throughout the state.

ST. PAUL CONVENTION
AND VISITORS BUREAU
101 Norwest Center, 55 E. Fifth St.
St. Paul, Minn. 55101   *297-6985*
                         (800) 627-6101

This bureau offers visitor assistance and tourism brochures. Its main office is staffed from 8 AM to 5 PM Monday through Friday. The bureau also operates information centers throughout downtown St. Paul: the World Trade Center, Wabasha and Seventh Place; the Landmark Center, 75 W. Fifth Street; City Hall and Courthouse, 15 W. Kellogg Boulevard; the Science Museum, Wabasha and Exchange Street; and the Minnesota State Capitol, Aurora and Constitution avenues.

GREATER MINNEAPOLIS CONVENTION
AND VISITORS ASSOCIATION
4000 Multifoods Tower, 33 S. Sixth St.
Minneapolis, Minn. 55402   *348-7000*

This tourism association, a source of valuable information on hotels, restaurants and attractions, may be reached at the above address or at its offices on the skyway level of the City Center, 40 S. Seventh Street. Hours at the City Center office are 9:30 AM to 8 PM Monday through Friday, 9:30 AM to 6 PM Saturday and noon to 5 PM Sunday.

Guided Tour Services

A bus tour can provide the first-time visitor with a basic orientation to Minneapolis and Saint Paul, their landmarks, lakes and lore. The following are reliable tour companies.

MEDICINE LAKE LINES/
GRAY LINE TOURS

835 Decatur Ave. N.
Golden Valley   469-5020

This company conducts sightseeing bus tours plus specialty tours to sporting events, shopping areas and the airport from early May through September. Bilingual guides are available. Fees for a four-hour guided tour of the Twin Cities are $18 for adults, $16 for seniors and $10 for children ages 7 through 14. Also available is a 6½-hour tour of the cities that includes a boat ride on the Mississippi aboard the paddlewheeler *Anson Northrup*. Fees for the latter are $28 for adults, $26 for seniors and $16 for children ages 7 through 14. Call the company for specific days and times of tours.

METRO CONNECTIONS

1219 Marquette Ave., Ste. 110
Minneapolis   333-8687

These tours feature commentary by experienced guides while you relax in a deluxe motorcoach. During summer two daily tours are offered seven days a week: a four-hour morning tour and a three-hour afternoon tour. In September tours are offered Wednesday through Sunday. In October tours run Friday, Saturday and Sunday, and a limited schedule is offered in November and December. Tours depart from several locales. The Sunday morning tour, originating from

Mall of America spotlights '30s gangster hideouts in St. Paul, as well as the usual itinerary. Fees are $17 for adults, $15 for seniors and $10 for children. Bilingual guides are available.

And For Something a Little Different . . .

ST. PAUL GANGSTER TOURS
292-1220

Dressed in double-breasted suits and fedoras, tour guides take you to the hideouts and watering holes of notorious gangsters who found safe haven in St. Paul in the 1930s. Under a unique pact devised by St. Paul political bosses, Prohibition-era gangsters were given free range in the "Saintly City" as long as they agreed to pay duty to the system and commit no crimes inside city limits. John Dillinger, Ma Barker, Baby Face Nelson and Alvin "Creepy" Karpis are just a few of the outlaws who visited town. Tours are offered on certain Saturdays in summer and fall. Call for a schedule. Prices are $20 for adults, $18 for senior citizens and $15 for children ages 6 to 15.

PADELFORD PACKET BOAT COMPANY
Harriet Island, St. Paul
Boom Island Park, Minneapolis
(For both locales)   227-1100

See the cities from the vantage point of the grand old Mississippi River on these sternwheel riverboats. The Padelford company operates five riverboats: The *Josiah Snelling*, *Jonathan Padelford* and the new *Harriet Bishop* sail from St. Paul's Harriet Island to Fort Snelling; the other two, the *Anson Northrup* and the *Betsy Northrup*, leave Minneapolis' Boom Island and navigate through the upper locks near downtown. Tours are given daily Memorial Day through Labor Day at noon

Best Entertainment Value in Town

- Nation's largest dinner theatre
- Lavish productions
- Choice of entree served tableside

• • • • •

Chanhassen
Dinner Theatres
**612-934-1525
or 800-362-3515**

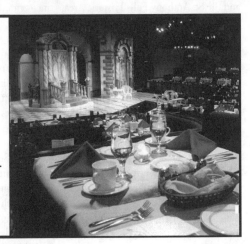

and 2 PM (no reservations needed). During May tours are limited to 2 PM Saturday and Sunday. Cost is $8.50 for adults, $7.50 for seniors, $5.50 children younger than 12 and free for ages 3 and under. Dinner and Sunday brunch cruises are also available (call for reservations). Fees for the latter range from $34.95 to $29.95.

CAPITAL CITY TROLLEYS
St. Paul   223-5600

In 1995 St. Paul added a colorful touch to the downtown panorama with the introduction of the Capital City Trolleys. The rubber-tired, natural gas-powered cars traverse downtown St. Paul in three main routes, stopping at such major attractions as the State Capitol, the Minnesota History Center, Rice Park, the Radisson Hotel, Lowertown, Town Square, Dayton's, the World Trade Center and the Science Museum of Minnesota. Rides cost a mere quarter (free for children 5 and younger) and pickups are about every 15 minutes from 11 AM to 11 PM. (Note: After 5 PM, the trolleys run on an abbreviated route.) To climb aboard, just look for bright red and green Trolley stop signs located near downtown parking ramps, bus stops and skyway access points. Trolley route maps are available at St. Paul Convention and Visitors Bureau information centers, hotel front desks and several other sites downtown.

RIVERCITY TROLLEYS
Minneapolis   673-5123

Across the river, Minneapolis is also getting into the act with its new RiverCity Trolleys, which travel a 40-minute route that encompasses the Minneapolis Convention Center, downtown, the Warehouse District

It's a special treat to watch Raptor Center staff members release a majestic bird into the wilds again.

Insiders' Tips

and the St. Anthony Falls Historic Area, including the recently reopened Stone Arch Bridge over the Mississippi. The trolleys leave the convention center on the hour and St. Anthony Main at 20 and 40 minutes after the hour. Hours of operation are 10 AM to 6 PM Monday through Thursday, 10 AM to 9 PM Friday and Saturday and noon to 6 PM Sunday. Cost is $1 for one round-trip ride (good for two hours and unlimited reboarding) and $3 for an all-day pass. Trolleys service other stops approximately every 20 minutes.

General Attractions

MINNESOTA HISTORY CENTER
345 W. Kellogg Blvd., St. Paul   296-6126

This new museum and research center on state history boasts hands-on exhibits, lively demonstrations and costumed interpreters. Grammar-school history was never like this. Visitors can view Prince's *Purple Rain* costume and a birch-bark voyageur's canoe, sit on a milking stool next to a full-sized plaster Holstein cow, run their fingers over a beaver trap, peek inside a model of a sod house, listen to Minnesota's own Andrews Sisters' recording of "Boogie Woogie Bugle Boy" — there's much more! These are all part of the center's popular "Minnesota A To Z" exhibit.

People of all ages can enjoy the History Center on many levels. While many of the exhibits seem targeted to adults, children will delight in climbing around and in two special exhibits: a real 24-ton boxcar, representative of Minnesota's railroad heritage, and the Grain Elevator, a play area that allows children to travel the same path that grain takes as it goes through processing.

In mid-November 1995 the museum opened "Families," a major new exhibit focusing on the stages families go through: the coming together, the growing apart, the memories, the hopes, the celebrations. This intriguing exhibit is set in a huge "house," with each room symbolizing a different theme. It will remain at the museum for several years.

The Minnesota History Center also has a restaurant, Cafe Minnesota, and two museum stores featuring Minnesota and Native-American books, games, toys, jewelry and more.

Every Sunday afternoon from 1 to 4 PM, the museum offers "History Hijinks," free programs in which visitors participate in activities such as bread-baking, beading and storytelling. Museum hours are 10 AM to 5 PM Tuesday, Wednesday, Friday and Saturday; 10 AM to 9 PM Thursday; noon to 5 PM Sunday (closed Mondays). Admission is free, except for parking.

SCIENCE MUSEUM OF MINNESOTA AND WILLIAM L. McKNIGHT-3M OMNITHEATER
30 E. 10th St., St. Paul   221-9488

This attractive, modern facility showcases the wonders of science with permanent exhibits in biology, paleontology, technology, geography and anthropology. Most of the displays are presented in a participatory, kid-friendly format. The Omnitheater shows nature films on a dome screen that puts you smack dab in the center of the action.

The Science Museum is open Monday through Friday from 9:30 AM to 9 PM, Saturday 9 AM to 9 PM and Sunday 10 AM to 9 PM. Admission is $5 for exhibits only, $6 for Omnitheater only and $7 for both exhibits and Omni. For children 12 and younger, admission is $1 less in all categories. For more information on the museum, see the Kidstuff chapter.

HISTORIC SUMMIT AVENUE
St. Paul's Summit Avenue is home to an

The riverboat Josiah Snelling *on the Mississippi River.*

Photo: Eric Miller, Pioneer Press

impressive stretch of stately mansions, built and owned by business and civic leaders during the Victorian era. Perhaps most impressive is the huge, fortress-like home of Great Northern Railway magnate James J. Hill (No. 240 and open for tours). From there, you can cruise by the rowhouse once inhabited by F. Scott Fitzgerald (No. 599), and where he completed his first book, *This Side of Paradise*, in 1919. The official residence of the state's chief executive, the Governor's Mansion (No. 1006) is open for free tours on Thursdays from May through October.

For more details on all three edifices, see the Architecture and Historic Sites chapter.

From downtown St. Paul, Summit Avenue begins at the majestic Cathedral of St. Paul and continues west for nearly five miles to the Mississippi. It's a grand drive.

JAMES FORD BELL
MUSEUM OF NATURAL HISTORY
17th Ave. and University Ave. S.E.
(On the U. of Minn. East Bank campus)
Minneapolis   624-7083

This museum houses more than 100 works of wildlife art, tracing the development of the art form from the early artist-naturalist through the sporting era to the modern age of ecological awareness. Recently the museum's collection was merged with that of the American Museum of Wildlife Art, and the result is an impressive, comprehensive display. In the children's Touch and See Room, everything is displayed at child height — the motto is "please DO touch." People of all ages will enjoy the museum's lifelike displays of animals in their natural habitat. Admission is $3 for adults, $2 for youths (ages 3 to 16) and seniors and free for children younger than 3. Admission is free on Thursday. Hours are 9 AM to 5 PM Tuesday through Friday, 10 AM to 5 PM Saturday and noon to 5 PM Sunday.

FOSHAY TOWER
821 Marquette Ave. S.
Minneapolis   341-2522

When baby boomers were wee tots, the 32-floor Foshay Tower was the tallest "skyscraper" in Minneapolis, and a visit to its observation deck for a panoramic view of the city was a grand outing. Completed in

1929 for $4.5 million by utilities magnate Wilbur B. Foshay and restored in 1992, the Foshay was the first skyscraper built west of the Mississippi and remained Minneapolis' tallest building until 1971. A splendid art deco showcase with ornate terrazzo floors and marbled walls, the Foshay was modeled after the Washington Monument. Upon its completion on August 30, 1929, John Phillip Sousa himself performed an original march dedicated to the edifice during lavish opening festivities. Alas, the hoopla was shortlived: two months later, Foshay lost a fortune in the great stock market crash and was later sentenced to prison on charges of mail fraud. The onetime entrepreneur died in a Minneapolis nursing home in 1957.

While nowadays the view is somewhat obstructed by the "big shoulders" of the 57-floor IDS Tower and its lofty cohorts, the top of the Foshay still affords a great panorama. The observation deck and Foshay Tower Museum detailing the history behind the colorful edifice are accessed through the 30th floor. Hours are noon to 4 PM Monday through Friday and 11 AM to 3 PM Saturday. Admission is $3 for adults and $2 for seniors and children.

THE AMERICAN SWEDISH INSTITUTE
2600 Park Ave., Minneapolis   *871-4907*

Founded in 1929 in the sprawling, ornate mansion of Swedish newspaper publisher and self-made millionaire Swan J. Turnblad, the American Swedish Institute is a tribute to more than 150 years of the Swedish experience in America. It houses everything from immigrants' trunks to more than 600 examples of exquisite Swedish art glass. The 33-room mansion alone, with a splendid grand entrance hall, ornate mahogany woodwork, sweeping staircases and 11 rare por-

celain fireplaces, is worth the trip. Two gift shops offer an extensive collection of Swedish-language books, music and handicrafts. Hours are noon to 4 PM Tuesday, Thursday, Friday and Saturday; noon to 8 PM Wednesday; and 1 to 5 PM Sunday. Admission is $3 for adults and $2 for senior citizens and students.

UPPER ST. ANTHONY FALLS LOCK AND DAM
Mississippi River at Portland Ave.
Minneapolis   *333-5336*

The legendary St. Anthony Falls and the Mississippi River have been tamed by a series of 29 locks that enable boat traffic to navigate the river over varying elevations from Minnesota to the Gulf of Mexico. The Upper Lock, at Minneapolis, lifts towboats, barges and other river craft 50 feet and above the falls — the highest lift of any lock on the Mississippi. The nearby Lower Lock lifts and lowers the water level about 25 feet.

There are many ways to view the locks, which are owned and operated by the Army Corps of Engineers. Visitors may observe the process from the Upper Lock Public Observation Deck, on the west bank of the river, just off Portland Avenue (immediately north of the Whitney Hotel at 150 Portland Avenue). Admission is free, and the view is nice. The observation deck is open 8 AM to 10 PM April 1 to December 1. Recent remodeling added restrooms and an elevator for those using wheelchairs. (Another interesting way to view the lock system up close and personal is to ride through the Upper Lock on the *Anson Northrup* riverboat. See the front of this chapter for more details.)

STONE ARCH BRIDGE
Mississippi River at Portland Ave., Minneapolis

For an spectacular view of the Mill City, take a stroll or trolley ride across the Mis-

METRODOME TOURS

HOURS: Public tours - Monday - Saturday 11:00 a.m. & 1:00 p.m.
Group tours - Scheduled 9:00 a.m. through 3:00 p.m.

PRICES: Adults $3.00 Students/Seniors $2.00
Groups of 15 or more adults $2.50

Appropriate for all ages. A fully accessible facility.

For information, call (612) 335-3309   **M E T R O D O M E**

sissippi on the historic Stone Arch Bridge, located just downriver from the Upper Lock and Dam. This 112-year-old limestone structure, originally a railroad bridge, was recently reopened for pedestrian and bicycle traffic and trolley rides. The picturesque span, built by railroad magnate James J. Hill, is the second-oldest bridge remaining on the Mississippi River. On the river's east bank, the bridge leads to Father Hennepin Park, believed to be where Father Louis Hennepin first viewed St. Anthony Falls in 1680. Adjoining the park to the west is the historic St. Anthony Main complex of shops and restaurants. Guided tours of the historic St. Anthony Falls district are offered by the Minnesota Historical Society on Saturday, Sunday and Thursday. Call 627-5433 for more information.

LOCK AND DAM NO. 1
Mississippi River at Minnehaha Pkwy.
Minneapolis   724-2971

About 3 miles downriver in South Minneapolis — take Minnehaha Parkway to the Mississippi — is Lock and Dam No. 1, providing another breathtaking view of Ole Miss from a modern, attractive visitors center and promenade. The center here is open April through October, 8 AM to 9 PM, and offers an interesting 45-minute tour. Visitors get a bird's-eye view of the lock, the 674-foot-long dam and the Ford Power Plant, one of only a handful of hydroelectric plants on the river.

NICOLLET MALL
Downtown Minneapolis

This 12-block pedestrian walkway, dotted with tree-shaded benches, sculptures and fountains, meanders through Minneapolis' world-class shopping district from Washington Avenue south to 13th Street. Built in 1967 and remodeled in 1991, the mall on any given summer day is home to street musicians, farmers market booths (Thursday), outdoor-cafe revelers and great browsing. Dayton's Department Store, at the 700 block, is a historic anchor and a favorite of locals. Nearby are the newer shopping complexes of Gaviidae Common (housing Neiman Marcus and Saks Fifth Avenue), The Conservatory (with Mark Shale and other quality shops), City Center and the IDS Crystal Court. See the Shopping chapter for a complete description of these stores.

MINNESOTA ZOO

13000 Zoo Blvd., Apple Valley   432-9000

Ecological awareness is the guiding theme of this attractive, modern zoological park in suburban Apple Valley. In fact, zoo planners were so successful in creating "natural habitat" settings for the animals that sometimes you can't see the ferrets for the trees! More than 2,700 mammals, birds, fish, reptiles and amphibians are found in this 500-acre zoo. Highlights include a coral reef exhibit, indoor tropical aviary and crowd-pleasing dolphins. Hours are 9 AM to 6 PM Monday through Saturday and 9 AM to 8 PM Sunday; winter hours are 9 AM to 4 PM daily. Admission is $8 for adults, $4 for children 12 and younger and $5 for seniors. To reach the zoo, take Minn. Highway 62, I-35E or I-494 to Minn. Highway 77, go south and look for zoo signs. For a more on the zoo, see the Kidstuff chapter.

COMO PARK ZOO
AND CONSERVATORY

Midway Pkwy. and Lexington Ave.
St. Paul   488-5571

This older zoo, the centerpiece of an expansive park in north St. Paul, has many charms (including Sparky the sea lion), is conveniently located and charges no admission. After you've grinned at the collection of 500 critters, escape into the lovely Victorian-style Conservatory and find your own secret garden. There is also a Japanese garden on premises. Zoo hours are 8 AM to 8 PM daily April through September; 8 AM to 5 PM the rest of the year. For more on the zoo, see the Kidstuff chapter.

MALL OF AMERICA, CAMP SNOOPY
AND UNDERWATER WORLD AQUARIUM

I-494 and Minn. Hwy. 77
Bloomington   883-8800

The largest shopping and entertainment complex in the United States attracts visitors from around the world. And why not? There's truly something for everyone in this indoor wonderland: You can shop 'til you drop, soar on a roller coaster in the Camp Snoopy indoor amusement park, play miniature golf or party into the wee hours in the fourth-floor nightclubs. Coming in '96 is the Underwater World aquarium, a 1.2 million gallon walk-through aquarium. For more on the mall and its attractions, see the Shopping and Kidstuff chapters.

FARMERS MARKETS

In St. Paul: 290 E. Fifth St.   227-6856
In Minneapolis: 312 Lyndale Ave. N.
(take the Hwy. 55 Exit off I-94)   333-1718

No Minnesota experience is complete without a bite into a juicy, red homegrown Big Boy tomato. Few culinary experiences compare with that sloppy, sensuous, flavorful indulgence. There are Big Boys aplenty at the Farmers Market, plus much more: exotic "designer" vegetables, organic breads, fish and meats, locally harvested honey and flowers galore. You'll also undoubtedly find members of the local Southeast Asian Hmong community selling their colorful embroidery at very reasonable prices.

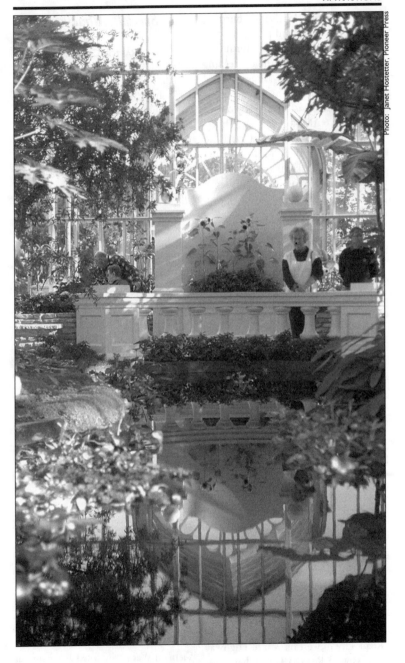

Photo: Janet Hostetter, Pioneer Press

The Como Park Conservatory.

The Farmers Market — bursting with vibrant color and pungent odors — is a Minnesotan's reward for suffering through nine months of freezing winter. Both markets are open April through October. The Minneapolis Farmers Market is open seven days a week from 6 AM to 1 PM. On Thursday, it moves to the Nicollet Mall and runs from 6 AM to 6 PM. In St. Paul, the Farmers Market is open Saturday and Sunday mornings. On Thursday, it is at Seventh Place in downtown St. Paul.

CANTERBURY PARK

1100 Canterbury Rd., Shakopee   445-7223

After a nearly three-year hiatus, live pari-mutuel horse racing returned to Minnesota's Canterbury Park in 1995. This attractive, state-of-the-art racetrack in the southwestern suburb of Shakopee offered 55 days of live racing last year and plans a similar season in the coming year. Live races are run Thursday through Sunday, with post time at 4 PM Thursday and Friday and 2 PM Saturday and Sunday. The facility also offers year-round pari-mutuel betting on simulcasts of races from around the country. The 353,000-square-foot grandstand area accommodates general admission and clubhouse seating. On Sunday, children enjoy free pony and trolley rides. Admission is $3 (plus $3 for clubhouse seating).

To reach Canterbury Park from Minneapolis, take I-35W south to Minn. Highway 13. Go west on 13 (which turns into Minn. Highway 101) to County Road 83. Continue south to track. From St. Paul, take I-35E south to County Road 42. Go west on Minn. Highway 42 to County Road 83. Go north to track.

Specialty Attractions

RAPTOR CENTER

1920 Fitch Ave., St. Paul   624-4745

The Gabbert Raptor Center, known informally as the Raptor Center, is a rehabilitation hospital and research center for eagles, hawks, owls, falcons and other raptors. The center, on the University of Minnesota-St. Paul campus, offers tours, by reservation, for groups of eight or more (individuals and smaller groups can usually be added to tour groups on Saturday). The facility has exhibits of live, unreleasable eagles, hawks and other birds and educational displays. Tours include a slide show and video on the history of the center and the rehabilitation process.

Hours are 9 AM to 4 PM Monday through Friday and 11 AM to 4 PM Saturday. Admission is $3.50 for adults, $2 for children and $2.50 for seniors.

SCHUBERT CLUB
MUSICAL INSTRUMENT MUSEUM

Landmark Center, 75 Fifth St. W.
St. Paul   292-3268

This small museum showcases an amazing collection of historic musical instruments and phonographs. Included are a 1542 harpsichord, a rare art deco piano made by Wurlitzer in 1935 and many more fine and rare creations. If only those keys could talk! Admission is free. Hours are 11 AM to 3 PM Monday through Friday.

MINNESOTA VIETNAM MEMORIAL
AND PEACE OFFICERS MEMORIAL

State Capitol Grounds, St. Paul

The Vietnam Memorial is a granite wall carved with the names of more than 1,000 Minnesotans who were killed in the Vietnam War or are listed as missing in action. The new Peace Officers Memorial, a large stone arch dedicated to the memory of all officers killed in the line of duty, was erected after two young policemen were killed during a manhunt in St. Paul in the summer of 1994.

DAKOTA COUNTY
HISTORICAL SOCIETY AND MUSEUM
130 3rd Ave. N., South St. Paul   451-6260

This museum contains more than 35,000 artifacts representing Dakota County history and traditions. But who cares about the numbers? What catches your eye here are the colorful murals and life-size dioramas depicting turn-of-the-century homes and shops — an apothecary, dental office, hat shop, blacksmith and more. The exhibits also include handicrafts of the Dakota Indians who inhabited what was once known as Kaposia Village in the present locale of South St. Paul. The museum is open from 9 AM to 5 PM Tuesday, Wednesday and Friday; 9 AM to 8 PM Thursday; and 10 AM to 3 PM Saturday. Admission is free. (Hungry? Head north on Concord Street to St. Paul's West Side and sniff out some honest-to-goodness Mexican cafes.)

THE BAKKEN: A LIBRARY AND
MUSEUM OF ELECTRICITY AND LIFE
3537 Zenith Ave. S.
Minneapolis   927-6508

Housed in a historic mansion overlooking Lake Calhoun, this collection is positively electrifying, featuring scientific instruments and rare books on electricity and medicine. Included are a first edition

of Mary W. Shelley's novel *Fr...* a 20-foot print of Raoul Dufy's *Spirit of Electricity* and electrical toys the 1800s. The attractive grounds also ha bor a medicinal herb garden. Museum hours are 9:30 AM to 4:30 PM Saturday. Admission is $3 for adults, $2 for students and seniors and free for children ages 8 and younger.

HENNEPIN HISTORY MUSEUM
2303 Third Ave. S., Minneapolis   870-1329

Housed in an old mansion kitty-corner from the world-class Minneapolis Institute of Arts, this museum has an impressive collection of historical memorabilia about the county, plus Ojibwa and Dakota Indian artifacts such as beadwork and a genuine birch-bark canoe. In 1994 a "City Kids" hands-on exhibit for children opened on the museum's second floor. While you're there, ask to see the award-winning, 10-minute video *Ghosts Along the Freeway*, which shows the impact of Interstate 94 construction on old Twin Cities neighborhoods. Hours are noon to 5 PM Tuesday through Sunday (archives are open noon to 5 PM Tuesday through Saturday). Admission is free.

HUMPHREY FORUM
U. of Minn., 301 19th Ave. S.
Minneapolis   624-5799

The life of Hubert Horatio Humphrey, one of Minnesota's most colorful and influential public servants, is showcased in this exhibit, which includes life-size photo murals, a replica of Humphrey's 1964 Sen-

A visit to the Farmers Market is a great way to spend a Saturday morning.

...is speeches and other ... Hours are 9 AM to 8 ... to 5 PM Tuesday ... AM to 1 PM Satur- ... Admission is free.

...EY METRODOME

...lis 335-3309

...he infamous inflatable domed stadium, home to Minnesota Twins baseball and Vikings football, offers tours Monday through Saturday at 11 AM and 1 PM. Tour participants get an upclose look at the press box, a walk on the baseball field and a peek into locker rooms. Fees are $3 for adults, $2 for children, students and seniors. No tours are offered on the days when the Twins play afternoon games. After the tour, check out a wacky little place called Dome Souvenirs Plus, where you'll find "The Original Baseball Hall of Fame of Minnesota," at 910 Third Street, just north of the Dome. Former Twins equipment manager Ray Crump runs this little shrine to baseball, Elvis and Hollywood. It's a one-of-a-kind attraction!

THE KERLAN AND HESS COLLECTION, RESEARCH CENTER FOR CHILDREN'S BOOKS

Walter Library, U. of Minn.
East Bank campus   624-4576

A book-lover's affinity for children's books was the source of this now-extensive literary collection. Included are original manuscripts, artwork and galleys for more than 5,000 children's books. The late Dr. Irvin Kerlan devoted decades to children's literature, collecting quality books, corresponding with authors and gathering original manuscripts and artwork. The collection is now housed at the University of Minnesota and may be viewed by the public upon request.

MUSEUM OF QUESTIONABLE MEDICAL DEVICES

219 S.E. Main St., Minneapolis   379-4046

More than 250 outrageous examples of medical quackery throughout history are showcased in this collection. Among the items are a piece of Martian-like headgear that judges your character, countless devices to change one's breast size, the infamous foot X-ray machines commonly found in shoe stores during the early '50s, plus fascinating literature on the tragic results of such "cures" as radium suppositories (alleged to boost one's sexual prowess). Museum curator Bob McCoy is a cheery extrovert brimming with stories about these supposed cure-alls. This museum is a real find. Hours are 5 to 9 PM Tuesday through Thursday, 5 to 10 PM Friday, noon to 10 PM Saturday and noon to 5 PM Sunday. Admission is free.

While you're here, take a few minutes to enjoy the view. Cobblestoned Main Street meanders past historic grain mills and old warehouses that are now home to Riverplace and St. Anthony Main, two complexes comprising restaurants, shops and offices. Across Main Street, down a rolling embankment, are the wide, churning waters of the mighty Mississippi. This is one of the loveliest views of the Minneapolis skyline. Historic St. Anthony Falls, the rapids that attracted the original settlers, have given way to an elaborate system of locks and dams, but the river is still a mesmerizing sight.

PAVEK MUSEUM OF WONDERFUL WIRELESS

3515 Raleigh Ave., St. Louis Park   926-8198

Founded by the late Joseph Pavek, an amateur radio authority and historian, this museum takes viewers back to the days when the wireless was king. Included are extensive displays of radio sets, primitive crystal sets and ham radio equipment. Admission is $3 ($2 for children younger than 13 and senior citizens). Hours are 10 AM to 6 PM Tuesday through Friday; 9 AM to 5 PM Saturday. It's closed Sunday, Monday and holidays.

BYERLY'S
3777 Park Center Blvd.
St. Louis Park   *929-2100*

In Byerly's, the Taj Mahal of supermarkets, shoppers stroll the carpeted aisles under glittering crystal chandeliers, perusing shelves stocked with everything from Wheaties to imported English water biscuits. One of many Byerly's stores in the Twin Cities, the St. Louis Park facility also features a fine-arts gift gallery, a candy store, a card shop, a liquor store and a popular restaurant. A visit to Byerly's makes grocery shopping an unforgettable experience. This Byerly's is northeast of the intersection of Excelsior Boulevard and Minn. Highway 100.

ELLINGSON CAR MUSEUM
20950 Rogers Dr., Rogers   *428-7337*

More than 70 automobiles, dating from between 1917 and 1973, plus a dozen motorcycles, are the centerpiece of this unique attraction in the northwest suburb of Rogers. The road warriors include a 1935 Mercedes SSK originally owned by the king of Sweden; a military tank built by Cadillac; a '56 Lincoln Mark II once owned by Harry Warner of Warner Bros.; Corvettes, GTOs and, granddaddy of 'em all, the Model T. It's enough to send chills and thrills up the spine of any car buff!

The museum is open from 10 AM to 6 PM Monday through Saturday; noon to 5 PM Sunday. Admission is $5 for adults and free for children age 12 and younger. To reach the museum, take I-94 northwest from Minneapolis and, when you get to Rogers, watch for the signs.

MINNESOTA AIR GUARD MUSEUM
Air National Guard Base
Mpls.-St. Paul International Airport (just south of Hwys. 55 and 62)   *725-5609*

Aviation buffs will delight in this out-of-the-way museum's collection of 15 vintage planes. An indoor gallery chronicles the history of the Minnesota Air Guard. Admission is free. Hours are 11 AM to 4 PM Saturday and Sunday from mid-April through mid-September and the second and third Saturdays of the month, October through March.

SIBLEY HISTORIC SITE
Minn. Hwy. 13, Mendota   *452-1596*

Fur trader Henry H. Sibley built this limestone and timber home near the confluence of the Mississippi and Minnesota rivers in 1836. Today visitors can view it and two other adjacent historic buildings filled with 19th-century furniture, costumes and artifacts. Sibley had a distinguished career, serving as Minnesota's first delegate to Congress, first justice of the peace and its first elected governor. The historic site is open May through October from 10 AM to 5 PM Tuesday through Saturday and noon to 5 PM Sunday. Admission is $3 for adults, $1 for children 6 to 16 and free for those 5 and younger.

PLANES OF FAME AIR MUSEUM
Flying Cloud Field, 14771 Pioneer Tr.
Eden Prairie   *941-2633*

Dedicated to preserving American aviation history, the Planes of Fame Air Museum harbors such famous flying machines as the P38 Lightning, British Spitfire, a B-25 Bomber and many more. Also displayed are combat films and aviation artifacts. For a real thrill, go for a spin in the open-cockpit Stearman trainer. Hours are 11 AM to 5 PM Tuesday through Sunday. Admission is $6 for adults, $3 for ages 7 to 12 and free for ages 6 and younger.

Inside
Annual Events and Festivals

Here's a true story: There was once a Twin Cities vegetarian who had an unusual ritual. For 364 days of the year he'd refuse to place meat in his mouth because of his health and humanitarian convictions. But once a year, during the waning days of August, with great deliberation and ceremony he'd make a trip to the Minnesota State Fair to eat a foot-long hot dog. He just couldn't make it through the year without that one juicy lapse.

Twin Citians of all convictions have their own reasons for attending any of the region's many annual events, and many of them are undoubtedly stranger than the vegetarian's. Nevertheless, we go again and again to these yearly happenings, getting our needed fixes of music, community spirit, holiday cheer, noise, crowds, people-watching or hot dogs.

And there's no shortage of opportunities. You'd need a very large personal calendar, not to mention several lifetimes of weekends, to log in all the festivals, carnivals, parades, holiday celebrations and music extravaganzas the Twin Cities offer. You couldn't possibly attend even most of them. But there's no harm in trying.

Consult the daily newspaper for specific dates, times and admission costs, if any, of these events. The Minnesota Department of Tourism also lists statewide

Photo: Marcj. Kawanishi, Pioneer Press

Minneapolis Aquatennial milk carton boat race.

festivals and events in its free, seasonal *Minnesota Explorer* publication. Call them at 296-5029 or (800) 428-4322.

January

ST. PAUL WINTER CARNIVAL
Downtown St. Paul and
other locations   *297-6953*

Launched in 1886 to rebut assertions in the eastern press that Minnesota was just another Siberia, the country's oldest and best-known winter festival annually runs from late January through early February. The Winter Carnival is a 12-day celebration of everything that non-Minnesotans and other people ignorant about the winter dread most about the frigid season: snow, ice, and windchill. If you've got it, you might as well make the most of it, right?

A distinctive, and some say peculiar, mythology has mushroomed alongside the carnival. According to the folklore, King Boreas, the ruler of snow and ice, and Vulcanus, the deity of fire, are rivals and enemies. When Boreas decides to make Minnesota his paradise and establish a celebration of the winter with his Queen of the Snows, Vulcanus mischievously makes repeated attempts to disrupt the proceedings and melt them to a puddle. All this explains why the St. Paul Winter Carnival has King Boreas and Queen of the Snows coronations, as well as frequent appearances by otherwise honorable citizens dressed as Vulcanus and his stooges who interrupt events, scream through town on fire engines and try to smear soot on people's faces.

Among the most popular Winter Carnival events are the two parades. The first, the daytime King Boreas Grand Day Parade, features marching bands, richly decorated floats, a bouncing girl (she's tossed aloft from a blanket) and a presiding grand marshal, usually a nationally known celebrity. The Vulcan's Victory Torchlight Parade, held at night, concludes with a fireworks show.

All told, about 1.5 million folks turn out for the 80 or so Winter Carnival events. Many of the activities take place out on the snow or ice: skating, tubing, team sports, ice-carving competitions, snow sculpting, kite flying, golf, even motorcycle racing. The closely followed hunt for the Winter Carnival Medallion, hidden somewhere in the city, gets people bundling up and digging holes in the darndest spots after they interpret clues printed daily in the *St. Paul Pioneer Press*. Often (though not every year), the carnival sponsors the construction of a spectacular ice castle that raises its chilly and colorfully lit walls high into the sky. Some of these castles have been among the largest such structures ever built.

But don't worry — not all the activities are held outdoors. Carnival-goers wishing a respite from the cold weather can attend such events as the Indoor Fun Fair, which has a county fair-like midway, and indoor concerts.

If you dislike the winter, the Winter Carnival can be a good incentive to change your attitude. If you already enjoy the cold season in the Twin Cities, the carnival can be one of the biggest reasons why.

March

ST. PATRICK'S DAY PARADES
Downtown St. Paul and Minneapolis

For several years now, the twin towns have both sponsored St. Patrick's Day parades. They're both impressive efforts, especially considering the risk of blizzard or ice storm each faces in mid-March. St.

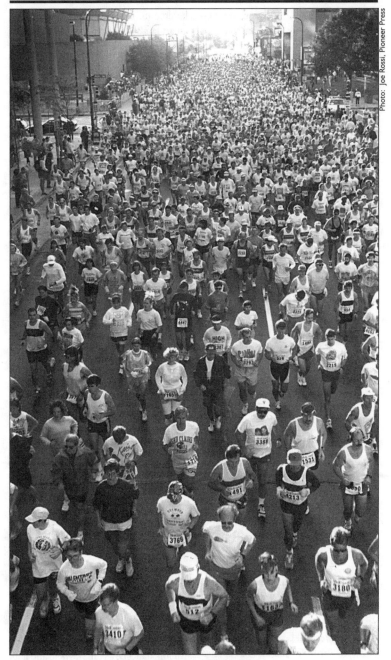

Photo: Joe Rossi, Pioneer Press

The Twin Cities Marathon is an annual event.

Paul's is the bigger, older and more established event, one that can count on the support of a sizable resident Irish-American community and many Irish-style pubs. In Minneapolis, the sudden splash of green still seems a bit out of place, but the parade is usually well-attended. They're both welcome breaks for downtown workers.

April

FESTIVAL OF NATIONS

St. Paul Civic Center, 143 W. Fourth St.
St. Paul 647-0191

The state's largest multi-ethnic event features great ethnic bands, continual folk dance performances, food from around the world, folk art demonstrations, arts and crafts exhibitions and an international bazaar.

May

HEART OF THE BEAST
MAY DAY PARADE

Bloomington Ave. S, near E. Lake St.
Minneapolis 721-2535

It's an unforgettable sight: enormous, 15-foot puppets marching down the street into Powderhorn Park, where a pageant performance takes place. More than 25,000 people come to watch this parade by the jumbo figures of the In the Heart of the Beast puppet troupe, traditionally held on the Sunday nearest May 1.

SCOTTISH COUNTRY FAIR

Macalester College, 1600 Grand Ave.
St. Paul 696-6239

There's so much tartan at this event that your eyes will be seeing patterns for days afterward. The fair also has bagpipers, highland dancing, a parade, sheep-herding and living history demonstrations, an art fair, kids' activities and food. Most notable are the athletic events — can those guys in kilts really throw telephone poles?

June

GAY AND LESBIAN PRIDE FESTIVAL

Loring Park, Minneapolis 377-8141

The Twin Cities' most free-spirited and raucous parade, marching down Franklin and Lyndale avenues to Loring Park, is the signature of this two-day festival. Vendors, artists and craftspeople, street entertainers and a huge crowd fill up Loring Park in celebration of gay and lesbian pride.

EDINA ART FAIR

50th St. and France Ave. S., Edina 922-4413

This annual arts and crafts fair began back in the mid-1960s and now attracts more than 250 exhibitors and crowds of buyers. Live music and food are other attractions.

GRAND OLD DAY

Grand Ave., St. Paul 224-3324

This is the biggest one-day street festival in the Midwest, and the Grand Day Parade is just one of its many highlights. Held annually on a Sunday in June, it features bands, street entertainers and plenty to eat and drink. Other features include a special kiddie parade and a family area. It's a fun day.

MIDSOMMAR CELEBRATION

American Swedish Institute, 2600 Park Ave.
Minneapolis 871-4908

This is a cheery and traditional Scandinavian-style summer celebration, complete with arts and crafts exhibitors, Swedish folk dancers, a real Maypole and a lot of food and music.

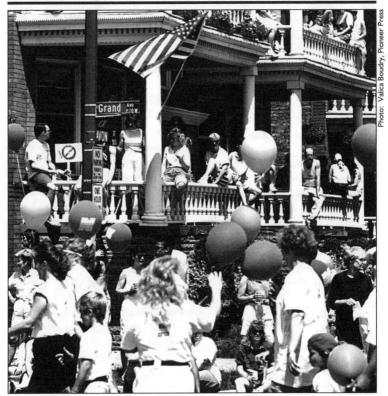

Photo: Valica Boudry, Pioneer Press

Grand Old Day Festival is an annual summer gathering and parade held on Grand Avenue in St. Paul.

MINNESOTA CRAFTS FESTIVAL

College of St. Catherine, St. Paul   333-7789

Traditionally held on the last weekend in June and sponsored by the Minnesota Crafts Council, this festival is regarded by many as the state's highest quality, though certainly not the largest, arts and crafts event. Representing artistry in ceramics, glass, wood, fiber and metal, 110 craftspeople from throughout the country come to display and sell their work to a quite discriminating crowd. Also on hand are food vendors and live entertainment.

SUMMERFOLK

Hyland Hills Park, Bloomington   338-8388

Red House Records, a St. Paul-based producer of folk and urban-folk music recordings, every year transforms a Sunday in June into a tuneful showcase of its best talent. Past artists in this festival have included Greg Brown, Shawn Colvin, Claudia Schmidt, John Gorka, Peter Ostroushko and many other nationally known artists.

TWIN CITIES JUNETEENTH CELEBRATION

Theodore Wirth Park, Minneapolis   377-7000

This annual event dating to 1986, which

includes a 5K run, live music, a parade, kids' activities and an African American Marketplace with hundreds of food and crafts vendors, celebrates the day, June 19, 1865, when African-American slaves in Texas finally learned they had been freed from bondage.

LIVE IN THE ZOO

Minnesota Zoo   432-9000

From June through September you can enjoy live concerts in the beauty of the great outdoors at the Minnesota Zoo's Weesner Family Amphitheater. Each year the line-up of nationally known acts ranges from blues to jazz and folk to pop. Recent artists have included John Hiatt, Tower of Power, Dr. John, Los Lobos, Little Feat and Steven Stills.

July

LYN-LAKE STREET FAIR

Lake St. at Lyndale Ave. S.
Minneapolis   822-4002

Only three years old, this south Minneapolis street festival has really taken root, drawing together artisans and craftspeople, kids, street entertainers, popular bands and big crowds. The fair includes a parade, food and refreshments.

ALL-STAR FESTIVAL OF THE BLUES

Municipal Stadium, 1771 Energy Park Dr.
St. Paul   922-9000

Since 1990 this event, sponsored by the Upper Mississippi Blues Society, has brought some of the bluest performers in the country to the Twin Cities. Past stars have included Lowell Fulson, Anson Funderburgh and Big Jay McNeely. Other highlights include food and arts and crafts.

MINNEAPOLIS AQUATENNIAL

Downtown Minneapolis and
other locations   331-8371

For more than 50 Julys, the Aquatennial has celebrated all the water Minneapolis has within its borders — with milk-carton boat races, two big parades, fireworks, a downtown block party, an arts and crafts fair, kids' events, a sand sculpture competition, music and 11 days of mirth. Communities from all around the state nominate young women who vie for the Queen of the Lakes crown. The 10-day celebration is one of Minneapolis' strongest traditions, and lately organizers have taken pains to make the event more culturally inclusive by adding youth arts events and a music festival.

It all started in 1939, when a group of Minneapolis business leaders witnessed a crowd of a million people who turned out to view the British royalty in Winnipeg, Manitoba. Convinced that their city could do just as good a job in attracting throngs to see homegrown royalty, the business people launched the Aquatennial to improve Minneapolis' public image. It was a success from the start, taking on an early emphasis in promoting the fight in World War II.

For many years, the festival's most popular attraction was the Aqua Follies, which until 1964 featured swimming, diving and water ballet. Over time the Aquatennial has also featured such celebrities as Jayne Mansfield, Jimmy Stewart, Aretha Franklin, and Hubert Humphrey. An annually changing theme gives the festival focus and direction.

Taking place throughout the city, Aquatennial includes skydiving shows, sports tournaments, art exhibitions, a gelatin slide, senior walks and dances, a sailing regatta, a kite flying contest, fishing clinics and a fishing derby, concerts, a

5K run and a fireworks finale. The two parades, the Grande Day Parade and the concluding Torchlight Parade, are the best-attended events. If you're alive and breathing, some part of Aquatennial will be of interest to you.

MINNESOTA HERITAGE FESTIVAL
Nicollet Island and vicinity
Minneapolis 874-0142

If you're interested in an entertainment- and food-filled couple of days devoted to the state's cultural diversity and heritage, this festival in downtown Minneapolis is for you. Set on Nicollet Island and old Main Street in the oldest part of Minneapolis, the four-day event includes exhibitions, dancing, historic tours and demonstrations, sports tournaments and a fireworks show. A lumberjack show, three music stages and an international bazaar of crafts from around the world are special highlights.

MOVIES AND MUSIC IN THE PARK
Loring Park, Minneapolis 375-7622

Walker Art Center sponsors this annual Monday-evening series, spanning July and August, that allows you to watch a movie outdoors in the company of hundreds of other people, with band music still ringing in your ears. The bands are on first, and they range from funk groups to folk-rockers. The film that follows is usually a cult favorite or crowd pleaser. It's all free.

RICE STREET FESTIVAL
Rice St., St. Paul 488-1039

Featuring one of the Twin Cities' longest parades, this festival, held in July, also includes a coronation of royalty, arts and crafts displays, food booths, kids' activities, sports tournaments and live music.

RONDO DAYS
Hallie Q. Brown/Martin Luther King Ctr.
270 N. Kent St., St. Paul

When the eight lanes of I-94 rolled across the Twin Cities in the 1950s and '60s, they split St. Paul's largest black neighborhood and obliterated its main street, Rondo Avenue. It took years for the community to recover from this disruption. Each year, the Rondo Days festival, held in July, seeks to recall the sights and sounds of the old neighborhood by bringing people together for a parade, arts and crafts displays, kids' activities and food.

A TASTE OF MINNESOTA
State Capitol Mall, St. Paul 228-0018

The most spectacular fireworks show in town is only one of the attractions of this annual Independence Day weekend extravaganza in the shadow of the State Capitol building. The name of the 13-year-old event tells most of the story: This gathering is about edibles. Each year some 35 Twin Cities restaurants band together to offer an incredible array of food from their booths. You can partake of cabbage rolls, ribs, chicken wings and many other types of traditional American and ethnic foods. At the same time, you can enjoy nationally known bands on the main stage, an arts and crafts fair, puppet shows and other kids' events, and, of course, the nightly fireworks. Proceeds benefit the St. Paul Downtown Council.

TWIN CITIES RIBFEST
Downtown Minneapolis 338-3807

Do you know the difference between pork back ribs, spareribs, country-style ribs and boneless ribs? The poor porkers themselves may not find delectable ribs a cause for celebration, but rib connoisseurs (and downtown workers on their lunch hour) smack their lips at this food event, held annually at the end of July. Chefs from around the country vie for the national barbecue rib championship. Also part of the festivities are a hog-calling contest and pig races (they have good reason to run).

VIENNESE SOMMERFEST

Orchestra Hall, 1111 Nicollet Mall
Minneapolis 371-5656

If you're interested in Brahms, Beethoven and bratwurst (and not necessarily in that order), read on. Viennese Sommerfest began in 1980 when the Minnesota Orchestra decided to create its own summer festival inspired by the music, food and spirit of Vienna. Now running four weeks in July and August, the event has grown into one of America's most engaging classical music festivals, one that attracts top-flight artists, local restaurateurs who prepare ethnic cuisine and folks who love music and like to hang out in the Marktplatz, the modest re-creation of a European common that takes shape on Peavey Plaza outside Orchestra Hall.

More than just music, the festival also includes dance, kids' events, tongue-in-cheek programming (last year there was "Late Night with David Zinman," hosted by the conductor and Sommerfest artistic chair) and movies. It's not stuffy at all — there's usually a candlelight recital and piano extravaganza — and even those who don't normally partake of classical music fall under its spell.

August

MINNESOTA RENAISSANCE FESTIVAL

Renaissance Festival Grounds, Minn. Hwy. 169
Shakopee 445-7361

Want to see jousting? Eager to hear olde-style musicians? Care to try your hand at dunking a foul-mouthed, insulting blackguard? Interested in gnawing a turkey leg? You can do all this, as well as enjoy arts and theater, crafts and other 16th-century diversions, at the Minnesota Renaissance Festival. One of the state's biggest attractions for the past 25 years, the festival runs successive weekends from mid-August through the end of September. You'll learn that Renaissance folks, while they had to deal with such diversions as 100-year wars and the plague, certainly had fun.

MINNESOTA STATE FAIR

Minnesota State Fairgrounds
Falcon Heights 642-2200

In the two weeks leading up to (and including) Labor Day, this marvelous, inter-species gathering — which simultaneously delights and torments the eye, ear, nose and stomach — manages to sum up the entire experience of living in Minnesota. Within the space of a day, you can experience a pig barn, a trout pond, an art gallery, a church diner, a salesman's spiel, a game operator's leer, a race car's whine, a tractor's rumble, mini-donuts, pronto pups, butter sculpture, sand sculpture, musicians on parade, talent show winners, vintage autos, monster-size squash, seed art, free carrots, bees in the hive, Ferris wheels in the air, cheese on a stick, pickle on a stick, gefilte fish on a stick and just about any other foodstuff that can be impaled with wood. You'll encounter he-men, hucksters, dazed tourists, proud sheep breeders, people selling silos, people carrying yardsticks, dairy princesses, TV news anchors, politicians who are all hands, barkers who are all voice, farm folks in overalls, teens in hardly anything, equestrians, cremation advocates, insemination specialists, weight guessers and weirdos. And everywhere kids: kids in strollers, crying kids, chewing kids, sticky kids, laughing kids.

Where else in the world can you: 1) drink all the milk you can for 50¢; 2) see the state's fattest hog; 3) lose your lunch on the Gravitron and still have fun; 4) eat, guilt-free, battered and fried cheese curds; 5) hear jazz in one ear and polka music in the other; 6) watch a dog being spayed; 7) see how slovenly those rock station DJs really are; 8) wait in line for a plastic bag imprinted with the name of a seed company; 9) see a sizable percentage of all the llama in Minnesota; 10) pet a water buffalo; 11) step in melted taffy (it could be worse); 12) meet a genuine chain-saw artist; or 13) learn the latest turkey recipes?

The fairgrounds, in the tiny St. Paul suburb of Falcon Heights along N. Snelling Avenue, are enormous, so come prepared to walk because you can't exactly drive through the place. (Special trams for those who can't or don't want to walk do inch through the crowds; the Alpine Lift ride, which connects two ends of the fairgrounds via cable-suspended cars, is a quick way to get from one place to another.) Official parking lots surround the grounds, and you can park for free if you have four or more in your car (others pay $3 to park). If you don't want to deal with that particular sea of cars, just park on the property of the many nearby homeowners who don't mind subjecting their lawns to hot tire treads; you'll pay handsomely for the privilege. Extensive MCTO bus service lets savvy riders bypass the traffic jam.

In 1995 tickets to the fair ran $5 for adults and $4 for kids ages 5 to 12 and seniors. Imps younger than 5 got in free. Discounted tickets are available in advance at the fairgrounds ticket office or at any Holiday gas station in Minnesota or western Wisconsin. On Senior Day senior citizens pay just $1, and on Kids Day those 12 and younger get in for a buck.

POWDERHORN FESTIVAL OF THE ARTS
Powderhorn Park, Minneapolis   823-0597

Powderhorn Park, a green oasis in a richly urban neighborhood of Minneapolis, hosts 170 artists from a four-state area, ethnic-food makers, multinational musicians, kids' activities and, in a recent year, a live Holstein cow in this early-August, two-day salute to the diversity of the city's arts.

UPTOWN ART FAIR
Vicinity of Lake St. at Hennepin Ave. S.
Minneapolis   827-8757

Minneapolis' trendiest neighborhood fills with 525 national artists, 400 volunteers and 350,000 visitors in this mammoth arts and crafts show, which is the largest in the Upper Midwest. Since the early-August fair's founding in the early 1960s, local residents have tended to feel overwhelmed by this three-day crush of people, but art lovers from around the region flock to it for its encyclopedic selection of handmade goods that range from

At the first St. Paul Winter Carnival in 1886, 200 workers erected a 140-foot-tall ice palace that weighed 100 tons and cost $5,210.

Insiders' Tips

schlock to masterworks. In addition to the artists, the fair features food, street performers, live music and children's activities. Each year it raises a quarter of a million dollars that funds neighborhood projects.

October

EUROPEAN OKTOBERFEST
E. Hennepin Ave., Minneapolis   379-3018

E. Hennepin Avenue in the Old St. Anthony district of Minneapolis, across the river from downtown, becomes a veritable Common Market of European cultures during the annual European Oktoberfest, held in September or October. The neighborhood's ethnic restaurants — representing German, Polish, Ukrainian, Rumanian, Italian and Russian cuisines, among others — tempt visitors with Old World food. Also on hand are ethnic bands, horse-drawn carriages and folk dancers. You can take a historic tour of the neighborhood, chomp on a perogie or visit the children's Gingerbread Village.

December

FOLKWAYS OF CHRISTMAS
Murphy's Landing, Shakopee   445-6901

Running on weekends from Thanksgiving through the end of the year at a living history museum, Folkways of Christmas gives visitors a chance to see the decorations and customs of a variety of 19th-century Minnesota ethnic groups. Some examples from past years: The Polish and Czech houses featured straw on the floor to honor Jesus' humble origins, as well as decorations paying tribute to the legend of St. Nicholas, and the German house had a Christmas tree and advent wreath. You can also hear a variety of ethnic holiday music and learn about the Scandinavian legends of Christmas elves who guard the house and the brightly lit menorah for the Jewish holiday of Hanukkah.

HOLIDAZZLE PARADES
Nicollet Mall, downtown
Minneapolis   338-3807

Between Thanksgiving and Christmas, downtown Minneapolis businesses mark the arrival of the holiday season with a quite spectacular series of lighted evening parades down Nicollet Mall. From your vantage point on the sidewalk or in one of the overhead skyways, you can hear electrically wired musicians, see spectacular floats and, of course, Santa. Kids love 'em.

INTERNATIONAL FESTIVAL OF TREES
Minnesota Landscape Arboretum
Chanhassen   443-2460

First celebrated in 1981, this annual holiday treefest runs from December through the first of the year at the Minnesota Landscape Arboretum. The festival features live evergreens bearing handmade holiday decorations from many cultures and centuries, including trees with Colonial American, Tahitian, Norwegian, English, Irish and Japanese themes. Other attractions are horse-drawn sleigh rides, kids' activities and family entertainment.

Inside
The Arts

The Twin Cities, it seems, has always bustled with the arts. As far back as 1856 — when St. Paul was still a dusty river town subject to cholera epidemics and Minneapolis was a frontier outpost less than a year old — the great Norwegian violinist Ole Bull, one of the most famous classical artists of the 19th century, came to the area accompanied by a 13-year-old Spanish girl named Adelina Patti, already on her way to becoming the best-known soprano of her generation. The duo gave a pair of recitals, but the performing conditions were not ideal. Before performing in Minneapolis, Bull had to insist that the floor of the concert hall, above Arthur McGhee's grocery store, be reinforced to prevent collapse. And because the owner of the only grand piano in town demanded the exorbitant fee of $50 to move the instrument to the hall, the touring musicians had to engage a smaller, much inferior, piano offered by another early settler.

Photo: Joe Rossi, Pioneer Press

Ghanian drummer Sowah Mensah performing with the Minnesota Orchestra.

Aside from the fact that big names like Bull and Patti still come to town, much has since changed in the artistic life of the Twin Cities. We've built outstanding facilities for enjoying the output of artists, places that include concert halls such as the Ordway Music Theatre and Orchestra Hall, theaters such as the Guthrie and Theatre de la Jeune Lune's stage, art museums such as the Weisman and Walker Art Center and other performing venues as diverse as Northrop Auditorium, the main stage at the Loft and the Chanhassen Dinner Theatres. We've grown into a metropolitan area that strongly supports the arts through patronage and philanthropy. Most important, we've long ago ceased being simply a stop in the touring schedules of out-of-state artists and have developed a homegrown and vital community of musicians, visual artists, dancers, film and video professionals and writers who attract national attention and influence the work of others.

Of course, some Twin Citians wouldn't be caught dead in a playhouse and yawn at the idea of waiting in line to see a groundbreaking art exhibit. They are viewed curiously by all the others in town who can't imagine not dipping into the artistic wealth that distinguishes the Twin Cities from so many other Midwestern communities.

The role of Old Man Winter in making this region an artistic mecca by freezing the outdoors five months a year is probably exaggerated; those arts organizations that maintain schedules during the glorious spring and summer, such as the Minnesota Orchestra and its spectacularly successful Viennese Sommerfest, report no problems getting crowds to attend such performances. Perhaps the annual freeze does give Twin Cities artists fewer distractions from their work, but more noteworthy is the encouragement and support — private, corporate and otherwise — that creative people find here. There's a reason why Minnesota outpaces 46 other states in the amount of federal support it receives for the arts: The money can sniff out the talent.

An excellent and free guide to the arts in the Twin Cities is *Art Town*, a directory published by the Metropolitan Regional Arts Council (call 292-8010 for a copy). And if you're a fan of automated telephone information lines, try calling ArtsPhone, a free and easy-to-use service that provides information on Twin Cities arts and performance events and can even connect you with the presenting organizations. ArtsPhone is updated every Friday afternoon; the number is 377-0241.

Dance

BALLET ARTS MINNESOTA
528 Hennepin Ave., Ste. 201
Minneapolis   340-1071

Ballet Arts Minnesota is a school and performance organization that uses such locations as Northrop Auditorium in

Insiders' Tips

Writer Anne Tyler, author of many novels about the American South, is a native of Minneapolis.

Photo: Sully Doroshow, Pioneer Press

Guthrie Theater in Minneapolis.

Minneapolis and O'Shaughnessy Auditorium in St. Paul to give traditional and contemporary ballet performances.

ETHNIC DANCE THEATRE

1940 Hennepin Ave.
Minneapolis　　　　　872-0024

Featuring skilled dancers, great costumes and unusual musicians, Ethnic Dance Theatre is dedicated to presenting the traditional dance and music of many world cultures. The group gives performances throughout the year at such locations as Orchestra Hall and O'Shaughnessy Auditorium and also offers workshops and school residencies.

MINNESOTA DANCE ALLIANCE

528 Hennepin Ave., Ste. 600
Minneapolis　　　　　340-1156

The Alliance is the state's largest organization supporting dance arts. It sponsors several dance performance series, which are presented on stage at Hennepin Center for the Arts, Walker Art Center and other locations. It also offers a newsletter and other services for dancers.

MINNESOTA DANCE THEATRE AND SCHOOL

528 Hennepin Ave., Ste. 5B
Minneapolis　　　　　338-0627

This ballet school for students of all ages is best-known to Twin Cities eventsgoers for its annual holiday presentation of Loyce Houlton's *Nutcracker Fantasy* at the Historic Orpheum Theatre in downtown Minneapolis. Over the past 27 years, this production — now the longest-running and most widely attended arts event in Minnesota history — has paired members of the Minnesota Orchestra and the Minnesota Dance Theatre in a magical combination of beautiful dancing and Tchaikovsky's beloved ballet music before audiences totaling more than 1 million.

NANCY HAUSER DANCE COMPANY AND SCHOOL

1940 Hennepin Ave.
Minneapolis　　　　　871-9077

Although the company's founder died several years ago, this organization remains a strong dance force in the Twin Cities, offering classes and presenting modern dance programs.

TAPESTRY FOLKDANCE CENTER

310 E. 38th St., Minneapolis　　825-3668

If you're anxious to learn how to dance a sher, cut a czarda or rock into a rhumba, check out this folkdance center, which provides instruction and the chance to take part in all kinds of ethnic and national dancing with like-minded people. Its programs take place in Sabathani Center in Minneapolis.

Literary Arts

THE LOFT

66 Malcolm Ave. S.E.
Minneapolis　　　　　379-8999

Housed in a former school building in Minneapolis' Prospect Park neighborhood, the Loft brings some of the world's finest writers to the Twin Cities for readings and other programs. Gary Soto, Andre Codrescu, Claribel Alegria and many others have mounted the Loft's stage to present their work, as have such area writers as Judith Guest, Kate Green, Carol Bly and Alexs Pate. Viewed as a whole, the organization's hefty schedule of writing classes is the finest in the region, and its grant programs, writing support groups and other services do much to strengthen the Twin Cities' active writing community. Special mentorship programs serve African American, Hispanic, Native American, Asian American and gay and lesbian writers.

MINNESOTA CENTER FOR BOOK ARTS
24 N. Third St., Minneapolis   338-3634

The Center for Book Arts, in the Minneapolis Warehouse District, promotes the practice of book arts and book design. It involves writers and book designers in innovative collaborations and offers classes and workshops on the art of the physical book. Its exhibitions explore the ways in which artists are changing the presentation of printed ideas.

THE PLAYWRIGHTS' CENTER
2301 E. Franklin Ave.
Minneapolis   332-7481

Itching to see some new plays — some *really* new plays? Several times each season, this nationally renowned organization holds informally staged or unstaged readings of playwrights' works in progress, providing a rare glimpse of the dramatic muse at work (or asleep at the wheel). The Playwrights' Center also offers grant support, workshops, classes and other performance opportunities for writers of plays.

SCREENWRITERS' WORKSHOP
P.O. Box 580800
Minneapolis 55458   331-3880

Participants in Screenwriters' Workshop programs are people interested in screenplays (and teleplays) or who want to improve their skills in writing them. This organization offers public readings of new works, classes, lectures, a newsletter and a competitive production program that brings members' scripts to the screen.

Moving Images

MINNESOTA MOTION PICTURE AND TELEVISION BOARD
401 N. Third St., Ste. 460
Minneapolis   332-6493

Funded by the state and from private donations, the film board works to attract movie and video projects to Minnesota and to assist film makers in a variety of ways once production begins. As a result of its efforts, 30 feature-length film projects have been undertaken in the state since 1990, creating thousands of jobs and bringing in millions of dollars. The film board also sponsors a couple of movie premieres each year, screening films made in Minnesota. The 24-hour tape-recorded film board hotline, 333-0436, lists upcoming opportunities for crew, talent and extras.

UNIVERSITY FILM SOCIETY
425 Ontario St. S.E.
Minneapolis   627-4431

Created and still directed by movie czar Al Milgrom, the U Film Society is the area's most ambitious and risk-taking presenter of international cinema. Films that never appear anywhere else between the coasts — including gems, soon-to-be classics and a few dogs — frequently land on this organization's screen in the Bell Auditorium on the University of Minnesota campus. The society also hosts the Rivertown Film Festival, an annual orgy of independently made and foreign films.

Multidisciplinary Arts

INTERMEDIA ARTS MINNESOTA
2822 Lyndale Ave. So.
Minneapolis   627-4449

Multimedia installations, performance art, video programs, sound sculptures and electronic music are all part of the territory of Intermedia Arts Minnesota, which sponsors exhibits, schedules classes and administers grants for artists working in a variety of new media and technologies. Among the Twin Cities mainstream arts organizations it has been one of the most active in presenting the work of artists of color.

Music

BACH SOCIETY OF MINNESOTA
P.O. Box 39292
Minneapolis 55439   649-4692

Embracing three separate performing groups — the Bach Society Chorus, the Sebastian Singers and the Motet Choir — this choral music organization gives several performances a year in different locations.

CEDAR CULTURAL CENTER
416 Cedar Ave. S.
Minneapolis   338-2674

This is one of the area's main folk, blues, international music and folk dance hangouts, with appearances by such artists as Greg Brown, Blind Boys of Alabama, Pierre Bensusan, Peter Ostroushko and Rory Block. A former movie theater, the facility has rather uncomfortable seating of the folding-chair variety, but everyone in the audience is up close to the stage, and the acoustics are fine. Every month the Center hosts several contradance and other footstomping events, and instruction is always provided.

THE FREDERICK CHOPIN SOCIETY
P.O. Box 8131
Minneapolis 55408   870-0604

If you like the music of Chopin — or Beethoven, Brahms, Bartók or anybody else who wrote for the piano — take advantage of the annual recital series that this keyboard-loving organization sponsors. Its recent concerts have spotlighted such well-known artists as Stephen Hough and Cynthia Raim, and rising stars in the classical-music scene also make frequent appearances. Most concerts take place at the Janet Wallace Fine Arts Center, Macalester College, St. Paul.

CORN PALACE PRODUCTIONS
1420 Washington Ave. S.
Minneapolis   340-1725

Each year, this feisty organization presents the Corn Palace Festival of Theatrical Music, a month-long set of musical theater shows that feature new tunes and collaborations between some of the area's most accomplished composers and librettists. It all takes place in the Southern Theater, a venerable old place built in 1909 and in a convenient spot, in the Seven Corners area of Minneapolis, that has seen everything from Swedish theater productions to avant-garde operas.

THE DALE WARLAND SINGERS
120 N. Fourth St., Minneapolis   339-9707

These vocalists, who together make up one of the region's best choral groups, often embark upon international concert tours and sponsor their own concert series in the Twin Cities. They've frequently appeared on radio, have recorded extensively and often commission new works. Their director, Dale Warland, is an internationally known vocal-music master.

EX MACHINA
230 Crestway Ln., West St. Paul   455-8086

Guided by the inventive mind of artistic director James Middleton, Ex Machina is a baroque opera company that stages productions that are always interesting and often eye-poppingly costumed and designed. See just one Ex Machina production, and you'll forever forget the notion that old music is sedate. The group's orchestra, performing on period instruments, is uniformly excellent, as are the singers who take on the sometimes bizarre roles that the featured baroque composers wrote.

MINNESOTA BLUEGRASS AND OLD-TIME MUSIC ASSOCIATION

P.O. Box 11419
St. Paul 55111   870-7432

The two biggest programs of this organization are a midwinter bluegrass fest held at a Twin Cities location and a much larger summer festival held outside the metropolitan area in Zimmerman usually in August. MBOTMA also publishes a monthly newsletter for members.

MINNESOTA CHORALE

528 Hennepin Ave., Ste. 211
Minneapolis   333-4866

Another of the Twin Cities' excellent professional-level choruses, the 150-voice Minnesota Chorale frequently performs with the Minnesota Orchestra and St. Paul Chamber Orchestra. It focuses on the great works of symphonic choral literature.

MINNESOTA COMPOSERS FORUM

332 Minnesota St., Ste. E145
St. Paul   228-1407

This is the nation's largest organization dedicated to the creation and appreciation of new music through the promotion of composers. Despite its name, MCF has members nationwide. It sponsors concerts of new music (often in collaboration with Walker Art Center), provides grants and performance opportunities to composers and connects composers with others who are seeking new works.

MINNESOTA GUITAR SOCIETY

P.O. Box 14986
Minneapolis 55414   374-4681

Fans of the guitar pay homage to this organization for bringing to town some of the country's finest players in the classical, jazz and blues styles. Its annual Classical Guitarathon, a spring fund-raising event, is a big audience favorite, as is the annual Jazz Guitarathon in the fall. Members receive a newsletter and other benefits.

MINNESOTA OPERA

620 N. First St., Minneapolis   224-4222

Once known nationwide for its productions of new opera, the Minnesota Opera now focuses on the classics, sometimes presented with a contemporary twist. Its shows, like recent productions of *La Boheme* and *Don Giovanni*, always look good and often boast impressive musical talent. Many of its productions use surtitles, English translations projected above the stage. It mounts its productions at Ordway Music Theatre and the Fitzgerald Theater, both in St. Paul. Ordway patrons can take advantage of Opera Insights, half-hour pre-show sessions that explore the opera's story, characters, staging and music. The Minnesota Opera also offers several types of opera classes.

MINNESOTA ORCHESTRA

1111 Nicollet Mall   371-5656
Minneapolis   (800) 292-4141

Founded in 1903 as the Minneapolis Symphony Orchestra, this world-renowned

When the Beatles appeared at Met Stadium in Bloomington in 1965, it was the only concert in their American tour that did not sell out.

Insiders' Tips

orchestra has worked under such music directors as Eugene Ormandy (1931 to 1936), Dimitri Mitropoulos (1937 to 1949), Antal Dorati (1949 to 1960; the orchestra made some of its best-known recordings under his baton), Stanislaw Skrowaczewski (1960 to 1979) and Sir Neville Marriner (1979 to 1986). Edo de Waart's nine-year tenure shaped the orchestra into a powerful ensemble that performs music of the 19th and 20th centuries most convincingly. During recent years, such composers as Strauss, Mahler and Berlioz have received the most sympathetic readings of their works from the Minnesota Orchestra. If not one of the nation's "big five" orchestras, the Minnesota Orchestra certainly ranks among the top dozen.

The 1995-96 season marks Eiji Oue's (pronounced AY-gee OH-way) debut as the Minnesota Orchestra's music director. Oue's appointment to the Minnesota post surprised the classical music world, especially because of his dramatic rise from a smaller regional orchestra in Pennsylvania, the Erie Philharmonic. An enthusiastic conductor committed to community service, Oue has made his mark quickly in the Twin Cities, and is expected to build upon the work of his predecessor de Waart.

In addition to its regular subscription-series concerts that run from the fall through the spring, the Minnesota Orchestra also performs Weekender Pops and summer Cabaret Pops concerts (former "Tonight Show" bandleader Doc Severinsen serves as principal pops conductor); offers informal Casual Classics concerts and plays at multicultural Kaleidoscope events; and sends each summer spinning with its annual, four-week-long Viennese Sommerfest. Led by artistic director David Zinman, Sommerfest is a high-energy music festival that features dozens of guest artists and more than its share of surprise events.

The Minnesota Orchestra uses Orchestra Hall in Minneapolis as its home field. Built in 1974, this hall is an acoustically amazing place that holds 2,262 people. Huge acoustical cubes on the ceiling and behind the stage scatter the sound in all directions, sometimes startlingly so. Some of the best sound is on the top tier, but many of the seats there suffer from obscured viewing. The view is best from Tier One. An adjoining parking ramp is connected to Orchestra Hall via a skyway.

Minnesota Public Radio offers live broadcasts of many orchestra concerts, and Public Radio International (formerly American Public Radio) carries them to stations around the country.

PLYMOUTH MUSIC SERIES
1900 Nicollet Ave.
Minneapolis   *690-6700*

For the past 26 years, the Plymouth Music Series has been exploring the world of music for voices and instruments. Directed by Philip Brunelle, a nationally prominent and Grammy Award-winning conductor, the series tackles fresh new compositions (including frequent world premieres), audience favorites and works that involve the talents of such guest artists as Garrison Keillor, James Earl Jones and Jubilant Sykes. Performances take place in several Twin Cities venues, including Orchestra Hall, Ted Mann Concert Hall on the University of Minnesota campus, the Ordway Music Theatre and Plymouth Congregational Church.

THE SAINT PAUL CHAMBER ORCHESTRA
Hamm Bldg., 405 St. Peter St.
Ste. 300, St. Paul   *291-1144*

People often wonder why the Twin Cities has two major orchestras. Compare the sound of The Saint Paul Chamber Orches-

Photo: Joe Rossi, Pioneer Press

Saint Paul Chamber Orchestra in Landmark Center.

tra with that of the crosstown ensemble, the Minnesota Orchestra, and you'll realize that the presence of both is due to more than plain sibling rivalry. Smaller and in possession of a jewel-like sound, the 37-year-old SPCO is the nation's only full-time chamber orchestra and is renowned worldwide for the caliber of its live performances and many recordings. In recent decades, its music directors have included Dennis Russell Davies, violinist Pinchas Zukerman and now Hugh Wolff, an increasingly prominent American conductor whose brightest years are still in the future. The ensemble has mastered an incredible range of material, from 16th-century works to brand-new pieces (winning several ASCAP awards for the performance of new music in the process). The SPCO's artistic strengths are particularly evident in its performances of new music as well as works by such composers as Vivaldi, Bach, Corelli, Haydn and Mozart.

Because the 32-member SPCO is smaller than a symphony orchestra and often plays in more intimate settings than the traditional cavernous concert hall, it sometimes seems more like a family than an orchestra. The players obviously like each other, work well together and have fun at what they're doing. Many members of the audience recognize SPCO musicians on the street and stop to talk with them.

Music Director Hugh Wolff heads an artistic staff consisting of Principal Guest Conductor Christopher Hogwood, Composer-in-Residence Aaron Jay Karnis and

Reserve Trust Creative Chair Bobby McFerrin. The SPCO presents more than 150 concerts and educational programs each year during a 40-week season, appearing frequently in the United States and abroad. In addition to performing at the Ordway Music Theatre and Orchestra Hall, the orchestra presents series at United Church of Christ and O'Shaughnessy Auditorium in St. Paul, Temple Israel and Ted Mann Concert Hall in Minneapolis and Wooddale Church in Eden Prairie. The SPCO is one of the most frequently broadcast orchestras in the country, heard weekly on 160 Public Radio International stations coast-to coast.

THE SCHUBERT CLUB

75 W. Fifth St., Ste. 302
St. Paul   292-3267

During the last decades of the 19th century, it was common for groups of music-minded citizens to band together to present enjoyable evenings of music, sometimes bringing in a renowned artist from outside the community. The Schubert Club is a miraculous holdover from that period that has expanded and adapted to the 20th century. For more than 100 years, it has invited the world's greatest classical musicians to the Twin Cities for recitals. In addition, the Schubert Club sponsors 40 other recitals each year, competitions and scholarships for young musicians and educational programs.

Insiders' Tips

Make sure you keep your ears open for information about the Guthrie's pre-performance rush tickets.

THURSDAY MUSICAL
1410 W. Skillman Ave.
St. Paul 333-0313

Like the Schubert Club, Thursday Musical originated during the 19th century as an organization founded by music lovers. It's evolved in its own distinctive way, however, emphasizing the showcasing of local musicians and ensembles and providing scholarships to young artists. Its concerts are performed at many venues around the Twin Cities.

TWIN CITIES GAY MEN'S CHORUS
528 Hennepin Ave., Ste. 701
Minneapolis 891-9130

Founded in 1981, this ensemble gives four major concerts a year in Twin Cities locations. It also commissions many new works and performs a great deal of contemporary music.

TWIN CITIES JAZZ SOCIETY
P.O. Box 4487
St. Paul 55104 633-0329

Jazz aficionados find this organization a good source of information on upcoming concerts. The society also sponsors its own jazz series and offers other programs. Its newsletter is an essential part of any jazz lover's monthly reading.

Theater

DUDLEY RIGGS BRAVE NEW WORKSHOP AND INSTANT THEATRE COMPANY
2605 Hennepin Ave.
Minneapolis 332-6620

Founded decades ago by Dudley Riggs, this group is one of the oldest comedy-and-satire companies in the country. Its productions, which invariably sport such playful titles as *Without a Clue: The Dumbing of America* and *Mixup in the Manger: Miracle on 26th Street*, routinely skewer conservative greed, liberal guilt and

"Minnesota nice" in shows that mix high hilarity and music. The group's Hennepin Avenue storefront theater is a worn and cramped cave perfectly suited for in-your-face entertainment.

BRYANT LAKE BOWL THEATER
810 W. Lake St., Minneapolis 825-8949

Here you can hear the crash of strikes and the agonized screams of those who throw gutter balls as you enjoy theater in an decidedly unorthodox setting. Satire and dark comedy are the normal fare in this surprisingly large theater that adjoins a popular bowling hangout. The tableside seats at the front of the theater are definitely better (and less prone to aural interruption from bowlers) than the rear row seating.

CHANHASSEN DINNER THEATRES
501 W. 78th St., Chanhassen 934-1525

About a half-hour drive southwest of Minneapolis is a large complex of theaters where cooks are employed as well as actors, waiters as well as lighting techs and bus help as well as box office staff. Since 1968 theatergoers have been coming to the Chanhassen Dinner Theatres to have their appetites for good food and stylishly produced plays satisfied simultaneously. Its high quality productions run the full gamut of popular theater and Broadway blockbusters — *Crazy for You* and *42nd Street* are some recent examples — and the setting, a semirustic building with fireplaces and snug alcoves, is memorable. Many TV and film stars, such as Loni Anderson and Linda Kelsey, started their climb to the big time here.

THE CHILDREN'S THEATRE COMPANY
2400 Third Ave. S.
Minneapolis 874-0400

One of America's largest and most highly respected producers of kids' theater, CTC stages new adaptations of classics such as *The Invisible Man*, Tomie dePaola's *Mother Goose*, and *Linnea in Monet's Garden*, as well as theater versions of such well-loved works as *Babar the Little Elephant* and Dr. Suess' *How the Grinch Stole Christmas*. High-quality productions are the norm, often with original music and outstanding child and adult actors. The company's modern theater, set in an arts complex it shares with the Minneapolis Institute of Arts, is designed with little viewers in mind (although adults typically constitute more than half of the audience) and features great sightlines, wide aisles and very comfortable seats.

CHILD'S PLAY THEATRE COMPANY
5701 Normandale Rd., Ste. 343
Edina   925-5250
The Twin Cities is lucky to have a second company dedicated to the production of childrens' theater. Usually presenting its programs at Eisenhower Community Center in Hopkins, Child's Play focuses on giving kids stage experience through performances and classes.

CRICKET THEATRE
821 Marquette Ave., Ste. 229
Minneapolis   337-0747
It's hard to believe that this groundbreaking theater company, which specializes in works by such living playwrights as Sam Shepard and Alan Ball, is already 26 years old. The 1995 season features five world premieres, four by Minnesota playwrights. With many near-bankruptcies in its past, the Cricket has always hung on to deliver high quality shows in locations all over Minneapolis. Currently most shows are being mounted at the Hennepin Center for the Arts.

GREAT AMERICAN HISTORY THEATRE
30 E. 10th St., St. Paul   292-4323
Charles Lindbergh, St. Paul's lost African-American Rondo neighborhood, Zelda and F. Scott Fitzgerald and other Minnesota figures and stories have been brought to the stage by this company specializing in musicals, dramas and comedies that detail the lives of people in this region. Many of its shows are world premieres. It gives its performances in the theater of the St. Paul Arts and Science Center. Finding a parking place can be tough, even with a few ramps in the area.

GUTHRIE THEATER
725 Vineland Pl.   377-2224
Minneapolis   (800) 848-4912, Ext. 2712
Although other Twin Cities theaters — most notably the Old Log and Theatre in the Round — antedate it, the Guthrie is the Big Bopper of the frisky local theater world, the institution that receives the most attention from the local press, the national media, funders and area theatergoers. It opened in 1963, the brainchild of British impresario Sir Tyrone Guthrie, who wanted to plant a high-quality repertory theater in the fertile ground of America's heartland. Nearly 200 productions later, Guthrie's dream has taken root with a vengeance: Some of the world's best directors, stage designers, costumers and actors work there, and its shows are invariably top-quality and thought-provoking. Recent seasons have included productions of classics such as *King Lear*, *The Royal Family*, *Firebugs* and *Babes in Arms*. The Guthrie's annual holiday production of Charles Dickens' *A Christmas Carol* is a decades-old tradition in the Twin Cities.

The Guthrie Theater occupies the west half of a cool and solid arts complex it shares with Walker Art Center at the southwest edge of downtown Minneapolis. The theater's recent exterior renovation displeased some patrons, but few can complain about the sightlines of the 1,500-seat interior. The best seats are on the main floor, because even some professionally trained voices can get lost up in the balconies. Areas 2, 3 and 4 allow seating for users of wheelchairs and their guests. Rush seats, available for most performances at $10, provide some great ticket bargains. The theater is also an excellent and frequently used concert venue.

Don't arrive at the last minute for Guthrie performances — traffic can get congested and parking can be hard to find in the largely residential neighborhood. There are pay lots next to the Minneapolis Sculpture Garden and on Groveland Avenue. The Guthrie is also accessible via bus lines 1, 4, 6, 12 and 28.

HEY CITY THEATRE ON HENNEPIN
824 Hennepin, Minneapolis   989-5151

For four years this theater mounted a lively production of *Forever Plaid* in the West Bank area of Minneapolis. Now, in its new location on Hennepin Avenue, Hey City Theatre draws crowds to a production of *Tony and Tina's Wedding*, complete with a nuptial feast.

ILLUSION THEATER
528 Hennepin Ave., Ste. 704
Minneapolis   338-8371

Presenting most of its shows in the Hennepin Center for the Arts, Illusion Theater is unusually focused on sparking personal and social change. It produces the work of many emerging and well-established contemporary playwrights and is perhaps best-known for its annual Fresh Ink Series, a weeks-long parade of new and in-progress plays by American writers of all kinds. Starting out in 1974 as a mime troupe, Illusion Theater

has grown into one of the Twin Cities' most intriguing and rewarding companies.

IN THE HEART OF THE BEAST PUPPET AND MASK THEATRE
1500 E. Lake St., Minneapolis   721-2535

If you've attended many parades or festivals in the Twin Cities, you've undoubtedly encountered an army of the Heart of the Beast's trademark jumbo puppet figures. It's an awesome sight. With permanent quarters in a former porn theater, the company employs puppets of many types to create surprisingly poignant shows for adults and families, often touching upon serious social issues. The group also offers many productions in various community settings.

JUNGLE THEATER
709 W. Lake St., Minneapolis   822-7063

One of the area's hottest and most successful playhouses is the Jungle Theatre. In just a few years it has exerted its own special influence. Its productions — including classic and contemporary works such as *The Swan*, *Waiting For Godot*, *The Glass Menagerie* and *Fool For Love* — are often outstanding. Situated in a storefront facility, the Jungle offers cramped (and very limited) seating that somehow increases the intensity and effectiveness of its shows. The Jungle's productions are for audiences who love expert directing, splendid acting and unforgettable theater.

LORING PLAYHOUSE
1633 Hennepin Ave. S.
Minneapolis   332-1617

Ensconced in a formerly elegant car dealership building (now also the quarters of the chic Loring Bar and Cafe), this avant-garde company presents irreverent and intriguing shows that resist simple categorization as comedies, dramas, etc.

They're all complex and playful, often arguments for different concepts of beauty or normalcy than mainstream theater usually presents.

MINNESOTA CENTENNIAL SHOWBOAT
Raspberry Island, St. Paul   624-2345

An old paddlewheeler moored on the banks of Old Man River may seem an unusual place to attend an old tearjerker like *Peg O' My Heart*, but decades worth of comedies, melodramas and musicals have strained the boards of this floating playhouse operated by the University of Minnesota's theater department. Open only during the summer, the Showboat, now anchored on St. Paul's Raspberry Island, features energetic and usually young casts, along with a gentle rise and fall that is certainly not part of your imagination.

MIXED BLOOD THEATER
1501 S. Fourth St., Minneapolis   338-0937

At one time the nation's largest employer of Equity actors of color, Mixed Blood is a company that has never shied away from controversial and thought-provoking productions. Its managing director, Jack Reuler, has long espoused a color-blind casting policy that only gradually have some other theaters imitated. Whether its shows are probing the causes and effects of the Crown Heights riots or examining the soul of Cyrano de Bergerac, they're always memorable.

MUSIC BOX THEATRE
1407 Nicollet Ave., Minneapolis   871-1414

After having served for years as the Cricket Theatre's home, this former cinema at the edge of downtown Minneapolis has been again refurbished to provide a congenial home for musicals and musical revues. One recent production, *The All Night Strut*, seamlessly paraded 27 favorite songs from the 1930s and '40s.

Audiences of a surprisingly wide range of ages have proven susceptible to this type of musical fare.

NEW CLASSIC THEATRE
1832 Carroll Ave., St. Paul   645-7547

Area premieres of new plays are the specialty of this company that puts together only one or two shows a year, usually presenting them at the Minneapolis Theater Garage or Mixed Blood Theater. Founded by artistic director Peter Moore, a well-known local actor, the company delivers strongly acted performances and challenging plays.

NORTHERN SIGN THEATRE
528 Hennepin Ave., Ste. 308
Minneapolis   338-7876, TTY 338-7549

The mission of this company is to spark dialogue between deaf and hearing people through the theater. Audiences can take in everything it produces — stage shows, touring productions, workshops and videos — in both American Sign Language and English.

OLD LOG THEATER
5175 Meadville St., Excelsior   474-5951

In business since 1941, Old Log is the oldest professional theater concern in the Twin Cities. Beautifully set near the shore of Lake Minnetonka, the current facility replaced the original theater decades ago and has more than 600 seats. (The old structure now serves as a scene shop.) The theatre presents productions such as *Beau Jest*, a romantic comedy making its area premiere after three years running in New York. This renowned and much-loved dinner theater boasts alumni who include movie star Nick Nolte.

PARK SQUARE THEATRE
253 E. Fourth St., St. Paul   291-7005

For years Park Square staged its

shows exclusively at the auditorium of the Minnesota Museum of American Art building in St. Paul, but now the company has begun using Seventh Place Theatre, 20 W. Seventh Place, St. Paul, as the home stage for its performances of classic plays from the European and American repertory. Its season runs winter through summer.

PENUMBRA THEATRE COMPANY
270 N. Kent St., St. Paul   224-3180

Penumbra, the Twin Cities' only professional company presenting works from an African-American perspective, performs at St. Paul's Martin Luther King Center. Long associated with Pulitzer Prize-winning playwright August Wilson (a former St. Paul resident), Penumbra has recently come into the public eye even more with solid stagings of plays by other writers. Each holiday season, Penumbra fills the Fitzgerald Theater with many performances of Langston Hughes' *Black Nativity*, an uplifting and music-filled retelling of the nativity story.

PLYMOUTH PLAYHOUSE
Hwys. 55 and 494, Plymouth   553-1600

With offerings such as *A Closer Walk with Patsy Cline*, *Pump Boys and Dinettes* and *The Lovely Liebowitz Sisters in a Krakatoa Homecoming*, this is a place to go for light musicals, nostalgia and cute comedy. The theater is a part of a Best Western Kelly Inn.

RED EYE COLLABORATION
15 W. 14th St., Minneapolis   870-0309

New multimedia theater works are Red Eye's bread and butter, and the group is well-known for its presentations of experimental, nontraditional and provocative shows. It also sponsors occasional music series and media exhibitions.

THE REFRESHMENT COMMITTEE
801 Dayton Ave., St. Paul   227-0775

The Refreshment Committee, a professional company that performs at Seventh Place Theatre in St. Paul, presents shows for adults and kids that illustrate biblical values and promote racial equality and social responsibility.

TEATRO LATINO DE MINNESOTA
3501 Chicago Ave. S.
Minneapolis   432-2314

This is a multicultural theater company that often presents issues-packed or exploratory Hispanic plays, many of them performed bilingually.

THEATER MU
3010 Hennepin Ave. S., Ste. 290
Minneapolis   824-0024

This theater company, specializing in plays that explore Asian-American issues, has made a fast entry into the Twin Cities' admittedly crowded stage scene. Its new productions include *Sam I Am*, while the Annual New Eyes Festival showcases emerging Asian America playwrights with staged readings of their work. Theatre Mu's productions are staged throughout the city

Take advantage of Walker Art Center's free admission policy on Thursday and the first Saturday of the month.

Insiders' Tips

at venues including the Southern Theater, Ordway and Hennepin Center for the Arts.

THEATRE DE LA JEUNE LUNE
105 N. First St., Minneapolis   *333-6200*

If the Guthrie Theater gets the lion's share of media and public attention among the Twin Cities' theaters, Theatre de la Jeune Lune challenges other venues for second place. An ensemble theater created by American and French actors, it stages richly imaginative and grandly conceived shows that are usually jointly created by many members of the company. For many seasons now, its productions, such as *Yang Zen Frogs* and *Don Juan Giovanni*, have drawn international raves. Jeune Lune performs in a stylish old downtown Minneapolis building, a former storage warehouse, that was partly designed by Cass Gilbert, architect of the U.S. Supreme Court building in Washington and New York's Woolworth Building. It gives the company the room it needs to mount productions that typically bulge with cast members and ideas. The company's name means "theater of the new moon," an oblique homage to the innovative Parisian Theatre du Soleil (Theater of the Sun).

THEATRE IN THE ROUND PLAYERS
245 Cedar Ave., Minneapolis   *333-3010*

Now creeping up on its 45th birthday, Theatre in the Round is the region's oldest community theater, and its stage certainly ranks among the busiest. Each year about 10 productions are mounted in the company's Seven Corners building; they range from classics to contemporary works and Broadway hits. Theatre in the Round also offers classes and training in theater crafts.

VENETIAN PLAYHOUSE
2814 Rice St., St. Paul   *484-1108*

This theater features extended-run productions of cabaret- and vaudeville-style shows, often staged by such companies as Troupe America. Dinner service is available before most shows. The playhouse is inside the Venetian Inn Restaurant.

The Visual Arts

BLOOMINGTON ART CENTER
10206 Penn Ave. S.
Bloomington   *887-9667*

This center supplies one of the best arguments that the suburbs are not arts-free deserts. It frequently exhibits the work of Bloomington-area artists and also offers art classes and workshops for kids and adults.

FREDERICK R. WEISMAN ART MUSEUM
333 E. River Rd. (East Bank of U. of Minn.)
Minneapolis   *625-9494*

Crossing the Washington Avenue Bridge or taking in the view across the Mississippi River, you can't miss this wonderful pile of improbably angled sheets of metal, designed by Los Angeles architect Frank Gehry, that sits atop the east bank and sends blinding reflections of sunlight in all directions. Named after its major donor, it's spectacular on the outside and very functional and friendly on the inside (although smaller than it appears from the exterior). This museum, run by the University of Minnesota, just opened a couple of years ago and has had a lot of visitors singing its praises. It houses the University's extensive art collection and also hosts visiting exhibitions from around the country. The permanent collection is especially strong in 20th-century American art. Recent showings have included *Imaging Women: Representations of Women in Art & Culture* and a photography exhibition titled *Faces of Sorrow: Agony in the Former Yugoslavia*. Parking is available in a ramp located beneath the museum. Admission to the museum is free.

MINNEAPOLIS INSTITUTE OF ARTS
2400 Third Ave. S., Minneapolis   *870-3266*

Back in 1911, a group of prominent Minneapolis citizens pooled their money to establish an ambitiously conceived art museum and classroom facility for the city. The original Beaux-Arts building, designed by the famed architectural firm McKim, Mead and White and completed in 1915, still stands, raising its columns to Fair Oaks Park across the street and the more distant skyscrapers of downtown. In recent decades, however, various additions have expanded the facility, creating one of America's great comprehensive art museums and luring art lovers from throughout the region.

The 80,000-item collection of the Art Institute is strong in many areas, particularly in decorative art, textiles and the art of ancient times, Asia, the United States before 1950 and Europe of the 14th through 19th centuries. Wandering its high-ceilinged galleries, you'll encounter works by Titian, Georgia O'Keeffe, Monet, Van Gogh, Grant Wood, Picasso, Miró and Magritte. You'll also see a 2,000-year-old mummy, a world-famous Oriental jade collection, the throne of a Chinese king, rooms representing many periods from American and European history, a fine collection of African masks, a remarkable hoard of prints and drawings, a photo gallery and a wondrous sand mural created on-site by a group of visiting Tibetan monks.

Don't miss Rembrandt's *Lucretia*, the gathering of French impressionist paintings, the American gallery ⸻ and the displays of the M⸻ Exhibition Program tha⸻ works of regional artis⸻ also boasts a gift shop, edu⸻ its, a coffee shop, video and film p⸻ and art classes for kids and adults.

A half-million people visit this museum every year. Like most art museums, the Institute is closed Mondays. Admission is free, except for some special or touring exhibitions usually displayed on the second floor.

MINNESOTA CRAFTS COUNCIL
528 Hennepin Ave., Ste. 308
Minneapolis   *333-7789*

This organization's most visible activity is a high-quality annual crafts fair, held in June or July at the College of St. Catherine in St. Paul. The Council, focused on promoting excellence in craft media and handmade objects, also sponsors other exhibitions and connects crafts artists with one another.

MINNESOTA MUSEUM OF AMERICAN ART
75 W. Fifth St., Second Fl.
St. Paul   *292-4380*

The Minnesota Museum of American Art has always operated in the shadows of its Minneapolis counterparts. It is less financially secure than the other art museums in town, which has recently prevented it from showing off the luster of its collection. Strong in American paintings (especially from the decades around the turn of the century) and the art of Asia, Africa and Oceania, the Minnesota Museum of American Art reserves the Landmark Center gallery space for temporary exhibitions, many of which focus on the work of contemporary artists. Recent exhibitions have included *Adventures in the Art Zone*, a family oriented interactive art experience, and *ness and Legacy: Contemporary Art about The Holocaust*, featuring the work of 22 artists and their response to the Holocaust.

NORTHERN CLAY CENTER

2375 University Ave. W.
St. Paul 642-1735

Get your wheels spinning and your fingers dirty at this ceramic arts center that sponsors classes and exhibitions of the work of regional and national artists.

WALKER ART CENTER

725 Vineland Pl., Minneapolis 375-7636

Sharing a building with the Guthrie Theater is one of the nation's greatest centers of contemporary art. Walker Art Center began, however, as the private collection of T.B. Walker, a Minneapolis lumber baron who collected Old Master paintings, Oriental pottery and jade carvings, musical instruments, ancient Greek vases and many other kinds of art objects. After Walker's death, the art foundation he had established decided to make 20th-century art the focus of its galleries at the foot of Lowry Hill in Minneapolis.

The thousands of pieces in the Walker's permanent collection now span the full range of American and European art movements in the 20th century, everything from Pop Art and Minimalism to Abstract Expressionism and Neo-Expressionism. Some of the nation's best touring contemporary art exhibitions also make a mandatory stop at the Walker.

The Walker, though, is much more than just an art museum. Through its renowned performing arts program, it sponsors or co-sponsors an amazing variety of events: film and video screenings, dance performances, concerts, appearances by performance artists, lectures, music and theater events, and children's programs. Many take place at the Walker, but others take the stage at venues around the area. Free First Saturday, on the first Saturday of every month, is a family event with special performances, art activities for kids and free gallery admission.

Across the street from the Walker and jointly operated by it and the Minneapolis Park Board is the 7-acre Minneapolis Sculpture Garden, an outdoor area that opened in 1988 and has rapidly become one of the Twin Cities' most popular hangouts for tourists, families and arts lovers. The beautifully landscaped Sculpture Garden contains exemplary works by such sculptors as Henry Moore and Frank Gehry, sprouts a great flower garden at its north end and includes a 52-foot-long sculpture and fountain that has become a symbol of Minneapolis' status as an arts-conscious city: Claes Oldenburg's and Coosje van Bruggen's *Spoonbridge and Cherry*. The Irene Hixon Whitney Bridge, a long and delicate connection between the Sculpture Garden and Loring Park, designed by Siah Armajani, is also a part of the collection.

Insiders' Tips

Night owls never miss late-night Saturday improv sessions at Dudley Riggs' Brave New Workshop.

Other Venues

HENNEPIN CENTER FOR THE ARTS
528 Hennepin Ave., Minneapolis   *332-4478*

This rugged sentinel at the corner of Fifth Street and Hennepin Avenue in downtown Minneapolis, built in 1890 as a Masonic Temple, houses many small arts organizations and contains two public performing spaces. The larger one, the 300-seat Bower Hawthorne Theatre on the top floor, is used by such companies as Illusion Theatre, Cricket Theatre, Lyric Theatre and Troupe America, as well as some music and dance groups. It suffers from the high elevation of the stage, which forces performers to look down at much of the audience. The second-floor Little Theater, a 140-seat space, is encumbered by poor lighting. In the works is a $2 million refurbishing of the building that would dramatically reconfigure the seating of the Bower Hawthorne Theatre and improve the technical equipment in the Little Theater. If the money is raised, it all could happen as early as 1996.

TED MANN MUSIC HALL
West Bank, University of Minnesota
Minneapolis   *624-2224*

Only a couple of years old, this concert hall has quickly become a major performing space for all kinds of musical organizations in addition to the many university ensembles that play there. Its acoustics are fine-tuned enough for a solo guitar recital and solid enough for a concert band. Sightlines are fine, especially from the side balconies.

MINNEAPOLIS THEATER GARAGE
711 W. Franklin Ave.   *870-0723*

This theater in the Wedge neighborhood, a former repair facility that now hosts occasional productions by the Jungle

Theater and other companies, is excellent from the audience's perspective. All seats are close to the stage, and sightlines are great. It's pretty small, perhaps accommodating a crowd of 100. Only street parking is available.

NORTHROP AUDITORIUM
University of Minnesota
Minneapolis   *624-2345*

This formidable auditorium, built in 1929 and capable of seating a crowd of 5,000, spent its early years mainly as a home of university events and as a classical-music concert hall where audiences cheered the likes of Vladimir Horowitz and Sergei Rachmaninoff. (The Minnesota Orchestra cut some of its most famous early recordings there, as well.) Nowadays Northrop does much of its own programming, putting on its stage some of the world's best ballet and dance ensembles and bringing in a variety of prominent pop and jazz musicians.

Two areas of the auditorium are best for dance performances: the first rows of the balcony and the side sections of the main floor, where you can follow the footwork without turning your head back and forth like a tennis fan. On the main floor, Row 25 has an advantage because its elevation over the preceding row is abnormally high. Northrop's balcony spotlights spill more light than their counterparts in other halls, so light-sensitive people may want to stick to the main floor. Acoustically, there are few advantageous seats; the stage's acoustical shell has improved the sound in the first 10 rows.

ORDWAY MUSIC THEATRE
345 Washington St., St. Paul   *224-4222*

The Ordway serves as the primary home of the Saint Paul Chamber Orchestra, the Minnesota Opera and the Schubert

Club, but it also offers interesting and ambitious programming of its own. Along with the Historic Orpheum Theatre in Minneapolis, it is the only place in town that can accommodate such gigantic and stage-busting Broadway shows as *Show Boat*, *Damn Yankees* and *West Side Story*. It also programs highly regarded (and well-attended) dance and music series, both of which have a strong international and multicultural component. The Ordway offers special programs for kids too.

Built in 1984 and reputedly inspired by the great concert halls of Europe, the Ordway has an 1,800-seat music hall that has never been as acoustically stunning as Minneapolis' Orchestra Hall but offers its own charms: a beautiful, old-world feel; comfortable seats with good sightlines; and a magical (especially during the winter) location at the edge of Rice Park, near the St. Paul Hotel, Landmark Center and the St. Paul Public Library. Seats to avoid are the first eight rows of the orchestra level, where the minimal slope makes viewing difficult. The side boxes of the balcony level offer only a partial view of the stage, but these seats are cheap, acoustically good and may allow you to see all the action if you're attending a chamber music concert or a piano recital.

The Ordway's McKnight Theater, with 300 seats, is equally handsome.

Several parking lots and ramps in the area serve Ordway patrons, but it almost always seems possible to find street parking (free at night and on Sundays) within a 10-minute walk.

O'Shaughnessy Auditorium
2004 Randolph Ave., St. Paul   690-6700

Until the arrival of the Ordway, O'Shaughnessy, on the campus of the College of St. Catherine, was St. Paul's biggest and best concert hall. It's seen everything in its 25 years: concerts by the Minnesota Orchestra and the Saint Paul Chamber Orchestra; pop, folk and bluegrass music; and dance. If you're attending a dance performance, the front of the balcony is the place to head, and these seats also put you right on top of the musicians during concerts. The back rows of the balcony, 125 feet from the stage, are too far away for nonbinocular vision. If the hall is notorious for anything, it's for the absence of any center aisle on the main floor or balcony levels. There can be as many as 63 seats unbroken by an aisle. So if you're expecting to leave in midperformance, pick an aisle seat to avoid climbing over 31 others.

Services for Artists and Audiences

Arts Midwest
528 Hennepin Ave., Ste. 310
Minneapolis   341-0755

Arts Midwest is one of the area's major funders and information providers for artists and arts presenters involved in everything from jazz to the visual arts. It administers, for example, the Midwest's Meet the Composers grants, which give money to arts organizations that have arranged visits from composers around the country. It's also active in helping develop organizations that serve artists of color.

Artspace Projects
400 First Ave. N., Ste. 518
Minneapolis   339-4372

This unusual and useful organization helps locate and construct living, working and exhibition space for artists in the Twin Cities area. Several of its cooperatives for low-income artists have been very successful.

ASIAN AMERICAN RENAISSANCE
1564 LaFond, St. Paul   *641-4040*

Presenting conferences, exhibitions, performances and lectures at several locations in the Twin Cities, this organization helps support Asian-American artists who are active in many disciplines.

BLACK MUSIC EDUCATORS OF THE TWIN CITIES
764 Dayton Ave., No. 2, St. Paul   *No Phone*

Created to advance the music of African-American composers and increase the number of performance opportunities for black musicians, this group sponsors scholarships, concerts and other programs.

CABLE ACCESS ST. PAUL
213 E. Fourth St., St. Paul   *224-5153*

St. Paul residents who want to try their hand at cable-TV video production should take advantage of the training, facilities and equipment offered by this organization.

CENTER FOR ARTS CRITICISM
2402 University Ave. W.
St. Paul   *644-5501*

Aspiring critics and people already accomplished in the world of arts criticism make use of the services of this organization, which provides grants, sponsors conferences and workshops and helps make criticism more accessible to artists and the public.

COMMUNITY CABLE CHANNEL 33
10816 Normandale Blvd.
Bloomington   *888-6702*

This is a public-access cable channel in Bloomington that offers residents the chance to produce and watch homegrown TV programs.

COMPAS
75 W. Fifth St., Ste. 304
St. Paul   *292-3249*

Artists can participate in this organization's school and community residencies, apply for its grants and take advantage of its other special programs. COMPAS, like several other St. Paul arts organizations, is downtown in Landmark Center, a former federal courts building renovated to house the arts.

FORECAST PUBLIC ARTWORKS
2324 University Ave. W.
St. Paul   *641-1128*

Public art projects and the public discussion of the arts is the business of FORECAST, which provides assistance to artists who are working for their communities. It also publishes a respected public-art publication.

INDEPENDENT FEATURE PROJECT/NORTH
119 N. Fourth St., Ste. 202
Minneapolis   *338-0871*

Serving independent filmmakers throughout the region, IFP/North offers classes and workshops as well as screenings of locally produced film and video work.

METROPOLITAN REGIONAL ARTS COUNCIL
2324 University Ave. W., Ste. 114
St. Paul   *645-0402*

Unlike most other states, Minnesota has established a group of regional arts councils to administer a chunk of state funds earmarked for the arts. The Metropolitan Regional Arts Council handles this administration for the seven-county Twin Cities area. It gives grants to arts organizations, encourages diversity in the arts, helps community groups generate arts activities and works to increase people's accessibility to the arts.

MIDWEST CENTER FOR ARTS, ENTERTAINMENT AND THE LAW

749 Simpson St., St. Paul   *644-1891*

This organization (nicknamed MiCAEL) helps connect artists with resources on the law and censorship.

MINNESOTA ASSOCIATION OF COMMUNITY THEATRES

521-5692

MACT's telephone hotline, a recorded message updated on Sundays, gives valuable information on community theater auditions and other theater activities in the seven-county metropolitan area.

MINNESOTA CITIZENS FOR THE ARTS

708 N. First St., Ste. 235D
Minneapolis   *338-2970*

This is a lobbying and advocacy group that strives to increase government funding for the arts and works within the government to improve the financial health of artists and arts organizations.

MINNESOTA CULTURAL MEDIA

4937 Aldrich Ave. N.
Minneapolis   *529-1435*

Minnesota Cultural Media concentrates on helping minority audiences gain access to the arts and assisting artists of color by sponsoring festivals and other arts programs in various communities and schools.

MINNESOTA STATE ARTS BOARD

400 Sibley St., Ste. 200
St. Paul   *215-1600*

This state-funded agency, whose arts-assistance budget has amazingly increased in recent years, gives a big boost to Minnesota artists and arts organizations by providing expertise, information and financial

assistance. Individual artists benefit from fellowships, career opportunity grants, cultural pluralism programs, support for folk artists and a variety of useful publications. The arts board also supports the work of artists who obtain residencies in schools.

NATIONAL WRITERS UNION, TWIN CITIES LOCAL

P.O. Box 50507
Minneapolis 55403   *879-4114*

This labor union helps writers of journalism, textbooks, fiction and poetry strengthen themselves economically by promoting model contracts, offering grievance assistance and providing contacts with other writers.

NATIVE ARTS CIRCLE

1433 Franklin Ave. E.
Minneapolis   *870-7173*

Promoting the artistic expression of people in the Native American community is the focus of this organization that sponsors exhibitions, writing workshops, film festivals and other programs.

RESOURCES AND COUNSELING FOR THE ARTS

429 Landmark Center
St. Paul   *292-4381*

Know a dancer who needs sharper bookkeeping skills? How about a sculptor in need of marketing tips or a musician seeking tax assistance? RCA helps by providing business and management assistance to artists of all kinds and to arts organizations. It offers workshops, individual counseling, job listings, publications and an artist loan program.

ST. LOUIS PARK COMMUNITY TELEVISION

5005 Minnetonka Blvd.
St. Louis Park   *924-2660*

This is another public-access TV station that serves a suburban community by helping residents produce their own programs and by ultimately airing them.

Very Special Arts Minnesota
528 Hennepin Ave., Ste. 305   *332-3888*
Minneapolis   *TTY 332-3888*

Very Special Arts strives to serve the needs of artists and arts patrons with disabilities by providing information on the physical accessibility of arts events, training and programs that raise awareness of the disabled.

Photo: John Doman, Pioneer Press

Downtown St. Paul's Rice Park with Landmark Center in the background.

Inside
Architecture
and Historic Sites

Perhaps a little more than most places, the Twin Cities has tended to undervalue the richness of its architecture and history. It's a reticence inspired not by modesty but by a mistaken interpretation of historical fact. After all, many Minnesotans reason, we've produced no U.S. presidents, have no nearby major battlefields, did not spawn any important architectural movements and have no landmarks that rank among the most visited (unless you count the Mall of America). Fortunately, however, politics, wars and postcard images do not define history any more than home-grown architectural movements necessarily produce memorable buildings.

Instead, what makes history interesting and buildings beautiful are people and structures that are full of life and can move us. These the Twin Cities have as much as any place. History is simply someone's story, and architecture is the translation of a personal story — or an emotion or philosophy — to the physical form of a structure. If people have dwelled here, there is good history and architecture here.

The best place to start any historical exploration of the Twin Cities, indeed, of the entire state, is the Minnesota History Center in St. Paul. This visionary and ambitiously conceived history museum — easily one of the best in the country — tells history largely in terms of people's personal stories. The experiences of the rich and prominent are given no more weight than the stories of the poor and common, to the extent that surviving historical materials allow the museum's staff to do so. The historical paths of African Americans, Native American and other Minnesotans of color are also receiving increasing attention there. For more information on the Minnesota History Center, see Attractions.

To state the obvious, architecture is best viewed by getting outside and looking. Look on foot, not by car. Get up close. Resist nostalgia. The Twin Cities has lost more than its share of great old buildings, most notably the Metropolitan Building in Minneapolis, but many worthless old dumps fell to the wrecking ball as well. By the same token, many newer structures speak well and with feeling (the Minnesota History Center is a good example).

Walk the streets of the Twin Cities and listen to its stories. You'll encounter plenty of great architecture and lots of wonderful history.

ARMSTRONG HOUSE
233-235 W. Fifth St., St. Paul

This startling and formerly elegant double-residence, built in 1886, is boarded up, so you'll have to be content with viewing it from the outside and imagining its grandeur. One of the last surviving houses anywhere in downtown St. Paul, it is owned by the State of Minnesota and has an uncertain future. Edward P. Bassford, an early Twin Cities architect whose other buildings are mostly demolished, designed it for the family of George Washington Armstrong, combining Romanesque features with elements of the Queen Anne style. The house will almost surely be razed in the coming years; moving it is not a possibility because its weight of 600 tons makes any travel an expensive and risky proposition.

FIRST NATIONAL BANK BUILDING
Minnesota and Fifth Sts., St. Paul

Long the most recognizable building on St. Paul's skyline (and still the classiest), this skyscraper was built in 1931 and renovated 40 years later. Indiana limestone, arranged in bands on the exterior, emphasizes its height. Don't miss the "1st" sign at the summit and the high-spirited sculpture by George Sugarman presiding over the main entrance.

F. SCOTT FITZGERALD HOUSE
599 Summit Ave., St. Paul

During the summer of 1919 at the age of 22, F. Scott Fitzgerald completed his first novel, *This Side of Paradise*, while living on the third floor of this rowhouse. He and his family had lived at several other St. Paul addresses, but this home, tantalizingly close to the residences of the city's ultra-rich, apparently provided ample fodder for the young author's literary preoccupation with class, social climbing and money. (In one of his works of fiction, Fitzgerald describes a Crest Avenue, obviously based on Summit Avenue, which he characterized as "a museum of American architectural failures.") Although a plaque details Fitzgerald's connection and the residence is registered as a National Historic Landmark, the in-

terior of the rowhouse is not open to public view.

FITZGERALD THEATER
10 E. Exchange St., St. Paul   290-1200

The Fitzgerald, which opened as the Schubert Theater in 1910, was never a really fancy place, but it gained national fame during the 1980s as the home base of Garrison Keillor's "A Prairie Home Companion" public radio show. A renovation during that period uncovered a long-lost upper balcony, moved the main entrance from Wabasha Street to Exchange, spiffed the place up and stopped the ceiling plaster from falling on people's heads. Long known as the World Theater, it was renamed in September 1994 in honor of native son F. Scott Fitzgerald. Nowadays the theater hosts concerts and shows, as well as Keillor's revived "A Prairie Home Companion" program.

FORT SNELLING
Fort Rd. at Hwys. 5 and 55
St. Paul   725-2413

Fort Snelling, a federal garrison established in 1820 to keep an eye on the northern portion of the land acquired years earlier with the Louisiana Purchase, was never attacked, which is one reason why the fort is around today for us to enjoy. Another reason, however, is the efforts of the Minnesota Historical Society, which shouldered the archaeological and preservational task of preventing the fort from crumbling into the Mississippi and Minnesota rivers, at the junction of which the military complex rises. Thanks to that work, we can now enjoy a site loaded with nationally significant history: Countless exploratory teams began there in missions to map and explore the frontier; Dred Scott, the slave whom the Supreme Court ultimately ruled a nonperson, lived there;

Civil War volunteers, bound for the Battle of Gettysburg, trained there; and Dakota Indians camped outside its walls during conflicts with the U.S. government in the 1860s.

Now a National Historic Landmark, the site uses a living-history approach in presenting itself to the public, with authentically costumed guides working in the re-created barracks, kitchens, laundry rooms, hospital, blacksmith shop and officers' quarters. Most of Fort Snelling is open to visitors during the spring and summer months, although a recently constructed on-site history center remains open year round.

ARD GODFREY HOUSE
University and Central Aves. S.E.
Minneapolis 870-8001

Open for summer public tours, this residence dates to 1848, when Maine native Ard Godfrey was active developing the dams and sawmills that tapped the immense energy of the St. Anthony Falls on the Mississippi River.

GOVERNOR'S RESIDENCE
1006 Summit Ave., St. Paul 297-8177

Designed by William Channing Whitney in the English Tudor Revival style and built for St. Paul attorney Horace Hills Irvine in 1910, this residence has only housed the families of the state's governors since the 1960s. Before that, governors lived in their own homes and the state booked space in hotels or the capitol building for official receptions.

The 20-room house has undergone several renovations and redesigns over the decades to accommodate the particular needs of the first families. Public tours are available during the spring and summer months.

HENNEPIN COUNTY GOVERNMENT CENTER
Fifth St. between Third and Fourth Aves. S.
Minneapolis 348-3848

So distinctive are the twin 24-story towers of this structure spanning Sixth Street and rising 24 stories into the air that they have been incorporated into the graphic logo that Hennepin County uses to identify itself. Designed to surrender more than half of the block to a welcome urban plaza and fountain, the complex also contains a striking 350-foot-high glass atrium. A tunnel connects it with the Minneapolis City Hall and Courthouse across Fifth Street. Inside are licensing bureaus, courtrooms and offices of the county commissioners and many other county agencies. Daily tours are offered.

JAMES J. HILL HOUSE
240 Summit Ave., St. Paul 297-2555

A visit to this dark, imposing and magnificent mansion — the most awesome of all the Victorian residences on St. Paul's Summit Avenue — will convince any doubters out there that the railroad business truly was a rewarding enterprise in the 19th century. James J. Hill, who purchased the sickly St. Paul and Pacific Rail-

Fort Snelling was nearly bulldozed in 1958 to make way for a highway, until the Minnesota Historical Society stepped forward to lead efforts to save the historic site.

Insiders' Tips

road and transformed it into the immensely successful Great Northern Railroad, invested nearly $1 million in his red-sandstone-faced house in 1891 and built it with size in mind. Designed by the Boston firm of Peabody, Stearns and Furber, it originally included 22 fireplaces and 13 bathrooms to accommodate the Hills and their eight children, as well as a massive reception room, full servants' quarters and a dining room (able to seat 40) whose furnishings must have been responsible for the clearing of several tracts of forest. After Hill's death in 1916 and that of his wife Mary five years later, the mansion fell into the hands of the archdiocese of St. Paul, becoming a National Historic Landmark in 1961. Now owned by the Minnesota Historical Society, the house is the setting for concerts and art exhibitions in the skylighted, pipe-organ-equipped gallery that Hill built for his own art collection. Guides give illuminating tours of the mansion and also lead occasional tours of the Summit Avenue neighborhood.

HISTORIC ORPHEUM THEATRE
910 Hennepin Ave., Minneapolis   339-7007

With nearly 3,000 seats at the time of its opening in 1921, the Minneapolis Orpheum (actually the second Orpheum Theatre to open its doors in the city) was the second-largest vaudeville house in the country, after New York's Lowe's State Theater. The Marx Brothers headlined the first bill of entertainers. The Orpheum has a fascinating past and a promising future, thanks to a city-sponsored renovation that returned the building to its former glory. Bestowing a new backstage area and improved dressing rooms and restrooms, the restoration also gave the Orpheum a cleaned-up exterior and a wonderful vertical neon sign that pulses

in purple. Once even owned by Bob Dylan, the theater now hosts a variety of Broadway, pop, jazz and rock events.

HISTORIC STATE THEATRE
805 Hennepin Ave., Minneapolis   339-7007

Across the street and a block away from the Orpheum is the Italian Renaissance-style State Theatre, an eye-popping palace of entertainment that has survived nearly 80 years as a movie theater and vaudeville house, church and vacant hulk. Fully restored in 1991, it now has 2,200 seats, period murals on the walls, glittering chandeliers, a golden proscenium arch above the stage and admirable sightlines from almost everywhere in the house. Concerts, dance events and Broadway shows fill its schedule.

IDS CENTER
777 Nicollet Mall, Minneapolis

Often hailed as one of the world's finest skyscrapers and perhaps architect Philip Johnson's best design, the IDS Center single-handedly transformed the Minneapolis skyline when it was completed in 1973. Now that the skyline has filled in and the IDS Center no longer appears to be a lonely digit stretching toward the heavens, the building nonetheless retains its supremacy. (In physical terms, that supremacy can be measured in inches, as other buildings have approached, but not surpassed, IDS' height.) Anyone who remembers "The Mary Tyler Moore Show" (and apparently 98.9 percent of Twin Citians do) can still picture the opening credits in which Mary rapturously descends the building's escalator before tossing her hat into the air outside on the Nicollet Mall. But the 51-story building and its revolutionary Crystal Court — a grand public space now largely empty except for

Photo: Scott Takushi, Pioneer Press

The historic State Theatre in downtown Minneapolis.

Jonathan Borofsky's sculpture *Hammering Man*, on loan from the Minneapolis Institute of Arts — have seen far more important events: presidential appearances, concerts of full symphony orchestras and thundering sports rallies. It has provided the setting for countless romantic trysts, as well — don't forget, this is the heart of a great city!

LANDMARK CENTER
75 W. Fifth St., St. Paul   292-3272

Nowadays, Landmark Center houses galleries of the Minnesota Museum of American Art and the offices of several other arts and community organizations, but in days past an intriguing assortment of gangsters, judges and postal officials walked through its doors. Back then, in fact until 1967, the granite building with the notable clock tower gathered together under one roof federal courts, the city's main post office and customs offices. When the federal offices vacated the building, it was threatened with demolition. Fortunately, community preservationists rallied together to preserve the

Neo-Romanesque castle, designed by Willowby J. Edbrooke and constructed in 1906. They mounted a 10-year, $12.5 million restoration, and now Landmark Center presides over Rice Park and the Ordway Music Theatre in one of downtown St. Paul's most visually attractive districts. It was the first building in the state to be nominated for the National Register of Historic Places.

LOWERTOWN HISTORIC DISTRICT
Vicinity of E. Sixth St. near Sibley St., St. Paul

Originally a bustling St. Paul neighborhood that sprouted off a Mississippi River landing and later a district of warehouses and merchandise distribution centers, Lowertown is now a unique mix of artists' lofts, residences, converted warehouses and commercial spaces. A 17-block area listed on the National Register of Historic Places, it includes Depot Place (1917 to 1923, formerly Union Depot, 214 E. Fourth Street), which handled millions of tons of rail freight and millions of passengers before closing down in 1971 to become a space for restaurants and retailers; First Trust Center (1914 to 1916, formerly the Railroad and Bank Building, 176 E. Fifth Street), a Classical Revival structure that was for decades the largest office building in the Twin Cities, recently restored for banking purposes; the Pioneer Building (1889, 340 N. Robert Street), boasting the only surviving open light court in the Twin Cities and a fascinating period elevator; and the First Baptist Church (1875, 499 Wacouta Street), whose original 190-foot-high spire, too heavy for the swampy ground, had to be removed in 1945. At the heart of the district is Mears Park, a plot of ground on which landscaping and history mix engagingly. An excellent brochure detailing a walking tour of the district is available from the St. Paul Heritage Preservation Commission, 266-6580.

LUMBER EXCHANGE BUILDING
425 Hennepin Ave., Minneapolis

In the halls that lumber barons once stalked now wafts the scent of aroma therapy, thanks to a 1980s restoration that infused the Lumber Exchange with new life and made it the home of such businesses as a Horst hair salon. A hunkering Richardsonian Romanesque structure designed by the renowned Twin Cities firm of Long and Kees and crafted in 1885 out of rough cut granite and Lake Superior brownstone, it is one of the few remaining signs that the lumber business, now much reduced in importance, built the state.

MILWAUKEE ROAD DEPOT
Washington Ave. S., Minneapolis

Yes, it's dirty and boarded up, and the clock in the tower hasn't worked for years, but this train depot and its accompanying shed are a historical treasure. Urban renewal projects of the 1950s and '60s, along with a couple of foolish razings right here in the 1990s, have erased most other traces of the working-class, down-and-out culture that formerly thrived in the Gateway district (not to romanticize it; the neighborhood was gritty, dangerous and the last stop for many of its residents). Virtually all the flophouses, saloons and bums' meeting places are long gone, leaving only this empty depot, the landing place of many unskilled workers who flocked to Minneapolis during the first half of the century. Designed by Charles Frost and built in 1898, the depot originally had a smashing rotunda, patterned marble floors and carved-wood ceilings. The 625-foot-long train shed is one of the very few such structures still standing in America. In its peak years, 29 scheduled trains departed daily. The depot closed to the public after a 1971 conversion to railroad office space and locked its doors for good about eight years later. Since then, the site has been considered for everything from a shopping mall to a gambling casino, but nothing ever seems to work out. The site remains in limbo.

MINNEAPOLIS ARMORY
500 S. Sixth St., Minneapolis

Empty and destined for future use as

Insiders' Tips

In 1888, Minneapolis architect LeRoy Buffington received the first U.S. patent for a method of skyscraper construction.

a film, video and sound recording studio, the Minneapolis Armory is at least not now threatened with demolition, a possibility that loomed large when Hennepin County coveted the site for a new jail. It would have taken quite a bit of force to bring this streamlined WPA-era building to its knees. Inside is a hangar-sized drill area with an 85-foot-high ceiling, seating for 4,500 and cavernous facilities that could swallow army trucks, other motorized vehicles and thousands of national defenders. Though sparsely ornamented and given rounded corners to make it resemble a military machine, the armory does have its cultured side, as well. Two large interior murals, created by artists Elsa Jemne and Lucia Wiley, illustrate Minnesota's origins and show scenes of peace and battle.

MINNEAPOLIS
CITY HALL AND COURTHOUSE
400 S. Fourth St., Minneapolis   673-3000

If you're looking at the Minneapolis skyline and you see an old building with a steeply pitched green roof and a big clock tower (the clock face is bigger than Big Ben's), you've caught sight of the Minneapolis City Hall and Courthouse. Get closer, because this magnificent and well-worn Romanesque building, faced with limestone and granite and filled with marble, pulses with the drama and frustration of everyday life. When completed in 1906, it signalled that Minneapolis was a metropolis of importance. The local architecture firm of Long and Kees designed it with a courtyard and a dignified entrance facing the Mississippi River, the direction in which most of the city then lay, but the subsequent demand for city services filled the courtyard with offices, removed the skylights and even flipped the main entrance to the opposite side.

But no matter, there's still history here — hangings, police investigations, payoffs to corrupt mayors. The building is best known for the 345-foot-high clock tower and its 15-bell carillon, along with the main lobby's *Father of Waters* statue, carved by Larkin Goldsmith Mead from the biggest block of Italian marble ever hauled out of the famous Carrara quarries.

MINNESOTA STATE CAPITOL
Cedar and Aurora Sts., St. Paul   296-2881

Architect Cass Gilbert, who later designed the U.S. Supreme Court building and New York's famed Woolworth Building, concentrated his formidable talents on Minnesota's third capitol structure (the first burned down, the second became too small after only a few years), even contributing to the design of the furniture. Just as it did when first built in 1905, the capitol building awes visitors with its monumental dome (modeled after St. Peter's in Rome), huge columns, stenciled ceilings, symbolic murals and vivid hues in the restored Senate and House chambers. On a bright day, few Minnesota sights are as grand as the sunlight glinting off the newly restored and reinstalled gold-leaf horses. They're part of a statue themed *The Progress of the State* that sits atop the main entrance. The sculpture, created by Daniel Chester French, was erected in 1907 and removed in 1994 for a $636,000 restoration. The Minnesota Historical Society offers free guided tours of the Capitol year round, and all galleries and legislative meetings are open to the public.

MINNESOTA WORLD TRADE CENTER
Wabasha and Eighth Sts., St. Paul

Easily the flashiest skyscraper in St. Paul, this 40-story office tower casts a warm glow over the city, thanks to its yellowish granite and bronze glass. Raised in 1987, it was the first international trade center built in the Midwest.

MISSISSIPPI RIVER
STONE ARCH BRIDGE

Mississippi River, near Main St., Minneapolis

Dating from 1883, this limestone and granite bridge was the brainchild of railroad magnate James J. Hill, who needed an improved rail link across the Mississippi River. His builders crafted it to last — its 23 arches and sound structure needed no major repairs for the next eight decades. Reminiscent of a Roman viaduct, the bridge remains the only stone-arch span ever built across the river. It closed as a railroad bridge in the early 1980s, but a recently completed restoration has given it new life as a pedestrian and bicycle crossing.

MURPHY'S LANDING

2187 E. Hwy. 101, Shakopee   445-6900

The Minnesota River, the region's other important waterway, cut a long valley in the southern part of Minnesota. Beginning in the middle years of the 19th century, settlers moved there, farmed there and built towns there. The Twin Cities' metropolitan spread has started to transform some of the valley towns into suburban communities, but Murphy's Landing re-creates what life was like before this change took place. Focusing on the years 1840 to 1890, this living-history museum brings back the rhythm of daily life in a typical Minnesota River Valley settlement, with historically dressed interpreters going about their tasks in a fur trader's cabin, farm and other village settings. In addition to offering period dinners, river boat excursions, trolley rides and an in-depth look at 19th-century ac-

tivities, Murphy's Landing sponsors seasonal events on the Fourth of July, Halloween and Christmas, as well as theme days that pay tribute to such icons of Americana as the Civil War, Tom Sawyer and Laura Ingalls Wilder. The site has a gift shop and restaurant.

NICOLLET MALL

Running from Washington Ave. S. to W. Grant St., Minneapolis

During the 1960s Minneapolis built the Nicollet Mall, a gently winding thoroughfare for pedestrians and buses that erased a congested business street, foisted the auto traffic upon neighboring avenues, drew international praise and reigned as the longest urban mall in the country. The millions it cost to build (and later to extend and redesign) have been well-spent, if only for the attention it has received and the controversy it has generated. Was the mall better as a winding route, as in the past, or relatively straight, as now? Who cares? Nowhere else in the Twin Cities can you regularly encounter street musicians (some of the regulars play cello, trumpet, sax, drums and bagpipes), street-corner evangelists, pushcart food vendors, illuminated holiday parades and wandering conventioneers.

NORWEST CENTER

Sixth St. and Marquette Ave., Minneapolis

Cesar Pelli, designer of this rosy and graceful 57-story office tower that appeared on the Minneapolis skyline in 1988, drew his inspiration from both the past and the present. For a half-century, Norwest Bank (formerly Northwestern National Bank) had occupied a venerable and well-loved structure on this same site, but a catastrophic fire on Thanksgiving Day 1982 reduced it to rubble. Pelli salvaged many artifacts from the old building — chandeliers, bronze medallions, cast railings — and built a modern setting in which they would look comfortable. Especially when dramatically lighted at night, Norwest Center plugs a gap in the skyline as it discreetly fails to overshadow the nearby IDS Tower. Don't miss the set of 16 vitrines in the main lobby that showcase Norwest's splendid collection of modernist decorative art, including pieces representing the arts-and-crafts, art nouveau, de Stijl, Bauhaus and art deco movements.

PILLSBURY "A" MILL

Third Ave. and Main St. S.E., Minneapolis

LeRoy Buffington, a prolific Minneapolis architect who worked on university buildings, hotels and office structures throughout the Upper Midwest, produced this limestone building that long symbolized the supremacy of flour milling in Minneapolis' economic life. Erected in 1881 and for years the largest and most productive mill on earth, it now houses limited storage and packing facilities. Even so, a sign still towers above the roof proclaiming "Pillsbury's Best Flour."

ALEXANDER RAMSEY HOUSE

265 S. Exchange St., St. Paul   296-0100

When Alexander Ramsey raised his home in 1872 at the St. Paul intersection of Walnut and Exchange streets, he already had an impressive political career behind him: He had served as the first territorial governor of Minnesota and the second governor after statehood, mayor of St. Paul, a U.S. senator and the U.S. secretary of war. Even so, Ramsey lived another 31 years in the house, leading an active social life and running his real estate affairs. The house, in the Irvine Park neighborhood, remained in the family until 1964, when the Minnesota Historical Society acquired and restored it. Today the Ramsey House still retains the carved walnut woodwork, marble fireplaces, and crystal chandeliers that make it one of the best preserved Victorian homes in the country. In addition, visitors can take in sparkling accumulations of silver and crystal and the Ramsey girls' remarkable doll house. Ramsey House is open April through December, and the Society's guides offer tours and operate a gift shop.

ST. ANTHONY FALLS HISTORIC DISTRICT

Nicollet Island and both sides of the Mississippi River, downtown Minneapolis   627-5433

A 165-acre area encompassing old flour mills, riverside warehouses, historic Main Street, one of Minnesota's earliest African-American neighborhoods and an entire island, the St. Anthony Falls Historic District provides a glimpse into the lives of some of the state's earliest urban dwellers. With many structures eligible for National Register listing and two National Historic Landmarks, the district is almost too much to take in and is best surveyed via walking tours organized by the Minnesota Historical Society. (The Society maintains an office in the district at 125 S.E. Main Street.) One tour covers the East Bank of the river, including old Main Street and other commercial areas; another traverses the West Bank and its rich milling history; and a third focuses on the industrial, residential and architectural history of Nicollet Island.

ST. PAUL CITY HALL AND COURTHOUSE

15 W. Kellogg Blvd., St. Paul   266-8500

Except perhaps for Mickey's Diner, few places in downtown St. Paul can so immediately transport you to another era as St. Paul's city hall and courthouse. The

41-foot-high Fourth Street lobby, which achieves striking effects with walls of blue Belgian marble (it appears nearly black), is one of the most enchanting art deco spots on the globe. Designed by Holabird and Root and Ellerbe Architects and completed in 1931, the building features the statue *God of Peace* by Carl Milles, which was carved from an enormous, 55-ton chunk of Mexican white onyx. The elevators are worth a view too because their doors are paneled with scenes from the city's history, painted by Albert Stewart.

JOHN H. STEVENS HOUSE
4901 Minnehaha Ave.
Minneapolis   722-2201

This house, the Twin Cities' first white-owned dwelling on the west side of the Mississippi River, dates from 1849. Originally occupying a site farther north, it is the building in which the name "Minneapolis" was first proposed and Hennepin County organized. Very simple in design, it is built in the New England Colonial style.

UNITED STATES POST OFFICE
100 S. First St., Minneapolis

They could film a 1930s movie in this place, because the interior public spaces of this Moderne-style behemoth, erected in 1933, seem to have changed little from the day it witnessed the selling of its first stamp. Handsome and clean-looking, the post office is a survivor of a massive urban renewal effort that cleared the Gateway district of many of its older buildings.

WAREHOUSE HISTORIC DISTRICT
Vicinity of First Ave. N. between Second and Seventh Sts., Minneapolis

Functionality can inspire beauty — that much is evident from the stone and brick structures that brush shoulders in Minneapolis' 14-block Warehouse District. Now housing restaurants, nightclubs, office buildings, artists' quarters and even theaters and galleries, many of the old edifices have been scrubbed, gutted and restored to produce a city district that remains as lively and prosperous as it was a century ago. The district, officially designated "historic" by the National Register of Historic Places, includes more than 150 buildings, cobblestone streets and a pair of steel bridges. Some of the most interesting structures are Butler Square (1906, 100 N. Sixth Street), the trailblazing renovation project that changed an enormous dry goods warehouse of questionable utility into a warm home for restaurants and offices; the Wyman Building (1896, 400 First Avenue N.), another design by the distinguished Minneapolis architecture firm of Long and Kees, a former warehouse that now counts galleries, designers and other small businesses among its tenants; and the former Minneapolis Van and Warehouse Company Building (First Street and First Avenue N., now the home stage of the Theatre de la Jeune Lune), a magnificent structure with an exterior that was altered early this century by the young Cass Gilbert. Many other buildings in the district deserve examination, however, and the Minneapolis Heritage Preservation Commission, 673-2422, offers highly recommended walking tours.

Inside
Ethnic Diversity

It's a cliche, but it's worth repeating: People of the Twin Cities come in all shapes, sizes, colors and places of national origin. They speak a hundred or more languages, wax nostalgic over an equal number of Old Countries and eat a rainbow of ethnic foods.

The U.S. Census, speaking in statistics, reports that German Americans are the largest single ethnic group in Minnesota. After them, in descending numbers, come the Norwegians, Swedes, Irish, "unclassified," "other groups," "race or Hispanic," Finns, English, Poles, "U.S./American," Italians, Czechs, the Dutch and Danes. Many other groups — Ukrainians, Ethiopians, Palestinians, Russians, Croatians — contribute to the Twin Cit-

ies as well, and this chapter can't possibly cover them all.

Even so, you can get to know many of them. Eat in their restaurants, attend their festivals, browse their shops, see their exhibits, visit their places of worship. At the same time, don't neglect to investigate your own ethnic background. How can you explain yourself to others if you don't know where you came from?

The African Americans

The number of African Americans living in the Twin Cities — 89,459, representing 3.9 percent of the population, according to 1990 census figures — has nearly doubled since 1980. Although that percentage is still small compared with

The Rondo Days Parade is named after Rondo Avenue, the center of the city's black community in the 1960s. The street was demolished to construct a freeway.

that of other American urban regions, African Americans have always had an important presence in the area.

As early as the late 18th century, African Americans were involved in the region's fur trade, and other black people arrived in succeeding decades as slaves owned by soldiers assigned to Fort Snelling. One of the latter group, Dred Scott, used his two years in residence at the fort (which was technically in free territory) as the basis of a legal suit to win his freedom. In the now-infamous 1857 case of Dred Scott vs. Sanford, the U.S. Supreme Court ruled that Scott was a noncitizen, an article of property who could not even file a legal suit.

The first Minnesota territorial census in 1849 determined that 40 free people of African ancestry lived in the region, most of them in St. Paul. That number gradually grew with the arrival of fugitive slaves. In 1868, two years before the 15th Amendment to the U.S. Constitution made it mandatory, Minnesota became one of a handful of states to voluntarily extend the vote to African-American men. The following year, the state legislature outlawed the racial segregation of public schools.

Up until about 1910, St. Paul remained the center of the Twin Cities' black community. An early group of free African Americans had settled near the Falls of St. Anthony, however, giving Minneapolis its own community. In both cities, they increased in numbers as they established churches, ran businesses and

formed social organizations. By 1930 the Rondo neighborhood of St. Paul and the near-north side and Seven Corners area of Minneapolis emerged as the hearts of the community.

Though not as overt as in Southern cities, discrimination existed in the Twin Cities, preventing African Americans from eating in many restaurants, renting halls in major hotels or earning wages comparable to those of whites. The black community was hit hard by the Great Depression, and 60 percent unemployment rates did not drop until the industrial mobilization of World War II. From 1950 to 1970 the African-American population of Minneapolis and St. Paul quadrupled, and a migration of black people from other northern industrial states has continued into the 1990s.

Nowadays about half of the Twin Cities' African Americans live in Minneapolis, with the remainder split between St. Paul and the suburbs. *Black Enterprise* magazine recently lauded Minneapolis as a hot spot for upwardly mobile African-American businesspeople, noting that the city has the highest number of black professionals per capita in the nation. At the same time, however, the percentage of people of color in poverty in the Twin Cities is higher than that of any other major metropolitan area.

A few notable members of the Twin Cities' African-American community, past and present, are Sharon Sayles Belton, mayor of Minneapolis; Alan Page,

Insiders' Tips

Nils Nyberg, a shoemaker who arrived in St. Anthony in 1851, is generally regarded as the first Swede to settle in Minnesota.

associate justice on the Minnesota Supreme Court and former Minnesota Vikings football star; William Finney, St. Paul chief of police; Roy Wilkins, a longtime national leader of the NAACP; and Curman Gaines, superintendent of the St. Paul Public Schools.

Organizations

COUNCIL ON BLACK MINNESOTANS
2233 University Ave., Ste. 426
St. Paul   642-0811
The council serves as a liaison between African-American Minnesotans and the state government, calling black issues to the attention of the governor and legislature and working to open access to state services and programs to all African Americans.

SABATHANI COMMUNITY CENTER
310 E. 38th St., Minneapolis   827-5981
A full range of counseling, education, senior, kids' and referral programs are offered by the several different agencies housed here.

SURVIVAL SKILLS INSTITUTE INC.
1501 Xerxes Ave. N.
Minneapolis   522-6654
This organization helps families and children of color by providing community-based family development programs.

PHYLLIS WHEATLEY COMMUNITY CENTER
919 Fremont Ave. N.
Minneapolis   374-4342
Providing a broad range of services, including education, counseling and assistance, to the primarily African-American residents of the near north side of Minneapolis is the primary focus of this community center.

Photo: Scott Takushi, Pioneer Press

St. Paul children celebrate the Hmong New Year's Day with the traditional ball-toss.

The Asians and Asian Americans

Like the Latinos who live in the Twin Cities, the Asians and Asian Americans in the region have greatly varied backgrounds and ethnicity. The 65,000 people of Asian descent in the metropolitan area (representing almost 3 percent of the population) trace their origins to Laos, Korea, Vietnam, China, India, the Philippines, Cambodia and Japan, among other countries. They are the Twin Cities' fastest-growing ethnic community.

The greatest in size are the Hmong (which means "free men"), a group that long lived in the mountains of Laos. During the 1960s and '70s, many Hmong aided the U.S. government in its fight against Laotian communists, and when the communists gained power, Hmong came to the United States in large numbers. The influx of Hmong into Minnesota has been steady since 1975, and the state has become the home of more

Hmong than any other except California. There is a sizable Hmong community in St. Paul. Among the Twin Cities' many notable Asian Americans is St. Paul school board member Choua Lee, the first Hmong elected to public office in the United States.

Other Southeast Asian people — from Laos, Cambodia and Vietnam — settled in the Twin Cities around the same time the Hmong did. Some were involved in the fighting of the Vietnam War, while others left to escape "re-education camps," government oppression, social abuse or poor economic opportunities.

About 10,000 of the state's Asian Americans are Koreans who were adopted by American families after the Korean War ended in 1953. Again following California, Minnesota ranks second nationally in the number of Korean children who have come for adoption. Many of the adoptees are now adults, and the South Korean government has drastically reduced the number of Korean children available for overseas adoption.

The Asian Indian, Chinese and Japanese communities in the Twin Cities have older roots. Chinese people arrived in Minnesota as early as the 1870s to establish businesses. In this century, more Chinese (from both China and Taiwan), as well as Asian Indians, arrived in Minnesota for university study and remained here. A group of Japanese workers came to the state around the turn of the century to work on the railroads, and the Japanese Americans increased their numbers during World War II when they settled in the Twin Cities after serving in the Military Intelligence Service Language School at Fort Snelling.

Organizations

ASSOCIATION FOR THE ADVANCEMENT OF HMONG WOMEN IN MINNESOTA

1518 Lake St., Ste. 209
Minneapolis   724-3066

Providing a connection between refugee women and Minnesota culture, this group helps Hmong women develop skills in self-sufficiency, leadership and self-respect.

CENTRE FOR ASIANS AND PACIFIC ISLANDERS

3702 E. Lake St., Minneapolis   721-0122

This agency helps Asians and Southeast Asians as they adjust to life in Minnesota. It offers legal aid, youth programs, a food shelf and health projects.

CHINESE AMERICAN ASSOCIATION OF MINNESOTA

P.O. Box 382584
Minneapolis 55458   No phone

This organization promotes the activities of Chinese Americans, offers programs that increase awareness of Chinese culture and keeps the Chinese-American community abreast of significant news.

Insiders' Tips

Many Finnish Americans in Minnesota celebrate St. Urho's Day, which commemorates the man who drove all the grasshoppers out of Finland.

FIL-MINNESOTA ASSOCIATION

7415 Fifth Ave. S.
Richfield   861-2397

The purpose of this group is to provide support and cultural offerings to the large community of Filipino Americans and educate others about the Philippines.

HMONG AMERICAN PARTNERSHIP

450 N. Syndicate, Ste. 35
St. Paul   642-9601

The main focus of this organization is helping Minnesota's Hmong become fully participating members of the community.

HMONG YOUTH ASSOCIATION OF MINNESOTA

379 University Ave. W., Ste. 214
St. Paul   225-9421

Hmong youth can receive educational assistance, job counseling and cultural support from this community organization.

JAPANESE AMERICAN CITIZENS LEAGUE

P.O. Box 582864
Minneapolis 55458   537-8076

This long-established organization works to protect the rights of Japanese Americans, preserve their culture and promote events of interest to members.

KOREAN INSTITUTE OF MINNESOTA

P.O. Box 8094, St. Paul 55208   644-3251

Classes in language, dance, culture, martial arts, cooking and art are offered by this Korean cultural organization.

LAO ASSISTANCE CENTER OF MINNESOTA

1015 Olson Memorial Hwy.   374-4967

This organization offers activities, progams in reemployment, job placement, interpretation and translation for adults and youth in the Lao community.

LAO FAMILY COMMUNITY OF MINNESOTA INC.

320 W. University Ave. 55103
St. Paul   221-0069

Created by Hmong people to assist other Southeast Asian refugees, this organization operates a variety of programs — focusing on literacy, youth, health, employment, legal aid and other areas — to foster self-sufficiency.

MINNESOTA ADOPTED KOREANS

P.O. Box 25852
St. Paul 55125   730-7563

This organization for adopted Koreans sponsors support groups and holds educational programs about Korean culture.

MINNESOTA CHINESE STUDENT ASSOCIATION

P.O. Box 14157
Minneapolis 55414   No phone

Through a variety of programs and special events, this group serves Chinese people in the area and promotes understanding between Americans and Chinese.

STATE COUNCIL ON ASIAN-PACIFIC MINNESOTANS

205 Aurora Ave., Ste. 100
St. Paul   296-0538

This council, created by the Minnesota Legislature, focuses on involving Asian-Pacific people in governmental decisions, giving them greater access to government services and providing them with increased opportunities.

VIETNAMESE CULTURAL ASSOCIATION OF MINNESOTA

2985 Northview St., Roseville   297-5451

Housed in a new building, this organization helps preserve Vietnamese culture

Performers at the Cinco De Mayo Festival.

Photo: Jeff Christensen, Pioneer Press

in Minnesota as it assists Vietnamese to adjust to life in the United States.

UNITED CAMBODIAN ASSOCIATION OF MINNESOTA INC.
1821 University Ave., Ste. 324S
St. Paul   645-7841

UCAM helps Cambodians in Minnesota by sponsoring youth programs, providing educational opportunities and employment services and preserving the Cambodian ethnic heritage.

The Chicanos and Latinos

Chicanos and Latinos in the Twin Cities account for the largest concentration of that group in the state, although there are sizable numbers in counties scattered throughout Minnesota. The biggest group of the 36,000 Twin Cities Chicanos and Latinos live in the suburbs, with 11,000 in St. Paul and 8,000 in Minneapolis. Their numbers, bolstered by a large number of recent arrivals from such places as Puerto Rico, Colombia, Cuba, Panama and El Salvador, have increased by two-thirds in the past decade alone.

The Twin Cities' first Spanish-speaking people came from Mexico and the U.S. Southwest. As late as 1910 there were only 52 people of Mexican origin in the entire state, but the availability of agricultural field work (mainly working with the sugar-beet crop) soon drew others, who arrived as migrant workers and later became permanent residents. These people primarily settled in St. Paul, occupying housing on the lower West Side. Their population increased tenfold during the 1920s, reaching more than 3,600. Hampered by high unemployment during the Depression, they still managed to launch places of worship, such as Our Lady of Guadalupe Church, and found social and service groups. Meanwhile, a much smaller community of Mexicans and Mexican Americans was kindled in Minneapolis.

Gradually these communities switched from seasonal to year-round work, their workers joining the staffs of such businesses as meat-packing plants and textile factories. An important change in St. Paul's Chicano community took place in the early 1960s, when most remaining families in the flood-plagued lower West Side moved to higher ground elsewhere on the West Side. During the next two decades, in both St. Paul and Minneapolis, the use of Spanish in the communities became more widespread.

Starting in the late 1970s, the community in the Twin Cities began to become more diversified with the arrival of people from Central and South America seeking better economic opportunities or fleeing political oppression. Even now, however, people of Mexican origin account for two-thirds of all Hispanics in Minnesota.

Organizations

CATHOLIC CHARITIES
HISPANIC OUTREACH
401 Concord St., St. Paul   224-0799

Catholic Charities offers referral services, financial assistance and other human services for the Hispanic and Latino community.

CENTRO CULTURAL CHICANO INC.
2025 Nicollet Ave. S.
Minneapolis   874-1412

This is a community cultural organization that provides employment assistance, educational programs, health counseling, activities for seniors and arts programs.

CENTRO LEGAL INC.
15 S. Fifth St., Ste. 1134
Minneapolis   338-4503
179 E. Robie St., St. Paul   291-0110

This organization is a source of legal assistance in the areas of immigration, family law and consumer law.

HISPANOS EN MINNESOTA
155 S. Wabasha, Ste. 128
St. Paul   227-0831

Health, chemical dependency and HIV

education services are the emphases of this community agency.

MINNESOTA
HISPANIC FEDERATION INC.
162 College Ave. W., St. Paul   224-4855

This is an advocacy and lobbying organization that seeks to educate the public and government officials on Hispanic cultures and their needs.

The Germans

More Minnesotans trace their ancestry to Germany than to any other country in the world. In the Twin Cities there are some very sizable Germanic pockets — Cottage Grove, 55 percent; Chaska, 58 percent; and Shakopee, 64 percent — but they've got nothing on Hamburg, Minnesota, where the German-American population stands at 92 percent. The metropolitan area's overall German share is 43 percent.

Unlike Irish immigrants, who primarily settled along the Atlantic seaboard, the majority of the 5 million immigrant Germans of the 19th century came to the Midwest, making such cities as Milwaukee and Cincinnati veritable burgs. They also came in large numbers to southern and central Minnesota. In the Twin Cities the German population swelled from 27 to more than 2,000 between 1850 and 1860, climbing further to about one-third of the population with the passage of another 10 years. St. Paul, in particular, acquired a strong German character, giving birth to more than 20 German-language newspapers in the 19th century.

Bringing more skills from their home country than many other immigrant groups, the Germans took up work in banking, brewing, shopkeeping and other nonmanual trades. They differed from other foreign-born groups in another important respect: They boasted a remarkable religious diversity, representing the Catholic, Lutheran, Methodist and Jewish faiths, among others.

Early on, German Americans established institutions of higher learning in the Twin Cities. They founded St. Paul's Luther Seminary, which later moved to Iowa. Concordia College in St. Paul, founded in 1892 by Missouri Synod Lutherans, long had a strong German atmosphere. Also carrying to Minnesota their deep musical traditions, they started most of the Twin Cities' major classical-music organizations. Emil Oberhoffer, the first music director of the Minnesota Orchestra (then called the Minneapolis Symphony Orchestra), was a native of Bavaria.

When World War I erupted, many German immigrants in the Twin Cities found themselves harassed by the Minnesota Commission of Public Safety, a hyper-patriotic organization created by the state legislature to aid the war effort. At the same time, the Minneapolis Board of Education restricted the teaching of German in public schools. Anti-German sentiment in Minnesota was greatly reduced during World War II.

Now, among many of the descendants of the German immigrants, nostalgia for the Old Country has faded. Even so, there is still quite a bit of enthusiasm for the preservation of German culture.

Organizations

VOLKSFEST ASSOCIATION OF MINNESOTA INC.

301 Summit Ave., St. Paul   222-7027

Germanic culture remains alive in the activities of this organization that sponsors language classes, music and dance groups, activities for seniors and social events.

The Irish

Although people of Irish origin make up a smaller percentage of the Twin Cities population than they do in many other U.S. metropolitan areas, they have always exerted a great influence in St. Paul, which became known as an Irish city even while Germans reigned as the capital city's largest ethnic group. When the Irish-born man of letters Oscar Wilde toured the country in 1882, St. Paul gave him one of the warmest welcomes he received anywhere in the United States. St. Paul has Irish pubs, Irish politicians, a huge St. Patrick's Day parade and reportedly has contributed more than its share to the coffers of the Irish Republican Army. Irish music and dance are popular throughout the Twin Cities, and Irish performers frequently make tour stops in these parts.

Minnesota, then a largely agricultural state, received only a small share of the great wave of Irish immigration in the 19th century. Some came as lumberjacks or soldiers in the U.S. Army, while others were railroad workers, craftspeople or domestics. Many settled in St. Paul because it was the headquarters of a Catholic archdiocese (one of the earliest arrivals was John Ireland, a native of County Kilkenny, who would eventually become the archbishop), and volunteer Irish laborers help erect the city's first Catholic school in 1851. That same year, the city reeled through its first St. Patrick's Day celebration. As the decades passed, the Irish spread more or less evenly throughout the city. In Minneapolis, the Irish lived primarily in the northeast portion of the city and downtown.

Many of the Irish went on to build careers in the civil service, law enforcement, politics and law. One of the state's most popular turn-of-the-century Irish politicians, Ignatius Donnelly, was a chronic party-switcher, lieutenant governor, member of the legislature, humorist, proponent of the existence of the lost continent of Atlantis and author of an internationally famous book about hidden cryptograms in the works of William Shakespeare. Nine out of the 10 mayors of St. Paul between 1932 and 1972 had Irish surnames.

Today, the Irish population of certain Twin Cities areas remains strong. Mendota Heights and Deephaven both have Irish concentrations of more than 20 percent, while Lilydale tops the charts at 25 percent. Overall, about 15 percent of Twin Citians claim some Irish blood.

Organizations

O'SHAUGHNESSEY-FREY LIBRARY
Department of Special Collections
University of St. Thomas, No. 5004
2115 Summit Ave., St. Paul   *962-5400*

This library contains a Celtic collection that includes more than 10,000 volumes on Irish folklore, history, literature, language and religion, as well as materials about the culture of Scotland and Wales.

The Native Americans

Many of the Twin Cities' Native Americans can trace their ancestry to people who have lived for centuries in the land now known as Minnesota. Through the mid-19th century, several native peoples had lived in the region, including the Dakota, Ojibwa, Assiniboin and Cheyenne. But when white soldiers, traders and settlers began arriving in significant numbers in 1819, the Dakota and Ojibwa had settled virtually all the land. The Dakota, spread out along much of the Midwest, were represented in southern Minnesota by four tribes — the Mdewakanton, Wahpekute,

Dancers at an American Indian Pow Wow.

Wahpeton and Sisseton — and had been in the area for several hundred years. The Ojibwa, who entered Minnesota from the east around 1700, occupied the more heavily forested northern regions. All told, approximately 15,000 American Indians dwelt here when the first whites arrived.

Starting in 1837, through a series of treaties and land successions, the tribes lost most of their territory. The area that now includes much of the Twin Cities was among the earliest chunks of Minnesota land lost to the Native Americans. In return for the land, the U.S. government paid the Ojibwa and Dakota bargain-basement prices and promised them reservations and other benefits. Often, however, the government was slow to pay, or Congress wouldn't establish the reservations. When the Dakota tired of these breaches of contract, they sometimes tried to resettle the lands they had given away. Disastrous conflicts of culture resulted, sparking the bloody U.S.-Dakota War of 1862 in which hundreds of people died and 38 Dakota Indians were hanged in Mankato, the largest mass execution in American history. Many Dakota fled Minnesota. In just a few years, the Dakota population in the state fell to only 176.

Meanwhile, the government concentrated on consolidating the various bands of the Ojibwa people on reservations. Seven reservations were created in the northern half of the state. Government bureaucrats, as well as some influential Indians, hoped that Native Americans would eventually assimilate into the dominant culture. Many reservation parcels, doled out to individuals, eventually fell into white hands.

In the late 19th and early 20th centuries, the Dakota began a return to Minnesota. They established small communities in the southern part of the state. By the time the post-World War II period arrived, Minnesota's Native Americans were ripe for a major migration to the Twin Cities, which the federal government officially encouraged. By 1960 one-fifth of Minnesota's Indians lived in the Twin Cities, a proportion that grew to more than one-third in the decades that followed.

Now about 23,000 Native American people live in the Twin Cities, representing 1 percent of the population. Most live in metro Minneapolis, where those of Ojibwa ancestry are the majority. More than 7,000 live in the suburbs. St. Paul's smaller Native American community includes many Winnebago people originally from Wisconsin, as well as Ojibwa and Dakota. Minneapolis, in particular, emerged as a center of American Indian activism, serving as headquarters of the American Indian Movement (AIM) and the Upper Midwest Indian Center. In recent years, Twin Cities Native Americans have also spearheaded a nationwide effort to convince school and professional sports teams to do away with their Indian names and mascots. (In 1993, the Minneapolis-based *Star Tribune* become only the second daily newspaper in the country to refuse to print the Indian names of such teams as the Cleveland and Atlanta baseball clubs and the Washington and Kansas City football clubs.)

Of the 11 reservations in Minnesota, only one — the Shakopee-Mdewakanton Reservation in Carver County, a Dakota community — lies within the Twin Cities metropolitan area. It owns the very successful Mystic Lake Casino complex (for more on casinos, see the Weekend and Daytrips chapter).

Organizations

MINNEAPOLIS AMERICAN INDIAN CENTER
1530 E. Franklin Ave.
Minneapolis 871-4555
This is a large cultural resource and community center that has programs focused on everything from social services to the arts.

MINNESOTA INDIAN AFFAIRS COUNCIL
1450 Energy Park Dr., Rm. 140
St. Paul 643-3032
Serving as the official liaison between Minnesota's Native American communities and the state government, the Indian Affairs Council involves itself in such issues as education, housing, the environment, tribal rights and health.

Photo: Scott Takushi, Pioneer Press

Festival of Nations, a multicultural event featuring folk dances, ethnic foods and an international bazaar.

RED SCHOOL HOUSE

643 Virginia St., St. Paul   488-6626

Offering an Ojibwa and Dakota culture-based curriculum for students in prekindergarten through the 12th grade, this alternative school has long served native families in the Twin Cities.

UPPER MIDWEST
AMERICAN INDIAN CENTER

1113 W. Broadway , Minneapolis   522-4436

Child welfare services, mental health programs, adult education, a learning center for high school students and an intergenerational program are a few of this center's offerings.

The Scandinavians

Lumped together (which you must never do, because the Norwegians, Swedes, Danes and Icelanders protest it vociferously), the Scandinavians dominate much of the ethnic scene in the Twin Cities. What Garrison Keillor says on the radio is true: There are a lot of Scandinavians here. It's actually common here to hear Norwegian/Swede jokes, have the opportunity to sample acquired-taste delicacies like lutefisk that have long vanished in the Old Country and major in Nordic languages at the University of Minnesota. And if you're looking for someone named, say, Donald Peterson, in the Minneapolis phone book, forget it — there are just too many of them. In the Twin Cities, 30 percent of the people claim some Nordic blood, with some areas — Richfield, Fridley and Ham Lake, to name a few — exceeding 40 percent.

The Norwegians in Minnesota outnumber the Swedes by a slight margin, with the Danes far behind. All three groups, however, originally came here because of economic troubles at home, an affinity for working the land and an oft-declared visual similarity between the new land and the old. More Norwegians came to Minnesota than to any other state. When they settled in, starting in the 1850s, they sent "America letters" back home that made their relatives and former townspeople feverish to join them.

By the 1880s many were heading for Minneapolis, which was destined to become the second-biggest Norwegian city in the world. At the start of World War I, Norwegians ran many of the city's banks, newspapers and churches. With the Swedes, they established a residential enclave along Cedar Avenue that was nicknamed Snooze Boulevard, after the reputedly heavy use of snuff by the residents. Later they moved to south Minneapolis and other sections of the city.

The Swedish immigrants, too, favored Minnesota more than any other state. They began their arrival just when the state was opening up for settlement, and they kept coming in substantial numbers for another 80 years. Much of this tide washed over the Twin Cities. At first Swedes tended to settle in the Phalen Creek area in St. Paul (which became known as Swede Hollow), St. Paul's East Side, the Snooze Boulevard neighborhood of Minneapolis and the shanties of Bohemian Flats along the Mississippi River. Later they migrated to northeast and south Minneapolis. By 1905 fully 7.5 percent of the Minneapolis population were natives of Sweden, and the city became a center of Swedish-American culture and life. Wherever they went, they formed businesses, music groups and social clubs.

The Danes did not come to the region in nearly as large numbers, and their migration ended sooner than the Norwegians or Swedes. The Danish were also more spread out, moving to Iowa and Wisconsin in large numbers. They began populating the Twin Cities in the 1880s, most of them living in Minneapolis. Dania Hall, in Minneapolis' Cedar-Riverside neighborhood, became a center of their community activities. Although all three groups are now largely assimilated in the Twin Cities, they maintain strong cultural ties through organizations and celebrations.

Organizations

AMERICAN SWEDISH INSTITUTE
2600 Park Ave. S., Minneapolis   871-4907

Founded by Swedish American newspaperman Swan Turnblad and housed in the fortress-like 1904 mansion he built as his home, the American Swedish Institute fosters an interest in Swedish settlers, the immigrant experience and the mingling of American and Swedish affairs. Its remarkable collection of more than 6,000 artifacts includes Swedish provincial costumes, a painting from 1712 by Gustaf Hesselius (the first Swedish-American artist), exquisite glassware, looms from the Old Country and Swedish books. Traveling exhibitions are also frequently on display. The building itself is a marvel, featuring a wall-sized enameled glass copy of a Swedish historical painting by Carl Gustav Hellqvist, 11 decorative and rare porcelain tile stoves and one of America's largest installations of carved African mahogany.

Insiders' Tips

Norwegians, Swedes, Danes and Icelanders make up the Twin Cities' large Scandinavian community.

DANISH AMERICAN FELLOWSHIP
4200 Cedar Ave. S., Minneapolis   729-3800

This organization preserves Danish culture through special events, cultural activities and educational programs.

SONS OF NORWAY INTERNATIONAL
1455 W. Lake St., Minneapolis   827-3611

This is the international headquarters of an organization that promotes Norwegian heritage and culture. Through its 50 district offices throughout the state, it sponsors educational programs, social activities and special events.

SWEDISH CULTURAL SOCIETY IN AMERICA
1150 Lois Court
Shoreview, Minn. 55126   481-9794

A promoter of Swedish culture and language in the United States, the society sponsors programs about the life and literature of Sweden.

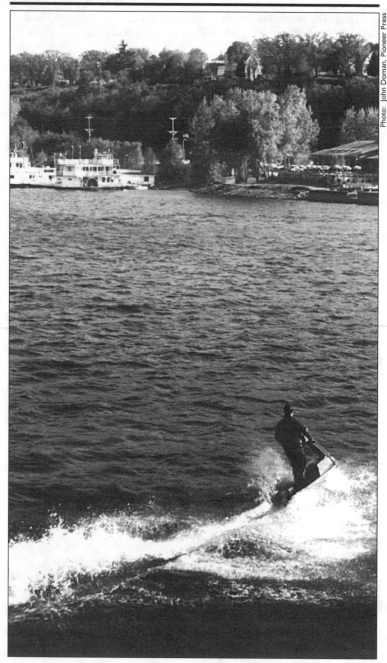

Photo: John Doman, Pioneer Press

The St. Croix River with Stillwater in the background.

Inside
Weekend and Daytrips

While the Twin Cities offer many weekend pleasures, sometimes the most diverting Saturdays and Sundays are spent miles away from the cities' borders, exploring Minnesota's small towns, lake resorts, dairy and wheat farms, river valleys or magnificent Lake Superior shoreline.

For some, getting away simply means going "up north" to the family's second home, a summer cabin on one of Minnesota's 10,000 lakes. A large number of Minnesotans own second homes — usually humble one-bedroom cottages — on lakes in the state's northern and northwestern resort areas. In many cases, owning a cabin is a matter of disposable income — many residents are sufficiently well-off to afford a second mortgage.

But we suspect the phenomenon is, at heart, based on tradition and culture, rather than economics. Many summer cabins have been in the same family for years and years. The lakeshore lot was purchased cheap decades ago, a makeshift cottage was built, and the deed was passed from generation to generation, in some cases, shared piecemeal by siblings or an assortment of relatives.

Owning a cabin keeps your feet on the ground and your priorities straight. What otherwise would be spent on a wild resort weekend or evening out instead is invested in that little shack in the woods.

Beyond the mortgage and property taxes, however, the cost of maintaining a cabin is minimal. Heaven knows, no one puts any money into furnishing these little hideaways. In fact, Minnesotans strive for the ultimate in tackiness when they "decorate" their cabins. If they replace anything in their primary homes, that castoff chair, rusty appliance or lumpy mattress finds a new home in the cabin.

It may be the '90s in the Twin Cities, but up north at the cabin, it's eternally the '50s and '60s — a world of gold shag carpeting, mismatched Melmac dishes, vinyl dinette sets and avocado green stoves. More often than not, the beds are covered with old sleeping bags (no Ralph Lauren comforters here) and the floors blanketed with wet bathing suits and sand. You'll find leeches (for bait) and beer in the fridge and a hot card game in progress at the table.

Truth be told, you wouldn't want it any other way. After all, the whole idea of going to the cabin is to shake off the city — all the burdensome cares, criteria, agendas, schedules, labels and expectations of civilization — and just hang out, preferably at the end of the dock with your toes in the water and a fishing pole in your hands.

Going up north to the summer cabin isn't so much a destination as it is a frame of mind.

Newcomers, if you happen to get yourself invited to somebody's cabin for a weekend or a day, accept without hesitation. (And if you don't get invited, invite yourself — "We'll be up in Alexandria this weekend. Maybe we'll stop over and see you at the lake." This is acceptable cabin etiquette. If your would-be hosts really don't want to see you, they'll just go fishing.) Then pack your swimsuit, grab some potato salad at the neighborhood deli — better yet, make a hot dish — and head on up. It's a Minnesota experience that's not to be missed.

On those rare weekends when Minnesotans aren't at the cabin, they're undoubtedly at a summer festival. Blame our long, cold winters, but when summer comes around, we find any reason to celebrate. Minnesota abounds in summer festivals. There's the **Woodtick Music Jubilee** in Akeley, the **Spam** (yes, Spam) **Jamboree** in Austin, **River City Days** in Red Wing, the **Waterfront Festival** in Duluth and the **Polka Fest** in Bird Island, not to mention **Sauerkraut Days** in Henderson.

The best reason to visit these festivals is to rediscover the soul of Minnesota — its small communities bursting with ethnic pride, its rambling river towns, romantic bed and breakfasts, the glory of Superior, the aching beauty of the St. Croix.

Fortunately, many of these destinations are just outside our back door — close enough to the Twin Cities for a day or weekend trip.

In this chapter, we make a few suggestions for short trips from Minneapolis and St. Paul. This is just a sampling. Many other fascinating locales are within reach, and, if you make the effort, you'll find your own favorite spot.

It's fun to plan your trip around a community festival. Check with the **Minnesota Department of Tourism**, 296-5029 or (800) 657-3700, for a schedule of year-round celebrations.

A word to the wise: If you have your heart set on staying in a specific bed and breakfast inn or eating at a popular historic inn, it's a good idea to make reservations ahead of time. Also, keep in mind that fall, with its blazing color displays, is as much a tourist season as summer in certain areas of the state, including Duluth and the North Shore Drive and the St. Croix, Mississippi and Minnesota river valleys.

A final note: Unless another area code is specifically mentioned, the destination listed here is within the 612 area code.

Rivertown Ramble

The St. Croix River, often called the Rhine of the Midwest, is a delightful destination just minutes from the Twin Cities. From its origins in northern Wisconsin, the waterway forms part of the Minnesota-Wisconsin border before joining the Mississippi River near the city of Hastings. Many interesting cities and towns sprouted on the banks of both rivers. Travelers may choose to ramble along the river banks and visit them all. The alternative is to throw out an anchor in any one of them for a day or two and soak up the ambiance. In an effort toward practicality, we will journey from north to south, from Taylors Falls to Red Wing.

Taylors Falls/St. Croix Falls

Taylors Falls (population 694) offers historic charm, small-town friendliness and the natural beauty of the Dalles of the St. Croix, a sublimely lovely gorge cut by the river. Like other St. Croix River burgs, Taylors Falls was a bustling lumbering community in the late 19th century, and its many existing Victorian homes are reflective of that boom period.

Tourism is nothing new to Taylors

ENJOY LOCALLY PRODUCED WINES AT

Northern Vineyards
W I N E R Y

FREE WINE
TASTING DAILY

A LARGE SELECTION OF VARIETAL & BLENDED WINES

THE CRUSH

- WINE ACCESSORIES
- MINNESOTA GOURMET PRODUCTS
- GREAT GIFT IDEAS • GIFT CERTIFICATES
OWNED AND OPERATED BY THE
MINNESOTA WINEGROWERS COOPERATIVE
LOCATED IN STAPLES SAWMILL
(612) 430-1032 • 402 N. MAIN ST., STILLWATER MN
Hours: Mon. - Sat. 10 a.m. - 5 p.m., Sun 12 p.m. - 5 p.m.

Falls. In the late 1880s, the town was the site of a log jam of monumental proportions: 30 feet high and more than 2 miles long. It took months to clear the mess, and, in the meantime, visitors came from far and wide to see the unbelievable phenomenon. It remains a source of local bragging rights. There's even a **Log Jam Restaurant**, where the historic event is depicted on placemats and historic photos.

Attractions here include the lovely old **Folsom House**, 465-3125, in the Angel Hill Historic District. This artifact-filled home of lumber baron William Folsom overlooking the St. Croix is open from late May through mid-October.

However, there's no denying Taylors Falls' real drawing card is the **Dalles**, strange formations of limestone and shale that tower dramatically over the rushing St. Croix. A fascinating stop is **Interstate Park**, where you can hike the park's infamous Pothole Trail, containing unusual, gaping holes drilled in rock by glacial waters, and enjoy breathtaking views from the river bluffs.

Many visitors choose to view the river up-close and personal by renting canoes at the **Taylors Falls Canoe Rentals** facility in the park, 462-6315. Other canoeing information is available across the river in St. Croix Falls, Wisconsin, at the **Riverway Headquarters Visitors Center**, Massachusetts and Hamilton streets, (715) 483-3284.

Water activity is also found at **Wild Mountain** outdoor amusement area, 465-6315, 7 miles north of Taylors Falls on County Road 16. This downhill ski park turns into a water park during the summer months, offering both water slides and dry slides down the slopes, plus a go-cart track, canoe rental and paddleboat tours of the river (see the Kidstuff chapter). Like any small town, Taylors Falls offers a rather limited range of restaurants; nonetheless, a few stand out. For instance, you can cruise back to the '50s at **The Drive-In**, on the north end of Main Street. Here you'll find carhops in poodle skirts delivering hamburgers and tasty homemade root beer to your car window à la *American Graffiti*.

Other dining options include the new **Romayne's** restaurant/bar, serving everything from sandwiches to grilled salmon in the indoors dining room or outside on the deck, and less-formal eateries, such as the **Log Jam Restaurant** and **Chisago House**.

Many an innocent tourist has spent the night in jail in Taylors Falls. No, this isn't a case of late-night revelry or an overzealous police department. One of the city's most unique guest houses is the two-story **Old Jail Co. Bed & Breakfast**, 465-3112, 100 Government Road. While the exterior has been authentically restored, the interior has been transformed into a comfortable living area, complete with modern kitchen and loft bedroom. Suites also are available next door in the historic Schottmuller Building.

If you're looking for something a bit more luxurious than the jail, the **St. Croix River Inn** in nearby Osceola, Wisconsin, is the ultimate. This 80-year-old Dutch Colonial home, on a bluff overlooking the St. Croix, boasts seven bed and breakfast rooms filled with antique-looking furniture, Jacuzzis and oodles of charm. Of course, charm comes with a price tag. Room rates range from $100 to $200 nightly. Call (715) 294-4248 for reservations and information.

As you head south to Stillwater, you may wish to stop at **William O'Brien State Park**, a very popular recreational area with bountiful campsites, beach, hiking and picnicking areas. It's 15 miles north of Stillwater.

Stillwater

Just 30 minutes northeast of the Twin Cities, Stillwater, a town steeped in history, sits picturesquely on the banks of the St. Croix. Founded in 1843, Stillwater lays claim to being Minnesota's oldest town. The state's territorial charter was drawn up here in 1848 and passed in Congress a year later, making the city the birthplace of the Minnesota Territory.

Stillwater was a thriving logging town until the industry dwindled in the early 1900s. Yet, through a rigorous preservation program, many of its historic buildings and homes have been painstakingly restored. And today, tourists, rather than logs, spill into this town of 14,000 to shop for antiques and oddities, dine overlooking the river or just enjoy its yesteryear pace.

Stillwater was once a contender to be the state capital but settled instead for the state penitentiary. The three-story Territorial Prison housed notorious criminals of its day, including Cole Younger, a member of the Jesse James gang. The sprawling old edifice still stands, but its prison days are over. Today, convicts are held in a much larger facility in neighboring Bayport.

Stillwater is known for its Victorian homes (many transformed into bed and breakfast inns), a picturesque Main Street lined with antique shops, galleries and bookstores, not to mention several good riverfront restaurants.

For antique buffs, the town has dozens of shops for browsing, including many dealers in the historic 1869 **Isaac Staples Sawmill Complex**, on North Main Street.

Book-lovers will want to check out the new **Stillwater Book Center**, at 229 S. Main Street, just across the street from another find, the **St. Croix Antiquarian Booksellers**. Housing 27 used-book sellers, the center also offers rare maps and prints, as well as hard-to-find books printed by university and small presses.

Dining ranges from casual to formal Victorian. For the former, try **The Dock**, 430-3770, 425 E. Nelson, where a riverfront deck attracts boaters and tourists, as well as locals, or **Savories**, 430-0702, 108 N. Main, a European bistro serving interesting sandwiches and soups.

The Freight House Restaurant, 439-5718, 305 S. Water Street, is steeped in railroad memorabilia and offers river views, plus an expansive outdoor deck. After your meal, go next door for a spin on the Rivertown Trolley, which offers 40-minute narrated tours of the town. If you enjoy mobile dining, check out the *Andiamo Showboat* dinner cruises, 430-1234, or enjoy a full-course meal aboard the *Minnesota Zephyr* train, 430-3000, as it rolls through the river valley.

Hedonists head for the Lowell Inn, 439-1100, 102 N. Second Street, which serves a generous fare in three elegant dining rooms of a graceful estate known as the Mount Vernon of the West. The inn also has 21 rooms for overnight guests. And you may need a room after that sumptuous repast!

Hike up the hill behind the Lowell Inn to Pioneer Park, offering a sweeping view of Stillwater and the St. Croix River valley.

Another interesting stop is the Joseph Wolf Brewery Caves, 439-3588, 402 S. Main Street, open Memorial Day through Labor Day. These hand-dug caves were originally used by fur trappers and later for beer storage by the Wolf Brewery. They are now the site of Vittorio's Restaurant. Call for tour information.

If wine rather than beer interests you, you can sample Minnesota wines — yes, *Minnesota* wines — at Northern Vineyards, 430-1032, 402 N. Main Street. Owned and operated by the members of the Minnesota Winegrowers Cooperative, Northern Vineyards offers 11 varieties for tasting and taking home.

Other sites include the Warden's Home Museum, 439-5956, 602 N. Main Street, an 1853 building that housed wardens of the first Territorial Prison, and the Washington County Historical Courthouse, 430-6233, 101 W. Pine Street, c. 1870, one of the oldest courthouses in the state.

Hudson

Just 12 miles east of St. Paul on I-94, this Wisconsin town on the St. Croix River was named for its physical resemblance to the Hudson River Valley in New York.

Founded in the 1840s by fur traders, Hudson was a thriving lumbering center in the 1850s and '60s. And today many grand Victorian homes built by lumber barons and wealthy merchants of the period still grace Hudson neighborhoods, especially along Third Street. Check in at the Hudson Chamber of Commerce, (715) 386-8411, 421 Second Street, for information on a self-guided tour of Hudson's old homes.

Or begin your sightseeing at the Octagon House, (715) 386-2654, 1004 Third Street. Listed on the National Register of Historic Places, the Octagon House — yes, it is truly eight-sided — contains a wealth of memorabilia, including a grand piano notable because it was dumped in the river twice on its way up the Mississippi to Hudson.

Across the street, at 1005 Third Street, is the historic 1884 Phipps Inn, a sprawling Queen Anne home divided into six comfortable, deluxe bed and breakfast suites. Call the inn at (715) 386-0800 for more information and reservations.

Picturesque Hudson is also home to the very modern, expansive Phipps Center for the Arts, (715) 386-2305, First and Locust streets, offering art exhibits, plays and popular and classical music concerts. Recently expanded, the Phipps boasts an awesome view of the St. Croix from the upper-floor gallery.

To get a real feel for the hometown appeal of this pretty city, just wander through Hudson's downtown, which centers on Second Street.

Pop into **Dick's Bar and Grill**, (715) 386-5222, Walnut and Second streets, an unpretentious eatery with concrete floors and wall murals, for some notoriously good down-home cooking, including "chicken-in-a-hubcap." This is baked or fried chicken served, just as it says, in a real hubcap.

Other good bets are **Sunsets**, (715) 386-4001, 500 First Street, for lunch or dinner (if the weather's good, grab an outdoor table on the deck) and the **North Shore Coffee Company**, (715) 386-4122, upstairs from **Valley Bookseller** at 112½ Walnut Street, for a steaming jolt of espresso and proprietress Maureen's freshly baked goodies.

Then walk off the calories at nearby Lakefront Park, which boasts a swimming beach, bandshell, walkways and a new amphitheater.

St. Croix Meadows Greyhound Park, just south of I-94, offers both matinee and evening races at a new, state-of-the-art track. Dining is available in the clubhouse. Call the racetrack at (715) 386-6800 for a racing schedule or dinner reservations.

Just northeast of Hudson, County Highway A leads to **Willow River State Park**, featuring a nature center, prairie land, a great trout stream, three dams, three lakes and a pleasant sandy beach.

North Hudson (population 3,100-plus) is a longstanding Italian enclave. Check out its Italian restaurants, or plan ahead and visit during the community's annual **Pepper Festival**, usually held in mid-August.

Red Wing

Pottery and work shoes have made the name Red Wing world-renowned, but you couldn't tell it from the looks of this pretty Mississippi River town. With its gorgeous 19th-century mansions, historic St. James Hotel and restored Main Street, Red Wing seems frozen in an earlier time of quiet elegance.

Located just 50 miles southeast of the Twin Cities, Red Wing (population 13,134) is nestled amid the craggy bluffs surrounding the Mississippi. A 1.5-mile climb up one of the most popular, Barn Bluff, affords a commanding view up and down the Mississippi.

The restored **T.B. Sheldon Auditorium Theatre**, 388-2806, Third Street at East Avenue, is not to be missed. This jewel box theater opened in 1904 and today hosts a variety of performances from films to plays to classical music concerts.

History buffs will want to visit the **Goodhue County Historical Society and Museum**, 388-6024, at 1166 Oak Street.

Be sure to take time for a stop at the **Red Wing Pottery Salesroom**, 388-3562, 1995 W. Main Street, where original pieces of the old Red Wing Pottery are still sold, along with other gifts and collectibles.

Pottery Place Outlet Center, 388-1428, 2000 W. Main Street, is a complex of factory outlets, shops and restaurants in a converted old stoneware factory.

Have lunch or dinner — or spend the night — in the elegant antiques-filled **St. James Hotel**, 388-2846, 406 Main Street, c. 1875, which also has an adjacent shopping mall.

Nearby **Frontenac State Park** (15 miles south on U.S. Highway 61) has been called the bird-watching capital of

Photo: Joe Oden, Pioneer Press

Stillwater, 20 miles northeast of St. Paul, is the birthplace of Minnesota.

southern Minnesota. And during the winter months, downhill skiers flock to Mount Frontenac and Welch Village ski resorts.

Treasure Island Casino, just outside of Red Wing off U.S. Highway 61, blasts the traveler back to the 20th century with its video slots, bingo and blackjack tables (see the "Casinos" section of this chapter).

Southern Stops

Rochester

There's always a doctor in the house in this bustling city where the claim to fame is the world-renowned Mayo Clinic.

About 80 miles south of the Twin Cities (via U.S. Highway 52) or about 46 miles south of Red Wing, Rochester is a city of roughly 70,000, with a thriving cultural and educational scene, thanks, in part, to its large concentration of doctors and other well-educated folk.

One of the jewels of Rochester is the sprawling **Mayowood** estate, former home of the famed Mayo family. Built in 1911,

this stately 57-room mansion overlooking the Zumbro River served as a social center for such visiting dignitaries as Franklin Roosevelt, Helen Keller and Adlai Stevenson. Reservations are required for tours; call (507) 282-9447. The **Mayo Clinic**, at 200 First Street S.W., also offers tours, and there's plenty to see: distinctive architecture, a well-adorned chapel, a carillon tower, not to mention those hallowed clinic halls visited by more than a quarter-million people every year. The tours are free and no reservations are required. Tours are given at 10 AM and 2 PM Monday through Friday. For more information, call (507) 284-2511.

Other attractions include **Quarry Hill Nature Center**, featuring a fossil-filled limestone quarry; **Whitewater State Park** with its climbing bluffs and trout fishing; **Olmstead County History Center and Museum**; and, to the west, the old town of **Mantorville**, containing many buildings listed in the National Register of Historic Places. Mantorville's **Hubbell House** draws diners from near and far. Housed in an 1854 inn, the restaurant serves traditional fare in a setting as comfortable as an old armchair. Call (507) 635-2331 for reservations.

New Ulm

Ninety miles southwest of the Twin Cities on the banks of the Minnesota River sits New Ulm, a little piece of Germany in the Midwest.

Traces of New Ulm's Teutonic heritage are everywhere, from the 45-foot Glockenspiel downtown to its neatly planned streets and the August Schell Brewery to the annual Oktoberfest revelry. Dominating this city of 13,000 is a statue of Hermann the Cheruscan, the 9th-century warrior who united Germany.

Highlights include the **Schell Brewery**, a family-owned brewery dating back to 1861, and surrounding gardens and deer park; the home of children's author/artist **Wanda Gag**; the **Harkin Store**, an 1870 general store; **Brown County Historical Museum**; and **Veigel's Kaiserhoff**, a restaurant renowned for its barbecued ribs.

To experience the town's *Gemütlichkeit* in full bloom, visit during **Oktoberfest** (usually the second week in October) when the polka music and the beer spill forth unceasingly for a rollicking good time.

St. Peter

In 1857 St. Peter was a contender to be the state capital, but a scheming legislator hid the crucial bill authorizing the capital's move from St. Paul. The deadline passed and so did St. Peter's chance for lasting glory — all because Legislator Joseph Roulette hated the idea of having to travel to St. Peter from his home in northern Minnesota.

This city on the Minnesota River 70 miles south of the Twin Cities is an interesting stop on the way to New Ulm or a good destination in its own right.

Dating to 1854, St. Peter (population 9,421) has several well-preserved historic buildings, including the home of St. Peter's first mayor, E. St. Julien Cox. This 1871 home is a magnificent example of Gothic Revival architecture.

Other interesting attractions include **Gustavus Adolphus College**, the **Nicollet County Historical Museum** and the **St. Peter Arts and Heritage Center**.

Stop for lunch or dinner at **Mitterhauser's Grill & Restaurant**, (507) 931-3833), 429 S. Minnesota Avenue, owned and operated by award-winning Austrian chef, Claus Mitterhauser.

Too tired for the drive home? Turn in at the **Park Row Bed & Breakfast**, (507) 931-2495, 525 W. Park Row, a cozy Victorian retreat.

New Prague

On your way back to the Cities, swing eastward and stop in the Czech town of New Prague (Minn. highways 13 and 19), which is noteworthy for its colorful wall murals, the copper-domed **St. Wenceslaus Church** and a delightful old inn, **Schumacher's New Prague Hotel**, 758-2133, 212 W. Main Street. The latter is an elegant Greek Revival brick building designed by famed architect Cass Gilbert in the late 1890s. Inside, the European-styled hotel features 11 lodging rooms, each individually decorated. Three cozy Old World-themed dining rooms serve home-style Czech and German specialties, accompanied by imported beers.

Northfield

Forty miles south of the Twin Cities at the junction of state highways 3 and 9, the town of Northfield (population 14,684) lays claim to two prestigious private colleges, **Carleton College** and **St. Olaf College**, and one colorful historic event: a foiled robbery attempt by the notorious Jesse James and his gang.

On September 7, 1876, James and his gang attempted to rob the First National Bank, but the cashier, Joseph Lee Heywood, refused to open the safe. He was shot to death, but the citizenry retaliated, killing two gang members and chasing the rest out of town. One other innocent bystander was killed in the melee. Three gang members were apprehended in Madelia, Minnesota, and sent to Stillwater State Prison. Six years later, Jesse James was murdered in Missouri. The foiled bank robbery is a source of community pride and is re-enacted every September during Defeat of Jesse James Days. The bank has been restored and is now a museum housing exhibits about the famous event.

In fact, Northfield contains many restored buildings and storefronts in its historic downtown, which is well worth a stroll. Also noteworthy is the **Archer House**, (507) 645-5661, 212 Division Street, a charming 1877, 38-room inn along the banks of the Cannon River.

Thanks to its two colleges, Northfield has a vibrant cultural scene, including several interesting art galleries. Both colleges are worth touring. The **Arboretum** at Carleton College offers hiking and jogging trails along the Cannon River and tours by reservation, 663-4309.

Just west of Northfield, on Minn. Highway 19, is **Fireside Orchard**, a great pie-and-cider stop before you hit I-35 back to the cities.

Northern Exposures

St. Cloud

St. Cloud, 65 miles northwest of the Twin Cities, has a population of about 80,000 (including suburbs), making it large enough to be interesting, yet small enough to be friendly.

In this prosperous city are found world-famous granite quarries; **St. Cloud State University** with its planetarium, anthropology and art museums; the **Stearns County Heritage Center**, 253-8424, 235 S. 33rd Avenue; distinctive gardens, such as the colorful **Munsinger Gardens** (Riverside Drive and Michigan Avenue); and several theater groups and art galleries.

Nearby **Collegeville** is home to **St. John's University**, the breathtaking **St. John's Benedictine Abbey** and the **Hill Monastic Manuscript Library**, 363-3514, possessing one of the largest collections of early manuscripts.

Well worth a side trip is the **Charles A. Lindbergh State Park**, 632-9050, about 26 miles north of St. Cloud at Little Falls. This secluded park in the woods skirting the Mis-

Weekend escapes to Stillwater or other St. Croix River Valley bed and breakfast inns are great fun.

Insiders' Tips

sissippi River contains the boyhood home of famous aviator and environmentalist Charles Lindbergh. Filled with his boyhood toys and period household furnishings, the comfortable old homestead with its big screened-in sleeping porch offers a fascinating look at the forces that shaped the man. The garage houses a Volkswagen Bug that Lindbergh drove on adventure trips throughout Africa.

Nearby, the park's visitors center offers films and exhibits on Lindbergh and his famous flight, as well as an interesting bookstore.

Brainerd

Brainerd, 125 miles north of the Twin Cities, is the hub of a region dotted with 450 lakes and more than 135 resorts, hotels and campgrounds. As such, it's a popular weekend destination for many Twin Citians. Most people come just to relax and recharge their batteries by lolling about on the beach, fishing, waterskiing or boating.

Apart from the dazzling lakes and serene woods, points of interest include the **Crow Wing County Museum**, (218) 829-3268, 320 Laurel Street; **Brainerd International Raceway**, (218) 829-9836, Minn. Highway 371, where Paul Newman has raced; **Paul Bunyan Fun Center** amusement park, (218) 829-6342, Minn. highways 210 and 371; **Lumbertown U.S.A.**, a re-creation of an 1870 logging camp, (218) 829-8872, at Madden's Resort on Gull Lake, 8001 Pine Beach Peninsula; and the **Paul Bunyan Arboretum**, (218) 829-8770, N.W. Seventh Street; not to mention various water-slide parks, mini-golf courses and shopping galore.

Duluth

Lake Superior gusts buffeting sea gulls off Canal Park, the boom of foghorns in the mist, old neighborhoods clinging to hillsides, others squatting on sandbars, the elegant Glensheen Mansion, falcons circling over Hawk Ridge.

These are but a few of the great reasons for visiting Duluth (population 85,493), bustling Lake Superior port city and gateway to the picturesque North Shore Drive. Duluth is the final stop on the St. Lawrence Seaway, which connects the Atlantic Ocean to the Great Lakes.

The heart of the city is the harbor and the aerial-lift bridge, through which thousands of domestic and foreign vessels arrive each year, lending an exciting international ambiance to the surroundings.

To get a real feel for Duluth, take a boat cruise of the harbor or tour the *William A. Irvin*, a retired ore carrier that's been transformed into a 610-foot floating museum.

The **Canal Park Marine Museum**, (218) 727-2497, operated by the U.S. Army Corps of Engineers, offers fascinating exhibits on maritime history and the Great Lakes, including dioramas of shipwrecks and models of famous shipping vessels, plus enough marine equipment to incite sailing fever in the most ardent landlubber.

Of course, no trip to the harbor and Canal Park is complete without a lunch or dinner stop at **Grandma's Saloon & Deli**, (218) 727-4192, with its convivial atmosphere, old-time decor and hearty sandwiches. Top off lunch with a brisk walk on Duluth's **Lake Walk**, a colorful walkway that skirts Lake Superior from Canal Park to just past **Fitger's Brewery**.

Children of all ages will enjoy **The Depot**, (218) 727-8025, 506 W. Michigan Street, a renovated 1892 railroad depot that now serves as an art center, housing several museums and performing arts spaces. The lower level contains a train museum with real, operating locomotives and historic storefront displays. This is great kidstuff — they love climbing all over the trains.

Drive north of town to **Glensheen Mansion**, (218) 724-8864, 3300 London Road, for a glimpse at how the other half lived in turn-of-the-century prosperity. Built on 22 acres in 1908 by attorney and legislator Chester Adgate Congdon, Glensheen is reminiscent of an English country estate with its elegant 39-room manor house and formal gardens overlooking Lake Superior. Call ahead for tour times and admission fees.

Other attractions include **Fitger's Brewery**, (218) 722-8826, 600 E. Superior Street, a complex of shops, restaurants and lodging, and for gamblers, **Fond-du-luth Gaming Casino**, (218) 722-0208, 129 E. Superior Street (see the "Casinos" section at the end of this chapter).

To take in the lovely sweep of city and water, drive along **Skyline Parkway**, a dramatic hilltop route in the western part of Duluth. In the fall, bird-watchers converge here at Hawk Ridge to watch migrating hawks and eagles soar over the city.

As you can see, Duluth, 150 miles north of the Twin Cities, is a destination in itself, or it can serve as a stop on your way up **North Shore Drive**, a breathtaking roadway that skirts crashing waves, verdant forests and crystalline streams for 150 miles to the Canadian border.

Plan your trip for a long weekend in order to do justice to the many attractions of Duluth and/or the North Shore. And make reservations. This area is a favorite destination for Twin Citians, especially in the summer and fall. You don't want to be stranded without a bed for the night. Among your choices are the **Spinnaker Inn**, 5427 North Shore Drive, (218) 525-2838; and **Fitger's Inn**, 600 E. Superior Street, (218) 722-8826. Another option is the very reliable **Radisson Duluth**, 505 W. Superior Street, (218) 727-8981.

Casinos

It's enough to make those Scandinavian immigrant farmers roll over in their graves. Minnesotans are becoming gambling fools!

They're flocking in droves to the glitzy, new American Indian-owned casinos to wager at the blackjack tables, pour quarters into video slots or dab bingo cards, then celebrate their winnings or mourn their losses at casino-operated restaurants and lounges.

It's a 1990s phenomenon with no end in sight. With more casinos than Atlantic City, Minnesota is the largest American Indian gaming market in the United States. The state has 17 Indian-operated casinos, and in 1993 they produced an estimated combined gross revenue of more than $3 billion.

We're not talking about cozy little country gambling halls. Many Minnesota facilities are big-time gaming complexes — some of the largest in the Midwest.

For example, Mystic Lake Casino in the Twin Cities suburb of Prior Lake measures 340,000 square feet, the biggest casino between Atlantic City and Las Vegas. Several other casinos are larger than 100,000 square feet. And it's not uncommon for every square foot to be absolutely packed, even on Saturday mornings!

All this action began in the late 1980s

and today — moral issues aside — it's become a major industry.

In this section we list various casinos in the Twin Cities area and those that are close enough for a daytrip or weekend outing. But first, here are some general characteristics of the gambling scene — Minnesota style.

• **Alcohol.** Unlike the scene in Vegas or Atlantic City, the booze doesn't pour from the bar like coins from the slots. Many of Minnesota's casinos are dry, including the big Mystic Lake complex in suburban Twin Cities. In other casinos, alcohol may be carefully controlled. Grand Casino Hinckley, for example, has a two-drink limit in the entertainment lounge. Other casinos sell alcoholic drinks, but not in the gaming areas.

• **Lighting Up.** The no-smoking movement is big in Minnesota and has extended to casinos, where several have set aside large no-smoking areas. Be aware of where you light up or you could face a large fine.

• **Food, Glorious Food.** Many casinos have initiated large buffets to lure gamblers. At bargain prices, these feasts may be worth the trip alone.

• **Blackjack and Slots.** Blackjack is currently the only table game allowed in Minnesota. It's played in the traditional Las Vegas fashion. Except for aces, double downs are permitted after splits, and dealers are required to stand on all 17s at most casinos. In Minnesota, as a general rule, video slots must return no less than 80 percent for non-skill games and no less than 83 percent for games with more player input, such as video poker.

A final note: Remember, the goal is to have fun, whether you win or lose. Bring your smile, loose change and your sense of perspective and you'll undoubtedly have a great time!

The casinos are listed alphabetically. We're concentrating on those close enough to be comfortable weekend destinations from the Twin Cities. For detailed information on other Minnesota casinos, contact the Minnesota Office of Tourism at 296-5029 or (800) 657-3700.

BLACK BEAR CASINO
Carlton   *(218) 878-2327*

Black Bear Casino, about 25 miles south of Duluth, is a new 87,000-square-foot facility operated by the Fond du Lac band of Ojibwa Indians. Inside the faux-limestone facility is a two-story main rotunda filled with 24 blackjack tables ($2 to $200 betting range), surrounded by 1,000 video slots and games. An upstairs 500-seat bingo parlor doubles as the casino's lunch and dinner buffet area.

Liquor is served in the gaming area, and the Blackbear Lounge offers a popular walleye fish dinner (entrees are in the $10 to $12 price range). The complex also has a sports bar and the Lady Slipper Lounge, with live music on weekends. The casino is open around the clock every day.

Directions: Go north on I-35 from the Twin Cities. After about 100 miles, as you near the Duluth area, take the Minn. Highway 210 Exit. You'll see the casino from the interstate.

FIREFLY CREEK CASINO
Granite Falls   *564-2121*

Set in a pleasant valley along the Minnesota River in southwestern Minnesota, this smaller casino has a friendly, down-home atmosphere, in addition to 350 slot and video games and 10 blackjack tables ($2 to $200). The Firefly also has a country-style cafe and a lounge.

The Firefly is open 24 hours on Fridays and Saturdays, 8 AM to 1 AM all other days.

When you tire of the action at the Firefly, you can hop in your car and head for Jackpot Junction Casino in Morton, just 40 miles away.

Directions: From the Twin Cities, take U.S. Highway 212 west to Granite Falls. From Granite Falls, take Minn. Highway 67 south for 5 miles to the casino. It's about 120 miles west of the Twin Cities.

FOND-DU-LUTH CASINO
129 E. Superior St.   *(218) 722-0280*
Duluth   *(800) 873-0280*

Run by the Fond du Lac band of Ojibwa, this casino offers 400 slot and video keno machines, plus an upstairs 525-seat bingo parlor. Due to a legal squabble between the Indians and the city of Duluth, no blackjack is currently offered.

The casino has a snack bar serving grilled food and an adjacent parking ramp (free parking with validation). The Fond-du-Luth is open 24 hours Fridays through Sundays and from 10 AM to 2 AM Mondays through Thursdays.

Directions: The casino is east of the intersection of County Highway 23 and I-35, on one of Duluth's major streets.

GRAND CASINO HINCKLEY
Hinckley   *(800) 472-6321*

A 75-minute drive from the Twin Cities brings you to the door of this deluxe gaming emporium. Inside are more than 1,500 slot and video games, 48 blackjack tables ($3 to $1,000), plus video craps and video blackjack tables and a computerized horse-racing game.

The casino is owned by the Mille Lacs band of Ojibwa, which also owns the nearby Grand Casino Mille Lacs.

This prosperous facility is growing like crazy. In 1995 this Hinckley complex added

a new hotel and an 18-hole golf course. The facility also has a 240-site RV park and 50-unit "chalet" (mini-mobile home) park.

Connected to the casino via an enclosed corridor is the Grand Grill Americana bar and restaurant. Inside the casino itself are the Silver 7s Lounge and the Grand Grill, where the buffet has received rave reviews. The casino lounge offers free entertainment nightly.

The casino also has a state-of-the-art Kid's Quest child-care center, for children between the ages of 6 weeks and 12 years. Grand Casino Hinckley is open 24 hours every day.

Directions: Go north on I-35 from the Twin Cities. Take the Hinckley Exit and go a mile east on Minn. Highway 48.

GRAND CASINO MILLE LACS
Onamia   *(800) 626-5825*

Grand Casino Mille Lacs, on the southwest shore of huge Lake Mille Lacs, is a smaller version of the Hinckley gaming complex and offers 1,200 slot and video games, 35 blackjack tables ($3 to $1,000), a 400-seat bingo parlor and a computerized horse-racing game.

Like its Hinckley sibling, Grand Casino Mille Lacs has on-site lodging (an attached 180-room hotel with pool), child-care facilities, a video arcade, plus one of the best buffets of any casino in the state. However, no liquor is served in the casino, which is open 24 hours a day.

Directions: From the Twin Cities, take U.S. Highway 169 north for about 100 miles. The casino is between Onamia and Garrison.

JACKPOT JUNCTION
Morton   *(507) 644-3000, (800) 538-8379*

Ironically, Jackpot Junction, one of the first successful Indian-run casinos in the state, sits near the site of the tragic Dakota

Conflict, a six-week war between Indians and whites more than 100 years ago that resulted in the forced exodus of the Sioux, or Dakota, tribes.

Today it seems the Dakota are exacting sweet justice at the gaming tables and slot machines.

Jackpot Junction offers 1,200 slot and video games, 63 blackjack tables ($2 to $1,000), using two- and four-deck shoes, plus a 385-seat bingo hall.

Because of its out-of-the-way location, 100 miles southwest of Minneapolis and St. Paul, Jackpot Junction offers regular low-cost busing from the Twin Cities and is generous with its coupon offers.

This large, sprawling facility has a full-service restaurant, Impressions, that is considered one of the better eateries in the area. Other areas include a buffet, three full-service bars and a concert area with nightly entertainment, including national celebrities. The casino operates a 90-site campground and RV park.

Jackpot Junction is open 24 hours daily.

Directions: From Minneapolis, take U.S. Highway 212 to Olivia, turn south on U.S. Highway 71 and follow the signs to the casino near Morton.

MYSTIC LAKE
ENTERTAINMENT COMPLEX
Prior Lake   445-6000, (800) 262-7799

Mystic Lake is the biggest casino complex in the Midwest. Technically, the complex comprises the Little Six Casino, the down-home Dakota Country Casino and the upscale Mystic Lake Casino. The latter two are huge domed gambling palaces connected by an enclosed mall. The Little Six, Mystic Lake's humble forerunner, is a half-mile away.

Mystic Lake Casino screams "Las Vegas" with its glitzy aura and giant chandeliers. At Mystic's high-stakes blackjack area, minimum bets are in the $100 range.

The adjacent Dakota Country Casino is designed to attract smaller-stakes gamblers, with tons of nickel slots, video poker machines and $3 blackjack tables. Overall, the complex has 2,100 slot and video games, 128 blackjack tables ($3 to $1,000), and a 1,200-seat bingo palace.

The casino's Four Seasons buffet is consistently top-rated. There's also the High Steaks Ranch House for meat-and-potatoes fans and the Minnehaha Cafe for lighter fare.

No liquor is served anywhere in the casino, but you'll find a wide selection of nonalcoholic cocktails and near-beers in Wild Bill's Saloon, which also features live entertainment. Mystic Lake's Celebrity Palace presents headliner acts.

The complex has a shopping mall of mainly American Indian arts and crafts.

Mystic Lake is open 24 hours daily.

Directions: From the Twin Cities, take I-35W south to County Highway 42. Take 42 west to County Highway 83. Turn south and go a mile to the complex. Alternative: Take Minn. Highway 13 west from I-35W, continuing when it becomes Minn. Highway 101. Turn south on County Highway 83 and go 5 miles.

TREASURE ISLAND CASINO
Red Wing   (800) 222-7077

This casino began in 1984 as the Prairie Island Bingo Hall and has since been greatly expanded to offer 1,250 slot and video games, 52 blackjack tables ($3 to $500), using two- to six-deck shoes, plus matinee and evening bingo sessions.

The complex features a recently built, lovely domed atrium with palm trees and the colorful Toucan Harry's bar, built to look like the bow of a wrecked pirate ship.

The older section of the casino, however, is made up of less-appealing, crowded gaming rooms. Treasure Island recently added riverboats that provide dinner cruises (no gambling on deck) departing from the casino's marina on the Mississippi.

Liquor is served in the casino and bar. Generous portions are offered up at the buffet. Child care is available at the Children's Center of Prairie Island, across the street; reservations are required: (800) 554-5473 or 385-0351.

The casino books stand-up comics and name acts every week as free entertainment. Treasure Island is open 24 hours daily. An RV park and a marina are on the property.

Directions: Take U.S. Highway 61 south from the Twin Cities and follow the signs to the casino, which is about 35 miles south of St. Paul and 8 miles north of Red Wing.

St. Croix Casino & Hotel
Turtle Lake, Wis.   (800) 846-8946

By big-city standards, the St. Croix is small, but it's got all the services — including two bars, nightly entertainment, a buffet room and a first-class restaurant. Here you'll find 700 slot and video games and 32 blackjack tables. The facility is open 24 hours and, if you really must get some shut-eye, there's a casino-owned hotel a block away (shuttle provided). The St. Croix is about 70 miles from the Twin Cities.

Directions: From Minneapolis and St. Paul, take I-35W north to U.S. Highway 8. Go east 28 miles to Turtle Lake, Wis.

Other Casinos

Here's a listing of other Minnesota casinos too distant for comfortable weekend trips but which may make an enjoyable stop during a longer vacation.

Fortune Bay Casino
Tower   (218) 753-6400
          (800) 992-7529

Grand Portage
Lodge & Casino Grand
Portage   (218) 475-2441
Hotel only   (800) 543-1384

Lake of the Woods Casino
1012 E. Lake St., Warroad   (218) 386-3381

Northern Lights Casino
Walker   (218) 547-2744
          (800) 252-7529

Palace Bingo and Casino
Cass Lake   (218) 335-6787
          (800) 228-6676

Red Lake Casino
Red Lake   (218) 679-2500

River Road Casino
Thief River Falls   (218) 681-4062

Shooting Star Casino
Mahnomen   (218) 935-2701
Hotel only   (800) 453-7827

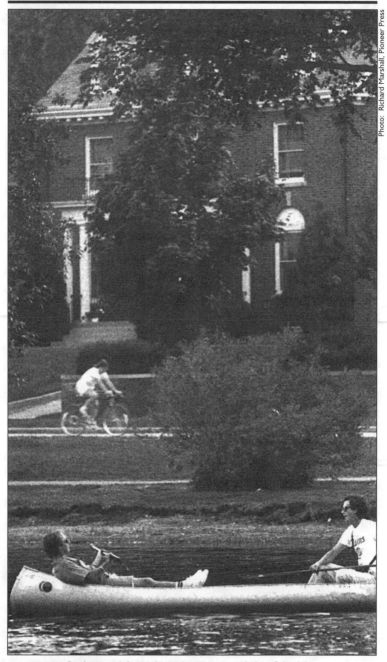

Big houses, bike paths and canoeists on Lake of the Isles.

Photo: Richard Marshall, Pioneer Press

Inside
Neighborhoods

From uptown penthouses to quaint Victorian homes nestled on shady city streets, from palatial lakeshore estates to "Leave it to Beaver" suburban ramblers, the greater Twin Cities area offers an amazing array of housing — for rent or for sale — to suit all personalities and pocketbooks.

At first glance, Minneapolis and St. Paul may look like one sprawling metropolis sliced by a river, but in reality the two cities are very different.

Even though it has its share of old, stately neighborhoods, Minneapolis, with a population of roughly 368,000, exudes a big, brash, modern image with its cutting-edge music scene, pro sports teams and bustling industry. St. Paul, with a population of approximately 272,000, possesses more of a small-town, traditional, old-monied, intellectual atmosphere — after all, seven colleges are located within its boundaries.

Minneapolis is, for the most part, laid out logically in a flat grid-like pattern, its streets sensibly patterned. St. Paul is a map maker's nightmare: Its roadways dance willy-nilly over hills and river bluffs. The Mighty Mississippi curves defiantly through its urban core, making the waterway a more dramatic presence in the Saintly City than in its sister city to the west.

While not immune to big-city problems of unemployment and crime, both cities, nonetheless, have relatively healthy economies, cultural treasures and extensive park land and lakes — qualities that greatly enhance their livability.

There's a park every eight blocks in Minneapolis — an acre of green for every 43 residents. While homes along Twin Cities lakefront boulevards command a hefty price, it is possible to find surprisingly affordable housing just a few blocks away, within walking distance of the water. It's devilish good fun to merrily jog around Lake Calhoun, wave at passersby and just pretend that the pink 20-room Tudor mansion over there — the one with the Ferrari in the driveway — is your home sweet home. Who's to know the difference, except you and your pocketbook?

In 1995 the National Association of Home Builders ranked Minneapolis No. 5 in the nation for affordable housing. Other national studies have echoed these findings for St. Paul as well. According to American Chamber of Commerce figures, the median cost of housing in Minneapolis in late 1994 was $118,987, compared to $104,000 in Kansas City, $143,359 in Denver and $187,490 in Los Angeles. While it's handy to keep that $118,987 figure in mind as a reference point, it's also wise to remember that Twin Cities area home prices vary greatly, depending on the neighborhood and, of course, living space and amenities. For those wishing to rent, the average monthly price of a rental unit in the metropolitan area is around $550. And within the city limits of either Minneapolis or St. Paul, rental units are even more affordable, at $485 and $499, respectively.

Still, finding the just-right home or apartment in the Twin Cities metropolitan area can be a daunting task, to say the least. After all, more than 2.3 million people make their home in this greater metropolitan area. Unless you're already familiar with the Twin Cities' neighborhoods and suburbs, you may wish to use the services of a reputable Realtor or apartment-search firm.

Two huge companies, Edina Realty and Burnet Realty, dominate the local real-estate scene. Yet there are many smaller realty firms with enough hustle and initiative to give the big guys a run for their money. See our Real Estate Resources chapter, following, for more information.

The housing industry is thriving in the Twin Cities, with new housing developments sprouting in suburbs, old warehouses being transformed into lofts and condos, and quaint Victorian homes undergoing restoration to their original splendor. Despite — or maybe because of — our dramatic climate of subzero winters and blistering summers, the Twin Cities is a sublimely livable locale. According to *Mpls.St. Paul Magazine*, about 75 percent of Minnesotans are natives who wouldn't think of living anywhere else, and more than half the state's 4.4 million population has not moved in the last five years. Thousands have come reluctantly and remained contentedly. Watch out, it could happen to you.

What follows is a brief overview of both cities, their neighborhoods and suburbs.

Minneapolis Neighborhoods

The Mississippi River is a good reference point for both cities. Minneapolis spreads out on both the east and west banks of the Mighty Mississippi as it rolls southeast toward St. Paul. The western and southern parts of the city are much larger, spreading over lake-dotted rolling landscape to join the suburbs of Brooklyn Center, Robbinsdale, Crystal, Golden Valley, St. Louis Park, Edina and Richfield. Beyond lie the second- and third-tier suburbs of Bloomington, Burnsville, Eden Prairie, Chaska, Chanhassen, Minnetonka, Maple Grove, Brooklyn Park, Plymouth and others.

On the eastern side of the Mississippi are Northeast Minneapolis and the neighborhoods surrounding the University of Minnesota to the southeast. Spreading out from Northeast Minneapolis are the suburbs of Fridley, Columbia Heights, St. Anthony, Coon Rapids and Blaine, among others.

Here's a look at some of Minneapolis' most colorful neighborhoods. Keep in mind that city housing can range from very affordable to very exclusive, reflecting Minneapolis' vibrant, diverse urban population.

Bryn Mawr, Kenwood and Calhoun-Isles

On the western edges of Minneapolis are the areas of Bryn Mawr, Calhoun-Isles and Kenwood, hilly neighborhoods of tree-lined streets and large, stately old and new homes. Bryn Mawr is bordered on the north by Glenwood Avenue and expansive Theodore Wirth Park, 957 acres of gardens and greenery encompassing Theodore Wirth Lake. On its southern end, Bryn Mawr veers southwest to encompass the genteel neighborhoods on the north and west shores of Cedar Lake.

Just south and southeast of Bryn Mawr are the areas of Kenwood and

Calhoun-Isles, prestigious neighborhoods surrounding Lake of the Isles and Cedar Lake. Kenwood is the home of the famous *Mary Tyler Moore* house from the popular TV sitcom of the 1970s. (It's at 2104 Kenwood Parkway.) Some of the old Kenwood homes have been divided into apartments, and the community has a lively population of old families and young professionals, many of whom can be seen jogging around the lakes. In 1994, the median housing price in Calhoun-Isles was $109,600.

Lowry Hill

Just east of Kenwood are the Lowry Hill, Lowry Hill East and East Isles neighborhoods, straddling Hennepin Avenue. This interesting area offers a pleasant mix of 19th-century mansions and old and new apartment buildings. Residents range from the very wealthy to struggling young professionals and bohemians. It's a choice locale for arts-lovers, containing the renowned Guthrie Theater, Walker Art Center, the Minneapolis Sculpture Garden, plenty of interesting restaurants and video stores. Lovely Loring Park and downtown are just a five-minute walk away.

Uptown

At the southern edge of Lowry Hill East and centered at Hennepin Avenue and Lake Street is the bustling Uptown area, a popular draw for young sophisticates and raging individualists. Close to the frenetic outdoor social scene at Lake of the Isles and Lake Calhoun, Uptown also is home to comedy clubs, bars, ethnic restaurants, coffee shops, boutiques and three movie theaters, of which two, the Uptown and The Lagoon, specialize in the latest foreign films. Calhoun Square, at Hennepin and Lake, is a popular shopping complex featuring one-of-a-kind shops and restaurants.

The Uptown Art Fair, held one weekend in August every year, is one of the most popular summer events in the cities.

Housing in Uptown includes affordable apartments and interesting big and small older homes. Many of the larger homes have been divided into apartments and condos.

Southwest Neighborhoods

Elegant homes, sprawling yards and lake views typify Minneapolis' southwest neighborhoods, fanning out around the south shore of Lake Calhoun and picturesque Lake Harriet. Here you'll find the neighborhoods of Linden Hills, Fulton, Lynnhurst and East Harriet. This is gentrified living, and many of its spacious and moderate size homes have been in the same families for years. The 1994 median housing price here was $111,500.

The area of 43rd Street and Upton Avenue, just three blocks west of Lake

Set aside a May weekend for the annual Minneapolis/St. Paul House Tour. It's fun and has great for ideas for your own home.

Insiders' Tips

Harriet, has a collection of charming little shops and ice cream stores. It's a great place to visit on Saturday afternoons.

Nokomis Neighborhoods

The residential areas surrounding Lake Nokomis and along Minnehaha Parkway in South Minneapolis are quiet, stable communities with an interesting mix of large and small homes. Lake Nokomis and Minnehaha Park are popular destinations for fishing, picnicking, walking and biking. In the Nokomis area in particular, housing is surprisingly affordable; the median housing price in 1994 was $79,432.

Powderhorn Community

Many young families who want to settle in the inner city find their first home in this old south-central city district. At its center is Powderhorn Park, a historic 65-acre park containing a small lake and a popular children's playground. The park is the scene of a colorful May Day Celebration, an annual event featuring gigantic puppets and banners, as well as the Powderhorn Arts Festival, an alternative-style art fair that coincides with the Uptown Art Fair.

Like any inner-city neighborhood, Powderhorn has its share of property crime and occasional drug-related incidences. "But we have a relatively low crime rate for an inner-city neighborhood," says Scott Hawkins, executive director of the Powderhorn Park Neighborhood Association. "People are very active in the neighborhoods. We have a lot of block clubs. We have a lot of younger families, senior citizens who've lived here 40 to 50 years and lots of youngsters, so there's lot of vitality."

Homes here sell fast, especially on the south side, according to Hawkins. The median housing price here is about $60,000.

North of Powderhorn is the Phillips neighborhood, bounded by Interstate 35W to the west, Hiawatha Avenue to the east, Franklin Avenue to the north and Lake Street to the south. The site of some of the highest poverty and infant mortality rates in the city, Phillips faces many challenges. Fueled by a strong neighborhood association, however, the community is working to fight the demons of crime and unemployment. Positive strides have been made. A former porn theater has been transformed into a youth art center. Children are painting colorful murals in the neighborhood park. An annual celebration, Phillips Power, Phillips Pride, commemorates the closing of a troublesome neighborhood liquor store. A series of weekly outdoor concerts celebrates the community's cultural diversity.

Seward Neighborhood

The Seward neighborhood, just south of the University of Minnesota's West Bank campus and south of I-94 and west of the Mississippi, is a stable mix of college intellectuals, professionals and working-class folk, plus a few leftover '60s activists who run a successful food cooperative and inhabit the egalitarian and colorful Seward Cafe on Franklin Avenue. The homes here are well-maintained, older two-stories and bungalows.

Campus Communities

University of Minnesota campus communities of Dinkytown and Stadium Vil-

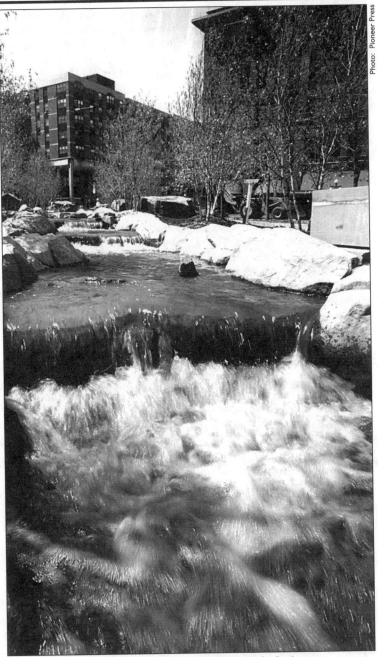

Photo: Pioneer Press

Mears Park in Lowertown in downtown St. Paul.

lage dominate southeast Minneapolis on the east bank of the river. This area also includes Prospect Park, a cozy residential area of winding streets whose landmark, the "Witch's Hat" tower, you can see as you drive east on I-94 over the Mississippi. This is one of the quieter neighborhoods in Minneapolis.

Northeast Neighborhoods

Northeast Minneapolis, on the northeast bank of the Mississippi, is a traditional, working-class ethnic district with roots in the Polish and Eastern and Southern European heritages. This old address suddenly has a new cachet. Many young families and couples, plus some artist types, are migrating northeast, attracted by its stability, affordable housing and proximity to downtown. Median housing price here is around $67,000.

North Minneapolis

North Minneapolis claims a rich, colorful history, housing that ranges from great old homes to depressed projects and everything in between, attractive parkland that includes the majestic Victory Memorial Drive and lovely Theodore Wirth Park, a culturally diverse population (34 percent African American, 10 percent American Indian and Asian American) and easy accessibility to downtown Minneapolis.

"Half of our housing stock is over 100 years old, and it's well-maintained," said Paula Saunders, director of the Jordan Neighborhood Association on the near north side.

At one time, North Minneapolis was a prestigious address, harboring thriving communities of Jewish and Eastern European heritage, and its schools were considered among the best in the city. Today, crime and poverty pose challenges, especially on the near north side. Yet Saunders believes the challenges are being overcome because of a strong program of block clubs and neighborhood activism.

Downtown

Minneapolis has 81 distinct neighborhoods, and we've only touched on a few. Not to be overlooked is downtown Minneapolis itself, which claims 25,000 residents living in apartments, condos and townhouses. Here the advantages are obvious: convenience, convenience, convenience! Within walking distance are major commercial centers, cultural offerings, retail stores, restaurants and the warehouse nightlife scene and concert halls, many of which are accessible via a state-of-the-art skyway system.

St. Paul Neighborhoods

None other than *Newsweek* magazine recently hailed St. Paul as one of the nation's "hottest cities" — and it wasn't referring to the weather! Despite its world-class industries, learning institutions and cultural offerings, the city possesses the "aw-shucks" atmosphere of a cozy, old small town, making it a very livable community.

We begin with downtown St. Paul, where around 6,000 people make their homes in high-rises and charming warehouses-turned-lofts, all within walking distance — in enclosed skyways, of course — to theaters, concert halls, churches, stores and a lively urban farmers market. The downtown district is, in fact, St. Paul's fastest-growing neighborhood.

Many neighborhoods in St. Paul draw home buyers like magnets because they offer a strong sense of community, stability, value and unique advantages. Here's a look at a few of these "hot" locales.

Western St. Paul

Well-maintained homes, stable, safe neighborhoods and the convenience of city living attract many buyers to the St. Anthony Park, Macalester-Groveland, Highland Park, Summit Hill and Crocus Hill areas of St. Paul.

Houses in these areas range in value from $70,000 to several hundred thousand dollars. In these neighborhoods are found good homes of all sizes and styles, from inexpensive bungalows to stately Victorians.

SUMMIT HILL

In the highly desirable Summit Hill neighborhood, west of downtown St. Paul, homes can sell for as much as $1 million. This area includes magnificent Summit Avenue with a breathtaking span of historically preserved 19th-century mansions. Today many of these grand edifices have been divided into townhouses and rental units, yet their stately exteriors remain unchanged. Interspersed among the estates are many charming, but smaller, turn-of-the-century homes inhabited by solidly middle-class folks. Residents cite as advantages the area's charming ambiance and its proximity to bustling Grand Avenue and downtown St. Paul.

CROCUS HILL

The prestigious Crocus Hill area, bounded roughly by St. Clair Avenue on the south, Lexington Parkway on the west, Grand Avenue on the north and Dale Street on the east, is graced with glorious Victorian mansions on quiet, shady, lamplit streets. This is where the great industrialists and civic leaders settled in the 1900s, and it remains a highly desirable residential area. The 1994 median housing price here was $131,500.

ST. ANTHONY PARK

St. Anthony Park, in the northwest corner of St. Paul, has a strong sense of small-town community spirit, abundant gardens and stable neighborhoods. Proximity to the University of Minnesota's St. Paul campus is an added plus. Homes here range in price from $60,000 to upwards of $200,000 for more spacious, typical dwellings with such amenities as old-fashioned woodwork and built-in buffets. St. Anthony is such a hot area that many homes sell privately, through word of mouth, without the assistance of a real-estate agent.

MERRIAM PARK

Merriam Park, between Hamline Avenue and the Mississippi River and University and Summit avenues to the north and south, was home to many large Irish

Locals love to attend the Fall Home and Garden Show every October at the Minneapolis Convention Center and the Home and Patio Show in February at the St. Paul Civic Center.

Insiders' Tips

families in the early 1900s. Mat Hollinshead, editor of the *Merriam Park Post* newspaper, likens the community to an "urban village that retains a lot of the atmosphere of the Victorian railroad and garden suburb it originally was 100 years ago."

The hilly community also affords a scenic panorama of the Mississippi River. This stable, predominantly middle-class district of single-family homes and apartments has an enviable reputation as one of St. Paul's safest neighborhoods. Homes range from cozy to luxurious, and in 1994 sold for a median price of $80,000. One real-estate agent says this is where you'll find many larger Victorian homes.

MACALESTER-GROVELAND

The Macalester-Groveland area, home to Macalester College, the University of St. Thomas and the College of St. Catherine, has a quiet, traditional "East Coast" ambiance with its housing stock dating back to the 1920s and '30s. This area is bounded by Summit Avenue on the north, Ayd Mill Road on the east, the river on the west and Randolph Avenue on the south. Its safe, stable neighborhoods are within walking distance to movie theaters, markets and the ever-popular Grand Avenue, with its arty boutiques and ethnic restaurants. Houses range from small two- or three-bedroom homes selling for as low as $70,000 on the east end to luxurious $400,000 estates on the Mississippi River. Median housing price here is around $100,000. Realtors say homes in the "Mac-Groveland" area have the best resale value in all of St. Paul.

HIGHLAND PARK

Highland Park, to the southwest, is home to a thriving Jewish community, as well as many non-Jewish residents. A major employer here is the Ford Motor Plant. This mature neighborhood offers quality housing that ranges from small homes to estate-like mansions and distinctive apartment buildings. Most were built in the 1940s and '50s. Amenities include well-maintained neighborhoods; distinctive recreational facilities such as a public golf course, sprawling Highland Park with its spacious swimming pool and new community recreation center; and high-quality schools. The median housing price here in 1994 was $104,600.

Como Area

You'll discover many handsome bungalows and two-story homes with quality touches such as built-in buffets and extensive woodwork in the residential areas surrounding lovely Lake Como and Como Park and extending directly eastward to I-35E. While much of the housing stock dates from the 1920s, some homes were built as early as the 1880s. They range from charming bungalows to Queen Anne-style mansions along the southern shore of Lake Como. Median housing price for Como is about $83,000.

Hamline-Midway

South and slightly west of the Como area is the Hamline-Midway district, bounded by University Avenue to the south, Cleveland to the west, Lexington to the east and Burlington Railroad tracks to the north.

Hamline-Midway is a safe area with stable, middle-class neighborhoods, where housing is affordable and of good quality. The majority of homes were built between 1890 and 1940, and some hold such sur-

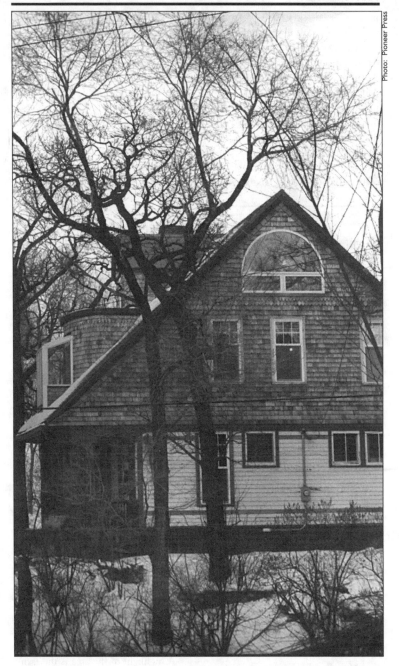

A home in the Prospect Park neighborhood of Minneapolis.

prises as leaded- and stained-glass windows and rich woodwork. Amenities include several parks, a neighborhood recreation center and proximity to both Minneapolis and downtown St. Paul. The eastern section has a concentration of Southeast Asian grocery markets and businesses, evidence of just one of many cultures represented in this neighborhood. This area is also heavily commercial/retail, and a growing community of artists have set up studios in many of the old converted warehouses here.

Payne Phalen

The Payne Phalen district, northeast of downtown St. Paul and west of I-35E, was for the most part developed around the same time as Highland Park — from the late 1930s through the '50s. The area has some charming neighborhoods, especially around and north of Maryland Avenue. Housing ranges from ramblers to 1½ stories and larger homes. Amenities include proximity to downtown St. Paul and recreational areas such as Lake Phalen and Keller Golf Course.

Reclaiming the City: the West Side

Across the river, just south of downtown, is the West Side (so named because it's on the west bank of the river), a vibrant community that prides itself on its cultural diversity. The predominantly Anglo population mingles with a strong Hispanic element (20 percent), ever-growing numbers of Asian Americans and some African Americans. This cultural stew is seen in the array of ethnic markets that dot the West Side: Mexican, Filipino, Asian-American grocery stores and even a Lebanese-Mexican deli. The community's Cinco de Mayo celebration annually draws thousands of spectators.

Housing is reflective of residents' economic profiles, ranging from rather well-off and solidly middle class to the poor. Enterprising individuals will make some real finds here.

Despite its stable families and cultural ties, the West Side has its share of joblessness, poverty and crime, concerns the community is addressing through social agencies and neighborhood groups.

DAYTON'S BLUFF

The picturesque Dayton's Bluff neighborhood, on the east bank bluffs of the Mississippi River and east of downtown St. Paul, is another stressed urban area undergoing difficult but hopeful transition. Enterprising individuals are moving into its neglected old houses — many dating to the 1880s — and restoring them to their original splendor. While there's no denying the problems of crime and poverty that plague the area, Dayton's Bluff residents possess an incredible community spirit and loyalty to this area. Median price of housing here is $65,500.

WEST SEVENTH STREET

This historic, working-class neighborhood — site of the birthplace of St. Paul — is southwest of downtown and north of the river. It too is undergoing exciting revitalization. West Seventh was settled by immigrants from Germany, Ireland, Poland, Bohemia and Italy, and, generations later, some of their descendants still make their homes in the neighborhood. Homes here, some c. 1880s, are being renovated, putting a fresh face on the community. And real "finds" can be had at very affordable prices.

A highlight of the area is the Irvine Park neighborhood, once St. Paul's finest residential community. Neglected for years, it was rediscovered in the '70s, and many of its elegant homes have been lovingly restored. The centerpiece park is located at Walnut Street and Ryan Avenue.

The Suburbs

In the wake of World War II, when thousands of Johnnys came marching home again, they and their families set their sights on the new suburban Camelots, just beyond city limits. Ideally suited to the postwar mood of prosperity and family togetherness, these semi-rural havens promised peace and contentment, affordable housing, green lawns and barbecue grills. What more could one want?

Like every major U.S. metropolitan area, the Twin Cities experienced a painful flight to the suburbs in the 1950s and '60s. In 1950 Minneapolis' population was 500,000; today it sits at around 368,400.

The following is a brief look at the suburbs, beginning on the western edge.

Lake Minnetonka Area

Just 12 miles west of Minneapolis is the renowned Lake Minnetonka. With its myriad bays and inlets, Minnetonka possesses the most shoreline of any lake in the state — measuring at least 100 miles.

Lake Minnetonka's long tradition as a resort and recreation center dates back into the 1800s, when people from throughout the country would vacation on its shores.

Today Lake Minnetonka is a residence of choice for Minneapolis' movers and shakers, some of whom live in the charming city of Wayzata along the lake's northwestern shore. Others reside in rambling estates in the Lake Minnetonka communities of Orono, Navarre, Excelsior, Deephaven, Minnetrista, Minnetonka Beach, Shorewood, Mound and Tonka Bay.

Lake Minnetonka living offers the best of both worlds, especially in summer. Minneapolis, with its employment and cultural offerings, is just 30 minutes away. And you can spend your evenings and weekends in your own private laid-back, sand-in-the-toes world of sailing, boating, lake sunsets and waterfront dining.

Such pleasures have their price, and, unless you're independently wealthy or a fast-track exec, Lake Minnetonka communities may be out of your reach. For example, in 1994 the median home price in the district encompassing Wayzata, Minnetonka Beach, Orono and Long Lake was $220,121. Occasionally, one may chance upon a real find — a modestly priced fixer-upper or older "cabin" situated a few blocks from the water — that won't dent the pocketbook.

Renters have more options, including attractive waterfront apartment complexes in Wayzata, Mound and Excelsior, plus apartments in private homes.

Both Wayzata, on the lake's north shore, and Excelsior, on its southeast shore, are picturesque cities offering lovely vistas of the legendary lake. Both possess

The Parade of Homes, held every September, features hundreds of newly built homes throughout the metro area. Even if you're not in the market, it's a smart way to borrow a few decorating ideas.

Insiders' Tips

a small-town ambiance with bustling main streets that have become slightly yuppified over the past 50 years.

For a taste of lake living, stop by the Excelsior Park restaurant in Excelsior on any summer night, choose a table outside on the deck overlooking the lake, and wait for the spectacle to begin. In a short time, boats — big and small — will queue up, ferrying their scantily clad, tanned occupants to choice outside tables for a round of merrymaking.

The Great Southwest

The suburbs of Chanhassen, Eden Prairie and Chaska, located along the Minnesota River southwest of Minneapolis, are hot areas of residential growth and economic development. Residents are attracted by the gently rolling landscape, well-planned neighborhoods of upper-bracket housing, plentiful lakes and relative proximity to Minneapolis.

Chaska is home to the Hazeltine National Golf Course (site of the 1991 U.S. Open) and a state-of-the-art, city-owned indoor water park. The median home sale price is $118,093.

Chanhassen claims the Minnesota Landscape Arboretum, a beautiful 905-acre preserve owned by the University of Minnesota, and Chanhassen Dinner Theatres, an award-winning entertainment complex. New upper-bracket developments are sprouting in this rural, lake-studded setting. The median home price here is $155,000.

Eden Prairie continues to draw residents with its lovely mix of parks, lakes, creeks and wooded areas amid well-planned upper-bracket neighborhoods. Average home sale price here is $167,000.

As the state's third-largest city and home to Mall of America, the southern suburb of Bloomington is a hopping, happening place these days! Many well-designed neighborhoods of moderate to expensive homes on large, wooded lots dot the rolling landscape of this attractive older suburb. Bloomington's eastern area was developed between 1945 and 1960 and features moderate size and smaller homes; its western regions are relatively new and still growing. Bloomington's most desirable residential areas border the expansive Hyland Lake Park Reserve, a popular recreational area. Median home sale prices: eastern Bloomington, $92,000; western Bloomington, $130,780.

Just to the north are the prestigious homes and gardens of the Edina, *la crème de la crème* of suburbia. An older, established community, Edina offers scenic, tucked-away neighborhoods of upper-bracket housing, plus pockets of moderately priced housing, a first-class school system, plentiful parks and tasteful commercial centers. Median home price is $180,192.

Northwest

As the metro area pops its buttons, outer-edge north and northwestern suburbs such as Maple Grove, Anoka, Plymouth,

Insiders' Tips

International Market Square, 338-6250, in the Minneapolis Warehouse District, is a home-decor showcase, featuring four floors of furniture and fixtures displays.

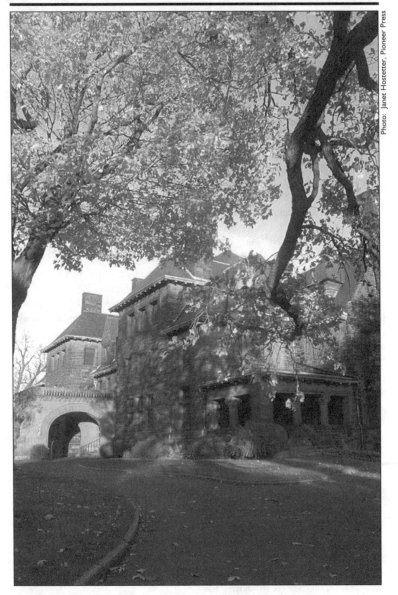

Photo: Janet Hostetter, Pioneer Press

James J. Hill Mansion on Summit Avenue in St. Paul.

Coon Rapids and Brooklyn Park experience burgeoning waves of new residents. Maple Grove and Plymouth especially are growing rapidly, with new housing developments sprouting in formerly open fields and woodlands.

Plymouth is bisected by I-494, promoting easy accessibility to other metro communities and businesses. Also within its borders are walking paths, several lakes and handsomely designed parks, such as French Regional Park on Medicine Lake and the swimming beach and park at Parkers Lake. The western edges of Plymouth are home to exclusive country manor-style estates on sprawling acreage with horse barns and pastures. The Luce Line bike trail begins in Plymouth and continues westward to Winsted. Ridgedale shopping center is close by. In 1994 Plymouth's median housing price was $170,000.

Maple Grove offers a solid mix of single-family homes, townhouses and condos, surrounded by several lakes, parks and biking paths, attracting younger families searching for a rural setting and relatively affordable housing. Median housing price here is $122,350.

Anoka possesses a charming small-town atmosphere with a thriving city center, many Victorian homes on well-maintained streets, plus some new homes and apartments. After all, former Miss America Gretchen Carlson and writer Garrison Keillor were once residents, so it must be "above average"!

Coon Rapids, spread along the Mississippi River northeast of Brooklyn Park, is also gaining in new residents and industry. Amenities include plentiful parks, such as Coon Rapids Dam Regional Park (site of the annual Carp Festival) and Bunker Hills Park Reserve. Its population (56,493) is youthful; the average age of residents is 28. Median housing price here is $97,400.

Brooklyn Park has grown steadily to become the state's sixth-largest city, and nearly half of its land is still undeveloped. Planners have painstakingly designed neighborhoods with generous room for parks and nature areas. Very attractive executive housing surrounds the recently built Edinburgh USA Golf Course. Median housing price here is $98,300.

First-tier suburban areas offer affordable housing dating from the late 1940s, '50s and '60s, cultural and age diversity, proximity to the cities and many individual charms. Plus, they're virtually totally developed with schools and utilities already in place, so property taxes aren't unreasonably high.

Northern inner-ring suburbs include Fridley, Columbia Heights and Brooklyn Center. The Mississippi provides a scenic western border for Fridley and enhances the city's recreational appeal. Fridley has a thriving business climate, good schools and easy accessibility to both Minneapolis and St. Paul. Median price of housing in Fridley is $88,100. Its neighbor, Columbia Heights, offers convenient shopping, an affordable housing stock and stable neighborhoods. Median housing price: $75,000. Brooklyn Center offers a range of housing, from affordable ramblers to riverfront estates. Its Earle Brown Heritage Center, a convention center based in a century-old farm, is a popular attraction. Median housing price here: $78,500.

The Near West

St. Louis Park, Robbinsdale and Crystal to the west and Richfield to the south all contain housing that ranges from rows of standardized post-World

War II homes and large, handsome homes in safe, tree-lined neighborhoods to myriad apartment complexes. You'll find a strong sense of community and stability in these fully developed suburbs and many long-standing residents. St. Louis Park and Richfield also have popular nature centers filled with hiking paths and wetlands. Median housing prices here are $80,000 in Robbinsdale and Crystal; $94,300 in St. Louis Park; and $90,700 in Richfield.

New Hope, immediately west of Crystal, is a planned community developed in the mid-'50s. You'll find wide boulevards, plentiful parklands and three industrial parks in this community where the median housing price is $102,000.

Golden Valley to the west has many attractive larger homes in woodsy neighborhoods. Part of Theodore Wirth Park is found in this community. The median housing price is $115,600.

Not to be forgotten is the western suburb of Hopkins, with its old-fashioned thriving Main Street, quiet tree-lined city neighborhoods of moderate housing and secluded upper-bracket woodland properties. It's almost like a small town that's been plopped right down in the middle of suburbia.

North by Northeast

St. Paul has more than its share of upper-bracket, country-club suburbs, especially in the north, notably the private community of North Oaks, as well as parts of Shoreview, White Bear Township, Gem Lake, Mahtomedi, Dellwood, Grant Township and the St. Croix River Valley. In these areas of rolling countryside and secluded lakes, property can and does sell for $1 million or more. Exclusive neighborhoods also surround Sunfish Lake

to the south and can be found in parts of Mendota Heights as well.

North Oaks, a private planned city of 3,516 residents, offers handsome homes on estate-size lots in a beautiful natural setting. Former Vice President Walter Mondale lived here; basketball great (and manager of the Minnesota Timberwolves) Kevin McHale is a current resident. Directly west are the suburbs of Shoreview, Arden Hills, New Brighton and Mounds View, with their attractive rolling hills and recreational lakes. Arden Hills offers attractive medium-size to executive-style homes in well-established neighborhoods. Median housing price here and in Shoreview is $138,200. Shoreview offers abundant recreational activities at its many lakes and parks, as well as its impressive city-owned indoor water park. New Brighton is more than 100 years old and offers a mix of moderate and executive homes and apartments. Median housing price here and in Mounds View is $107,200.

White Bear Lake also offers a mix of modest, midpriced homes, as well as expensive ones, and then there's that spectacular lake, with an intriguing history all its own. Like Minnetonka, it was once a popular summer resort locale. White Bear Lake has a well-preserved, old-fashioned downtown that oozes charm. Median housing price here: $106,700.

Closer to St. Paul and more down to earth are the inner-ring suburbs of Roseville, Falcon Heights, Little Canada, Maplewood and North St. Paul, offering solid neighborhoods and a range of affordable housing. Roseville is blessed with both natural attractions, in the form of abundant park land and lakes, and a thriving industrial/retail base. It is home to Rosedale, a major shopping center. Median housing price in Roseville and Falcon

Heights is $105,200. The latter suburb lays claim to the State Fairgrounds and the University of Minnesota St. Paul campus.

Maplewood offers older, middle-class neighborhoods on its eastern edge and new, attractive developments of medium-size to executive-style homes along its hilly, woodsy western edge. It is home to world-famous 3M Corp. Median housing price here and in nearby North St. Paul is $91,220. The latter suburb is one of the few Twin Cities suburbs with an intact downtown, which, along with its plentiful lakes and well-maintained housing, enhances its appeal.

Stillwater and Environs

Situated on the hills and bluffs overlooking the St. Croix River 20 miles northeast of downtown St. Paul, Stillwater is as pretty as a Victorian picture. The historic rivertown offers a colorful Main Street, rambling Victorian homes, a friendly small-town atmosphere and easy accessibility to the Twin Cities. In fact, many Stillwater residents work in the St. Paul area. The area is fully developed, and houses sell rather briskly, many by word of mouth. The median home price is $123,200.

Eastern and Southern Suburbs

Woodbury, a suburb just east of St. Paul, is growing like corn in July; its population almost doubled between 1980 and 1990, and there's no signs of it slowing. Here you'll find a mainly white-collar, professional community housed in upper-bracket homes ranging anywhere from $125,000 to $250,000 and more. A magnificent natural setting of rolling hills, lakes and woods lends a country feel to this suburb. The median housing price is $156,700.

Cottage Grove, near the confluence of the Mississippi and St. Croix rivers, is an older suburb that is experiencing renewed popularity, with developers adding new upper-bracket homes to the mix of moderately priced older homes. The median housing price for Cottage Grove and nearby St. Paul Park and Newport suburbs is $94,400.

West St. Paul, south of St. Paul's West Side, and South St. Paul, located east of West St. Paul (we know, the directions are screwy!), are among the city's first ring of suburbs and have stable neighborhoods and nice, affordable homes. Because they are in Dakota County, rather than Ramsey County, their property taxes are significantly lower. Median home sale prices are $87,000 in West St. Paul and $79,100 in South St. Paul.

Inver Grove Heights to the south offers a full range of housing on large lots and a country-living atmosphere. The average home sale price here is $115,000.

Eagan, directly south of St. Paul, is a booming suburb attracting young families and singles with a mix of modest to upper-bracket housing, duplexes and fourplexes. The median age of residents is 30. The average home sale price is $138,300.

The south suburbs in general, especially Burnsville, Apple Valley and Rosemount, seem to be growing with an influx of young families who are attracted by their new, affordable housing, plentiful parks and lakes, open spaces and freeway access. Median housing prices: Burnsville, $124,300; Apple Valley, $123,200; and Rosemount, $114,000.

Historic Mendota and Mendota Heights, at the confluence of the Minnesota and Mississippi rivers, were thriving

See the Possibilities...

...at every Lundgren Bros. Neighborhood

A pond or stream for fishing. Big shady trees. Friendly neighbors...And the perfect home. Our homes are built with character and drama, and tailored to fit your individuality and dreams.

Founded in 1969, Lundgren Bros. is a Twin Cities builder that is still locally owned and managed. Our reputation for distinctive designs, sensitive land planning, quality, and personal service is unmatched in the industry. So if you're looking to build or buy a new home — and build a relationship with a company you can trust — call Lundgren Bros., your neighborhood builder.

BROS.

ur Neighborhood Builder

935 East Wayzata Blvd.
Wayzata, MN 55391
612-473-1231

Builder License #0001413

Lundgren Bros. neighborhoods are open daily in: Apple Valley • Chanhassen • Eden Prairie • Maple Grove • Medina • Minnetonka • Plymouth

Please call 473-1231 for a current directory of our neighborhoods and models.

settlements for the early Dakota Indians and then the fur traders who supplanted them in the 1800s. Today, Mendota Heights is home to young families living in attractive medium-size and larger properties along picturesque riverfront and hillsides. The median housing price is $163,000.

Inside
Real Estate Resources

To the delight of local real estate agents and builders, the Twin Cities really do sell themselves.

Minneapolis and St. Paul's natural beauty, vital economy and highly rated quality of life make these cities and their suburbs very desirable places to live. Our bustling real estate market is proof that the rest of the country is rediscovering us. We're actually becoming a trendy destination!

In this chapter, we'll offer some practical information to help you in your search for a new home — be it an apartment or a custom-built house. Included are listings of real estate firms, relocation companies, apartment locators, tenant unions, senior housing resources, builders and mortgage companies.

Buying and Selling Homes

The local real estate scene is dominated by two giants, Edina Realty and Burnet Realty, both with offices scattered throughout the cities. They are joined by hundreds of other smaller companies that manage to grab a fair share of the market. When seeking out a real estate company to help you in your home search, don't shortchange the smaller firms. What they lack in size, they many times make up for in innovation, experience and good old-fashioned hustle.

Overall, the real estate scene in Minnesota is above-board and well-regulated, thanks in part to new laws that encourage openness between agents and potential clients, be they buyers or sellers.

Photo: John Doman, Pioneer Press

A view of downtown St. Paul with the Mississippi River in the foreground.

Real Estate Companies

What follows is sampling of real estate firms in the Twin Cities. It is by no means comprehensive. For a more extensive listing, check the telephone directory or call the Realtor associations listed later.

BURNET REALTY
(at least 37 offices)
Corporate office, 7550 France Ave. S.
Edina 844-6400

CENTURY 21
(at least 25 independent offices)
Headquarters, 7900 International Dr.
Ste. 155, Bloomington 854-8776

COLDWELL BANKER
(about 20 offices)
St. Paul office
604 Snelling Ave. S. 699-6666

COUNSELOR REALTY
(six offices)
Edina/Bloomington office
5810 W. 78th St., Edina 921-0911

EDINA REALTY
(at least 50 offices)
Headquarters, 6800 France Ave.
Edina 928-5900

ROGER FAZENDIN REALTORS
1421 E. Wayzata Blvd., Wayzata 473-7000

RE/MAX REALTY
(at least 17 independent offices)
Regional office, 3800 W. 80th St.
Ste. 550, Bloomington 897-0447

REALTY WORLD
(at least 7 offices)
Regional headquarters
Tess Daily, Realty World Executive
Calhoun Beach Club, 2925 Dean Pkwy.
Minneapolis 928-7610

Real Estate Associations

To receive more information on the real estate market in the Twin Cities, call one of the following associations.

MINNEAPOLIS AREA ASSOCIATION OF REALTORS
933-9020

ST. PAUL AREA ASSOCIATION OF REALTORS
774-5206

CONSUMER CREDIT COUNSELING SERVICES
1111 Third Ave. S., Ste. 336
Minneapolis 349-6953

This agency can counsel consumers before they make home-purchase or rental decisions and help in cases of loan delinquency or financial mismanagement. Charges are based on ability to pay.

DIVISION OF ENFORCEMENT AND LICENSING
State Department of Commerce
113 E. Seventh St., St. Paul 296-2488

This office investigates complaints about real estate agents, lenders, building contractors and appraisers. It also provides information on home-owners insurance and tips on buying real estate.

COMMUNITY ASSOCIATIONS INSTITUTE
4248 Park Glen Rd., St. Louis Park 927-9220

This national, nonprofit organization can provide information on individual condominium, co-op or home-owners associations, plus general information on issues pertinent to community associations.

WITHIN REACH

If a new home is in your future, consider Wedgewood, the Twin Cities' premier master planned community. Within easy reach of St. Paul, Minneapolis or the airport — as well as your real estate budget — Wedgewood offers so much more . . . eight select builders, an 18-hole championship golf course, biking trails, city parks, landscaping allowances and an unmistakable sense of neighborly pride. Visit Wedgewood and compare. It's everything you're looking for in a new home community.

NOWHERE ELSE
BUT WEDGEWOOD.

A master planned community in Woodbury, developed by Minnesota Mutual and marketed by LCA Marketing, Inc. 2-1/2 miles south of I94 on Woodbury Drive (County Road 19). Homes and townhomes from the $170s. Call 1-800-549-4588 for model home hours and a free Buyer's Guide. An equal housing opportunity.

WEDGEWOOD

Live The Life You Have Imagined . . .

Distinguished Single Family Home Neighborhoods:
John Mitchell Preserve   Vadnais Heights

Custom Townhome Neighborhoods:
Birch Lake Ponds   White Bear Lake

Coming Soon! - Woodbury Villas

PRATT
H O M E S

429-8032
Builder License No. 0000001

BLACK RELOCATION ASSOCIATION
P.O. Box 58220
Minneapolis 55458   623-4362

This is a business, professional and social relocation service tailored to meet the needs of African Americans new to the Twin Cities. It works with many local corporations, providing a newcomer's connection from a black perspective.

Relocation Assistance

Buying a home is one of the most important — and most stressful — milestones of your life.

The process becomes even more challenging if you are relocating across the country instead of merely across town. Transplanted into a totally new city, you may feel like a 20th-century explorer, searching out everything from the right neighborhood school for your child to the nearest hardware store. Depending on your attitude, it's either a grand adventure or a royal pain.

This is where relocation specialists can help. Many of the larger real estate firms have these specialists who, at a moment's notice, can provide prospective newcom-

ers with a plethora of information on schools, churches, newcomers associations, neighborhood housing costs and other concerns.

Relocation departments at many of the larger realty companies can accelerate the sale or purchase of property around the country by plugging into national marketing networks.

Here are some very busy relocation offices in the Twin Cities.

EDINA REALTY
RELOCATION DEPARTMENT
1400 S. Hwy. 100, Golden Valley   591-6400

BURNET REALTY
RELOCATION SERVICES
7550 France Ave. S., Ste. 215
Edina   844-6500

ROGER FAZENDIN REALTORS
1421 E. Wayzata Blvd., Wayzata   473-7000

Apartments

If you're in the market for apartments, help is available. Two free apartment directories are available at grocery stores,

Relocating To Minneapolis Area?

May We Assist You?

PLEASE CALL

Patricia Broyles

Director of Relocation

- Full Time Relocation Director
- Certified Relocation Professional
- Member of the National Relocation Director's Council
- Member of the National Organization Employee Relocation Council

We have a National reputation and over 30 years of real estate experience.

Let us help you become familiar with Minneapolis and its suburban areas and assist you in finding your new home.

Roger Fazendin REALTORS

ESTABLISHED 1965

**The Right Size
The Right Experience**

(612) 473-7000

Fax (612)--473--3127

libraries and shopping centers throughout the Twin Cities: *Apartment Living Guide*, 884-2980, and *For Rent* magazine, 830-0515.

Or you can let an apartment-search company do the legwork for you. Here are several.

APARTMENT SEARCH
7200 France Ave. S.   830-0500
Edina   (800) 989-8780

This company will help find the right apartment for you. It has 11 branch offices in the Twin Cities and does not charge you a fee.

APARTMENT RENTER'S CHOICE
1935 W. County Rd. B2, Ste. 160
Roseville   636-5414

This company has three offices in the Twin Cities.

APARTMENT RENTAL SERVICES
4141 Parklawn Ave., Edina   921-9455

This firm specializes in the rental of privately owned townhouses and condos.

Tenants Unions

These organizations help resolve disputes between landlords and tenants. Volunteers offer advice and make referrals to legal services, housing or reconciliation courts. Membership fees are minimal, ranging from $10 to $15 a year. The *Tenants Rights Handbook* is available for $5.35 ($6.85 by mail) from either the Minneapolis or St. Paul tenants union or from the Minnesota Public Interest Research Group (MPIRG), 2512 S.E. Delaware Street, Minneapolis 55414.

MINNEAPOLIS TENANTS UNION
1513 E. Franklin Ave., Minneapolis   871-7485

This is also known as the Minnesota Tenants Union. If you're in desperate need of a quick answer, you can call its pay-per-call hotline number, (612) 976-8888. Cost is $1.25 for the first minute and 99¢ for every additional minute.

ST. PAUL TENANTS UNION
500 Laurel Ave., St. Paul   221-0501

This organization answers tenants' inquiries from 9 AM to 5 PM weekdays.

ST. PAUL HOUSING
INFORMATION OFFICE
21 W. Fourth St., St. Paul   266-6000

Under the auspices of the city of St. Paul, this office provides free information on all sorts of housing issues, from mortgage programs, foreclosure preventions and tenant-landlord issues to rental opportunities (market and subsidized) and rehabilitation loans.

MINNESOTA MULTI-HOUSING
ASSOCIATION HOTLINE
858-8222

This nonprofit organization offers information and assistance to both landlords and tenants. You can call its free hotline between 2 and 5 PM Monday through Friday.

HOME LINE
Renters line   933-0017
Foreclosure info line   933-1993

This nonprofit housing service offers help to renters with questions or problems and to homeowners who are facing foreclosure. It is for residents of suburban Hennepin County.

Home Construction

The Minneapolis and St. Paul greater metropolitan area is one of the largest, most active home-building communities in the nation. According to the National Association of Home Builders, the Twin Cities ranks ninth for volume and dollars

Looking for an Apartment?

Apartment Search will help you!
It's Fast and it's Free!

- Over 100,000 choices on color video
- Apartments, town-homes, condos
- All prices and locations
- Short term and furnished
- One-stop apartment shopping
- Save time and money

11 convenient locations
Call 333-RENT

**OPEN 7 DAYS
AND 4 EVENINGS
CALL TOLL FREE**

Mpls 1-800-989-8780
St. Paul 1-800-989-4005
Fax 1-612-897-1063

Serving the Twin Cities since 1965

spent on home construction and third for volume and dollars spent on home remodeling.

There are a whopping 1,200 members in the Builders Association of the Twin Cities, with 600 members comprising 75 percent of the local building marketplace. To help you begin your search for the builder that will be a good match for you, we've listed some Twin Cities home-construction companies below. Here too are a few guidelines on how to select a good builder.

• Ask friends or acquaintances who've recently built their own homes for recommendations.

• Drive by a builder's construction site. If the work area is orderly and neat, that's one indication of a good builder.

• Inspect one of the builder's model homes. Are ceramic tiles evenly spaced? Does the wood trim along floors, windows and doors fit snugly against the walls? Are the floors quiet?

• Call the Builders Association of the Twin Cities and ask whether your prospective builder is licensed or has been the subject of any consumer complaints.

• Ask builders for references and make follow-up calls.

The Builders Association sponsors two new-home showcases every year: the Parade of Homes Spring Preview, in late February and early March, and the Parade of Homes, in September. Both events showcase hundreds of newly constructed Twin Cities homes in a variety of price ranges.

If you haven't been bitten by the remodeling bug yet, you will be once you've visited International Market Square, in Minneapolis' Warehouse District at the corner of Glendale and Lyndale avenues. A showplace of building products and home furnishings housed in the historic Munsingwear — yep, we're talking under-

wear, folks — Building, the IMS is filled with attractive displays of furniture and appliances from traditional to ultramodern. The building is open to the general public, but purchases must be made through an interior designer.

Builders

BREAM BUILDERS INC.
961 Grand Ave., St. Paul   298-1044

CENTREX HOMES
12400 Whitewater Dr., Ste. 120
Minnetonka   936-7833

CHARLES CUDD CO.
1802 Wooddale Dr., Woodbury   731-3153

COUNTRY HOME BUILDERS
800 Ivy Ln., Eagan   452-0336

GOOD VALUE HOMES
9445 East River Rd., Coon Rapids   780-HOME

HANS HAGEN HOMES
941 N.E. Hillwind Rd., Fridley   572-9455

LANDICO
7835 Telegraph Rd., Bloomington   829-0555

LUNDGREN BROS. CONSTRUCTION INC.
935 E. Wayzata Blvd., Wayzata   473-1231

McNULTY HOMES
400 Second Ave. S., No. 650
Minneapolis   339-0674

ORRIN THOMPSON HOMES
8421 Wayzata Blvd., Golden Valley 544-7333

PEMTOM LAND CO.
14180 Hwy. 5, Eden Prairie   937-0716

PRATT HOMES
4225 White Bear Pkwy., Ste. 100
Vadnais Heights   429-8032

The McNulty Company

Designers and Builders of Fine Custom Homes Since 1945

Custom Designed
Homes and Townhomes

Deephaven * Eden Prairie * Shorewood
Edina * Orono

Or on the site of your choosing

call us today for more information

339-0674 — 474-5231

400 Second Avenue South, Minneapolis, MN 55401

PULTE HOMES CORP.
1355 Mendota Heights Rd., No. 300
Mendota Heights   452-5200

ROTTLUND HOMES
2681 Long Lake Rd., Roseville   638-0500

SHAMROCK BUILDERS INC.
3200 N.W. Main St., Coon Rapids   421-3500

TOWN & COUNTRY HOMES
6800 France Ave. S., Edina   925-3899

VINTAGE BUILDERS
8401 73rd Ave. N., Ste. 90
Minneapolis   535-5225

WEDGEWOOD CUSTOM HOMES
3040 Woodbury Dr., Woodbury   731-4588

Information on Building

For more information on building, contact one of the following associations.

BUILDERS ASSOCIATION OF MINNESOTA
646-7959

BUILDERS ASSOCIATION
OF THE TWIN CITIES
851-9242

BUILDING CODE DIVISION
State Administration Department
Metro Square Bldg., St. Paul   296-4639
   This division establishes the State Building Code and can provide free information on all types of building codes.

Mortgage Companies

Once you find that perfect lot or home, you'll probably need to arrange financing. Here are some local companies with good reputations to get you started on your search for the mortgage lender that best suits your needs.

EASTERN HEIGHTS STATE BANK
7525 Currell Blvd., Woodbury   736-9992

FIRSTAR MORTGAGE
3900 Sibley Memorial Hwy., Eagan   454-3301

FLEET MORTGAGE
7760 France Ave. S., Edina   921-0330

HOMESTEAD MORTGAGE CORP.
4105 Lexington Ave. N.
Arden Hills   490-5555

MARQUETTE MORTGAGE
7401 Metro Blvd., Edina   830-9305

NORWEST MORTGAGE
733 Marquette Ave., Minneapolis   339-7905

ROSEPOINTE
2555 Hamline Ave. N., Roseville   639-1000

Seniors Housing

The Twin Cities have numerous retirement apartment complexes offering such assisted-living amenities as meal service, on-site nursing services, housekeeping and activity programs. Some may be listed with the previously mentioned apartment-referral firms. Here are other helpful resources.

EBENEZER SOCIETY
15 locations   879-2200

EDINA PARK PLAZA
3330 Edinborough Way, Edina   831-4084

FRIENDSHIP VILLAGE
8100 Highwood Dr., Bloomington   831-7500

REMBRANDT RETIREMENT COMMUNITY
3434 Heritage Dr., Edina   920-9145

WALKER METHODIST
13 locations
Call ElderLine for information   827-8310

Other helpful groups include:

SENIOR RESOURCES INC.
2021 Hennepin Ave. E.
Minneapolis   331-4063

This organization can provide information on senior housing, volunteer programs, transportation services and other issues.

MINNESOTA SENIOR FEDERATION
1885 University Ave. W.
St. Paul   645-0261

This advocacy organization also provides information on retirement living.

Inside
Schools and Child Care

Minnesota is justifiably proud of its public school system. According to the U.S. Department of Education, the state has the highest commencement rate — 89 percent — in the nation. And a whopping 90 percent of Minnesota's high-school graduates go on to receive some form of post-secondary education.

The North Star State has a long tradition of academic excellence, from preschool through college, in both the public and private sectors. This is especially true in the greater Twin Cities, where per-pupil funding is, on average, higher than it is in other areas of the state and the nation.

Although Minneapolis and St. Paul proper have their share of big city problems, their public schools are among the nation's best urban schools. In addition to traditional neighborhood schools, both

districts have a range of magnet schools offering specialized study areas along with the basics. Such programs promote de-segregation by attracting students from diverse neighborhoods. Both city school districts pride themselves in their solid academics and, like other districts throughout the state, allow motivated students the option of taking university-level courses while attending high school.

"Choice" is the keyword in Minnesota's innovative open-enrollment program, which has garnered national attention. The open-enrollment policy permits students in kindergarten through 12th grade to apply to attend any public school district in the state. The district to which the student is applying may approve or reject the application, based on available space. In Minneapolis and St. Paul, students also must receive permis-

Outside Mounds Park All-Nations Magnet School in St. Paul.

sion from their home districts to leave, and such permission may be denied if the departure would harm desegregation.

Of course, it's always best for parents and students to visit several districts personally before making any enrollment decisions. The Minnesota Department of Education has published a guide for parents, titled "How to Select a School for Your Child," For more information on open enrollment, call the Enrollment Options Hotline at (800) 657-3990 or, in the Twin Cities, 296-1261.

Minnesota also is in the process of adopting rigorous standards to ensure that every high-school graduate possesses the knowledge and skills necessary to succeed in the global economy.

Another innovative program is the above-mentioned post-secondary option, a program that allows students to take college courses — usually tuition-free — while still in high school. This gives students a valuable head start in the great diploma race.

In the area of special needs, Minnesota schools offer students with disabilities a full range of services to create the least-restrictive learning environment. For more information, contact local school districts or call the state Department of Education at 297-2843. Also, virtually all school districts offer enrichment programs for the gifted and talented.

In all, the greater Twin Cities are home to 48 independent public-school districts offering kindergarten through 12th grade education and more than 250 private elementary and secondary schools. The following is an overview of public and private K through 12 educational offerings in the Twin Cities. Space limitations prohibit listing all public and private schools. A great resource for more complete information is *Schoolhouse*

Magazine ($7.95 from Advertising Sales Inc., 35 W. Water Street, Suite 201, St. Paul, Minnesota 55107; 227-1519), an annual directory of Twin Cities public and private schools.

Also, recognizing the importance of early childhood education and quality child care, we've also included important information for parents of preschoolers. You'll find it at the end of this chapter.

Public Schools

ST. PAUL PUBLIC SCHOOLS
360 Colborne St., St. Paul   293-5208

St. Paul has 47 elementary schools, five middle schools (grades 6 through 8), four junior highs (grades 7 and 8), six high schools, three alternative secondary schools, a K-12 open school and a technical college within the St. Paul Independent School District.

Student population is around 40,000. Of that, 49 percent are students of color, primarily Asian Americans (22 percent), African Americans (19 percent) and Hispanics (6 percent).

Variety is a key element: St. Paul offers magnet, neighborhood and specialty schools; programs for the gifted and talented; special education; and an extensive community education program. While all St. Paul schools offer the basic subjects, the magnets and specialty schools have special emphases in certain areas. They are part of the district's voluntary desegregation plan, attracting students from throughout the city. One of St. Paul's most unusual schools is the American Indian Magnet School, which focuses on the history and culture of the American Indian, especially the Ojibwa, Lakota and Winnebago tribes, and stresses such values as racial harmony,

We don't teach kids what to think. We teach them how.

Mounds Park kids don't just memorize facts; they learn to think for themselves. To find out more about a fully accredited college preparatory school (K-12) that cares about kids, call (612) 777-2555.

Mounds Park Academy

environmentalism and cooperation rather than competition.

Another is the Jackson Preparatory Magnet School, emphasizing strong reading, math, computer and thinking skills. Other magnets concentrate on the environment, outcome-based education, Spanish and other languages, gifted programming, science, math and technology, humanities and creative arts. Students also have an option to attend neighborhood schools, which, in some cases, may also be magnets.

St. Paul secondary schools also vary in format and subject focus. Students may choose from a number of specialty options, including media/communications, business/math/science, graphic communications (printing), performing arts, Chinese language and the International Baccalaureate program. The latter is a rigorous two-year, pre-university program for motivated students.

Overall, the district promotes a "High Five" set of goals: higher readiness, higher achievement, higher graduation rate, higher parent participation and higher adult literacy. The application process for the magnet, specialty and secondary schools begins in February, with deadlines in March. For information on the various school options, call the Student Placement Center at 293-5413.

MINNEAPOLIS PUBLIC SCHOOLS
807 N.E. Broadway, Minneapolis   627-2199

In 1993 Minneapolis Public School District took a bold step and selected as its superintendent Peter Hutchinson, the head of a management consulting firm with virtually no formal training in education. It's just one example of the district's no-holds-barred approach to education.

There are 59 elementary school programs, seven middle schools (grades 6 through 8) and seven senior highs, serving a total of 45,315 students, in the Minneapolis School District. Class size is limited as follows: 19 in kindergarten through grade 2, 25 in grades 3 through 8 and 26 in grades 9 through 12.

In 1995 the Minneapolis school board approved spending $274 million over the next five years to construct a few new schools and renovate existing buildings, in some cases adding new science labs and media centers.

At the elementary level, parents and students are offered a plethora of educational alternatives, ranging from the traditional classrooms to continuous-progress programs (ungraded multi-age classrooms with team teachers) and Montessori-style schools. There also are several learning centers focusing on specific curriculum themes, such as international and fine arts; math, science and technology; urban/environmental; Spanish immersion; American Indian immersion; and French immersion. Ninety-three percent of students applying for specific programs receive first choice.

Middle schools offer such innovations as team teaching and an interdisciplinary approach. Students also may specialize in areas such as urban/environmental; math, science and technology; and a pre-International Baccalaureate. All seven high schools offer the traditional curriculum plus one or more magnet programs, such as American Indian, arts and communication, automotive, aviation and aerospace, health careers/medical, and international studies. One specialty, the Metropolitan Learning Alliance, holds classes at the Mall of America! In addition, the system has two open-school programs.

High schoolers may choose from among the following foreign languages: Chinese, Japanese, French, German, Latin, Ojibwa, Spanish and Russian.

ANOKA-HENNEPIN PUBLIC SCHOOLS
11299 N.W. Hanson Blvd.
Coon Rapids   422-5521

This large north-suburban district, with a student population of about 37,400, operates 27 elementary schools, six middle schools, four high schools, two alternative secondary programs and a technical college. A new kindergarten center

opened in the fall of 1995. The district encompasses all or parts of Andover, Anoka, Blaine, Brooklyn Center, Brooklyn Park, Burns Township, Champlin, Coon Rapids, Dayton, Fridley, Ham Lake, Oak Grove and Ramsey.

The elementary level is characterized by self-contained classrooms, although there is some team teaching. A strong writing program is emphasized in all grades (after all, radio personality/writer Garrison Keillor is a graduate of the Anoka school system). In 1995 the school system introduced a new math program, based on hands-on use of manipulative materials, at the elementary level.

The district is proud of its strong emphasis on basic skills, while offering a wide choice in elective subjects. Language choices include Spanish, French and German, beginning in 7th grade. It has received state recognition for its discipline-based elementary art program.

BLOOMINGTON PUBLIC SCHOOLS
8900 Portland Ave. S., Bloomington   885-8454

This sprawling southern suburban district boasts nine K-4 elementary schools, an intermediate school (grades 5 through 6), Hillcrest Community School (an elective K-6 school with multi-age instruction), a junior high, a Bravo school (an alternative for grades 7 and 8), and two senior highs. Enrollment is around 11,500.

While the elementary level emphasizes self-contained classrooms and team teaching, intermediate-level students are clustered in groups of about 160, working with teams of six teachers. The alternative programs — Hillcrest and Bravo — feature small groups, interdisciplinary study and multi-age grouping.

Senior highs offer French, German, Japanese, Latin, Russian and Spanish. All

*Providing high quality education
integrating the Christian faith and learning.*

Coed Christian day school for students in grades preschool through twelve.

Call or write Admissions Officer at 612-729-8326
3107 47th Avenue South, Minneapolis, MN 55406

subject areas incorporate computers, and all schools have computer labs.

Site-based management guides the curriculum, which emphasizes critical thinking, problem-solving and interdisciplinary studies.

Five Bloomington schools have been named National Schools of Excellence by the U.S. Department of Education. The district also was recognized by an Ohio school-selection consulting firm for offering a "parent-pleasing" curriculum.

BROOKLYN CENTER PUBLIC SCHOOLS
6500 Humboldt Ave. N.
Brooklyn Center   561-2120
This modest-size district, encompassing the city of Brooklyn Center and surrounding areas, enrolls 1,815 students in its elementary school and a high school.

Here's a telling statistic: Brooklyn Center is reported to have the highest open-enrollment numbers in the state, attracting transferring students with its drama, sports and music programs. The high school (grades 7 through 12) offers four years of French and Spanish with independent learning enhanced by a language lab. The elementary school has two

computer labs; the high school offers four. A College in the Schools program offers advanced courses in writing and modern fiction.

BURNSVILLE-EAGAN-SAVAGE
PUBLIC SCHOOLS
100 River Ridge Ct., Burnsville   895-7212
This district serves 10,900 students in parts of Burnsville, Eagan, Savage, Apple Valley and Shakopee with nine elementary schools, two junior highs, a traditional and an alternative senior high, plus the new Dakota County Technology Careers Academy. A recently passed bond referendum will add a new elementary school and junior high, as well as upgrading all existing school buildings.

The district boasts a strong, wide-ranging curriculum, which includes French, German, Spanish, Latin and Russian, plus a highly lauded computer-literacy program. Its elementary computer program has been replicated worldwide. Apple Computers has named the district a "Classroom of Tomorrow" consulting site.

CENTENNIAL PUBLIC SCHOOLS

4707 North Rd., Circle Pines   780-7607

Serving the northern areas of Circle Pines, Lexington, Lino Lakes, Centerville and northeast Blaine, the Centennial district has four elementary schools, a junior high and a senior high. A new sports arena and fine-arts center are obvious drawing cards for this district's student population of 5,500.

At the elementary level, classes are self-contained and encompass such subjects as chemical health and computer technology, as well as the basics. A highlight of the junior high program is a state-of-the-art industrial technology curriculum. The high school has been named a National School of Excellence.

CHASKA-CHANHASSEN-VICTORIA-CARVER PUBLIC SCHOOLS

110600 Village Rd., Chaska   368-3607

With a student population of 5,000, this district in the burgeoning southwestern suburbs serves Chanhassen, Carver, Chaska, East Union and Victoria with an early childhood center, five elementary schools, a middle school (grades 6 through 8) and a high school. A new high school will open in 1996.

The elementary schools stress basic skills, which are reinforced in the middle schools in a supportive setting where students meet daily with advisors. The high school offers more than 250 courses in 14 departments. Secondary students may take as many as four classes in daily 90-minute periods. This allows students to take more classes in a year, while deepening the student-teacher relationship.

In 1993 Chaska placed second in the nation in the High School Quiz Bowl, and, over the last decade, its debate team has competed seven times at the national level. The school is one of the first five districts named by the National Education Association as an NEA Learning Lab.

COLUMBIA HEIGHTS PUBLIC SCHOOLS

1400 49th Ave. N.E.
Columbia Heights   574-650

This inner-ring suburban district enrolls more than 3,000 students from Columbia Heights, southern Fridley and Hilltop. The system has three elementary schools, a middle school (grades 6 through 8) and a high school. The elementary schools employ a variety of teaching methods, including team teaching, multi-age classrooms and self-contained classes. The high school offers four years of French, German and Spanish. Computers are used throughout all grades, and a fully equipped TV studio allows students to explore the world of broadcasting.

EDEN PRAIRIE PUBLIC SCHOOLS

8100 School Rd., Eden Prairie   937-3648

This district, in the upscale southwestern suburb by the same name, serves 8,600 students with a kindergarten center, four elementary schools (grades 1 through 4), an intermediate school (grades 5 and 6), middle school (grades 7 and 8) and a high school.

The intermediate school offers foreign-language instruction on an exploratory basis, and the higher grades offer five years of French, German and Spanish. Additional courses in Chinese, Japanese and Russian are available via interactive cable TV. Computer literacy is stressed at all levels.

The intermediate school groups children into "neighborhood" clusters, allowing them to circulate among small groupings of classrooms. Middle school students are grouped into eight teams of approximately 150 students each. The high school was recently remodeled and expanded to include a new football/track stadium.

EDINA PUBLIC SCHOOLS

5701 Normandale Rd., Edina   920-2980

This district, in an affluent suburb just south of Minneapolis, boasts a long tradition of academic excellence. Six K-5 elementary schools, two middle schools (grades 6 through 9) and a senior high serve a student population of 6,000.

Four of the district's schools have received excellence awards from the U.S. Department of Education. The high school especially has been named among the nation's top schools in such magazines as *Money, People, Parade* and *Town and Country.*

A French-immersion program is available in the elementary grades, and an variety of languages — German, French, Latin, Spanish, Russian, Japanese and Chinese — is offered in high school. The curriculum has a strong college-prep emphasis.

The high school has been recognized for its literary magazine, choir, concert band and its winning athletic program.

FRIDLEY PUBLIC SCHOOLS

6000 N.E. West Moore Lake Dr.
Fridley   571-6000

With two K-5 elementary schools, a middle school (grades 6 through 8) and a high school, the Fridley district, north of Minneapolis, numbers 2,500 students. One of its elementary schools and its middle school have been named National Schools of Excellence. Fridley High School was a recent finalist for the honor.

In addition to offering an extensive college-prep curriculum, Fridley High School also provides vocational training with such features as state-of-the-art technology, manufacturing apprenticeships and an on-site greenhouse. The district's K-12 computer literacy program is directed by a technology coordinator, and computer literacy is a graduation requirement.

HOPKINS PUBLIC SCHOOLS

1001 Minn. 7, Hopkins   988-4024

With a student enrollment of about 7,800 drawn mainly from Hopkins and Minnetonka, this district has seven elementary schools, two junior highs and a senior high. Students in grades 4 through 6 may take French, German and Spanish; in high school, the choices expand to include Chinese, Japanese and Russian. The high school also offers many accelerated college-level courses.

The high school and middle schools have been named National Schools of Excellence, and the district has been designated a National Technology Lighthouse. Each school has its own computer center.

INVER GROVE HEIGHTS PUBLIC SCHOOLS

9875 Inver Grove Tr.
Inver Grove Heights   457-7210

In this southeastern suburb of St. Paul, a total of 4,000 students attend five elementary schools, a middle school (grades 6 through 8) and a senior high.

The IGH elementary schools feature self-contained classrooms with flexible groupings in reading and math. In the middle school, interdisciplinary classes merge social studies, English, math and science. An innovative program, Quest, is used in the 7th grade to help build student self-esteem and decision-making skills.

All schools boast computer labs, and computer literacy is a high priority. All schools are connected to the Northern Dakota County Cable TV network.

MAHTOMEDI PUBLIC SCHOOLS

1620 Mahtomedi Ave., Mahtomedi   426-3224

Serving 2,500 students in the northeastern suburbs of St. Paul, this district has two elementary schools (K-2 and grades 3 through 5), a middle school (grades 6 through 8) and a senior high. Extensive remodeling and expansion of school facilities, including a new fine-arts auditorium, was undertaken in 1990. Mahtomedi stresses "individual attention with a world view."

Elementary schools stress whole language, mathematics, technology and critical thinking skills. Following the Carnegie Commission Report on Middle Level Education, the middle school incorporates daily advisor sessions, team teaching, flexible scheduling and interdisciplinary units. High school students choose from a broad academic curriculum and extensive extracurricular opportunities.

MINNESOTA CENTER FOR ARTS EDUCATION

6125 Olson Memorial Hwy.
Golden Valley   591-4700

The center, also known as the Arts High School, was established in 1989 and is a tuition-free, statewide public high school for 11th and 12th graders who are selected through a competitive application and review process. Enrollment numbers around 250. Arts offerings include dance, literary arts, media, music, theater and visual arts. These are taught in addition to a full range of academics, and special emphasis is placed on creative and analytical thinking, problem-solving and decision-making. Two-thirds of students live on campus in dormitories.

MINNETONKA PUBLIC SCHOOLS

261 School Ave., Excelsior   470-3406

This award-winning district in the western suburbs enrolls 7,000 students in six K-5 elementary schools, two middle schools (grades 6 through 8), and a high school.

Elementary schools emphasize basic skills, including a fourth "R": responsibility. New to this district is an elementary-level world-language program, consisting of two 30-minute weekly classes in French, Spanish or German (depending on the school).

The middle school emphasizes academic skills while nurturing students' self-confidence and self-esteem. The high school is a National School of Excellence.

MOUNDS VIEW PUBLIC SCHOOLS

2959 Hamline Ave., Roseville   636-3650

This school system has eight K-5 elementary schools, three middle schools (grades 6 through 8), two traditional senior highs and two alternative senior highs, all serving a student population of 12,000, in this suburban district north of St. Paul.

The district stresses site-based management with each of its schools choosing its own organizational structure and teaching methods. Parents are active participants in school advisory committees.

Technology is a high priority in Mounds View; schools have interactive cable TV and computer labs.

The secondary schools offer advanced-placement classes and College in the Schools courses. Students perform above national averages in standardized tests.

NORTH ST. PAUL-MAPLEWOOD-OAKDALE PUBLIC SCHOOLS

2055 Larpenteur Ave. E.
Maplewood   770-4600

Schools in this district include an early childhood-kindergarten center, nine K-5 elementary schools, two middle schools (grades 6 through 8), and two high schools.

Choose the very Best.

Catholic • Co-educational • Grades 9-12 • College Preparatory • Comprehensive

Cretin-Derham Hall
550 S. Albert Street St. Paul, MN 55116 690-2443

The system serves an enrollment of 10,500 students. In the works are a new high school, elementary and middle schools and system-wide technological improvements.

This district pioneered the concept of outcome-based education, requiring that all of its students meet a certain level of competency in the basics.

Foreign languages offered at the secondary level include French, German, Russian and Spanish. Secondary schools have a strong college-prep curriculum, and students may opt for a vocational education program and have an opportunity to attend a nearby technical college.

ORONO PUBLIC SCHOOLS
685 N. Old Crystal Bay Rd., Orono   449-8300

Serving 2,500 students in the western communities of Independence, Maple Plain, Medina, Long Lake, Orono and Minnetonka Beach, this district has a primary school (early childhood, kindergarten and 1st grade), an elementary school (grades 1 through 4), a middle school (grades 5 through 8) and a high school.

At the elementary level, self-contained and multi-age classrooms are educational options. Foreign languages include Spanish, German and Japanese.

Computer-literacy is stressed at all grade levels, and Orono students have pioneered keyboarding units that are replicated around the country.

OSSEO PUBLIC SCHOOLS
11200 93rd Ave. N., Maple Grove   425-4131

The fifth-largest school district in the state, Osseo educates 21,000 students in the growing northwestern suburbs, including all or parts of Brooklyn Park, Maple Grove, Plymouth, Brooklyn Center and Osseo. The district has 20 elementary schools, four junior highs and two senior highs. A third high school will open in 1996, and two present elementary schools will be relocated to new buildings in the near future.

One unique feature of this school system is weekly multidisciplinary seminars at the elementary level. These are conducted in a variety of subject areas.

Osseo's Cedar Island School has been named a National School of Excellence. And Northview Junior High is a National Drug-Free School. Osseo is a solid contender in the Odyssey of the Mind competition, placing in the top 10 in international competition.

RICHFIELD PUBLIC SCHOOLS
7001 Harriet Ave. S., Richfield   861-8244

Four elementary schools, a junior high and a senior high serve a student population of 4,400 in the Richfield district, one of eight districts in the nation to participate in the Quality Districts Project of the National Center for Outcome-Based Education.

Reinforcement in basic skills is stressed in the elementary grades. A great educational tool here is a nearby city-run nature center. Also, 6th graders spend a week at an environmental camp in northern Minnesota.

Computer literacy begins in kindergarten and is reinforced throughout all grades. Other highlights of the district include strong journalism and writing programs in the senior high and extensive interscholastic athletic programs.

ROBBINSDALE PUBLIC SCHOOLS
4148 Winnetka Ave. N.
New Hope   533-2781

With 12 elementary schools, four middle schools, two high schools and an alternative high school, Robbinsdale serves a student population of 14,000 in the northwestern inner-ring suburbs. Linda Powell, who went on to become the state commissioner of education, is a former Robbinsdale principal.

Strengths of this district include a commitment to outcome-based education, a belief that every child can succeed and innovative teaching methods such as language immersion and continuous progress/applied skills program.

The middle schools offer adviser relationships and interdisciplinary learning teams. One middle school is devoted to

technology and its uses in all subject areas. The high school offers extensive courses, including Japanese.

Five district schools have been named National Schools of Excellence.

ROSEMOUNT-APPLE VALLEY-EAGAN PUBLIC SCHOOLS
14445 Diamond Path, Rosemount   423-7775

This sprawling southern district has nearly 25,000 students in 18 K-5 elementary schools, five middle schools (6 through 8), three high schools and an alternative secondary program. A sixth middle school will open in 1996 and a fourth high school in 1997.

Each school has a computer lab with extensive instruction in technology. Foreign languages include Spanish, French, German, Russian and Japanese. In fall 1995 the district opened a School of Environmental Studies for juniors and seniors at the nearby Minnesota Zoo.

The district prides itself on a comprehensive curriculum, committed teachers and a supportive community. Four of its schools have been named National Schools of Excellence. Three schools have received awards for excellence in the arts.

ROSEVILLE PUBLIC SCHOOLS
1251 W. County Rd. B2, Roseville   635-1600

Seven elementary schools, a K-8 school, a middle school and a senior high serve about 5,300 students in the Roseville district, which prides itself on its grass-roots community involvement and cooperative-learning methods. Changes are under way both in physical buildings (remodeling, updating) and in curriculum, where a new emphasis is being placed on fostering community values.

The middle school groups students into "houses," small comfortable learning units. The high school offers a strong college-prep and vocational-education programs.

ST. ANTHONY-NEW BRIGHTON PUBLIC SCHOOLS

3303 33rd Ave. N.E., St. Anthony   782-1000

With 1,150 students, this district is one of the area's smallest, a factor that enhances individualized learning and teacher-student rapport. The district has one elementary school, a middle school (grades 6 through 8) and a high school.

A unique feature at the elementary level is the extended-day program on certain weekdays and Saturdays, offering more learning opportunities for students and parents. The high school offers four years of French and Spanish.

The district boasts strong community involvement, high learner expectations and an emphasis on emotional growth in addition to academic learning. Its proximity to Minneapolis and St. Paul cultural attractions complements its curriculum.

ST. LOUIS PARK PUBLIC SCHOOLS

6425 W. 33rd St., St. Louis Park   928-6064

This district, in the inner-ring western suburb of St. Louis Park, has four elementary schools (two K through 3, two 3 through 6), a junior high (grades 7 through 8) and a senior high. Its total enrollment is more than 4,300.

In 1993 the district jumped aboard the information superhighway with a telecommunications program that linked its schools to a worldwide network. St. Louis Park has recently remodeled its school libraries into media centers to incorporate the latest video and computer equipment. These centers are open to the community at night.

In addition to stressing the basics, the district strives to help students develop critical thinking, research skills and a familiar-

ity with a broad range of technology. Highlights at the elementary level include multiage classroom alternatives, whole language and a new Spanish language program. French and German are added at the junior high level and Japanese is taught in senior high.

St. Louis Park alumni include *New York Times* journalist Thomas Friedman and Hollywood filmmakers Ethan and Joel Coen (*Raising Arizona, Miller's Crossing, The Hudsucker Proxy*).

All of St. Louis Park's schools have been named National Schools of Excellence by the U.S. Department of Education. The district and city have initiated a Children First program, a communitywide partnership dedicated to strengthening families and enhancing life for children.

SHAKOPEE PUBLIC SCHOOLS

505 S. Holmes St., Shakopee   496-5000

This district in a semi-rural southern suburb has nearly 3,000 students with two K-4 primary schools, an intermediate school (grades 5 through 6), a junior high (grades 7 through 9) and a senior high.

Hands-on learning in core subjects characterizes the elementary curriculum. In junior high, emphasis is placed on basic skills, accelerated math and an array of extracurricular offerings toward the goal of nurturing independence and initiative.

Also noteworthy is instruction in Dakota language offered at the high-school level. All schools are linked via computer networks.

A recent referendum upgraded elementary buildings and improved technology offerings.

SOUTH ST. PAUL PUBLIC SCHOOLS

700 N. Second St., South St. Paul   457-9400

With a student population of 3,500,

South St. Paul district has two elementary schools, a high school (grades 7 through 12) and the Area Learning Center, an alternative secondary program.

At the elementary level, self-contained classrooms prevail, and options include student groupings, team teaching and co-operative learning. In the high school, 7th and 8th graders learn in a middle-school setting. The district places special emphasis on developing writing skills. Language instruction includes French, German, Spanish and Russian, and the district participates in the International Baccalaureate program.

SOUTH WASHINGTON COUNTY SCHOOLS
8040 S. 80th St., Cottage Grove   458-4200

This mushrooming district in the rural, southeastern suburbs of St. Paul serves all or parts of Newport, St. Paul Park, Cottage Grove, Afton, Denmark, Grey Cloud and Woodbury and has a student population of around 14,500.

The district has 11 elementary schools, four junior highs (grades 7 and 8), two of which opened in fall 1995, two senior highs and a secondary alternative learning program.

The district is a showcase of outcome-based education, providing written learner outcomes for all subjects taught. Other highlights include an extensive gifted program, accelerated and advanced-placement classes in many subjects, intensive computer and keyboard training, Junior Air Force ROTC programs in the high schools and an academic awards program that bestows school letters for scholastic achievement.

Of course, strong community support for schools is not surprising in Washington County, which was listed among the top-20 fastest-growing, wealthiest and most-educated areas in the country by the *Wall Street Journal*. It shares the distinction with nearby Dakota County.

SPRING LAKE PARK SCHOOLS
8000 N.E. Minn. 65
Spring Lake Park   786-5570

Encompassing the northern 'burb of Spring Lake Park and parts of Blaine and Fridley, this district of approximately 4,200 students has four elementary schools, a middle school and a senior high.

The basics of reading, writing, language, spelling and math, as well as computer literacy, are stressed at the elementary level. In middle school, highlights include a seven-period day, two sophisticated computer labs, exploratory courses in a range of subjects and a strong advisory program. Students at this level are grouped in "families" to provide a more friendly learning environment.

Spring Lake Park secondary students have won top state honors in math and chemistry. Also notable is the district's award-winning medical and allied health program.

WAYZATA PUBLIC SCHOOLS
210 N. County Rd. 101, Wayzata   476-3100

This western suburban district has 7,800 students in seven elementary schools, two junior highs (grades 7 through 9) and a high school. Its students come from Corcoran, Maple Grove, Medicine Lake, Medina, Minnetonka, Orono, Plymouth and Wayzata.

Thirteen 1994 Wayzata graduates were named National Merit semifinalists, the second-highest number of any school in the state.

At the elementary level, self-contained classrooms with limited team teaching are the norm. Reading is taught through a

Consider BRECK...

an Episcopal, coeducational, college-preparatory day school enrolling students of diverse backgrounds and abilities in grades preschool through twelve.

Breck

123 Ottawa Avenue North, Minneapolis, Minnesota 55422   Michael Weiszel, Admissions
(612) 347-9202

literature-based program that integrates phonics. The district places a high emphasis on computer literacy and all schools have computer labs.

All secondary schools have been named National Schools of Excellence, and one elementary school has been named a Minnesota School of Excellence.

WESTONKA PUBLIC SCHOOLS
5600 Lynwood Blvd., Mound   472-0306

Encompassing all or parts of Independence, Lyndale, Minnetrista, Mound, Navarre, Orono, Shorewood and Spring Park, Westonka serves 2,400 students with two primary schools (K through 4), a middle school (grades 5 through 7), a high-school prep program (grades 8 and 9) and a high school.

Both primary schools have been named National Schools of Excellence. At this level, the schools have primarily self-contained classrooms with flexible groupings while team teaching and interdisciplinary learning characterize the middle-school level. The unique high-school prep program (grades 8 and 9) stresses academic and social skills and offers team teaching and a strong counseling program. The high school curriculum includes college-prep coursework.

WEST ST. PAUL PUBLIC SCHOOLS
1897 Delaware Ave., West St. Paul   681-2300

This system has five elementary schools, a junior high and a senior high, serving 4,800 students in the West St. Paul district, which encompasses Lilydale, Mendota, Mendota Heights, Sunfish Lake, West St. Paul and parts of Eagan and Inver Grove Heights.

Elementary schools stress the basics with special emphasis on math. Frequent visits to a nearby nature center enhance the schools' environmental education. The junior high emphasizes science and math, enhanced by a Macintosh computer lab. College prep and vocational courses are available in high school, which boasts a new IBM computer lab along with Macintosh technology. Foreign-language instruction is offered in French, German, Russian and Spanish.

The high school fine-arts program has won national recognition, and four schools have received Elementary School of Excellence Awards.

WHITE BEAR LAKE PUBLIC SCHOOLS
2399 Cedar Ave., White Bear Lake   773-6000

This large northeastern district serves about 9,700 students in 10 K-5 elementary schools, two middle schools (grades 6 through 8) and a senior high that is divided into two campuses. Students come from all or parts of Birchwood, Gem Lake, Hugo, Little Canada, North Oaks, Vadnais Heights and White Bear Lake.

In addition to the traditional self-contained classroom model, the district offers an elementary alternative program called Centerpoint, characterized by multi-age groupings, hands-on instruction and flexible curriculum. The high school offers a wide range of college-prep and vocational classes to meet the varied needs of all students.

The district stresses education in the basic skills and higher-order thinking skills, and an innovative community program links schools with local business and industry.

Private Schools

More than 250 private elementary and secondary schools, many with a religious affiliation, serve the greater Minneapolis and St. Paul area. Here's a brief overview of some of the area's finest.

ACADEMY OF THE HOLY ANGELS
6600 Nicollet Ave., Richfield   866-8762
Tuition: $3,400-$4,800

Founded in 1931 as a Catholic girls school, the academy today is coeducational — football team and all — providing quality academic instruction in a Christian environment.

The academy comprises grades 7 through 12 and has an enrollment of about 700 students. At the middle school level, the student-teacher ratio is 17-to-1.

Holy Angels has a modern computer lab and offers an array of computing courses. The academy offers five years of French and German and four years of Spanish and Russian.

The academy offers athletics for boys and girls, including soccer, track, football, hockey, basketball and tennis, and its extracurricular activities include dance line, cheerleading, math league and speech, among others.

BENILDE-ST. MARGARET'S
2501 S. Minn. 100, St. Louis Park   927-4176
Tuition: $3,995 - $4,970

This coeducational Catholic school is the happy result of a 1974 merger of two well-respected parochial schools, Benilde Catholic boys school and St. Margaret's Catholic girls school.

With a junior high and high school, Benilde-St. Margaret's has an enrollment of 821 students. Religious affiliation is not a factor in the admission process; however, religion classes are required as part of the curriculum.

The school emphases academic excellence in a Christian setting. In 1992-93 Benilde-St. Margaret's had the largest number of National Merit semifinalists of any private school in the state. A full range of college-prep academic courses is offered, and foreign languages taught here include French, German and Spanish. Computers are available in labs and classrooms.

The school recently added a $1.8 million physical education center with a gym, weight room and locker rooms.

BLAKE SCHOOL
511 Kenwood Pkwy., Minneapolis   338-2586
Tuition: $5,185 to $10,180

This highly regarded nonsectarian private school offers a strong program of academics in a supportive environment. Approximately 1,150 students are enrolled in preschool through 12th grade at Blake, which has been named a National School of Excellence by the U.S. Department of Education.

Blake is divided into three separate campuses in Minneapolis, Hopkins and Wayzata. At the elementary level, the emphasis is on small classes, student-teacher interaction, cooperative learning and positive self-esteem. French, German and Spanish are offered in the lower grades. Blake Lower School was included in *Child* magazine's 1991 listing of the "10 best schools in America."

In the middle school grades 6 through 8, students are grouped into supportive "families," and classes stress academics, independent learning and critical thinking. The high school offers several advanced courses in math, the sciences and the humanities. The teacher-to-student ratio in high school is 1-to-10.

BRECK SCHOOL
123 Ottawa Ave. N., Golden Valley   377-5000
Tuition: $5,815 to $8,750

Breck School, which sits on a rolling 47-acre campus in Golden Valley, just west of Minneapolis, is an Episcopal, co-educational, college-preparatory day school encompassing preschool through 12th grade.

With a student population of 1,105, Breck considers its strengths to be solid academics taught in a nurturing environment. Breck has been recognized as a National School of Excellence, and in 1991 two of its seniors were among 13 students nationally to achieve a perfect SAT score.

Elementary instruction stresses a whole-language approach to reading and writing. Foreign languages include French, Chinese, German and Spanish.

A unique feature at the middle school level (grades 5 through 8) is Project Adventure, a course of physical, emotional and moral challenges that includes games, problem-solving and high- and low-rope obstacle courses.

CONCORDIA ACADEMY
2400 N. Dale St., Roseville   484-8429
Tuition: $2,406 to $4,355

This coed Lutheran high school is attended by 225 students in grades 9 through 12.

The school offers an Apple computer lab, German and Spanish language courses and optional vocational courses at nearby Northeast Metro Technical School for those who choose not to go on to college.

Concordia lists its strengths as a small teacher-to-student ratio, commitment to academic excellence and a Christian environment. It is supported by 20 area Lutheran congregations.

CONVENT OF THE VISITATION
2455 Visitation Dr., Mendota Heights 454-6474
Tuition: $2,815 to $6,890

Founded by the Sisters of the Visitation in 1873, this Catholic day school enrolls 370 students in lower, middle and upper levels. While the lower and middle schools are coed, the upper school is for girls only, the only all-girls secondary school in Minnesota.

Ninety-nine percent of upper-school graduates continue on to college. Self-esteem and leadership are nurtured in a family-like environment.

CRETIN-DERHAM HALL
550 S. Albert St., St. Paul   690-2443
Tuition: $4,450

This coed Catholic high school has a student enrollment of 1,160 and offers a varied curriculum at honors, advanced, college-prep and basic levels. Languages include German, French and Spanish.

The school is equipped with two computer labs. Emphasis is on the academic, spiritual and emotional education of the total person.

DE LA SALLE

25 W. Island Ave., Minneapolis   379-1105
Tuition: $4,150

Administered by the Christian Brothers, De La Salle is the only coed Catholic high school in Minneapolis proper. Enrollment is 350 at this school situated on picturesque Nicollet Island in the Mississippi River.

Features include two computer labs (in both Apple and IBM), computer-assisted design programs, college-prep academics, small classes, campus ministry and a culturally diverse student population (25 percent minority; 18 percent non-Catholic). The school recently conducted a major fund-raising campaign to renovate buildings and build scholarships.

FIRST BAPTIST SCHOOL

14400 Diamond Path, Rosemount   423-2271
Tuition: $1,750

Affiliated with the First Baptist Church of Rosemount, this K-12 school enrolls 210 students in a rigorous academic program presented within a Christian environment.

Self-contained classrooms are the norm at the elementary level, which also boasts art and science specialists. The secondary level has eight daily class periods. The 20-year-old school has won awards for its band and choir.

FOURTH BAPTIST CHRISTIAN SCHOOL

1250 W. Broadway, Minneapolis   522-3620
Tuition: $1,680

This 27-year-old school enrolls 510 students in kindergarten through 12th grade.

Emphasis is on self-contained classrooms, individualized attention, solid academics, a strong volunteer program and parental involvement. The school recently rebuilt its computer lab to provide one computer for every four students. An in-house FM radio station helps augment students' speech skills.

HILL-MURRAY HIGH SCHOOL AND MIDDLE SCHOOL

2625 Larpenteur Ave. E.
Maplewood   777-1376
Tuition: $3,600 to $4,500

This coed Catholic school is the result of the 1971 merger of Archbishop Murray Memorial High School for girls and Hill High School for boys. Guided by its Benedictine and LaSallian roots, the school emphasizes "work, prayer, service, hospitality and love that acts justly."

Serving 660 students in grades 7 through 12, Hill-Murray offers a college-prep, interdisciplinary curriculum; fully equipped computer labs; technology education, including engines, plastics and woodworking; and a full range of sports. Its hockey team is a serious contender in state tournaments.

More than 89 percent of Hill-Murray grads go on to college.

INTERNATIONAL SCHOOL

6384 Beach Rd., Eden Prairie   941-3500
Tuition: $7,700

This nonsectarian school, part of a worldwide school system founded in 1886, serves 385 students in preschool through grade 12. Befitting its global outlook, the school offers daily instruction in French and Spanish beginning at age 3. It also emphasizes math, science and computer literacy.

Other features include a gym, pool, tennis courts, a soccer field, playgrounds and nature trails on a 55-acre lakeshore campus.

MEADOW CREEK CHRISTIAN SCHOOL

3037 N.W. Bunker Lake Blvd.
Andover   427-4595
Tuition: $2,200 to $2,600

This coed, K-12 private school is housed in the interdenominational, evangelical Meadow Creek Church and has an enrollment of 630 students.

The school strives to offer a quality education based on biblical principles. Other features include a computer lab for secondary levels, Spanish beginning at grade 7 and a strong music program. The staff includes a full-time special-education teacher.

MINNEAPOLIS JEWISH DAY SCHOOL

4330 Cedar Lake Rd.
St. Louis Park   374-5650
Tuition: Approx. $4,000

This 10-year-old private elementary school, within the Jewish Community Center, offers a high-quality academic program that includes a healthy dose of Hebrew studies. Enrollment is around 150 in kindergarten through grade 6.

MINNEHAHA ACADEMY

32nd St. and West River Pkwy.
Minneapolis   729-8326
Tuition: $5,350 to $6,250

Founded in 1913 by the Northwest Conference of the Evangelical Covenant Church, this coed private school enrolls 970 students on two campuses: Upper School (grades 9 through 12), at 32nd Street and W. River Parkway, and Middle and Lower Schools, at 4200 W. River Parkway.

The school welcomes students of many denominations and offers quality academics in a strong spiritual setting. A high percentage of its graduates go on to college. Foreign languages include French, German, Latin and Spanish. Computer literacy is encouraged in all grades and a so-

phisticated communications system includes CD-ROM systems and internet access.

The school has a well-rounded athletic program and facilities that include three gyms, three fields, tennis courts and an indoor ice arena.

MINNESOTA WALDORF SCHOOL

2129 Fairview Ave. N., Roseville   636-6577
Tuition: $3,885 to $5,200

This school is one of more than 500 worldwide following the Waldorf system, which relies heavily on imagination, play, art, mythology, song and nature to help children develop their full potential in body, mind and spirit. The school encompasses kindergarten through the 8th grade.

Children begin each day with a two-hour main lesson, concentrating on one subject for a period of three to four weeks. Lessons are imaginatively presented; for example, music and movement may enhance the teaching of math.

Students remain with the same teacher from 1st grade through 8th grade. Classes are small, ranging from 10 to 20 students. Foreign languages include French and German. The City of Lakes Waldorf School, at 3450 Irving Avenue S., Minneapolis, offers a similar program. Its telephone number is 822-1092.

MOUNDS PARK ACADEMY

2051 E. Larpenteur Ave., St. Paul   777-2555
Tuition: $7,450 to $8,730

This coed, college-prep school enrolls 640 students in kindergarten through 12th grade. Mounds Park emphasizes individualized learning through small classes, creative teachers and extensive fine arts offerings in addition to a challenging core curriculum and foreign languages (French and Spanish) in all grades. Japanese is taught in high school. A new theater-gymnasium wing, which includes fine-arts classrooms, was added to the school in 1994.

NEW LIFE ACADEMY

6758 Bailey Rd., Woodbury   459-4121
Tuition: $1,500 to $3,400

This nondenominational Christian school (prekindergarten through grade 12) has an enrollment of 502. Features here include a computer lab, career center with computers and guidance software, German and Spanish instruction, Bible courses, small classes and a high-quality music program, all provided in a personable setting.

ST. AGNES SCHOOL

530 Lafond Ave., St. Paul   227-1886
Tuition: $3,400

This coed K-12 Catholic school encourages academic and spiritual development in a Christian setting. The school offers courses in Latin, German and Spanish and a range of math (including calculus), as well as advanced-placement courses for gifted students. Both IBM and Apple computers are available for use by students. Enrollment is around 550.

ST. BERNARD'S HIGH SCHOOL

170 Rose Ave., West St. Paul   489-1338
Tuition: $3,450

This Catholic high school offers advanced math and religion courses and four years of French, German and Spanish, as well as the usual secondary-level curriculum. The school considers its strengths to be its Christian emphasis, small classes and individualized learning. Enrollment is around 350.

ST. CROIX LUTHERAN HIGH SCHOOL

1200 Oakdale Ave., West St. Paul   455-1521
Tuition: $2,500 to $4,000

Established in 1958, this high school stresses intellectual, spiritual and physical development in a caring Christian community. The school offers Spanish, German and Latin courses and computer training. The school is known for its high standards, small classes and individualized instruction. Enrollment is around 283.

ST. PAUL ACADEMY
AND SUMMIT SCHOOL

1712 Randolph Ave., St. Paul   698-2451
Tuition: $6,360 to $9,790

This nondenominational, coed school enrolls 859 students in kindergarten through grade 12.

Summit School, the lower school, is on a separate campus at 1150 Goodrich Avenue, St. Paul. Summit offers both self-contained classes and multi-age groupings.

The Academy boasts a traditional college-prep curriculum, taught in a flexible, interdisciplinary setting. The teacher-student ratio is 1-to-9, and the average class size is 15. Foreign languages include German, French, Latin and Spanish. Seventh graders participate in a week-long environmental education course in northern Minnesota.

Typically, one-fourth to one-third of SPA seniors earn recognition in the National Merit program. In recent years, 100 percent of graduates have gone on to college.

ST. THOMAS ACADEMY

949 Mendota Heights Rd.
Mendota Heights   454-4570
Tuition: $6,775 to $7,275

The only all-male high school in the Twin Cities, St. Thomas Academy has an enrollment of 650 in grades 7 through 12 and offers a rigorous college-prep academic and religious curriculum. The teacher-to-student ratio is 1-to-15.

Ninety-eight percent of the class of 1994 went on to college. Students may earn advanced-placement college credit through a program with local colleges. Every student is required to take a Junior Reserve Officers Training Corps course. Strengths include small classes, challenging academics and emphases on leadership and self-discipline.

TALMUD TORAH DAY SCHOOL
636 S. Mississippi River Blvd.
St. Paul 698-8807
Tuition: $5,000

This private K-6 elementary school offers an academic program that encourages students to explore various subject areas via a multidisciplinary approach that integrates math, science, history, writing and art. Students are from all Jewish backgrounds: affiliated, unaffiliated and secular. Hebrew is used throughout the day. The enrollment is around 160.

Talmud Torah also offers an afternoon school for youth in grades 2 through 7, as well as a Midrasha educational program for teens in grades 8 through 12. There is also a preschool program on premises.

TESSERACT SCHOOL
3800 Tesseract Place, Eagan 454-0604
Tuition: $6,290 (preschool rates vary)

This private, nondenominational school provides instruction in preschool through 8th grade. Strengths include a low student-teacher ratio, rigorous academic curriculum, Spanish instruction and strong parental involvement.

With its philosophy based on research gathered by Control Data Corp., Tesseract stresses individualized, active learning. At Tesseract, no student is labeled as a failure; instead, instruction is customized to each student's needs.

Oh, yes, that strange name. "Tesseract" was inspired by Madeline L'Engle's classic children's book, *A Wrinkle in Time*, where the word describes a fifth-dimensional corridor for traveling to otherwise unreachable destinations.

TORAH ACADEMY
2800 Joppa Ave. S., St. Louis Park 920-6630
Tuition: Approx. $5,000

This full-day Jewish school provides secular and Jewish studies coursework for 260 students in prekindergarten through grade 8. While the school is based on Orthodox principles, its students come from all types of Jewish backgrounds.

TOTINO-GRACE HIGH SCHOOL
1350 Gardena Ave. N.E., Fridley 571-4675
Tuition: $4,600

This coed Catholic high school (grades 9 through 12) offers a challenging curriculum in a Christian community. Enrollment is 955. Foreign languages include German, French and Spanish. Computers are available in classrooms, two labs and a media center, and the school participates an international computer consortium.

A recent remodeling project added a second gym, art rooms, choir and band facilities, and an industrial arts room. A campus ministry program offers worship, retreats and social-justice projects.

The Early Years

Education doesn't begin at the kindergarten door. The preschool years are a time of bold discoveries, grand adventures and blossoming friendships. More and more, we're discovering just how smart babies are and how they absolutely thrive on mental, emotional and physical stimulation — delivered, of course, in a loving, secure setting.

To meet the challenge, the state of Minnesota sponsors an educational program called Early Childhood Family Education (ECFE) for children from birth through age 4 and their parents. Administered locally through 369 Minnesota school districts and tribal schools, ECFE consists of weekly parent/child classes that incorporate creative play, adult discussion and peer support. More than 258,000 parents and children participate in the ECFE program. Information about local ECFE programs may be obtained by calling your local school district or the state Department of Education at (612) 296-8414.

Options in Child Care

Finding good child care is a never-ending struggle for working parents. Where's June Cleaver when you need her? Hello. Wake-up call. It's the '90s, and today's June is chasing a paycheck and chauffeuring "the Beav" to the nearest day-care center.

Parents today have many options in child care. Some parents seek out licensed home-care providers because they prefer a more family-like setting. Others opt for licensed commercial child-care centers, finding security in the professional staff and standardized no-surprises setting.

Whatever your choice, do your homework. Contact a local child-care referral agency or your city or county offices for guidance and a listing of licensed centers and home-based providers (see the contact numbers listed below). Also, friends, relatives and neighbors are great sources for child-care referrals. Another place to turn is your neighborhood public school, where the staff usually can provide a list of reliable caregivers.

Call ahead and schedule your first visit to a prospective child-care provider and then stop by again unannounced during hours of operation to see her or him in action. Ask questions. What is the adult-to-child ratio? What is the staff members' turnover rate and educational training? Check out the play areas, bathrooms, kitchen and the supply of age-appropriate toys. Observe how the provider interacts with children. And trust your instincts. If something just doesn't seem right, it probably isn't. Move on to the next facility.

Perhaps the most comfortable arrangement of all is to hire a nanny or an au pair (a foreign nanny who comes to the United States on a one-year visa). While the latter lives with the host family and earns an average stipend of $100-plus a week, in addition to room and board, nannies may be hired on either a live-in or day-care basis. There are many referral agencies for both nannies and au pairs. For more information, look in the Yellow Pages under "Nannies."

As children age, child-care needs naturally lessen. School-age children often require only before- and after- school care. Fortunately, more and more schools are offering these extended-day services. They're worth looking into. In most cases, the staff is well-qualified, and your child will feel right at home in the comfortable school setting among his or her peers. As another plus, many extended-day programs also offer care during school-release days and summer vacations.

Increasingly, Minnesota employers are getting into the act and supporting harried parents in a number of ways, from opening child-care centers at the job site to offering such benefits as flextime and job sharing. A leader in this area is the St. Paul Companies, which in 1991 built a $1.6 million child-care facility at its headquarters in downtown St. Paul.

Other companies offer working parents such benefits as flextime, job sharing, work-at-home options, tax-exempt child-care savings plans, liberal sick-day and parental-leave policies and resource and referral services.

Despite such innovations, finding the just-right caregiver remains a daunting task — and a major investment. In the Twin Cities, child-care costs vary according to the age of your child and whether you use an in-home provider or a center. Centers may charge anywhere from $101 a week for preschoolers to $141 a week for infants. Licensed in-home care providers charge an average of $85 a week for preschoolers and $95 a week for infants.

Because of the high cost of quality day care, Minnesota has established a Child Care Fund to provide child-care assistance to eligible families. Parents are required to pay a portion of the child-care costs while receiving assistance through the fund.

Referral and Information Services

The following are child-care referral and information services for various geographic areas of the greater Twin Cities.

Greater Minneapolis Day Care Association
Information   *341-1177*
Referral   *341-2066*
(This organization also has information on local summer camps and programs.)

Resources for Child Caring
  (serving Ramsey County)   *641-0332*
Community Action Council
  (serving Dakota County)   *431-2424*
Anoka County Community Health
  and Social Services   *422-7146, 422-7153*
Carver County Licensing
  Department   *448-3661*
Scott County Child Care
  Resource and Referral   *431-7752*
Washington County Community
  Social Services   *439-6901*

Parent Hotlines

Here are helpful numbers for parents who need emotional support or just some good advice.

FIRST CALL FOR HELP

Minneapolis   *335-5000*
St. Paul   *224-1133*

First Call for Help is a United Way service that offers crisis counseling and referrals to parents.

CRISIS NURSERY

Crisis Nursery of Ramsey and
  Washington counties   *641-1300*
Minneapolis Crisis Nursery   *824-8000*
Crisis Nursery of Anoka   *785-1181*
Crisis Nursery of Dakota County   *432-5578*

This service provides temporary child care for parents in crisis who need a respite from their children. Most limit service to children younger than 12.

University of St. Thomas, St. Paul.

Photo: Joe Oden, Pioneer Press

Inside
Higher Education

In a region where kids graduate from high school at an extraordinarily high percentage and people of all ages are notoriously heavy users of the library systems and area book stores, is it any wonder that institutions of higher learning are everywhere you look? The Twin Cities boasts an enormous range of opportunities in higher education, from two-year community colleges to renowned private institutions to one of the nation's largest public universities.

Among the educational choices are one of the largest public universities in the nation (the University of Minnesota); the liberal-arts college with the second-highest endowment in the nation (Macalester College); a school that blazed a trail in allowing working people to attain college degrees (Metropolitan State University); an institution with a program in jewelry-making (Minneapolis Technical Institute); and one of the country's best-known art schools (Minneapolis College of Art and Design). Some are old, some new, some tiny and others sprawling. They all, however, offer proof that Twin Citians love to learn — whether for fun or for profit.

In addition to the institutions listed here, dozens of professional schools give training in careers that include accounting, acupuncture, electronics and radio broadcasting, veterinary medicine, acting and modeling, and truck driving. They are listed in the phone directory.

Four-Year Colleges and Universities

AUGSBURG COLLEGE
731 21st Ave. S., Minneapolis   330-1000

It's easy to inattentively drive by this Lutheran-affiliated liberal arts college, with its compact 25-acre campus squeezed between the sprawl of the University of Minnesota and the rush of I-94. Founded in 1869, Augsburg is primarily an undergraduate residential college, with only about a third of the 2,900 students living off-campus or commuting. The college offers pre-professional programs in such fields as medicine, law, veterinary science and theology, and the most popular majors are business, education and communication.

BETHEL COLLEGE AND SEMINARY
3900 Bethel Dr., St. Paul   638-6400

About 1,800 students attend this 124-year-old private college, about a 20-minute drive from both downtowns and affiliated with the Baptist General Conference. Despite Bethel's vintage, its campus is the newest in the state, with up-to-date academic, recreational and housing facilities. Business, nursing, education and psychology number among the most popular majors. Christian spiritual development receives much emphasis in the form of chapel services, Bible study groups and on- and off-campus ministry activities. The adjacent Bethel Seminary has a 70,000-volume theological library.

COLLEGE OF ASSOCIATED ARTS
344 Summit Ave., St. Paul   *224-3416*

There are no sports teams or dormitories for the 150 students enrolled in this private art school ensconced within one of America's greatest neighborhoods of turn-of-the-century Victorian residences. The college offers majors and a Bachelor of Fine Arts in communication design, fine arts and illustration, as well as study-abroad opportunities in Australia, Ireland and England. The college is not accessible to physically disabled students.

COLLEGE OF ST. CATHERINE
2004 Randolph Ave., St. Paul   *690-6000*
601 25th Ave. S., Minneapolis   *690-7700*

St. Cate's, as the institution is affectionately nicknamed, is a Catholic-affiliated college with 3,900 students who attend classes at campuses in St. Paul and Minneapolis. Founded as an undergraduate institution for women in 1905 by the Sisters of St. Joseph of Carondelet, the college was the first Catholic school in the United States to be awarded a Phi Beta Kappa chapter. Students at the well-groomed St. Paul campus, all women, focus on liberal-arts and professional programs. The bachelor's degree is offered in more than 30 disciplines.

At the Minneapolis campus (formerly known as the St. Mary's campus), a co-educational student body pursues associate degrees and certificates in such health-related fields as holistic therapy, medical transcription, nursing, respiratory therapy, and chemical dependency family treatment. St. Catherine's also offers master's degree programs in education, library science, nursing, theology and other areas, and a Weekend College program for women who want to continue working as they learn.

CONCORDIA COLLEGE
275 N. Syndicate St., St. Paul   *641-8278*

Concordia, a private college affiliated with the Lutheran Church (Missouri Synod), recently celebrated its centennial. It has a tidy 26-acre urban campus that serves as academic home for approximately 1,200 students. Nearly half the students study business, with others majoring in such fields as education, social sciences and humanities.

HAMLINE UNIVERSITY
1536 Hewitt Ave., St. Paul   *641-2800*

Hamline is Minnesota's oldest private institution of higher education, having been established in 1854 as a college affiliated with the United Methodist Church. Its 50-acre campus, conveniently close to the state fairgrounds and the Midway district of St. Paul, bridges a business/retail district and a quiet residential neighborhood. The atmosphere of the university is progressive, and its 2,500 students (who include about 1,000 graduate students, quite a few of them 35 and older) are considered a pretty sharp bunch. Undergraduates primarily major in social sciences, arts and humanities and business.

MACALESTER COLLEGE
1600 Grand Ave., St. Paul   *696-6000*

Long before it added hundreds of millions of dollars to its endowment several years ago due to a windfall from the estate of alumnus DeWitt Wallace (the founder of *Reader's Digest*), Macalester was a college worthy of attention. Academically strong and home to international students from some 75 nations during a typical year, Macalester boasts a spirited appreciation of diversity and dissent. Walter Mondale went to school there, and Hubert Humphrey taught there.

Founded in 1874 by the Presbyterian church (although today the church connection is nominal), this liberal-arts college has the necessary financial strength, academic rigor and multicultural orientation to keep it prominent for a long time. About 1,700 students, all undergraduates, attend.

METROPOLITAN STATE UNIVERSITY
700 E. Seventh St., St. Paul   772-7777

When the Minnesota State University system created this institution in 1971, the school was leading a pack of universities grappling with the needs of working adults who wanted to further their education. Initially marketed as a "college without walls," it continues to offer programs for students unable to find a comfortable place within other post-secondary schools. Today the median age of its 5,000 students is the mid-30s, and classes meet at locations throughout the Twin Cities. Popular majors are an individualized study program and nursing.

MINNEAPOLIS COLLEGE
OF ART & DESIGN
2501 Stevens Ave. S., Minneapolis   874-3700

Everyone calls this fine-arts college MCAD (pronounced EM-cad), and its location next to the extensive museum holdings of the Minneapolis Institute of Arts places the works of Rembrandt, Titian, O'Keeffe and Grant Wood within easy reach. Founded in 1886 (the renowned children's book illustrator and author Wanda Gág was an early alumna),

the college now has 600 students seeking degrees at the bachelor's level. Many members of the faculty — the student-faculty ratio is a tiny 12-to-1 — are prominent practitioners of such disciplines as sculpture, architecture, painting, animation, video and clothing design. Well-known visiting artists teach as well. The MCAD Gallery, in the main building, mounts outstanding exhibitions of artworks from around the world.

WILLIAM MITCHELL COLLEGE OF LAW
875 Summit Ave., St. Paul   290-6326

This law school's noted alumni include retired U.S. Supreme Court Chief Justice Warren Burger, former Minnesota Supreme Court Chief Justices Douglas Amdahl and Peter Popovich, and nearly one-third of Minnesota's current judges. Ranging in age from 20 to 60, William Mitchell's 1,150 students benefit from the school's renowned legal writing program, a highly respected clinical law program, the availability of an unusual Master of Laws in Taxation degree, and the recently added Warren E. Burger Library. Forty-four percent of the students are women.

NATIONAL COLLEGE —
ST. PAUL CAMPUS
1380 Energy Ln., St. Paul   644-1265

National College, one of the newest (founded in 1975) and smallest of the Twin Cities' post-secondary schools, has an open admission policy. Its 240 students prima-

Although a charter for the University of Minnesota was drawn up and approved by the legislature in 1851, the school did not offer its first college-level classes until 18 years later.

Insiders' Tips

rily study business administration and management, and all are commuters.

NORTH CENTRAL BIBLE COLLEGE
910 Elliot Ave. S., Minneapolis   *332-3491*

Affiliated with the Assemblies of God, North Central Bible College has about 1,000 students pursuing such areas as pastoral studies, youth ministries and elementary education. Other academic fields include biblical languages, broadcasting, children's ministries, church business administration, urban studies, drama and journalism. Most students live on campus, and two-thirds are from outside Minnesota. The campus is small and close to downtown Minneapolis.

NORTHWESTERN COLLEGE
3003 N. Snelling Ave. N., St. Paul   *631-5100*

Northwestern, a nondenominational Christian liberal-arts college founded in 1902, offers a full range of majors, from accounting to youth ministries. Most of its 1,300 students, however, focus on education, arts and humanities, business and social sciences. The 95-acre campus is close to the Rosedale shopping mall. Students desiring to venture further afield can take advantage of study-abroad opportunities in Greece, Israel, Japan and England.

ST. MARY'S COLLEGE OF MINNESOTA
2510 Park Ave., Minneapolis   *874-9877*

St. Mary's is the graduate-level branch of a liberal-arts college in Winona, Minnesota. Affiliated with the Catholic Church, it serves more than 2,000 adult students who take part in 11 master's degree programs in day, evening and weekend classes.

UNIVERSITY OF MINNESOTA
Minneapolis   *625-5000*
St. Paul   *625-5000*

Truly a city within a city, the Twin Cit-ies branch of the University of Minnesota almost defies description. It's big: Nearly 45,000 students (undergrads and grad students) scatter their studies throughout a 1,730-acre campus that spans the Mississippi River and leapfrogs to the north edge of St. Paul. It's venerable: Founded in 1851, U of M includes a central mall originally conceived by Cass Gilbert (later much altered in design) that now typifies the Big 10 university look. It's academically distinguished: Only half of the undergrad applicants are offered admission (and it says a lot for academic quality that 40 percent of the entering students come from out of state), the libraries contain some 8 million items, and the graduate programs include a nationally renowned medical school, a law school, the Hubert Humphrey Institute of Public Affairs and the Carlson School of Management.

Among the newest buildings are an eye-popping art museum and the ear-pleasing Ted Mann Concert Hall; the Science Building in the Medical School is under construction. As a Big 10 university, of course, the U of M boasts plenty of pennant-waving intercollegiate athletics. The women's and men's Gopher basketball teams have done particularly well lately (see the Spectator Sports chapter).

UNIVERSITY OF ST. THOMAS
2115 Summit Ave., St. Paul   *962-5000*

St. Thomas, a coeducational liberal-arts university established in 1885 by the Roman Catholic Church, enrolls about 10,000 students — a group evenly divided between undergrads and graduate students. The 78-acre main campus sits squarely within a residential area that constitutes St. Paul's "college belt"; the College of St. Catherine and Macalester are close at hand, and even Hamline is not too distant. The university offers a kaleidoscopic range of academic majors, although more than a third of the undergrads opt to concentrate on business. Graduate students also frequently pursue M.B.A.s and other business-related advanced degrees. Even among undergrads, living off campus or commuting is the norm (which, in the past, has contributed to conflicts with neighborhood residents over parking congestion). St. Thomas has two branch campuses, one in Chaska and a recently constructed facility in downtown Minneapolis that has one of the largest fresco paintings in North America, a work (on the ceiling) by Minnesota-born artist Mark Balma.

Community Colleges

These public two-year institutions are enormously important in the grand scheme of the Twin Cities' higher educational offerings. For some students, the community colleges provide a way to learn and improve career skills at night and on weekends, outside the boundaries of the normal work day. For others, these schools pave the way for enrollment in four-year institutions. And some students simply use the colleges as a non-intimidating route to a subject of interest. All of these colleges offer three different two-year degrees: the Associate of Applied Science, providing career-related skills; the Associate of Arts, which transfers to four-year schools; and the Associate of Science, which transfers to technical programs.

• **Anoka-Ramsey Community College**, 11200 Mississippi Boulevard N.W., Coon Rapids; 427-2600

• **Inver Hills Community College**, 2500 E. 80th Street, Inver Grove Heights; 450-8500

• **Lakewood Community College**, 3401 N. Century Avenue, White Bear Lake; 779-3200

• **Minneapolis Community College**, 1501 Hennepin Avenue, Minneapolis; 341-7000

• **Normandale Community College**, 9700 France Avenue S., Bloomington; 832-6000

• **North Hennepin Community College**, 7411 N. 85th Street, Brooklyn Park; 424-0702

Public Technical Colleges

The area's many technical colleges emphasize career skills, offering such majors as accounting, apparel and upholstery, aviation mechanics, barbering, cosmetology, child development, culinary skills, commercial art, retail sales and machine tool technologies. At a technical college you can learn how to overhaul an engine, use airline reservation software, manage a small business, construct necklaces and bracelets, edit videos, practice reflexology or tailor clothing. Tuition fees are moderate, and virtually anyone older than 18 can enroll. People 62 or older receive special discounts.

Here are a few to contact about programs.

• **Anoka-Hennepin Technical College**, 1355 W. Highway 10, Anoka; 427-1880

• **Hennepin Technical College**, Suburban Technical Institute, 1820 N. Xenium Lane, Plymouth; 559-3535

• **Minneapolis Technical College**, 1415 Hennepin Avenue, Minneapolis; 370-9400

• **Northeast Metro Technical College**, 3300 Century Avenue N., White Bear Lake; 770-2351

• **Rosemount-Dakota County Technical College**, 145th Street and Akron Road, Rosemount; 423-2281

• **St. Paul Technical College**, 235 Marshall Avenue, St. Paul; 221-1370

Adult Continuing Education

Most of the public school districts in the Twin Cities area offer low-cost continuing education classes for adults. Courses range from the esoteric (How to Review a Movie) to the practical (How to Make Your Will). In between lie classes in foreign languages, sports instruction, yoga, writing, music, financial planning, self-defense, cooking and computers. The instructors can be genuinely knowledgeable or merely enthusiastic. For more information, contact your local school district.

MACPHAIL CENTER FOR THE ARTS
1128 LaSalle Ave., Minneapolis   321-0100

After 28 years as part of the University of Minnesota's Continuing Education program, MacPhail became in 1994 an independent, nonprofit arts education institution serving both adults and children. Founded in 1907 by violinist William S. MacPhail, the school had been a degree-granting institution for decades. Now MacPhail offers a huge choice of instrumental and vocal music instruction, as well as sponsors master classes, music ensembles and music history and theory classes. The children's Suzuki programs and adult class piano courses are especially highly regarded. MacPhail, in downtown Minneapolis near Orchestra Hall, is one of the nation's largest community arts schools.

OPEN U
706 N. First St., Minneapolis   349-9273

Open U is a private and for-profit provider of continuing education classes, which are held at locations around the area. Prices tend to be a bit steeper than the courses that school districts offer but are still reasonable. Open U is particularly strong in classes about relationships, intimacy, career development, local history, the film business, the arts and travel. It often flies in nationally known experts to teach.

Inside
Business

For years, despite the occasional defection of some local manufacturer to low-tax South Dakota, the Twin Cities have consistently been ranked among the nation's healthiest business centers. Seventeen of the Fortune 500 industrial companies are based in the area, along with several of the nation's largest privately held firms.

Several ingredients contribute to the region's robust commercial climate: a diversified business base, a skilled and well-educated workforce, an unemployment rate that is consistently better than the national average and a healthy per capita income. Residents of the Twin Cities earned $24,145 per capita in 1993, which was 14 percent above the U.S. average.

Deep in the past are the days when three businesses — railroads, lumber and

Photo: Joe Oden, Pioneer Press

Corporate headquarters for the 3M Company is located in Maplewood, a suburb of St. Paul.

flour — dominated the Twin Cities economy. Since the end of the 19th century, the railroads have declined in power, the timber has vanished and most of the flour has been milled elsewhere, but a great many other industries have stepped in to fill the void.

Starting in the 1950s, for example, computers became big business in the Twin Cities. At the same time that Minneapolis-based Control Data went through a spectacular rise (and eventual decline), other local high-technology companies such as Univac and Cray Research were making their mark. The Twin Cities also carried technology into the medical-devices business, providing a home for Medtronic, St. Jude Medical, Cardiac Pacemakers and other companies.

The Twin Cities' placement in the heart of a rich agricultural region ensures that food processing remains an important commercial activity here. The former milling giants General Mills and Pillsbury are still going strong, although they have extended their reach into such areas as yogurt, frozen meals, ready-to-eat breakfast cereals and restaurants. (And Pillsbury is owned by a corporate entity in the United Kingdom.)

Two other regional industrial behemoths, 3M and Honeywell, have weathered defense cuts by strengthening their international business and stressing innovation.

Probably the most distinctive aspect of business in the Twin Cities has been a remarkable commitment to community involvement. Scores of firms, large and small, annually give 2 or 5 percent of their pre-tax income to charitable arts and social service organizations, and the area is nationally renowned for the number of big-business families that have endowed foundations to annually give money to community causes and nonprofit groups. Corporate-sponsored employee volunteerism is a powerful force, as well, and the Points of Light Foundation recently gave three of its six national community involvement awards to Twin Cities companies: Dayton Hudson, Honeywell and General Mills.

Corporate Profiles

American Express Financial Advisors Inc.

IDS Tower, Minneapolis   *671-3131*

This is the new name of an old Twin Cities firm long known as IDS Financial Services. This financial planning company commissioned the area's most famous skyscraper, the IDS Tower, although it no longer owns the building. American Express Financial Advisors provides financial planning services throughout the country and offers several types of insurance, mutual funds, investment certificates and other investments. It employs more than 4,400 people in Minnesota. Annual earnings are $3.2 billion.

Insiders' Tips

J. Paul Getty, who accumulated a fortune of $4 billion by the time of his death in 1976, was born in Minneapolis.

Made or Invented
in the Twin Cities

Rollerblades were invented in Minnesota.

Photo: Joe Oden, Pioneer Press

Every day, whether they know it or not, people around the world use products or services that come from the Twin Cities. Going back to the 19th century, Twin Cities businesses and inventors have developed more than their share of neat and innovative stuff. Here's a sampling.

ARMORED CARS
In 1919 a Minneapolis factory turned out the nation's first.

BETTER BUSINESS BUREAU
This organization traces its origins to an effort to crack down on deceptive advertising in Minneapolis in 1911.

BETTY CROCKER
Way back in 1921, when it was still called the Washburn-Crosby Company, General Mills invented Ms. Crocker to respond to people's baking questions. She's since graced countless food packages, appeared on the radio and undergone a half-dozen facial updates.

BREATHE RIGHT
That hot-selling bandage-like thing that helps people breathe easier while they sleep was developed by CNS Inc. of Chanhassen.

The Pillsbury Doughboy is a hometown boy in the Twin Cities.

BROADCAST SATELLITE

In 1993 United States Satellite Broadcasting, of the Twin Cities, launched the world's first high-power direct-broadcast satellite. Subscribers with satellite dishes can receive 150 TV channels.

BURMA-SHAVE

Minneapolis was long the home of Burma-Shave, and all those highway signs were cooked up in the Twin Cities.

CARAMEL APPLES

A food vendor at the 1916 Minnesota State Fair introduced them.

CHEERIOS

Along with dozens of other cereals, this is one of General Mills' key contributions to America's morningtime culture. It first hit the store shelves in 1941 under the brand name "Cheerioats." Thirteen years later, General Mills introduced Trix, one of the first presweetened cereals. (The Trix Rabbit came later, in 1960.)

COOTIE

Minneapolis postal worker Herb Schaper invented this louse-inspired game in 1948, and his firm, Schaper Manufacturing Company, went on to develop such other toys as Stadium Checkers, Ants in the Pants and Inch Worm.

CORTLAND, HARALSON AND WEALTHY APPLES

They were all developed by Twin Cities apple specialists between 1885 and 1935.

CRAY SUPERCOMPUTERS

Used all over the globe, they're manufactured in Eagan.

CREAMETTES MACARONI

You can bet your noodle that this pasta originated in Minneapolis.

DELUXE CHECKS

A goodly number of the personal checks we write are printed by Deluxe Corp., which is based in Shoreview.

ENCLOSED SHOPPING CENTER

Southdale, which opened in Edina in 1956, was the country's first indoor shopping center.

GLASS MEATCASE

A now-forgotten Minneapolis butcher installed in his shop the country's first glass case for meats, around 1897.

GRAIN BELT, LANDMARK, PIG'S EYE AND SUMMIT BEERS

Twin Cities breweries produce all of them.

HAMM'S BEAR

Hamm's, purveyors of the brew made in "the land of sky blue waters," turned a white-bellied cartoon bear into a national celebrity with its ads in the 1950s and '60s.

HAPPY TO BE ME DOLL

The doll that raises the self-esteem of girls comes from High Self Esteem Toys in Woodbury.

HEART-LUNG MACHINE

University of Minnesota scientists built the first one in 1955. Twenty-two years later they followed up with the first total-body computer tomagraphy scanner.

HEART PACEMAKER

Medtronic, based in Minneapolis, became the first company to market wearable, battery-operated heart pacemakers in 1957. It later followed with the first implantable pacemakers. St. Jude Medical in Little Canada has built its international business on mechanical heart valves.

HOME THERMOSTAT

You can thank the tinkerers at Honeywell in Minneapolis for developing the first ones (c. 1885).

HYDROELECTRICITY

The western hemisphere's first hydroelectric generating plant was built in 1882 at Minneapolis' Falls of St. Anthony.

LAND O'LAKES BUTTER

And cheese, too — they're both the bread and butter of the Arden Hills dairy cooperative.

LOG CABIN SYRUP

It first dripped out of the Twin Cities around 1920.

MINI DONUTS

Lil' Orbits Doughnut Machines in Plymouth manufactures the gizmos that make them.

MALT-O-MEAL

More than 75 years ago, Malt-O-Meal began producing its cereals in Minneapolis.

MMPI

Now used as an employment screening tool around the country, the Minnesota Multiphasic Personality Inventory was invented by University of Minnesota psychologists in 1939.

MUNSINGWEAR UNDERWEAR

Now they market everything from kitchenware to household novelties, but Munsingwear in Minneapolis once produced the clothes that were close to everyone's skin.

NORDICTRACK

If Americans have grown more fit in the past decade, NordicTrack in Chaska is partly responsible.

NUT GOODIE

Something of a cult following keeps this candy alive.

PEANUT BUTTER PARFAIT

Along with Slurpees and other Dairy Queen treats, they're prepared everywhere, but Dairy Queen International is based in Bloomington.

PILLSBURY DOUGHBOY

That pudgy little dude, invented in 1965 by an ad agency for Minneapolis-based Pillsbury, has endured countless pokes in the belly.

POST-IT NOTES

3M scientist Art Fry invented them in 1974, and they first reached the market four years later. Now they're stuck all over.

PUFFED RICE

University of Minnesota professor Alexander Anderson invented the puffing process in 1901.

ROLLERBLADES

Blame your strong ankles and bruised knees on Scott Olson and Brennan Olson of Minneapolis, who invented Rollerblades in 1980. The company they founded is now based in Minnetonka.

SATELLITE TOILETS
No construction site or outdoor event would be complete without them. Satellite is headquartered in Plymouth.

SCOTCH TAPE
3M developed the first cellophane tape in 1928. Not by coincidence, the first rolls of masking tape also came out of 3M's labs in 1925.

SHOPPING BAG
St. Paul grocer Walter Duebner invented the nation's first commercially produced shopping bag with handles in 1916.

THINSULATE
It's another 3M invention.

TOASTER
In 1926 McGraw Electric Company of Minneapolis began marketing the first electric toaster for use in the home.

TONKA TRUCKS
They were developed and long manufactured in Minnetonka.

YEARBOOKS AND CLASS RINGS
Odds are that Jostens in Bloomington produced your class ring, and there's a good chance they printed your school yearbook too.

CARGILL INC.
15407 McGinty Rd., Minnetonka   742-7575

Many Twin Citians are surprised when they learn that this low-profile giant is the world's largest privately held company, with revenues approaching $50 billion. Its business is the trading of such commodities as wheat, vegetable oil, corn, meat, animal feeds, fertilizers, salt, steel and resins. Founded in 1865, Cargill Inc. employs more than 3,400 people in Minnesota and about 70,574 worldwide.

CARLSON COMPANIES INC.
Carlson Pkwy., Minnetonka   540-5000

Founded in 1938, this diversified and privately-held firm has made its chairman and CEO, Curtis L. Carlson, one of the wealthiest men in the Upper Midwest. Carlson Co. Inc. employs about 41,000 people in Minnesota and 112,000 worldwide and operates Carlson and Neiman Marcus travel agencies, corporate incentive programs, the Radisson Hotels, Colony Hotels and Resorts and TGI Friday's and Country Kitchen restaurants. Company revenues top $2 billion annually.

DAYTON HUDSON CORPORATION
777 Nicollet Mall, Minneapolis   370-6948

One of the nation's largest retailers, Dayton Hudson operates three store groups: Target, the upscale discounter;

Mervyn's, which concentrates on midprice apparel and linens; and a department store division that includes Dayton's, Hudson's and Marshall Field's stores scattered throughout the nation's midsection. The company began in 1902 when George Draper Dayton opened his first Dayton's store at the corner of Seventh and Nicollet in Minneapolis (the store is still there, albeit much enlarged), but Marshall Field's and Hudson's corporate roots are even older. Minnesotans fondly think of the company as strictly a local product, but only a small fraction of Dayton Hudson's 900-plus stores are in the state. With $21 billion in sales, it is the state's largest publicly held company. Dayton Hudson's charitable largesse is legendary: Since 1946 it has donated 5 percent of its pre-tax earnings to community organizations through the Dayton Hudson Foundation and funds administered by each store group.

FINGERHUT
4400 Baker Rd., Minnetonka   932-3100

Fingerhut, founded in 1949, is a direct-to-the-consumer marketing company, selling a broad range of products and services through catalogs, television and other media. The company employs approximately 9,500 people. Total revenues for 1994 exceeded $1.9 billion.

GENERAL MILLS INC.
1 General Mills Blvd., Golden Valley   540-2311

Much more than Cheerios and Betty Crocker mixes come out of this place. General Mills also produces Bisquick, Yoplait yogurt and Gold Medal flour (a very old Twin Cities product), as well as operating Red Lobster and Olive Garden restaurants. Everyone knows that Big G is one of the three heavy hitters in the highly competitive breakfast cereal market, but few realize that the corporate head-

quarters in Golden Valley is the site of some great outdoor sculptures; Jonathan Borofsky's *Man with a Briefcase* is a fine example. General Mills is a prominent (and progressive) donor to charitable causes; in recent years it has been named by various publications and organizations as one of the nation's best workplaces for African-American employees, one of the most admired food companies and one of the country's best equal-opportunity employers. Annual sales are more than $8 billion.

HONEYWELL INC.
Honeywell Plaza, Minneapolis   951-1000

Once a major defense contractor, Honeywell has in recent years focused on building its international business in developing and producing control systems. There's a good chance that your home thermostat or security system is a Honeywell product, and the company also markets gas valves, sensors of all kinds and energy management devices. A space and aviation systems division manufactures guidance systems and controls for use in military and commercial aircraft and spacecraft. Honeywell's annual revenues of $5.9 billion make it the fifth-largest publicly held company in Minnesota.

LAND O'LAKES INC.
4001 Lexington Ave. N.
Arden Hills   481-2222

Founded in 1921, this food processing, marketing and farm supply cooperative is owned by 300,000 farmers (1,020 member associates and 7,812 individual members) in 15 midwestern and northwestern states. Land O'Lakes distributes farm supplies to its members, while processing and marketing their farm commodities. The company is best-known for its food products, including butter (Land

O'Lakes was the nation's first firm to offer butter made from "sweet cream" and in quarter-pound sticks), cheese and dried and fluid milk. With $2.8 billion in net sales, Land O'Lakes employs more than 2,000 people in Minnesota.

NORWEST CORPORATION
Sixth St. and Marquette Ave.
Minneapolis   *667-1234*

Norwest, headquartered in downtown Minneapolis' beautiful Norwest Tower (see Architecture and Historic Sites), is the state's largest banking institution, providing mortgage, trust and investment services. With annual earnings of $800 million, Norwest owns banks in 16 states stretching from Arizona to Indiana and has been aggressive in acquiring new banks and savings and loans.

NWA INC.
5101 Northwest Dr., Eagan   *726-2111*

NWA, the parent company of Northwest Airlines and several other travel-related businesses, was the second-largest privately held company in Minnesota until it recently went public. It now seems solidly in the black after a few financially disastrous years in which bankruptcy appeared possible. Northwest Airlines uses the Twin Cities as its home base and one of its hubs, giving the community unusually good air access to other cities around the world. About 18,000 Minnesotans work for NWA.

PILLSBURY
Pillsbury Center, Minneapolis   *330-4966*

Founded in 1869 and originally known as Pillsbury Flour Mills, this $4 billion company has been owned since 1988 by London-based Grand Metropolitan, a multinational giant. It produces some of the best-known brand names in the food business: Green Giant, Hungry Jack, Totino's, Jeno's and Joan of Arc, not to mention the Pillsbury line of cake mixes and dough products. Pillsbury also provides restaurants and other commercial food services with baked and frozen products. Of the 16,000 employees, 2,300 are Minnesotans.

THE ST. PAUL COMPANIES
385 Washington St., St. Paul   *221-7911*

The occupant of one of the newest and flashiest business headquarters in St. Paul happens to be the state's oldest corporation. One of the most amazing features of the St. Paul Companies' facilities is a palatial in-house child-care center for employees' kids, which promptly earned the company kudos in *Working Mother Magazine*. Founded in 1853 as St. Paul Fire and Marine Insurance Company, the company is the nation's biggest underwriter of medical liability insurance and also handles property liability insurance, reinsurance and insurance brokerage services. Its annual revenues are $4.5 billion.

SUPERVALU INC.
11840 Valley View Rd.
Eden Prairie   *828-4000*

Supervalu is one of the nation's biggest food wholesalers, serving more than 2,500

Minnesota leads the nation in the production of sugar beets.

Insiders' Tips

independently operated supermarkets around the country — stores that use the Supervalu, Cub Foods, NewMarket, IGA and County Market names, among others — and 100-plus corporate-owned food marts. With $16.1 billion in revenues, it ranks as Minnesota's second-largest publicly held company.

3M COMPANY

3M Center, Maplewood   733-1110

Also known as Minnesota Mining and Manufacturing, 3M is Minnesota's most profitable publicly held business, in 1994 reporting $15 billion in sales. Perhaps not by coincidence, it out-spends all other U.S. manufacturers in research and development, a practice that resulted in sales of more than $1 billion in first-year products, up more than 15 percent from 1993. (Since its founding in 1902, 3M has developed more than 60,000 products.) The company's goal is to generate 30 percent of its sales from products that are less than 5 years old. Scotch Tape, Post-it Notes and other adhesives still make up a big part of the company's sales, but 3M is also into electronic pain blockers used by dentists, fingerprint identification systems and other high-tech devices. Half of its business is overseas. The company employs 23,000 people in Minnesota.

Business Organizations

Need to know more about a Twin Cities business? Want to check out its record with consumers? These organizations can help.

IMPORTANT PHONE NUMBERS

Better Business Bureau	699-1111
Chambers of Commerce:	
Greater Minneapolis	370-9132
Minnesota African American	374-5787
Minnesota American Indian	222-8623
Minnesota Hispanic	222-0569
Northern Dakota County	452-9872
St. Paul Area	223-5000
Suburban Area (St. Paul suburbs)	483-1313
Twin West (western suburbs)	540-0234

Inside
Worship

Even more than the determination of where to eat, shop or find entertainment, the decision of where to worship is personal and often based on intangibles. We each seek out places of worship (or choose not to go to them) in accordance with our upbringing, moral positions, craving for a particular spiritual atmosphere, habits, family situation, ethnic background and even political beliefs.

In the Twin Cities, the choices seem virtually unlimited. The region has a national reputation as a bulwark of Lutheranism, and indeed the dominantly German and Scandinavian ethnic makeup of the population has made the Twin Cities one of North America's largest communities of Lutherans. Religious membership figures, which are notoriously unreliable when it comes to report-

ing true religious affiliation, actually point to Roman Catholics as the state's largest religious group, followed (in order of descending numbers) by members of the Evangelical Lutheran Church of America, Missouri Synod Lutherans, Methodists, Presbyterians, Lutherans in the Wisconsin Evangelical Synod, Assemblies of God church members, Baptists, Jews, Episcopalians and Black Baptists. The number of agnostics and atheists is unknown.

The Twin Cities have many notable places of worship, and not all of them are in buildings. Many people, of course, worship at home and outdoors. Consider what follows as the sketchiest outline of places of worship in the area — a thumbnail guided tour that requires your own spiritual investigation and participation to become genuinely helpful.

Photo: Joe Rossi, Pioneer Press

Cathedral of St. Paul.

African Methodist Episcopal

ST. PETER'S A.M.E. CHURCH
401 E. 41st St., Minneapolis   825-9750

St. Peter's congregation can trace its roots back to the 1880s, when it broke away from St. James A.M.E. Church, which was founded in 1869. The long history of the church is immediately apparent: In front of the building sits a 2-foot-square foundation stone from the congregation's first home.

Baptist

ZION BAPTIST CHURCH
621 Elwood Ave. N., Minneapolis   377-5436

This church provides religious support and social programs for the African-American Baptist community in Minneapolis.

Buddhist

TWIN CITIES BUDDHIST ASSOCIATION
No address   545-2211

This organization sponsors English-language Buddhist services several times each year, with a minister from the Chicago Midwest Buddhist Temple presiding, at First Universalist Church, 3400 Dupont Avenue S., Minneapolis.

GYUTO WHEEL OF DHARMA MONASTERY
687 Second Ave. N.W.
New Brighton   633-8020

Tibetan and American teachers offer a variety of classes on basic Buddhist philosophy, meditation training and monthly ritual observances.

Congregational

PLYMOUTH CONGREGATIONAL CHURCH
1900 Nicollet Ave., Minneapolis   871-7400

Built in 1908 in the English Gothic style, this church has a socially active congregation and a fine performing arts center that hosts theater performances and concerts of all kinds. The Plymouth Music Series uses the church as its home base.

Episcopal

CATHEDRAL CHURCH OF SAINT MARK
519 Oak Grove St., Minneapolis   870-7800

Since 1908 this Gothic Revival fortress has faced Loring Park in Minneapolis. The church is filled with stately art: a detailed carving of John the Baptist by Isaac Kirchmeyer, stone carvings by Twin Cities artist John Rood, lovely carved wood throughout and vibrant Renaissance-style stained-glass windows by Charles J. Connick. Following the plan of many English churches, it has a long nave, side aisles and a deep choir space. The square crenellated tower, damaged by a lightning strike, has been repaired. The church is the home of an Episcopal congregation founded in 1852.

Greek Orthodox

SAINT GEORGE GREEK ORTHODOX CHURCH
1111 Summit Ave., St. Paul   222-6220

St. Paul's Greek Orthodox community receives religious, educational and cultural benefits from this spiritual bulwark, which sponsors classes in the Greek language, dance and music, as well as conducts spiritual services.

SAINT MARY'S GREEK ORTHODOX CHURCH
3450 Irving Ave. S., Minneapolis   825-2247

Walkers and bikers circumnavigating Lake Calhoun can see the gold dome of this Byzantine church peeking above the trees. St. Mary's, which was built in 1957,

WORSHIP DOWNTOWN

WESTMINSTER PRESBYTERIAN CHURCH
A TELLING PRESENCE IN THE CITY

10:30 a.m. - Sanctuary Worship
with
Westminster Choir
8:30 a.m. - Chapel Service
9:15 a.m. - Education Hour for all
Free parking on Sunday morning at Orchestra Hall Ramp

NICOLLET MALL AT TWELFTH STREET 332-3421 DOWNTOWN MINNEAPOLIS

CENTRAL LUTHERAN CHURCH

Join us this Sunday!

9 and 11 am Worship in the Sanctuary

10 am Contemporary Praise Worship

7 pm Evensong at Central

333 12th St. S. • One block east of the Convention Center

HENNEPIN AVENUE UNITED METHODIST CHURCH

511 Groveland, Minneapolis / 871-5303
I-94 West, Lyndale Exit
Sunday Worship 8:30 am, Informal; 9:30 & 11am, Traditional
6:00 pm, Praise & Prayer

PLYMOUTH
CONGREGATIONAL CHURCH
Sunday Service 10:30 a.m.
(10:00 a.m. in summer)
8:30 a.m. Chapel Communion

NICOLLET AT NINETEENTH, MINNEAPOLIS   871-7400

serves as the heart and soul of the Greek Orthodox community in Minneapolis.

Islam

ISLAMIC CENTER OF MINNESOTA
1401 Gardena Ave. N.E.
Fridley   *571-5604*
Islamic people of all backgrounds come to this center for worship, cultural programs, exhibits and other activities.

Jewish

MOUNT ZION TEMPLE
1300 Summit Ave., St. Paul   *698-3881*
This Reform synagogue houses Minnesota's oldest Jewish congregation, which was established in the 1850s. The temple itself dates from 1955 and was designed by Eric Mendelsohn. Other St. Paul area synagogues include Temple of Aaron (Conservative), 698-8874, and Adath Israel Orthodox, 698-8300.

TEMPLE ISRAEL
2324 Hennepin Ave., Minneapolis   *377-8680*
Temple Israel, completed in 1928, is the third Minneapolis home of this congregation and the largest Reform synagogue in the state. Outside, the building is a stately example of the columned Classical Revival style, but the interior betrays the theatrical leanings of its architect, Jack Liebenberg, who designed movie theaters throughout the Upper Midwest. There's a wide balcony, great sightlines and incredible acoustics that make the syna-gogue a favored venue for such ensembles as the Saint Paul Chamber Orchestra. Among the eight other synagogues in Minneapolis and its suburbs are Adath Jeshurun Congregation (Conservative), 545-2424; Beth El Synagogue (Conservative), 920-3512; Beth Jacob (Conservative), 452-2226; Bet Shalom Reform Congregation, 933-8525; Kenesseth Israel Congregation (Orthodox), 920-2183; and Bais Yisroel (Orthodox), 926-7867.

Lutheran

CENTRAL LUTHERAN CHURCH
333 12th St. S., Minneapolis   *870-4416*
Before the growth of the suburbs, Central was the dominant Lutheran church in the Minneapolis area. Located downtown and affiliated with the Evangelical Lutheran Church of America, it still draws many people, is a well-liked concert venue and has a large membership.

LA IGLESIA LUTERANA DE CRISTO EL REDENTOR
784 Jackson St., St. Paul   *291-2757*
Services and classes are mainly in Spanish at this St. Paul Lutheran church in the Hispanic community.

MOUNT OLIVET LUTHERAN CHURCH
5025 Knox Ave. S., Minneapolis   *926-7651*
The size of this southwest Minneapolis church's parking lot testifies to the enormity of its congregation. Mount Olivet, in fact, boasts one of the largest memberships

Insiders' Tips

Minnesota's first church, raised by French priest Lucian Galtier, was completed in St. Paul in 1841.

of any Lutheran church on the continent. Practically every weekend includes several weddings at the church, and services at Christmas and other peak times create traffic jams along 50th Street.

NORWEGIAN LUTHERAN MEMORIAL CHURCH (MINDEKIRKE)
10th Ave. S. and E. 21st St.
Minneapolis   874-0716

This Norwegian church offers Sunday services, social and cultural programs and an annual festival paying tribute to the accomplishments of Leif Eriksson.

Maronite Catholic

ST. MARON'S MARONITE CATHOLIC CHURCH
219 Sixth Ave. N.E., Minneapolis   379-7647

This church, which offers weekly services in the Maronite Catholic tradition and an Aramaic mass, primarily serves people of Lebanese descent. It sponsors classes in Arabic studies, as well as English courses for recent immigrants. Another Maronite Catholic Church in the Twin Cities is Holy Family Maronite Catholic Church in St. Paul, 291-1116.

Metropolitan Community

ALL GOD'S CHILDREN METROPOLITAN COMMUNITY CHURCH
3100 Park Ave. S., Minneapolis   824-2673

The name of this church tells a lot about it. Located in a solidly urban south Minneapolis neighborhood, it opens its doors to people regardless of their economic status, ethnic background or sexual persuasion. Most of its members, in fact, are gay and lesbian, and for the past 20 years the church has been the site of countless holy unions among same-sex couples. In most respects, however, the services at All God's Children are no different from those at many other conservative Christian houses of worship in the Twin Cities, and visitors are often surprised to discover that.

Presbyterian

CENTRAL PRESBYTERIAN CHURCH
500 Cedar St., St. Paul   224-4728

Central Presbyterian dates back to 1889, when St. Paul's downtown was considerably less built up than it is today. Nowadays, commercial buildings butt right up to the church, but the rustic and spacious interior is a welcome sanctuary from the bustle of the city.

WESTMINSTER PRESBYTERIAN CHURCH
1201 Nicollet Mall, Minneapolis   332-3421

The Paul Granlund sculpture at the front of this Nicollet Mall church, *Birth of Freedom*, provides a soaring statement that this is a church that reaches out to the community. Erected in 1897 in the English Gothic style, the church boasts active public programming that includes the Westminster Town Hall Forum, a series of noontime lectures by speakers of national reputation on topics of current interest. The talks are free, open to the public and broadcast on radio nationwide.

Roman Catholic

ASSUMPTION CATHOLIC CHURCH
51 W. Ninth St., St. Paul   224-7536

Built in 1873 for a German-speaking congregation and modeled after the Ludwigskirche in Munich, this downtown church, the oldest Catholic house of worship in St. Paul, raises twin towers that have long been a city landmark. Viewed from the outside, its German Romanesque Revival face appears almost plain, but inside is a gorgeous sanctuary full of murals, statues and a sea of votive candles in richly colored holders. Its designer was Joseph Reidl, who served as architect to the King of Bavaria.

BASILICA OF SAINT MARY
88 N. Seventh St., Minneapolis   333-1381

The Vatican has designated only 31 basilicas in the United States, and this was the first, achieving that rank from Pope Pius XI in 1926. (A basilica is a church that has been singled out for its special religious or historical significance. You can recognize them by the pavilion and silver-belled standard in the sanctuary.) When construction began in 1907, the nave was reputed to be the widest of any church in the world. The neo-Baroque church, which took 18 years to build, has greatly benefited from a recent renovation that brightened up the copper dome and from a rerouting of roads that makes the approach to the building much more attractive. A statue of Father Louis Hennepin stands in front of the basilica, placed there in 1930 to celebrate the 250th anniversary of the missionary's visit to Minnesota.

CATHEDRAL OF SAINT PAUL
239 Selby Ave., St. Paul   228-1766

This great cathedral, a domed structure situated on a hill overlooking downtown St. Paul, is certainly the most famous house of worship in the Twin Cities. Completed in 1915 after nine years of construction, through the dedicated fund-raising and vision of Archbishop John Ireland, it was designed in the Renaissance style by the Parisian architect E.L. Masqueray. It seats 3,000 people and draws crowds not only for religious services but also for organ recitals and choral concerts (avoid the seats behind the pillars). The dome is 175 feet high and 96 feet in diameter.

OUR LADY OF GUADALUPE CHURCH
401 Concord St., St. Paul   228-0506

St. Paul's Hispanic community and Our Lady of Guadalupe are inextricably intertwined, and the church has long been a mainstay of the city's Mexican and Mexican-American people.

OUR LADY OF LOURDES CHURCH
1 Lourdes Pl. S.E., Minneapolis   379-2259

Out Lady of Lourdes, in the heart of old St. Anthony, the birthplace of Minneapolis, is the oldest continuously operated church in the city. It was built in 1854 as a Universalist church and purchased 23 years later by a French-Canadian Catholic congregation, which came to town to mill logs and grain, and now is recognized as a U.S. Historic Landmark. You can still hear French carols there at Christmas, and the church offers guided tours that showcase the original tapestries, stained-glass windows and statues. The church also prepares and sells tourieres, a type of French meat pie.

SAINT LAWRENCE CATHOLIC CHURCH
1201 Fifth St. S.E., Minneapolis   331-7941

Serving southeast Minneapolis for more than 100 years, Saint Lawrence Catholic Church is in Dinkytown, near the University of Minnesota. Its Paulist Fathers focus on reconciliation, evangelization and ecumenism, and they are particularly interested in reaching out to people who feel separated from the Church. Known for its good preaching and spirited music, the church is home to a parish enrollment of about 1,200 diverse people who include many young families, college students and young adults.

SAINT LOUIS CATHOLIC CHURCH
506 Cedar St., St. Paul   224-3379

St. Paul's French Catholics built this

Photo: Chris Polydoroff

The icy landscape creates a memorable sunrise.

church in 1909, and it has always operated in the shadow of the magnificent Cathedral of Saint Paul, less than a mile away. (Emmanuel Masqueray designed both buildings, as well as the Basilica of Saint Mary in Minneapolis.) Nevertheless, it is a venerable parish church built of limestone and brick, with a cruciform interior plan and a pair of beloved towers.

SAINT OLAF CATHOLIC CHURCH
215 S. Eighth St., Minneapolis   332-7471

This church, raised by Scandinavian Catholics in the 1950s, maintains a strong community presence in downtown Minneapolis. Its subdued architecture also presents an interesting contrast to the older and more ornate churches that German, Irish and French Catholics erected elsewhere in the Twin Cities. A Chapel on the Street along Second Avenue S. was added in 1972.

Romanian Orthodox

SAINT MARY'S
ROMANIAN ORTHODOX CHURCH
854 Woodbridge St., St. Paul   488-5669

This historic house of worship, built in 1913 and since designated a historic landmark, is modeled after the church of Sanicolaul Mare in Romania. In addition to a striking carved iconostasis and altar, the church contains archives and old books of church liturgies.

Russian Orthodox

RUSSIAN ORTHODOX CHURCH
OF THE RESURRECTION OF CHRIST
1201 Hathaway Ln. N.E.
Fridley   574-1001

A focal point of the Twin Cities' Christian Russian community, this church offers

language classes and cultural programs, as well as worship opportunities.

Ukrainian Catholic

SAINT CONSTANTINE
UKRAINIAN CATHOLIC CHURCH
515 University Ave. N.E.
Minneapolis   379-2394

Ukrainians and Ukrainian Americans have lived for generations in northeast Minneapolis, and this church is an active member of that ethnic community. Offering Byzantine Ukrainian rites, Saint Constantine's also sponsors Ukrainian social and cultural events and has a sizable and historic collection of Ukrainian art.

Ukrainian Orthodox

SAINT MICHAEL'S
UKRAINIAN ORTHODOX CHURCH
505 N.E. Fourth St., Minneapolis   379-2695

With nearly 200 families in its congregation, this is one of several Ukrainian Orthodox churches in the Twin Cities. It supplements its worship services with the sponsorship of music groups and other cultural organizations.

Unitarian-Universalists

THE FIRST UNITARIAN
SOCIETY OF MINNEAPOLIS
900 Mount Curve Ave.
Minneapolis   377-6608

Founded in 1881, the First Unitarian Society occupies a handsome building two blocks south of Walker Art Center and the Guthrie Theater. It offers Sunday Assemblies renowned for their music featuring the First Unitarian Orchestra and Chorus, Sunday Morning Forums covering a wide range of current events and topics, children's programs, and religious education for kids and young adults, as well as social activities, support for the Twin Cities' Tibetan community and transgenerational events. The Twin Cities has one of the largest concentrations of UUs outside of Boston, and many prominent figures in Minneapolis' history were Universalists.

United Church of Christ

SPIRIT OF THE LAKES
UNITED CHURCH OF CHRIST
2930 13th Ave. S., Minneapolis   724-2313

This is one of a small number of openly gay and lesbian churches in the Twin Cities. Spirit of the Lakes celebrates holy unions and involves itself in efforts to help people with AIDS, combat homophobia and provide a spiritual home for people who have been cast out of other churches.

United Methodist

HENNEPIN AVENUE
UNITED METHODIST CHURCH
511 Groveland Ave., Minneapolis   871-5303

At night you can see a slender, dramatically illuminated spire reaching for the sky near downtown Minneapolis. The spire, 238 feet high, belongs to this Gothic-style church, erected in 1916. The church seats 1,000 people, with an octagonal sanctuary design inspired by the central core of the Cathedral at Ely, England. Charles J. Connick of Boston, who also created the windows at the Cathedral of Saint Mark just down the block, designed this church's fine stained-glass art. In a second floor art gallery is one of America's largest collections of religious paintings owned by a church. Spanning the 16th through 19th centuries and donated early in this century by a church member, lumber baron (and founder of Walker Art Center) T.B. Walker, the collection includes *Ecce Homo* by Antonio Ciseri, *The Annunciation* by Juan Correa de Vivar and *Abraham and the Three Angels* by Pieter Pourbus. The gallery also hosts temporary exhibitions.

Wicca

MINNESOTA CHURCH OF WICCA
No address   827-4474

Wicca adherents are numerous in the Twin Cities, and some of them do not like the pejoratively intended "pagan" or "witch" labels others try to slap upon them. But other Wicca people wear those badges with pride. Falling cleanly outside the Judeo-Christian tradition, Wicca believers follow nature-based practices that have existed in various cultures for millennia.

HealthPartners Clinics.

It's Easy To Find Us
Near Home, Near Work,
Or Somewhere In Between.

If you're looking for a new clinic, you should take a close look at HealthPartners clinics.

Because no matter where you live in the Twin Cities, a HealthPartners clinic isn't far away. From Apple Valley to Coon Rapids, we have 19 clinics throughout the metro area.

And with more than 350 health care professionals practicing in 30 separate specialty areas, we offer a full range of primary and specialty care services.

Our clinics also feature on-site pharmacy, dental, radiology, laboratory and optical services. All to help improve your health.

To learn more, call (612) 883-7000.

HealthPartners

HealthPartners clinics are available to members of HealthPartners, Group Health and Choice Plus health plans.

©1995 HealthPartners

Inside
Healthcare

Not quite at the top of the list of things people associate with Minnesota, but somewhere in the top 10 — behind the cold weather, Garrison Keillor, lakes, loons, wild rice and mosquitoes — is great healthcare. More than a century ago, people with tuberculosis, cholera and other diseases headed here because they believed the climate would help them recover. At the same time, the birth of the celebrated Mayo Clinic in Rochester (about 80 miles south of the Twin Cities) contributed to our healthy image, but it is the statewide excellence of the healthcare system that makes headlines these days. After all, Minnesota boasts the second-highest life expectancy of all the 50 states (behind Hawaii and its warm weather — try to explain it), and the Mayo Clinic can't take credit for all that.

Reduced to its essentials, good health in Minnesota probably boils down to skilled healthcare providers, creative healthcare organizations and government agencies, and few local opportunities for the population to engage in such hazardous activities as cliff diving, oil rig work and eating fresh shellfish.

Overall, if you're sick, this is a good

Photo: Chris Polydoroff, Pioneer Press

Hazelden Treatment Center for alcohol and drug rehabilitation near Center City.

place to be, and if you're well, it's a good place to stay well. A recent *Money Magazine* study placed two of the Twin Cities' health maintenance organizations, Group Health and MedCenters, among the top 10 nationwide. In addition, *U.S. News and World Report's* annual survey of the nation's top hospitals included the University of Minnesota Hospital and Clinic as well as the Mayo Clinic.

For a medical emergency anywhere in Minnesota, call 911. For nonemergency information or help, check out the Twin Cities hospitals and organizations listed here. Remember that the quality of a hospital or HMO (health maintenance organization), in particular, can be difficult to gauge. The best way to determine how well a healthcare organization will meet your particular needs is to ask doctors, former patients and the people who work there. The *Twin Cities Hospitals' Community Service Directory*, which contains information on hospital hotlines, primary care programs, community services, and charity care policies, can also help; to receive a copy call 641-1121.

Hospitals

ABBOTT-NORTHWESTERN HOSPITAL/SISTER KENNY INSTITUTE
2727 Chicago Ave. S.
Minneapolis   863-4000
TTY   863-5165

Among the Twin Cities' private hospitals, the 960-bed Abbott-Northwestern is by far the largest. It offers 24-hour emergency care, inpatient and outpatient treatment, chronic care rehabilitation and cardiac care. Behavioral health programs are a particular strength, with inpatient, residential and outpatient care available for children, adolescents and adults needing treatment for chemical dependency and mental health problems. The Sister Kenny Institute is a specialized acute-care facility that has programs for people with brain injuries, strokes, spinal cord injuries and chronic pain; its phone number is 863-4400.

BETHESDA LUTHERAN MEDICAL CENTER
559 Capitol Blvd., St. Paul   232-2000

Bethesda Lutheran, a member of the HealthEast hospitals group, the largest such health-care aggregate in St. Paul, is a chronic and rehabilitative acute-care facility that provides general medical, respiratory and transitional care services. The facility is near the State Capitol.

CHILDREN'S HOSPITAL
345 N. Smith Ave., St. Paul   220-6000

Children's Hospital offers a range of specialized services for kids, as well as pediatric emergency services and a physician referral service.

CHILDREN'S MEDICAL CENTER OF MINNEAPOLIS
2525 Chicago Ave. S.
Minneapolis   813-6100

This is another highly regarded hospital for kids, with a center devoted to Sudden Infant Death Syndrome, behavioral services, teenage medical services and a physician referral line.

FAIRVIEW RIDGES HOSPITAL
201 E. Nicollet Blvd., Burnsville   892-2000
TTY   892-2077

One of three Fairview hospitals in the Minneapolis area, Fairview Ridges offers adult chemical dependency treatment, pediatric services, prenatal care and 24-hour emergency care. It is just north of the I-35W and I-35E fork off County Road 42.

FAIRVIEW RIVERSIDE MEDICAL CENTER

2450 Riverside Ave., Minneapolis   672-6000
TTY   672-6273

The most centrally located of the Fairview facilities, with easy access from I-94, Fairview Riverside has an institute for athletic medicine, a multiple sclerosis clinic, chemical dependency services for adults and adolescents, MS services, obstetrics, senior care and mental health treatment.

FAIRVIEW SOUTHDALE HOSPITAL

6401 France Ave., Edina   924-5000
TTY   924-5066

Fairview Southdale, with a high reputation for the quality of its treatment, is an acute short-term hospital that provides adult mental health services, adult chemical dependency treatment, senior services, a wound care center, a spine care center, an eating disorders program, preventive cardiology treatment, maternity care and a sleep center.

GILLETTE CHILDREN'S HOSPITAL

200 University Ave. E., St. Paul   291-2848
TDD   229-3928

Gillette offers treatment, rehabilitation and family counseling — as well as customized braces, breathing ventilators and wheelchairs — for kids and teens with brain and spinal cord injuries, cerebral palsy, epilepsy, scoliosis and orthopedic problems and spina bifida.

HENNEPIN COUNTY MEDICAL CENTER

701 Park Ave., Minneapolis   347-2913
TTY   347-6219

A virtual microcosm of the Twin Cities and its people, HCMC, in downtown Minneapolis, is a bustling and pulsing facility, the site of both family pain and personal triumph. As a Level 1 trauma center and burn center, it receives many of the area's most serious and violent emergency cases. Among HCMC's best-known facilities are a regional sleep disorders center, a regional kidney disease program, nurse and midwife services, a head injury program and an arthritis and orthopedic specialty center. A full range of outpatient services includes allergy, endocrine, eye, infectious disease, pediatrics, plastic surgery, psychiatry and speech treatment.

MERCY HOSPITAL

4050 Coon Rapids Blvd.
Coon Rapids   421-8888

Mercy is part of the HealthSpan organization, offering 24-hour emergency care, general medical and surgical treatment, and behavioral healthcare in the northern suburbs.

METHODIST HOSPITAL

6500 Excelsior Blvd.
St. Louis Park   932-5500

Minneapolis' western suburbs are well-served by Methodist Hospital, which has 24-hour emergency service, ReadyCare treatment for minor injuries, a Parkinson's Disease clinic, hospice care, a sleep disor-

---

In 1985, a 40-year-old woman became the world's first female to receive an artificial heart, at Abbott-Northwestern Hospital in Minneapolis.

Insiders' Tips

ders center, a back and neck clinic and a good reputation for treating cardiac cases.

MIDWAY HOSPITAL

1700 University Ave., St. Paul   232-5000

Midway, the most westerly of HealthEast's hospitals, is an acute-care institution that offers full medical and surgical, maternity with special care nurseries, pediatrics, emergency, diagnostic and lab services.

NORTH MEMORIAL MEDICAL CENTER

3300 Oakdale Ave. N.
Robbinsdale   520-5200
TTY   520-5775

North Memorial, the largest hospital in the northern suburbs of Minneapolis, has 24-hour emergency services, a cancer center, a hospice program, a pain institute, perinatal treatment, speech pathology services and an institute for athletic medicine.

ST. FRANCIS
REGIONAL MEDICAL CENTER

325 Fifth Ave., Shakopee   445-2322

For the far western end of the metropolitan area, St. Francis provides about 100 hospital beds and a full range of services.

ST. JOHN'S NORTHEAST HOSPITAL

1575 Bream Ave., Maplewood   232-7000

St. John's, which sits near the intersection of I-694 and Highway 61, is a 140-bed hospital that offers acute-care in a wide range of areas: pediatrics, maternity, surgical and general medical, as well as a variety of outpatient services.

ST. JOSEPH'S HOSPITAL

69 W. Exchange St., St. Paul   232-3000

Now a HealthEast institution, St. Joseph's is the state's oldest hospital. It sprang into being suddenly in 1853 when a cholera epidemic ravaged St. Paul, then a hamlet of barely 1,000 people. Four nuns, sisters in the order of St. Joseph of Carondelet, shouldered the burden of helping the sick. They established their first infirmary in a log church built in 1841, near today's intersection of Minnesota Street and Kellogg Boulevard. Within a year the facility moved to its current site at Ninth and Exchange (then the outskirts of town) and built several structures on the block. St. Joseph's began St. Paul's first ambulance service and, in 1886, was the site of America's first successful gall bladder removal. Now, after much new construction in the 1970s, the oldest part of the medical complex dates from 1922. St. Joseph's is an acute-care hospital offering a broad range of inpatient and outpatient services.

ST. PAUL-RAMSEY MEDICAL CENTER

640 Jackson St., St. Paul   221-3456

Renowned for its emergency services, St. Paul-Ramsey is a teaching hospital with physicians in almost every field of medicine. The only Level 1 trauma center of the Twin Cities' eastern area, it is home to a burn center and participates in the LifeLink III network for local, regional and national medical emergency transport. A ReadyCare clinic treats minor illnesses and injuries as well. The hospital's main building is in downtown St. Paul, with easy access from I-35E and I-94.

SHRINERS HOSPITAL

2025 E. River Rd., Minneapolis   335-5300

Shriners Hospital is a philanthropic rarity: an institution that provides — usually at no charge — pediatric and orthopedic care for kids from qualified families. The money for treatment comes from

Shriners fraternal organizations and their fund-raising efforts.

UNITED HOSPITALS

333 N. Smith Ave., St. Paul   220-8000
TDD/TTY   220-8757

United, close to town, just a block from Children's Hospital of St. Paul, provides all-day/all-night emergency services, prenatal care, and full medical and surgical treatment. It also operates smaller Urgent Care Centers in Eagan, 454-7809, and Roseville, 488-9815.

UNITY HOSPITAL

550 Osborne Rd., Fridley   421-4222

A hospital in the HealthSpan network, Unity provides a full range of medical services, including behavioral health treatment and around-the-clock emergency care.

UNIVERSITY OF MINNESOTA HOSPITAL AND CLINIC

412 Union St. S.E., Minneapolis   626-6000
TDD   626-0990

Whoa, this place is big! With 700 beds and top-flight teaching, research and technological resources, the U of M Hospital is one of the best medical centers in the country. Well-known for its cancer center, heart and lung institute, transplant center and children's hospital, it also has more than 150 other specialty clinics dealing with a wide range of medical problems in audiology, dermatology, ophthalmology, hemophilia, HIV treatment, psychiatry and psychology, women's health and oncology, to name a few. The hospital, on the university campus, also has special clinics for women's cancer, teens at risk, sports medicine and hand rehabilitation, spinal cord injuries and therapeutic radiology.

VETERANS MEDICAL CENTER

1 Veterans Dr., Minneapolis   725-2000

Serving a half-million vets in the entire Upper Midwest region, the Veterans Medical Center offers short-term and extended care, chemical dependency treatment, cardiac care, and many other types of services. If you're a veteran, you probably already know all about it.

Chemical Dependency Programs

Around the world, Minnesota has a reputation as a center of chemical dependency treatment — and the tongue-in-cheek "Land of 10,000 Treatment Centers" label is probably not too far off the mark. Actors, politicians, authors, artists and plenty of people in other occupations have flocked here from far and wide for short- and long-term dependency care.

Literally dozens of dependency treatment centers are scattered throughout the region, and the decision of which to use should be based on such factors as doctors' recommendations, cost, location, treatment philosophy and reputation. Because of its size and fame, however, one treatment provider merits individual mention.

HAZELDEN

P.O. Box 11   (612) 257-4010
Center City, MN 55012   (800) 257-7800

Hazelden, founded in 1949, is a nonprofit organization that offers many techniques to assist people in recovering from chemical dependency. It provides rehabilitation care for adolescents and adults, aftercare and family services, dependency counseling training, and a variety of publications and educational materials.

The main campus is in Center City, a community about a 45-minute drive north of the Twin Cities; another local Hazelden facility is in Plymouth (a Center for Youth and Families). The organization's rehabilitation program, based on the Twelve Steps of Alcoholics Anonymous, typically requires a stay of 10 to 40 days, using individual counseling, group treatment techniques and aftercare. Hazelden's publishing department produces and distributes 1,500 books, videos and audio cassettes for chemically dependent and nondependent people. Many of these materials are available in area bookstores.

Health Maintenance Organizations (HMOs)

The Twin Cities have been fertile ground for the HMO, a prepaid system of healthcare involving physicians and other healthcare providers working in a group practice in conjunction with the services of affiliated hospitals, pharmacies, opticians and other providers. Group Health, now part of the hefty HealthPartners organization, was one of the nation's first HMO groups when it began in 1957. Since then, many other HMOs have sprouted here, and some experts have lauded HMOs as being partly responsible for the high quality and relatively low cost increases of medical care in the state.

Most Twin Citians who receive services from HMOs gain their membership as an employee or retiree benefit. Typically they'll select their HMO from a limited choice that the employer offers. The location of the HMO clinics and costs are often important factors in the enrollment selection.

The Twin Cities area is also out front in the creation of new types of managed medical care organizations. ChoicePlus, an HMO built from scratch in 1992 by some of the region's largest private employers, seems to be succeeding in lowering costs while giving members good care. It includes employees from such businesses as General Mills, 3M, Honeywell, Dayton's and Target stores, and First Bank Systems.

Often, though, it is difficult to evaluate and compare HMO services. A consortium of public and private organizations is currently working on gathering comparable data from HMOs in preparation for the creation of an ambitious guide that will allow consumers to really measure one organization's quality and services against another's. Until that information is available, consumers can do some of their own comparison shopping by checking out two publications. One is a free report on HMO operations in Minnesota, published by the HMO division of Minnesota Department of Health. It includes some basic statistics and performance indicators and can be ordered by calling 282-5649. The second publication is *Minnesota Managed Care Review*, which compares the enrollments, expenses and services of HMOs. It costs $45 and is available by calling 925-9121.

HMOs in Minnesota have undergone frequent mergers and reorganizations in recent years. The largest HMO group in the Twin Cities is Allina Health System with 950,000 Medica and Select Care Health Plan enrollees. Next in size is Health Partners, whose Group Health and Health Partners plans have 652,000 enrollees.

Blue Plus	456-8000
HealthPartners	
Group Health	883-6000
Health Partners	883-6000
Allina Health System	992-2900

Community and Government Health Organizations and Services

AIDS EMERGENCY FUND
P.O. Box 582943, Minneapolis   331-7733

When people living with AIDS encounter financial problems, they can turn to this community fund for assistance.

ALIVENESS PROJECT
730 E. 38th St., Minneapolis   822-7946

People with AIDS or who are HIV-positive can take advantage of the Aliveness Project's massage and chiropractic services and support groups.

AMERICAN CANCER SOCIETY
3316 W. 66th St., Edina   925-2772

This is the Twin Cities chapter of the national health organization focused on eliminating cancer through education, research, services and preventive measures.

CHILDREN'S HEALTH PLAN
444 Lafayette Rd., St. Paul   297-3862

This plan provides outpatient medical and dental care for children from low-income families.

COMMUNITY CLINIC CONSORTIUM
450 N. Syndicate St., St. Paul   644-6555

Sixteen clinics in Ramsey, Hennepin and Washington counties fall under the umbrella of this consortium, each offering health services on a sliding scale of fees. People of all ages can take advantage of the services. The physicians and other healthcare professionals are often volunteers treating their patients out of a dedication to community service.

COMMUNITY UNIVERSITY HEALTHCARE CENTER
2016 16th Ave. S., Minneapolis   627-4774

This clinic offers medical, dental and mental health services, along with access to treatment at the University of Minnesota Hospitals, all on a sliding fee scale. Often the program is fully subscribed and can take no newcomers.

HENNEPIN COUNTY BUREAU OF HEALTH ASSURED CARE PROGRAM
525 Portland Ave., Minneapolis   348-6141

Assured Care provides discounted, income-based access to services offered by the Hennepin County Bureau of Health: medical clinic treatment, dental care, mental health services, eye care, pharmacy, emergency-room treatment and others. The renewal membership is for a year, and it costs nothing to apply.

INDIAN HEALTH BOARD
1315 E. 24th St., Minneapolis   721-9800

Anyone — not only Native Americans — can use the Indian Health Board's medical care, dental care and counseling services, as well as the special programs for diabetics, smokers trying to stop and pregnant women. It bases its fees on the patient's income.

MEDICAL ASSISTANCE
Hennepin County
400 S. Fifth St., Minneapolis   348-2722
Ramsey County
160 E. Kellogg Blvd., St. Paul   266-4007

You must come in person to apply for Medical Assistance, Minnesota's program for people on low incomes.

MINNEAPOLIS HEALTH DEPARTMENT
250 S. Fourth St., Minneapolis   673-2301

The Health Department provides a variety of low-cost services for people in need of nutrition and health education, immunizations, prenatal care and child healthcare.

MINNESOTA AIDS PROJECT
1400 Park Ave. S., Minneapolis 341-2060

An AIDS organization that's been around a while now, Minnesota AIDS Project helps HIV-positive people and those with AIDS in such areas as housing, support groups, referrals and legal aid. The Aids Line at 373-2437 offers information on additional services.

MNCARE
297-3862

A couple of years ago, Minnesota beat the Clintons to the draw and made U.S. history by becoming the first state to create a comprehensive health coverage package for uninsured and underinsured people. Inpatient and outpatient coverage is available for lower and moderate income individuals and families. The program bases its charges on a sliding scale in accordance with the insured's income, and the processing time is supposed to be quick. Call for current rates and qualifications.

MINNESOTA COMPREHENSIVE HEALTH ASSOCIATION
P.O. Box 64566, St. Paul 456-5290

People whom other insurers turn down as "uninsurable" can receive medical coverage through this organization's plan, even those with pre-existing conditions and in high-risk occupations. The rates are not cheap (about 25 percent higher than other forms of health insurance), but low-income people receive some breaks.

PILOT CITY HEALTH CENTER
1313 Penn Ave. N., Minneapolis 520-8800

Charging fees based on a sliding scale,

this health clinic offers medical, dental, mental health and social service assistance to people in the community.

PLANNED PARENTHOOD OF MINNESOTA
1965 Ford Pkwy., St. Paul 698-2406

Five Planned Parenthood clinics in the Twin Cities provide women with a variety of healthcare, counseling and reproductive health services.

RED DOOR CLINIC
525 Portland Ave., Minneapolis 348-6363

Operated by Hennepin County, this clinic specializes in the detection of sexually transmitted diseases and in health counseling.

WOMEN'S AND CHILDREN'S HEALTH PROGRAMS
6601 Shingle Creek Pkwy.
Brooklyn Center 569-2670

Services available for women here include family planning, prenatal care and delivery, Pap and pelvic exams, nutrition and health information and pregnancy testing. For kids, developmental, vision, hearing and speech screenings are offered, as well as immunizations, referrals and exams. Patients pay fees based on their income and family size.

Healthcare Phone and Referral Services

These phone lines provide information on specific health problems or give out referrals to doctors, usually physicians on the staff of the sponsoring hospital or part of a group practice or professional group. If you're looking for a physician, don't hesitate to ask friends and co-workers for referrals, as well.

American Board of
Medical Specialties (800) 776-2378

Children's Hospital of St. Paul	
Physician Referral Service	220-6880
Fairview HealthWise	
Connection	672-7272
HealthEast Tele-Health	232-2600
Hennepin County Medical	
Center Poison Control	347-3141
Methodist Hospital Health	
Directions	932-5500
North Memorial Medical	
Center's The Professionals	520-5555
Ramsey Poison Center	221-2113
Ramsey Tel-Med	221-8686
United Hospital Medformation	863-3333
University of Minnesota Hospital	
and Clinic Cancer Line	626-5555
University of Minnesota Hospital and	
Clinic Physician Referral	626-6000
Women's Cancer Resource	
Center	338-8544

Inside
Community Service and Volunteerism

Minnesotans may have cold noses and frostbitten fingers (at least six months a year), but our hearts are warm and giving.

Volunteerism is thriving in the Twin Cities area, where thousands of individuals pull up their shirt sleeves and lend a helping hand to social service agencies, charities and arts organizations. They organize high-falutin' symphony balls, walk their soles bare for AIDS, read to the blind, befriend troubled teens, deliver meals and smiles to shut-ins, accompany 3rd-graders on field trips and even clean the kennels at the animal shelters. Hey, somebody's got to do it!

Perhaps the impulse to reach out and help is partly a natural response to our living conditions. The truth is, our winters can be life-threatening and cruel — just ask anyone who's been stalled on a desolate Minnesota highway on a 30-below night. Minnesotans think nothing of pulling over to share jumper cables or push a car out of a snowbank.

Likewise, when tornadoes threaten and occasionally strike entire communities, neighbors help neighbors without a second thought. During the cataclysmic Mississippi River floods of spring 1993, hundreds of Twin Citians flocked to the aid of stressed-out Iowa river towns. Boarding bus caravans and free Northwest Airlines flights, they headed south to pack sandbags, clean up mud-laden homes and console residents.

Superbowl 1992, held in Minneapolis during a frigid January, was a rousing success mainly because of the hearty goodwill of thousands of local residents who volunteered as guides, greeters and hosts to the throngs of visitors.

That spirit of altruism seems to have carried over into other aspects of daily living. In study after study, Minnesota is recognized as a place where people volunteer at a higher rate than the national average.

As the adage goes, when you volunteer, you help yourself as well as helping others. In addition to the satisfaction that comes from giving of yourself, volunteering is a way to make new friends, learn about your community and develop leadership and people skills.

To find the volunteer slot that's right for you, call around to local hospitals, nursing homes, social service agencies, churches, senior citizens centers and schools. They're all crying for help. Nature centers and parks, too, always need volunteer tour guides, hosts and cleanup crews in the summer and cross-country trail guides in the winter. Or, if you're feeling overwhelmed by it all and need a little guidance, call one of the following agencies that can refer you to the right organization.

THE UNITED WAY VOLUNTEER CENTER

404 S. Eighth St., Minneapolis   340-7621

This referral service matches individuals to more than 5,000 volunteer opportunities in 600 Twin Cities agencies and charities. It predominantly serves the Minneapolis/west metro area. The Volunteer Center also regularly publishes lists of specific volunteer opportunities in the Minneapolis-based Star Tribune, as well as in several suburban newspapers.

ST. PAUL VOLUNTEER CENTER

2485 Como Ave., St. Paul   644-2044

Like its counterpart in Minneapolis, this center also refers individuals to volunteer opportunities — predominantly in the St. Paul/east metro area. Its database includes more than 4,000 opportunities in 600 agencies. The St. Paul Volunteer Center also publishes lists of volunteer opportunities in the St. Paul Pioneer Press and east-metro suburban newspapers.

Other Volunteer Resources

COMMUNITY VOLUNTEER SERVICE

2300 Orleans St. W., Stillwater   439-7434

This agency refers volunteers to agencies and charities throughout Washington County. It also operates a senior center and a bureau for holiday volunteering.

MINNESOTA OFFICE OF CITIZENSHIP AND VOLUNTEER SERVICES

Department of Administration
117 University Ave., St. Paul   296-4731

The MOCVS is an information clearinghouse and resource center for materials about the management of volunteer programs and the engaging of citizens in the public policy process.

RETIRED & SENIOR VOLUNTEER PROGRAM

(For Minneapolis)   331-4467

RETIRED SENIOR VOLUNTEER PROGRAM

(For St. Paul)   221-2820

Brother, Can You Spare a Dime?

For some, community service may simply take the form of signing a check or making a financial pledge. In the Twin Cities, studies show that 25 percent of all employees contribute funds to charities. The generosity doesn't stop at the office, but continues at home. *NonProfit Times*, a publication on nonprofit management, has rated the Twin Cities the nation's most responsive area for telemarketing appeals for charity. The magazine also ranks the area ninth nationally in terms of its overall fund-raising climate. The following is a good source of information for those who are faced with financial requests from charities.

THE MINNESOTA CHARITIES REVIEW COUNCIL

46 E. Fourth St., Ste. 636   224-7030
St. Paul   (800) 733-4483

This private, nonprofit organization serves as an independent source of information about national and local charities. It can be a real help for consumers who are inundated by telephone solicitors and confused about where their valuable dollars are going. The council's database contains information on more than 3,000 charities.

Photo: Joe Oden, Pioneer Press

Garrison Keillor's radio program "A Prairie Home Companion" is broadcast from St. Paul's Fitzgerald Theater.

Inside
Media

You may not realize it, but the Twin Cities is a media powerhouse of sorts. Skeptical? For starters, it's one of the few metropolitan areas of its size that still has competing daily newspapers. It also has competing alternative weeklies and a pair of battling city magazines. The area boasts the nation's largest public-radio system and is the headquarters of a public-radio network that out-distributes National Public Radio. And in the realm of moving images, movie fans have rushed to the theaters to see such made-in-Minnesota movies as *Untamed Heart*, *The Mighty Ducks*, *Grumpy Old Men*, *Iron Will* and *Little Big League*.

What do you expect from a city where winter sets in for a five-month stay starting in November — that people will sit outside and revel in the chill? (Well, some do. See the chapter on Winter's Wonderland.) Instead, Twin Citians are prodigious readers, listeners and viewers, and this town offers plenty to engage their eyes and ears.

Publications

Daily Newspapers

ST. PAUL PIONEER PRESS

345 Cedar St., St. Paul	222-5011
Home delivery	222-1234

This paper, the morning daily that is a publisher of this *Insiders' Guide*®, can trace its origins to some of the earliest ink spilled in Minnesota Territory. Among its direct ancestors are the *Minnesota Pioneer*, the state's first newspaper, founded in 1849; the *St. Paul Daily Democrat*, which arrived on the scene soon afterward; and the *St. Paul Daily Press*, spawned by the Civil War. Nowadays the *Pioneer Press* is part of the Knight-Ridder newspaper group, has a daily circulation of more than 200,000 (nearly 300,000 on Sunday) and is the primary paper serving the 40 percent of the Twin Cities that lies in the east metropolitan area — Ramsey, Washington and Dakota counties — along with parts of western Wisconsin. No home delivery is available to most addresses in Minneapolis and points west, although the *Pioneer Press* is widely available at newsstands and vending machines throughout the Twin Cities.

The paper is best-known for its thorough and award-winning sports coverage, its high-quality and wide-ranging feature writing (which earned the paper two Pulitzer Prizes during the 1980s), and its attractive, reader-friendly design.

Another popular feature of the *Pioneer Press* is its Bulletin Board section, an indescribable collection of reader-supplied gossip, rant, cute kid stories and general observations of life displaying varying levels of couth and intelligence. It has proven so popular that the paper has published three anthologies. Also take note of The Line, the newspaper's telephone audiotext service, which supplies movie reviews, stock prices, sports scores, historical sound clips and, perhaps uniquely, bird calls; the number is 222-1000. In late 1995 the paper became Minnesota's first commercial daily newspaper fully available on the Internet at http://www.pioneerplanet.com.

STAR TRIBUNE
425 Portland Ave. S.
Minneapolis   673-4000

The sole survivor of 130 years of journalistic wars, cannibalism and mergers in Minneapolis, this morning daily is one of the nation's only metropolitan papers lacking the name of a city on its masthead. The reason is that the *Star Tribune* publishes separate editions for Minneapolis, St. Paul and outstate Minnesota, generating a daily circulation of more than 400,000 (nearly 700,000 on Sunday). Consequently, home delivery is available throughout the Twin Cities area. Owned by the Cowles publishing empire, the paper has dour columnists (excepting the deliciously irreverent C.J., the purveyor of gossip), solid entertainment and business reporting, spirited food writing, a page called News with a View that mixes journalism and personal essay and enough syndicated advice columnists to satisfy the cravings of the worst addict. The paper's Minnesota Poll has taken important opinion samplings of the state's residents for many decades, and the *Star Tribune* earned a Pulitzer Prize in 1990 for investigative reporting.

Like its crosstown rival, the paper offers several services to readers over the phone, including stock prices, music clips, movie reviews, late-breaking news updates and fax-on-demand information. The *Star*

Tribune launched a complete newspaper and backfile service for online subscribers in 1995.

Other Newspapers

THE AMERICAN JEWISH WORLD
4509 Minnetonka Blvd.
Minneapolis   920-7000

The World is an award-winning weekly publication that has served as the voice of Minnesota's Jewry for decades. It includes local news, international news with a local slant, religious reports, profiles, events listings and commentary.

ASIAN AMERICAN PRESS
422 University Ave., St. Paul   224-6570

Members of Minnesota's Asian and Pacific Islander community are the audience of this weekly newspaper, which boasts a surprisingly high number of news stories from the international realm. Topics include business, the arts, politics and education.

ASIAN PAGES
P.O. Box 11932, St. Paul 55111   869-1232

With readers throughout Minnesota, Iowa and Wisconsin, the biweekly Asian Pages features softer news than *Asian American Press*, serving as a resource in the areas of immigration, personal finance, the arts, cooking and education.

CITY PAGES
401 N. Third St., Ste. 550
Minneapolis   375-1015

One of two alternative news week-

Insiders' Tips

Twin Citians will never admit it, but it's true: C.J.'s column is the first thing they read in the *Star Tribune*.

Tune in Your Radio Favorites

For folks out there in radio land who might want a complete listing of where to tune to meet their up-to-the-minute radio mood, here's a handy one for you.

AM Stations

KTCJ	690	Progressive rock
WMIN	740	Hits of the '40s, '50s and '60s
KUOM	770	College alternative
WCCO	830	News, general interest
KTIS	900	Inspirational music, talk
KMJZ	950	Smooth jazz
KMZZ	980	Hard rock
WCTS	1030	Religious music, news
KFAN	1130	Sports
WIMN	1220	Nostalgia
WWTC	1280	For children
WMNN	1330	News, information
KLBB	1400	Nostalgia
KQRS	1440	Album-oriented rock
KDWA	1460	'50s and '60s music
KBCW	1470	Country music
KSTP	1500	News, talk
KKCM	1530	Christian music
KYCR	1570	Religious programming
WIXK	1590	Country music

FM Stations

KBEM	88.5	Jazz
WCAL	89.3	Classical music, news
KMOJ	89.9	Soul, blues, gospel, reggae, jazz
KFAI	90.3	Music, news, talk shows
KNOW	91.1	News, information
KQRS	92.5	Album-oriented rock
KEGE	93.7	Modern rock
KSTP	94.5	Adult contemporary music
KNOF	95.3	Religious programming, music
WLKX	95.9	Country music
KTCZ	97.1	Progressive rock
KTIS	98.5	Religious programming, news
KSJN	99.5	Classical music
WBOB	100.3	Country music
KDWB	101.3	Contemporary hit music
KEEY	102.1	Country music
WLTE	102.9	Light rock
KMJZ	104.1	Smooth jazz
WREV	105.1/105.3	Alternative
KCFE	105.7	New adult contemporary
WIXK	107.1	Country music
KQQL	107.9	Golden oldies

lies in the Twin Cities, *City Pages* is a bit more of a muckraker than its rival, *Twin Cities Reader*, more often featuring exposés and investigative reporting. *City Pages* also seems aimed at a somewhat younger audience, with strong coverage of the arts (especially music) and sports, along with good cartoons. Free, it's available throughout the area in racks.

FINANCE AND COMMERCE

615 S. Seventh St., Minneapolis   333-4244

This weekly newspaper is the place to look for legal notices and lists of real estate transactions, bankruptcy petitions, legal judgments, liens and new business openings. Each issue also contains several news stories, mainly wire service articles.

INSIGHT NEWS

1815 Bryant Ave N., St. Paul   588-1313

In-depth stories, sports news, arts coverage and commentary are the strengths of this weekly newspaper for the African-American community. *Insight* also features business and employment news, health stories and a community calendar. It is available free at points throughout the Twin Cities.

MINNEAPOLIS ST. PAUL CITYBUSINESS

527 Marquette Ave. S., Ste. 300
Minneapolis   288-2100

CityBusiness presents a thorough weekly roundup of the business news of the Twin Cities, with a sprinkling of humor, company profiles, opinion and commercial statistics, along with an every-issue top-25 list sketching the movers and shakers in a variety of business endeavors. It's available at newsstands and by subscription.

MINNEAPOLIS SPOKESMAN/ ST. PAUL RECORDER

3744 Fourth Ave. S., Minneapolis   827-4021
909B Selby Ave., St. Paul   224-4886

These weekly papers for the Twin Cities' African-American community, produced by the area's oldest black publishing firm (founded in 1935), offer local and national news, business stories, sports reports, a church directory and the opinions of several columnists.

MINNESOTA CHRISTIAN CHRONICLE

1619 Portland Ave. S.
Minneapolis   339-9579

Established in 1978, this weekly newspaper presents local and national Christian news, pro-life commentary and an extensive events calendar.

THE MINNESOTA WOMEN'S PRESS

771 Raymond Ave., St. Paul   646-3968

This thoughtful and well-written biweekly newspaper aims to approach the news through personal perspectives, relating the diversity as well as the shared experiences of women. Many of the stories focus on individual women and their work, and there are also articles on finance, the arts, politics and lifestyles. Some of the most provocative writing is in columns and first-person pieces. *The Women's Press* is distributed free at more than 350 locations throughout the area.

THE NATIVE AMERICAN PRESS

7800 Metro Parkway, Ste. 300
Bloomington   851-0010

Heavy with local and national news about Native Americans and their communities, the weekly *Press* packs a lot of information into each issue. It includes opinion pieces and the writings of columnists as well. It's free and available at several locations in the area.

SKYWAY NEWS/FREEWAY NEWS

15 S. Fifth St., Minneapolis   375-9222

These free weeklies, available in racks in downtown and suburban Minneapolis and downtown St. Paul, serve a readership mostly made up of commuter office workers. They consider themselves the community papers of their areas, and their coverage of business, retail and development issues within their geographic realms is good. Downtown arts and entertainment coverage is also commendable. Special issues each year devoted the St. Paul Winter Carnival and the Minneapolis Aquatennial are great introductions to these big events and often offer historical perspective as well. Both of the Minneapolis and St. Paul Skyway News print useful maps of its city's skyway system in each issue.

TWIN CITIES READER

10 S. Fifth St., Ste. 200
Minneapolis   321-7300

The *Reader* is a longtime staple of consumers of so-called alternative news, although the publication has grown more respectable with age. Long gone are the explicit ads seeking sexual encounters; they've been replaced by the area's biggest selection of tastefully written "eligibles" ads, along with an editorial emphasis on city and state politics, media coverage and the arts. The paper (available free at racks in office buildings, restaurants and places of entertainment) also contains thorough events listings.

Magazines and Other Publications

COLORS

2608 Blaisdell Ave. S.
Minneapolis   874-0494

Self-described as a "journal of opinion by writers of color" in Minnesota, *Colors* is skillfully written, attractively designed and always interesting to read. Recent issues have presented interviews, first-person essays, examinations of social issues, a lively letters page and a calendar of events.

COMPUTERUSER

220 S. Sixth St., Ste. 500
Minneapolis   339-7571

Once strictly a Twin Cities publication, the monthly *ComputerUser* now boasts distribution in several other areas of the country. The tabloid covers computer technology, software and office equipment with grace and wit, allowing even non-nerds to gain something from reading it. Its listings of user groups and BBS linkups are especially useful. *ComputerUser* is free and available at public libraries, computer stores and other pick-up points.

CORPORATE REPORT MINNESOTA

105 S. Fifth St., Ste. 100
Minneapolis   338-4288

Often subdued in tone and quite corporate-looking, this monthly magazine profiles CEOs, provides in-depth examinations of Minnesota industries and keeps up with business trends throughout the

Reading the *Pioneer Press'* Bulletin Board is a great way to start the day.

state. It is well-written, though not often explosive. Each year it publishes an encyclopedic and highly successful directory of Minnesota's public and privately held businesses.

FAMILY TIMES
2912 Xenwood Ave. S.
St. Louis Park   922-6186

Family Times, a monthly tabloid focusing on issues concerning Minnesota's families, has a circulation of 65,000 and is distributed free at stores, restaurants, medical offices and clinics, libraries and other public facilities. It covers such topics as foster parenting, child rearing, children's education, family medicine, entertainment and new products and services.

LAVENDER LIFESTYLES MAGAZINE
2344 Nicollet Ave. S., Ste. 50
Minneapolis   871-2237

With the demise of the *Gaze* newspaper in 1995, *Lavender Lifestyles Magazine* became the Twin Cities' most influential publication for gay men and lesbians. A bimonthly, it offers personality profiles and coverage of the arts, sports, astrology, community events, social issues and popular culture. It's free and available at racks around the region.

MINNESOTA HISTORY
345 Kellogg Blvd. W., St. Paul   296-6126

A quarterly magazine published by the Minnesota Historical Society, *Minnesota History* presents longish and satisfying explorations into the state's past, covering everything from architecture, politics, ethnic history, popular culture and transportation to new books and prominent personalities. The photos and maps, largely drawn from the Society's own collection, are gorgeous.

MINNESOTA MONTHLY
10 S. Fifth St., Ste. 1000
Minneapolis   371-5800

Award-winning in its design and distinguished in its writing, *Minnesota Monthly* covers the state's (primarily the Twin Cities') lifestyle, venturing into the arts, home design and planning, politics, current affairs and profiles, with occasional forays into semi-investigative reporting. Each year, the magazine sponsors a writing competition and a photography contest. Available on newsstands, *Minnesota Monthly* is also sent free to members of Minnesota Public Radio, and the network's radio schedule occupies the last quarter of the magazine.

MINNESOTA PARENT
401 N. Third St., Ste. 550
Minneapolis   375-1203

Each month, *Minnesota Parent* serves up an assortment of articles on living with kids. No facet of the family experience seems unturned: Food, entertainment, shopping, books and software, health, art and travel are all present in abundance. The free tabloid publication is distributed throughout the region.

MINNESOTA SPORTS
15 S. Fifth St., Ste. 800
Minneapolis   375-9045

If you run, bike, golf, swim, lift weights, ski, skate or camp, you should check out this monthly publication full of events listings, nutrition advice, gear reviews, motivational techniques and sports news. It's crammed with information and is available free at pickup points throughout the area.

MINNESOTA'S JOURNAL OF LAW AND POLITICS
527 Marquette Ave., Ste. 2301
Minneapolis   338-8808

This is a brash, smart, funny and irreverent magazine about attorneys and politicians, and you should find a copy even if you normally have no interest in the machinations that take place in the capitol or in our legal system. Its writing is great and its covers are often outrageous.

MPLS.ST.PAUL

220 S. Sixth St., Ste. 500
Minneapolis   339-7571

With a long string of national city-magazine awards and a hefty circulation, *Mpls.St.Paul* is influential, often-quoted and well-read. Its directories of the best in everything from doctors to restaurants to schools are sensible and accurate, and the magazine also delivers good celebrity coverage, travel reporting and profiles.

TWIN CITIES BUSINESS MONTHLY

220 S. Sixth St., Ste. 500
Minneapolis   339-7571

A newcomer in the area's crowded field of business publications, this one has made its mark by offering snazzy design and an emphasis on the people in business. Its regular columns, however, are devoted to such topics as personal finance, home businesses and (no kidding) the prostate gland. The feature articles are long, but they'll generally hold your interest.

Television

TV Stations

KARE (CHANNEL 11)
546-1111

This station is the local NBC affiliate.

Its news department, traditionally strong in weather (which is by no means a topic of peripheral interest in temperature-challenged Minnesota) and seemingly aimed at a slightly younger viewership than some other stations, sometimes tends toward the sensationalistic but offers strong on-air talent.

KLGT (CHANNEL 23)
646-2300

KLGT, a Warner Network station, is the rerun capital of the TV dial. "I Love Lucy," "Designing Women," "Newhart," "Andy Griffith" and "Saved by the Bell" are some of the current offerings. It carries some pretty good old movies late at night too. In 1995, KLGT began airing a WCCO-TV alternative newscast that highlights "softer" news.

KMSP (CHANNEL 9)
944-9999

KMSP is the biggie among the area's independents. Its weekday evening schedule is dominated by an hour-long 9 PM newscast, giving the station added time to present local stories in more detail. Because of KMSP's limited resources in the past, its reporters had the reputation of often being the last to arrive at a news scene, but this may be changing.

KSTP (CHANNEL 5)
645-5555

KSTP, the ABC affiliate, has a distinguished history of innovation. During the 1940s it became the first TV station in the

Twin Citians *love* to hate sports curmudgeon Sid Hartman on WCCO-AM Radio and in the *Star Tribune*.

Insiders' Tips

Midwest to air a daily newscast and later was the first full-color station in the world. In reporting, its strength has traditionally been its quick response to spot news — disasters, fires and other emergencies. KSTP was also the only station in the state to keep complete archives of its news stories going all the way back to 1948, and this valuable collection was recently donated to the Minnesota Historical Society for public access.

TWIN CITIES PUBLIC TELEVISION
KTCA (CHANNEL 2)
KTCI (CHANNEL 17)
222-1717

Headquartered since 1989 in a new television center in downtown St. Paul, Twin Cities Public Television is an active producer of programming and enjoys a devoted following. Its self-produced shows include "Newton's Apple," "Arts on 2," "Almanac," "Tape's Rolling!" and "NewsNight Minnesota," the latter a news show introduced in 1994 that aims to explore meaty issues and avoid fluff. Channel 2, which usually goes off the air at 1 AM, airs the bulk of the programming, while Channel 17, shutting down at midnight, broadcasts a continuous radar weather summary during the day and repeats KTCA airings at night.

KXLI (CHANNEL 41)
(612) 262-8666

Broadcasting from the St. Cloud area, KXLI is an independent station with programming that includes movies, reruns and Christian shows.

WCCO (CHANNEL 4)
339-4444

The Twin Cities' longtime CBS affili-ate, WCCO has evolved into a community-oriented station with a news department strong in in-depth reporting, crime stories and sports. In 1994, it introduced family-sensitive newscasts, in addition to its regular news shows. The innovation gained national attention. The station also recently began offering an alternative-style news show on Channel 23.

WFTC (CHANNEL 29)
424-2929

The region's FOX affiliate, WFTC airs "Star Trek: The Next Generation" and "Seinfeld" reruns, as well as NFL and Viking Football games, National Hockey League games and, during football season, "The Warren Moon Show."

Cable TV

Several cable TV firms serve the Twin Cities' municipalities. Rather surprisingly, considering the long winter in these parts and the need to burrow in, the Twin Cities has one of the nation's lowest cable TV subscription percentages — fewer than half the households.

AMERICAN WIRELESS SYSTEMS
452-8010

This small, upstart company offers cable services within 30 miles of downtown Minneapolis.

MEREDITH CABLE
483-9999

This company serves the northern suburbs of Roseville, Columbia Heights and Anoka.

MIDWEST SPORTS CHANNEL
330-2678

This is a local all-sports cable channel.

PARAGON CABLE TV
522-2000

Paragon serves Minneapolis and many of the western suburbs.

CONTINENTAL CABLEVISION
222-3333

Continental is the cable company for St. Paul and suburbs.

Radio

With a few notable exceptions, radio stations in the Twin Cities are much like they are any place else in the United States. At last count, we have 42 places to park on the AM and FM dials, and listeners have the usual choices of formats: country-western (shop around among five stations), album-oriented rock, classic rock, top 40, alternative rock, oldies, urban contemporary, adult contemporary, gospel, contemporary Christian, classical, jazz, news and sports/talk.

A few of the stations, however, do stand out as distinctive, either for historical, cultural or program-related reasons.

KBEM 88.5 FM
627-2833

If not for this little noncommercial station that broadcasts from studios in Minneapolis' North High School (the station is operated by the Minneapolis Board of Education), we'd have precious little jazz to hear on the radio. The station also airs a fine bluegrass show on Saturday mornings and is the absolute best source of traffic information, courtesy of reports from the Minnesota Department of Transportation.

KFAI 90.3 FM
341-3144

The "fresh air" slogan of this community supported station is no lie. You can pick up French, African, urban folk, bluegrass, Greek and Russian music off its airwaves, along with tunes from many other parts of the globe. Its signal doesn't always carry far, and its on-air folks are sometimes discombobulated, but a generous spirit and appreciation for diversity are apparent in its broadcasting.

KMOJ 89.9 FM
377-0594

Though frequently beset by organizational troubles, this noncommercial station has successfully served as the voice of the Twin Cities' African-American community for many years. Frequently described as "urban contemporary" in format, its programming actually ranges from gospel to rap, with some very savvy DJs calling the shots.

MINNESOTA PUBLIC RADIO
KNOW 91.1 FM
KSJN 99.5 FM
290-1500

Who would have thought that public radio, formerly the bastion of ill-clothed techno-geeks, classical music eggheads and paroled campus radicals, could evolve into an efficient, well-organized, financially strong and popular medium? To everyone's surprise, it happened years ago in Minnesota.

Minnesota Public Radio, a network of 27 stations scattered throughout the Upper Midwest (there's even one in Idaho!), has grown into the nation's biggest producer of shows, gatherers of listeners and raisers of money among the nation's public radio enterprises. Its nationally distributed programs include "St. Paul Sunday Morning," Garrison Keillor's "A Prairie Home Companion," "Sound Money," "Pipedreams" and broadcasts of Minnesota Orchestra and Saint Paul Chamber Orchestra concerts.

It's also a founder of Public Radio International (headquartered in Minneapolis and formerly called American Public Radio), a program distributor whose shows match — and perhaps surpass — the listenership of National Public Radio's programs. In the Twin Cities, MPR operates three stations: KSJN (99.5 FM), a primarily classical music station that dabbles in eccentric popular-music programming during the morning drive time; and KNOW (91.1 FM), whose all-news format, international programming and intelligent, award-winning reporting make it one of the best sources of information among all the choices in the Twin Cities media.

WCAL 89.3 FM
(800) 222-9225

An improved signal now makes WCAL accessible to most Twin Cities radios. Broadcasting from St. Olaf College in Northfield, this public radio station (which is not part of the Minnesota Public Radio network) is a great place to tune in to hear amiable voices and the relaxing complexities of Baroque fugues. Founded more than 75 years ago, WCAL is one of the nation's first publicly supported stations, so you can blame them for every listener support drive that's ever been broadcast.

WCCO 830 AM
370-0611

Although its legendary Arbitron ratings have slipped some over the years, WCCO remains one of the most dominant stations in any radio market in the nation. When a blizzard threatens, you can bet that nearly 100 percent of the parents in the Twin Cities tune in to hear about district school closings. And when folks anywhere in the Upper Midwest want to find out Minnesota's take on an issue — the station's signal really carries — they tune in as well.

On the air since 1922, WCCO has had plenty of time to perfect its approach. Its on-air talent conveys a warm and neighborly persona, not too intellectual and not too cynical. Its talk shows sometimes sound more like family reunions than the cutting, ego-powered exercises that can take place elsewhere on the dial. In recent years, the "Good Neighbor" has become more like other stations, but folks still tune in for weather and Twins baseball.

WWTC 1280 AM
926-1280

This spot on the dial is reserved for kids. The home of Radio AAHS, this station delivers children's music, commentary and other programming, and 25 percent of the kids in the Twin Cities listen to it. Satellites carry its signal to 16 other full-time children's radio stations around the country.

Inside
Public Services

If you're just moving to the Twin Cities, you'll need to get your phone and electric service started. If you've lived here awhile, you may want to complain about a dog on the loose, find out where to register to vote or learn the location of the nearest public library. Whatever the crisis or reason, and for better or worse, we rely on those indispensable services of government and utility companies to help us get through the day.

Especially in the Twin Cities, where two large metropolises lie side by side, the responsibilities of each level of government can be confusing. In addition to the federal-state-county-city hierarchy that exists all over the country, we can boast an additional layer of metropolitan councils, multicounty agencies that oversee certain government services for the whole metropolitan area. You'll find more about that later in this chapter.

One important thing to remember: For any fire, police or medical emergency, call 911 from anywhere in Minnesota. That's the fastest way to receive help in life-threatening situations.

Government junkies will find the Citizens League's frequently updated *Public Affairs Directory* a useful resource. Call 338-0791 for more information.

A final note on one Minnesota political peculiarity: The names of our political parties. The Democratic party is called the Democrat-Farmer Labor Party, or DFL. It reflects the Democrats' merger with the left-leaning Farmer Labor Party a half-century ago. Until recently, Republicans here were called Independent Republicans, or IR — a name originally in-

Minnesota State Capitol in St. Paul.

Photo: Joe Rossi, Pioneer Press

tended to distance Minnesota Republicans from the national Republican party, a souvenir of the Republican-bashing days of the late '70s.

U.S. Senators and Congressional Representatives

Minnesota sends two senators and eight representatives to the U.S. Congress. If you want to urge your representative to support legislation, oppose legislation or pay attention to your governmental views and concerns, these are the people to contact.

Senators

ROD GRAMS (R)
U.S. Senate, 261 Dirksen Senate Office Bldg.
Washington, DC 20510
Local office   427-5921
Washington office   (202) 224-3244

PAUL WELLSTONE (DFL)
U.S. Senate, 717 Hart Senate Office Bldg.
Washington, DC 20510-2303
Local office   645-0323
Washington office   (202) 224-5641

Congressional Representatives

GIL GUTKNECHT
(R, FIRST DISTRICT)
425 Cannon House Office Bldg.
Washington, DC 20515
Local office   (507) 252-9841
Washington office   (202) 225-2472

DAVID MINGE
(DFL, SECOND DISTRICT)
115 Longworth House Office Bldg.
Washington, DC 20515
Local office   (612) 269-9311
Washington office   (202) 225-2331

JIM RAMSTAD
(R, THIRD DISTRICT)
103 Cannon House Office Bldg.
Washington, DC 20515
Local office   881-4600
Washington office   (202) 225-2871

BRUCE F. VENTO
(DFL, FOURTH DISTRICT)
2304 Rayburn House Office Bldg.
Washington, DC 20515-2304
Local office   224-4503
Washington office   (202) 225-6631

MARTIN OLAV SABO
(DFL, FIFTH DISTRICT)
2336 Rayburn House Office Bldg.
Washington, DC 20515
Local office   348-1649
Washington office   (202) 225-4755

WILLIAM P. LUTHER
(DFL, SIXTH DISTRICT)
1419 Longworth House Office Bldg.
Washington, DC 20515
Local office   730-4949
Washington office   (202) 225-2271

COLLIN PETERSON
(DFL, SEVENTH DISTRICT)
1314 Longworth House Office Bldg.
Washington, DC 20515
Local office   (218) 847-5056
Washington office   (202) 225-2165

JAMES L. OBERSTAR
(DFL, EIGHTH DISTRICT)
2366 Rayburn House Office Bldg.
Washington, DC 20515
Local office   (218) 727-7474
Washington office   (202) 225-6211

Federal Government Services

Uncle Sam maintains Federal Courts Buildings at 110 S. Fourth Street, Minneapolis, and 316 N. Robert Street, St. Paul. For general information on any aspect of U.S. government services, call the Federal Information Center at (800) 688-9889.

Other Libraries
That Speak Volumes

In addition to the dozens of public libraries in the Twin Cities, other libraries in the region have valuable holdings in a multitude of fields. Every college and university, for example, has a library of some kind, and most are open to the public (with school alums often retaining borrowing privileges). The holdings of the University of Minnesota are particularly impressive, with special collections devoted to African-American literature, World War I, architectural history, ballooning, the YMCA of the U.S.A. archives, mathematical astronomy, and Greek literature, to name a few.

Here are some Twin Cities libraries especially worthy of checking out:

AMERICAN SWEDISH INSTITUTE
2600 Park Ave. S., Minneapolis   871-4907

The institute's library is a large repository of historic information on Swedish immigration to the United States. Much of it, of course, is written in Swedish.

ANDERSON HORTICULTURAL LIBRARY
Minnesota Landscape Arboretum
Chanhassen   443-2440

Come and root out all the information you need on plants and horticulture. This collection of books, magazines and seed and nursery catalogs is the only horticultural library in the Upper Midwest.

BAKKEN LIBRARY
3537 Zenith Ave. S., Minneapolis   927-6508

Here's a truly one-of-a-kind collection of materials about the history of electricity and magnetism in the life sciences. It includes a fascinating selection of publications on quack electric cures.

GOLDSTEIN GALLERY
FASHION PHOTOGRAPHY AND ILLUSTRATIONS COLLECTION
University of Minnesota
St. Paul Campus   625-2737

This is a horde of fashion magazines, illustrations, photos, catalogs and costumes, deep but not too large. It's used by writers, fashion designers, historians and theater costumers.

JAMES J. HILL REFERENCE LIBRARY
Fourth and Market Sts., St. Paul   227-9531

Sharing a building with St. Paul's Central Library, this facility is exceptionally user-friendly (and privately funded) for people who seek business information. Here you can find business periodicals, annual reports, electronic databases and books, along with some of the most helpful librarians in town.

KERLAN AND HESS COLLECTIONS

University of Minnesota
Minneapolis Campus   624-4576

These children's literature research collections, containing more than 120,000 kids' picture books, story books, manuscripts, photos, drawings and press proofs for all types of children's volumes, constitute one of the world's finest accumulations of its kind.

MINNESOTA HISTORICAL SOCIETY

345 Kellogg Blvd. W., St. Paul   296-2143

The Society's Minnesota History Center — palatial in all other respects as well — contains a beautiful Research Center that sets historians' mouths watering. People researching genealogy and house histories like it too. It contains vast holdings of manuscripts, books, maps, business records, photographs, periodicals and oral-history tapes, along with just about every newspaper ever printed in Minnesota (on 70,000 reels of microfilm). To avoid crowds, the best time to go is on weekdays.

MINNESOTA LIBRARY FOR THE BLIND AND PHYSICALLY HANDICAPPED

Minnesota State Academy for the Blind
Faribault   (507) 332-3279, (800) 722-0550

Although this library is in southern Minnesota, well outside the Twin Cities area, it distributes its materials via the U.S. Mail to patrons throughout the state who can't read conventional printed materials because of blindness or other disabilities. Its collection includes cassette tapes, computer disks, Braille books and large-print books.

QUATREFOIL

1619 Dayton Ave., St. Paul   641-0969

Materials about gay men, lesbians and other sexual minorities are the focus of this lending library, which also sponsors book discussions and art shows.

REPRODUCTIVE HEALTH LIBRARY

Planned Parenthood, 1965 Ford Pkwy.
St. Paul   698-2401

Open by appointment only, this collection includes materials on birth control, reproduction, sexually transmitted diseases, infertility, abortion and sexual assault.

SMALL-PRESS LIBRARY

The Loft, 66 Malcolm Ave. S.E.
Minneapolis   379-8999

The Loft, one of the nation's foremost organizations for writers, maintains a substantial small-press library that includes literary journals, poetry chapbooks and works of fiction and criticism, all issued by publishers not catering to the mass market.

WOMEN'S HEALTH LIBRARY

Melpomene Institute for Women's
Health Research
1010 University Ave., St. Paul   642-1951

Materials in this collection cover all aspects of women's health: fitness, aging, pregnancy, body image and osteoporosis, for example.

PASSPORTS

Several facilities in the area accept applications for U.S. passports. They include the Hennepin County Government Center, 348-8240, and the main Minneapolis Post Office, 349-4736.

UNITED STATES POSTAL SERVICE
349-9100, 293-3777

These numbers connect you to Postal Answer Line, an automated postal information service that requires you to use a touch-tone phone. To speak with a real live person, call 349-4711. For ZIP code information, call 349-3535.

OTHER SERVICES

Consumer Product	
Safety Commission	290-3781
Immigration and Naturalization	
Service	854-7754
Internal Revenue Service	644-7515
Social Security	
Administration	(800) 772-1213
Veterans Administration	(800) 366-2998

State Government Services

St. Paul is the state capital, making access to state services, or at least to state work-ers, relatively easy for most in the Twin Cities. The center of state government activity is the Capitol complex, a prominent grouping of buildings at the north edge of downtown St. Paul. Call 296-6013 for general information on state services.

MINNESOTA STATE LOTTERY
635-8100

If you dream of effortlessly striking it rich, the state lottery might be one of the government "services" you'll enjoy the most. After voters authorized a state lottery in 1988, the Minnesota Legislature approved lottery legislation a year later. Now we have two kinds of lottery games to play: instant, or scratch-off, games and computerized number games. Some 4,000 retailers throughout Minnesota sell instant or online tickets, so you should have no problem finding someone willing to take your wager. Winning numbers are announced on TV, radio and in newspapers, or you can call the 24-hour Player Hotline at 297-7371. About 55 percent of players' wagers are returned to lottery winners, with the rest of the money going to the state's general fund and an environment and natural resources trust fund. The state's proceeds from the lottery annually amount to about $70 million.

MOTOR VEHICLE SERVICES
296-6911

If you have a car, the Driver and Vehicle Services Division of the Department of Public Safety wants to know about you and your auto. To get a driver's license, you must take an exam at one of the many exam stations throughout the Twin Cities area. If you're a new Minnesota resident, you must register your car within 60 days of your arrival. In the Twin Cities, you are required to register your car and renew the registration annually; if you own an older vehicle, this process may require you to take the vehicle to an emissions test station, many of which are scattered around the area. The emissions checkers tend to get swamped toward the end of the month, when last-minute renewers all rush in at once, so the least crowded time to go is in the first half of the month, especially on weekdays.

OTHER SERVICES

Arts Board	297-2603
Health Dept.	623-5000
Human Rights Dept.	296-5663
Job Service	296-3644
Revenue Dept.	296-3403
Road Condition Information	296-3076
Veterans Affairs	296-2562

Metropolitan Services

Because the Twin Cities metropolitan area now embraces seven counties, several metro-wide agencies provide services that cross county lines. For general information on metropolitan services, call 291-6359.

Metro Airports Commission	726-8100
Metro Mosquito Control District	645-9149
Metro Parks and Open Space Commission	291-6363
Regional Transit Board	229-2700

County Government Services

Here's where things start to get complicated. We have seven counties in the Twin Cities, each providing the same basic services to its residents.

ANOKA COUNTY

General Information	421-4760
County Commissioners	323-5680
Highway Department	754-3520
Job Training Center	783-4800
Parks and Recreation	757-3920
Sheriff	323-5000

CARVER COUNTY

General Information	361-1500
Community Health Services	442-4493
Community Social Services	361-1600
Highway Department	361-1010
Parks	361-1000
Sheriff	361-1231

DAKOTA COUNTY

General Information	437-3191
Community Services	450-2742
Employment and Economic Assistance	450-2611
Highway Department	891-7101
Job Training	438-8345
Parks	437-6608
Public Health	552-3100
Sheriff	438-4700

HENNEPIN COUNTY

General Information	348-3000
Children and Family Services	348-2324
Child Protection Services	348-3552
Community Health	348-3925
County Commissioners	348-3081
Economic Assistance	348-5198
Licenses	348-8240
Parks	559-9000
Sheriff	348-3744
Social Services	348-4806
Voter Registration Information	348-5151

RAMSEY COUNTY

General Information	266-8500
Auto Impound Lot	482-5212
Community Human Services	266-4444

County Commissioners	266-8350	General Information	673-3000
Garbage	773-4444	Animal Control	348-4250
Job Training Program	770-8900	Animal Licenses	673-2050
Parks and Recreation	777-1707	Auto Impound Lot	673-5777
Public Health	266-2400	City Council information	673-2200
Public Works	266-2600	Civil Rights	673-3012
		Elections and Voter Registration	673-2070
SCOTT COUNTY		Fire Department Emergencies	911
General Information	445-7750	Fire Department	
Highway Engineer	496-8346	Non-emergencies	673-2890
Human Services	445-7751	Garbage Collection	673-2917
License Bureau	496-8448	Health Department	673-2301
Sheriff	496-8300	Housing Complaints	673-5858
		Mayor's Office	673-2100
		Park and Recreation Board	661-4800
WASHINGTON COUNTY		Police Department Emergencies	911
General Information	439-3220	Police Department	
Community Services	439-6901	Non-emergencies	673-2853
Parks	731-3851	Public Works	673-2352
Public Works	430-4300	Recycling	673-2917
Sheriff	430-7600	Snow Emergency Information	348-SNOW
		Water Works	673-2404

City Government Services

The municipal governments of Minneapolis and St. Paul provide the most comprehensive city services in the Twin Cities, but every suburb and town does its own part. Scores of other cities and towns are scattered throughout the Twin Cities area; consult your phone book to find out more about municipal services outside of Minneapolis and St. Paul.

MINNEAPOLIS

Minneapolis city government is led by Sharon Sayles Belton, the first African-American and first woman mayor in the city's history. The 13-member city council meets every two calendar weeks in Room 317 of City Hall, 350 S. Fifth Street.

ST. PAUL

St. Paul's mayor, Norm Coleman, presides over a seven-member City Council that meets Tuesday and Thursday in the Council Chambers, Third Floor, City Hall.

General Information	266-8989
Animal Control	645-3953
Animal Licenses	645-5451
Employment and Training Center	266-6515
Fire Department Emergencies	911
Fire Department	
Non-emergencies	224-7811
Health Center	292-7711
Housing Information	266-6000
Human Rights	266-8966
Mayor's Office	266-8510
Parks and Recreation	266-6400
Police Department Emergencies	911
Police Department	
Non-emergencies	291-1111

In Minnesota, women first got the vote — in school board elections only — in 1875.

Insiders' Tips

Public Works	292-6600
Voter Registration	266-2717
Water Utility	266-6274

Public Libraries

Minnesota is blessed with good and heavily used public library systems — some county libraries are even open on Sundays! — and the best part is that if you have a library card from any of the state's 101 public library systems, you can check out materials from any other public system in Minnesota. By the same token, you can return most materials to any library, regardless of where you checked them out. So whip out your St. Paul library card in Minneapolis, your Dakota County card in Anoka County or your Hennepin County card in Duluth!

A warning for the computer-phobic: Not one of these library systems maintains a card catalog system any more. All instead use online computer catalogs or microfiche catalog listings. Don't be afraid of those computer terminals. They make it a lot easier to find materials.

MINNEAPOLIS PUBLIC LIBRARIES
Central Library
300 Nicollet Ave., Minneapolis 372-6500

The 15 libraries in the Minneapolis Public Library System, evenly scattered throughout the city, hold nearly 2.5 million items. More than 1.6 million of those items are housed in the Central Library, a four-floor, 1960s-vintage downtown building that is becoming increasingly crowded — so crammed, in fact, that only 16 percent of its books and other materials are visible on open shelves (you have to request the rest from closed stacks). Despite the lack of space, the Central Library remains the best public library in the Twin Cities to do most kinds of research, and the librarians who staff the reference desks in the library's 10 departments know their areas of the collection inside out.

Departments of especially notable strength are business and economics, children's books and history and travel. Certainly the most heavily circulated part of the collection is the movie videos, which you can borrow for a week at a time for free. Most departments also have InfoTrack periodical search terminals that have made the old and unwieldy *Reader's Guide to Periodical Literature* a relic of the past.

The third floor of the Central Library contains the valuable Minneapolis Collection, an aggregation of books, clippings, photos, maps and other materials covering the city's history, and special book collections that focus on North American Indians, natural history, travel and exploration, fables, World War II, the antislavery movement and Mark Twain's works.

During the summer of 1994, the library inaugurated InfoLine, a free telephone reference service that answers callers' inquiries about everything from addresses to weather facts. You can reach InfoLine at 372-6633.

Library users with computers and modems can access the Minneapolis Public Library's online catalog by calling 332-5135 (1200 bps) or 332-5223 (2400 bps).

ST. PAUL PUBLIC LIBRARIES
Central Library
90 W. Fourth St., St. Paul 292-6311

Of all the public libraries in the Twin Cities, the St. Paul Public Libraries' downtown Central Library is the greatest architectural gem. Constructed in 1916 from slabs of pink Tennessee marble and blocks of Kettle River sandstone, it's an Italian Renaissance palace that rises at the edge of Rice Park. (The St. Paul Library shares the building with the James J. Hill Reference Library; see the sidebar for more information.) Inside is a wonderful marble staircase that most patrons apparently eschew in favor of the elevators.

As a place to read and do research, the 99,000-square-foot Central Library leaves much to be desired. It is cramped, poorly signed and cold, and the collection (or what little of the collection is available on open shelves) is confusingly organized in far-flung rooms. A baffling online catalog doesn't make it easy for patrons to find materials. While an access-minded renovation succeeded in making the building simpler for people with disabilities to navigate, the interior redesign also closed off the splendid original entrance and replaced it with an uninspiring ground-floor reception area.

With a collection significantly smaller than Minneapolis', the 400,000-volume Central Library's greatest strength is its librarians, who meet patrons' needs even while working under an obviously tight budget. The library has a good audiovisual department, Children's Room and literature collection, as well.

Twelve other branch libraries make up the St. Paul system, which has a total collection of about 700,000 items. People with computers and modems can access the online catalog by calling 292-6376.

County Libraries

For Twin Citians in suburban or outlying areas, the seven county library systems place books, audiovisual materials and information within easy reach. Many of the county libraries are very heavily used. Just go inside the recently enlarged Southdale-Hennepin Area Library in Edina on a typical weeknight during the school year, and you'll see what a busy library really looks like. The Dakota County Libraries, in fact, have the Twin Cities' highest per capita circulation despite the relatively small size of their collection.

ANOKA COUNTY LIBRARIES
Central Library
707 Hwy. 10 N.E., Blaine   784-1100

This system has 10 branches and a collection of more than 500,000 items. Remote access to the online catalog is available at 784-8950.

CARVER COUNTY LIBRARIES
448-9395

Carver County's diminutive system serves the southwest part of the Twin Cities and has fewer than 100,000 items in its collection. Computer/modem access to the catalog is shared with the Scott County Libraries, 496-8235.

DAKOTA COUNTY LIBRARIES
688-1500

The five Dakota County libraries serve neighborhoods in West St. Paul, Eagan, Burnsville, Farmington and Apple Val-

The Twin Cities suburbs of Brooklyn Park, Coon Rapids, Plymouth, Minnetonka and Edina rank as the sixth- through tenth-largest Minnesota cities, respectively.

Insiders' Tips

ley. Computer/modem access to the online catalog is available at 452-6008.

HENNEPIN COUNTY LIBRARIES
541-8530

The Hennepin County Library system includes 27 facilities with 1.4 million items and an annual circulation of 8.9 million — the highest of any public library system in the region. Access the dial-in catalog by calling 540-8200.

RAMSEY COUNTY LIBRARIES
631-9435

The seven libraries in this well-trafficked system, holding some 600,000 items, are in the non-St. Paul areas of the county. Call 486-2222 for dial-in catalog access.

SCOTT COUNTY LIBRARIES
873-6767

Second-smallest of the metro-area library systems, Scott County's has seven branches. Dial-in access to the catalog is at 496-8235.

WASHINGTON COUNTY LIBRARIES
459-2040

The Washington County system has 300,000 items in its collection. Call 739-9647 for dial-in access.

Utility Services

In general, Twin Cities area water and sewer service is provided by local municipalities. But if you want natural gas, electricity and phone service, you'll have to deal with these guys.

MINNEGASCO
372-4727

Minnegasco is the utility that supplies natural gas to Minneapolis and its surrounding suburbs. Call 372-5050 to report gas leaks or emergencies.

NORTHERN STATES POWER (NSP)
282-1234

They've got the volts, and they also provide the natural gas to St. Paul and its suburbs. Call 221-4411 for electric emergencies and 221-4421 if you smell gas.

U S WEST COMMUNICATIONS
(800) 244-1111

For 99 percent of the Twin Cities area, call U S West if you want to order new home phone service, to ask billing questions, or to change existing home phone service. The person you'll speak with will probably be in Englewood, Colorado, which is where U S West is headquartered. For home phone repairs, call (800) 573-1311. To receive copies of the White or Yellow Pages, call (800) 422-8793.

Inside
Service Directory

The following is a list of useful Minneapolis and St. Paul telephone numbers for both the traveler and new resident.

Keep in mind, however, that despite our best efforts to be up-to-date, some of these organizations and businesses are staffed by volunteers and/or are just testing the waters to try to fill a need, so may have ceased operations by the time of this volume's publication. And don't forget that sometimes the best information comes via word of mouth — from neighbors, hotel concierges and taxi drivers.

See our Public Services chapter for other helpful numbers, and if you are interested in getting involved in helping your community, our Community Services and Volunteerism chapter is a good resource. Also, the Healthcare chapter has a list of referral services.

Emergency Numbers

Public Safety

AMBULANCE, FIRE AND POLICE
911

Poison Control

MINNESOTA REGIONAL POISON CENTER
St. Paul	221-2113
Hennepin County	347-3141

General Crisis Hotlines

SUICIDE HOTLINE
347-2222

MINNESOTA CRISIS INTERVENTION CENTER
347-3161

CRISIS CONNECTION
379-6363

DAKOTA COUNTY SOCIAL SERVICES CRISIS LINE
891-1414

UNITED WAY'S FIRST CALL FOR HELP
(General referral services)
St. Paul	224-1133
Minneapolis	335-5000
Anoka	783-4880

Child Care

GREATER MINNEAPOLIS DAY CARE ASSOCIATION
(Serving North Minneapolis and Hennepin County suburbs) 341-2066

EARLY CHILDHOOD RESOURCE CENTER
(Serving South Minneapolis) 721-0265

RESOURCES FOR CHILD CARING
(Serving Ramsey County) 641-0332

CHILD CARE RESOURCE AND REFERRAL
(Washington County)	430-6488
(Scott and Carver counties)	496-2321
(Dakota County)	431-7752

Services for the Disabled

MINNESOTA STATE
COUNCIL ON DISABILITY
296-6785, (800) 945-8913

This state office serves as a general referral agency for people with disabilities, providing information on everything from housing to employment training to financial assistance.

METRO MOBILITY
221-0015

This company provides transportation for the handicapped in converted vans and buses.

ARC MINNESOTA
827-5641

With 55 chapters in Minnesota, this organization provides education and support to people with developmental disabilities.

COURAGE CENTER
520-0520

This is a Golden Valley-based rehabilitation center for people with physical disabilities.

METROPOLITAN CENTER
FOR INDEPENDENT LIVING
646-8342, 603-2001 (TTD)

This organization promotes independent living for people with disabilities.

Entertainment

TWIN CITIES JAZZ SOCIETY'S JAZZLINE
633-0329

CITY LINE
645-6060

THE CONNECTION
922-9000

Legal Services

LAWYER REFERRAL SERVICE
(Hennepin County)   339-8777

LEGAL AID SOCIETY
332-1441

This is a referral service for low-income people who need legal help.

RAMSEY COUNTY ATTORNEY REFERRAL
224-1775

VOLUNTEER LAWYERS NETWORK
339-9139

Newcomer Services

SUBURBAN WEST
AREA NEWCOMERS CLUB
473-8588, 449-0038

WELCOME WAGON
General number   332-6231

WELCOME WAGON
OF THE SOUTHWEST SUBURBS
934-7995

Travel and Transportation

Trip Planning

MINNESOTA OFFICE OF TOURISM
296-5029, (800) 657-3700

These folks can give you information about every area of the state.

DEPARTMENT OF NATURAL RESOURCES
296-6157

The DNR provides information on outdoors issues, including Minnesota hunting seasons and laws.

NORTHERN LIGHTS TOURISM ALLIANCE
(800) 664-9453

Northern Lights provides tourism information on Duluth, Minnesota's North Shore of Lake Superior and other Northern Minnesota attractions.

CANADIAN CONSULATE
332-4314

The Canadian Consulate provides information on traveling in Canada.

Road Condition Information

DEPARTMENT OF TRANSPORTATION
ROAD-CONDITION HOTLINE
296-3076

Bus Lines, Local

METROPOLITAN COUNCIL
TRANSIT OPERATIONS
373-3333

Bus Lines, Long Distance

GREYHOUND
(800) 231-2222

JEFFERSON LINES
332-3224

Carpooling

MINNESOTA RIDESHARE
349-RIDE

Taxicabs

AIRPORT TAXI
721-0000

SUBURBAN TAXI
(south)   884-8888
(west)   545-1234
(north)   781-1111
(east)   222-2222

ST. PAUL YELLOW CAB
222-4433

Trains

AMTRAK
(800) 872-7245

Airlines and Charter Flights

HUBERT H. HUMPHREY TERMINAL
(for charter flights)   726-5800

NORTHWEST
(800) 225-2525

TWA
333-6543

AMERICAN
(800) 433-7300

CONTINENTAL
332-1471

DELTA
339-7477

UNITED
(800) 241-6522

USAIR
(800) 428-4322

Helplines

AIDS and Sexually Transmitted Diseases Information

AIDS HOTLINE
373-AIDS

MINNESOTA AIDS PROJECT
341-2060

Minnesota Sexually Transmitted Diseases Hotline

(800) 783-2287

This hotline also provides family planning information and referrals to area clinics.

Child Abuse

Hennepin County Child Protection

348-3552

Minnesota Committee for the Prevention of Child Abuse

641-1568

Ramsey County Social Services

266-4500

Parenting

Parent Warmline

813-6336

This line, staffed by trained volunteers, answers questions on parenting and childhood. However, it is *not* an emergency hotline. For parenting crises, call First Call for Help, 335-5000, the Crisis Nursery listed below or, in life-threatening situations, call 911.

Metro Crisis Nursery Program

646-4033

Dedicated to reducing the incidence of child abuse, this program provides emergency child care for parents in crisis.

Children's Home Society Crisis Nursery

(For Ramsey County residents)   641-1300

Crime Victims

Citizens Council Victim Services

340-5400

Domestic Abuse, Rape and Sexual Assault

First Call for Help

Minneapolis	335-5000
St. Paul	224-1133

Alexandra House Inc.

646-0994

Rape and Sexual Assault Center

825-4357

Family Planning

Minnesota Family Planning Hotline

(800) 783-2287

Drugs and Alcohol

Cocaine Hotline

(800) 262-2463

Alcohol, Drug and Pregnancy Helpline

(800) 638-2229

Center for Substance Abuse Treatment

(800) 662-4357

Al-Anon

(For families of alcoholics)   920-3961

Alcoholics Anonymous

Minneapolis	922-0880
St. Paul	227-5502

Gambling Addiction

Minnesota Compulsive Gambling Hotline

(800) 437-3641

Gay, Lesbian Issues

GAY AND LESBIAN HELP LINE
822-8661

Banks

We've listed the larger banks, those with convenient locations throughout the Twin Cities. But remember, it's not size, but service, that counts.

FIRST BANK
(nearly 60 locations)   973-1111

FIRSTAR BANK
(47 locations)   784-5100

MARQUETTE BANK
(34 locations)   661-4000

NORWEST BANKS
(76 locations)   667-9378

TCF BANK
(51 locations)   823-2265

Animal Services

Humane Societies

**ANIMAL HUMANE
SOCIETY OF HENNEPIN COUNTY**
522-4325

This modern, attractive facility provides refuge to abandoned animals, offers obedience classes and education on animal welfare. The facility is at 845 N. Meadow Lane, Golden Valley.

HUMANE SOCIETY OF RAMSEY COUNTY
645-7387

Kennels and Pet Sitters

Here are several of the area's care cen-

ters for your pet. There are others as well; consult your veterinarian or the telephone directory.

PETS ARE INN

North Minneapolis and suburbs	544-4104
South Minneapolis and suburbs	888-3545
St. Paul and suburbs	292-8933

HOME AND PET SITTERS
459-6091

PAWS PLUS
537-6159

ANIMAL INN BOARDING KENNEL
777-0255

DOG HOUSE BOARDING KENNELS
473-9026

KOLSTAD'S K-9 ACRES
934-3884

GOLDWOOD KENNELS
429-0648

Veterinarian Referral

**MINNESOTA VETERINARY
MEDICAL ASSOCIATION**
645-7533

General Information

TIME AND TEMPERATURE
224-8463

WEATHER FORECAST
375-0830

ZIP CODE INFORMATION
452-3800

Index of Advertisers

Index

H

ORDER FORM
Fast and Simple!

Mail to:	**Or:**
Insiders Guides®, Inc.	**for VISA or**
P.O. Drawer 2057	**MasterCard orders call**
Manteo, NC 27954	**(800) 765-BOOK**

Name _____

Address _____

City/State/Zip _____

Qty.	Title/Price	Shipping	Amount
	Insiders' Guide to Richmond/$14.95	$3.00	
	Insiders' Guide to Williamsburg/$14.95	$3.00	
	Insiders' Guide to Virginia's Blue Ridge/$14.95	$3.00	
	Insiders' Guide to Virginia's Chesapeake Bay/$14.95	$3.00	
	Insiders' Guide to Washington, DC/$14.95	$3.00	
	Insiders' Guide to North Carolina's Outer Banks/$14.95	$3.00	
	Insiders' Guide to Wilmington, NC/$14.95	$3.00	
	Insiders' Guide to North Carolina's Crystal Coast/$12.95	$3.00	
	Insiders' Guide to North Carolina's Mountains/$14.95	$3.00	
	Insiders' Guide to Myrtle Beach/$14.95	$3.00	
	Insiders' Guide to Atlanta/$14.95	$3.00	
	Insiders' Guide to Boca Raton & the Palm Beaches/$14.95	$3.00	
	Insiders' Guide to Sarasota/Bradenton/$14.95	$3.00	
	Insiders' Guide to Northwest Florida/$14.95	$3.00	
	Insiders' Guide to Tampa Bay/$14.95	$3.00	
	Insiders' Guide to Mississippi/$14.95	$3.00	
	Insiders' Guide to Lexington, KY/$14.95	$3.00	
	Insiders' Guide to Louisville/$14.95	$3.00	
	Insiders' Guide to Cincinnati/$14.95	$3.00	
	Insiders' Guide to the Twin Cities/$14.95	$3.00	
	Insiders' Guide to Boulder/$14.95	$3.00	
	Insiders' Guide to Denver/$14.95	$3.00	
	Insiders' Guide to Branson/$14.95	$3.00	
	Insiders' Guide to Civil War in the Eastern Theater/$14.95	$3.00	

Payment in full (check or money order) must
accompany this order form.
Please allow 2 weeks for delivery.

N.C. residents add 6% sales tax _____

Total _____